T0310744

Virtual and Augmented Reality in Education, Art, and Museums

Giuliana Guazzaroni
Università Politecnica delle Marche, Italy

Anitha S. Pillai
Hindustan Institute of Technology and Science, India

A volume in the Advances in Computational
Intelligence and Robotics (ACIR) Book Series

Published in the United States of America by
    IGI Global
    Engineering Science Reference (an imprint of IGI Global)
    701 E. Chocolate Avenue
    Hershey PA, USA 17033
    Tel: 717-533-8845
    Fax: 717-533-8661
    E-mail: cust@igi-global.com
    Web site: http://www.igi-global.com

Copyright © 2020 by IGI Global. All rights reserved. No part of this publication may be reproduced, stored or distributed in any form or by any means, electronic or mechanical, including photocopying, without written permission from the publisher. Product or company names used in this set are for identification purposes only. Inclusion of the names of the products or companies does not indicate a claim of ownership by IGI Global of the trademark or registered trademark.

Library of Congress Cataloging-in-Publication Data

Names: Guazzaroni, Giuliana, 1968- editor. | Pillai, Anitha S., 1967-
  editor.
Title: Virtual and augmented reality in education, art, and museums /
  Giuliana Guazzaroni and Anitha S. Pillai, editors.
Description: Hershey, PA : Engineering Science Reference, an imprint of IGI
  Global, [2020] | Includes bibliographical references and index. |
  Summary: "This book explores the strategic role and use of virtual and
  augmented reality in shaping visitor experiences at art galleries and
  museums and their ability to enhance education"-- Provided by publisher.

Identifiers: LCCN 2019034137 (print) | LCCN 2019034138 (ebook) | ISBN
  9781799817963 (hardcover) | ISBN 9781799817970 (paperback) | ISBN
  9781799817987 (ebook)
Subjects: LCSH: Virtual reality in education. | Museums--Educational
  aspects.
Classification: LCC AM7 .V56 2020 (print) | LCC AM7 (ebook) | DDC
  069/.15--dc23
LC record available at https://lccn.loc.gov/2019034137
LC ebook record available at https://lccn.loc.gov/2019034138

This book is published in the IGI Global book series Advances in Computational Intelligence and Robotics (ACIR) (ISSN: 2327-0411; eISSN: 2327-042X)

British Cataloguing in Publication Data
A Cataloguing in Publication record for this book is available from the British Library.

All work contributed to this book is new, previously-unpublished material. The views expressed in this book are those of the authors, but not necessarily of the publisher.

For electronic access to this publication, please contact: eresources@igi-global.com.

Advances in Computational Intelligence and Robotics (ACIR) Book Series

Ivan Giannoccaro
University of Salento, Italy

ISSN:2327-0411
EISSN:2327-042X

MISSION

While intelligence is traditionally a term applied to humans and human cognition, technology has progressed in such a way to allow for the development of intelligent systems able to simulate many human traits. With this new era of simulated and artificial intelligence, much research is needed in order to continue to advance the field and also to evaluate the ethical and societal concerns of the existence of artificial life and machine learning.

The **Advances in Computational Intelligence and Robotics (ACIR) Book Series** encourages scholarly discourse on all topics pertaining to evolutionary computing, artificial life, computational intelligence, machine learning, and robotics. ACIR presents the latest research being conducted on diverse topics in intelligence technologies with the goal of advancing knowledge and applications in this rapidly evolving field.

COVERAGE

- Artificial Life
- Machine Learning
- Automated Reasoning
- Cognitive Informatics
- Synthetic Emotions
- Brain Simulation
- Algorithmic Learning
- Adaptive and Complex Systems
- Agent technologies
- Computational Intelligence

IGI Global is currently accepting manuscripts for publication within this series. To submit a proposal for a volume in this series, please contact our Acquisition Editors at Acquisitions@igi-global.com or visit: http://www.igi-global.com/publish/.

The Advances in Computational Intelligence and Robotics (ACIR) Book Series (ISSN 2327-0411) is published by IGI Global, 701 E. Chocolate Avenue, Hershey, PA 17033-1240, USA, www.igi-global.com. This series is composed of titles available for purchase individually; each title is edited to be contextually exclusive from any other title within the series. For pricing and ordering information please visit http://www.igi-global.com/book-series/advances-computational-intelligence-robotics/73674. Postmaster: Send all address changes to above address. © © 2020 IGI Global. All rights, including translation in other languages reserved by the publisher. No part of this series may be reproduced or used in any form or by any means – graphics, electronic, or mechanical, including photocopying, recording, taping, or information and retrieval systems – without written permission from the publisher, except for non commercial, educational use, including classroom teaching purposes. The views expressed in this series are those of the authors, but not necessarily of IGI Global.

Titles in this Series

For a list of additional titles in this series, please visit:
https://www.igi-global.com/book-series/advances-computational-intelligence-robotics/73674

AI and Big Data's Potential for Disruptive Innovation
Moses Strydom (Emeritus, France) and Sheryl Buckley (University of South Africa, South Africa)
Engineering Science Reference • © 2020 • 405pp • H/C (ISBN: 9781522596875) • US $225.00

Handbook of Research on the Internet of Things Applications in Robotics and Automation
Rajesh Singh (Lovely Professional University, India) Anita Gehlot (Lovely Professional University, India) Vishal Jain (Bharati Vidyapeeth's Institute of Computer Applications and Management (BVICAM), New Delhi, India) and Praveen Kumar Malik (Lovely Professional University, India)
Engineering Science Reference • © 2020 • 433pp • H/C (ISBN: 9781522595748) • US $295.00

Handbook of Research on Applications and Implementations of Machine Learning Techniques
Sathiyamoorthi Velayutham (Sona College of Technology, India)
Engineering Science Reference • © 2020 • 461pp • H/C (ISBN: 9781522599029) • US $295.00

Handbook of Research on Advanced Mechatronic Systems and Intelligent Robotics
Maki K. Habib (The American University in Cairo, Egypt)
Engineering Science Reference • © 2020 • 466pp • H/C (ISBN: 9781799801375) • US $295.00

Edge Computing and Computational Intelligence Paradigms for the IoT
G. Nagarajan (Sathyabama Institute of Science and Technology, India) and R.I. Minu (SRM Institute of Science and Technology, India)
Engineering Science Reference • © 2019 • 347pp • H/C (ISBN: 9781522585558) • US $285.00

Semiotic Perspectives in Evolutionary Psychology, Artificial Intelligence, and the Study of Mind Emerging Research and Opportunities
Marcel Danesi (University of Toronto, Canada)
Information Science Reference • © 2019 • 205pp • H/C (ISBN: 9781522589242) • US $175.00

Handbook of Research on Human-Computer Interfaces and New Modes of Interactivity
Katherine Blashki (Victorian Institute of Technology, Australia) and Pedro Isaías (The University of Queensland, Australia)
Engineering Science Reference • © 2019 • 488pp • H/C (ISBN: 9781522590699) • US $275.00

701 East Chocolate Avenue, Hershey, PA 17033, USA
Tel: 717-533-8845 x100 • Fax: 717-533-8661
E-Mail: cust@igi-global.com • www.igi-global.com

Editorial Advisory Board

Davide Borra, *The Italian University for Design (IAAD), Italy*
Laura Carletti, *University of Nottingham, UK*
Paolo Clini, *Polytechnic University of Marche, Italy*
Emanuele Frontoni, *Polytechnic University of Marche, Italy*
Alex James, *Nazarbayev University, Kazakhstan*
Vasile Palade, *Coventry University, UK*
Roberto Pierdicca, *Polytechnic University of Marche, Italy*
Maria Paola Puggioni, *Polytechnic University of Marche, Italy*
Mario Savini, *University of Teramo, Italy*

List of Reviewers

Cecilia Maria Bolognesi, *Polytechnic University of Milan, Italy*
Sergio Casas, *University of Valencia, Spain*
Ali Geris Manisa Celal, *Bayar University, Turkey*
Giorgio Cipolletta, *University of Macerata, Italy*
Nesrin Özdener Dönmez, *Marmara University, Turkey*
Yowei Kang, *National Taiwan Ocean University, Taiwan*
Antonios Kargas, *National and Kapodistrian University of Athens, Greece*
Nikoletta Karitsioti, *University of Peloponnese, Greece*
Ajinkya Rajendrakumar Kunjir, *Lakehead University, Canada*
Patrizia Schettino, *AgID, Italy*
Nazime Tuncay, *Cyprus Science University, Cyprus*
Kenneth C. C. Yang, *The University of Texas at El Paso, USA*

Table of Contents

Section 2
Virtual and Augmented Reality in Art and Museums

Section 3
Virtual and Augmented Reality in Education, Art, and Museums: Case Studies

Detailed Table of Contents

Section 1
Virtual and Augumented Reality in Education

Chapter 1
Design Models for Developing Educational Virtual Reality Environments: A Systematic Review 1
Ali Geris, Manisa Celal Bayar University, Turkey
Nesrin Özdener, Marmara University, Turkey

Virtual reality, although not a new technology, has rapidly increased its popularity in the last few years. As a result, their use in educational environments has been a topic of interest in academic research. One of the first questions asked by education researchers has been, "How can we design an effective virtual reality environment?", which led to the development of many design models for the preparation of educational virtual reality environments based on various approaches. These design models have been systematically examined in terms of themes and codes within this study, in hopes this chapter may be of importance for guiding researchers who want to design an educational virtual reality environment or create a design model.

Chapter 2
Role of Immersive (XR) Technologies in Improving Healthcare Competencies: A Review 23
Prabha Susy Mathew, Bishop Cottons Women's Christian College, India
Anitha S. Pillai, Hindustan Institute of Technology and Science, India

Immersive technology refers to technology that enhances reality by blending the physical environment with virtual content or by completely taking the user to a virtual world far away from reality. Different immersive technologies are augmented reality (AR), virtual reality (VR), and mixed reality (MR). As immersive technology is becoming more affordable, user-friendly, pervasive, and ubiquitous, it's been adopted and embraced by several industries. Though its early adopters were from the gaming industry, now it's explored and used by many other industries such as mining, healthcare, and medicine, retail, education, automotive, manufacturing, etc. Using these technologies, medical professionals can improve their competencies, and they will be able to effectively transfer the skill acquired through simulations to the operation theatre. This chapter focuses on uses, benefits, and adoption challenges of Immersive technologies with specific reference to healthcare training.

Chapter 3

Derya Uzelli Yilmaz, Izmir Kâtip Çelebi University, Turkey
Sevil Hamarat Tuncalı, Izmir Kâtip Çelebi University, Turkey
Yusuf Yilmaz, Ege University, Turkey

Today's new technologies have impacted many different areas of education, with nursing education one such area. Nursing education, as a learning process, targets the combination of cognitive, affective, and psychomotor learning domains. However, traditional teaching methods may not meet all of the Y and Z generations' learning needs. Today's learners are accustomed to multimedia learning environments and have come to expect a certain level of technology integrated into their curricula. Virtual Reality (VR) technology enables students to become immersed within a 360-degree view experience of scenes that have been completely digitally created, whilst no longer viewing the real world around them. Virtual simulation has been used to teach communication, disaster relief, teamwork, and interviewing techniques, among other skills; and can also provide immersive personalized learning experiences. This chapter presents some of the many facets of VR in today's nursing education.

Chapter 4

Nazime Tuncay, Bahçeşehir Cyprus University, Cyprus

Radio channels lack visuality and virtual reality platforms are designed to overcome this problem. Virtual objects are very common these days and people get used to virtual platforms. Does this mean people are ready to be involved in such a system? Is this necessary? How to make sounds visible? Use of Virtual Reality is growing rapidly in industry as well as in education area. This chapter is about the virtual radio center construction necessities, usefulness, and its adaptability to real life and to courses.

Chapter 5

Biancamaria Mori, MenteZero, Italy

This chapter will discuss Gamification and video games, analyzing their peculiarities. After a brief historical introduction to the disciplines that intertwine the design of Gamification applications, such as User interaction, User Interface, and Game Design, authors analyze the real areas in which Gamification can be applied with verifiable results, citing scientific studies and examples of applications. We will see then how from the video games Toca Boca for children, to the "tourist" version of Assassin's Creed Oringis presented at the British Museum, up to the latest interactive applications for business training, the techniques of the game are exceeding the playful areas to make more deep human interaction with the real surrounding it.

In 2013, the Oxford Dictionaries announced "selfie" as the word of the year. The dictionary defined it as "a photograph that one has taken of oneself, typically one taken with a smartphone or webcam and uploaded to a social media website." Selfies are also a complex form of social interaction, an emerging aesthetics, thus having an irrevocable impact on self-portraiture. All visual culture revolves around the body and the body par excellence is the face. The 21st century portrait represents a kind of black mirror where we project ourselves into a kind of blindness. Mask and face are confused by an omnipresent multividuality in which the shield reveals itself and reveals other possible worlds. The face-mask melts in between Real and Virtual and the self becomes augmented.

Section 2
Virtual and Augmented Reality in Art and Museums

The forthcoming Industry 4.0 is expected to change not only manufacturing and industrial services, but will rearrange how services are offered in a variety of sectors, including museum's services. Museums will inevitably be led to more digital (VR & AR) and promoting (Social Media) paths. A forthcoming "digital convergence" between VR & AR technologies and social media's promoting logic could enlarge museums' potentialities in attracting more visitors, younger visitors, while new patterns for connecting learning effects and amusement should be established. This chapter contributes to the following: • Presenting existing theoretical and empirical research on Virtual Reality and Augmented Reality technological implementation in Museums. • Presenting current tensions on social media's usage from cultural organizations. • Exploring how VR & AR applications can incorporate various elements coming from social media operational logic.

Chapter 8

The global AR, MR, and VR markets will reach USD$40.6 billion in 2019. As a result, digital reality technologies have become a key component of promoting art exhibition and museum industries to the general public around the world. Emerging applications such as ARCHEOGUIDE, ARCO, and 3D-MURALE have allowed museum-goers to access archeological artefacts and sites remotely without physically visiting the museums. Digital reality technologies have therefore been perceived to have the great potential to promote (creative) cultural industry contents, because of the characteristics of these platforms (e.g., interactivity, realism, and visualization). This chapter employs a case study approach to discuss the current state of digital reality technology applications in museums and art exhibitions around the world. The study provides several best practice examples to demonstrate how digital reality technologies have fundamentally transformed the art exhibitions and museums.

Chapter 9

Ajinkya Rajendrakumar Kunjir, Lakehead Univeristy, Canada
Krutika Ravindra Patil, MES College of Engineering, Pune, India

In Today's digital world, AR is a tech which imposes layers of virtual segments on the real world. Research Practitioners and Designers in all applications seem to be more concerned about the learning facilities than keeping the visitors engaged in public art exhibitions, Museums, and holiday tourist locations. These ignored circumstances have provoked studies to emphasize more on the usability of Mobile Augmented Reality (M.A.R.) at Art galleries and Museums. According to the recent surveys, the current M.A.R. applications at target locations focus on healthy people without any disabilities, and not on those with disabilities. This chapter recommends major design elements of M.A.R. at museums and art galleries, and highlights all the challenges faced by visitors suffering from visual, speech, and Learning Disorders. The research discusses the 11 vital elements which include Usability, Design, Motivation, Interaction, Perceived control, Satisfaction, Attention, and others involving engagement of M.A.R. necessary for building an effective M.A.R. application for disabled people.

Chapter 10

Giuliana Guazzaroni, Università Politecnica delle Marche, Italy

Virtual reality (VR), augmented reality (AR), and artificial intelligence (AI) are increasingly being used by educational institutions and museums worldwide. Visitors of museums and art galleries may live different layers of reality while enjoying works of art augmented with immersive VR. Research points out that this possibility may strongly affect human emotions. Digital technologies may allow forms of hybridization between flesh and technological objects within virtual or real spaces. They are interactive processes that may contribute to the redefinition of the relationship between identity and technology, between technology and body (Mainardi, 2013). Interactive museums and art galleries are real environments amplified, through information systems, which allow a shift between reality, and electronically manipulated immersive experiences. VR is emotionally engaging and a VR scenario may enhance emotional experience (Diemer et al., 2015) or induce an emotional change (Wu et al., 2016). The main purpose of this chapter is to verify how art and VR affect emotions.

Chapter 11

Paolo Clini, Università Politecnica delle Marche, Italy
Ramona Quattrini, Università Politecnica delle Marche, Italy
Paolo Bonvini, Università Politecnica delle Marche, Italy
Romina Nespeca, Università Politecnica delle Marche, Italy
Renato Angeloni, Università Politecnica delle Marche, Italy
Raissa Mammoli, Università Politecnica delle Marche, Italy
Aldo Franco Dragoni, Università Politecnica delle Marche, Italy
Christian Morbidoni, Università Politecnica delle Marche, Italy
Paolo Sernani, Università Politecnica delle Marche, Italy
Maura Mengoni, Università Politecnica delle Marche, Italy
Alma Leopardi, Università Politecnica delle Marche, Italy
Mauro Silvestrini, Università Politecnica delle Marche, Italy
Danilo Gambelli, Università Politecnica delle Marche, Italy
Enrico Cori, Università Politecnica delle Marche, Italy
Marco Gallegati, Università Politecnica delle Marche, Italy
Massimo Tamberi, Università Politecnica delle Marche, Italy
Fabio Fraticelli, Università Politecnica delle Marche, Italy
Maria Cristina Acciarri, Università Politecnica delle Marche, Italy
Serena Mandolesi, Università Politecnica delle Marche, Italy

Digit(al)isation of Cultural Heritage is a multidimensional process that helps in the rescue of European Cultural Identity, and the paradigm of Digital Cultural Heritage (DCH) is a valid instrument for social and cognitive inclusion of museum visitors. In light of disseminating and validating new paradigms for the enjoyment and exploitation of Cultural Heritage (CH) artifacts, this chapter shows main first results from CIVITAS (ChaIn for excellence of reflectiVe societies to exploit dIgital culTural heritAge and museumS). The project develops virtual/augmented environments, through the multisensorial interaction with virtual artworks, to satisfy needs and overcome limitations in a larger CH scenario, applying a bottom-up approach. The research presented show a robust and interdisciplinary approach applied to Ducal Pace at Urbino: key activities and faced challenges demonstrated to test cross-fertilization strategies, involving multilayered issues.

Chapter 12

Roberto Pierdicca, Università Politecnica delle Marche, Italy
Emanuele Frontoni, Università Politecnica delle Marche, Italy
Maria Paola Puggioni, Università Politecnica delle Marche, Italy
Eva Savina Malinverni, Università Politecnica delle Marche, Italy
Marina Paolanti, Università Politecnica delle Marche, Italy

Augmented and virtual reality proved to be valuable solutions to convey contents in a more appealing and interactive way. Given the improvement of mobile and smart devices in terms of both usability and computational power, contents can be easily conveyed with a realism level never reached in the past. Despite the tremendous number of researches related with the presentation of new fascinating applications of ancient goods and artifacts augmentation, few papers are focusing on the real effect these tools have on learning. Within the framework of SmartMarca project, this chapter focuses on assessing the potential of AR/VR applications specifically designed for cultural heritage. Tests have been conducted on classrooms of teenagers to whom different learning approaches served as an evaluation method about the effectiveness of using these technologies for the education process. The chapter argues on the necessity of developing new tools to enable users to become producers of contents of AR/VR experiences.

Section 3
Virtual and Augmented Reality in Education, Art, and Museums: Case Studies

Chapter 13

3D real time game technologies create an opportunity to design interactive immersive experiences developing affordable, easy-to-use, and incredible virtual worlds for Museums. This chapter presents the potential of these technologies for the development of edutainment content for their visitors at MAIO - Museum of Art Taken Hostage in Cassina de' Pecchi (Milan). The Museum presents the story of 1,623 masterpieces such as Michelangelo, Tiziano, Raffaello, and Canaletto that were stolen in Italy during World War II and never found again. Visitors can explore the artworks through 2 installations: MAIO Virtual Museum, through VR inside an oniric 3D environment, and MAIO Play, a multiplayer video game.

Chapter 14

The experimentations described here concern the virtualization of the Studio Museo Achille Castiglioni, a small museum that hosts important artefacts designed by one of the most famous architects and designers of the 20th century, winner of 7 "Compasso d'oro" awards. The digitization process creates two virtual experiences to enjoy the place and the design objects to give visibility to the small context far from the big museum. The first (less complex and immersive) experimentation deals with the semantic implementation of 360° panoramic photographs, giving rise to a virtual tour of the museum available on the web with no interaction: it is the description of the state of the art of this place. The second one (a real VR simulation) derives from a more complex workflow based on digital surveying, digital modelling, and developing of virtual environments and interactions. The two proposed case studies demonstrate how new technologies can represent indispensable instruments for the safeguard, enhancement, and communication of Cultural Heritage.

The chapter presents the interpretative strategies used by designers of an immersive environment on Hindu mythology and Hampi, an archaeological site in India, and their own knowledge of Hindu deities and their attributes. The process of animating an Indian Hindu deity for a potentially international audience means not only mastering 3D computer graphics and producing high-quality panorama of the sacred and historical place, but also working carefully on the interpretation and representation. The chapter uses concepts and theories from different disciplines (iconology, hermeutics, design research, museums studies, etc.) with the aim to describe, deconstruct, and understand the design choices. The study uses as main method the grounded theory: data are interviews and observations and the patterns emerging from qualitative data are compared with previous theories, during the process of theoretical comparison.

Virtual interactive experience created for the Picture gallery of Jesi (Italy). Namely, three interactive works realized with Unreal Engine 4 to give the spectator a greater immersiveness on the immortal pictures of Lorenzo Lotto. The goal was achieved by creating three choreographies with audio supervised by a historian, recreation of the works with three-dimensional graphics and a specially composed soundtrack by Tecla Zorzi. The augmented reality (AR) application was realized specifically for Android tablets.

Foreword

GIVE ME A LEVER AND I CAN LIFT THE WORLD

The impact that immersive technologies - Virtual Reality, Augmented Reality and Mixed Reality - have on 21st century society is increasingly strong.

The application fields of these technologies evolve at a frenetic pace, as does the market for devices that represent them. *Goldman Sachs estimates that in 2025 this market can reach a value of 80 billion dollars.*

An important value considering that in 2014, after an experimentation phase lasting over 50 years, immersive technologies officially entered the market.

Beyond the estimates, the fact is that these particular technologies, together with quantum computers and artificial intelligence, create new approaches to solving iper-complex problems in all areas of human experience.

Architecture, art, aerospace, automotive, publishing, educational, entertainment, gaming, information technology, security, medicine, military, psychology, robotics, telecommunications, tourism, sports are just some of the application fields where immersive technologies are used today. These technologies are used in public and private research centers around the world.

For me, some of these application fields are more important than others. They have been accompanying my life for several years and allow me to meet interesting people and visit special places. They allow me to expand my wealth of personal and professional knowledge.

One of the interesting people known during the Virtual Reality activities is Giuliana Guazzaroni. Giuliana, together with Anitha S. Pillai, edited this Book entitled *Virtual and Augmented Reality in Education, Art, and Museum.*

A book of notable impact that includes the valuable contributions of Professors, Researchers, Entrepreneurs and Educators from seven different States of the Earth, located in three continents.

This book is the demonstration that immersive technologies have the power to create a thought, a vision, a common mission shared by all of us to release a healthy culture of scientific and/or academic matrix towards professionals, entrepreneurs and educators who want to improve their understanding of the strategic role offered by immersive technologies in the fields of education, art and museum environments.

In the last 3 years I have met thousands of very young people, students, athletes, associations, teachers, entrepreneurs and ordinary people. I did my job with them. I have divulged the importance and the role that immersive technologies like Virtual, Augmented and Mixed Reality have today in the society.

I also focused the spotlight on the opportunities that these technologies offer to the younger generations in the fields of videogame, education, teaching and art.

That's why when Giuliana and Anitha asked me to write the foreword to the Book, i accepted with great pleasure and without hesitation. I am deeply honored.

This book is a concentration of scientific information, research and valuable data that allow the reader to get a realistic and current overview of immersive technologies and their present and future potential, in particular in the evolution of educational, artistic and museum environments and systems .

Each chapter of the book is full of data, studies, analyzes, information on projects and research. From the application of immersive technologies to teaching up to museum systems, the book touches on related topics such as gamification, social media, best practices, digital aesthetics, digital itineraries, personal assistance, neuroscience, the use of symbols and much more. This Book is a great and interesting work.

With this Book it is really possible to enrich the knowledge and understand those which can become real strategic levers of human growth and development that the most aware and young generations can catch today and immediately.

As Archimede also said:

Give me a lever and I can lift the World

Enjoy reading

Nicola Bandoni
VR Land, Italy

Preface

The advances in Virtual and Augmented Reality have brought various changes in our day to activities. By using Virtual reality (VR) an artificial environment is created with software and presented to the user in such a way that the user feels it as a real environment. VR is capable of creating sensory experiences like sight, touch, hearing, and smell. VR presents a complete 3-Dimensional virtual representation of the actual world or of objects within it. Software like AutoCAD allows architects, engineers, and design professionals to create precisely 3-D drawings of actual buildings before they make changes to them. Well-known companies like Walmart, Chipotle and Verizon are now using VR as a tool to train for potentially dangerous situations like armed robberies, a dangerous scenario that could be difficult to imagine (https://gcn.com/articles/2019/07/24/vr-active-shooter-training.aspx). Virtual 360-degree tours enable people to visit faraway sites. The website of the Metropolitan Museum of Art (the Met) in New York, gives visitors a virtual tour of the works of van Gogh and di Bondone. Of late it is noticed that VR museums have become a hot topic in the art world. Museum curators realized the ability of VR to immerse visitors and many museums have created virtual reality programs to share their collections across the globe. VR is also widely used in the Education sector to teach various subjects at all levels. VR can be used in Healthcare for Training Medical Practitioners, Reduce Stress and Pain, Counseling, Cognitive Rehabilitation and Physical Therapy (Pillai & Matthew, 1970). VR can also be used in medical fields like Dentistry, Autism, Mental Health and Surgery, rehabilitation. Conventional MRI or CT scans can reveal only very little information about what a patient's brain looks like, but when those images are fed into VR technology, surgeons can see the brain—all the ridges and fissures, lobes, and veins—in 3D, so they can simulate surgery before stepping into the operating room (https://fortune.com/2019/01/09/virtual-reality-surgery-operating-room/?xid=gn_editorspicks). Different organizations, researchers and educators have been involved in the study and realization of VR solutions to be used as therapy, training, and support for individuals with Autism (Guazzaroni & Pillai, 2019). According to Guazzaroni and Pillai (2019) previous researches and experiments showed that it is possible to ameliorate the level of concentration, coordination, socialization, communication, self-awareness, and memory in school children treated with these tools and VR environments may offer a total physical involvement of the Autism Spectrum Disorders that may see the world through virtual immersion and active practice. The University of Alberta has created an educational App known as Cell 101 VR app to give cell biology students a virtual reality perspective of the inner workings of cells and their interactions, allowing them to visualize cell biology in a way they never could before. Students can get a clear understanding of the cell and its functions by rotating the components and view them from different angles (https://www.folio.ca/vr-app-gives-medical-students-a-new-way-to-see-inner-workings-of-cells).

On the other hand Augmented reality (AR) is a direct or indirect live view of a physical, real-world environment whose elements are augmented by computer-generated sensory input such as sound, video, graphics or GPS data (Grier et al., 2012). AR refers to the integration of the actual world with digital information about it. Actual objects and people cast an information shadow: an aura of data which, when captured and processed intelligently, can offer extraordinary value to consumers (O'Reilly & Battelle, 2009). AR can be used by museums to help the visitors, in particular, those with sensory impairments or learning disabilities. ARs the result of using technology to superimpose information - sounds, images, and text - on the world we see (https://www.indiatoday.in/education-today/featurephilia/story/role-of-augmented-virtual-reality-in-education-1417739-2018-12-67). One of the most popular ways AR has infiltrated everyday life is through mobile games. In 2016, the AR game 'Pokémon Go' became a sensation worldwide, with over 100 million estimated users at its peak, according to CNET and it ended up making more than two billion USD and counting, according to Forbes (https://www.indiatoday.in/education-today/featurephilia/story/role-of-augmented-virtual-reality-in-education-1417739-2018-12-67).

The main difference between Virtual reality and Augmented reality is that VR creates a totally simulated environment whereas AR uses the prevailing environment and enhances new information on top of it. AR and VR can be used in many areas like: Medicine, Navigation, Education and Training, Real Estate, Retail, Art, Museums etc. to name a few.

AR and VR technologies coupled with Internet of Things and Artificial intelligence have infinite potential in various sectors listed above. Virtual reality, augmented reality and Artificial Intelligence is increasingly being used today by more and more Educational institutions, Tourism industries, Museums, Art galleries, Manufacturing and Healthcare sectors worldwide. In near future schools, museums and art galleries, Universities, healthcare etc. will need to change outmoded ways of working and conventional thought processes to fully embrace the potential of artificial intelligence, virtual reality, mixed reality and augmented reality facilities. There are many subsets of Artificial Intelligence research, ranging from speech recognition and natural language understanding to machine learning and deep learning essential to business analytics and systems designed to make sense of big data. Museums have long dealt with virtual and augmented reality in their exhibitions, such as experiential tours. The consequence is that technology has opened up new possibilities for learners/users who are eager to have a part in shaping the museum-going experience. Many cultural tourism sites such as art galleries, museum or cultural heritage sites have discovered AR and VR in the past few years. They have enhanced their visitor experiences with innovations ranging from virtual enhancements to re-live historical sites and events, engage with content in museums, or to visit remote destinations in virtual environments (Han, Weber, Bastiannsen, Mitas, & Lub, 2018). Thirty-five major art museums in France cooperated in the project eMotion to animate art exhibitions and let the visitor travel around the world (Han, Weber, Bastiannsen, Mitas, & Lub, 2018). Animated characters come to life in a symbiosis of photo, art, and digital animation to tell stories and let the visitor explore the virtual world (De Paola, 2018). Commercial projects often aim at engaging potential visitors in the pre-travel phase to trigger their interest. Microsoft's HoloMaps and HoloTour, for instance, use 360-degree video content and spatial sound to encourage the user to move around the CG-augmented places such as Machu Picchu or the Colosseum in Rome without traveling to the actual location. Although virtual and augmented reality is receiving increasing attention in tourism and cultural heritage, the effect of mixed reality on museum visitors' experience has still not been fully answered, and research on this topic is still in its infancy (https://www.indiatoday.in/education-today/featurephilia/story/role-of-augmented-virtual-reality-in-education-1417739-2018-12-67). Many Museums across the globe are using VR to give life to their exhibits. The Peterson Automotive Museum in

Los Angeles used Microsoft HoloLens in 2017 to create excellent VR experience by letting the visitors interact with a classic American sports car, the Ford GT40. The HoloLens allowed visitors to see the car up close, alongside a modern 2017 Ford GT for comparison (https://www.museumnext.com/article/how-museums-are-using-virtual-reality/). Some of the limiting factors in using VR is cost. VR Design and management or VR programs can be very costly and depending on the size of the project. The larger the size, costs also increase. Another challenge is how to maintain the cleanliness of headset when multiple people use it?

Classroom teaching/learning is embracing new technologies like AI, VR, AR and progressing at an unprecedented rate. The subject area includes the use of augmented reality, virtual reality, mixed reality and artificial intelligence in education (e.g. schools, professional training, etc.), museums or art galleries. Mobile phones and tablets offer the possibility of interacting and staying fluidly connected to the mobile Internet. The consequence is that mobile Internet may facilitate the development and the popularity of informal learning environments (e.g. in museums or galleries). Especially, teenagers and young adults have adopted a new mobile culture and have been identified as "archetypal mobile superusers" (Ling, 2004). In fact, the mobile is not seen as a mere device to phone, but a social instrument to stay always connected with the network. (Bressler, 2006). Nowadays, social media are no longer seen as an autonomous space from material reality. They may be seen as a place of collective action, in urban and nonurban areas and, in particular, during the gathering, that transforms an aggregate of individuals in a collective actor. Social media are tools for a "choreography of the gathering". In the future, the experiences that make some use of augmented reality, virtual reality, robots, wearable technologies, and creativity will be more and more diffused. The practice of mobile Internet will lead to more and more people to connect in the streets and to enact the new urban ritual. Moreover, memories and digital storytelling will be increasingly used to build rich experiences for citizens, students or tourists as demonstrated by the challenges posed by the new smart cities, and its inhabitants' needs of different narrations.

This book has chapters relating to the use of VR and AR in Education, Art, Museums and case studies mentioning how / where they were implemented, mentioning the various methodologies, software, and hardware used. Researchers will be able to identify research problems to enhance the user experiences in education, art or museums. Computer professionals and scientist would also find the book useful in exploring new areas. The main advantage of this book is that it is not limited to a subset of people – Anyone who is interested in learning about VR / AR and its application will find the book useful. Education sector can improve the teaching-learning process by incorporating these new technologies in the way classes are being conducted. Healthcare sector can harness the benefits in medicine, surgery, dentistry, nursing, etc. Some of the existing applications are mentioned in the chapters so that the readers understand the benefit of using these innovative methods. It will be a boon for the art and museum curators as they get to know how these technologies have been used to attract large audience. Many of us even get to understand some of the museums, educational institutions, hospitals, etc. where these technologies are currently being used.

ORGANIZATION OF THE BOOK

The book is organized into three sections. The first section comprises papers related to VR and AR in Education, the second section is Chapters related to Art and Museum and the third section presents Case Studies regarding the application of VR and AR. A brief description of each of the chapters follows:

Section 1: Virtual and Augmented Reality in Education

Chapter 1, "Design Models for Developing Educational Virtual Reality Environments," aims to make a systematic review of design models developed in accordance with the process of designing virtual reality environments. Authors feel that this review may serve as a resource that can help the researchers in selecting the most suitable design model for an educational environment making use of virtual reality technology or even develop a new design model. In-Depth literature the review was made, and design models that were included in the findings section were separated according to their themes and codes established as a result of content analysis.

Chapter 2, "Role of Immersive (XR) Technologies in Improving Healthcare Competencies: A Review," discusses the use of Immersive Technology in medical education. As Immersive technology is becoming more affordable, user-friendly, pervasive and ubiquitous, it's been adopted and embraced by several industries. This paper focuses on uses, benefits and adoption challenges of Immersive technologies with specific reference to healthcare training.

Chapter 3, "Nursing Education in the Era of Virtual Reality," discusses the use of VR to improve the combination of cognitive, affective, and psychomotor learning domains. Authors feel that traditional teaching methods may not meet all of the Y and Z generations' learning needs since today's learners are accustomed to multimedia learning environments and have come to expect a certain level of technology integrated into their curricula. This chapter presents some of the many facets of VR that can be seen in today's nursing education.

Chapter 4, "Constructing Virtual Radio Center: Virtual Platforms," is about the virtual radio center construction necessities, usefulness and its adaptability to real life and to our courses. According to the author, many educators support the view that virtual reality will give learners an opportunity to experience environments which, for reasons of time, distance, scale, and safety, would not otherwise be available and having a virtual radio center in a university is sure to take lots of students' attraction.

Chapter 5, "Gamification: To Engage Is to Learn," discusses Gamification and video games, and analyzing their peculiarities. After a brief historical introduction to the disciplines that intertwine the design of Gamification applications, such as User interaction, User Interface and Game Design, authors analyze the real areas in which Gamification can be applied with verifiable results, citing scientific studies and examples of applications.

Chapter 6, "Ubiquitous Self: From Self-Portrait to Selfie," discusses selfie as a complex form of social interaction, an emerging aesthetics, thus having an irrevocable impact on self-portraiture. All visual culture revolves around the body and the body par excellence is the face. According to the author the 21st century portrait represents a kind of black mirror where we project ourselves into a kind of blindness and the face-mask melts in between Real and Virtual and the self becomes augmented.

Section 2: Virtual and Augmented Reality in Art and Museums

Chapter 7, "Reinventing Museums in the 21st Century: Implementing Augmented Reality and Virtual Reality Technologies Alongside Social Media's Logics," address talks about how forthcoming Industry 4.0 is expected to change not only the manufacturing and industrial services, also how it will rearrange how services are offered in a variety of sectors, including museum's services. Museums will inventible be led to more digital (VR & AR) and promoting (Social Media) paths. The authors feel that the forthcoming "digital convergence" between VR & AR technologies and social media are promoting logic could enlarge museums potentialities in attracting more visitors, younger visitors, while new patterns for connecting learning effects and amusement should be established.

Chapter 8, "Employing Digital Reality Technologies in Art Exhibitions and Museums," uses a case study approach to discussing the current state of digital reality technology applications in museums and art exhibitions around the world. The study provides several best practice examples to demonstrate how digital reality technologies have fundamentally transformed the art exhibitions and museums.

Chapter 9, "Challenges of Mobile Augmented Reality in Museums and Art Galleries for Visitors Suffering from Vision, Speech, and Learning Disabilities," highlights the learning facilities and methods of keeping the visitors engaged in public art exhibitions, Museums, and holiday tourist locations. This chapter aims at the major design elements of Mobile Augmented Reality (M.A.R.) at museums, art galleries, and highlights all the challenges faced by visitors suffering from visual, speech, and Learning Disorders. The research discusses the eleven vital elements which include Usability, Design, Motivation, Interaction, Perceived control, Satisfaction, Attention, and others of engagement of M.A.R. necessary for building an effective M.A.R. application for differently-abled people.

Chapter 10, "Role of Emotions in Interactive Museum: How Art and Virtual Reality Affect Emotions," discusses how VR, AR and artificial intelligence (AI) are increasingly being used by educational institutions and museums worldwide. According to the author digital technologies may allow forms of hybridization between flesh and technological objects within virtual or real spaces.

Chapter 11, "Digit(al)isation in Museums: Civitas Project – AR, VR, Multisensorial, and Multiuser Experiences at the Urbino's Ducal Palace," presents the main first results from CIVITAS (chain for the excellence of reflective societies to exploit digital cultural heritage and museums). The chapter talks about the project developed using virtual/augmented environments, through the multisensorial interaction with virtual artworks, in order to satisfy needs and overcome limitations in a larger CH scenario, applying a bottom-up approach.

Chapter 12, "Evaluating Augmented and Virtual Reality in Education Through a User-Centered Comparative Study: SmartMarca Project," focuses on assessing the potential of AR/VR applications specifically designed for cultural heritage. Tests have been conducted on classrooms of teenagers to whom different learning approaches served as an evaluation method about the effectiveness of using these technologies for the education process. The chapter will even argue on the necessity of developing new tools to enable users to become producers of contents of AR/VR experiences.

Section 3: Virtual and Augmented Reality in Education, Art, and Museums – Case Studies

In Chapter 13, "Employing Real-Time Game Technology for Immersive Experience (VR and Video-games) for All at MAIO Museum: Museum of WWII Stolen Artwork," the authors present the potential of these technologies for the development of edutainment content for their visitors at MAIO - Museum of Art Taken Hostage in Cassina de' Pecchi (Milan). The Museum presents the story of 1623 masterpieces such as Michelangelo, Tiziano, Raffaello and Canaletto that were stolen in Italy during World War II and never found again.

Chapter 14, "Through Achille Castiglioni's Eyes: Two Immersive Virtual Experiences," described concern the virtualization of the Studio Museo Achille Castiglioni, a small museum that hosts important artifacts designed by one of the most famous architects and designers of the twentieth century, winner of 7 "Compasso d'Or" awards. The digitization process aims at creating two virtual experiences. The first (less complex and immersive) experimentation deals with the semantic implementation of 360° panoramic photographs, giving rise to a virtual tour of the museum available on the web with no interaction: and the second one (a real VR simulation) derives from a more complex workflow based on digital surveying, digital modeling, developing virtual environments and interactions.

Chapter 15, "Where Is Hanuman? Hindu Mythology, Transmigration, and Design Process of Immersive Experiences in Museums," presents the interpretative strategies used by designers of an immersive environment on Hindu mythology and Hampi, an archaeological site in India, and their own knowledge of Hindu deities and their attributes. The paper uses concepts and theories from different disciplines (iconology, hermeneutics, design research, museums studies, etc.) with the aim to describe, deconstruct and understand the design choices.

Chapter 16, "An Augmented Reality (AR) Experience for Lorenzo Lotto," explores three interactive works realized with Unreal Engine 4 to give the spectator a greater immersiveness on the immortal pictures of Lorenzo Lotto. The goal was achieved by creating three choreographies with audio supervised by a historian, recreation of the works with three-dimensional graphics and a specially composed soundtrack by Tecla Zorzi. The Augmented reality (AR) application was realized specifically for Android tablets.

The book comprises of 16 chapters detailing the use of AR and VR in Education, Art, and Museums. The chapters are written by experts across the globe. This is an essential research book that explores the strategic role and use of VR and AR in shaping visitor experiences at art galleries and museums and their ability to enhance education. Highlighting a range of topics such as online learning, digital heritage, and gaming. This book is ideal for museum directors, tour developers, educational software designers, 3D artists, designers, curators, preservationists, conservationists, education coordinators, academicians, researchers, and students.

REFERENCES

De Paola, F. (2018). La destination France s'anime en realite augmentee [Online]. Retrieved from https://www.lechotouristique.com/article/la-france-se-montre-en-realite-augmentee

Grier, R. A., Thiruvengada, H., Ellis, S. R., Havig, P., Hale, K. S., & Hollands, J. G. (2012). Augmented reality—implications toward virtual reality, human perception, and performance. *PsycEXTRA*.

Guazzaroni, G., & Pillai, A. S. (2019, Jan. 1). *Virtual reality (VR) for school children with autism spectrum disorder (ASD): A way of rethinking teaching and learning*. Retrieved from https://www.igi-global.com/chapter/virtual-reality-vr-for-school-children-with-autism-spectrum-disorder-asd/215827

Han, D., Weber, J., Bastiaansen, M., Mitas, O., & Lub, X. (2018). Virtual and augmented reality technologies to enhance the visitor experience in cultural tourism. In M. Claudia, T. Dieck, & T. Jung (Eds.), The power of augmented and virtual reality for business. Springer.

Pillai, A. S., & Mathew, P. S. (1970, Jan. 1). *Impact of virtual reality in healthcare: a review*. Retrieved from https://www.igi-global.com/chapter/impact-of-virtual-reality-in-healthcare/215819

Acknowledgment

We wish to thank all the authors for having shared their precious research, work and experiences.

We wish to express sincere thanks to all the Editorial Advisory Board members.

We also thank all the reviewers who prepared accurate evaluations of the chapters and helped us with their constructive reviews.

Finally, a very special thank you goes to our families and friends for their loving encouragement to complete this work.

Giuliana Guazzaroni

Anitha S. Pillai

Section 1
Virtual and Augumented Reality in Education

Chapter 1
Design Models for Developing Educational Virtual Reality Environments:
A Systematic Review

Ali Geris
https://orcid.org/0000-0003-2136-5490
Manisa Celal Bayar University, Turkey

Nesrin Özdener
Marmara University, Turkey

ABSTRACT

Virtual reality, although not a new technology, has rapidly increased its popularity in the last few years. As a result, their use in educational environments has been a topic of interest in academic research. One of the first questions asked by education researchers has been, "How can we design an effective virtual reality environment?", which led to the development of many design models for the preparation of educational virtual reality environments based on various approaches. These design models have been systematically examined in terms of themes and codes within this study, in hopes this chapter may be of importance for guiding researchers who want to design an educational virtual reality environment or create a design model.

INTRODUCTION

The concept of virtual reality can be broadly defined as the ability of a user to perceive and interact with a real-world environment in a three-dimensional simulation on the computer with particular technologies that the user wears on his body (Freina & Ott, 2015; Neguţ, Matu, Sava, & David, 2016). Recently, educational research has shown an increased interest in virtual reality technology because of its ability to simulate real-world conditions. According to Fowler (2015), virtual reality technology is among the

DOI: 10.4018/978-1-7998-1796-3.ch001

Copyright © 2020, IGI Global. Copying or distributing in print or electronic forms without written permission of IGI Global is prohibited.

most promising up-to-date technologies in terms of potential for being effectively used in education and training activities. As a matter of fact, the advantage of using virtual reality environments in education has been noticed by numerous researchers and many studies have been carried out.

Monahan, McArdle, and Bertolotto (2008) point out that students can feel good about the presence of their classmates and teachers in a virtual reality environment; where they receive immediate feedback and have the opportunity to live in the same environment with their friends even though they are not physically in the same environment. According to Goodwin, Wiltshire, and Fiore (2015), virtual reality environments offer educational and experiential opportunities that can positively affect learners. In their study Freina and Ott (2015) identify some advantages of virtual reality as the ability to safely engage in real-world activities that involve risk, or the ability to experience situations that are physically inaccessible or that require high costs. The general conclusions obtained from research on the use of virtual reality in learning environments by different researchers can be listed as follows:

i. Virtual reality supports peer cooperative learning (Huang, Rauch, & Liaw, 2010)
ii. Virtual reality develops the ability of learners to solve problems and discover new concepts (Huang et al., 2010; Leite, Svinicki, & Shi, 2010),
iii. Virtual reality increases student motivation (Freina & Ott, 2015; Limniou, Roberts, & Papadopoulos, 2008; Ott & Tavella, 2009),
iv. Virtual reality offers a high level of interaction (Chittaro & Ranon, 2007; Lau & Lee, 2015)
v. Virtual reality enables learners to gain knowledge with less effort than traditional learning environments (Chittaro & Ranon, 2007),
vi. Virtual reality makes teaching processes more realistic and secure (Brasil et al., 2011; Dalgarno, Hedberg, & Harper, 2002; Johnson & Levine, 2008).

A fundamental aspect of educational virtual reality environments is their design phase, wherein practitioners strive to achieve the goal of enabling training in virtual reality environments that can be at least as effective as face-to-face education (Beaumont, Savin-Baden, Conradi, & Poulton, 2014). C. H. Chen, Yang, Shen, and Jeng (2007) have asked the question "What is the right model and theory that can be used to design virtual reality learning environments suitable for individuals." Chuah, Chen, and Teh (2011) argues that the development of virtual reality environments is a challenging process that requires accurate planning and design, pointing out that traditional instructional design models do not have the components and methods appropriate for current technologies. Similarly, Goodwin et al. (2015) claim that it is difficult to apply traditional teaching methods and strategies in virtual reality environments.

Hanson and Shelton (2008), who started with the question "How can I design an environment to teach what I am trying to teach on," suggest that in the process of designing virtual reality environments, the first step is to determine learning objectives. On the other hand, Grajewskia, Górskia, Hamrola, and Zawadzkia (2015) points out that virtual reality environments have a different structure than other computer simulations and that the greatest of these differences is the peripherals used. Also, many researchers have stated that realistic objects and avatar structures have an essential role in the effectiveness of virtual reality environments. (Ahmad, Wan, & Jiang, 2011; Dalgarno & Lee, 2010; Jong, Shang, Lee, & Lee, 2010).

Because of all that has been mentioned so far, it can be seen that researchers have different perspectives on the design of educational virtual reality environments. This chapter aims to make a systematic review of design models developed in accordance with the process of designing virtual reality environments. It is hoped that this review may serve as a resource that can help the researchers in selecting the most suitable design model for an educational environment making use of virtual reality technology or even develop a new design model. In this context, an in-depth literature review was made, and design models that were included in the findings section were separated according to their themes and codes established as a result of content analysis. In the conclusions section, an evaluation of content analysis for the included design models has been made.

BACKGROUND

Virtual Reality

Nowadays, the educational activities in which learning and teaching activities are carried out at predetermined times and environments are replaced by three-dimensional virtual worlds designed to reflect the real world in which learning and teaching activities can be done independently of time and place. Three-dimensional (3D) virtual environments are defined as environments in which the real world environment can be simulated to a great extent and where participants can have the opportunity to interact with each other (Wang, Laffey, Xing, Ma, & Stichter, 2016). 3D environments can motivate learners by providing a safe and realistic experience to learners (Omale, Hung, Luetkehans, & Cooke-Plagwitz, 2009) and allow them to transfer what they have learned to real life (Wagner, 2008). Thanks to 3D environments, learners have the opportunity to apply their theoretical knowledge in the closest way to reality (Bulu, 2012). These simulation-based environments in which learners can experience more allow individuals to take a risk by developing critical thinking skills and support independent decision-making mechanisms. (Chow, 2016). As a result of the researches, the contributions of three-dimensional virtual environments to the learning-teaching process are as follows; (1) cooperative learning possibility, (2) visualization, (3) behavioral synthesis, (4) presence, containment, and learning, (5) simulation of high cost and hazardous activities (Bailenson et al., 2008). The concept of virtual reality has started to gain importance as a result of the contributions made by the three-dimensional virtual environments to the learning-teaching process and the sense of being provided for the learners and to increase the perception of reality.

The concept of virtual reality is defined as the fact that a real-world environment can be perceived and interacted in a three-dimensional simulation created on a computer by the help of special technologies that the user wear on his body (Freina & Ott, 2015; Neguţ et al., 2016). There are two types of the virtual reality approach that immersive and non-immersive according to the way of reflecting the real world (Figure 1). Non-immersive virtual reality, also called desktop virtual reality, is defined as three-dimensional virtual environments that can be interactively created using multimedia tools in computers, such as monitors, keyboards, mice, or joysticks. (C. J. Chen, Toh, & Fauzy, 2004; Gazit, Yair, & Chen, 2006). 3D games, simulations, and virtual worlds (SecondLife, etc.) can be given as examples of non-immersive virtual reality environments. Immersive virtual reality environments are defined as being in the real world by breaking away from the consciousness of time in three-dimensional virtual environments (Bailenson et al., 2008). Participants can experience intense emotion in their immersive virtual environment and feel psychologically as if they were in this environment. (Adams, 2004; Blascovich & Bailenson, 2005). This is defined as the feeling of presence and is the main characteristic of the surrounding virtual reality (Passig, Tzuriel, & Eshel-Kedmi, 2016; Yeditepe, 2015). In addition to these opportunities, virtual reality can be seen as a popular educational tool with the help of computer graphics that can be improved and updated (Chuah et al., 2011).

Figure 1. Immersive virtual reality

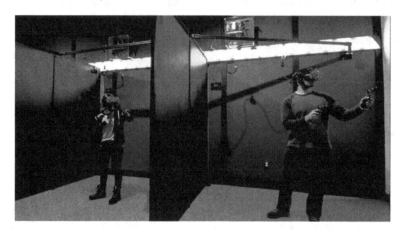

Virtual Reality in Education

Virtual reality, one of the most up-to-date technologies with the potential to be actively used in education and training activities (Fowler, 2015; Kavanagh, Luxton-Reilly, Wuensche, & Plimmer, 2017); it should be considered as a platform where teaching content can be presented regularly, with a high level of user interaction and a high level of presence (Osuagwu, Ihedigbo, & Ndigwe, 2015). As a matter of fact, these opportunities and potentials provided by virtual reality have been noticed by many educational institutions, and learning environments have started to be created on virtual worlds (Bulu, 2012; Chow, 2016; Minocha & Reeves, 2010). According to Lee and Wong (2014), there is a growing trend towards virtual reality-based education in schools and universities.

Many types of research emphasize that virtual reality makes important contributions to education. According to Goodwin et al. (2015), virtual reality teaching environments offer educational opportunities and experience opportunities that can positively affect learners. Monahan et al. (2008) stated that students, classmates, and teachers could feel the presence of students in a virtual reality environment, get instant feedback and have the opportunity to live in the same environment as their friends even though they are not physically in the same environment. It has been determined that problems such as mobility, inclusive perception, interaction, and spatial limitations that learners can live in three-dimensional virtual environments can be overcome in virtual reality environments. (Appelman, 2005). Freina and Ott (2015) also emphasized that it is important for learners to experience virtual reality, which is important in learning environments, in real environments and risk-related activities, enabling them to experience situations that are physically inaccessible or require high costs. The two main constraints of the physical world were revealed by researchers; the inability to have the opportunity to experience in the real environment due to distance, time, price or security and the difficulty of observing the limitless possibilities in the real environment can be overcome in virtual reality environments and these environments can support the development of learning. (Ramasundaram, Grunwald, Mangeot, Comerford, & Bliss, 2005). The general conclusions obtained from research on the use of virtual reality in learning environments by different researchers can be listed as follows: (i) virtual reality supports peer cooperative learning (Huang et al., 2010), (ii) virtual reality develops the ability of learners to solve problems and discover new concepts (Huang et al., 2010; Leite et al., 2010), (iii) virtual reality increases student

Figure 2. An instructional design framework for virtual reality environments (Chen et al., 2004)

motivation (Freina & Ott, 2015; Limniou et al., 2008; Ott & Tavella, 2009), (iv) virtual reality offers a high level of interaction (Chittaro & Ranon, 2007; Lau & Lee, 2015), (v) virtual reality enable learners to gain knowledge with less effort than traditional learning environments (Chittaro & Ranon, 2007), (vi) virtual reality make teaching processes more realistic and secure (Brasil et al., 2011; Dalgarno et al., 2002; Johnson & Levine, 2008).

Design Models for Virtual Reality Environments

Thanks to the benefits and facilities provided by the learners of virtual reality environments, there is another point in the face of increasing use in education. A fundamental aspect of educational virtual reality environments is their design phase, wherein practitioners strive to achieve the goal of enabling training in virtual reality environments that can be at least as effective as face-to-face education (Beaumont et al., 2014). Goodwin et al. (2015) stated that it is difficult to apply traditional teaching methods and strategies in virtual reality supported learning environments. Chuah et al. (2011) point out that virtual reality-based teaching environments are a challenging process that requires accurate planning and design, while traditional instructional design models do not have components that are up to date. These shortcomings in the process are thought to lead to the inability of researchers to determine effective experiences for students (Appelman, 2005). This situation brings to mind the question of what is the right model and theory that can be used for designing virtual learning environments suitable for individuals (C. Chen, 2007).

The researchers, who dealt with the correct design model and the theory that could be used in the design of three-dimensional virtual reality environments, pointed out different points. C. J. Chen et al. (2004) developed a model of Macro and Micro-strategies, based on the design of virtual reality environments based on Mayer's multimedia components and constructivist paradigm (Figure 2). As a micro-strategy, based on Mayer's principles of multimedia design, researchers have integrated macro strategies in addition to their micro-strategies in the form of integrative goals, objectives, enterprise scenarios, and supporting tools.

Appelman (2005) states that it is necessary to focus on the perception of the learner to examine the effectiveness of the method and teaching experienced in three-dimensional virtual reality environments. The experimental method, in which Appelman (2005) refers to the perception of the learner, rather than to a particular technology or methodology, provides a flexible approach to address the learner's perceptions in a way that is appropriate for each research. Within the scope of the experimental method, the main aim is not to stick to a model during the focusing of the design process, but to accurately control the learners' perceptions.

During their work on virtual reality, Hanson and Shelton (2008) first revised the analysis and design steps of the ADDIE instructional design model by the design-based research methodology. The researchers formed the initial stage of the design process with the questions they included under the steps of analysis and design. Then, in the light of the questions in this analysis and design step, the researchers who designed their environments discussed the design process in four stages. These stages are (1) determination of expectations, (2) familiarity with virtual reality, (3) evaluation of design factors, and (4) evaluation of necessary resources. The researchers based the design process on meeting the expectations of the learners and responding to these expectations. Researchers' approach to the design process focuses on the learner's perception similar to the experimental method of Appelman (2005).

Dalgarno and Lee (2010) identified several characteristics that should be considered in the design of virtual reality environments and provided a general framework for the design process. The researchers discussed the design process and the features that the design should have in terms of both technical and learner interaction. Although they discussed the design process from the perspective of the learner, Dalgarno and Lee (2010) also considered the process technically, unlike the previous researchers. Researchers, including the real image of the medium, fluency in moving objects, consistency of object behaviors, spatial sound, kinesthetic and tactile feedback, also recommend that attention to these components may be helpful in learning.

Goodwin et al. (2015) stated that the most important point for the design of virtual reality environments is that the human body can grasp the right equipment and provide the maximum level of learning. From this point of view, and by introducing a model based on cognitive science, researchers have looked at the design of virtual reality environments from another dimension. The researchers, who presented a five-stage design process consisting of analysis of instructional content, publication, and revision of teaching environment, implementation of teaching and analysis, evaluation and revision of teaching achievements, stated that each stage has different focal points. In these focal points, the researchers, who have also learned the learning dimension as well as the learning dimensions, have also included the technical aspects such as the determination of the tools, technology, and settings to be used, environment inclusiveness, artificial tutorials, and the possibility of active experience in the design process.

As seen in the literature review, the importance of using virtual reality environments in education increases day by day, and the answers to the questions about the right design process are discussed with different approaches.

DESIGN MODELS: THEMES AND CODES

Searching and Selection

The scope of the design process of virtual reality and educational virtual reality environments was determined before accessing the design models to cover within the scope of the chapter. Virtual reality environments have been considered as environments where the real-world environment can be simulated to a great extent within the three-dimensional space and participants can find the opportunity to interact with each other (Wang et al., 2016). In this context, design models have been identified as models that shed light on the design process of a three-dimensional educational virtual reality environment.

Table 1. Searching details

Keywords	Databases					
	Web of Science	Science Direct	Scopus	ERIC	IEEE Explore	CoHE Th. C.
Virtual Reality & Instruction	542	548	60	100	16	-
Virtual Reality & Model	984	1921	659	51	4	-
Virtual Reality & Designing	102	476	31	19	101	-
Virtual Reality & Design Model	10	45	3	3	2	-
Virtual Reality & Instructional Design	16	33	2	33	13	-
Virtual Reality	-	-	-	-	-	198

Figure 3. Determination of themes and codes

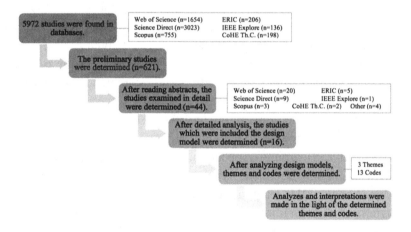

"Virtual Reality & Instruction", "Virtual Reality & Model", "Virtual Reality & Designing", "Virtual Reality & Design Model" and "Virtual Reality & Instructional Design" keywords were searched in the databases of "Web of Science", "Science Direct", "Scopus", "ERIC", "IEEE Explore" and "CoHE Thesis Center". As a result of the surveys conducted between 01.03.2018 - 31.05.2018, the studies which are open to access were examined.

The keywords' search was done on the titles and keywords of the studies. Abstracts of a total of 621 studies, which include all of the keywords, were examined. As a result of the abstract reviews made, it is determined that 44 studies are suitable for detailed analysis in terms of design models developed for virtual reality environments. After a detailed review of the 44 studies in which full texts were accessed, it was found that there was a model for the design of virtual reality environments in 16 studies. A summary of the process can be seen in Figure 3.

Themes and Codes

It is known that researchers have different perspectives for design models, and models are taken with different approaches. The fact that many different components influence the design process of virtual reality environments is one of the most important challenges for researchers. In order to properly manage the design process or create a design model, attention should be paid to multiple points. For this reason, in the scope of this chapter, themes, and codes that can shed light on the design process of virtual reality environments and new design models to be developed have been produced with the common aspects of the current design models and the contribution of literature.

Hanson and Shelton (2008) who started with the question "How can I design an environment to teach what I am trying to teach on," suggest that in the process of designing virtual reality environments, the first step is to determine learning objectives. Zhou, Ji, Xu, and Wang (2018) also stated that learning design, learning styles, learning activities, and learning outcomes would be appropriate in the design process. Other points to be considered in the design process are; problem state, scenario, learning styles, goals, activities, tasks, socialization, and evaluation. (Appelman, 2005; Dalgarno & Lee, 2010; Freitas, Rebolledo-Mendez, Liarokapis, Magoulas, & Poulovassilis, 2009; Goodwin et al., 2015; Pattanasith, Rampai, & Kanperm, 2015; Zhou et al., 2018). Many of these elements put forward by the researchers have found themselves in the educational models under the educational title. In this context, the first theme was named as the "Educational Framework". Within the scope of the educational framework; problem and objectives, scenario, learning, socialization, and evaluation are also identified as the codes of this theme.

According to Jonassen (1999), the problem in constructivist learning environments is of great importance to learners. Presenting a problem to learners in virtual reality environments as in real life and solving the problem is effective in learning. (Appelman, 2005; C. J. Chen, 2009). The fact that the objects and avatars in the environment have a realistic structure in the realization of the virtual reality environment has a share (Ahmad et al., 2011; Dalgarno & Lee, 2010; Jong et al., 2010). Besides, the fact that the virtual reality environment has an immersive structure and that the learner can break the connection with the real life is another important point (Dalgarno & Lee, 2010; Grajewskia et al., 2015; Hanson & Shelton, 2008). According to Dalgarno and Lee (2010), the design element defined as presence is the ability of the learner to capture a real-life sense in a virtual reality environment. Another important point in the interaction of the learner, who can capture the feeling of presence, with the virtual reality environment and objects (C. J. Chen, 2009; Grajewskia et al., 2015; Hanson & Shelton, 2008; Shih & Yang, 2008). These elements, which many researchers have dealt with, are usually in the design stage of the models studied. In this context, the second theme is named as "Design Framework". Within the scope of the educational framework; authenticity, immersion, presence, fidelity, and interaction are also identified as the codes of this theme.

Grajewskia et al. (2015) stated that virtual reality environments have a different structure than other computer simulations and that the largest of these differences are due to the peripherals used. The hardware components used to take part in virtual reality environments are also important for the effectiveness of the environment. At the same time, modeling techniques, object behaviors, object properties, and programming infrastructure to be used are also factors affecting the effectiveness of the environment (C. J. Chen, 2009; Dalgarno & Lee, 2010; Grajewskia et al., 2015). In the studies examined, it has been determined that the items in question are generally included in the topics where the technical infrastructures of virtual reality environments are discussed. In this context, the third theme is named

Table 2. Themes and codes

Themes	Codes	References
Educational Framework	Problem and objectives	Appelman (2005), Hanson and Shelton (2008), Freitas et al. (2009), Dalgarno and Lee (2010), Goodwin et al. (2015), Zhou et al. (2018).
	Scenario	
	Learning	
	Socialization	
	Evaluation	
Design Framework	Authenticity	Shih and Yang (2008), C. J. Chen (2009), Jong et al. (2010), Dalgarno and Lee (2010), Ahmad et al. (2011), Grajewskia et al. (2015).
	Immersion	
	Presence	
	Fidelity	
	Interaction	
Technical Framework	Peripheral devices	C. J. Chen (2009), Dalgarno and Lee (2010), Grajewskia et al. (2015).
	Modeling	
	Programming	

Table 3. Design models that have been educational framework themes and codes

Themes	Codes	Number of models with codes (%)	Number of models without codes (%)
Educational Framework	Problem and Objectives	14 (87,5%)	2 (12,5%)
	Scenario	11 (68,7%)	5 (31,3%)
	Learning	12 (75,0%)	4 (25,0%)
	Socialization	10 (62,5%)	6 (37,5%)
	Evaluation	9 (56,2%)	7 (43,8%)

"Technical Framework." Within the scope of the technical framework; peripheral devices, modeling, and programming are also identified as the codes of this theme. Three themes and thirteen codes identified in this chapter are given in Table 2.

The evaluations of the design models examined within the scope of this section based on the themes and codes given in Table 2 are explained under the theme headings.

Educational Framework

When the design models and literature prepared for the development of virtual reality environments are examined, it is possible to see that the educational framework has an important place in these models. However, it is not correct to say that the educational perspective is fully implemented in all models analyzed under this chapter. The results of the evaluation of the titles included in the educational steps of the studied design models are given in Table 3.

When Table 3 is examined, it is seen that the code which is primarily in the design models is problems and targets. Jonassen (1999) stated that a problem transferred from real life is effective in learning. The content of the problem, the presentation of the problem, and the application area of the problem are the basic elements that should be considered in the learning environments. The problems should be considered as the source of the skill desired in learning environments. Each learning environment is designed to solve a problem. For this reason, what the problem to be chosen is and what it aims to make learners gain is important. In this context, it is seen that most of the design models (14, 87.5%) developed for the virtual reality environments examined have included problems and objectives.

C. J. Chen (2009) stated that virtual reality environments provide the learner with the opportunity to easily discover the area of application of the problem, to interact with objects and to manipulate the problem as they wish, and to support the learner-centered approach. It is possible to be able to manipulate the problem in the learning environment and to be comprehended by the learner by a correct scenario. The effect of the problem presented in a complex scenario on learning may not be desirable (C. J. Chen, 2009). In this context, the number of models that include the scenario item evaluated within the educational framework from the examined design models is 11; 68,7%. This ratio shows that many models consider the scenario.

Based on the study of Bloom taxonomy, Zhou et al. (2018) stated that educational frameworks consist of learning objects, learning styles, learning activities, and tasks. Similarly, many researchers mentioned the importance of learning techniques, learning styles and learning activities in virtual reality environments (Ahmad et al., 2011; C. J. Chen, 2009; Dalgarno & Lee, 2010; Shih & Yang, 2008). Virtual reality environments offering various learning opportunities to learners such as; learning by experience (C. J. Chen, 2009; Dalgarno & Lee, 2010), self-directed learning (Shih & Yang, 2008; Zhou et al., 2018), learning by observing (Zhou et al., 2018), knowing and doing learning (Hanson & Shelton, 2008), building knowledge and sharing knowledge (Karaman & Özen, 2016; Shih & Yang, 2008). The fact that virtual reality environments allow many different learning experiences emerges as a reason for researchers to focus more on the design process. In this context, it was determined that 12; 75,0% of the studied design models had a step on learning.

The situation in which learners can interact with each other or with instructors in learning environments is examined under the heading of socialization (Figure 4). Karaman and Özen (2016) stated that it is a design step that the learners can interact with virtual profiles in virtual reality environments. Shih and Yang (2008) also stated that it is important for personal learners to cooperate and interact with each other, and that socialization will affect learning. Considering that social interactions support social learning and social learning can be provided in virtual reality environments, it is thought that it may be positive to include socialization in design models (Zhou et al., 2018). In this context, it is seen that 10; 62,5% of the design models examined included socialization.

The study of the effectiveness of education and the learning environment in a learning environment is another important point for researchers. The evaluation of virtual reality environments and education in these environments is also a prominent issue for researchers. Conducting usability studies and analyzing the virtual reality environment are the factors affecting learning effectiveness (C. J. Chen, 2009; Grajewskia et al., 2015). Activities such as feedback from learners, results of the evaluation of learner performances, validation studies, evaluation of conformity of design elements are some of the methods that can be used in examining the learning environment (C. J. Chen, 2009; Hanson & Shelton, 2008). Almost half (9; 56.2%) of the design models evaluated within the context of examining the learning

Figure 4. Individuals in a virtual reality environment

Table 4. Design models that have been designed framework themes and codes

Themes	Codes	Number of models with codes (%)	Number of models without codes (%)
Design Framework	Authenticity	8 (50,0%)	8 (50,0%)
	Immersion	8 (50,0%)	8 (50,0%)
	Presence	3 (18,7%)	13 (81,3%)
	Fidelity	6 (37,5%)	10 (62,5%)
	Interaction	14 (87,5%)	2 (12,5%)

environment and the effectiveness of the training in this environment have been identified as a remarkable point in terms of the fact that the ratio is not high enough.

Design Framework

One of the most important points in the development of a virtual reality-supported educational environment is the design stage. Questions such as which elements to be used during design, which design criteria to pay attention to are important for researchers. In this context, the conditions of the models analyzed within the scope of the design framework are presented in Table 4.

In the section of problems and objectives discussed within the scope of the educational framework, the importance of transferring problems from real life is mentioned. Authenticity comes to the fore in the stage of presenting the problems in a virtual reality environment (Figure 5). Authenticity is one of the most important features that virtual reality environments offer (Appelman, 2005; Dalgarno & Lee, 2010; Grajewskia et al., 2015; Shih & Yang, 2008). According to Dalgarno and Lee (2010), three-dimensional and high-quality models in virtual reality environments provide a realistic view and provide real-life flow to learners. This allows learners to increase their sense of living in a real-world environment (Hanson & Shelton, 2008) and provide more realistic learning opportunities (Ahmad et al., 2011). Considering

Figure 5. Authentic design

the importance of authenticity in virtual reality environments and the studies of researchers on these issues, it is one of the most important points to be considered in the design process. In this context, the authenticity step was examined within the scope of the design framework in the related models. However, only half of the design models (8; 50,0%) were found to have authenticity.

One of the most important features that distinguish virtual reality environments from other learning environments is that it can take the individual away from real life with the help of peripheral units and fully integrate it into the virtual environment. This allows the individual to fully experience the learning universe in the virtual reality environment (Appelman, 2005; Dalgarno & Lee, 2010; Grajewskia et al., 2015; Shih & Yang, 2008). The importance of this situation, which is called immersion, has been mentioned many times by researchers and found its place in the design models. The number of models with the immersion step was determined as 8; 50%.

Presence refers to the feeling of being in real life in a realistically designed virtual reality environment. While immersion is more of a feature provided by the environment and its peripherals, presence is a feeling that the individual lives in a virtual reality environment. The level of presence experienced by students in virtual reality environments is one of the factors affecting learning (Dalgarno & Lee, 2010; Hanson & Shelton, 2008). The sense of presence that a virtual reality environment gives to learners is one of the issues to be considered during the design phase, and this step has been found in only 3; 18,7% of the models.

Another feature of learning environments that are designed with realistic design elements, supported by virtual reality tools that provide proper immersion, and that fully reflect the sense of presence, is that it has a good level of fidelity. Fidelity means that a real problem presents realistic design elements and realistic learning experiences in real life. Even though the problems and design elements are realistic, the yields of training that cannot be provided properly may not be at the desired level. It can be said that learning environments designed in accordance with the original are more effective on the desired learning level (C. J. Chen, 2009; Dalgarno & Lee, 2010). It was determined that the fidelity step was present in 6; 37,5% of the design models.

The last step taken by the researchers within the scope of the design framework is the interaction. Unlike socialization, which is considered within the framework of the educational framework, when the interaction element is examined, it is seen that the basic point is the interaction of the learners with the

Table 5. Design models that have been technical framework themes and codes

Themes	Codes	Number of models with codes (%)	Number of models without codes (%)
Technical Framework	Peripherals	7 (43,8%)	9 (56,2%)
	Modelling	5 (31,2%)	11 (68,8%)
	Programming	5 (31,2%)	11 (68,8%)

objects in the virtual reality environment. The high level of interaction of the learners with the objects in the educational environment is among the factors that affect the learning positively (C. J. Chen, 2009; Grajewskia et al., 2015; Hanson & Shelton, 2008; Shih & Yang, 2008). The interaction step has been taken into account by many researchers and found a place in most of the design models. It was determined that 14; 87,5% of the design models examined had an interaction element.

Technical Framework

In the process of developing a virtual reality-supported educational environment, perhaps the most important step is the technical elements to be used technical factors such as peripherals, models, and programming elements to be used. During the implementation of virtual reality, the environment is the main factors affecting the efficiency of the educational environment. In this context, the current situation of the design models analyzed under the technical framework is given in Table 5.

The most important elements that will ensure that all steps and virtual reality environments discussed within the scope of the educational framework and design are effective are the peripherals. The primary necessary peripherals to experience the virtual reality environment are usually virtual reality glasses and Wearable Technologies. Grajewskia et al. (2015) stated that the peripherals which will be used in virtual reality environments have a great effect on the problem, scenario, and containment. In this context, design models were examined, and it was determined that the number of studies that touched on the importance of peripherals and integrated into the model was 7; 31,2%.

The object models to be used in the development of virtual reality environments and the programming infrastructure of the environment are also important in terms of learning scenes and stage flows. Similar to Dalgarno and Lee (2010), who emphasized the importance of realistic design and realistic scene flow, C. J. Chen (2009) also stated that the modeling phase and the programming stage affected the efficiency of the virtual reality environment. Although it is not appropriate for researchers to designate a complete modeling and programming technique for the design phase of virtual reality environments; it is important to consider these processes at the design stage, to determine the relevant techniques in advance and to determine the appropriate teams at the beginning of the process. In this context, the modeling and programming steps taken into consideration were determined in 5; 31,2% of the design models.

DISCUSSION AND CONCLUSION

In this section, a systematic review of the design models prepared for the development of virtual reality-supported educational environments was conducted. In the process of examining the design models, firstly the general information of the studies (year, model test status, development area), and then the common approaches in the models using the thematic analysis method are divided into themes and codes. As a result of the analyzes, the current situation of the design models was revealed, and remarkable results were obtained. An evaluation was made on the results examined under the previous title.

Although the use of virtual reality environments has increased in recent years, the simulations used in the military field in the 1960s are the first examples (Kavanagh et al., 2017). In later periods, especially in the 1990s, different institutions and companies worked on it, but virtual reality technologies made their main rise in the late nineties with the emergence of immersive units. After this period, the virtual reality technology, which attracted more attention of researchers, was tried in many areas. In this context, the basic question which the educators paid attention to is how to design an effective virtual reality environment. Many researchers have mentioned that traditional teaching models for an appropriate design may be inadequate (Appelman, 2005; C. H. Chen et al., 2007; Chuah et al., 2011; Goodwin et al., 2015). In order to design an effective virtual reality environment, researchers have tried to develop the right design model and have developed many models with different perspectives. Upon analyzing the years when these models were developed, it was determined that 7; 43,8% design model studies were carried out in the years 2005 – 2009, which were the first periods in which virtual reality technology entered educational environments. It is seen that the next jump was between 2015 – 2018 and 7; 43,8% models were put forward. This situation is thought to be due to the widespread use of virtual reality technologies and its increasing popularity in recent years (Fowler, 2015; Kavanagh et al., 2017).

After examining the distribution of design models according to years, investigations were made according to the scientific field, they were developed and whether the model was tested or not. Taçgın (2017) stated that first of all, the boundaries should be determined for the training to be given in a virtual reality environment, and pointed out to the design for which teaching. Although the design models examined were determined for educational environments, it was found out that the studies could be from different fields. Although most of the design models are studies conducted in the field of education or by educational researchers 12; 75.0%, 1; 6,0% study was conducted in the field of health and 3; 19,0% studies were conducted in the field of engineering. When the developed design models are examined within the scope of the study, we can see that the vast majority 12; 75,0% has been tested. As a result of both studies, it was determined that the researchers tested the virtual reality technology and made improvements with the interdisciplinary studies not only with the studies in the field of education. It is thought that this situation is due to the fact that virtual reality environments have the potential to be used in many different areas.

Firstly, codes were created within the scope of the educational framework, which is the first theme. When the problem and objective code, which is the first one of the codes formed based on the literature and design models, was examined, it was determined that most of the design models had this code. Considering that a problem transmitted from real life and appropriate targets for this problem are effective in learning (Appelman, 2005; C. J. Chen, 2009; Jonassen, 1999), it is important that most of the design models contain this step because the problems are the primary source of the skill required to be acquired in learning environments. It should not be forgotten that it is designed to solve a problem based on each learning environment. The scenario is the second code of the educational framework, but it is the step of how the problem is presented in the virtual reality environment. It should be kept in mind that the education environment, which is not designed with a correct scenario, may not provide the desired problems and objectives (C. J. Chen, 2009). Considering this situation, the importance of the scenario is increasing for designers. Another code dealt within the scope of the educational framework is learning. Learning code includes topics such as learning styles, learning activities, learning objects, and tasks. Many researchers emphasize the importance of the mentioned topics in virtual reality environments and teaching environments (Ahmad et al., 2011; C. J. Chen, 2009; Dalgarno & Lee, 2010; Shih & Yang, 2008). At the same time, this step increases the importance of virtual reality environments by providing learning opportunities to learners by learning by experience, self-directed learning, observing learning, knowing and doing learning, knowledge building (C. J. Chen, 2009; Dalgarno & Lee, 2010; Hanson & Shelton, 2008; Karaman & Özen, 2016; Zhou et al., 2018). As a result of the examinations conducted in this context, it is seen that the majority of the design models are expected to have a learning code and are considered to be a significant criterion. The ability of learners to work with each other in learning environments and their interaction with each other has a positive effect on learning (Karaman & Özen, 2016; Shih & Yang, 2008). Considering that socialization can be provided at an advanced level in virtual reality environments and socialization has a positive effect on learning, it is considered important to include the socialization code in the educational framework (Zhou et al., 2018). As in every learning environment, the evaluation of educational studies and the environment in virtual reality environments is one of the most important steps. Evaluation is a necessary study to examine both learning effectiveness and the efficiency of the environment. In this context, the researchers mentioned the diversity of the studies that can be done and stated that such activities as learner feedback, learner performance evaluation results, evaluation of conformity of design elements are the methods that can be used at this stage (C. J. Chen, 2009; Grajewskia et al., 2015; Hanson & Shelton, 2008). Considering the importance of evaluation and the variety of studies that can be applied, it is noteworthy that there are only half of the design models examined. It should be kept in mind that every educational environment and every design model can only be developed with adequate and accurate assessments.

When the design framework and codes, which are the second theme determined within the scope of this chapter, are examined, interesting results were encountered. Authenticity, the first code identified within the scope of the design framework, defines the transfer of the real-life environment to the virtual reality in the same way (Appelman, 2005; Dalgarno & Lee, 2010). Authenticity helps learners to live in a real-life environment and offers a more realistic learning opportunity (Ahmad et al., 2011; Hanson & Shelton, 2008). Considering the importance of authenticity by researchers and the effect on learning, it is also crucial that the design models contain this step. As a result of the analyzes, it is an important result that authenticity is found in half of the studied design models. It should not be forgotten that the realistic presentation of the problems chosen from real life in a virtual reality environment has a significant impact on learning. Immersion, which is the concept that enables individuals to fully experience the learning universe in virtual reality environments, (Grajewskia et al., 2015; Shih & Yang, 2008) is defined as the second code of the design framework. Immersion is one of the most important features provided by virtual reality environments. Because, with the immersion feature, the individual can be completely disconnected from real life and fully integrated into the virtual environment. This helps to fully experience the learning environment. The real world feeling that individuals live in virtual reality environments is defined as presence. The level of the presence experienced by learners in virtual reality environments is another factor affecting learning (Dalgarno & Lee, 2010; Hanson & Shelton, 2008). Considering that the feeling of presence can help the learner internalize the environment, it is thought that this situation should be taken into consideration during the design phase of the environment. The fourth code, which is determined as fidelity, is the fact that the elements and problems in virtual reality environments can behave in real life. If authenticity can be summarized as the design of all the design elements as one-to-one, the fidelity can be defined as ensuring that all of the activities that may occur during the presentation of these elements and problems can be experienced in real life. According to C. J. Chen (2009), fidelity is one of the features that virtual reality environments must provide in order to provide learning at the desired level. Similarly, Dalgarno and Lee (2010) pointed out the importance of fidelity. The interaction of learners with objects in the virtual reality environment is different from socialization. The interaction under the design framework examines the individual - object relationship rather than the individual - individual relationship. Many researchers stated that a high level of interaction with objects in learning environments positively affects learning. (C. J. Chen, 2009; Grajewskia et al., 2015; Hanson & Shelton, 2008; Shih & Yang, 2008). In the scope of this chapter, the analysis of the interaction status was also conducted in the design models examined. As a result of the analyzes, it was found that the majority of the models included the interaction element, and this was seen as a positive result. It should be kept in mind that increasing the level of interaction of learners with objects positively affects learning.

Within the scope of the third theme, which is called the technical framework, firstly the identified code was the peripheral units. Peripherals are the means by which the learner can enter the educational environment prepared within the framework of educational and design frameworks. Grajewskia et al. (2015) stated that the peripherals to be used have a significant effect on educational virtual reality environments. Failure to identify the right peripherals and ignore the impact on the educational environment will be one of the greatest mistakes researchers can make. Modeling and programming codes do not state which modeling techniques and programming languages should be used in virtual reality environments. The main objective of these two codes is to address modeling and programming at the very beginning of the design phase, to select the appropriate methods and to determine the appropriate teams. Considering the importance of realistic design and stage flow (Dalgarno & Lee, 2010), modeling and programming steps are also factors affecting this situation (C. J. Chen, 2009). Therefore, it is considered important to include these codes at the beginning of the design process or in the design model.

CONCLUDING REMARK

In this chapter, a systematic review of the design models prepared with the content analysis method for the development of educational virtual reality environments was made by the themes and codes created in the light of the literature. The results of the analyzes and evaluations can be summarized as follows:

The first result of a systematic review of design models is that the majority of the studies on design models have been realized in the early periods of the emergence of virtual reality environments and in the last period when the peripheral units became widespread. These periodic increases show that the tools used in virtual reality environments and their costs are important for researchers. According to the first findings, it is the case that only educators are not involved in the development of design models. The existence of design models developed through studies in the field of health and engineering is possible through interdisciplinary studies. Similar to this positive result, the fact that most of the developed design models were tested within the scope of the research was an important point.

The analysis of three themes and thirteen codes identified within the context of thematic content analysis resulted in both positive and negative results. As a result of the analyzes made within the context of the educational framework, it is possible to say that the researchers gave the most importance to this step. It is an important result that even the lowest rate level is at least half of the design models. Especially the learning and problem codes in the models examined were the two most important steps of the researchers. Within the scope of the design framework, the most important point that researchers take into consideration is the interaction stage. In contrast to the interaction step in almost every model, it is remarkable that other important points, such as authenticity, presence, and fidelity, remain at meager rates. It can be said that this situation is due to the lack of a holistic approach to the design framework. The technical framework was the least considered step among the design models. Technical framework in one-third of the models and the codes of this framework is actually as important as the other two themes. The reason for this importance is that the elements within the technical framework are the basis for the creation and effective use of educational virtual reality environments.

As a result, it can be seen that the majority of the steps involved in the design models of virtual reality environments are based on Mayer's multimedia design components. However, the main point that separates the virtual reality environment from other multimedia elements is that the environment can be experienced by encircling units from the real world. At this point, it is of great importance to use the peripheral devices, the appropriate platform for these peripherals, the right design, and coding elements to develop the environment.

FUTURE RESEARCH DIRECTIONS

In future studies, it is recommended to pay attention to the themes and codes examined in detail in this chapter at the stage of selecting the most suitable design model for training in a virtual reality environment or during the development of a new design model. Considering that all of the themes and codes that are identified are created in the light of the literature, it should be taken into consideration that designing virtual reality environments with many different directions is a challenging process. It is recommended to pay particular attention to the codes specified in the educational framework. Besides, the authenticity, presence, and interaction steps in the design framework have an important place. However, attention to the right technical framework is important for the management of the process. It should not be forgotten that focusing only on the educational framework or design elements in the educational environment to be developed will not be effective unless the right technical framework is determined. It is the most important advice that can be given to the researchers to pay attention to all these themes and codes which are mentioned separately.

REFERENCES

Adams, E., (2004). Postmodernism and the three types of immersion. *Gamasutra: The art & business of making games, 9.*

Ahmad, N. S. H. N., Wan, D. T. R., & Jiang, P. (2011). Health course module in virtual world. *Procedia Computer Science, 3*, 1454–1463. doi:10.1016/j.procs.2011.01.031

Appelman, R. (2005). Designing experiential modes: A key focus for immersive learning environments. *TechTrends, 49*(3), 64–74. doi:10.1007/BF02763648

Bailenson, J. N., Yee, N., Blascovich, J., Beall, A. C., Lundblad, N., & Jin, M. (2008). The use of immersive virtual reality in the learning sciences: Digital transformations of teachers, students, and social context. *Journal of the Learning Sciences, 17*(1), 102–141. doi:10.1080/10508400701793141

Beaumont, C., Savin-Baden, M., Conradi, E., & Poulton, T. (2014). Evaluating a second life problem-based learning (PBL) demonstrator project: What can we learn? *Interactive Learning Environments, 22*(1), 125–141. doi:10.1080/10494820.2011.641681

Blascovich, J., & Bailenson, J. (2005). Immersive virtual environments and education simulations. In P. Cohen & T. Rehberger (Eds.), *Virtual Decisions: Digital Simulations for Teaching Reasoning in the Social Sciences and Humanities.* Mahwah, New Jersey: Lawrence Earlbaum Associates, Inc.

Brasil, I. S., Neto, F. M. M., Chagas, J. F. S., de Lima, R. M., Souza, D. F. L., Bonates, M. F., & Dantas, A. (2011). *An intelligent agent-based virtual game for oil drilling operators training.* Paper presented at the 2011 XIII Symposium on Virtual Reality (SVR).

Bulu, S. T. (2012). Place presence, social presence, co-presence, and satisfaction in virtual worlds. *Computers & Education, 58*(1), 154–161. doi:10.1016/j.compedu.2011.08.024

Chen, C. (2007). Formative research on the instructional design process of virtual reality-based learning environments. *ICT: Providing choices for learners and learning. Proceedings ascilite Singapore*, 149-156.

Chen, C. H., Yang, J. C., Shen, S., & Jeng, M. C. (2007). A desktop virtual reality earth motion system in astronomy education. *Journal of Educational Technology & Society, 10*(3), 289–304.

Chen, C. J., (2009). Theoretical bases for using virtual reality in education. *Themes in Science and Technology Education* (Special Issue), 71-90.

Chen, C. J., Toh, S. C., & Fauzy, W. M. (2004). The theoretical framework for designing desktop, virtual reality-based learning environments. *Journal of Interactive Learning Research, 15*(2), 147.

Chittaro, L., & Ranon, R. (2007). Web3D technologies in learning, education, and training: Motivations, issues, opportunities. *Computers & Education, 49*(1), 3–18. doi:10.1016/j.compedu.2005.06.002

Chow, M. (2016). Determinants of presence in 3D virtual worlds: A structural equation modeling analysis. *Australasian Journal of Educational Technology, 32*(1). doi:10.14742/ajet.1939

Chuah, K.-M., Chen, C.-J., & Teh, C.-S. (2011). Designing a desktop virtual reality-based learning environment with emotional consideration. *Research & Practice in Technology Enhanced Learning, 6*(1).

Dalgarno, B., Hedberg, J., & Harper, B. (2002). The contribution of 3D environments to conceptual understanding. In 19th annual conference of the Australasian society for computers in learning in tertiary education, Winds of change in the sea of learning (pp. 1-10). Auckland, New Zealand: UNITEC Institute of Technology.

Dalgarno, B., & Lee, M. J. (2010). What are the learning affordances of 3-D virtual environments? *British Journal of Educational Technology*, *41*(1), 10–32. doi:10.1111/j.1467-8535.2009.01038.x

Fowler, C. (2015). Virtual reality and learning: Where is the pedagogy? *British Journal of Educational Technology*, *46*(2), 412–422. doi:10.1111/bjet.12135

Freina, L., & Ott, M. (2015). *A literature review on immersive virtual reality in education: state of the art and perspectives.* In The International Scientific Conference eLearning and Software for Education (Vol. 1, p. 133).

Freitas, S. d., Rebolledo-Mendez, G., Liarokapis, F., Magoulas, G., & Poulovassilis, A. (2009). Developing an evaluation methodology for immersive learning experiences in a virtual world. In *Proceedings of the Conference in Games and Virtual Worlds for Serious Applications.* 10.1109/VS-GAMES.2009.41

Gazit, E., Yair, Y., & Chen, D. (2006). The gain and pain in taking the pilot seat: Learning dynamics in a non-immersive virtual solar system. *Virtual Reality (Waltham Cross)*, *10*(3-4), 271–282. doi:10.100710055-006-0053-3

Goodwin, M. S., Wiltshire, T., & Fiore, S. M. (2015). Applying research in the cognitive sciences to the design and delivery of instruction in virtual reality learning environments. In *Proceedings of the International Conference on Virtual, Augmented and Mixed Reality.* 10.1007/978-3-319-21067-4_29

Grajewskia, D., Górskia, F., Hamrola, A., & Zawadzkia, P. (2015). Immersive and haptic educational simulations of assembly workplace conditions. *Procedia Computer Science*, *75*, 359–368. doi:10.1016/j.procs.2015.12.258

Hanson, K., & Shelton, B. E. (2008). Design and development of virtual reality: analysis of challenges faced by educators. *Journal of Educational Technology & Society*, *11*(1), 118–131.

Huang, H.-M., Rauch, U., & Liaw, S.-S. (2010). Investigating learners' attitudes toward virtual reality learning environments: Based on a constructivist approach. *Computers & Education*, *55*(3), 1171–1182. doi:10.1016/j.compedu.2010.05.014

Johnson, L. F., & Levine, A. H. (2008). Virtual worlds: Inherently immersive, highly social learning spaces. *Theory into Practice*, *47*(2), 161–170. doi:10.1080/00405840801992397

Jonassen, D. H. (1999). Designing constructivist learning environments. In C. M. Reigeluth (Ed.), Instructional-design theories and models: a new paradigm of instructional theory (Vol. 2, pp. 215-239). New Jersey: Lawrence Erlbaum Associates.

Jong, M. S. Y., Shang, J., Lee, F., & Lee, J. H. M. (2010). An evaluative study on VISOLE—virtual interactive student-oriented learning environment. *IEEE Transactions on Learning Technologies*, *3*(4), 307–318. doi:10.1109/TLT.2010.34

Karaman, M. K., & Özen, S. O. (2016). A survey of students' experiences on collaborative virtual learning activities based on the five-stage model. *Journal of Educational Technology & Society, 19*(3), 247–259.

Kavanagh, S., Luxton-Reilly, A., Wuensche, B., & Plimmer, B. (2017). A systematic review of virtual reality in education. *Themes in Science and Technology Education, 10*(2), 85–119.

Lau, K. W., & Lee, P. Y. (2015). The use of virtual reality for creating unusual environmental stimulation to motivate students to explore creative ideas. *Interactive Learning Environments, 23*(1), 3–18. do i:10.1080/10494820.2012.745426

Lee, E. A.-L., & Wong, K. W. (2014). Learning with desktop virtual reality: Low spatial ability learners are more positively affected. *Computers & Education, 79*, 49–58. doi:10.1016/j.compedu.2014.07.010

Leite, W. L., Svinicki, M., & Shi, Y. (2010). Attempted validation of the scores of the VARK: Learning styles inventory with multitrait–multimethod confirmatory factor analysis models. *Educational and Psychological Measurement, 70*(2), 323–339. doi:10.1177/0013164409344507

Limniou, M., Roberts, D., & Papadopoulos, N. (2008). Full immersive virtual environment CAVE TM in chemistry education. *Computers & Education, 51*(2), 584–593. doi:10.1016/j.compedu.2007.06.014

Minocha, S., & Reeves, A. J. (2010). Design of learning spaces in 3D virtual worlds: An empirical investigation of second life. *Learning, Media, and Technology, 35*(2), 111–137. doi:10.1080/1743988 4.2010.494419

Monahan, T., McArdle, G., & Bertolotto, M. (2008). Virtual reality for collaborative e-learning. *Computers & Education, 50*(4), 1339–1353. doi:10.1016/j.compedu.2006.12.008

Neguţ, A., Matu, S.-A., Sava, F. A., & David, D. (2016). Task difficulty of virtual reality-based assessment tools compared to classical paper-and-pencil or computerized measures: A meta-analytic approach. *Computers in Human Behavior, 54*, 414–424. doi:10.1016/j.chb.2015.08.029

Omale, N., Hung, W. C., Luetkehans, L., & Cooke-Plagwitz, J. (2009). Learning in 3-D multi-user virtual environments: Exploring the use of unique 3-D attributes for online problem-based learning. *British Journal of Educational Technology, 40*(3), 480–495. doi:10.1111/j.1467-8535.2009.00941.x

Osuagwu, O., Ihedigbo, C., & Ndigwe, C. (2015). Integrating virtual reality (VR) into traditional instructional design. *West African Journal of Industrial and Academic Research, 15*(1), 68–77.

Ott, M., & Tavella, M. (2009). A contribution to the understanding of what makes young students genuinely engaged in computer-based learning tasks. *Procedia: Social and Behavioral Sciences, 1*(1), 184–188. doi:10.1016/j.sbspro.2009.01.034

Passig, D., Tzuriel, D., & Eshel-Kedmi, G. (2016). Improving children's cognitive modifiability by dynamic assessment in 3D immersive virtual reality environments. *Computers & Education, 95*, 296–308. doi:10.1016/j.compedu.2016.01.009

Pattanasith, S., Rampai, N., & Kanperm, J. (2015). The development model of learning through virtual learning environments (VLEs) for graduate students, department of educational technology, faculty of education, Kasetsart University. *Social and Behavioral Sciences, 176*, 60–64.

Ramasundaram, V., Grunwald, S., Mangeot, A., Comerford, N. B., & Bliss, C. (2005). Development of an environmental virtual field laboratory. *Computers & Education*, *45*(1), 21–34. doi:10.1016/j.compedu.2004.03.002

Shih, Y.-C., & Yang, M.-T. (2008). A collaborative virtual environment for situated language learning using VEC3D. *Journal of Educational Technology & Society*, *11*(1), 56–58.

Taçgın, Z. (2017). Ameliyathanede Kullanılan Cerrahi Setlerin Öğretimine Yönelik Bir Sanal Gerçeklik Simülasyon Geliştirilmesi ve Test Edilmesi[Development and evaluation of a virtual reality simulation to teach surgical sets used in the operating room]. Doctoral Thesis, Marmara University.

Wagner, C. (2008). Learning experience with virtual worlds. *Journal of Information Systems Education*, *19*(3), 263.

Wang, X., Laffey, J., Xing, W., Ma, Y., & Stichter, J. (2016). Exploring embodied social presence of youth with Autism in a 3D collaborative virtual learning environment: A case study. *Computers in Human Behavior*, *55*, 310–321. doi:10.1016/j.chb.2015.09.006

Yeditepe, B. B. (2015). Digital games: Design requirements and player psychology. *AJIT-e*, *6*(19), 7–21. doi:10.5824/1309-1581.2015.2.001.x

Zhou, Y., Ji, S., Xu, T., & Wang, Z. (2018). Promoting knowledge construction: a model for using virtual reality interaction to enhance learning. *Procedia Computer Science*, *130*, 239–246. doi:10.1016/j.procs.2018.04.035

ADDITIONAL READING

Chen, C. J., Lau, S. Y., Chuah, K. M., & Teh, C. S. (2013). Group Usability Testing of Virtual Reality-based Learning Environments: A Modified Approach. *Social and Behavioral Sciences*, *97*(6), 691–699.

Chen, C. J., & Teh, C. S. (2013). Enhancing an instructional design model for virtual reality-based learning. *Australasian Journal of Educational Technology*, *29*(5). doi:10.14742/ajet.247

Chuah, K. M., Chen, C. J., & Teh, C. S. (2008). Incorporating Kansei Engineering in instructional design: Designing virtual reality based learning environments from a novel perspective. *Themes in Science and Technology Education*, *1*(1), 37–48.

Cochrane, T., Cook, S., Aiello, S., Christie, D., Sinfield, D., Steagall, M., & Aguayo, C. (2017). A DBR framework for designing mobile virtual reality learning environments. *Australasian Journal of Educational Technology*, *33*(6), 54–68. doi:10.14742/ajet.3613

Jones, M. G., Hite, R., Childers, G., Corin, E., Pereyra, M., & Chesnutt, K. (2016). Perceptions of presence in 3-D, haptic-enabled, virtual reality instruction. *International Journal of Education and Information Technologies*, *10*, 73–81.

Kopcha, T. J., Schmidt, M. M., & McKenney, S. (2015). Editorial 31 (5): Special issue on educational design research (EDR) in post-secondary learning environments. *Australasian Journal of Educational Technology, 31*(5), 5. doi:10.14742/ajet.2903

Martín-Gutiérrez, J., Mora, C. E., Añorbe-Díaz, B., & González-Marrero, A. (2017). Virtual technologies trends in education. *EURASIA Journal of Mathematics Science and Technology Education, 13*(2), 469–486.

Tsiatsos, T., Andreas, K., & Pomportsis, A. (2010). Evaluation Framework for Collaborative Educational Virtual Environments. *Journal of Educational Technology & Society, 13*(2), 65–77.

KEY TERMS AND DEFINITIONS

Authenticity: Authenticity defines the transfer of the real-life environment to the virtual reality in the same way.

Fidelity: Fidelity, is the fact that the elements and problems in virtual reality environments can behave in real life. If authenticity can be summarized as the design of all the design elements as one-to-one, the fidelity can be defined as ensuring that all of the activities that may occur during the presentation of these elements and problems can be experienced in real life.

Immersion: Immersion, which is the concept that enables individuals to fully experience the learning universe in virtual reality environments.

Interaction: The basic point is the interaction of the learners with the objects in the virtual reality environment.

Peripheral Devices: Peripherals are the means by which the learner can enter the educational environment prepared within the framework of educational and design frameworks.

Presence: Presence refers to the feeling of being in real life in a realistically designed virtual reality environment.

Socialization: Socialization is that the situation in which learners can interact with each other or with instructors in learning environments.

Virtual Reality: The concept of virtual reality can be broadly defined as the ability of a user to perceive and interact with a real-world environment in a three-dimensional simulation on the computer with particular technologies that the user wears on his body.

Chapter 2
Role of Immersive (XR) Technologies in Improving Healthcare Competencies:
A Review

Prabha Susy Mathew

Bishop Cottons Women's Christian College, India

Anitha S. Pillai

iD https://orcid.org/0000-0002-3883-8234

Hindustan Institute of Technology and Science, India

ABSTRACT

Immersive technology refers to technology that enhances reality by blending the physical environment with virtual content or by completely taking the user to a virtual world far away from reality. Different immersive technologies are augmented reality (AR), virtual reality (VR), and mixed reality (MR). As immersive technology is becoming more affordable, user-friendly, pervasive, and ubiquitous, it's been adopted and embraced by several industries. Though its early adopters were from the gaming industry, now it's explored and used by many other industries such as mining, healthcare, and medicine, retail, education, automotive, manufacturing, etc. Using these technologies, medical professionals can improve their competencies, and they will be able to effectively transfer the skill acquired through simulations to the operation theatre. This chapter focuses on uses, benefits, and adoption challenges of Immersive technologies with specific reference to healthcare training.

DOI: 10.4018/978-1-7998-1796-3.ch002

Copyright © 2020, IGI Global. Copying or distributing in print or electronic forms without written permission of IGI Global is prohibited.

INTRODUCTION

As a result of technological advancements industries and consumers are inundated with technology choices that they can use it to their advantage. One such technology is immersive technology or extended reality (XR) that's been recently transforming the healthcare training by reducing medical errors, improving medical practitioners' competency, reducing training costs and providing immersive and interactive learning environment. Immersive technologies such as augmented reality (AR), virtual reality (VR) and mixed reality (MR) are increasingly used in Healthcare education to train medical professionals' complex procedures by simulating it, making the scenario interesting and realistic. Right from training medical doctors, it is used in treatment planning, pharmacy- specific training and in surgery. (Michael, Simon & Nicholas, 2018). These immersive technologies-based training programs focus on procedural skill thereby improving patient safety and competencies of medical practitioner. Compared to traditional tools for training, immersive learning tools can greatly improve the quality of training, reduces costs, provides deeper understanding opportunities and improves patient satisfaction through better care from healthcare professionals.

IMMERSIVE TECHNOLOGIES

Immersive technology refers to technology that provide users with an experience of immersing oneself in simulated world that users can interact with. Immersive technology or extended reality (XR) is a term used for collectively referring technologies such as AR, VR and MR each of these have some key differences. (Reality Technologies, n.d.) The AR, VR ecosystem can be largely classified in to components, Head Mounted Devices (HMD) and Applications (Goldman Sachs, 2016). The Landscape for Immersive technology is as indicated in Figure1.

Virtual reality refers to fully immersive virtual world environment which substitutes the real world. An important pieces of virtual reality kit are the VR Head-Mounted Device (HMD) which is the similar to glasses and may or may not require a PC/Smartphone/Console to power the content being produced. The tethered VR headset / HMD needs to be connected to a PC via cable for the VR experience, while untethered does not require a PC or a console to be connected as it has in-built processor, memory, battery, sensor, display etc. The Virtual learning experience is enhanced, when the VR HMD is worn along with Headphones, special gloves, tracking devices and other optional devices such as bio controller. The HMD has several sensors to aptly simulate the visual, aural and haptic senses of the user through sensory feedback integrated with the output devices. (Oluleke & Xuming, 2013). The three categories of VR based on the level of immersion they provide are: Non-immersive simulations which is the least immersive technology achieved using conventional desktop, Semi-immersive simulations give user a partial immersive experience using High performance computing systems and Fully immersive simulations give user fully immersive experience through HMD and tracking devices. Some of the VR headsets used are Occulus Rift, Occulus Go, HTC Vive, PlayStation, Google Daydream and Cardboard, Samsung Gear, Lenevo Mirage solo (Greenwald, 2018). (Bhone, 2019) in their systematic review, assessed the effectiveness of VR interventions for education of Health Professionals. They found evidence showing a small improvement in knowledge and moderate-to-large improvement in skills of learners taking part in VR interventions compared to traditional or other forms of digital learning. For VR HMD, trackers (head, motion, eye) and sensors with modern graphic processing unit (GPU) will give learners better im-

Figure 1. Immersive technology landscape

IMMERSIVE TECHNOLOGY – LANDSCAPE

APPLICATION

Healthcare
PrecisionOs
VIPAAR
ORama

Museums
Viking VR
Story of forest
Skin and Bone

Education
Google Expeditions
Wonderscope
Metaverse

Games
PokemonGO
Ghostbusters World
Egg, Inc

Tourism
Marriot's YouVisit, Vroom service
Mindful Touch VR Spa Treatment
at Nobu Hotel in LA

Arts Gallery
ReBlink
Invasive Species

Military
Tactical Augmented Reality (TAR)
Synthetic Training Environment (STE)

Manufacturing
FIVE (Ford Immersive Vehicle Environment)
Common Augmented Reality Platform (CAP)

HMD

AR, VR & MR
• Microsoft HoloLens • Google Glass • Magic Leap •Epson Moverio BT-2 • Atheer • Osterhout Design Group • Facebook Oculus
• Samsung Gear VR • Google Cardboard • HTC Vive • Sony PSVR • Vuzix iWear • VR Union Claire •Google daydream & Cardboard
• Lenevo Mirage solo •Eyesight Raptor • ODG R-7 • Samsung HMD Odyssey • Acer windows MR • Dell Visor • Meta2

COMPONENTS

Audio
TI, Wolfson, Realtek, Ossic

Camera
360Heros, GoPro, Odyssey, Nokia OZO,
Jaunt NEO, Matterport Pro 3D

Display
Samsung, JDI, Himax,
Crystal

3D Lens
Wearality, Zeiss, Canon,
Nikon, Largan

Haptics
Alps, AAC, Nidec,
cypress

Memory
Micron, Samsung, SK Hynix,
Toshiba

Position & Gesture Tracker
PSVR, Oculus insight, WorldSense,
SLAM, HTC, ManoMotion,
LeapMotion

Motion Sensor
Leap Motion, InvenSense,
Motion Engine, Holosuit,
MS Kintec

Development Platforms
Unity, Unreal

Content Management
Augment, Blippar, Layar
creator

SDK/Tools
Vuforia, ARKit, ARCore, Kundan,
Wikitude, EasyAR, Onirix studio,
Lumin, DeepAR, MRToolKit

Processors – CPU, GPU, HPU
Qualcomm, MediaTek, Intel i7, Nvidia,
AMD, Qualcomm, Microsoft

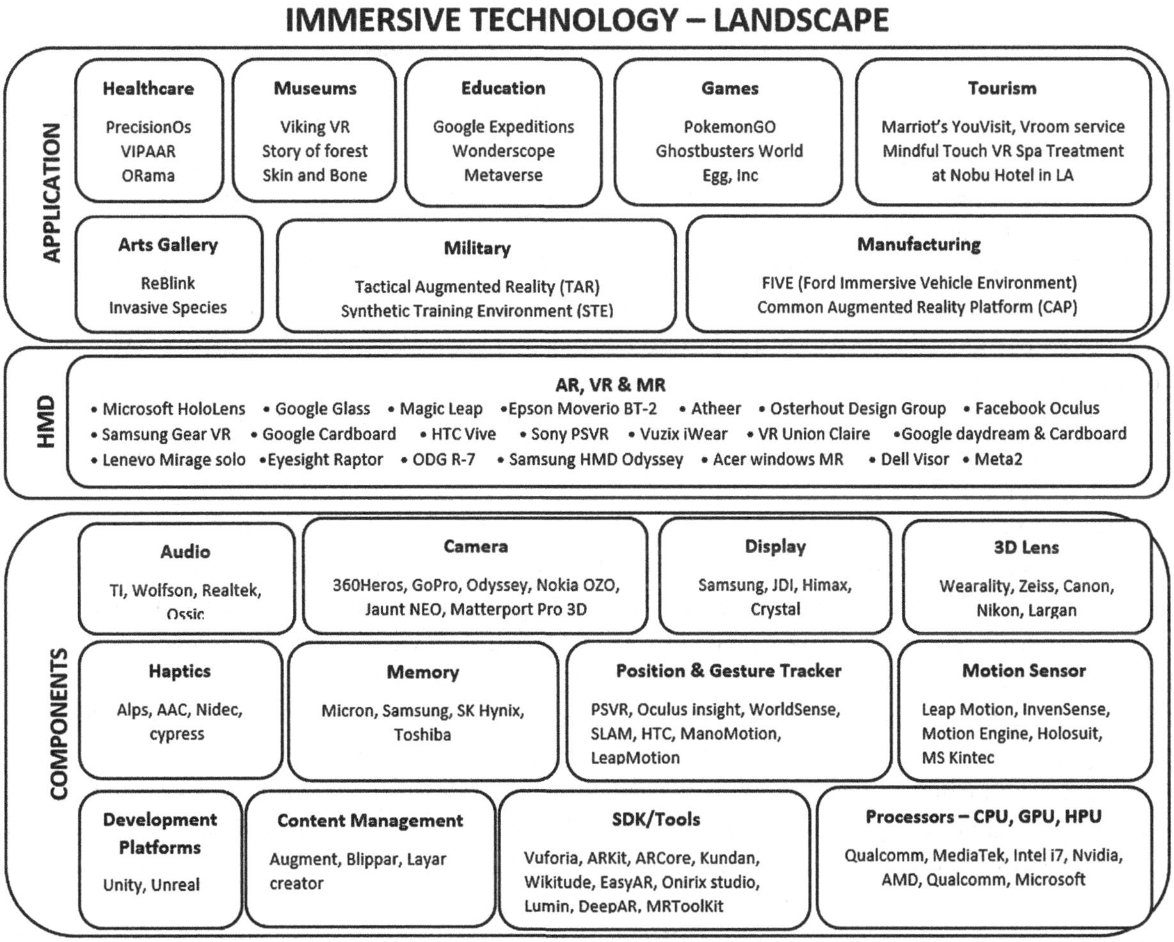

mersive experience (Hamacher, Kim, Cho, Pardeshi. Lee, Eun & Whangbo., 2016) However they found VR has few challenges such as lack of accurate head-tracking and motion sickness experienced by users.

Augmented reality refers to superimposing digital/virtual content on to user's physical world thereby enhancing user's reality. Smartphones, Tablets, Smart Glasses, Tethered AR HMDS etc. to give user the immersive experience. Google Glass and Epson Smart Glasses are the most frequently used devices, newer devices, such as Hololens (Microsoft) are used in many of the recent applications. Apart from the basic devices such as glasses and tablet, it also requires components such as camera, projector, sensor, trackers. Oculus tracker uses infrared tracking systems while HTC VIVE uses a laser-based system to identify users' position in the environment, device such as Microsoft HoloLens is used for interactions which does not require additional programming as it is a part of the system itself. (Hamacher et al., 2016). Few categories of AR are: Marker based AR and Markerless AR. Marker based AR, it uses camera to recognize visual markers such as an image or a QR code. It allows users to view image from all directions in detail, while Markerless AR is a widely accepted and it uses simultaneous localization and mapping (SLAM) technology, which is an advanced AR technology that uses GPS, digital compass etc. to provide location-based data. The Smithsonian's National Museum of Natural History uses Skin & Bones App that allow their visitors to point the camera of their mobile device at one of 13 skeletons displayed and view those animal's come to life "with its skin on". Some of the animals that come to life via the app are vampire bats, a 150-pound Mississippi catfish, giant sea cows, rattlesnakes. The visitors are able to learn everything about that animal as to how it sounded, lived and preyed on other animals, its anatomy and evolution. This is made possible through advanced technologies of 3D AR and 3D tracking. ("Smithsonian", 2015) AR enhanced T-shirt can be used to learn human anatomy through a user-friendly interface. It has a printed code on it which is recognised by AR application that allows user to visualize and explore organs that look real. (Wee Sim, Benjamin, Kavit, Adrian, Ketan, & Jason, 2016) PokemonGo is an example of most popular location-based AR game. The game uses GPS technology to superimpose digital character Pokemon into user's real-world location. Users smart phone camera is used as a guide to find those creatures hidden in the real-world location. Projection based AR, projects artificial lights on real world environment or even to project 3D interactive hologram into thin air and superimposition-based AR works by either fully or partially replacing the original view of an object with the new augmented view of the same object. it provides graphical overlay-based guidance to medical professionals. (Reality Technologies, n.d.) There are a wide variety of Smart Glasses available in market such as Sony, Epson, Vuzix Blade AR, Google Glass Enterprise Edition, Eyesight Raptor, ODG R-7, Magic Leap, Microsoft HoloLens to name a few. (Steve Noble., 2019). In educational training set up AR has been used in several places such as ImmersiveTouch surgical simulation uses HMDs, patient-specific anatomy, and haptic feedback to train surgeons and educate patients. An AR based Vein viewing system, AccuVein is used to help professionals locate veins for IV placement, which is great in reducing the rate of multiple needle pricks on patient. It uses a handheld scanner that superimposes map of patient's veins over his/her skin surface in real time. Accuvein even helps the cosmetic physicians to view and avoid veins while giving Botox treatment to their patient's. A similar system Augmedix allows physicians to enter patient centric data in a hands-free way by just wearing google glass. All the information is passed through the glass to the Augmedix software and is automatically inputted into the patient's electronic health records (EHR). It reduces the physicians administrative work of entering patient details in to the system, thereby giving them more time to interact with patients. VIPAAR (Virtual Interactive Presence and Augmented Reality) is a remote mentoring system. VIPAAR is used with Smart Glass which allows a skilled surgeon in a remote location to communicate and instruct a surgeon in another location by projecting mentor's augmented "hands" into the surgeon's display. (Jasmine Sanchez, n.d.; Smith, Nelson, & Maul, 2018).

Mixed Reality on the other hand intertwines the digital as well as the real world thereby allowing interactions between the digital and the real-world objects. There are not many MR headsets available when compared to AR and VR headsets. Some of the MR headsets are Microsoft's HoloLens, Magic Leap, Samsung HMD Odyssey, Acer windows MR, Dell Visor, HP windows MR headsets, Lenovo explorer etc. (Steve Noble., 2019) Mixed reality ultrasound simulation solution with Microsoft HoloLens used by CAE healthcare team allows learners to examine the 3D anatomy inside the body of Vimedix mannequins. Learner can understand a concept better by getting a detailed view of the hologram. Even physicians will be benefitted as they can practice placing implants or other complex procedures before they perform a procedure on their real patients. (CAE Healthcare, 2017). MR applications are not just used for training the learners, it can also be used as an effective tool for preoperative communications by surgeons. With MR technology the surgeon can simulate the operation that enables patient and the caregivers clear understanding of the patient condition, surgical process and risks involved improving the doctor-patient understanding. MR surgical simulators such as MR simulator for ventriculostomy procedure and a subclavian central venous access (SCVA) can boost confidence of surgeons when dealing with a complex and unfamiliar technique as it provides real-life experience mimicking the procedures. (Hong-zhi, Xiao-bo, Zeng-wu, Mao, Song, Xing-huo & Zhe-wei, 2019)

USE CASES OF XR IN MEDICAL AND HEALTHCARE TRAINING

Medical training requires more realistic training approach. To provide such realistic training without putting the real patients at risk mannequins have been used since long. These Mannequins that were used for learning did not give options of reusability as well as initial investment was often costly. Till recent past medical students have relied on human cadavers to identify, locate and understand different organs in human anatomy. (John, 2017). In recent times technologies such as extended reality (XR) is embraced by healthcare sector and there are multitude of use cases that proves its worth in the industry. XR which also consists of AR, VR and MR is well suited to provide realistic simulation-based training to medical professionals at a reduced cost when compared to the traditional approach. XR technologies are reusable, can be reconfigured, dependence on live subjects is eliminated and improves learning curve by providing better visualization of human body.

Surgical Training

In a traditional set up, practicing a complex surgical procedure was limited as it relied majorly on the availability of cadavers. Oranges or faux skin was used to learn incision and suturing Surgical training which was a decent option, but it was not useful to simulate more complex procedures. Given the complex nature of training required in surgery some of earliest VR applications in medical training was for the surgical domain. There are several companies that provide AR/VR/MR based training option for a surgical skill practice before actual surgery. Some of the semi-immersive surgical simulators like Osso VR, Immersive touch, MIST VR, LapSim, ProMIS allow surgeons to practice a complex procedure any number of times using VR headsets and haptic technology till they perfect the skill (Scott Christian., 2018). (Kamarudin & Zary, 2019). VR and AR based surgical simulators such as Touch Surgery which is an innovative and cost-free app for mobile devices can help learners to understand surgical procedures in a more realistic and interactive way. It has been used to simulate surgical procedure for orbital floor construction (Khelemsky, Hill & Buchbinder, 2017). Touch surgery has also been identified as a serious game approach and an effective tool in teaching medical students chest tube insertion procedure and self-assess their training performance.(Haubruck, Nickel, Ober, Walker, Bergdolt, Friedrich, Müller-Stich, Forchheim, Fischer, Schmidmaier, & Tanner, 2018) some of the surgery domains that use XR as their training tools are discussed below:

a. Plastic and reconstructive surgery

AR used in plastic and reconstructive surgery, can give the patient a 3D simulation of the final facial appearance and can help the trainee in understanding technically complex aesthetic procedures and overlaying patient-specific 3D model of the desired facial reconstruction onto the operative field during surgery to reduce the risk of error. (Khelemsky et al., 2017). Crisalix Surgeon is a simulator for visualizing plastic surgery results. (Younjun, Hannah, & Yong Oock., 2017) in their paper categorized AR/VR based plastic surgery into surgical planning, navigation and training. According to their review it helped surgeons with preoperative surgical planning for more accurate prediction of outcomes, Intraoperative navigation reduced the complications improving surgical performance, 3D human anatomy provided a great learning and training platform for plastic and reconstructive surgery. Surgeons can understand their surgical plans in 3D with XR better. Surgeons trained using immersive technologies completed their procedures 29% faster and made 6 times fewer mistakes than surgeons trained traditionally made. (Armando, 2019). A marker-based AR system that used already existing devices, free software and libraries for improvements of the body surface, important for plastic surgery was devised and evaluated. (Mitsuno, Daisuke, Ueda, Koichi, Itamiya, Tomoki, Nuri, Takashi, Otsuki, & Yuki, 2017). The system used Moverio BT-200 smart glasses for visualizing the 3D image, Blender for 3D image processing, Unity app development software with an IDE. Vuforia, a free software development kit was incorporated as neither Unity nor Moverio has program for marker recognition. The 3D Image of the body surface and the bone were superimposed, onto the surgical site. Overlapping the 3D image on the Actual surgery site is essential for guided surgery on the planned position and to perform cutting procedure precisely.

b. Laparoscopic Surgery

Laparoscopic AR provides intraoperative guidance for identification of targets such as tumors, infection etc. and critical structures such as organs, nerves etc. Laparoscopic AR would help surgeon match information (mostly images) from different sources to the scene and are able to increase their spatial awareness. Minimally Invasive Surgical Trainer-Virtual Reality (MIST-VR) is a low fidelity simulator which does not support force-feedback option and also lacks stereoscopic visualization. It is used to learn basic laparoscopic skills such as suturing and tying knots. LapVR simulators uses haptic technology that lets the learners acquire the tactile laparoscopic surgical skills such as suturing, knot-tying, cutting, clipping and loop ligation. LapVR module has basic laparoscopic techniques as well as modules for gallbladder removal, laparoscopic cholecystectomy, ectopic pregnancy and bilateral tubal occlusion with alternative cases and level of difficulty. Instructor can customize case parameters to match each learner's performance (Panteleimon, Angeliki, Ioanna, Georgios, Christos, Thrasyvoulos, Georgios & Michail, 2017; CAE Healthcare, 2017) The ProMIS AR simulator (Haptica, Ireland) is used for training laparoscopic tasks including navigation, object positioning, suturing, traction, knot tying and sharp dissection (Barsom, Graafland, & Schijven, 2016) LapSim(Surgical Science, Sweden) which is a high fidelity simulator includes basic skill modules, anastomosis and suture and laparoscopic cholecystectomy scenarios, and one case is dedicated to gynecology. LAP Mentor (3D System, USA) is a high fidelity, haptic feedback-based simulator that targets both learners and experienced surgeons, teaching from basic laparoscopic skills to complete operations. The modules include basic laparoscopic skills, suturing, laparoscopic cholecystectomy, ventral hernia, gastric bypass, and gynecology cases. A relatively cheap AR simulator LTS3-e (LTS) is capable of training and assessing the technical laparoscopic skills of Fundamentals of Laparoscopy (FLS) program. It is an electronic evolution of McGill inanimate system for training and evaluation of laparoscopic skills (MISTELS) and offers a few more tasks. It provides validated exercises and scenarios that are assessed electronically with McGill metrics. (Panteleimon et al., 2017). VBLaST a laparoscopic skill training simulator is used for learning laparoscopic tasks peg transfer, pattern cutting, ligating loop and suturing. It provides automatic and immediate assessment of skill but gives learners less immersive experience. To improve surgical immersion VatsSim-XR a versatile simulator that performs multiple surgical training scenarios in different simulation modes (VR, CVR, AR, and MR) on a single device was developed for patient-specific training environment. The experiments conducted by both professional and novice thoracic surgeons show that the (cognitive virtual reality) CVR trainer shows a better result than that of the traditional VR trainer. The AR trainer can provide visuo-haptic fidelity and accuracy in training environment, while the box trainer and MR trainer both demonstrated the best 3D perception and surgical immersive performance. However, the box, VR, and AR simulators provide less immersive experience compared to its MR counterpart which may not be perfect in operation time (T), surgical clamps track length (CL), endoscope track length (EL), surgical clamps angle accumulation (CA), endoscope angle accumulation (EA), and the numbers of block drop (ND) but provides highly realistic operating rooms for the trainers. (Zhibao, Yonghang, Chengqi., Jun, Xiaoqiao, Zaiqing, Qiong & Junsheng, 2019). Biophotonics based AR system guarantees alignment between the augmentation and laparoscopic image thereby eliminating the need for camera calibration. In laparoscopy, this technique has been used to monitor blood supply in intestinal MIS. (Bernhardt., Nicolau, Soler & Doignon, 2017).

c. Robotic Surgery

In recent past robotic surgery has become preferred choice for surgical procedures because of faster recovery, lesser complication, minimal scarring and decreased blood loss. As a result of such demand surgeons are in constant need to improve and retain their skill without compromising on patient safety. Using simulators could help surgeons in perfecting their skill and recuing error rates. The most popular use of XR technology is in robotic surgery. Some of the simulators available are Robotic surgery VR trainers (RoSS), SimSurgery Educational Platform (SEP), ProMIS, Mimic dV Trainer (MdVT), Surgical SIM RSS, RobotiX Mentor (RM) and the da Vinci Skills Simulator (dVSS). Educational impact has been there for all the simulators except for SEP (Omar M, 2019). RoSS and DV-Trainer have shown face and content validity. DV-Trainer, along with SEP Robot (SimSurgery) and da Vinci Skills Simulator, provides metrics about the trainees' performance with construct validity. RoSS™ is the only one that incorporates whole procedural tasks (Panteleimon et al., 2017), (Hertz, George, Vaccaro, & Brand, 2018) in their comparative study on 3 most commercially available VR robotic simulators provided statistically significant evidence that all the 3 demonstrated face and content validity. Although dVSS had the highest scores and is least expensive of all 3. The dVT and RM have similar cost and availability, training modules available on these models may be a differentiating feature between them.

d. Orthopedic Surgery

The ImmersiveTouch simulator is used in a variety of spine surgery procedures. ImmersiveSim and ImmersiveTouch platforms are the training and education simulators that provide high fidelity, haptic feedback along with realistic user interface. The simulator provides a realistic environment for surgeons and residents, giving them ability to feel the layers of the spinal cord while performing procedures. The system provides immediate feedback for relevant parameters in each module within the chosen surgery, enabling trainees to identify their weaknesses and evaluate their performance. Phantom haptics interface is used for spinal needle insertion. In a comparative study of VR models used for training in arthroscopy, it was found that Arthro MENTOR and ArthroSIM displayed face, content, and construct validity. ArthroS (Virtamed) has demonstrated greater face validity than Arthro MENTOR and ArthroSIM (Panteleimon et al., 2017). Osso VR, a VR surgical training platform uses handheld technology to provide immersive coaching for a robotics-assisted device. This solution offers the largest knee portfolio aided by robotics and offers the accuracy of robotics-assisted technology for bi-cruciate retaining total knee implant. It is Haptic-enabled to provide an immersive training environment. (Justin, 2019). Precision OS is an orthopaedic surgical training using immersive virtual reality. It gives detailed performance metrics to the surgeon at any step of the procedure in order to evaluate him or her on the procedure being performed. Precision OS offers three different simulation platforms: Arthroplasty Platform, Patient Specific Anatomy and Trauma Platform. The first platform allows surgeons to become familiar with patient anatomy, identify precision metrics and perform virtual surgery. The second platform allows surgeons to use advance imaging to perform surgery of a specific upcoming procedure with relevant data before the actual procedure. The third Platform focuses on fracture configuration, screw trajectory and plate position about trauma surgery. (Kristi, 2018).

e. Neurosurgical Procedures

ImmersiveTouch is AR simulation-based surgical training systems. It is a high-fidelity simulator with haptic technology that allows trainees to perfect their skills in a risk-free environment which replicates a real surgery experience for neurosurgery residents. This simulator is used in many surgical disciplines, including spine surgery, ophthalmology, ENT surgery, and neurosurgery (Panteleimon et al., 2017). (Barsom et al., 2016) mentions that an AR setup in neurosurgery that requires basic equipment such as personal computers (PC), a monitor, a camera, tracking tools and 3D image editing software. PC is used for preoperative editing of clinical images and for projection of the augmented image to the real scene. The Augmented images are displayed on Monitors for the surgical team. After evaluating the system, it was found to be a valid training method not only for thoracic pedicle screw placement (face and predictive validity) and clipping aneurysms (face validity) but also for percutaneous trigeminal rhizotomy (construct validity). Besides, it had positive effect on learning, reduced time taken to hone their skill in many neurosurgical procedures, such as ventriculostomy, bone drilling percutaneous treatment for trigeminal neuralgia, lumbar puncture, pedicle screw placement and vertebroplasty. (Wright, Ribaupierre & Eagleson, 2017).

NeuroVR is a neurosurgical training and assessment platform with complex computer-generated metrics in 13 categories. It simulates procedures such as microdissections, tumour aspiration, and hemostasis. variation of this is Neurotouch cranio a virtual reality simulator for select cranial microsurgery procedures that uses stereovision and bimanual tool handles with forced feedback. It computes real-time interactions between surgical tools and tissue, using contact algorithms and tool-specific interaction models for doing neurological procedures. (Panteleimon et al., 2017). (Wright et al., 2017) designed an easy to use and affordable endoscopic third ventriculostomy (ETV) simulator using Unity, Vuforia and the leap motion (LM) for an AR environment. The LM-based system was compared with NeuroTouch for its usability and training efficiency on two parameters task speed and accuracy. From the study it was observed that LM-based system provides a more intuitive 3D interactive experience than the stylus, experts showed higher targeting success rate than the novices and had almost similar task completion times. The PerkStation is a training platform for image-guided interventions. Trainees perform AR image overlaying while training on a phantom,. The PerkStation measures total procedure time, time inside phantom, path length, potential tissue damage, out-of-plane deviation and in-plane deviation. The procedures such as facet joint injections and lumbar puncture has been taught by using PerkStation. Studies conducted to validate the performance of perk station revealed success rate of facet joint injections was significantly higher in comparison with the control group, with significantly less tissue damage and in another study lumbar punctures carried out by Perk Station group outperformed the control group with a shorter period of needle insertion time and less tissue damage (Barsom et al., 2016). UpSim neurosurgical box is a simulator for the advanced training in neurosurgery. It is a physical scenario which interact with a mobile App for AR. With this system it is possible to replicate all the steps of a microsurgical procedure combining a physical scenario with an augmented reality simulation, from the skin incision to microsurgical manipulation of deep neuroanatomy, providing the mental and manual skills required to learn neurosurgical procedures. ("hybrid neurosurgical simulator", n.d.) Some of the other VR/AR simulators mentioned in (Panteleimon et al., 2017) are RoboSim, Vascular Intervention SimulationTrainer (VIST), EasyGuide Neuro, ANGIO Mentor, VIVENDI, Dextroscope and Anatomical Simulator for Pediatric Neurosurgery (ASPN)

f. Ocular Surgery

A study on efficacy Eyesim, a high-fidelity ophthalmic training simulator application developed for intraocular surgery training, demonstrated that it was effective in refining surgical skills of trainees on capsulorhexis of high-tension capsules. The system is more effective in improving surgical skills of the novice surgeons who have less skills. (Panteleimon et al., 2017; Anuradha, 2019). Training modules include ocular anatomy, pupil simulator, ocular motility simulator, and a visual pathway simulator. It is available on Mobile Platforms, Desktop, Ibench Mobile, and Icatcher. Instructors using the simulator can select from any number of functions and have their students perform a diagnosis, providing learners with an opportunity to practice and understand different cases (Pfandlera, Marc, Stefan, & Weigl, 2017). Some other cataract surgery simulators are PhacoVision (Melerit Medical), and MicroVisTouch (ImmersiveTouch). (Panteleimon et al., 2017).

g. Spine Surgery

(Pfandler et al., 2017) in their study identified various AR, VR and MR simulators used for training, assessment, and planning in spinal surgery. Virtual Protractor (AR) is used for Percutaneous vertebroplasty, Medtronic Surgical Technologies (MR), Immersive Touch Simulator (VR) is used for Thoracic pedicle screw placement, Percutaneous spinal needle placement, Pedicle screw placement, Sensable Phantom Premium1.5 (VR) is used for Lumbar puncture, Stealth 3D navigation unit (Medtronic) (MR) is used for Placement of lateral mass screw, PerkTutor; Sonix Touch US system in conjunction with the SonixGPS (AR) is used for facet joint injection, Torso Mannequin, Micron Tracker2 optical tracking system, PHANToM haptic device, graphical user interface (AR) is used for Spinal needle insertion, NovintFalcon (MR) is used for Vertebroplasty, PerkStation (AR) is used for Percutaneous facet joint injection, Phacon Corporation (MR) for Posterior cervical laminectomy and foraminotomy. The quality of the studies mentioned were assessed with the Medical Education Research Study Quality Instrument (MERSQI) The six domains of study quality of the MERSQI (study design, sampling, type of data, and validity of evaluation instrument, data analysis, and outcomes) were rated. From the study it was observed that the simulator-trained group(s) outperformed the non–simulator trained group proving that simulator-based training and assessment of surgical skills in spinal surgery can significantly improve the success rate with less potential tissue damage and reduces completion time of a procedure.

h. Cardiac Surgery

INSIGHT HEART is an AR and MR app for medical education. Learners can take a MR tour of heart anatomy, zoom, rotate, and scale the high-quality 3D MR holograms that floats in front of them and they are able to control the app via voice control or gestures. The 3D holograms of the heart beats in real time is reproduced through audio visual simualtion along with visual effects of artery hypertension, partial fibrillation, and myocardial infraction. The SentiAR is a Microsoft HoloLens-enabled intraprocedural 3D augmented reality platform. Other healthcare companies have been using HoloLens for holographic MR training simulations, however SentiAR differs from them by offering a real-time holographic image of the patient's actual anatomy over the patient in the operation room, allowing surgeons to see patient specific details. (Tagaytayan, Kelemen, & Sik-Lanyi, 2018). The EchoCom is an AR based echocardiography training system for neonates consisting of a 3D tracking system attached to a mannequin to identify congenital heart diseases using sonographic information. The system was tested on experts, intermediates and beginners and it has achieved Face validity and construct validity. (Barsom et al., 2016). The CAE VIMEDIX is an AR system for echocardiography training consisting of a mannequin and a transducer. It can be used to train transthoracic echocardiography or transesophageal echocardiography. It has displayed face validity. (Barsom et al., 2016; Panteleimon et al., 2017).

Other simulators are ANGIO Mentor system is used in conjunction with standard guidewires, catheters, balloons, stents, and similar devices for monitoring the patient's vital signs. It is used in many endovascular procedures, such as carotid stenting and renal, iliac, and other vascular interventions. Vascular Intervention Simulation Trainer (VIST) is like the ANGIO Mentor. Where along with endovascular procedures, it has an electrophysiology module for training in pacemaker lead placement. Nakao Cardiac Model is a VR for training in surgical palpitation of the beating heart. It supports haptic feedback. It does not provide any metric for evaluation. A VR Lobectomy Simulator includes video-assisted thoracoscopic surgery resection, lobectomy; it supports haptic feedback and has metrics tools that can evaluate surgical performance. (Panteleimon et al., 2017).

i. Dental Training and Surgery

The Voxel-Man a surgical simulator is used for training in a variety of disciplines such as ENT, Voxel-Man Tempo for ear surgery and Voxel-Man Sinus for endoscopic sinus surgery. The Voxel-Man Dental is used for dental training. This device allows the learners to use High and low speed burs with matching haptics and sound, provides virtual dental mirror and magnification of teeth, Drilling with realistic haptic feedback and additional cross-sectional images. Microtomography is used to derive high-resolution tooth models from real teeth. The software allows students to work with realistic cases like remove of caries, preparation of cavity with automatic skill assessment for immediate feedback on their performance. A surgical navigation system "3D Tooth Atlas 9", IGI (DenX Advanced Dental system) assists the dental clinicians during preoperative and intraoperative phases of dental implant surgery. During the procedure the clinician can navigate implant to precise location and depth, assisted by audio and visual feedback, thereby avoiding mistakes and performing the surgery with high level of accuracy (Bogdan, Dinca & Popovici, 2011). In an evaluation study oral surgery simulator, Forsslund system was suggested to be an effective training tool to improve dental education. Iowa Dental Surgical Simulator (IDSS) is developed by the College of Dentistry at the University of Iowa. It has a joystick and a modified handle from an explorer, a dental instrument that allows the students to explore tooth surfaces for carious lesions. It's a cost-effective system that uses force feedback to teach and assess the tactile skill of the learner. (Wee Sim et al., 2016)

Anatomy Training

Currently medical students studying anatomy can access the cadaver lab only during the specific allotted hours, getting detailed understanding and view of organs is tough. XR based clinical anatomy curriculum could be far more engaging compared to traditional method. It will help students to understand spatial concepts better and provide them access to educational resources without geographic constraints. Tools like Microsoft HoloLens enables learners to view individual organs in motion from different perspectives, see its functioning and hear heartbeat sound providing a more realistic learning experience. It provides students an opportunity to learn at their own pace, access training outside of Lab and to delve into details that further interests them (Zweifach & Triola, 2019). Several AR/VR related software used for anatomy education such as Blender, Occulus Rift, Vuforia V5, DextroBeam, Aurasma and Magicbook, ARTHRO, dVSS, MistVR, LapSim, ProMIS etc used for medical education were reviewed by (William, Brandon, Perez & Sarah, 2017) which suggests that these simulators are noninferior to standards of practice with regard to learning anatomy. However, Radiation oncology would benefit from the integration of AR/VR technologies, as it provides a cost effective, scalable solution that improves quality of patient care and individual proficiency. At Case Western Reserve, replaced their cadaver lab and 2D illustrations in medical books with HoloLens headsets. HoloAnatomy app is being used which allows medical students to rotate and virtually dissect a body to see and understand the structures, systems, and organs. (Emory & Maya, 2017; "3D Tooth Atlas 9",2018) developed by University of the Pacific's Arthur A. Dugoni School of Dentistry in collaboration with eHuman Digital Anatomy is a VR based dental training system, that will enable dentists to get in-depth understanding of the tooth structure and aliments. The VR model will give students a realistic representation of each type of tooth, how they grow and why they develop cavities and other issues. The improved version of 3D model of teeth with AR capabilities is organized into five sections: Periodontology, Anthropology, Odontogenesis, Dental Embryology and Clinical Access. The Clinical Access section includes over 550 Holographic models of teeth considering every known anatomical pathology and development. (Ta-KoHuang, Chi-HsunYang, Yu-HsinHsieh, Jen-ChyanWang & Chun-ChengHung, 2018)

Clinical Skills Training

Another application of AR/VR has been the use of virtual patients to practice clinical skills such as taking patient history, diagnosing medical condition and prescribing medicines (Scott Christian, 2018). Immersive practice with XR based Think F.A.S.T. (Face, Arms, Speech, Time) training simulation is a powerful and engaging VR simulation that puts learners in a medical emergency. Medical students use VR to educate themselves on how to recognize symptoms of a stroke using the F.A.S.T. system while interacting in real-time with a virtual patient. It uses the Qualcomm® Snapdragon™ 835 VR development kit; a standalone all-in-one mobile XR headset with a single panel AMOLED head mounted display (HMD) and an integrated Snapdragon 835 mobile platform, 3D audio tools, Unity 3D to build the training platform which is compiled to an Android package and Leap Motion for precisely tracking the hand movement (Leilani, 2017). An interactive educational program Virtual Hernia Clinic (VHC) uses virtual patient simulations model to provide learners with clinical scenarios to identify, assess, diagnose and treat patients with hernias. It provides surgeon with opportunities to practice and make the clinical judgment required to perform hernia surgery ("Virtual Health Clinic", n.d.). VR based HumanSim system enables doctors, nurses and other medical personnel to interact and engage in a training scenario with a patient or healthcare professional within a 3D environment only. It provides an immersive experience by measuring the participant's emotions with the help of sensors (Moisaka solutions, 2017). HoloPatient is a MR project undertaken through Pearson's partnership with Microsoft HoloLens. Both Texas Tech University Simulation Program and San Diego State University School of Nursing are working with Pearson. It uses Holographic Capture (HCAP) technology from Microsoft. Actors simulate the real-world scenario which is then transferred as video into Holograms placed into any environment to let students conduct patient assessments and make a diagnosis. (Emory & Maya, 2017). some of the dental simulators for improving future dentists' clinical skills are DentSim an AR based advanced dental training simulator, the system allows the students to train individually and evaluates the work, thus enhancing their clinical skills. Individual Dental Education Assistant (IDEA) simulator provides haptic feedback to the trainee while they practice. The system offers modules for Manual Dexterity, Caries Detection, Oral Med, Scaling and Root Planning. A study in ("3D Tooth Atlas 9", 2018) reported that the system provides a platform for gaining crucial clinical experience. However, they reported that scoring system and the tactile sensation needed to be improved for more realistic experience. The Simodont Dental Trainer a 3D VR based system by Moog industrial group. The training modules offer simulation for manual dexterity, cariology, crown and bridges exercises with different dental burrs. Like forsslund system, the Simodont trainer also has been incorporated to the training curriculum of Academic Centre for Dentistry in Amsterdam (ACTA) (Elby, Bakr, & Roy, 2017). PerioSim is a VR based haptic simulator aimed to improve skills in diagnosing and treatment of periodontal diseases. It is a part of dental training curriculum of University of Illinois in Chicago. Though the easy access to the system via internet and the provision through which instructor can upload a dental procedure and students can replay it at any later time are things that makes it most appropriate to be used for educational training. It was identified that the realism of the tactile feedback had some issue that needs further work. ("3d Tooth Atlas 9",2018; Bogdan, Dinca & Popovici, 2011) Preparation of primary tooth stump is an important skill for performing the dental restorations. For improvising the skills of trainees in fixed prosthetics preparation, a virtual and augmented reality technologies-based simulator (VirDenT) system can be used. Nvint Technologies and the Harvard School of Dental Medicine together developed Virtual Reality Dental Training System (VRDTS). With this system students can practice cavity preparations, work with a virtual decayed tooth, use a drill for cavity repair, fill the prepared cavity with amalgam, and carve the amalgam to match the original tooth contour. VRDTS enables the learner to feel the difference between enamel, dentin, caries, amalgam, and pulp throughout the procedure unlike how it is in the conventional plastic teeth used for training. The student's procedure can be tracked and quantified with feedback to both student and teacher. VR Haptic dental system HAP-DENT is a multi-layered virtual tooth model with different mechanical hardness that allows learners to feel tooth cutting which is like that with a real tooth. The learners can operate a stylus of the haptic device in six degrees of freedom to control dental turbine movement and to feel a tactile force. (Wee Sim et al., 2016) Oculus and Children's Hospital Los Angeles (CHLA) jointly developed a virtual reality software that is used to efficiently train residents, existing clinicians and staff in handling pediatric emergencies. The Oculus Go headset used for this simulation is portable and convenient to use. (Tagaytayan et al., 2018)

Remote Training

In many countries people living in rural areas have less or limited access to healthcare facilities. Shortage of medical practitioners, healthcare facilities, less preventive cares and longer waiting in case of emergencies are typical challenges of remote areas. AR as a Telemedicine Platform for Remote Procedural Training enables the learners or novice practitioners to perform complex medical procedures such as Point of Care Ultrasound (PoCUS) without visual interference. (Wang, Parsons, Stone-McLean, Rogers, Boyd, Hoover, Meruvia-Pastor, Gong, & Smith, 2017) Their proposed system uses the HoloLens to capture the view of a simulated remote emergency room (ER) through mixed reality capture (MRC), mentor's hand gestures are captured using a Leap Motion and virtually displayed in the AR space of the HoloLens to support remote procedural training. Comparison of the system with the full telemedicine set-up did not show any statistical difference. The results were not negative which suggests that these types of AR systems have the potential to become a helpful tool in telemedicine, just like the full telemedicine set-up, provided it is made more robust and lightweight. In several studies, HoloLens which is a MR technology has been used for medical training, training for patients with Alzheimer's disease to improve the short-term memory of patients, viewing magnetic resonance imaging (MRI) images on a HoloLens for MRI-guided neurosurgery. Implementation of E-consultation system leveraged on holographic and augmented reality systems, in a typical intensive care unit (ICU) environment, for remote consultancy services. It was found very beneficial in providing care to critically ill ICU patients and in reducing the rate of morbidity and mortality. (Sirilak, & Muneesawang, 2018). While performing a shoulder surgery using AR a local surgeon was able to interact with a remote surgeon and was able to receive live feedback. The University of Alabama, Birmingham developed Virtual Interactive Presence and Augmented Reality (VIPAAR) system that allowed the remote surgeons to parallelly view the procedure and participate in virtual interactions with the local surgeon. The local surgeon sees the virtual interaction from the remote surgeon through the Google glass. The report suggested that the surgery performed using VIPAAR resulted in no complications and provided an additional support for complex procedures and high-risk surgeries. (Herron, 2016). Use of AR shows a promising new development in telemedicine systems as it can be used by inexperienced doctors who can consult and obtain advice from specialist practitioners who is in a remote location. ORamaVR is redefining medical education through cutting edge VR techniques. With ORamaVR, trainees can improve their skills and remember complex surgical procedures in a virtual environment by collaborating with up to seven remote users and carrying out operations on virtual patients. Recently, some of the medical schools such as Stanford Medical School, the USC Keck School of Medicine, the New York University Langone Medical School and the Aristotle University Medical School participated in ORamaVR demonstration for collaborative surgical training. Surgeons and medical residents collaborated to perform a Total Hip arthroplasty operation out of which five participants were located remotely. A cooperative system like this training multiple young surgeons simultaneously within the same virtual space can reduce the time it takes to train medical students as well as the cost. Proximie, is a cloud-based AR platform used to remotely connect surgeons and students from anywhere in the world via live video feed and Augmented interaction. Economically weaker countries and conflict zones are currently using this platform to train their surgeons remotely. Proximie is being used in an educational setting to teach medical students at Yale University Medical School (New Haven, Connecticut, USA), the Royal Free Hospital, Chelsea and Westminster Hospital and St Tomas' Hospital (London, United Kingdom) giving positive feedback and encouraging results (Perkins Coie LLP, 2019).

Equipment Operation Training

(Bifulco, Narducci, Vertucci, Ambruosi, Cesarelli & Romano, 2014) in their paper presented an application prototype based on AR to train untrained users, with limited or no knowledge, to effectively interact with an ECG device and to place ECG electrodes on patient's chest which was achieved by presenting text, graphics and audio messages to the user. The system when tested, was found to be intuitive and easy to use.

Benefits and Hurdles of XR Adoption in Medical and Healthcare Training

Over the last decade healthcare sector has adopted and benefitted from the immersive technologies. In healthcare, Immersive 3D environments have been used to teach medical students, train new staff members and improve current medical professionals' clinical skills. These immersive training models have been found to be more engaging and effective compared to the traditional teaching models. However, there may be several adoption challenges faced by educational institutions which cannot be ignored.

Benefits of XR Adoption in Medical and Healthcare Training

Remote Learning and collaboration

XR technologies can bridge the distance between the trainer and trainees. Trainees can learn remotely from an expert. The immersive technologies make the whole experience of remote learning very engaging. Virtual interactive presence and augmented reality (VIPAR) simulator allows a remote surgeon to provide assistance and training by projecting their hands into the display of another surgeon wearing a headset. (Herron, 2016). A recent trend of educational meetings is to incorporate live surgery as part of the programme. "VR in OR" application enable medical students around the world to see and learn surgeries or complex procedures broadcasted live on their smartphone. (Monsky, James, & Seslar, 2019; Eran Orr., 2018).

Real Life Concepts with Greater Retention

XR tools promotes learning by doing as opposed to passive learning thereby helping the learners retain or absorb the procedure or skill learned. According to Dr. Narendra Kini, CEO at Miami's Children Health System, VR training programs offer a better retention compared to a traditional education. From his observations, trainees retain 80% of the information after one year of training, while only a 20% retention rate was observed when trained with traditional methods. (Matthew & Shailee, 2017). XR technologies can make learners job-ready through simulations before attending the real patients.

Reduced Cost and Risk

Medical training often involves investment into material or cadaver that has to be disposed after a single training. Simulators reduce this cost by allowing the trainees to practice procedure any number of times till they perfect the procedure without putting actual patients at risk. The initial investment cost will pay off after a short period of time. (William et al., 2017) The tracheal insertion training cost per employee is $3,000 at an elderly care facility in America. While the same training on VR based Next Galaxy's tracheal insertion system costs only $40 per employee, it also saves them the travel cost to other training centres and the need to depend on live subjects. The training can be done remotely and repeatedly with no additional costs (Monsky et al., 2019)

Reduced Learning Curve

Simulation allows training that is independent of place and time. One does not have to wait for the cadaver's lab or the operation room to be free to practice a procedure. It is available 24/7 and a greater number of procedures can be practiced within a limited time providing a more comfortable learning curve. Case Western medical school's dean, Pamela Davis, explained that "students have commented that a 15-minute session with HoloLens could have saved them dozens of hours in the cadaveric lab." (Monsky et al., 2019)

Significant Improvements in the Operating Room

Training with original instruments and 3D graphics makes the surgeon familiar with the devices and eases the transfer of skills from the simulator to the operating room. It has been observed that surgeons trained on a simulator take less time to complete procedures and tend to make fewer mistakes. Socpis developed MR based Holographic Navigation system, which incorporates a Microsoft HoloLens that is worn by the surgeon to enhance the spatial presentation to track pedicle screws and other surgical markings. It significantly improves their speed, precision and reduces errors. Berlin Humboldt Hospital's Spinal Surgery Clinic Chief Christian Woiciechowsky believes that "solutions such as these has the potential to make surgery more effective, safe, and precise" (Monsky et al., 2019)

HURDLES THAT HINDER XR ADOPTION IN HEALTHCARE TRAINING

Content Offering

The key challenge that healthcare sector faces now lack in quality content and its availability for engaging the user in VR applications. For this reason, the right talent in areas including skilled 3D artists, VR programmers, experienced designers and other specialists needs to be identified to craft quality and engaging content needed to bring in to make the user experience more immersive. Recent survey conducted by VR Intelligence and SuperData revealed that 52% of respondents felt that lack of content is a great barrier against the adoption of VR. (Cardiff, 2018; Peter H.,2019).

Uncomfortable Hardware

The other barrier to adoption of immersive technology is lack of good user experience design. The VR and AR HMDs available are cumbersome to use (Cardiff, 2018). For most high-quality VR experience requires the trainees to be tethered to the desktop. Operators have reported being dizzy, disoriented, or nausea like motion sickness. (Marta, 2018). Shiyao Wang et al. in their study found several problems with the HoloLens that impacted the user experience. Some of the issues mentioned by trainees about the device were that they found HoloLens to be heavy and painful to wear, nose pad was not comfortable, some participants could not find a suitable fit to their head available in the device. (Wang et al., 2017)

Technological Glitches

1. **Battery Life:** Most of the training and collaborative AR/VR apps available does not have battery life that can sustain for longer at least during the entire training session. In a system that used HoloLens for telementoring it was found that HoloLens could last for only approximately four participants or about 100 minutes before having to be charged again. (Wang et al., 2017)
2. **Latency**: VR latency is the time taken between initiating a movement and a computer-generated response. In the study of a telementoring system, it was noticed that, the latency, was the key reason for poor performance. 5G devices can reduce latency Enhancing real-time connectivity. (Wang et al., 2017)
3. **Field of View (FOV):** It is the angle of observable view from a VR headset. FOV greatly influences the user experience. In the study (Wang et al., 2017) many users felt FOV was narrow, though the HoloLens has a field of view of 120 degrees horizontally. Other high-end headsets such as ODG R-9, Magic Leap one has limited FOV, original HoloLens FOV was around 35 degrees, HoloLens 2 is around 70 degrees while meta 2 has a reasonably better FOV of 90-degree rate but require a cable attachment. (Adrienne, 2015).
4. **Vergence Accommodation Conflict**: This is a viewing problem for VR HMDs. It is the difference between the physical surface of the screen and the focal point of the simulated world the user views. Such display of 3D images in VR goggles creates conflicts that are unnatural to the eye, which can cause visual fatigue and discomfort resulting into headaches and nausea in users. A good VR user experience (UX) design can reduce or evade VAC-induced discomfort. (Adrienne, 2015).
5. **Eye-Tracking Technology:** VR head-mounted displays haven't been adequate at tracking the user's eyes for computing systems. Advances in eye tracking techniques and eye tracking hardware add-ons and software to AR/VR headsets, decreases systems demand by tracking a user's eye and rendering only in the fovea region, may soon reduce power consumption and increase responsiveness of the system. (Smith et al., 2018; Adrienne, 2015).
6. **Interoperability issue:** With more and more AR and VR systems being used, and multiple devices Connecting to form a system, there is a varying degree of compatibility issue that one needs to work on. (Eran Orr., 2018).
7. **Privacy and Security Concerns:** Perkins Coie LLP and the XR Association in their survey results show that consumer privacy (47%) and data security (42%) top the charts for legal risks concerning immersive technologies. Data confidentiality is also a major concern when recording data on to HMDs, stricter means of data protection must be devised to protect it from being hijacked. The seven principles of storing and handling must be known by all the health professional dealing with them. (Eran Orr., 2018).

Other issues are computational power, cost of immersive technologies, high-quality graphics resolution, User Interface and the ability of the system to tackle computational loads. (Smith et al., 2018)

FUTURE DIRECTIONS

In spite of advancements in technology and demand from across the industries, immersive technology still needs to evolve in order to give its users improved seamless immersive experience. Some areas which need to evolve are discussed below:

Security, Safety, Health, Hygiene and Comfort: The AR and VR HMD's constantly tracks the minute details of the user to give them personalized experience. In this process security and privacy of the user should not be compromised, so appropriate means must be implemented to ensure it. Injuries have been reported while the users were using fully immersive HMD's. As the user's real-world view is replaced with virtual or augmented view user as a result user may end up colliding with real world objects. Other possible cause of injury could be user tripping over the wire that connects the HMD to the computer. Safety of the user from such injuries should be provided. When AR and VR HMD's are used by large number of users especially in Museum's it becomes a breeding ground for infection causing organisms and often the design of HMD makes it difficult to sanitize. Some economic means must be devised to keep the device clean and hygienic. The size, weight and fit of the HMD are very important to factors to improve user experience. In past several research works have mentioned about simulator driven sickness such as nausea, headache, dizziness experienced by users. The physical discomfort can be reduced by designing HMD's that are light weight and comfortable for the users to seamlessly wear it. Perhaps use contact lenses instead of smart glass. (Guy, Gareth, Nicole, Martin, Dawn, Jonathan, Damian, Julian & Lewis, 2018).

Performance enhancement through Edge computing: Hosting the AR and VR services on mobile edge computing instead of cloud architecture can help deal with issues such as latency, processing speeds, high energy consumption affecting battery life and user experience. Edge computing keeps data closer to the user by storing it at Mobile edge computing (MEC) servers thereby increasing the processing speed and reducing latency as opposed to cloud computing where reaching data centres would take long time. Newer architecture using edge computing can tackle existing performance related issues of Mobile Augmented Reality (MAR). (ETSI, 2018; Alisha, 2019).

XR enhanced with AI and ML: Immersive (XR) and emerging technologies such as Artificial Intelligence (AI) and Machine Learning (ML) provides enhanced multidimensional and interactive AR experience. AI and ML algorithms can bring sophistication and cognitive functionality to the existing XR based systems. Already many social media applications like Snapchat, Facebook and Instagram are using AI and AR for either image enhancements or to design realistic avatars based on the image captured for fun, experimental and personalized user experiences. AI when combined with XR systems for medical education can improve training as more data facts can be included and the system will provide more interactive and personalised virtual environment for learners. (Nilima, 2019; Yitzi, 2018)

Improved connectivity through 5G: The current 4G system has limited bandwidth resulting in to AR systems that is not very effective for shared or multiuser experiences. As the concurrent users increase the efficiency of the network drops. The laggy connection often ruins the user experience and often leave the user feeling physically sick which can have detrimental effect on its adoption by user. 5G is one disruptive technology that will offer low latency, better network performance, higher bandwidth with 6Dof (Degree of freedom) which will allow users to walk through the environment. These features of 5G will provide consistent user experience and will enable real- time collaborations with a greater number of concurrent users. The HMD devices need to evolve in order to incorporate the 5G chipset to deliver the 5G benefits which are very critical for the XR applications. (Qualcomm, 2017)

Future enhancements can be in the topics mentioned but not limited to it, as there are many more areas that needs to be explored such as sensory enhancement, benefits of IoT and AR, Improving the field of view (FOV), enhanced multi-sensation rendering framework, Mobile Content for AR apps etc. that can make digital reality more powerful and immersive. (Yitzi, 2018).

CONCLUSION

Immersive technology is a boon to next-gen medical education. Simulations that immersive technology provide, transports the students into an emergency or allows students to view organs in all perspectives from close angles. It exposes medical students to real-life situations without putting patients at risk. Advancements in technology constantly up the quality of users training experience.

From the paper it can be well summarized that immersive technology provides a very strong and positive impact on its learners. The residents and surgeons can benefit as it reduces the learning curve, allows learners to practice complex procedures at their convenience any number of times till they master a skill and for surgeons' time taken to complete a procedure is reduced as they can overlay images on the patient for improved navigation during surgery. However, the challenges identified need to be addressed for adoption rates to improve. Healthcare training can leverage form the immersive technologies as in future with technological advancements, price drops and developers creating newer and richer contents -teaching modules, its use in healthcare training appears almost definite.

REFERENCES

Aboumarzouk, O. M. (2019). *Blandy's urology*. Hoboken, NJ: John Wiley & Sons; Available at https://books.google.co.in/books?isbn=1118863372

ARpost. (2018, August). *3D tooth atlas 9: The virtual reality training system for dentists of the future.* Available at https://arpost.co/2018/08/14/3d-tooth-atlas-9-the-virtual-reality-training-system-for-dentists-of-the-future/

Bamodu, O., & Xuming, Y. (2013). Virtual reality and virtual reality system components. In *Proceedings of the 2nd International Conference on Systems Engineering and Modeling (ICSEM-13)*. Paris, France: Atlantis Press.

Barad, J. (2019). *Reality training for robotics-assisted surgery*. Available at https://healthiar.com/osso-vr-creates-first-virtual-reality-training-for-robotics-assisted-surgery

Barsom, E. Z., Graafland, M., & Schijven, M. P. (2016). Systematic review on the effectiveness of augmented reality applications in medical training. *Surgical Endoscopy*, *30*, 4174. doi:10.100700464-016-4800-6

Bernhardt, S., Nicolau, S. A., Soler, L., & Doignon, C. (2017). *The status of augmented reality in laparoscopic surgery as of 2016*. Medical Image Analysis 37, 66–90. http://dx.doi.org/ 1361-8415/doi:10.1016/j.media.2017.01.007

Bifulco, P., Narducci, F., Vertucci, R., Ambruosi, P., Cesarelli, M., & Romano, M. (2014). Telemedicine supported by Augmented Reality: An interactive guide for untrained people in performing an ECG test. *Biomedical Engineering Online, 13*(1), 153. doi:10.1186/1475-925X-13-153

Bogdan, C. M., Dinca, A. F., & Popovici, D. M. (2011). A brief survey of visuo-haptic simulators for dental procedures training. In *Proceedings of the 6th International Conference on Virtual Learning* (pp. 28-29).

CAE Healthcare announces first mixed reality ultrasound simulation solution with Microsoft HoloLens. CAE Healthcare Inc. Orlando, FL: CAE Healthcare; (2017). Available at https://www.cae.com/news-events/press-releases/cae-healthcare-announces-first-mixed-reality-ultrasound-simulation-solution/

Cardiff, E. (2018). *Response to local surgical challenges.* Available at https://eu.augmentedworldexpo.com/sessions/proximie-augmented-reality-providing-a-global-response-to-local-surgical-challenges/

Christian, S. (2018, March 22). *Using virtual, augmented, and mixed realities for medical training.* Available at http://designinteractive.net/using-virtual-augmented-mixed-realities-medical-training/

Craig, E., & Georgieva, M. (2017, Aug. 30). *VR and AR: Driving a revolution in medical education & patient care.* Available at https://er.educause.edu/.blogs/2017/8/vr-and-ar-driving-a-revolution-in-medical-education-and-patient-care

DeLeon, L. (2017, Oct. 26). *ForwardXP: XR Training for a F.A.S.T. Response.* Available at https://developer.qualcomm.com/blog/forwardxp-xr-training-fast-response

Diamandis, P. H. (2019). *5 breakthroughs coming soon in augmented and virtual reality.* Available at https://singularityhub.com/2019/05/10/5-breakthroughs-coming-soon-in-augmented-and-virtual-reality/

ETSI. (2018). *AR and VR at Glance.* Available at https://www.etsi.org/images/files/ETSITechnology-Leaflets/Augmented_VirtualReality.pdf

Greenwald, W. (2018). *The best VR headsets of 2018.* Available at https://in.pcmag.com/consumer-electronics/101251/the-best-vr-virtual-reality-headsets

Hamacher, A., Kim, S. J., Cho, S. T., Pardeshi, S., Lee, S. H., Eun, S. J., & Whangbo, T. K. (2016). Application of virtual, augmented, and mixed reality to urology. *International Neurourology Journal, 20*(3), 172.

Haubruck, P., Nickel, F., Ober, J., Walker, T., Bergdolt, C., Friedrich, M., ... Tanner, M. C. (2018). Evaluation of app-based serious gaming as a training method in teaching chest tube insertion to medical students: Randomized controlled trial. *Journal of Medical Internet Research, 20*(5), e195. doi:10.2196/jmir.9956

Herron, J. (2016). Augmented reality in medical education and training. *Journal of Electronic Resources in Medical Libraries, 13*(2), 51–55. doi:10.1080/15424065.2016.1175987

Hertz, A. M., George, E. I., Vaccaro, C. M., & Brand, T. C. (2018). Head-to-head comparison of three virtual-reality robotic surgery simulators. JSLS. *Journal of the Society of Laparoendoscopic Surgeons, 22*(1). doi:10.4293/JSLS.2017.00081

Hlova, M. (2018). *What does it take to develop a VR solution in healthcare.* Digital Health. Available at https://www.mddionline.com/what-does-it-take-develop-vr-solution-healthcare

Hu, H. Z., Feng, X. B., Shao, Z. W., Xie, M., Xu, S., Wu, X. H., & Ye, Z. W. (2019). Application and Prospect of Mixed Reality Technology in Medical Field. *Current medical science, 39*(1), 1-6. https://doi.org/ doi:10.100711596-019-1992-8

Huang, T. K., Yang, C. H., Hsieh, Y. H., Wang, J. C., & Hung, C. C. (2018). Augmented reality (AR) and virtual reality (VR) applied in dentistry. *The Kaohsiung Journal of Medical Sciences, 34*(4), 243–248.

Hunter, A. (2015). *Vergence-accommodation conflict is a bitch — here's how to design around it.* Available from vrinflux-dot-com/vergence-accommodation-conflict-is-a-bitch-here-s-how-to-design-around-it.

Jin, W., Birckhead, B., Perez, B., & Hoffe, S. (2017, December). *Augmented and virtual reality: Exploring a future role in radiation oncology education and training. applied radiation oncology.* Available at https://appliedradiationoncology.com/articles/augmented-and-virtual-reality-exploring-a-future-role-in-radiation-oncology-education-and-training

Kamarudin, M. F. B., & Zary, N. (2019, April). Augmented reality, virtual reality, and mixed reality in medical education: A comparative web of science scoping review. doi:10.20944/preprints201904.0323.v1

KhannaA. (2019). *EyeSim.* Available at https://www.eonreality.com/portfolio-items/eyesim- ophthalmology/

Khelemsky, R., Hill, B., & Buchbinder, D. (2017). Validation of a novel cognitive simulator for orbital floor reconstruction. *Journal of Oral and Maxillofacial Surgery, 75*(4), 775–785.

Khor, W. S., Baker, B., Amin, K., Chan, A., Patel, K., & Wong, J. (2016). Augmented and virtual reality in surgery—the digital surgical environment: Applications, limitations and legal pitfalls. *Annals of Translational Medicine, 4*(23), 454. doi:10.21037/atm.2016.12.23

Kim, Y., Kim, H., & Kim, Y. O. (2017). Virtual reality and augmented reality in plastic surgery: a review. *Arch Plast Surg. 44*(3), 179–187. Published online. doi:10.5999/aps.2017.44.3.179

Kosowatz, J. (2017, May 1). *Mixed reality replaces cadavers as teaching tool.* Available at https://aabme.asme.org/posts/mixed-reality-replace-cadavers-as-teaching-tool

Kyaw, B. M., Saxena, N., Posadzki, P., Vseteckova, J., Nikolaou, C. K., George, P. P., ... Car, L. T. (2019). Virtual reality for health professions education: Systematic review and meta-analysis by the Digital Health Education collaboration. *Journal of Medical Internet Research, 21*(1).

Lloyd., M., Watmough, S., & Bennett, N. (2018). Simulation-based training: applications in clinical pharmacy. *The Pharmaceuticals Journal-A royal pharmaceuticals society publication.*

Mitsuno, D., Ueda, K., Itamiya, T., Nuri, T., & Otsuki, Y. (2017). Intraoperative evaluation of body surface improvement by an augmented reality system that a clinician can modify. *Plastic and Reconstructive Surgery. Global Open, 5*(8). doi:10.1097/GOX.0000000000001432

Monsky, W. L., James, R., & Seslar, S. S. (2019). Virtual and augmented reality applications in medicine and surgery-the fantastic voyage is here. *Anatomy & Physiology, 9*(1), 313.

Noble, S. (2019, March 25). *The 10 best augmented reality smartglasses in 2019.* Available at https://www.aniwaa.com/best-of/vr-ar/best-augmented-reality-smartglasses/

Onkka, K. H. (2018). *Precision OS allows surgeons to practice before taking on real surgery.* Available at https://healthiar.com/precision-os-allows-surgeons-to-practice-before-taking-on-real-surgery

Orr, E. (2018). *Virtual reality as an effective medical tool.* Available at https://www.xr.health/virtual-reality-effective-medical-tool.html/

Ortiz, A. (2019). *Welcome to extended reality: Transforming how employees work and learn.* Available at https://www.ibm.com/blogs/insights-on-business/ibmix/welcome-to-extended-reality/

Pantelidis, P., Chorti, A., Papagiouvanni, I., Paparoidamis, G., Drosos, C., Panagiotakopoulos, T., . . . Sideris, M. (2017, Dec. 20). *Virtual and augmented reality in medical education, medical and surgical education - past, present and future,* IntechOpen, doi:. Available at https://www.intechopen.com/books/medical-and-surgical-education-past-present-and-future/virtual-and-augmented-reality-in-medical-education doi:10.5772/intechopen.71963

Perkins Coie LLP. (March 2019) *Industry insights into the future of immersive technology.* Perkins Coie LLP and the XR Association VOLUME 3.

Pfandlera, M., Lazarovici, M., Stefan, P., & Weigl, M. (2017). Virtual reality-based simulators for spine surgery: A systematic review. *The Spine Journal,* ▪▪▪, 1529–9430. doi:10.1016/j.spinee.2017.05.016

Qin, Z., Tai, Y., Xia, C., Peng, J., Huang, X., Chen, Z., ... Shi, J. (2019). Towards virtual VATS, face, and construct evaluation for peg transfer training of Box, VR, AR, and MR trainer. *Journal of Healthcare Engineering, 2019.* doi:10.1155/2019/6813719

Qualcomm. (2017). *Augmented and virtual reality: The first wave of 5G killer apps.* ©2017 ABI Research. Available at https://www.qualcomm.com/media/documents/files/augmented-and-virtual-reality-the-first-wave-of-5g-killer-apps.pdf

Roy, E., Bakr, M. M., & George, R. (2017). The need for virtual reality simulators in dental education: A review. *The Saudi Dental Journal, 29*(2), 41–47. Published online March 6, 2017. doi:10.1016/j.sdentj.2017.02.001

Sachs, G. (2016). *Virtual reality and augment reality: Understanding the race for next computing platform.* The Goldman Sachs Group, Inc. Available at https://www.goldmansachs.com/insights/pages/technology-driving-innovation-folder/virtual-and-augmented-reality/report.pdf

Sanchez, J. (n.d.). *Augmented reality in healthcare.* Available at https://www.plugandplaytechcenter.com/resources/augmented-reality-healthcare/

Schofield, G., Beale, G., Beale, N., Fell, M., Hadley, D., Hook, J., . . . Thresh, L. (2018, June). Viking VR: Designing a virtual reality experience for a museum. In Proceedings of the 2018 Designing Interactive Systems Conference (pp. 805-815). ACM. https://doi.org/10.1145/3196709.3196714

Seam, A. (2019). *AT&T unlocks the power of edge computing: delivering interactive VR over 5G.* Available at https://about.att.com/innovationblog/2019/02/edge_computing_vr.html

Shah, N. (2019). *The next big thing: Integrating AI into augmented and virtual reality.* Available at https://www.cygnet-infotech.com/blog/integrating-ai-into-augmented-and-virtual-reality

Short, M., & Samar, S. (2017). *Transforming healthcare and saving lives with extended reality (XR).* Available at https://www.accenture.com/us-en/blogs/blogs-extended-reality-for-enterprise-health-care

Sirilak, S., & Muneesawang, P. (2018). *A new procedure for advancing telemedicine using the HoloLens.* IEEE; doi:10.1109/ACCESS.2018.2875558

Smith, T., Nelson, J., & Maul, R. (2018). *Digital reality in life sciences and health care.* Available at https://www2.deloitte.com/content/dam/Deloitte/us/Documents/life-sciences-health-care/us-lshc-tech-trends-digital-reality.pdf

Smithsonian. (2015). *Smithsonian brings historic specimens to life in free "skin and bones" mobile app.* Available at https://www.si.edu/newsdesk/releases/smithsonian-brings-historic-specimens-life-free-skin-and-bones-mobile-app

Solutions, M. (2017, Oct. 26). *Virtual reality and augmented reality in healthcare.* Available at http://moisaka.com/virtual-reality/

Tagaytayan, R., Kelemen, A., & Sik-Lanyi, C. (2018). Augmented reality in neurosurgery. *Archives of Medical Science, 14*(3), 572–578.

The first hybrid neurosurgical simulator based on physical and augmented reality. (n.d.). Available at https://upsim.upsurgeon.com/discover/the-first-hybrid-neurosurgical-simulator-based-on-physical-and-augmented-reality-.kl

The ultimate guide to understanding augmented reality (AR) technology. (n.d). ©RealityTechnologies.com Diversified Internet Holdings LLC. Available at https://www.realitytechnologies.com/augmented-reality/

Virtual Health Clinic. (n.d.). Society of american gastrointestinal and endoscopic surgeons (Sage). Available at https://www.sages.org/virtual-hernia-clinic/

Wang, S., Parsons, M., Stone-McLean, J., Rogers, P., Boyd, S., Hoover, K., ... Smith, A. (2017). Augmented reality as a telemedicine platform for remote procedural training. *Sensors (Basel), 17*(10), 2294. doi:10.339017102294

Weiner, Y. (2018). *39 ways AR can change the world in the next five years.* Available at https://medium.com/thrive-global/39-ways-ar-can-change-the-world-in-the-next-five-years-a7736f8bfaa5

Wright, T., de Ribaupierre, S., & Eagleson, R. (2017). Design and evaluation of an augmented reality simulator using leap motion. *Healthcare Technology Letters, 4*(5), 210–215. doi:10.1049/htl.2017.0070

Zweifach, S. M., & Triola, M. M. (2019). Extended reality in medical education: Driving adoption through provider-centered design. *Digital Biomarkers, 3*(1), 14–21. doi:10.1159/000498923

ADDITIONAL READING

Chen, L., Thomas W Day., Wen Tang., & Nigel W. John. (2017). *"Recent Developments and Future Challenges in Medical Mixed Reality"* IEEE International Symposium on Mixed and Augmented Reality (ISMAR). DOI: 10.1109/ISMAR.2017.29

Gavaghan, K. A., Peterhans, M., Oliveira-Santos, T., & Weber, S. (2011). A portable image overlay projection device for computer-aided open liver surgery. *IEEE Transactions on Biomedical Engineering*, *58*, 1855–1864.

Heather, A. Tudor Chinnah., & Vikram Devara. (2019). *"The Use of Virtual and Augmented Reality in Anatomy Teaching"*. MedEdPublish. DOI: Available from: https://www.mededpublish.org/manuscripts/2195 doi:10.15694/mep.2019.000077.1

Krigsman, M. (2018). *"This medical pioneer trains digital doctors with AR and VR"*. Beyond IT Failure. Available from: https://www.zdnet.com/article/virtual-reality-medical-pioneer-trains-digital-doctors/

Maddox, T. (2018). *"Extending Reality to the Operating Room"*. HEALTH Tech, Tech Trends, VR Tech. Available from: https://techtrends.tech/tech-trends/xr-medical-visualization-tools-reduce-cognitive-load-and-enhance-learning/

Sarah, M. Zweifach & Marc M. Triola. (2019). *"Extended Reality in Medical Education: Driving Adoption through Provider-Centered Design"*. Digit Biomark 2019; 3:14–21, DOI: , © 2019 The Author(s). Published by S. Karger AG, Basel. www.karger.com/dib doi:10.1159/000498923

P. Vávra., J. Roman., P. Zonča., P. Ihnát., M. Němec., J. Kumar., N. Habib., & A. El-Gendi. (2017). *"Recent Development of Augmented Reality in Surgery: A Review"* Hindawi. Journal of Healthcare Engineering Volume 2017, Article ID 4574172, 9 pages https://doi.org/ doi:10.1155/2017/4574172

Workman, S. (2018). *"Mixed Reality: A Revolutionary Breakthrough in Teaching and Learning"*. EDUCASE. Available from: https://er.educause.edu/articles/2018/7/mixed-reality-a-revolutionary-breakthrough-in-teaching-and-learning

KEY TERMS AND DEFINITIONS

Augmented Reality (AR): It is a technology that blends the user's view of real world with digital information on top of it, to provide the user an enhanced version of reality.

Extended Reality (XR): It refers to a continuum, which combines all real and virtual world environments. It encompasses virtual, augmented and mixed reality technologies to provide users a better immersive experience.

Haptics: It refers to the technology that uses tactile (touch) sensation to interact with the computer applications in order to improve user experience.

Head Mounted Display (HMD): It is a computer display system that is mounted on a helmet or a set of goggles.

Immersive Technology: It refers to technology that enables users to interact with simulated environments and objects, blurring the line between the real world and the digital world. It covers a range of technologies such as AR, VR, MR.

Marker Based Augmented Reality: It is a term used to represent an AR application that needs prior knowledge of a user's environment to identify/ locate part of real world that needs to be augmented. This is achieved by placing a marker in the real world where the digital image must overlay.

Markerless Augmented Reality: It is a term used to represent an AR application that does not need prior knowledge of a user's environment to identify/ locate part of real world that needs to be augmented and hold it to a fixed point in space. it is also known as location-based AR. It functions using such technologies as GPS, accelerometer, digital compass and SLAM (simultaneous localization and mapping technology).

Mixed Reality (MR): It brings together real and digital environments that co-exist and interact with each other to produce new environment which allows user to immerse in the world around while interacting with the virtual world.

Virtual Reality (VR): It is a technology that creates a simulated environment that can be similar or completely different from the user's environment. The VR headset gives the user a fully immersive visual experience.

Chapter 3
Nursing Education in the Era of Virtual Reality

Derya Uzelli Yilmaz
Izmir Kâtip Çelebi University, Turkey

Sevil Hamarat Tuncalı
Izmir Kâtip Çelebi University, Turkey

Yusuf Yilmaz
Ege University, Turkey

ABSTRACT

Today's new technologies have impacted many different areas of education, with nursing education one such area. Nursing education, as a learning process, targets the combination of cognitive, affective, and psychomotor learning domains. However, traditional teaching methods may not meet all of the Y and Z generations' learning needs. Today's learners are accustomed to multimedia learning environments and have come to expect a certain level of technology integrated into their curricula. Virtual Reality (VR) technology enables students to become immersed within a 360-degree view experience of scenes that have been completely digitally created, whilst no longer viewing the real world around them. Virtual simulation has been used to teach communication, disaster relief, teamwork, and interviewing techniques, among other skills; and can also provide immersive personalized learning experiences. This chapter presents some of the many facets of VR in today's nursing education.

INTRODUCTION

Traditional teaching methods may not meet all of the Y and Z generations' learning needs (Somyürek, 2014). Today's learners are accustomed to multimedia environments and have come to expect technology to be integrated into their curricula (Lee & Wong, 2016). Nursing education is one of the fields that has benefitted from Virtual Reality (VR) being incorporated within teaching and learning methods. VR technology enables students to become immersed in a 360-degree view experience of a scene that

DOI: 10.4018/978-1-7998-1796-3.ch003

Copyright © 2020, IGI Global. Copying or distributing in print or electronic forms without written permission of IGI Global is prohibited.

is completely digitally created (Izard et al., 2018). Particularly in nursing education, VR has been used to provide virtual scenarios in a simulated environment in order to teach communication, disaster relief, teamwork, and interviewing, among other skills; as well as to provide an immersive personalized learning experience (Ferguson et al., 2015). VR-based learning provides learners with experiences in contextually rich environments that encourage reflection. Environments that support learning activities designed to authentically replicate clinical practice settings can be used to replicate clinical environments. Such environments may support and provide a foundation for learning during students' future clinical nursing experiences (Gore & Loice, 2014; Korhan et al., 2018). VR has become one such technique by creating a higher degree of fidelity in nursing education by employing realistic methods. Therefore, the aim of this chapter is to discuss the intended and unintended results of nursing education with VR, and to emphasize the importance of VR in the context of cognitive, psychomotor, and affective outcomes that guide today's clinical teaching and evaluation of nursing students.

BACKGROUND

VR-based learning provides learners with experiences in contextually rich environments that encourage reflection. Environments that support learning activities designed to authentically replicate clinical practice settings should be seen and treated as clinical environments. Such environments are seen to support and provide a foundation for learning during future clinical experiences (Chen & Teh, 2013; Gore & Loice, 2014). Practitioners engaged in VR are required to integrate knowledge of anatomy and physiology whilst performing and validating clinical competency in specific procedures such as intravenous catheterization, nasogastric tube placement, urinary catheterization, and pain management (Choi, 2017; Guo, Deng & Yang, 2014; İsmailoğlu & Zaybak, 2018; Jöud et al., 2010). In 2017, Wolters Kluwer Health published results of a survey on technology utilization within nursing education. The study showed a significant increase in the use of virtual simulation. Specifically, the "Future of Technology in Nursing Education" report revealed that 65% of nursing education programs employed virtual simulation, with VR utilization predicted to increase from 10% to as much as 45% over the next 5 years in response to a worsening shortage of clinical training sites (Wolters Kluwer, 2017). The VR teaching approach has become recognized as one of the most effective clinical teaching/learning strategies currently available to ensure caregiver competency in terms of clinical knowledge and critical thinking, as well as the technical application of psychomotor skills through the use of technology. Regardless, the VR approach has great potential as a powerful tool in healthcare education of the future. This chapter aims to present some of the many facets of VR in the scope of nursing education.

Nursing Education

Education is a process that primarily involves teaching, but also facilitates the gaining of certain behaviors, values, and attitudes by learners, helping them to form a lasting view of the world, and to learn how best to approach problems (Hacıalioğlu, 2011). Nursing education is a combination of theoretical and practical elements that involve cognitive, affective, and also psychomotor fields of learning, and as such necessitates the integration of theory and practice specific to the field (Eker, Açıkgöz, & Karaca, 2014).

Nursing education has evolved throughout history. In Ancient Egypt, Mesopotamia, the Hittite Empire, and in Rome, nursing education started with the concept of training based on the master-apprentice relationship, with healer women who offered patient care and various other healthcare services, which then progressed to a more scientific approach with Florence Nightingale (Topuksak & Kublay, 2010). In 1860, the Florence Nightingale School of Nursing was established at St. Thomas' Hospital in London, England, as the first modern School of Nursing, and is accepted as the foundation of formal nursing education. In the school, nursing students received 1 year of education taught in the classroom and also through applied teaching in the hospital. A registration and reporting system was used in order to evaluate the nursing students' development (Ergül, 2011). In 1860, Nightingale's nursing school founded the first criterion for nursing to be considered as a profession, with the provision of systematic formal education, selection of students according to various set criteria, and a set uniform to be worn by those providing care to patients. After the First World War (1914-1918), hospital nursing, community health nursing, and private nursing became specialized as three separate sub-branches of the profession. During the Second World War (1939-1945), the value of the nursing profession was strengthened with nursing education extended to the undergraduate level (Kıran & Taşkıran, 2014).

In the development of Nursing Science, master's and doctoral postgraduate programs in nursing were first started at Columbia University in the United States of America (USA) in 1933. Since the 1960s, particularly in the USA, the United Kingdom (UK), Canada and in Australia, strong trends in the extension of nursing practices in the provision of healthcare across many countries worldwide led to the development of postgraduate education and more advanced nursing roles in western countries (Ergül, 2011; Kıran & Taşkıran, 2014; Ökdem, Abbasoğlu, & Doğan, 2000; Topuksak & Kublay, 2010).

From the time of Florence Nightingale until the present day, nursing educators have worked on establishing the most effective methods to help students become competent in their profession. After determining that learning takes place through cognitive, affective, and psychomotor domains, nursing education was transferred to professional ability laboratories and healthcare institutions. Modern nursing education includes not only knowledge and clinical experience, but also the teaching of basic nursing skills, techniques, and practices towards the aim of becoming a proficient nurse in practice. For this reason, the training process should contribute to the students internalizing knowledge, skills, attitudes, and ethical standards related to their discipline, and to adopt them as part of their professional behavior (Karaöz, 2003).

Since nursing care includes cognitive, affective, and psychomotor domains, training programs should be developed based on evaluating the learning outcomes of nurses in order to develop their ability to provide individual-specific care. When cognitive learning outcomes in nursing education are examined; in the first years of nursing education, nurse educators used evidence to teach basic knowledge about human life, nature, and science, and to apply this knowledge from simple to complex, easy to difficult, and from easy to abstract, and also as a precondition to remember, understand, apply, analyze, evaluate, and create processes (Brown, 2011; Krathwohl, 2002). In more advanced nursing education, individuals are coached to be able to make more complicated and effective decisions about patient care, as well as the assessment of basic information in order to provide nursing care to patients as individuals, and also their family and friends through the teaching of pathophysiology, diagnosis, the treatment of diseases, and interventions for patient care. The aim is to conduct the various stages of understanding, implementation, analysis, and synthesis based on the knowledge gained during their early nursing education (Kaddoura, VanDyke, Cheng, & Shea-Foisy, 2016).

Positive and negative emotions, attitudes, values, interests, as well as the personal and social characteristics of the individual are evaluated in the affective field. Learning depends on the individual's abilities and interaction with their environment, and is therefore difficult to determine, express, and evaluate the results of learning outcomes related to this field (Gömleksiz & Kan, 2012). Learning deficiencies in this area may lead to the disregard of the individual's psychosocial needs in nursing care. In the process of nursing education, identifying the outcomes related to the affective area and the teaching of these skills enables nurses to better evaluate the personal reactions of patients, and other nursing staff, and to therefore plan and implement more effective interventions. This helps to improve self-support by reducing self-criticism and fostering empowerment skills; to choose the most effective evaluation tools to identify patients' dilemmas and responses; to determine responses so as to alleviate non-adaptive emotions; to increase awareness of the responses that affect objectivity; and to understand the reactions of colleagues in order to improve their professional performance (Gorman & Sultan, 2007).

In the process of making cognitive and behavioral skills gains in nursing education, students are expected to exhibit the expected behaviors instinctively. The psychomotor domain focuses on physical skills that involve the coordination of brain functions and muscular movements. Evaluations in this area are more concrete and measurable, and therefore observable, than the cognitive and psychosocial domains; focusing on outcomes rather that the process (Brown, 2011; Stroup, 2014). Skills laboratories and simulated applications can be employed in the teaching and development of psychomotor skills in nursing education. The aim is for students to acquire the necessary skills through modeling, small rough modeling, or simulators at different levels of reality prior to practicing in the actual patient care environment.

In line with the learning objectives determined for cognitive, attitudinal, and psychomotor outcomes, students should be provided with cognitive, psychomotor, and affective learning, which is the main objective of clinical teaching in clinical practice areas; and to exhibit clinical performance in these areas, which occurs through behavioral change (Anderson, 2005). In classical nursing education, patients are determined in a clinical setting and students work alongside a nursing educator. Expectations of the latest generations in clinical education are still changing day by day, and as such new technologies have become increasingly integrated within nursing education, as detailed in the following section.

Education Technology in Nursing Education

Nursing students are expected to apply skills acquired in their academic course and laboratory environment to actual patients during clinical applications. During this process, faculty members are confronted with many factors such as issues of patient safety, limited possibilities for clinical application and shortening of hospital stays, and an increasing student numbers. Students often experience a sense of insecurity about their communication skills and nursing practices, as they do not know how to integrate their acquired skills into patient care (Stroup, 2014).

Nursing care is not only related to providing quality care, but also requires critical thinking and detailed attention to the profession. In order to provide quality and safe nursing care to patients, nursing students are required to successfully pass clinical skills training throughout their nursing education. No matter how much importance is attached to gaining clinical experience, it will continue to remain difficult for students to gain skills if they have inadequate opportunity to experience clinical procedures (Şengül, 2010). These concerns in nursing education require the use of different methods to be applied for their teaching and learning.

In addition to these problems faced in nursing education, schooling in the profession has started to include nontraditional teaching methods. In order to increase students' learning experiences, educational technologies are being employed in the teaching of nursing. The attractiveness of innovative technologies offers educators new ideas and new approaches in the teaching process. In addition to the traditional methods of lecture and demonstration, other teaching approaches have been introduced for the acquisition of skills in nursing education through technological developments affecting the educational environment.

One such method is web-based learning, which is defined as educational technology integrated with informational technology in the learning and teaching environment whereby information is shared and used via the Internet. The web-based training method has been proposed as alternative or complementary to traditional education methods for the acquisition of clinical nursing skills, which is an important part of undergraduate education in the nursing profession (Bahar, 2015; Lu, Lin, & Li, 2009). Another method employed in nursing education is video-based instruction. Video-based teaching is carried out by preregistration of the skills, with the aim of providing students with information about psychomotor skills. Video-based teaching is a method that enables students to visualize nursing skills at any time in order to reinforce their learning and thus contribute positively to their skills training (Korhan, Tokem, Uzelli Yılmaz, & Dilemek, 2016).

Today, mobile learning (m-learning) is one of the most frequently employed methods in nursing education. Interest in e-learning environments in nursing education has now moved more towards m-learning environments. M-learning is defined as students and instructors accessing learning resources anywhere and anytime using mobile telephony devices (e.g., smartphones and tablet personal computers). M-learning affords users flexibility in time and space, thereby increasing their independence and sense of responsibility for learning. In addition, m-learning enables students to become self-motivated to learn using new technologies and teaching methods. M-learning is a method that is readily available to support and complement traditional nursing education with a student base who are themselves predominantly already mobile device users. Therefore, the use of m-learning in nursing education is increasing (Mann, Medves, & Vandenkerkohf, 2015). M-learning through the advances seen in mobile device technology includes VR.

Simulation Technologies in Nursing Education

One intensively applied area of technology used in nursing education is simulation. Simulation applications are used as a training method in which students are immersed in a situation that reflects real-life conditions, and thereby gain a virtual or artificial experience without need to adopt the risks associated with learning in the physical clinical environment (Cannon-Diehl, 2009; Unver et al., 2017). Simulation is not just the usage of technology, but can be used to replace real-world experiences in order to contribute to the students' academic development. It is completely interactive in a way that mimics the real world, and can be a teaching method that also includes experienced guides integrated within the environment (Gaba, 2004). The simulation teaching process involves four main aspects of nursing education: (1) improvement of students' technical competence with the application and reapplication of psychomotor skills; (2) provision of expert training tailored to students' needs; (3) inclusion of learning objectives in emotional components; and, (4) improvement of students' abilities to reach valid clinical decisions (Khorshid et al., 2002). Historically, the emergence of simulation started with the aim of determining situations which could have potentially serious negative training consequences for sectors such as aviation, the automobile industry, and the nuclear industry which could arise from human error

Table 1. Simulation applications used in teaching nursing principles

Low-tech simulations	High-tech simulations
Three-dimensional (3D) organ models	Screen-based simulations
Basic plastic mannequins	Realistic, high-fidelity procedural simulators
Animal models	Realistic high-tech interactive human simulators
Simulated / standardized patients with human cadavers	Virtual reality (VR), augmented reality (AR), and haptic systems

(Gore & Loice, 2014). In health sciences, simulators are used in skills laboratories and have become an indispensable part of today's training programs (Kuzu-Kurban, 2015).

Simulation applications range from the simplest to the most complex. While a simple level simulation application can be a discussion of a case study written by an instructor through gamification, today's technology can also provide students with the opportunity to provide patient care through a computer-assisted patient simulator (Decker, Sportsman, Puetz, & Billings, 2008). Simulation applications include high-tech, advanced simulation equipment. Table 1 presents the range of simulations used in nursing education, categorized as low-tech or high-tech simulations (Kızıl & Şendir, 2019).

Low-tech simulation tools are used in nursing education to teach basic anatomy skills with three-dimensional organ models in anatomy laboratories. Basic plastic-made mannequins and basic skills trainers are used for the development of psychomotor skills (injection application, catheterization application, etc.). Animal models are used for the teaching of advanced life support, tracheostomy applications, surgical skills training, and in physiology laboratories for medical education. Human cadavers are the real-life simulations that are often used in anatomy and pathology laboratories (Ziv, 2005). Actor-patients who are simulated or standardized are trained to accurately describe and tell the story, symptoms and emotional state of a real patient. This approach is often used for the development of nursing students' communications skills (Bradley, 2006).

Advanced technology simulators are models developed using computer hardware and software, offering a high level of realism in students' training through the application of interventional simulation tools, especially for basic psychomotor, procedural, and technical skills training. Hybrid models feature integrated simulators, with part or whole-body models, coupled with computer-based technologies that enable students to work with the human physical structure and the associated physiological factors. Unlike other simulators, the high reality simulator is capable of showing a physiological response, with advanced features including chest movements, electrocardiography, monitorization, eye movements, pupil reflex, and speech according to the nature of heart and lung sounds. These simulators can even react to actual physiological responses without need for control by the trainer (Kardong-Edgren, Lungstrom, & Bendel, 2009).

Educational environments that are supported by visual materials and reality foster and maintain learners' attention, and help to embody concepts and to simplify issues that are otherwise difficult to understand. In this sense, in recent years, education environments have been improved, with virtual and touch-based high-tech systems offering simulated applications that have reduced the time requirement for certain aspects of nursing education.

Augmented Reality (AR) is the simultaneous and interactive representation of visual elements and real life through the application of advanced computer software. AR technology provides an environment in which students can interact with a variety of virtual objects placed in the real world (Ferguson,

Davidson, Scott, Jackson, & Hickman, 2015). AR teaching environments encourage students to use their imagination and creativity by creating a deeper form of learning, providing different aspects of objects that are difficult to learn, and in drawing their attention to the subject being taught. In addition, AR helps students to create objects that cannot be achieved in the real world by transforming them into 3D objects, and thereby providing a learning environment that best fits their learning speed and learning style (Vaughn, Lister, & Shaw, 2016).

Haptic systems can be introduced into the virtual environment through communication with the learner or user in a tactile sense. Information about virtual environment components changed as a result of technology-based interventions are transmitted to the user through tactual feedback. Haptic technology also provides human-computer interaction by providing auditory, visual, and textual feedback to the user through a simulation interface (Butt, Kardong-Edgren, & Ellertson, 2018). This approach enables students to experience a more realistic level of experience through haptic technology components included in the virtual environment. Haptic systems can also be added to VR environments, enabling learners to increase their sense of reality. VR is explained in detail in the following section.

Virtual Reality

Often referred to simply as "VR," Virtual Reality is a term derived from the Latin "Virtualis" and was used for the first time by Jaron Lanier in 1989 (Oppenheim, 1993). Although there have been a number of definitions put forward in the literature, there is still a lack of standardization or consistency (Kardong-Edgren, Farra, Alinier, & Young, 2019). In summary, VR can be defined as 3D simulation applications that provide users with a sense of presence in a given environment with different hardware that interacts with haptic tools (Kaleci, Tepe, & Tüzün, 2017).

There are three basic features that distinguish VR technology from other multimedia applications: navigation, interaction, and immersion (Stary, 2001; Trindade, Fiolhais, & Almeida, 2002). "Navigation" allows users to move efficiently and comfortably across distances and between locations. "Interaction" between users and the environment offers interactivity in real-time. Simultaneous interaction with 3-D objects creates the perception for the user of being physically present. "Immersion" is where the user feels they are within and can act within the depicted environment. The level of reality offered by VR increases in line with the levels of presence and immersion comprehended by the user in their VR experience (Hanson & Shelton, 2008).

The feeling of presence is defined as the subjective experience in which an individual is present in a particular place or environment, even though physically located elsewhere (Gökoğlu & Çakıroğlu, 2019). Presence and immersion, which are two separate components of the virtual environment, are closely related. In other words, the more a virtual environment creates a sense of immersion, the higher the level of presence comprehended by the user (Witmer & Singer, 1998).

VR applications offer a computer-generated, 3D simulation of a real-world situation, whereby the user can perceive the simulated environment as esthetic and can interact in the environment through the use of special devices worn on the body (Ausburn & Ausburn, 2004; Serrano, Baños, & Botella, 2016). VR consists of advanced computer technologies that deliver instantaneous human-computer interaction. There are two basic types of VR, the immersive and non-immersive approach, based on a real-world projection situation. Non-immersive VR is defined as 3D visuals created by multimedia tools on personal computers that can be explored interactively using a monitor, keyboard, mouse or joystick (Chen, Toh, & Wan, 2004). Immersive VR provides users with the ability to function within that environment by feeling like they are actually a part of an environment (Passing, David, & Eshel-Kedmi, 2016). In this way, users can perceive their virtual environments as if they are in the real world.

In the context of these features, studies have shown that immersive VR applications can create positive learning outcomes in education. Freina and Ott (2015) stated that research on VR is mostly conducted under the disciplines of computer sciences, engineering, or medicine, where the use of immersive VR education has shown considerable advantages and potential. The same study emphasized that VR makes learning more fun and evocative when used for educational purposes in which there is no risk, whereas implementing similar training in the real world is often not possible. Based on these aspects, the teaching of nursing skills applications through VR is considered to be extremely important and beneficial in terms of improved educational experiences as providing near real-world conditions that would otherwise not be feasible. Thanks to VR, students can not only learn scientific facts faster and better, but can also attain close to real life experiences by practically taking part and experimenting (Dreesmann, 2018). Applications of VR in the area of nursing education are discussed in detail in the following section.

VIRTUAL REALITY IN NURSING EDUCATION

Nursing education aims to transfer theoretical knowledge within a course teaching environment to psychomotor skills applied in the clinical environment. The traditional methods used in nursing education are no longer sufficient to develop and evaluate today's students' problem-solving, critical thinking, and communication skills. In this sense, it is significantly important to address the gap between transferring what students learn in the classroom to their daily clinical practice (Karaöz, 2003).

The VR approach, which is one of the methods used to address such problems in the teaching and learning process, was initially limited by earlier technology that were simulation-based, and were also prohibitively costly. However, VR technologies will likely be included in healthcare teaching programs within the next 5 years, and especially in the field of research and development (Wolters Kluwer Health, 2017). In addition, it is inevitable that today's student population, which is predominantly Z generation, has an increasing tendency towards VR-based education. Additionally, VR has become relatively easier to apply within educational environments, along with more cost-effective solutions, and the development of portable technologies such as VR glasses.

VR technology helps to improve learning outcomes in the healthcare field, through helping to make learning permanent whilst affording users the opportunity to practice their skills (Graafland, Schraagen, & Schijven, 2012). VR applications can effectively visualize complex healthcare environments. With the help of VR, theoretical knowledge in the field of health education can be integrated into the clinical environment by educators employing the visualizing options of VR technology.

VR applications used in nursing education are composed of two levels (Khalifa, Bogorad, Gibson, Peifer, & Nussbaum, 2006). The first level is simple VR, which is limited to a computer interface that does not use a real-world scene, artificial intelligence or other technological support systems. Anatomical atlases can be considered as an example of a first level VR application. Students can examine human anatomical structures seen in textbooks through VR anatomic atlases in 3D, and thereby see the relationships between structures in a concrete way. The second level includes advanced VR with visual and haptic user interfaces. Virtual suture disposal practices, especially used in the development of surgical skills, can be given as an example of this level. VR applications in nursing education can be examined as: the application of nursing skills within a laboratory setting, and the application of clinical teaching in nursing.

Virtual Reality – Nursing in a Skills Laboratory

The aim of nursing education is to provide students with the required basic knowledge, skills, and attitudes in cognitive, sensory, and psychomotor fields, to internalize these gains, and then to transform them into behaviors (Şen, 2012). The skills laboratories used in the teaching of psychomotor skills are considered safe and controllable environments which complement rather than substitute for actual clinical training, but which aim to provide students with the necessary professional skills (Öncü, 2014). While it is aimed for students to reach the required level of competence in the vocational skills laboratory, these skills are also strengthened with additional practice conducted under the supervision of trainers in clinical education (Kolcu et al., 2017). Although psychomotor skills teaching performed by the demonstration method is a teaching method that must be used in order to gain basic practice skills, this method alone may be inadequate in achieving the required professional behaviors such as critical thinking and decision-making (Gore & Loice, 2014). For this reason, other teaching methods are also employed in order for students to reach the necessary learning goals required within the nursing profession.

Difficulties that may be experienced in the transfer of theoretical knowledge to the application of health education can be overcome through the use of VR applications. The ability to show and manipulate is among the distinct educational benefits of VR technology, as reported in the literature. The ability to perform learning tasks in the real-world environment, and to experience situations that are difficult or even impossible to experience are considered among the educational benefits of VR-based training (Bricken & Byrne 1994; Pantelidis, 1993). VR-based training environments provide non-stationary experiential environments that can positively affect students' learning outcomes (Goodwin, Wiltshire, & Fiore, 2015).

VR offers a high-end user interface with real-time simulations and interactions that can address multiple sensory channels (Osuagwu, Ihedigbo, & Ndigwe, 2015). It is an important component that requires the appropriate implementation of teaching designs as the basis of the interface. A study by Chuah, Chen, and Teh (2011) on the use of VR in education focused on the cognitive effects of a given specific situation on the emotional level of students. The results of the study reported that a significant relationship was found between the students' feelings and the design components of a computer-based VR learning environment.

In VR technology, it is possible for users to navigate, look around, and interact with the VR environment and with objects in this virtual world, just as they would in the real world. Therefore, the underlying interrelationship on the basis of VR primarily needs to be the teaching of psychomotor skills, and which is then used in order to achieve an experimental active learning environment (Osuagwu et al., 2015)

VR can be divided into three groups, which are: 1) 3D simulations and micro-worlds within the scope of learner interaction; 2) 3D environments with multi-user support; and 3) environments where teaching resources are projected through 3D interfaces (Chen & Teh, 2013; Chen, Toh, & Wan, 2004). Virtual simulations are used in teaching complex and difficult skills in nursing, and are defined as electronic systems in which the applied interventions are perceived by sensors within the simulated system and their mechanical effect, and the physiological response that occurs based on touch (haptic). For example, the sensor inside the pelvic model in a simulated system used in pelvic inspection training can detect the pressure of touch during the pelvic inspection process and thereby provide feedback to the learner. In this way, the trainer provides information about whether or not the application is being performed correctly (Seropian, Brown, Gavilanes, & Driggers, 2004; Ziv, Small, & Root-Wolpe, 2000).

In addition, VR simulations reflect real-life events within virtual environments and interactive scenarios. In this way, it can be ensured that students perform the necessary skills applications and that they are evaluated objectively at the end of the application, both by themselves and their educators. These systems can provide an effective learning environment, especially where the educator may otherwise be unable to fully assess their students' initiatives. VR simulations also include virtual representations (e.g., patient, doctor, student, instructor, other hospital personnel, etc.) that portray individuals in real life within a virtual hospital environment in three dimensions (Davis, 2015). These representations can be customized by changing the facial expressions, skin color, body shape and size, hair style or color, and the clothing worn (Wiecha, Heyden, Sternthal, & Merialdi, 2010). VR applications can contribute to increasing student motivation and success by allowing unrestricted implementation of clinical scenarios in a risk-free environment, and thereby reducing student anxiety whilst improving self-confidence, helping to develop clinical decision-making skills, and learning the correct techniques by providing feedback at the end of the practice (Cook, 2005; Jenson & Forsyth, 2012; Sarıkoç, 2016).

Virtual Reality – Clinical Teaching of Nursing

Clinical education in nursing aims to integrate theoretical knowledge with practical knowledge in real life situations, and also to help students develop the necessary problem-solving skills. In order to achieve these goals, students should be provided with cognitive, psychomotor, and affective learning, which is the main purpose of clinical teaching in clinical practice areas, and to foster behavioral changes in these areas.

Clinical learning environments provide students with the opportunity to observe, decide and apply patient care, patients' clinical tables, role models, and to work alongside future colleagues and other healthcare team members. However, clinical environments where clinical education is conducted take place in a complex social environment, unlike the classroom environment where theoretical education is conducted. As a result, there may be difficulties in controlling environmental conditions based on the need to integrate cognitive, psychomotor, and sensorial skills in order for students to provide competent healthcare services to patients, the need to assure the safety of students and the recipients of healthcare services, and the varying different individual needs of learners (White & Evan, 2002).

Due to patient safety issues and ethical considerations in the clinical field, students' direct experience in patient care and the opportunities available to them to cope with problem-based clinical situations are somewhat limited. These factors make clinical teaching naturally difficult and challenging.

Simulation-based clinical training is therefore a useful andragogical approach that offers nursing students the opportunity to practice clinical and decision-making skills through real-life situational experiences, but without unnecessarily compromising patient safety (Shin, Park, & Kim, 2015). Therefore, the use of simulation-based VR applications is considered important for the development of clinical skills in nursing education.

In VR technology employed in nursing education, it is possible to interact with virtual objects created in the environment just as though in the real world. The use of VR technology in the teaching of psychomotor skills is now primarily based on VR applications, and the provision of such an experiential learning environment for the practicing of these skills is considered one of the most significant gains in nursing education (Osuagwu et al., 2015).

The clinical learning environment in nursing education has an important effect on the development of quality nursing education, and therefore the students' learning. In order to ensure a positive contribution, the clinical environment requires the necessary features that make learning easier. VR is acknowledged to make learning of difficult to understand and complex concepts that much easier (Goodwin et al., 2015). VR environments also support communication, decision-making, and understanding because they have the potential to help students test out certain scenarios (Ramasundaram, Grunwald, Mangeot, Comerford, & Bliss, 2005).

The use of the VR approach in the development of clinical skills was initially somewhat limited because the devices used were only simulator-based and also prohibitively costly. However, as Lee and Wong (2014) pointed out, there has been an increasing trend towards VR-based education both at the secondary and higher education level. Nowadays, VR can be experienced by a more widespread audience, especially in conjunction with more cost-effective and portable technologies such as VR glasses. In particular, the use of technologies such as VR glasses can now be more easily accessed, and are more cost-effective compared to simulators.

In addition to these obvious advantages, there may also be certain disadvantages of using VR in nursing education. One disadvantage of VR technology is that it requires considerable financial investment in the long term to be used different units. Adapting VR to the field of nursing requires expertise just as it requires technical knowledge (Kaleci, Tepe, & Tüzün, 2017). When working with such applications, a multidisciplinary process must be managed with the necessary experts in the field. In the development of clinical teaching skills in nursing schools, the use of game-based VR applications, especially in virtual patients simulating the clinical environment, can be integrated into the teaching process (Ma, Jain, & Anderson, 2014).

OUTCOMES OF VIRTUAL REALITY IN NURSING EDUCATION

VR is conceptual, perceptual, and interactive, and enables instant feedback within highly beneficial learning environments that enable students to explore (Jarmon, Traphagan, Mayrath, & Trivedi, 2009). In the literature related to the use of VR in education, these environments have been shown to provide students with a social and entertaining environment for group learning, thus providing students with skills such as learning with groups, thinking at higher levels, and acting upon decisions (Downey, 2011; Duncan, Miller, & Jiang, 2012). Dickey (2005) stated that in addition to learning in collaboration, VR also provides students with the opportunity to practice what they learn; that is, it enables them to learn by gaining experience. The research concluded that VR facilitates role-playing, placing the student at the center of the learning-teaching process, and thereby increasing social communication, interaction, and collaboration. It also offers simultaneous communication and interaction between instructors and students. Based on these pedagogical benefits, VR also contributes to increases in students' internal motivation levels (Dreher, Reiners, Dreher, & Dreher, 2009).

It is difficult to state that the environment in which face-to-face relationships are maintained and face-to-face communication as the real social space have the same meanings and lead to the same actions (Kaleci, Tepe, & Tüzün, 2017). For example, it can be easily and directly read when a person is upset, angry, delighted, or happy, and from both opinions stated and as seen in relationships with others. Therefore, there is a more unmediated relationship in which it is easier to obtain information about human actions so as to understand their intentions. In fact, continuity of communication is limited when

Figure 1. Distribution of Studies on Use of VR in Nursing by Years (Google Scholar)

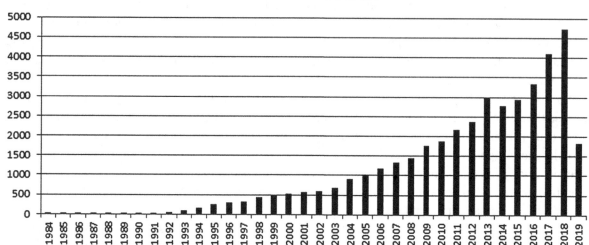

switched just to the virtual environment. Depending on these evaluations, it may be thought that time spent in real socialization decreases and that time spent within Internet-based environments will be affected by moral development through social environments and in the virtual environment, especially when considering the development of skills such as empathy and subjective responsibility will be interrupted (Tanhan & Alav, 2015).

Nurses critically need to develop effective communication skills, to be aware of their emotions, to manage their emotions and be empathic in order to establish and maintain a good relationship with their patients. Nursing is a profession where human relations are experienced intensively, and as such empathy is one of the most basic components of primary nursing care (Nazik & Arslan, 2011). Since the 2000s, a number of studies have indicated that university students have decreased their empathy skills and that new communication technologies may be seen as a reason for this decline (Konrath, O'Brien, & Hsing, 2011). In addition, long-term immersion in technology-related areas negatively affects mirror neurons which play an important role in human empathy (Tanhan & Alav, 2015).

Interaction with virtual people or patients in a VR environment can affect students' attitudes for taking responsibility and approaching others. Although this may be seen in the future, it is thought that such instances related to VR in nursing education are preventable by using VR as a support to skills teaching and for the development of interaction with real patients. In nursing, ethical values should be safeguarded and educators should be made fully aware of the effects of nursing on the upholding of professional values whilst keeping pace with the latest technologies.

In the literature, studies with an increasing trend have been conducted more and more with regards to the effects of VR in the field of nursing on the teaching and learning process. Its contribution to the field of nursing has become more visible among the nursing educators. The results of studies have contributed rigorous teaching and learning methods in the field. The distribution of studies in the field of nursing in the literature by years is given in Figure 1 and Figure 2.

Figure 2. Distribution of Studies on Use of VR in Nursing by Years (PubMed)

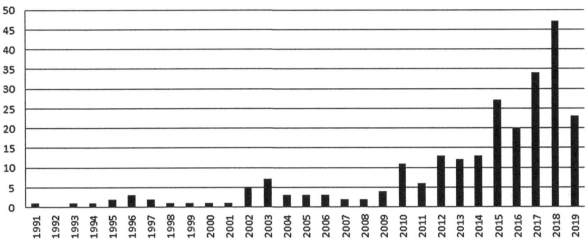

The results of research examining the effects of VR technology on nursing education in a general context, and the virtual simulation methods used in basic nursing skills training have positively impacted on academic achievement and skills performance. The relationship between students' academic achievement and their skill score in VR practice was examined by Engum, Jeffries, and Fisher (2003) and also by Reyes et al. (2008); however, no significant difference was found between VR educated experimental study groups and the corresponding traditionally educated control groups.

When research results are examined; Smith and Hamilton (2015) determined that VR simulation group students in their basic nursing skills education learned more easily about urinary catheter practice skills than their non-VR peers. Tsai et al. (2015) noted that the VR system contributed positively to the ability to administer an intravenous catheter. Similarly, İsmailoğlu and Zaybak (2018) found that intravenous catheter application skill scores and satisfaction scores of nursing students were significantly higher for a group educated with virtual simulation system (IV Virtually) than the study's control group. Jamison et al. (2006) observed a significant increase in the intravenous catheterization skill performance and final test scores of students using VR simulation (Cath Sim). Bowyer et al. (2005) observed that the occurrence of pain and hematoma in the patients of students who performed phlebotomy skills training with virtual simulation method was less than students in the corresponding control group of the study, but that the successful application of this method was more than the students in the control group.

In a study conducted on the effect of VR on students' anxiety levels, it was determined that the status anxiety level of students educated through the computer-based VR method in the area of intravenous catheterization skills training was lower compared to the control group (Chang, Chung, & Wong, 2002). The study by Tsai et al. (2015) in the care of Chronic Obstructive Pulmonary Disease (COPD) patients who are playing the game revealed that the student's knowledge and skills were increased, and anxiety was reduced.

Game-based VR application is one of the teaching methods used in nursing education. When different research results related to this method are examined, Noyudom Ketpichainarong, and Ruenwongsa (2011) used VR game-playing for a tracheostomy aspiration skills application, and found that VR-educated students' knowledge levels increased. Chia (2013) stated that a virtual game prepared for the management of COPD increased the knowledge level of students (Chia, 2013; Noyudom et al., 2011); whilst Lancaster's (2014) game-based VR application for post-op morphine treatment also increased students' knowledge levels. Similarly, Butt (2015) stated that a game-based VR application used in urinary catheterization skills application was found to be both interesting and entertaining. Finally, in a study conducted by Smith et al. (2016), it was stated that students who used a game-based VR application in decontamination teaching showed very high levels of knowledge and skill, and that the students stated that the game was good.

ETHICAL ISSUES OF VIRTUAL REALITY NURSING EDUCATION

Training forms a concerted effort to create changes in human behavior that are necessary for the realization of the required rules and norms. One of the most important criteria of professionalism is to obtain a qualified education, whilst another is to adopt professional ethical principles. Professionalism requires ethical awareness and sensitivity. Ethical education is considered of vital importance in the development of ethical awareness and sensitivity in professionalism, as well as its practice across the board. Today, ethical education within the scope of health sciences has become intertwined with the concept of professionalism, which can be summarized as understanding and learning the role, duties, and responsibilities of health professionals, as well as recognizing and respecting patients as human beings (Vanlaere & Gastmans, 2007). Nurses require the necessary knowledge and skills to provide quality care, to be sensitive to the human and moral aspects of patient care, and to provide services in accordance with established professional ethics (Grady et al., 2008). In this section, the ethical actions and sensitivity changes considered pertinent to the application of VR-based training are discussed so as to evaluate the differentiation of communication within the VR environment from real life.

The use of simulation learning and VR is considered to enrich the five elements of global nursing; universal esthetics, universal knowledge, universal ethics, universal politics, and universal health (Baumann, Sharoff, & Penalo, 2018). However, concerns have been raised in the literature that communication within VR environments differ from real-world interaction, and that ethical sensitivities may change as a result.

FUTURE RESEARCH DIRECTIONS

As an emerging technology, VR has a potential to transform nursing education (Forondo et al., 2017). The development of VR technology and the portability of VR systems offer a very promising broad use and potential implementation in nursing curriculum for the future training (Bracq, Michinov, & Jannin, 2019). In the literature, the use of VR in nursing education has an increasing trend, and more research studies have been conducted more and more with regards to the effects of VR in the field of nursing on the technical skills process. The use of virtual technology for nontechnical skills of nurses has increased since 2010 (Bracq, Michinov, & Jannin, 2019).

On the other hand, according to Knew et al. (2019) future research should examine effectiveness of VR technology on how students' attitudes, behaviour and satisfaction change in clinical practice by the use of VR. In particular, future research should be conducted for the transfer of skills to the clinical practice, and impact to the quality of nursing care. Nurse Educators can design learning interventions to maximize the benefits of VR applications and so they can determine the most effective way to implement virtual application into curriculum. In this context, the impact of VR technology on nursing education will largely depend on future technological advancements.

CONCLUSION

This chapter aimed to explore the use and impact of VR in nursing education. According to the literature, virtual technologies can facilitate students' knowledge retention, clinical reasoning, as well as their improved satisfaction with learning, and their self-efficacy. Studies have shown that VR practice is a teaching method that can be applied to nursing education, especially when new generation students have a natural predisposition to the use of technology and today's individuals each have different learning styles. Skills applications that are prepared with VR technologies make it possible for students to repeat their skills with virtual patients as many times as they need, without unduly risking patient safety, by feeling as if they are practicing within a real-world clinical environment prior to their actual clinical experience. For these reasons, it is suggested that in order to increase the quality of education provided, institutions that provide nursing education should adapt to today's technological developments, and to incorporate VR applications into educational content and to expand their usage and application.

REFERENCES

Anderson, L. W. (2005). Objectives, evaluation, and the improvement of education. *Studies in Educational Evaluation*, *31*(2-3), 102–113. doi:10.1016/j.stueduc.2005.05.004

Ausburn, L. J., & Ausburn, F. B. (2004). Desktop virtual reality: A powerful new technology for teaching and research in industrial teacher education. *Journal of Industrial Teacher Education*, *41*(4), 33–58.

Bahar, A. (2015). Temel hemşirelik becerisi eğitiminde yenilik: Web tabanli eğitim (*An innovation in nursing basic skills education: web-based education*). [Journal of Anatolian Nursing and Health Sciences]. *Anadolu Hemşirelik ve Sağlık Bilimleri Dergisi*, *18*(4), 304–311.

Baumann, S. L., Sharoff, L., & Penalo, L. (2018). Using simulation to enhance global nursing. *Nursing Science Quarterly*, *31*(4), 374–378. doi:10.1177/0894318418792877 PMID:30223748

Bracq, M. S., Michinov, E., & Jannin, P. (2019). Virtual reality simulation in nontechnical skills training for healthcare professionals: A systematic review. *Simulation in Healthcare*, *14*(3), 188–194. doi:10.1097/SIH.0000000000000347 PMID:30601464

Bradley, P. (2006). The history of simulation in medical education and possible future directions. *Medical Education*, *40*(3), 254–262. doi:10.1111/j.1365-2929.2006.02394.x PMID:16483328

Bricken, M., & Byrne, C. M. (1994). Summer students in virtual reality: A pilot study on educational applications of virtual reality technology. In A. Wexelblat (Ed.), *Virtual reality: Applications and explorations* (pp. 199–218). Boston, MA: Academic Press.

Brown, L. P. (2011). Revisiting our roots: Caring in nursing curriculum design. *Nurse Education in Practice*, *11*(6), 360–364. doi:10.1016/j.nepr.2011.03.007 PMID:21459042

Butt, A. L. (2015). *Exploring the usability of game-based virtual reality for development of procedural skills, in undergraduate nursing students*. (Doctoral Dissertation), Boise State University, Idaho.

Butt, A. L., Kardong-Edgren, S., & Ellertson, A. (2018). Using game-based virtual reality with haptics for skill acquisition. *Clinical Simulation in Nursing*, *16*, 25–32. doi:10.1016/j.ecns.2017.09.010

Cannon-Diehl, M. R. (2009). Simulation in healthcare and nursing: State of the science. *Critical Care Nursing Quarterly*, *32*(2), 128–136. doi:10.1097/CNQ.0b013e3181a27e0f PMID:19300077

Chang, K. K.-P., Chung, J. W.-Y., & Wong, T. K.-S. (2002). Learning intravenous cannulation: A comparison of the conventional method and the CathSim Intravenous Training System. *Journal of Clinical Nursing*, *11*(1), 73–78. doi:10.1046/j.1365-2702.2002.00561.x PMID:11845758

Chen, C. J., & Teh, C. S. (2013). Enhancing an instructional design model for virtual reality-based learning. *Australasian Journal of Educational Technology*, *29*(5), 699–716. doi:10.14742/ajet.247

Chen, C. J., Toh, S. C., & Wan, M. F. (2004). The theoretical framework for designing desktop virtual reality-based learning environments. *Journal of Interactive Learning Research*, *15*(2), 147–167.

Chia, P. (2013). Using a virtual game to enhance simulation-based learning in nursing education. *Singapore Nursing Journal*, *40*(3), 21–26.

Choi, K. S. (2017). Virtual reality in nursing: Nasogastric tube placement training simulator. *Studies in Health Technology and Informatics*, *245*, 1298. PMID:29295381

Chuah, K.-M., Chen, C.-J., & Teh, C.-S. (2011). Designing a desktop virtual reality-based learning environment with emotional consideration. *Research and Practice in Technology Enhanced Learning*, *6*(1), 25–42.

Cook, L. J. (2005). Inviting teaching behaviors of clinical faculty and nursing students' anxiety. *The Journal of Nursing Education*, *44*(4), 156–161. PMID:15862048

Davis, A. (2015). Virtual reality simulation: an innovative teaching tool for dietetics experiential education. *The Open Nutrition Journal*, *9*(1), 65–75. doi:10.2174/1876396001509010065

Decker, S., Sportsman, S., Puetz, L., & Billings, L. (2008). The evolution of simulation and its contribution to competency. *Journal of Continuing Education in Nursing*, *9*(2), 74–80. doi:10.3928/00220124-20080201-06 PMID:18323144

Dickey, M. D. (2005). Three-dimensional virtual worlds and distance learning: Two case studies of ActiveWorlds as a medium for distance education. *British Journal of Educational Technology*, *36*(3), 439–451. doi:10.1111/j.1467-8535.2005.00477.x

Downey, S. (2011). i-MMOLE: Instructional framework for creating virtual world lessons. *TechTrends*, *55*(6), 33–41. doi:10.100711528-011-0539-z

Dreesmann, N. (2018). Virtual reality check, are you ready? *Journal of Gerontological Nursing, 44*(3), 3–4. doi:10.3928/00989134-20180213-01 PMID:29470583

Dreher, C., Reiners, T., Dreher, N., & Dreher, H. (2009). Virtual worlds as a context suited for information systems education: Discussion of pedagogical experience and curriculum design with reference to Second Life. *Journal of Information Systems Education, 20*(2), 211–224.

Duncan, I., Miller, A., & Jiang, S. (2012). A taxonomy of virtual worlds usage in education. *British Journal of Educational Technology, 43*(6), 949–964. doi:10.1111/j.1467-8535.2011.01263.x

Eker, F., Açıkgöz, F., & Karaca, A. (2014). Hemşirelik öğrencileri gözüyle mesleki beceri eğitimi (Occupational skill training through the eyes of nursing students). [Dokuz Eylul University Faculty of Nursing Electronic Journal]. *Dokuz Eylül Üniversitesi Hemşirelik Elektronik Dergisi, 7*(4), 291–294.

Engum, S. A., Jeffries, P., & Fisher, L. (2003). Intravenous catheter training system: Computer-based education versus traditional learning methods. *American Journal of Surgery, 186*(1), 67–74. doi:10.1016/S0002-9610(03)00109-0 PMID:12842753

Ergül, Ş. (2011). Türkiye'de Yükseköğretimde Hemşirelik Eğitimi (Higher education of nursing education in Turkey). [Journal of Higher Education and Science]. *Yükseögretim ve Bilim Dergisi, 1*(3), 152–155.

Ferguson, C., Davidson, P. M., Scott, P. J., Jackson, D., & Hickman, L. (2015). Augmented reality, virtual reality and gaming: An integral part of nursing. *Contemporary Nurse, 51*(1), 1–4. doi:10.1080/103761 78.2015.1130360 PMID:26678947

Foronda, C. L., Alfes, C. M., Dev, P., Kleinheksel, A. J., Nelson, D. A. Jr, O'Donnell, J. M., & Samosky, J. T. (2017). Virtually nursing: Emerging technologies in nursing education. *Nurse Educator, 42*(1), 14–17. doi:10.1097/NNE.0000000000000295 PMID:27454054

Freina, L., & Ott, M. (2015). A literature review on immersive virtual reality in education: State of the art and perspectives. In I. Roceanu, F. Moldoveanu, S. Trausan-Matu, D. Barbieru, D. Beligan, & A. Ionita (Eds.), *Proceedings of the International Scientific Conference e-learning and Software for Education (eLSE 2015), Rethinking education by leveraging the eLearning pillar of the Digital Agenda for Europe!* (Vol. 1, pp. 133-141). "Carol I" National Defence University, Bucharest, Hungary.

Gaba, D. (2004). The future of simulation in healthcare. *Quality & Safety in Health Care, 13*(suppl_1), 2–10. doi:10.1136/qshc.2004.009878 PMID:14757786

Gökoğlu, S., & Çakıroğlu, Ü. (2019). Measurement of presence in virtual reality based learning environments: Adapting the presence scale to Turkish. *Education Technology: Theory and Practice, 9*(1), 169–188.

Gömleksiz, M. N., & Kan, A. Ü. (2012). Affective dimension in education and affective learning. Turkish Studies-International Periodical for the Languages. *Literature and History of Turkish or Turkic, 7*(1), 1159–1177.

Goodwin, M. S., Wiltshire, T., & Fiore, S. M. (2015). Applying research in the cognitive sciences to the design and delivery of instruction in virtual reality learning environments. In R. Shumaker, & S. Lackey (Eds.), *Proceedings of the International Conference on Virtual, Augmented and Mixed Reality* (pp. 280-291). Cham, Switzerland: Springer. 10.1007/978-3-319-21067-4_29

Gore, T. N., & Loice, L. (2014). Creating effective simulation environments. In B. Ulric & B. Mancini (Eds.), *Mastering simulation: a handbook for success* (pp. 49–86). USA: Sigma Theta Tau International.

Gorman, L. M., & Sultan, D. F. (2007). *Psychosocial nursing for general patient care* (3rd ed.). Philadelphia, PA: F. A. Davis.

Graafland, M., Schraagen, J., & Schijven, M. P. (2012). Systematic review of serious games for medical education and surgical skills training. *British Journal of Surgery*, *99*(10), 1322–1330. doi:10.1002/bjs.8819 PMID:22961509

Grady, C., Danis, M., Soeken, K. L., O'Donnell, P., Taylor, C., Farrar, A., & Ulrich, C. M. (2008). Does ethics education influence the moral action of practicing nurses and social workers? *The American Journal of Bioethics*, *8*(4), 4–11. doi:10.1080/15265160802166017 PMID:18576241

Guo, C., Deng, H., & Yang, J. (2014). Effect of virtual reality distraction on pain among patients with hand injury undergoing dressing change. *Journal of Clinical Nursing*, *24*(1), 115–120. PMID:24899241

Hacıalioğlu, N. (2011). Basic concepts of education and training. In N. Hacıalioğlu (Ed.), *Nursing teaching in learning and education* (pp. 10–17). Istanbul, Turkey: Nobel Medical Bookstores.

Hanson, K., & Shelton, B. E. (2008). Design and development of virtual reality: Analysis of challenges faced by educators. *Journal of Educational Technology & Society*, *11*(1), 118–131.

İsmailoğlu, E. G., & Zaybak, A. (2018). Comparison of the effectiveness of a virtual simulator with a plastic arm model in teaching intravenous catheter insertion skills. *Computers, Informatics, Nursing*, *36*(2), 98–105. doi:10.1097/CIN.0000000000000405 PMID:29176359

Izard, S. G., Juanes, J. A., García Peñalvo, F. J., Gonçalves Estella, J., Sánchez-Ledesma, M. J., & Ruisoto, P. (2018). Virtual reality as an educational and training tool for medicine. *Journal of Medical Systems*, *50*(42), 50–54. doi:10.100710916-018-0900-2 PMID:29392522

Jamison, R. J., Hovancsek, M. T., & Clochesy, J. M. (2006). A pilot study assessing simulation using two simulation methods for teaching intravenous cannulation. *Clinical Simulation in Nursing*, *2*(1), e9–e12. doi:10.1016/j.ecns.2009.05.007

Jarmon, L., Traphagan, T., Mayrath, M., & Trivedi, A. (2009). Virtual world teaching, experiential learning, and assessment: An interdisciplinary communication course in Second Life. *Computers & Education*, *53*(1), 169–182. doi:10.1016/j.compedu.2009.01.010

Jenson, C. E., & Forsyth, D. M. (2012). Virtual reality simulation: Using three-dimensional technology to teach nursing students. *CIN: Computers, Informatics, Nursing*, *30*(6), 312–318. PMID:22411409

Jöud, A., Sandholm, A., Alseby, L., Petersson, G., & Nilsson, G. (2010). Feasibility of a computerized male urethral catheterization simulator. *Nurse Education in Practice*, *10*(2), 70–75. doi:10.1016/j.nepr.2009.03.017 PMID:19443272

Kaddoura, M., VanDyke, O., Cheng, B., & Shea-Foisy, K. (2016). Impact of concept mapping on the development of clinical judgment skills in nursing students. *Teaching and Learning in Nursing*, *11*(3), 101–107. doi:10.1016/j.teln.2016.02.001

Kaleci, D., Tepe, T., & Tüzün, H. (2017). Üç Boyutlu Sanal Gerçeklik Ortamlarındaki Deneyimlere İlişkin Kullanıcı Görüşleri (Users' opinions of experiences in three dimensional virtual reality environments). [Turkish Journal of Social Sciences]. *Türkiye Sosyal Araştırmalar Dergisi*, *21*(3), 669–689.

Karaöz, S. (2003). An overview of clinical teaching in nursing and recommendations for effective clinical teaching. *Journal of Research and Development in Nursing*, *5*(1), 15–21.

Kardong-Edgren, S., Lungstrom, N., & Bendel, R. (2009). VitalSim® Versus SimMan®: A comparison of BSN student test scores, knowledge retention and satisfaction. *Clinical Simulation in Nursing*, *5*(3), e105–e111. doi:10.1016/j.ecns.2009.01.007

Kardong-Edgren, S. S., Farra, S. L., Alinier, G., & Young, H. M. (2019). A call to unify definitions of virtual reality. *Clinical Simulation in Nursing*, *31*, 28–34. doi:10.1016/j.ecns.2019.02.006

Khalifa, Y. M., Bogorad, D., Gibson, V., Peifer, J., & Nussbaum, J. (2006). Virtual reality in ophthalmology training. *Survey of Ophthalmology*, *51*(3), 259–273. doi:10.1016/j.survophthal.2006.02.005 PMID:16644366

Khorshid, L., Eşer, İ., Sarı, D., Zaybak, A., Yapucu, Ü., & Gürol, G. (2002). Hemşirelik öğrencilerinde invaziv ve invaziv olmayan işlemleri ilk kez yapmaya bağlı korku semptom ve belirtilerinin incelenmesi (The examination of the fear symptoms and signs while performing first invasive and noninvasive nursing procedures in nursing student). [Journal of Anatolian Nursing and Health Sciences]. *Anadolu Hemşirelik ve Sağlık Bilimleri Dergisi*, *5*(2), 1–10.

Kıran, B., & Taşkıran, E. G. (2014). Overview of nursing education and manpower planning in Turkey. Mersin University School of Medicine. *Journal of History of Medicine and Folk Medicine*, *5*(2), 62–68.

Kızıl, H., & Şendir, M. (2019). Innovative approaches in nursing education. *International Journal of Human Sciences*, *16*(1), 118–125. doi:10.14687/5437

Kolcu, G., Başaran, Ö., Sandal, G., Saygın, M., Aslankoç, R., Baş, F. Y., & Duran, B. E. (2017). Mesleki beceri eğitim düzeyi: Süleyman Demirel Üniversitesi tıp fakültesi deneyimi (Vocational skill education level: experience of the Süleyman Demirel University faculty of medicine). [Smyrna Medical Journal]. *Smyrna Tıp Dergisi*, *3*, 7–14.

Konrath, S., O'Brien, E., & Hsing, C. (2011). Changes in dispositional empathy in American college students over time: A meta-analysis. *Personality and Social Psychology Review*, *15*(2), 180–198. doi:10.1177/1088868310377395 PMID:20688954

Korhan, E. A., Tokem, Y., Uzelli Yılmaz, D., & Dilemek, H. (2016). Hemşirelikte psikomotor beceri eğitiminde video destekli öğretim ve OSCE uygulaması: Bir deneyim paylaşımı (Video-Based teaching and OSCE implementation in nursing psychomotor skills education: Sharing of an experience). İzmir Katip Çelebi Üniversitesi Saglık Bilimleri Fakültesi Dergisi (İzmir Kâtip Çelebi University Faculty of Health Sciences Journal), 1(1), 35-37.

Korhan, E. A., Yılmaz, D. U., Ceylan, B., Akbıyık, A., & Tokem, Y. (2018). Hemsirelikte Psikomotor beceri ogretiminde senaryo temelli ogrenme: Bir Deneyim Paylasimi (Scenario based teaching in nursing psychomotor skills education: Sharing of an experience). Izmir Katip Celebi Universitesi Saglik Bilimleri Fakultesi Dergisi (İzmir Kâtip Çelebi University Faculty of Health Sciences Journal), 3(3), 11-16.

Krathwohl, D. R. (2002). A revision of Bloom's taxonomy: An overview. *Theory into Practice, 41*(4), 212–218. doi:10.120715430421tip4104_2

Kuzu-Kurban, N. (2015). Teaching in nursing and role of trainers. In S. Arslan & N. Kuzu-Kurban (Eds.), *Nurse Educator Becoming Process* (pp. 1–7). Ankara, Turkey: Anı Publications.

Kyaw, B. M., Saxena, N., Posadzki, P., Vseteckova, J., Nikolaou, C. K., George, P. P., ... Car, L. T. (2019). Virtual reality for health professions education: Systematic review and meta-analysis by the digital health education collaboration. *Journal of Medical Internet Research, 21*(1). doi:10.2196/12959 PMID:30668519

Lancaster, R. J. (2014). Serious game simulation as a teaching strategy in pharmacology. *Clinical Simulation in Nursing, 10*(3), 129–137. doi:10.1016/j.ecns.2013.10.005

Lee, E. A.-L., & Wong, K. W. (2014). Learning with desktop virtual reality: Low spatial ability learners are more positively affected. *Computers & Education, 79*, 49–58. doi:10.1016/j.compedu.2014.07.010

Lu, D.-F., Lin, Z.-C., & Li, Y.-J. (2009). Effects of a web-based course on nursing skills and knowledge learning. *The Journal of Nursing Education, 48*(2), 70–77. doi:10.3928/01484834-20090201-10 PMID:19260398

Ma, M., Jain, L. C., & Anderson, P. (Eds.). (2014). *Virtual, augmented reality and serious games for healthcare 1* (Vol. 1). Berlin, Germany: Springer. doi:10.1007/978-3-642-54816-1

Mann, E. G., Medves, J., & Vandenkerkohf, E. G. (2015). Accessing best practice resources using mobile technology in an undergraduate nursing program. *Computers, Informatics, Nursing, 33*(3), 122–128. doi:10.1097/CIN.0000000000000135 PMID:25636042

Nazik, E., & Arslan, S. (2011). The investigation of the relations between empathic skills and self-compassion of the nursing students. *Journal of Anatolian Nursing and Health Sciences, 14*(4), 69–77.

Noyudom, A.-N., Ketpichainarong, W., & Ruenwongsa, P. (2011). Development of a computer-based simulation unit on tracheal suctioning to enhance nursing students' knowledge and practical skills. In C. Denpaiboon, P. Pipitkul, A. Phitthayayon, S. Ondej, & S. Soranastaporn (Eds.), *Proceedings of the Thai Simulation (ThaiSim) 2011 3rd Annual International Conference* (pp. 65-76). Bangkok, Thailand: ThaiSim: The Thai Simulation and Gaming Association, Thonburi University.

Ökdem, Ş., Abbasoğlu, A., & Doğan, N. (2000). Nursing history, education and development. *Ankara Üniversitesi Dikimevi Sağlık Hizmetleri Meslek Yüksekokulu Yıllığı, 1*(1), 5–11.

Öncü, S. (2014). *The CIPP model example in clinical skills education evaluation.* (Doctoral dissertation), Institute of Health Science, Ege University.

Oppenheim, C. (1993). Virtual reality and the virtual library. *Information Services & Use, 13*(3), 215–227. doi:10.3233/ISU-1993-13303

Osuagwu, O., Ihedigbo, C., & Ndigwe, C. (2015). Integrating virtual reality (VR) into traditional instructional design. *West African Journal of Industrial and Academic Research, 15*(1), 68–77.

Pantelidis, V. S. (1993). Virtual reality in the classroom. *Educational Technology, 33*(4), 23–27.

Passing, D., David, T., & Eshel-Kedmi, G. (2016). Improving children's cognitive modifiability by dynamic assessment in 3D immersive virtual reality environments. *Computers & Education, 95*, 296–308. doi:10.1016/j.compedu.2016.01.009

Ramasundaram, V., Grunwald, S., Mangeot, A., Comerford, N. B., & Bliss, C. (2005). Development of an environmental virtual field laboratory. *Computers & Education, 45*(1), 21–34. doi:10.1016/j.compedu.2004.03.002

Reyes, S. D., Stillsmoking, K., & Chadwick-Hopkins, D. (2008). Implementation and evaluation of a virtual simulator system: Teaching intravenous skills. *Clinical Simulation in Nursing, 4*(1), e43–e49. doi:10.1016/j.ecns.2009.05.055

Sarıkoç, G. (2016). Use of virtual reality in the education of health workers. *Journal of Education and Research in Nursing, 13*(1), 243–248.

Şen, H. (2012). Hemşirelikte psikomotor beceri öğretiminde rehber ilkeler: Kalp masajı örneği (Guide principles of psychomotor skills teaching in nursing: Sample of chest compression). [Dokuz Eylul University Faculty of Nursing Electronic Journal]. *Dokuz Eylül Üniversitesi Hemşirelik Elektronik Dergisi, 5*(4), 180–184.

Şengül, F. (2010). *The effect of nursing education models on the critical thinking dispositions of the students: A multicenter study.* (Master's Dissertation), Institute of Health Science, Çukurova University.

Seropian, M. A., Brown, K., Gavilanes, J. S., & Driggers, B. (2004). Simulation: Not just a manikin. *The Journal of Nursing Education, 43*(4), 164–169. PMID:15098910

Serrano, B., Baños, R. M., & Botella, C. (2016). Virtual reality and stimulation of touch and smell for inducing relaxation: A randomized controlled trial. *Computers in Human Behavior, 55*, 1–8. doi:10.1016/j.chb.2015.08.007

Shin, S., Park, J.-H., & Kim, J.-H. (2015). Effectiveness of patient simulation in nursing education: Meta-analysis. *Nurse Education Today, 35*(1), 176–182. doi:10.1016/j.nedt.2014.09.009 PMID:25459172

Smith, P. C., & Hamilton, B. K. (2015). The effects of virtual reality simulation as a teaching strategy for skills preparation in nursing students. *Clinical Simulation in Nursing, 11*(1), 52–58. doi:10.1016/j.ecns.2014.10.001

Smith, S. J., Farra, S., Ulrich, D. L., Hodgson, E., Nicely, S., & Matcham, W. (2016). Learning and retention using virtual reality in a decontamination simulation. *Nursing Education Perspectives, 37*(4), 210–214. doi:10.1097/01.NEP.0000000000000035 PMID:27740579

Somyürek, S. (2014). Öğretim sürecinde z kuşağının dikkatini çekme: Artırılmış gerçeklik (Gaining the attention of generation Z in learning process: Augmented reality). [Educational Technology Theory and Practice]. *Eğitim Teknolojisi Kuram ve Uygulama, 4*(1), 63–80.

Stary, C. (2001). Exploring the concept of virtuality: Technological approaches and implications from tele-education. In A. Riegler, M. F. Peschl, K. Edlinger, G. Fleck, & W. Feigl (Eds.), Virtual reality: Cognitive foundations, technological issues & philosophical implications, (pp. 113-128). Peter Lang.

Stroup, C. (2014). Simulation usage in nursing fundamentals: Integrative literature review. *Clinical Simulation in Nursing*, *10*(3), 155–164. doi:10.1016/j.ecns.2013.10.004

Tanhan, F., & Alav, Ö. (2015). Siber kimliklerin kişiliğe yansıması: Proteus etki (Tanımı, nedenleri ve önlenmesi) (The effect of ciber personalities on personality: Proteus effect (Definition, causes and prevention). *Online Journal of Technology Addiction & Cyberbullying*, *2*(4), 1–19.

Topuksak, B., & Kublay, G. (2010). Florence What has changed from Florence Nightingale to present in nursing education? Modern nursing education in Europe and Turkey (Nightingale'den Günümüze Hemşirelik Eğitiminde Neler Değişti? Avrupa ve Türkiye'de Modern Hemşirelik Eğitimi). *Maltepe Üniversitesi Hemşirelik Bilim ve Sanatı Dergisi (Maltepe University Journal of Nursing Art and Science)*, 298-305.

Trindade, J., Fiolhais, C., & Almeida, L. (2002). Science learning in virtual environments: A descriptive study. *British Journal of Educational Technology*, *33*(4), 471–488. doi:10.1111/1467-8535.00283

Tsai, S. L., Chai, S., & Chuang, K. H. (2015). The effectiveness of a chronic obstructive pulmonary disease computer game as a learning tool for nursing students. *Open Journal of Nursing*, *5*(7), 605–612. doi:10.4236/ojn.2015.57064

Unver, V., Basak, T., Watts, P., Gaioso, V., Moss, J., Tastan, S., & Tosun, N. (2017). The reliability and validity of three questionnaires: The student satisfaction and self-confidence in learning scale, simulation design scale, and educational practices questionnaire. *Contemporary Nurse*, *53*(1), 60–74. doi:10.1080/10376178.2017.1282319 PMID:28084900

Vanlaere, L., & Gastmans, C. (2007). Ethics in nursing education: Learning to reflect on care practices. *Nursing Ethics*, *14*(6), 758–766. doi:10.1177/0969733007082116 PMID:17901186

Vaughn, J., Lister, M., & Shaw, R. J. (2016). Piloting augmented reality technology to enhance realism in clinical simulation. *Computers, Informatics, Nursing*, *34*(9), 402–405. doi:10.1097/CIN.0000000000000251 PMID:27258807

White, R., & Evan, C. (2002). *Clinical teaching in nursing* (2nd ed.). Springer.

Wiecha, J., Heyden, R., Sternthal, E., & Merialdi, M. (2010). Learning in a virtual world: Experience with using second life for medical education. *Journal of Medical Internet Research*, *12*(1), e1. doi:10.2196/jmir.1337 PMID:20097652

Witmer, B. G., & Singer, M. J. (1998). Measuring presence in virtual environments: A presence questionnaire. *Presence (Cambridge, Mass.)*, *7*(3), 225–240. doi:10.1162/105474698565686

Wolters Kluwer Health. 9AD, Summer (2017, May 15). *65% of nursing education programs adopting virtual simulation*. Retrieved from http://healthclarity.wolterskluwer.com/nursing-education-programs-virtual-simulation.html

Ziv, A. (2005). Simulators and simulation-based medical education. In J. Dent, & R. M. Harden (Eds.), A practical guide for medical teacher (pp. 211-220). London, UK: Elsevier.

Ziv, A., Small, S. D., & Root-Wolpe, P. (2000). Patient safety and simulation-based medical education. *Medical Teacher*, *22*(5), 489–495. doi:10.1080/01421590050110777 PMID:21271963

ADDITIONAL READING

Bracq, M. S., Michinov, E., & Jannin, P. (2019). Virtual reality simulation in nontechnical skills training for healthcare professionals: A systematic review. *Simulation in Healthcare*, *14*(3), 188–194. doi:10.1097/SIH.0000000000000347 PMID:30601464

Butt, A. L., Kardong-Edgren, S., & Ellertson, A. (2018). Using game-based virtual reality with haptics for skill acquisition. *Clinical Simulation in Nursing*, *16*, 25–32. doi:10.1016/j.ecns.2017.09.010

Foronda, C., Budhathoki, C., & Salani, D. (2014). Use of multiuser, high-fidelity virtual simulation to teach leadership styles to nursing students. *Nurse Educator*, *39*(5), 209–211. doi:10.1097/NNE.0000000000000073 PMID:25137445

Foronda, C., Gattamorta, K., Snowden, K., & Bauman, E. (2014). Use of virtual clinical simulation to improve communication skills of baccalaureate nursing students: A pilot study. *Nurse Education Today*, *34*(6), 53–57. doi:10.1016/j.nedt.2013.10.007 PMID:24231637

Foronda, C. L., Alfes, C. M., Dev, P., Kleinheksel, A. J., Nelson, D. A. Jr, O'Donnell, J. M., & Samosky, J. T. (2017). Virtually nursing: Emerging technologies in nursing education. *Nurse Educator*, *42*(1), 14–17. doi:10.1097/NNE.0000000000000295 PMID:27454054

Gore, T. N., & Loice, L. (2014). Creating effective simulation environments. In B. Ulric & B. Mancini (Eds.), *Mastering Simulation: A Handbook for Success* (pp. 49–86). USA: Sigma Theta Tau International.

Hudson, K. W., Taylor, L. A., Kozachik, S. L., Shaefer, S. J., & Wilson, M. L. (2015). Second Life simulation as a strategy to enhance decision making in diabetes care: A case study. *Journal of Clinical Nursing*, *24*(5-6), 797–804. doi:10.1111/jocn.12709 PMID:25421741

Kyaw, B. M., Saxena, N., Posadzki, P., Vseteckova, J., Nikolaou, C. K., George, P. P., ... Car, L. T. (2019). Virtual reality for health professions education: Systematic review and meta-analysis by the Digital Health Education collaboration. *Journal of Medical Internet Research*, *21*(1), e12959. doi:10.2196/12959 PMID:30668519

Menzel, N., Willson, L. H., & Doolen, J. (2014). Effectiveness of a poverty simulation in second life®: Changing nursing student attitudes toward poor people. *International Journal of Nursing Education Scholarship*, *11*(1), 39–45. doi:10.1515/ijnes-2013-0076 PMID:24615491

KEY TERMS AND DEFINITIONS

3D: Stands for three dimensions or three-dimensional in which provides perception of depth in computerized environment.

Augmented Reality: Combination of real world and computer-generated information on objects to provide perceptual reality through the digital screens or head mounted devices.

Immersion: A psychological sense of being in a virtual environment.

Simulation: A technique that creates a situation or environment to represent similar or exact conditions of reality to provide training and learning experiences for novice learners.

Virtual Reality: An artificial 3D environment in which learner can interact and discover through computer technologies and headsets.

Virtual Reality Simulation: A type of simulation which incorporates with computerized 3D environment for immersive and engaging learning.

Chapter 4
Constructing Virtual Radio Center:
Providing Visuality to Sounds

Nazime Tuncay
Bahçeşehir Cyprus University, Cyprus

ABSTRACT

Radio channels lack visuality and virtual reality platforms are designed to overcome this problem. Virtual objects are very common these days and people get used to virtual platforms. Does this mean people are ready to be involved in such a system? Is this necessary? How to make sounds visible? Use of Virtual Reality is growing rapidly in industry as well as in education area. This chapter is about the virtual radio center construction necessities, usefulness, and its adaptability to real life and to courses.

Constructing Virtual Radio Center

This chapter provides information about the process of creating a virtual radio center and the experiences that the author had after delivering courses in the center. We are going to discuss virtual radio center construction necessities, usefulness of such centers and its adaptability of these to real life situations and to our courses. It's not very common to hear virtual centers being used even in this 21st century, especially in undeveloped or developing countries. Therefore, this chapter provides a different vision in the radio technology and offers visuality and even mobility to sounds. Making sounds visual is not providing visual scenes to them but providing visual platforms as an alternative to the real-world platforms. We are going to discuss **how, where and why** we should create virtual radio centers.

DOI: 10.4018/978-1-7998-1796-3.ch004

Copyright © 2020, IGI Global. Copying or distributing in print or electronic forms without written permission of IGI Global is prohibited.

Figure 1. Radio facilities

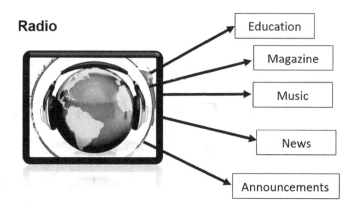

What is Radio?

It is a technology that delivers electromagnetic waves that passes through the atmosphere and helps communication. Since 1900s Radio is one of the simplest and most widely used technological invention for communication. It transfers sound or binary data wirelessly and it is a powerful machine that helps delivery of data to many people from all walks of life. In 21th century radio is used together with many Smart technologies. Non-verbal communication technological opportunities are very important for people`s improving their imagination. Radio is essential for education, it is one of the earliest forms of distance education; it's a good source of magazine, its cheap and easy to reach to many audiences. Radio is one of the simplest and cheapest technologies for listening to music. It gives you the opportunity to listen to News around the world as well as making some announcements yourself with a very low price. Figure 1 illustrates some of the important usage areas of "Radio".

There are some software for virtualizing the monitoring and control of broadcast IP (AoIP) has become the standard for broadcast facilities, allowing broadcast plants to be more powerful, less expensive to buy and maintain, and faster to build (The Tellos Alliance, 2019). Although its not so common we have some researches in this area in the literature also. Virtanen and his friends wrote a paper about virtual version of audio installation in a historic building consisting of audio clips and creating a virtual radio (Virtanen, et.al., 2018). The external appearance in virtual worlds can change the brain mechanisms involved with the occasion and, ultimately, affect human behavior towards it. Virtual Radios are a way of simulating or replicating an environment and giving the user a sense of being there, taking control, and personally interacting with that environment with his/her own body. With the emergence of speech-controlled virtual agents (VAs) in consumer devices such as Amazon's Echo or Apple's HomePod, large public interest in related technologies is seen(Schmidt, et. al., 2019). Figure 2 shows an example of Virtual Radio Software.

Virtual reality makes reality more abstract and easier to be visually acceptable. Radio technology lacking visuality may be taken as an abstract resource for education. 3D interactive environments provide constructivist learning activities by allowing learners to interact directly with information from a first-person perspective (Dede, 1995). Virtual Radio Platforms may help sounds be "visible" and students more "creative"! Increasing one's imagination is sure to increase their involving in different activities

Figure 2. Virtual radio software (The Tellos Alliance, 2019)

which will increase the chance of their coming with more accurate solutions to the problems at hand and with many creative ideas.

Virtual Radio Centers may also bring coding, inventing and imagining to the students world and will help them to visualize the sounds as a tool for multi-purpose activities with multiple people. It will involve entertainment in the education courses related with radio ethics. Use of personalized avatars in virtual radio system may change the way that people emotionally respond to music and radio news.

Does 3D interactive environments allow learners to interact directly with the people from a first-person perspective? Or do they fail to provide the necessities of social life. The important thing is being the first person or the third person or may be none of these and only the feeling as the first person in life! Which one is more appealing? Does 3D interactive environments allow learners to interact directly from a first-person perspective? Is virtual reality an experience in which a person is surrounded by a three-dimensional computer-generated representation, and is able to move around to see it from different angles and reshape it? Since radio channels lack the visuality, why not make it more visual? Many educators support the view that virtual reality will give learners an opportunity to experience environments which, for reasons of time, distance, scale, and safety, would not otherwise be available. Having a virtual radio center in an university is sure to take lots of students' attraction. Use of Virtual Reality is growing rapidly in industry as well as in the education area. Are we ready to be involved in such a system? 10 years before answer to this question may be "no", however virtual objects are very common these days and people get used to virtual platforms. So, why not make sounds visible?

THE WORD "VIRTUAL"

When you see the word virtual, you must do a little research to understand what it really means. These days the word virtual may be used in variety of different meanings:

Online

When you see virtual education delivered in an university, this may mean that they are saying you have to register online and enter to the courses online. You have to have an internet access in this case. There are many virtual radio sites on Internet which are mainly webpages that has an icon that when you click you access to the radio channels online.

3D-Video

Some intuitions by using the word "Virtual Campus" or "Virtual Faculty" they mean that when you click you may reach to a 3D video of the campus or the faculty. You have to have a good internet access for this. If your internet is slow, it will take more time for you to watch the video and it may be interrupted several times while playing.

User-Interactive Platform

Some intuitions use the word "virtual" to mean that you can also interact and decide what you want to see or hear. Such platforms may be Web 2.0 or Web 3.0 technologies. You have to have a good internet access for this.

Virtual World

It is an online environment that is built as a representative of the real life conditions and two-dimensional or three-dimensional graphical models called avatars are used in these environments as a representative of human beings. You can not enter into such systems without creating an avatar of yourself. In this chapter, **by the word "Virtual" we mean by the environment where you use your own avatars that the virtual world provides.** You have to have a very good internet access and a high-quality technological tool like an Intel i7/i9 Laptop or a latest technology SmartPhone for this.

What is Virtual Reality ?

Virtual Reality can be defined as an artificial environment generated through software and presented on a computer-generated display, where the observer's actions produce actions in the artificial environment leading to a sense of being in the environment (McConville & Virk, 2012). There are many virtual reality applications that universities and museums use to make their students/ visitors to experience the real feeling of being there. Virtual reality offers an artificial environment that makes almost everything possible everywhere and anytime.

What is a Virtual World?

It's an online world (a world that you create on Internet) that you can enter with your avatar and you can behave as you behave in the real world. There are more than 500 active virtual worlds available on internet in many different languages. Some of these are Second Life, Active Worlds, Sansar, Lady Popular, Fantage, Meez, Multiverse, My Hospital, Big Farm, Kaneva, There, Club Penguin, Dofus, Gaia,

WoozWorld, ourWorld, There, Roblox, Small and Worlds. These all can be classified into education oriented, social-orientated or game-orientated.

The virtual world generation is done in two steps; a first one in which the output is a 2D floor plan, and a second one which generates a 3D representation of the virtual world (Trescak, Esteva & Rodriguez, 2010). Many virtual worlds provide its users with many communication scenarios, developing tools for improving platforms, chances of exhibition, virtual campuses for delivering courses and research studies. The combination of virtual worlds and virtual reality systems has been proposed as one of the most important challenges during the next years to facilitate a user's full immersion experience (Griol, Sanchis, Molina & Callejas,2019). There are many virtual museums as well as virtual campuses these days. Some universities for example Bahçeşehir Univeristy, California State University, Coventry University, Columbia University, Edinburgh University, Harvard University, Middle East Technical University, Sheffield University and Stanford University have virtual campuses; their students have virtual avatars and can sign in and enter to the virtual environment with their avatars. Some universities like Birmingham City University, The University of Kent, MiddleSex University, University of Oxford, University of Westminister, University of York has virtual reality applications and provides virtual tours and videos to show their facilities.

How We Can Construct a Virtual Radio Center?

There are many options for constructing a Virtual Radio Center. What I did was using a virtual world, called Second Life. You can join to Second Life by using the following Link: https://join.secondlife.com/. I had bought a land and started writing codes for creating and placing the necessary items in the room. Second step was teaching students how to enroll to the system and inviting them to the radio room. Combining this with a program called ooVoo (https://www.oovoo.com/oovoo/) resulted in augmented reality system. Virtual Radio Center had more facilities to offer than a non-virtual one. Making changes on virtual platforms was easier than making changes to the real-life platforms. Walking in the virtual center was very exciting for the students because they were able to click on music boxes and choose their favorite songs to listen. They were even singing and recording their own songs as well as their poems for their loved ones. It was a worth-trying experience for me and for my students.

About Second Life

The virtual world of Second Life, a computer-driven, simulated three-dimensional virtual world inhabited by graphic avatars is developed by Linden Lab (Boellstorff, 2008; Berger, 2012; LaPensée & Lewis, 2014; Martin, 2014; Abdullah, 2015; Locher et al., 2015; Berger, et al.). It is widely being used by many distance educators as well as people from all folks of life for many purposes. Second Life is a Virtual Platform that you can easily search and install on internet. There is no registration fee if you want to create an avatar and transfer to the virtual platforms. You can choose to be a woman, man or an animal depending on your purpose of usage. Your outfit completely depends on how you want it to be. However, you have to pay for owning a land and creating centers. Also, for the interior decoration you will have to buy some virtual objects. You can earn, save and use Linden money in the virtual world which can be exchanged with real life money. It's very common to see many people writing codes for selling tools in Second Life. This is also future of the coding technology and a new area of business. The platform itself has "Learning Island" in itself which teaches you how to use it. You can see an avatar that I have

Figure 3. TunNaz in the learning platform

created, called "TunNaz" in the Learning Island in Figure 3. When you first create your avatar, you enter into the learning land and practice the allowed movements in the platform. You can also search whatever you want to go in the search bar and "transfer" there. It is also possible joining to many different communities on Second Life. For example, you can see in the figure that there is another community called "Virtual Public Radio", you can click "Join Now" button and join it.

There are many Islands, Universities, Shopping Centers and Multi-Purpose Centers in Second Life as well as user-created ones. You can see in Figure 4, TunNaz is in "TrigiTec Radio" Platform. This is a virtual platform for listening to music, meet with musicians, search for information by clicking to the bulletin boards.

The most beautiful part of this program is that it provides you the opportunity to use your own programming knowledge. In other words, you can write your own codes for owning your own objects. In the Figure you can see the avatar "TunNaz", she is in the Learning Land.

VirtualNEU Radio center

VirtualNEU Radio Centre rooms built in Second Life can be seen in Figures 5 & 6 &7. The construction steps are just like the real-world cases: **Buy a land, start building and decorate.** I have written codes for having Bulletin Boards, interactive Search Engine Windows and bought carpets, curtains and sofas that you see on Figures 5 & 6 &7. The boxes were free and I made chairs for my students with that boxes and colored them with different colors.

Carefully selected decorative mobiles such as carpets, windows, speakers that were arranged in the center can be seen in Figure 5, 6 & 7. Here like real life, a land is bought and the center was decorated. After buying sofas, they were resized and recolored and programmed to speak or show some text when someone touches. Everything that is needed and imagined in a real center was programmed here.

Figure 4. TunNaz in the learning platform

Figure 5. Virtual avatars and virtual radio center (Room1)

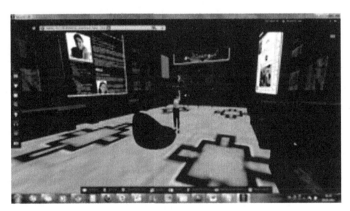

When someone clicked on the bulletin board called "SEMINERLER" on Figure 5, he could reach to the seminar records that I had given via Radio Channel.

Figure 6 represents a virtual environment where real students and virtual students are in the same classroom. On the right you can see that 6 students that are connected online and shared their own cameras with their classmates while they are participating to the class activities. Some other students that you see on the Figure 6 had created their own avatars and sat on the boxes and they are answering

Figure 6. Virtual avatars and virtual radio center (Room2)

Figure 7. Virtual avatars and virtual radio center (Room3)

teachers' questions. (The teacher is me with my TeacherNazime avatar standing in the middle of the class, and asking questions). Here students could answer the teachers' questions by voices, however they had not very good internet access, they could not use their microphones for answering the questions, so they were writing their answers.

Figure 7 is a meeting room, where students can sing and record their sounds. The pictures on the walls are all linked to related channels and webpages.

We were using the Center in Figure 7 for group works. Students were searching from the web browser and recording their meetings.

There were various decorations and all the necessary tools for an educative environment, radio buttons for channel choices, bulletin boards, information saving areas where students were living live messages and recording their voices. What can be done more? All the rest is up to your imagination and students' creativity. It is possible to give some permissions to your students for writing codes and creating some of their own staff in the center.

Why We Should Have a Virtual Radio Platform?

Virtual Radio platforms can be used by education institutes to attract 20th century students' attention to the courses. Digital games and platforms can be used as instructional tools to improve students learning through enhancing learning interest and motivation (Chan et al., 2017; Groff, Howells, & Cranmer, 2010; Groff, McCall, Darvasi, & Gilbert, 2015; Hsu, Tsai, Chang, & Liang, 2017, Kim & Sun,2018).

These platforms provide Easiness in many means. Internet is available in most cafes and restaurants and it is not as expensive as it was 10 years before. Today nearly %90 youth are interested in Internet activities. Many people carry Smartphones with them which are reasonably cheap, realistic, entertaining and educative. Fastness to reach to the center and not having transportation problems makes it a good choice.

These days many people, specially youth, are recording their voices and having their own Youtube Channels. A Center will collect all the separate Youtube channels in a platform and help people to have more audience. With virtual radio centers, one can easily record voices and they can save time. The fast access of internet is sure to make access to these centers fast. Not all people may want to come to the real radio centers, however virtual radio centers gives a chance to new identities. In a virtual community information sharing is faster than any real radio center. Virtual centers help virtual communities to grow, more than real centers do.

SUGGESTIONS FOR FUTURE DESIGNS

Easy Designs are Needed

The easier that it is, the more people will use it; when the more people use it, the more they will benefit from it. Designs can be simplified for easiness. Not everyone have programming talent so it must not contain complicated parts in which participants would find hard to understand. People get afraid of things that they find too complicated to understand.

Reachable Platforms

There are many restrictions in these platforms. If virtual systems are designed such that they are more reachable to a great audience it would be more interesting and more popular. Although some parts which needed interactive communication may not be easily reachable, the general meeting areas should be more open to outsiders.

The internet access problems may also make these platforms hard to reach. In these platforms Internet speed is important for users being able to transport to different lands easily. It would be good if virtual platforms use objects that require less memory space and are uploaded more easily.

CONCLUSION

In a café, in a journey or while you are driving a car, radio may be a good choice, however no one watches a radio on Internet these days when they have a chance of watching a TV channel. Virtual Radio Centers, including access to several radio channels and compatible with mobile phones should be more common in future. These centers will help people to visualize what's going on and will give them a chance to participate both physically and virtually. Nonetheless, a Virtual Radio Center will make the sounds visible!

REFERENCES

Berger, M., Jucker, A. H., & Locher, M. A. (2016). Interaction and space in the virtual world of second life, *Journal of Pragmatics* 101, 83-100.

Chan, K. Y. G., Tan, S. L., Hew, K. F. T., Koh, B. G., Lim, L. S., & Yong, J. C. (2017). Knowledge for games, games for knowledge: designing a digital roll-and-move board game for a law of torts class. *Research and Practice in Technology Enhanced Learning*, *12*(1), 7. doi:10.118641039-016-0045-1 PMID:30613256

Dede, C. (1995). The evolution of constructivist learning environments: immersion in distributed virtual worlds. *Educational Technology*, *35*, 46–52.

Griol, D., Sanchis, A., Molina, J. M., Callejas, Z. (2019). Developing enhanced conversational agents for social virtual worlds, *Neurocomputing*, 354, 27-40.

Groff, J., Howells, C., & Cranmer, S. (2010). *The impact of console games in the classroom: Evidence from schools in Scotland*. UK: Futurelab.

Groff, J., McCall, J., Darvasi, P., & Gilbert, Z. (2015). Using games in the classroom. in K. Schoenfield (Ed.), Learning, education and games Vol. 2: Bringing games into educational contexts (pp. 19-41). Pittsburgh, PA: ETC Press.

Hsu, C. Y., Tsai, M. J., Chang, Y. H., & Liang, J. C. (2017). Surveying in-service teachers' beliefs about game-based learning and perceptions of technological pedagogical and content knowledge of games. *Journal of Educational Technology & Society*, *20*(1), 134–143.

Kim, Y. R., & Park, M. S. (2018). Creating a virtual world for mathematics. *Journal of Education and Training Studies*, *6*(12), 172. doi:10.11114/jets.v6i12.3601

McConville, K. V. M., & Virk, S. (2012). Evaluation of an electronic video game for improvement of balance. *Virtual Reality (Waltham Cross)*, *16*(4), 315–323. doi:10.100710055-012-0212-7

Schmidt, S., Bruder, G., & Steinicke, F. (2019). Effects of virtual agent and object representation on experiencing exhibited artifacts. *Computers & Graphics*, *83*, 1–10. doi:10.1016/j.cag.2019.06.002

The Tellos Alliance. (2019), *The Tellos Alliance virtual radio is the future, the future is here*, Retrieved from https://www.telosalliance.com/Radio-Solutions/Virtual-Radio

Trescak, T., Esteva, M., & Rodriguez, I. (2010). A virtual world grammar for automatic generation of virtual worlds. *The Visual Computer*, *26*(6-8), 521–531. doi:10.100700371-010-0473-7

Virtanen, J.-P., Kurkela, M., Turppa, T., Vaaja, M. T., Julin, A., Kukko, A., ... Hyyppa, H. (2018). Depth camera indoor mapping for 3d virtual radio play. *The Photogrammetric Record*, *33*(162), 171–195. doi:10.1111/phor.12239

Chapter 5
Gamification:
To Engage Is to Learn

Biancamaria Mori
MenteZero, Italy

ABSTRACT

This chapter will discuss Gamification and video games, analyzing their peculiarities. After a brief historical introduction to the disciplines that intertwine the design of Gamification applications, such as User interaction, User Interface, and Game Design, authors analyze the real areas in which Gamification can be applied with verifiable results, citing scientific studies and examples of applications. We will see then how from the video games Toca Boca for children, to the "tourist" version of Assassin's Creed Oringis presented at the British Museum, up to the latest interactive applications for business training, the techniques of the game are exceeding the playful areas to make more deep human interaction with the real surrounding it.

INTRODUCTION

Interactivity, that is, the working relationship of reciprocal reference or exchange, is at the basis of the way in which the human being interfaces (another word not by chance used in reference to computer contexts) with the world that surrounds it.

Every day, we understand what is outside of us with the use of the five senses, developing one or two of preference to others according to the historical period and the geographical location in which we grow up. We smell, taste, listen, but above all, we see and touch objects, changing our reality.

Precisely referring to the predominance of these two senses (sight and touch), when the computers sale became possible even for private buyers, the need was to make user-machine communication easier for people who lacked technical knowledge by creating graphical interfaces (UI).

Although the first interfaces were organized on their own text character sets, using graphic symbols such as straight lines, angles, and arrows, the result of a still primitive technology, graphic icons soon made their entrance with the advent of enhanced machines., virtual objects that reproduced the elements we can find on or around a desktop, such as the trashcan, document sheets, pencils and calculators.

DOI: 10.4018/978-1-7998-1796-3.ch005

Copyright © 2020, IGI Global. Copying or distributing in print or electronic forms without written permission of IGI Global is prohibited.

These precautions were the first step towards a user-friendly computing device, which also allowed the novice an intuitive approach to IT tools.

The user interface is a discipline based on the design of user interfaces for machines and software, which has extended over the years from computers to mobile devices, from websites to applications, reaching cars, embracing all fields of human interaction machine and claiming for itself the role of a bridge between the humanities and computer sciences. It is in fact through a well-designed interface that we acquire and learn the information necessary for using a software or hardware.

The user interface is supported by a complementary discipline called User Interaction, which deals with how the user and the machine interact on each other.

Put simply, if the User Interaction are the actions that the machine and the user perform on each other, the User Interface is the words and symbols with which they communicate.

These two disciplines wisely used define a better educational experience for most users of any age (Antin, 2012; Kim et al., 2015).

USER INTERACTIVITY AS A LANGUAGE TO UNDERSTAND

With the emergence of the gaming industry as an entertainment giant, which has undermined and transformed the concept of play that has always been linked to childhood and sports, expanding the concept of gaming to Experience also and often addressed only to adults, we see planting the first seeds for a new discipline that will be intertwined with the aforementioned: Gamification, which will be able to mix user interaction and user interface with the language and dynamics of the game, exploiting the new language used by video games together with the mechanics of the Game Design, combining the use of technological means and the learning of notions or procedures the entertainment of the game.

Here, we explore how Gamification can be useful in the pedagogical area.

Through Gamification, which can make use of different ways for the medium (based on, for example, the twelve intelligences theorized by Gardner), we can transmit a skill or a notion, so that the subject can experience learning in a more personalized way, allowing him to experiment several times and find different ways to solve an experience that could arise in the real world, with the benefit of the protected environment that the game experience creates, so as to put into practice solutions applicable later in the experience daily.

The educational apps of Toca Boca are an example of "learning by playing", in fact, through the mechanics of the game, the child acquires knowledge through a pedagogical and engaging use of the technological medium, stimulating the imagination and bringing it closer to the world and its dynamics. Scratch is another exquisite example, a site that allows you to learn how to program by combining pieces of code as if they were pieces of a puzzle, where the child (or a novice programming student) understands how to connect programming blocks and how to structure a function thanks to the intuitive connections and colors that help in classifying the code according to its purpose.

If in the child the approach to Gamification is to abstract from the notional learning by immersing it in an involving reality through pedagogical techniques that facilitate learning, in the adult the discourse evolves: thanks to the adult maturity, more advanced means can be exploited in which abstraction is not necessary and learning techniques are enhanced, using achievements, scores, goals and rewards without neglecting emotional involvement and storytelling.

Learning in the adult world even if more complex does not lack of customization, they can in fact decide which learning method is most suitable for them, when to learn, at what pace and with what difficulty. Babbel and Duolingo are the two most used applications in the linguistic field thanks to the excellent user interface, integrated with Game Design: a quiz with multiple answers in multiple languages (verbal, phonetic and figurative), levels, goals and gratification.

Thanks to a series of learning techniques and methods studied by Pimsleur, learning a new language becomes easier if you prioritize the learning of the sounds of words and sentences and then learn the meaning, after the phonics, only later. and without placing a clear distinction between grammar, vocabulary and pronunciation. Babbel and Duolingo exploit these dynamics very well, making use of a quiz game and a skill tree where the user progresses as he learns the language. Users gain skill points or tokens when they complete the lessons and "level up" when the user completes all the actions associated with a skill. Each lesson consists of a series of small challenges, such as translation, repetition of a sound and anticipation: reaching the correct sentence when it is confirmed.

With the lives, the score, the progressive unlocking of levels and the reminders that invite the user to play, they are stimulated and put into competition thanks to the rankings, playing an important role on the constancy of the same user (Barata et al., 2013; Kuh, 2009).

BETWEEN VIDEO GAMES AND GAMIFICATION

Nowadays mass cultural phenomena and despite many detractors, it is a fact highlighted by science (one among many, the study of action games and cognitive abilities of Daphné

Bavelier) that Video Games since 1958 have positively influenced our vision and our approach to the world, favouring a greater understanding of the other and stimulating the imagination.

The videogamer is put to the test by the videogame through numerous challenges, puzzles or experiences: the videogame is a unique medium that makes the player interact, multiplying the possibilities of learning and exercising a potential of immersivity and attraction that other media, lacking of the interactive component, just don't.

The videogame universe is not dictated by the laws of physics, but by the most important sphere of the rules of the game that determines both the approach between the player and the game, and the ability of the game itself to communicate through the actions that the player must (or try) to accomplish: the gameplay. These are the building blocks that go into creating the gaming experience in the video game, and in Gamification make learning happen.

More and more studies[1] show that gamers have much more mnemonic learning skills and are able to react faster to situations than those who are not accustomed to virtual games. In particular, gamers are better at learning and retaining in their memory the knowledge they have learned, because the activity of the hippocampus is stimulated, the part of our brain responsible for transforming short-term memories into long-term memories. It should also be noted that the stress of the hippocampus brings long-term benefits like preventing senile dementia.

Playing video games therefore stimulates the ability to learn quickly, regardless of the specific message of the video game.

Thanks to the narrative system the videogame is capable of touching the emotional sphere and it is not uncommon for it to take on a moral: all the properties that a book or a film can have are enhanced by immersion, allowing the user to feel involved in first person in the events that follow one another during the adventure. A clear example is the scandal caused by the videogame Mass Effect 3 when it was released, in which the protagonist driven by the player, a space captain intent on disentangling himself in disparate events for the salvation of the worlds, could, however, entertain with other characters also homosexual relationships. This happened in 2012, where the concept of homosexuality in Western culture had already been cleared and queer culture flourished and spread to other art channels, from cinema to television to literature. Why then if a film and a video game deal with the same issues, in the first case is it perceived by the public as something acceptable and cultural, while the second product ends up under public trial?

In my opinion the answer is very simple to deduce. In the first case, that is in the film, we have a passive observation of a narrative: we are witnessing a succession of events that can be narrative or documentary, which allow us to reflect from an external point of view on the subject dealt with. In the video game, on the other hand, despite the fact that the regulations on PEGI[2] have been in force for many years, parents and institutions fell into a panic at the idea that our children, our young people, could personally choose to have homosexual relationships with NPCs. In this case, therefore, free choice comes into play, the possibility of choosing to play a homosexual character involves taking on responsibility that the simple external observation that the cinema proposed could not simply propose. This example, however unfortunate, denotes how much the masses perceive the communicative power that the video game carries with it.

The same potential can also be observed on the implementation of game mechanics, each goal can be achieved in different ways, allowing the player to choose which path to take and accept the consequences, based on the rules of the system and the skills of the player himself. The function of the Game Over is not negligible: if in the Western society, (in particular European) the failure is perceived as something irreparable and that must be avoided, during the game you have the freedom to lose and start again. The "game over" therefore assumes the positive meaning of trying again to refine the technique and learning to lose becomes a potential to face defeats in a positive way, in the game as in life.

If these gameplay elements are combined with education, learning and / or achieving a goal all becomes easier and more satisfying, adding value to experience.

Gamification takes its cue from the rules of the game and its achievements to create an educational environment, where everyone can choose the tools within the game mode that is most functional for learning certain techniques.

There are games that use various game mechanics to ensure that each user chooses the method that best suits them to get to the goal, thus enhancing the critical spirit, awareness of their abilities and enhancing their talents.

Many games, in order to transmit the learning of a skill, increase the engagement through the use of a laboratory part, implementing the gestures in video games, increasing interaction at narrative and environmental level, making learning less stressful and notional creating an atmosphere full of emotion thanks to a wise interweaving of actions, visual environments and sounds, in order to create experiences that allow to stimulate the association of images and mnemonic exercise (Kim, 2014).

THE POWER OF THE GAME

In the introduction to her "reality is broken" book, Jane McConigal (2011) begins by reporting study data that defines a veritable exodus of gamers in virtual worlds, which in the United States alone amount to 183 million people playing on average thirteen hours a week, thus being able to be defined as active gamers. To explain why this phenomenon is the power that the game brings with it, she cites Herodotus, reporting an example of how in the history of games the sphere has been fundamental for development and often for the survival of civilizations:

When Atys was king of Lydia in Asia Minor some three thousand years ago, a great scarcity threatened his realm. For a while people accepted their lot without complaining, in the hope that times of plenty would return. But when things failed to get better, the Lydians devised a strange remedy for their problem. The plan adopted against the famine was to engage in games one day so entirely as not to feel any craving for food . . . and the next day to eat and abstain from games. In this way they passed eighteen years, and along the way they invented the dice, knuckle-bones, the ball, and all the games which are common.

It is clear from this excerpt of "the Histories" how much the game, as McGonigal (2011) also underlines, thanks to its immersive component has been fundamental in the development and even in the survival of many civilizations.

We are wrongly accustomed to perceiving the game, above all the video game, as a passive escape from the surrounding reality, an entertainment that alienates the player making him forget the real world, when in truth the game plays an important role in helping us overcome the difficulties .

The game, transporting us into a world that is not dictated by the rules of society and physics but dictated by a specific sphere of rules, allows us to develop empowering about ourselves and our community when the logic of reality is lacking.

In fact escaping into the video game is often, if the subject is aware, an intentional and active choice where the gamer does not lose consciousness of himself: in a western world where the people the first shortage is no longer the primary need for food, but the lack of stable reference points and the continuous and frenetic technological development that leads to an acceleration of life itself, the need that we try to fill in virtual worlds is the search for stability, certainties and logical rules for a present and a future that makes us feel better about ourselves and our environment.

Video games make the difficulties of life of the new millennium bearable, calming the thirst for meaning towards a, perhaps, more superficial world.

The game, if exploited in positive terms, is the apple that the doctor prescribes us to eat every day.

Taking note of the facts and data available to us, it would now be totally out of place not to recognize the communicative power and attraction it has for the masses of the video game. We can decide to ignore this potential, thus losing a great opportunity, or we can decide to start producing with awareness of the medium games and experiences that are intertwined with reality going to improve it (McGonigal, 2011).

EDUCATION, MUSEUM AND BUSINESS: PLACES WHERE GAMIFICATION LIVES

One of the areas that surely naturally approaches the concept of play and experience is that of infant training.

Through play, younger children learn to distinguish geometric shapes, to count and memorize words that are increasingly more and more complex during growth, but also to collaborate with companions and friends, to assimilate values and morals. The child, therefore, no longer considered an empty vessel to be filled, is educated to understand through the stimulus of the game, making learning always diversified and rich, prepared to become a human inserted in an interactive social context.

Already in the thirties John Dewey American philosopher and educator, theorized pedagogical activism, a current that starts from the conception of the child as an active subject and protagonist in learning processes.

Being an important factor in the growth of the child, as a process by which the individual assimilates knowledge, techniques and habits of life from birth, education must invest in all aspects of the educational process, such as socialization, content cultural and school organization itself.

For Dewey (1938) the latter must be conceived as a democratic social environment that stimulates the spirit of participation and co-responsibility, making each child play a decisive role, preparing him to face future life by amplifying his potential and seeking continuity with future experiences. In fact, Dewey (1938) believes that an experience, to be educational, cannot exist as an isolated case, but to be part of a broader project that stimulates the child to learn and have the necessary curiosity to research other educational experiences in the future[3].

If at first the video game was not seen as an educational experience because it did not include the movement and the laboratory and social experimentation that was sought in the training experiences, today thanks to the new technological means and the more in-depth attention to the social aspect of design of the last generation games, combined with devices that involve not only the mind but also physical activity and gestures, the video game undoubtedly places itself in educational experiences, allowing also to go beyond the concept of here and now.

Studying theoretical subjects in this way becomes easier and more engaging if it becomes possible to visit places and eras that are impossible to experience differently or to visualize and interact with physical functions and laws, reducing the abstraction of these concepts and bringing them closer to a more understandable environment for the educator.

Precisely this concept makes us understand how Gamification can be important also in the field of cultural heritage and tourism.

It is no coincidence that in recent years museums have increasingly approached multimedia and interactive techniques to bring visitors closer to the museum heritage.

A concrete example of the potential of Gamification is that of the *Pavilhão do Conhecimento*, the interactive museum of science and technology of Lisbon, whose purpose is to make physical and natural phenomena accessible to all, stimulating exploration and experimentation and spreading the technological culture and scientific.

The Pavilhão is organized in 4 large exhibition areas, each of which presents different interaction methods: Hit and Run Modules, a large area dedicated to physical installations, Explore, an area dedicated to the exploration of natural phenomena, Dóing enlarged workshop, an 500 m² area dedicated to 3D printing workshops and mechanical play activities, and finally an area dedicated to temporary exhibits.

Each installation can be played and the visitor, both child and adult, can directly manipulate the physical event, making it unleash whenever it wants.

The pavilion organizes events for families every month, reviving adult curiosity and stimulating the child to discover the world and the phenomena that surround it.

In 2017, the Pavilion organized a temporary exhibition / event in collaboration with the video game Angry Birds[4], produced for Rovio Entertainment's mobile devices, with huge catapults, slides and modules where visitors could throw the protagonist birds towards the enemy green pigs, realizing the phenomena of gravity and acceleration, involving children and adults in physical experiments. The installation was divided into several areas: on the one hand a group of children was building a wall of soft bricks, on the other there was another group of children ready to demolish it by throwing angry birds with large slings.

The child, having fun, learns through the experience of applied science the fundamental physical principles, such as the principles of Newton's dynamics.

An example relating to the humanities is that of Ubisoft, which in the month of February 2018 presented the Assassin's Creed: Origins[5] Discovery Tour mode at the British Museum, given the large amount of Egyptian finds inside, offering the possibility to explore the Egypt of the Pharaohs era thanks to a meticulous reconstruction carried out thanks to the efforts of wise digital and historical artists, freely following their entire surface and discovering the customs of its inhabitants: the form of the video game in this example becomes the maximum expression of potential of educational content. Just like on a tourist trip, the visitor will be guided by historians and Egyptologists in Ancient Egypt in a world devoid of legal pressures to the normal dynamics of the game. In each guided tour the tourist can follow the golden line on the ground and listen to the guide at the stops, marked with a brilliant point near the destinations and always remaining free to move at will.

Thanks to this new way of exploration, learning becomes subjective, adapting to the rhythms of each user and allowing them to experience sites that are now unapproachable or no longer available.

Making the museum within reach is a broad end, of which gamification can only be one of the steps.

At the base of this transformation, as has already been observed in recent years, the museum must become from an exclusive and elite to an inclusive and family place, eliminating the austere aura reserved only for a sphere of intellectual people but rather opening the doors to families, children, disabled people and all those categories who want to educate themselves, through new technological and accessible means.

Subsequently, like any place and tourist agency, the museum needs to bring its heritage closer to people so that they can feel involved in a comfortable environment in order to exploit the potential of the place to stimulate a deeper cultural learning. And it is in this specific case that gamification can be used in the most profitable way.

Thanks to Gamification we can indeed restore life and context to historical finds or splinters, which simply exposed would risk not being readable or interesting, as children of a society and a costume no longer adherent to our reality. Failing to link them to an environment and a specific use, the visitor will most likely only see an alien object that is difficult to understand.

Given the potential of the experiences in the field of marketing, the Customer Experience is born: the customer's perception of his interaction with the company, ever more carefully and personalized. The feeling that the satisfied customer receives after interacting with the company is an opportunity and a promise of continuity between the two.

Therefore, the market eye is not only attentive to the product but also to its experience and presentation, to how it sells and to the journey the customer makes up to its purchase, to the atmosphere that breathes in the store and the palette that beautifies the site.

For example, customers who want to book a trip have at their disposal customized and varied experiences, such as gastronomic experiences, organized meetings and personalized tourist trips, as if to make the memories of a trip as unique as possible.

In this new trade of memories, the analogical and digital experience seem to exchange: if before the virtual reality sold the maximum customization with the evolution of the market, the analogical experiences have become it too, with the difference that the latter leave memories to put on show.

Also, in the field of business gamification has found interesting applications, for example by retaining the end customer through awards, achievements, experiences and video games, creating a continuous link with the brand. On Aliexpress and Wish, two platforms reserved for online sales, there is a roulette that releases prizes every day, encouraging daily access to the app and making the customer earn points to spend on purchases, convincing him to return to the platform again.

Customer involvement and loyalty can be improved both locally and remotely: the video game is an excellent choice to enhance the engagement of a chain of pizzerias or shops: the customer can register the QR code after a purchase printed on the receipt and unlock virtual prizes to continue the gaming experience.

In Covet Fashion, an app for Android and iPhone, the player is subjected to look challenges that, if positively voted by other users, will earn prizes in clothes and virtual accessories. The clothes reflect the real fashion lines of some brands to which the app is connected, thanks to an online sales platform where you can physically buy clothes, with discounts accessible only through winnings and daily accesses within the video game.

Mirrors in augmented reality, in-store mini-games and technological toys, such as mixed reality applications and interactive catalogues, are on-site Gamification solutions, an interactive way to learn about and present the brand's products, such as the IKEA mini-game where the user could choose the arrangement of the furniture in a living room, available both in the shops and on their site.

Within the company's production, Gamification can focus mainly on two points: increasing engagement in the work of its employees and improving product development and production procedures.

In the first case the employee can be encouraged, through a scoring system among employees, made of real goals and prizes to improve his performances thanks to the competition created by the rankings of the most deserving employees (techniques used above all by American gamification) and awards that encourage and reward the most productive worker.

In the second case, the employee is helped in his work, made easier and more enjoyable thanks to technological devices that have the task of guiding him in complex procedures making it easily accessible to the guided assistance and consultation of the operations to be completed: his services will increase and be rewarded accordingly (Baard, 2004; Kim, 2014).

For all sectors, the most important and interesting aspect is feedback: Gamification gathers a huge amount of data. Through a video game or an interactive app, the company can know how much customers have been involved using the application. From an entrepreneurial point of view, one can monitor the performance of each employee and measure the deficits in the workflow of the company, having direct feedback with data that allows the development of a better work pipeline.

AR, VR & MIXED REALITY: LAST FRONTIERS OF GAMIFICATION

Thanks to new software and hardware technologies, the user can experience ever more immersive and tangible experiences from our senses.

Using some special viewers that isolate the user from the surrounding environment, Virtual Reality allows to enter an immaterial space, digitally created and to live it not through the perception of a luminous rectangle, like the screen, but through a spherical projection that develops around the user. Through these new devices, the user can turn his head and look at this world from the angle he prefers, moving inside thanks to joysticks or more advanced devices that allow the real movement of the body. Thanks to gesture technology and hand recognition, the experience becomes even more realistic and immersive, bringing the user to have a "tactile" relationship with virtual objects: although he cannot actually touch them, he is able to manipulate them with same gestures that he would carry out in reality. VR is used in entertainment and gaming, creating more and more engaging gaming experiences.

Initially used to build HUDs[6], the latest Augmented Reality technology is very different, allowing us to enrich the world around us with digital content. In this way, the user is not estranged from the real world, never losing visual contact with it, but rather enriching it with digital interactive content.

The fields of application of AR are manifold, from the simple display of useful information in places like stations and roads (let's think of Google Maps AR), up to the interaction between public and work in a museum.

Recent examples are the Google Street View AR, which recognizes buildings and streets and allows orientation through digital road signs, and Google Lens, a tool that allows the recognition of texts, their translation, the recognition of objects and products.

The Mixed Reality superimposes the virtual reality to the physical one observing the real world by drawing information in AR or allows to see and move virtual objects that interact with the analogic world perfectly integrated with the environment.

The landing on the market is still far away but in recent years many experiments have been made, one of these is Microsoft's HoloLens: a device, similar to a helmet for VR technology, which includes transparent lenses that allow the visualization of one's field visual and information about it in AR. HoloLens can be adapted to different types of applications, from assistance in the construction and maintenance of any project to playful applications such as the visualization of the Minecraft world on one's home table, allowing for complete interaction.

AN EXPLANATION OF DIGITAL REALITIES

Interactions between humans and digital worlds have now been temporarily classified into 3 types: Virtual Reality, Augmented Virtuality, Augmented Reality, the combination of these three technologies is called [7]Mixed Reality.

Virtual Reality is the one in which the user finds himself in a world completely simulated by the stranger from physical Reality, completely immersing him in a simulated environment that replaces the senses of sight and hearing with the real ones created in an exclusive interaction with cyberspace.

Augmented reality is instead a superposition of digital data in the real world, providing the user with real-time contextual information in the surrounding environment, creating, as explained in the previous chapter, a useful interaction in the analogic world.

The Augmented Virtuality is little known, it is a superposition of real parts over a digital world, for example of real hands that can interact with the simulation.

So what is the bond that unites the parts of mixed reality? The search for the solution to the interaction between human machine that is as natural as possible, or the possibility of using the senses simulating interactions considered humanly normal, sight, hearing and touch.

All of them solve interactions by simulating the senses with digital substitutes, such as the screen for visual perception, sound amplifiers for hearing and finally specific hardware or digital detections to simulate hands, even if this point needs to be done considerations regarding touch.

Touch is a sensory perception that is still missing inside mixed reality, in fact, solutions that the user can perceive in the shape of the virtual world on his fingertips have not yet been found. When this happens, the hardware simulation will be complete, going first towards a progressive improvement that will lead to a more realistic perception of the virtual world up to a 1: 1 resolution with the analogic world.

After this approach of Mixed Reality to the real world, what will be the next step? Probably the answers to this question are in science fiction, such as something shown in the film *Matrix*, or when the digital world will be directly perceptible by our central nervous system, replacing everyday reality.

REFERENCES

Antin, J. (2012). Gamification is not a dirty word. *Interaction*, *19*(4), 14–16.

Appleton, J. J., Christenson, S. L., Kim, D., & Reschly, A. L. (2006). Measuring cognitive and psychological engagement: Validation of the student engagement instrument. *Journal of School Psychology*, *44*(5), 427–445. doi:10.1016/j.jsp.2006.04.002

Baard, P. P., Deci, E. L., & Ryan, R. M. (2004). Intrinsic need satisfaction: A motivational basis of performance and well-being in two work settings. *Journal of Applied Social Psychology*, *34*(10), 2045–2068. doi:10.1111/j.1559-1816.2004.tb02690.x

Barata, G., Gama, S., Jorge, J., & Goncalves, D. (2013). Engaging engineering students with gamification. In *Proceedings 5th International Conference on Games and Virtual Worlds for Serious Applications*, pp. 1-8. IEEE.

Bartle, R. (1996). Hearts, clubs, diamonds, spades: Players who suit MUDS. Available at https://mud.co.uk/richard/hcds.htm

Chopin, A., Bediou, B., & Bavelier, D. (2019). Altering perception: The case of action video gaming. *Current Opinion in Psychology.*, *29*, 168–173. doi:10.1016/j.copsyc.2019.03.004 PMID:30978639

Dewey, J. (1938). *Experience and education*. New York: Macmillan.

Gardner, H., & Hatch, T. (1989). Multiple intelligences go to school: Educational implications of the theory of multiple intelligences. *Educational Researcher*, *18*(8), 4–9.

Kim, A. J. (2014). *Innovate with game thinking*. Retrieved from http://amyjokim.com/blog/2014/02/28/beyond-player-types-kims-social-action-matrix

Kim, Y., Glassman, M., & Williams, M. S. (2015). Connecting agents: Engagement and motivation in online collaboration. *Computers in Human Behavior, 49*(1), 333–342. doi:10.1016/j.chb.2015.03.015

Kuh, G. D. (2009). The national survey of student engagement: conceptual and empirical foundations, *New Directions for Institutional Research,* 141, pp. 5-20. doi:10.1002/ir.283

McGonigal, J. (2011). *Reality is broken: Why games make us better and how they can change the world.* New York, NY: Penguin Press.

ADDITIONAL READING

Abramovich, S., Schunn, C. and Higashi, R.M. (2013), "Are badges useful in education? It depends upon the type of badge and expertise of learner", Educational Technology Research and Development: A Bi-Monthly Publication of the Association for Educational Communications & Technology, Vol. 61 No. 2, pp. 217-232.

Attali, Y., & Arieli-Attali, A. (2015). Gamification in assessment: Do points affect test performance? *Computers & Education, 83*(1), 57–63. doi:10.1016/j.compedu.2014.12.012

Bergstrom, K., Fisher, S., & Jenson, J. (2016). Disavowing that guy: Identity construction and massively multiplayer online game players. *Convergence (London), 22*(3), 233–249. doi:10.1177/1354856514560314

Brualdi, A. C. (1996). *Multiple Intelligences: Gardner's Theory. ERIC Digest.* Eric Digests.

Bruner, J. (1960). *The Process of Education.* Cambridge, Mass.: Harvard University Press.

Gardner, H. (1975). *The Shattered Mind.* New York: Knopf.

Keeler, A. (2014). *Beyond the worksheet: playsheets, GBL, and gamification* (pp. 1–3). Edutopia; www.edutopia.org/blog/beyond-worksheet-playsheets-gbl-gamification-alice-keeler

Keeler, A. (2015), "Gamification: engaging the students with narrative", Edutopia, pp. 1-3, www.edutopia.org/blog/gamification-engaging-students-with-narrative-alice-keeler Kiang, D. (2014), "Edutopia", Using gaming principles to engage students, October 14, www.edutopia.org/blog/using-gaming-principles-engage-students-douglas-kiang Kingsley, T.L. and Grabner-Hagen, M.M. (2015), "Gamification: questing to integrate content, knowledge, literacy, and 21st-century learning", Journal of Adolescent & Adult Literacy, Vol. 59 No. 1, pp. 51-61, doi:10.1002/jaal.426

Koivisto, J., & Hamari, J. (2014). Demographic differences in perceived benefits from gamification. *Computers in Human Behavior, 35,* 179–188. doi:10.1016/j.chb.2014.03.007

Kolb, L. (2015). *Epic fail or win? Gamifying learning in my classroom* (pp. 1–5). Edutopia; www.edutopia.org/blog/epic-fail-win-gamifying-learning-liz-kolb

Kumar, B., & Khurana, P. (2012). Gamification in education: Learn computer programming with fun. *International Journal of Computers and Distributed Systems, 2*(1), 46–53.

Smith, L. G., & Smith, J. K. (1994). *Lives in Education. A narrative of people and ideas 2e.* New York: St Martin's Press.

Sternberg, R. J. (1985). *Beyond IQ: A triarchic theory of human intelligence.* New York: Cambridge University Press.

Sternberg, R. J. (1996). *Successful intelligence.* New York: Simon & Schuster.

White, J. (1998). *Do Howard Gardner's multiple intelligences add up?* London: Institute of Education, University of London.

Williams, W. M., Blythe, T., White, N., Li, J., Sternberg, R. J., & Gardner, H. (1996). *Practical intelligence for school.* New York: HarperCollins College Publishers.

KEY TERMS AND DEFINITIONS

Augmented reality: It is a superposition of digital data in the real world, providing the user with real-time contextual information in the surrounding environment, creating, as explained in the previous chapter, a useful interaction in the analogic world.

Customer Experience: the customer's perception of his/her interaction with a company.

Cyberspace: A virtual environment in which people interact with each other. This is the place in which online games occur.

Gamification: Mix user interaction and user interface with the language and dynamics of the game, exploiting the new language used by video games together with the mechanics of the Game Design, combining the use of technological means and the learning of notions or procedures the entertainment of the game.

Mixed-Reality: It is the combination of Virtual Reality, Augmented Virtuality, Augmented Reality.

Videogame Universe: It is not dictated by the laws of physics, but by the most important sphere of the rules of the game that determines both the approach between the player and the game, and the ability of the game itself to communicate through the actions that the player must (or try) to accomplish: the gameplay.

Virtual Reality: It is the one in which the user finds himself in a world completely simulated by the stranger from physical Reality, completely immersing him in a simulated environment that replaces the senses of sight and hearing with the real ones created in an exclusive interaction with cyberspace.

ENDNOTES

[1]   study conducted by Ruhr-University Bochum, in Germany.
https://news.rub.de/english/press-releases/2017-09-29-neuroscience-gamers-have-advantage-learning

[2]   PEGI, abbreviation of Pan European Game Information is the first pan-European classification system based on age and content for video games. https://pegi.info/it/node/47

[3]   Experience and Education - John Dewey, 1938

[4]   https://www.pavconhecimento.pt/4422/angry-birds-a-exposicao

[5]   https://support.ubi.com/it-IT/Faqs/000031846/Discovery-Tour-Mode-of-Assassin-s-Creed-Origins-ACO

[6]   Head Up Display: military devices that allowed aircraft pilots and tanks to display useful information without shifting attention from the surrounding environment

[7]   https://en.wikipedia.org/wiki/Mixed_reality

Chapter 6
Ubiquitous Self:
From Self–Portrait to Selfie

Giorgio Cipolletta
University of Macerata, Italy

ABSTRACT

In 2013, the Oxford Dictionaries announced "selfie" as the word of the year. The dictionary defined it as "a photograph that one has taken of oneself, typically one taken with a smartphone or webcam and uploaded to a social media website." Selfies are also a complex form of social interaction, an emerging aesthetics, thus having an irrevocable impact on self-portraiture. All visual culture revolves around the body and the body par excellence is the face. The 21st century portrait represents a kind of black mirror where we project ourselves into a kind of blindness. Mask and face are confused by an omnipresent multividuality in which the shield reveals itself and reveals other possible worlds. The face-mask melts in between Real and Virtual and the self becomes augmented.

INTRODUCTION

The face is a metonymy of the body (Belting, 2017). According to psychologist Michael Argyle, the closer we get to a person, the more the face appears independent from the rest: we are not so much surrounded by bodies but by faces that are constantly changing. In fact, we have a face, but we "mill and mold" it, we manipulate it, we create it and recreate it through mimicry (Argyle, 1975). A mask can either cover a face, substitute it or be separated from it. For example, when a face is painted, modified with make-up, or decorated, it becomes a sort of mask or a picture. Metaphorically we say that a person hides behind a 'mask', Maya's veil, an illusion that doesn't show one's true personality. In everyday life individuals never show themselves for the whole of what they really are, but wear multiple masks that, according to Pirandello, turn them into characters. Nowadays, we could say that they become their multiple performative *personae*. In common sense, that is closed to Pirandello's point of view, a mask is simply a mystification, a symbol of alienation, a sign of depersonalization and blasting of the Self into multiple identities. But it can also be a form of adapting to a context or social situation.

DOI: 10.4018/978-1-7998-1796-3.ch006

Copyright © 2020, IGI Global. Copying or distributing in print or electronic forms without written permission of IGI Global is prohibited.

In response to the endless metamorphosis of the face, ancient funerary masks wanted to provide one image: the real "true face" and not a corpse one. The mask - magic element par excellence - sums up an individual while also suggesting his/her end. It is the face of each one, but it is also the face among other faces, a face that becomes one when it gets in touch with other faces looking or being looked at. Belting continues his analysis highlighting how the face does not only resemble the mask, but it also produces its own masks, influencing other faces or reacting to them (*Maskengesicht* = face-mask). Belting points out that the portrait-medium is a key moment for the emancipation of the subject. In fact, modernity is enclosed in the passage from icon to portrait, from the sacred Face of Christ to many faces of individual paintings. Instead, contemporary art gathers and collects all digital and ubiquitous masks acknowledging the typical phenomenon of our facial society (Macho, 1996), where the self is expanded and extended in a plural dimension.

The definition of 'portrait' states that it is the representation of a person considered in itself but not for its attributes or attributions, nor for its acts or for the relationships it is engaged in. In other words, the aim of the portrait is to return a self in itself and for itself; it resembles me, it addresses and engages me (Nancy, 2000). Unlike the icon, the portrait allows the relationship to be equal because there is a dialogue. Nonetheless, during the Enlightenment the link between mask and lie was accentuated with the birth of physiognomy - the science of faces that claims to reveal the character that lies behind facial features and mimicry. The ritual power of masks is therefore lost. They no longer represent a synthesis of the self, but they bear the social fictions, they are worn to turn oneself into something else. Western thought will then treat masks as found evidence, hoping to exorcise their suggestion of death. It is only in the twentieth century that, according to German philosopher Thomas Macho (1996), we began to "live in" a facial society that produces faces nonstop. At every street corner, on every billboard, advertisements haunt us with faces to the point that "without a face nothing dares to invade the space reserved for billboards".

We can assume that in our contemporary age mask and face crossbreed and produce another surface, putting aside the "sacral" sense of mortuary masks: together they conquer a digital 'smooth' surface. Today, if photography – by either analog or digital cameras- produced first and foremost masks, whereas painting – by method, forms and intentions- produced portraits of faces, the mask-face adapts to this new state of hybridization and representation, from cinema to virtual reality. In this paper I will use the term 'mask' and 'visage' as synonyms; the contact between mask and visage is a face-to-face that has transferred into a digital, open and ubiquitous territory. New technologies and their possibilities take the mask off the face and vice versa…

BACKGROUND (ETYMOLOGIES)

At this point, it seems important to clarify a few recurrent terms: person, face, visage and derivatives.

The term 'person' has its Latin etymology in the word "persona", that is the mask worn by theatre actors to intensify their voices in order to be heard even by far away audience members. making it person. Hence, the term in Stoic philosophy is used to refer to all persons, considered as actors-in-life due to playing the role given to them by God, destiny, and society. Therefore the term "person" identifies the one who's the subject of an action, the cause of his/her actions.

The English word 'face' comes from Old French *face* "face, countenance, look, appearance"[1], from Vulgar Latin **facia* (source also of Italian *faccia*), from Latin *facies* "appearance, form, figure," and secondarily "visage, countenance," which probably is literally "form imposed on something" and related to *facere* "to make". The face is not a simple part of the body – as Emmanuel Lévinas affirms; the face is where presence is accomplished and transcends any representation that could be made of the face itself. A synonym of face, "visage" is a form with a certain surface, limited by features, as the geometric meaning of the term suggests; however, this delimited surface is characterized by expressions, therefore it's also full of meaning on which the observer's gaze acts. According to semiologist Patrizia Magli (1995) the face is the result of the constant action of focalization and cropping onto this surface by an observer; it is the part that stands for the whole. In Italian there is a third term (the first two being *faccia* and *viso*) indicating the face: volto, coming from Latin *Vultus*, the oldest Latin term for face.

In the age of facial society, the face-to-face contact is transferred to the Internet–Facebook where the digital dimension strips the face of its bodily presence, thus modifying one of the fundamental habits of our perception that involves the need to recognize faces. In our global era, facial features have been freed from national or local definitions, as well as from economic contexts, to turn into facial masks. We are overwhelmed by facial masks, writes Belting. Thomas Macho reiterates that the proliferation of faces is the effect of modern techniques of portrait reproduction. At this point, one might wonder how self-portrait could survive the contemporary.

When photographic portrait was the trend, Man Ray, in example, immortalized Marcel Duchamp in disguise as Rrose Sélavy, a woman with makeup, wig and hat. Rrose Sélavy is just a face, that turns into a mask which exist in photography. This frameshot marks not only a limit to the 'external' space, but it is also a symbolic border that allows us to peep inside (Belting, 2017, p. 204). Man Ray also had Jean Cocteau pose while holding an empty frame in front of his face, so that Cocteau turns into an image even before Ray took the picture: the direct shot of the mask and the frame thus becomes the symbol of the time interval that separates the viewer from any photograph (*Ibidem*). The operation of Portuguese photographer Jorge Modler in some of his self-portraits turns unpredictable the attempt to take possession of his person in a photograph, because he always generates masks, thus ending up taking a picture of the form of "an essence suspended" between the I and the other. With the turning point of the digital, the technological production of faces creates cyberfaces - a new kind of synthetic hybrid faces, often detached from a living body - that spread, overlap and overexpose, losing their cultural value (Benjamin, 1936).

In Facebook and Photoshop era the face is reduced to its mere value of "exposure" (face), it's a set of features without any "aura of the glance", it is a commodity form of the human face (Han, 2015, p. 22). The faces that are produced and reproduced no longer belong to anyone, they lose their link with history and resemblance to real faces. Cyberfaces represent only interfaces in the midst of an infinite number of images, flat and smooth surfaces, where the face "unmasks" only through the action of morphing, but it just gives us a non-alive, synthetic, hybrid, science fiction, posthuman face in its digital appearance (Flusser, 2000). In his book *For a Philosophy of Photography*, Flusser states that photographers use the camera in an attempt to find the possibilities not yet discovered within it, but it is as if we created ourselves to seek an ideal version of ourselves and, in this process, we try to exhaust the photographic program by realizing all our possibilities. Perhaps we are afraid that our images - our "I" – will run out and therefore we produce ourselves in excess (Ibid, p. 26). It was perhaps unexpected that people would generate an astronomical amount of themselves and that our desire to capture and share selves would become a global phenomenon. This longing for selves seems to (perhaps) lean towards the myth of Narcissus, as media theorist Marshall McLuhan explains: "men are immediately fascinated by any extension of themselves in any material other than themselves". In contrast to the popular version of the myth of Narcissus, McLuhan (1994) points out that Narcissus did not fall in love with himself, but rather, insensitive to his image, he cannot recognize his reflection as his own. It seems that we are experiencing a similar situation of misrecognition when using different apps such as Instagram.

It's like not knowing that we are looking at ourselves, makes us insensitive to our own self-portraits and produce many different versions of ourselves. On the English-speaking web the word selfie begins to circulate in early 2000s - making appearances since 2002 on the *Oxford English Corpus*). The first lexicographic appearance (spelled as *selfy*) is in 2005 by users in the *Urban Dictionary*, a famous online dictionary compiled by the users themselves: this confirms an already widespread use, especially on websites and social networks then used for sharing photos (e.i.: Flickr and MySpace). Since 2009 we can find *selfie* in *Wiktionary*; in August 2013 it is registered as a neologism and elected "word of the year" by the *Oxford Dictionaries*. *Selfie* is not exactly a synonym of either automatic shutter release - as in a "device for delaying the shooting of a camera"- or self-shot - as in a "photo where the shooter is also the subject", or self-portrait. In the Oxford Dictionaries Online the term means '*a photograph that one has taken of oneself, typically one taken with a smartphone or webcam and uploaded to a social media website*'. Hence, it is not a coincidence that the practice of selfie boomed at the same time as the introduction of front cameras in smartphones.

FACIAL SOCIETY

Faces are omnipresent, they're everywhere and they constantly produce new masks either of anonymous masses or dictators. The desire to find a "real face" clashes with our metropolitan alienation. The same crisis can be observed in the fact that portrait loses all value of epistemic recognition. According to psychoanalyst Bollas, in early 21ˢᵗ century computer age has caused an extreme disorientation of the humanistic self by offering new ways of thinking, being and relating (Bollas, 2018). In the era of multiple collapsing (Belpoliti, 2005), the contemporary detaches itself from itself by being extremely transitory, facial mimicry transforms the face into masks, the gaze loses its landmarks. The falling down of the Twin Towers is the ultimate destructive act that provokes a space closure and a claustrophobic reaction. We shall start from reflecting on 9/11 and its descriptions: its symbolic and actual, global and explosive meaning; the stories of ordinary people; general pain and bewilderment; disbelief; and that extreme sense of vulnerability that everyone has felt deeply when watching the images of suicides' bodies throwing themselves from the towers - black dots, slightly bigger than ants, falling down the façade of the sky-scraper (Belpoliti, 2005: 50). 9/11 represents a thin line of demarcation where even the contemporary dissolves into something more complex and transitory we could call the trans-contemporary (Cipolletta, 2014: 79). It represents the mandatory transition towards a different way of looking at, an "out of control" gaze, where the act of looking has swarmed onto everything (Cousins: 2017).

Even the linguistic act is continuously supported by facial expressions and gaze. The face draws from facial expressions, from gaze and language, thus storing many images. The face is not only an image, but it also generates images, shifting from passive to active, from image to vector of images (Belting, 2017). The history of the human face goes back to Stone Age masks that represented or reconstructed faces. Basically, we could say that the mask is the reverse of words. Words are used for direct communication between two human beings, whereas the mask "interrupts" this communication: it establishes a different type of communication producing engagement or correspondence, but not an exchange. In other words, the physiognomy of the face opens up to visual communication. From photography to cinema, all visual cultures revolve around the body, and the most important thing is the face.

When we consider the visual grammar of cinema, Massimo points out that, when editing started, the alternation of close-up, foreground, background, etc. was not immediately comprehensible to viewers who had to modify their mode of perception - that was considered 'natural' even though actually culturally determined and variable.

The mask is no longer that sign, perhaps it also changed in its "nature", but it has not dissolved yet. (Canevacci, 2017, pp. 121-125).

It is exactly the cinematic close-up that reinvents a model of facial representation that is peculiar of the mask now. Somehow cinema shifts the nature of the close-up from being a borderline moment to being an almost constant presence in the narrative module of tv-series. In other words, the camera impoverishes – yet at once universalizes – our visual grammar. Again according to Canevacci, for a curious rebalancing of the many codes emitted by reproducible visual communication, the increasing dose of close-ups reduces the demand for facial-mime skills.

The new distinguishing mark in the visual hierarchy created by the present acting in cinema is a paradoxical combination of exaggerated fixity and – linked to it – of extreme expressiveness: as the face fixes itself like it did in the original masks, it becomes ever-moving. The foreground in television turns into a mask more and more. The *visus* – at once all that you see and a real and proper face – provokes both a dilation and a contraction: the face turns into the landscape and the *visus* becomes an "environment". Tv-series style accentuates close-ups as it stretches sequence shots towards infinity; editing is almost abolished in this reversing of the codes of visual communication that "fixes", reifies and paralyzes the *visus* (Ivi, p. 131).

The face is an open form that crosses the boundaries between presentation (presence) and representation (absence), between closeness and distance (Belting, 2017, p. 135). The viewer looks at the screen and consumes faces on which society projects its power structure. The public face has produced its own mask. Photography and cinema, despite their claim to exact reproduction, only create other masks. On the one hand, the absolute reproducibility of the faces generates a control tool (the police archive, the passport photos); on the other hand, it makes it possible to impose magnified faces, where "a single face subdues the multitude of faces of passers-by". The face has its own story, it is the fulcrum of the perception of the self, of the attention towards others, of the rituals of civil society. The face speaks through non-verbal language. Gavin Turk's face in *Portraits of Something that I'll never Really See* (1997) is reminiscent of a corpse, causing a distance to be drawn from any apparent relationship, in this case, with the camera, and the viewer doesn't really know if the artist is dead or pretends to be dead. This episode immediately takes us back in time to the portrait of Hyppolyte Bayard, a mysterious *Self-portrait as a Drowned Man* (1840) in which we see an apparently deceased, collapsed figure. This portrait portrays Bayard as a suicide, a life pushed to drown because of the refusal of the French authorities to attribute to him some scientific discoveries in the field of photography. The two self-portraits compared refer us to an intense self-referentiality questioning the value and authorship of their work, highlighting the ambiguity of the Self in a self-portrait, where it is never exclusive to the Self, but also implies the other.

SELFIES

In the cinema, the face is filmed in close-ups where the framing in the foreground makes the body appear in its approach in a pornographic way, depriving it of language, as Roland Barthes would say a single photograph (the display of only one thing) (Barthes, 1981, p. 42). With the close-up, agreeing with both Canevacci and Byung-Chul Han (2017b), as well as with Walter Benjamin, it expands into space, while with the slow motion shooting it expands the movement. If in the cinema the close-up "looks good" on screen. *Visus* is the view of the foreground that on the one hand dilates the only face of the actor and on the other hand restricts the field of view to the face itself.

The close up of cinema with its "sacred" function anticipates the television visus, while the digital selfie democratizes, drawing a narcissism without boundaries.Today everyone can have a vision and communicate it to the world as a selfie. In the contemporaneity of the "excessive" self, every click is a impulse. The facial exposure times in front of the camera are longer.

In the close-up of society, according to Byung-Chul Han, the face presents itself as a prisoner of itself, becoming self-referential, thus losing the "significance of the world" and its relative expressiveness. Here the selfie becomes an empty face, deprived of its expression, indicating the intimate void of the self (Han, 2017b, p. 22). It is in the smoothness of the face, without interiority, that the face becomes the facade, the interface, the smoothed and exposed screen. In the state of crisis of a body in continuous mutation (metrobody) (Cipolletta, 2014), it disintegrates, shatters in the digital age, in-forming, date-transforming (dataism) (Harari, 2015). The body is transparent, additive, composed of data, of its digital connection in a networked world and irrevocable (*Ver-Netze*). The digital retina transforms the world into a screen of images and control. In this autoerotic space, in this digital interiority no wonder is possible. (Han, 2017b, p. 38). The portrait moves its frame within the representation of oneself through another activity in a democratization of portraiture (Bonini, 2014) that began with the irruption of the camera, defined by John Berger as a box to carry "appearances". What if we see today are no longer faces, but masks? In 1980 Roland Barthes in *Camera Lucida* explains how photography can mean, or rather define, a generality only by assuming a mask, evoking also *The adventure of a photographer*, a novel by Italo Calvino (1970). The Italian writer traces in the mask what makes a face the product of society and its history.

During the twentieth century, August Sander's undertaking with *Men of the twentieth century*, where the German photographer portrayed men and women as masks of time and society, causing concern, in fact, in 1934, the Nazis censored Sander, because his faces did not correspond to the Nazi archetype of the race (Barthes, 1981, p. 36). From Sander we catapult the masks of time to Warhol, who overturns the identity by rehabilitating the characteristic serial mechanics to automatic inserting it in a context reproducible technologically. The American pop art artist, obsessed by his image, opens the door to what today we will call selfie-mania, self-celebrating and reducing even those famous fifteen successful minutes, in a few seconds. Savini (2015) wrote:

In the work entitled Selfie (2013) by Jesse Darling, a mirror reflects the image of the English artist while photographing with a smartphone. Below, a phrase captures the viewer's attention: "You, you and you". The reference inevitably goes to the cover that the American weekly Time dedicated to the character of the year in 2006, the user of the Net. On that page a computer monitor was replaced with a reflective surface similar to a mirror that highlighted the word "You". The viewer became "person of the year" and its centrality was confirmed by another message: "Yes, you. You control the Information Age. Welcome to your world". Both underline the psychological significance of hyper-mediation (Bolter & Grusin, 1999) and confirm that today we are in the hybrid era, a new sociotechnological era that emerges as technologies merge with human beings (Khanna, Khanna, 2012, p. 6; Savini, 2015).

It is evident that today, in the infosphere (Floridi, 2017), we are subject to an unprecedented inflation of images, a symptom of a cultural and political pathology, within which the post-photographic phenomenon breaks out.

Post-photography refers to photography that flows into the hybrid space of digital sociality and is a consequence of visual overabundance (Fontcuberta, 2018, p. 4). We live the image and the image lives there. Images acts, they look at us, (Bredekamp, 2015) are immersed in the capitalism of images, in the *Society of the Spectacle* (Debord, 1967), where the real world is transformed into simple images, simple images become real beings. As we have seen, the roots of selfie are placed in the history of photographic practices. The first selfie in history dates back to 1839 by Robert Cornelius, an American, considered the pioneer of international photography, in his studio in Philadelphia. The one who made the selfie a real mania was Anastasia Nikolaevna, daughter of the last Russian tsar, Nicholas II. In the photo next door, she is shooting with her Kodak Brownie. He seems to have repeatedly taken self-shots in front of large mirrors in different poses and settings. In the early twentieth century, precisely in 1920 in New York, you take the usages (or group selfie), the first vintage photo taken self-taught, was taken by the five Lords of the Byron Company. Also in New York, three photographers pose together for a selfie on the roof of Studio Marceau. Barack Obama's famous hug with his wife Michelle on the day of his re-election, November 6, 2012, signed with Four More Years, also changes social communication, as well as the selfie by young people with Pope Francis posing during an audience. This photo as soon as it was it was posted on Twitter has immediately traveled around the world, as well as the one of December 10, 2013 during the funeral of Nelson Mandela in which they are portrayed together with the Danish Prime Minister Helle Thorning-Schmidt, U.S. President Barack Obama and British Prime Minister David Cameron, changing the cold official photo in favor of a popular format. A couple of weeks later, the famous actors Ellen DeGeneres at the 2014 Oscars ceremony appeared with a selfie taken by Bradley Cooper, becoming the most popular tweet so far.

The selfie, writes Nicholas Mirzoeff, is a digital performance that brings together the self-image, the tradition of the artist's self-portrait as a hero and the mechanical image of modern art, creating a different way of thinking about the history of visual culture as the history of self-portrait (Mirzoeff, 2015, p 26), starting with the famous and enigmatic painting by Velázquez, *Las Meninas* and its wonderful game of representation (Foucault, 1967). We need to mention the fundamental contributions by Raphael in the *School of Athens* (1509), and those by Masaccio, Lippi, Mantegna, Botticelli, and the self-portrait with fur by Albrecht Dürer (1500), those of Bernini, Poussin, Artemisia Gentileschi, the head of Goliath where Caravaggio (1606-1610) portrays himself. We arrive at the infinite self-portraits of Rembrandt, then Goya, Courbet, Van Gogh, Degas touching then "troubled" up to the compulsive and massacring hysteria of Francis Bacon, for exploding in the Andy Warhol's "serialization", in the audacity and intimacy of Larry Clark (1943) and Nan Goldin (1953), the muscular and aesthetic of Mapplethorpe and the expressive therapies of Villinger and Newton, those "disturbed" of Francesca Woodman, and finally those "irreverent" of Günter Brus during the period of Viennese actionism (1960).

During 2017 at the Saatchi Gallery in London with the exhibition *From Selfie to Self-Expression*, the self-portrait as the ancestor of selfie is exhaustively investigated, the exhibition attempts to redeem its historical authority and establish it as an authentic artistic form. From the frame of the painting to the printed film of the camera to the "cold and smooth" surface of the screen. Self-portrait has become the artistic genre that distinguishes our era – writes Hall (2014) – the countless number of contemporary self-portraits is impressive. Hypertechnological developments have made the selfie public by mixing with the private for a "third hybrid territory" without borders. The device "get deviced" its own body (Cipolletta, 2014) to put us in the window ("showcaseization") so that we can get the right recognition, to experience the like in paleoselfism (Bonami, 2019). We have all the technological means to desire in the excited society (Turcke, 2012) the exact likeable. Selfie allows you to "show off" yourself (Codeluppi, 2015), to "eternalize" yourself without having a mediator (as the photographer was), they are themselves photographers of themselves, becoming simultaneously device and content at the same time. The body-device exposes itself, fixes its presence of "grateful" recognition inside the liquid windows. The need to belong, to present oneself and to promote oneself (Nadkarni, 2012) makes any medium a vehicle of narcissism and low self-esteem (Mehdizadeh, 2010; Malik, 2015).

Individuals with high traits of narcissism are inclined to positively consider the publication of their own selves and to be involved in feedback from others, as well as to observe the selves of others. The level of narcissism does not mediate the relationship between observing others' selves and the likelihood of giving you a comment or a "like". Interesting research has shown the relationship between narcissism and Smartphone Addiction. The higher the levels of narcissism, the more likely it is to be to create a Smartphone Addiction (Hussain, Pearson, 2016).

Paraphrasing Fontcuberta in the his book the *The Fury of Images*, one could say that if the photograph was elfic, the post photography is becoming selfic. Precisely in this selfic dimension, it is not a passing fashion, on the contrary, it is consolidating a kind of images that has arrived to remain, such as portraits for the passport, wedding photos or tourist photographs (Fontcuberta, 2018, pp. 83, 97). As unpleasant as their diagnosis may be, selfies are the "raw" material that allows us to understand and correct ourselves, so we can no longer do without them. In the game of seduction that takes place in social networks and in its rituals, the photographs become gestures of sharing and approval, of exchange and self-award. We have the desire "to always" have our camera at our disposal in order to not miss any opportunity to represent us (Ivi, p. 134).

Selfie makes possible, on the one hand, the ostentation of the disembodied corporeity and, on the other one, the centrality of the gaze of oneself and of the other. What appears in the creative photographic self-portrait is not the body that was inherited at birth without being able to choose it, but a possible reinvention of it. We strive to be a copy without an original (Baudrillard, 1988). In the selfie body image manipulation there is the same need shown, even if in a more radical way, by the artists of body art, and confirmed at another level by the practice of tattoos, piercings and cosmetic surgery, through which the body is customized by the subject to regain its property (Barbieri, 2016).

In the ergonomics of the selfie, the exploration of reality is not done with the eye leaning against the viewfinder of the machine. The physical and symbolic distance between the subject and the camera – often accentuated by the ridiculous selfie-stick, i.e. the loss of physical contact between the eye and the viewfinder – deprives the camera of its condition as an ocular prosthesis, an orthopedic device integrated into our body. There is no longer any proximity, reality appears here in a projection outside the body, detached from direct perception, in an already elaborate image that occupies a small digital screen (Fontcuberta, 2018, p. 97). According to Savini (2015), *the diffusion of the selfie phenomenon is the daily practice of a total hybridization with the device, establishing a relationship of intimacy and developing new pathologies such as nomophobia, i.e. the uncontrolled fear of not having one's mobile phone at hand and therefore remaining disconnected from the Net (Khanna, Khan, 2012, p. 5). The technological object has increasingly become an object parlant, with its own soul and at hand (Savini, 2015).*

Selfie has somehow reinvented and potentially extended to everyone the desire to have a visible vision for all or almost all, democratizing it making it globally irresistible, drawing a digital narcissism without borders (Canevacci, 2017, p. 135).

FROM TECHNOLOGICAL UNCONSCIOUS TO DIGITAL UNCONSCIOUS

According to Savini (2015),

at the end of the 1960s, the Italian artist Franco Vaccari developed the concept of real-time exhibition, presenting exhibitions that were "self-made" through photography: the public, in fact, was invited to "destroy the space of contemplation to open that of action" (Vaccari, 2011, p. 27). In 1972 Vaccari presented at the XXXVI Biennale d'Arte in Venice the work entitled Esposizione in tempo reale N. 4. Through an inscription in four languages, clearly visible on the wall, visitors were invited to build the work: Leave a photographic trace of your passage on these walls. A Photomatic booth was installed in the room, a passport camera that people used during the period of the exhibition to document their presence and to contribute to the realization of the work. The walls were filled like a collective fresco with small photos depicting grimaces, smiles and original poses. Vaccari's work could very well be thought of as an anticipation of the practice of selfie (Savini, 2015).

The artist limited himself to starting the process, leaving the public free to act. Vaccari's exhibition is a growing organism that interacted with every aspect of the environment (Vaccari, 2011, p. 85).

Savini in an article published in the magazine Wired (Selfie, la rappresentazione di se stessi è affermazione dell'essere hic et nunc, 2015) continues his reflection on selfie, highlighting how *in 1996 "the American collective Surveillance Camera Players, creatively posed the problem of video-control: the performances were carried out strictly in public spaces in front of cameras. In these short shows, the signs take the place of the sound and passers-by are involved in the actions"* (Savini, 2015). The electronic device with its lightness of apparatus and quality of liveness has been used as a mirror in which to look at oneself, to look at oneself in the image on the monitor in the act of looking at one's own reflected image. The selfie is to be understood as an experience characterized by a precise aspect, that is the complex of actions performed by the upper limbs and the extremities of the body of the subject in performing the act of photography: the arm that moves away from the torso, the hand that holds and orients the device, the fingers that "press" on the virtual buttons on the display, and then again the arm that "withdraws" again towards the body, the hand that redirects the device towards the subject, the fingers that operate on the display to apply filters, correct contrast and lighting and either in any case save or share the final product of this complex act. After the technical reproducibility has sanctioned a substantial alternation of the gesture of the stroke with that of the shot, the motility of the gesture within the neo-medial self-portrait space has assumed, for the most part, highly mechanical connotations, which have to do with the automation of the click, with the dragging of the mouse, or with the forms of interaction between manual skills and graphic interfaces made possible by touchscreen devices. According to Walter Benjamin in his *A short History of Photography* (1931), if the nature that speaks to the camera is a different nature from the one that speaks to the eye, then it will be different especially for this reason. Photography makes aware for the first time the optical unconscious, just as psychoanalysis discloses the instinctual unconscious. (Benjamin, 1999, p.63). Vaccari shifts the attention of the unconscious to the moment of the photographic shot in which they intervene with a symbolically structured process where at the same time there is a technological unconscious of the medium, a social one and then all the types of unconscious found in the person of the photographer and finally the personal and conscious motivation (Vaccari, 2011, p. 12).

According to sociologist and communication theorist Derrick de Kerckhove (2016), in the era of transparency and Big Data, online emotions are a new way of interpreting everyday reality. Social networks constitute an integrated system of impulses, desires and frustrations that circulate at the speed of light, modifying perceptions. In the age of transparency we do not tolerate gaps in information or vision (Han, 2015, p. 15), but only the existing one is confirmed and optimized, where the society's judgment of the positive says "I like" (Ivi, p. 16). In this ubiquitous, instantaneous digital condition, a new, very special form of virtual community is being created, in which our smartphones make us nodes within a global hypertext, as in the interactive architectures of networks. Living concentrated on a screen for most of our time leads to a reversal of mental orientation, instead of interiorizing information in the silence of reading, meditating on it within us, we publish it on the "windows" of Facebook and Twitter. The space of the Net is essentially relational and shifts the attention and the communication outside of us, in fact in the social media the identity is constituted as projection and distribution of the self outside the place of the body. We are somehow aware, perhaps, of being completely traced, but we underestimate this additive condition of data storage (Big Data) by the "big five" (GAFAM: Google, Apple, Facebook, Amazon and Microsoft) of the ITC (Information and Communications Technology). This presence of potentially extractable data on each of us is what is called the "digital unconscious" by De Kerckhove. It comes to life and develops through the different forms of knowledge and information that circulate on the Net, orienting the definition of the daily reality of each of us and of the social world in a connective process that feeds on the modes of interaction between individuals. In some way we overcome Freud's unconscious, the instincts, impulses and desires that do not manifest on a rational level, and therefore arte not immediately controllable. The digital unconscious is characterized by its global reach, by the extraordinary speed through which it allows access to information, by the instantaneous possibility of collecting and bringing out on a conscious level a considerable collection of data, correlated in different configurations in near real time. The digital person will not only want to get climate answers from his technological gadget, but will also want to know how the world is. The future is an app that keeps us informed about the world's health (De Kerckhove, 2016).

TOUCHSCREEN AESTHETICS

The new mirror-device (the screen) that we confront every day for a touch-screen aesthetic. The screen becomes the new skin through which we touch the other and empathy is replaced by screen-empathy. The screen constructs the new environment in which the human being meets, constructing an "emotional geography", where the human being establishes an empathic relationship with the body, activating a process of communication. The screen becomes wearable, portable and plays with the body that embodies it. In other words, the screen is the new flesh, while the body becomes a device, it arranges the bodily system in relation to new technologies and is placed in a process of communication by activating information (info-aesthetics), data, downloads that generate continuous connections and exchanges between users. Contemporary man produces technology, but at the same time he is its technological "product". The diffusion of new digital trends involves all disciplines and influences the status of the body at various levels, both psychological and physical, cultural and biological. A new subjectivity is born from this digital experiential contamination based on the possibility of being connected and of "touching" us virtually. It develops, what I call a "touch-screen" aesthetic. As we have seen the philosophy of feeling expands and multiplies through tactile activity. Each of us tries to touch the other daily, to reach him, to "feel" him through technological devices, thus overcoming the limit of the body itself. The skin has a fundamental role, it is a catalyst of all the externalizations of the world and constitution of the psychic self. The incredible amount and spread of smartphones, the multiplication of reading devices such as the IPad, e-book, all come with a touch screen system. Our body in relation to the use of technological innovations produces info-aesthetics through icons, applications, thus reconfiguring the communication architecture. The touch produce communications-sensations: it is the screen that "enjoys" our emotions through the electrical impulse that we provoke everytime we touch the screen. But every touch produces a message, the opening of a program, the downloading of an application, any movement we make with our hands activates an incredible process of meta-communication and aestheticization of the media circuits. Bodies multiply (avatars) "wear" new plural identities through the process of "embodiment" that "digital surgery" puts in place. The mirror of contemporary reality turns out to be an instrument of contemplation and reflection and gives us back the sense of mutation. Today, devices increasingly "incorporate" not only our "double I" (physical/virtual), but also our mind (embodiment). We have never seen a world more tactile than the digital one.

The mirror is the metaphor of the technological device that "re-media" our reality (re-mediatization". Its power is to open up to the digital logic of the Net. Today the new threshold of the body is no longer the skin, but the screen: the mirror-device. Given the different relationship that we establish with the screen, it is no longer a simple window from which look and interface and look inside empty screens. For Umberto Eco, initially the mirror is a channel-prosthesis. It is able to extend the radius of action of the eye, it allows us to grasp the visual stimulus where the eye could not reach. The mirror as a prosthesis is a channel, a material medium that allows the passage of information (Eco, 1985, p.16). The Italian semiologist argues that the image reflected in the mirror is not a sign because, simply, it is not for the body that causes it. It exists only in the presence of the object (or subject, reflection). As far as the use of extensions of the body is concerned, the selfie-stick is used by placing a smartphone or a camera on a support present on one of the hands, so that these devices can be used beyond the normal spectrum of movement of the arm, which through it assumes different possibilities. According to Paolo Fabbri's reflections on the stick (2006), the auction for selfie can be considered transitively as an operator of the relationship between the body, the devices supported at a distance, the natural world. The selfie can thus be considered in the context of different phenomena related to technical prosthesisation, in relation to practices, forms of self-portrait socially travelled through the mobile, in relation to the concept of syncretic text, stories shared through different languages, the relationship with the medium, which becomes increasingly dereferentialized and semiotically reworked. Posing in front of the lens (I mean: knowing I am posing, even fleetingly), I do not risk so much as that (at least, not for the moment) (Barthes, 1981. p. 12).

Photography critic Susan Bright, in her book *Autofocus. The Self-Portrait in Contemporary Photography* (2010) wrote:

What is depicted in a Self-Portrait? Historically, self-portrait (especially in paintings) has always been conceived as a representation of emotions, as an exteriorization of intimate feelings and as a profound self-analysis and self-contemplation that would have the power to confer a kind of immortality to the artist. (...) When we observe a photographic self-portrait (...) we rather see a demonstration of self-love (Bright, 2010, p. 10).

Bright argues that anyone with a camera, whether they are an artist or not, has the urge to point it at themselves and photographers or artists who have never portrayed themselves are a rarity. The popularity of "selfie" as a social and aesthetic practice is not the result of an increase in narcissism in our society, but rather the consequence of the mix of democratization of photographic technologies, increasingly miniaturized and at hand in our phones and spread of sites where you can easily share photographic images such as Flickr, Facebook, Twitter, Pinterest, Instagram. The phenomenon of selfie can be traced not so much to an increase in narcissism due to the spread of new technologies of the self as to a generalized increase in awareness of one's own image in digital ecosystems, due to the democratization of social networking tools. Selfie is related to self-presentation practices. If, therefore, on the one hand the classic self-portrait was narcissistic (self-admiration), today selfie becomes, on the contrary, a much more social practice, not directed towards oneself, but towards others, influencing the way in which others see us. Selfie are made to be transmitted, not for private consumption. On the one hand, there is the desire to showcase, which encapsulates the tradition of self-portraiture, on the other hand there is instead the new awareness of its own digital image, filtered, modified, in a frozen time where the intentionality of the exhibition destroys that of the interior (Han, 2015, p. 40). Selfie does not look at anything, the screen does not admit any desire, if not that of the other.

FOR AN ARTISTIC PRACTICE OF SELFIE

In conclusion, after having met the desire to represent oneself through selfie, the loss of sight, in this last part we propose some examples of how, first the portrait and then the self-portrait, become aesthetic practice through some artistic projects.

Self-portrait has become part of our daily lives and its popularity has increased with the spread of sites for sharing photographic images. Photography plays an important role in digital communication. However, we must ask ourselves if these are really self-portraits or simple images that people make of themselves. Many artists and photographers have investigated new forms of artistic research into the "augmented" self.

Let's start talking about the "technological" portrait with the mechanical performance created by the French artist Patrick Tresset, with the robotic installation *Paul the Robot* (2011). Starting from the simplicity of the design of Tinguely's creative machine, the drawings he makes can be considered here as part of a performance made by the machine, but designed by the artist. Using a webcam, the robotic arm called *Paul* collects in visual training on the appearance of the models, it performs through the algorithmic and robotic procedures necessary for drawing. The creative act, i.e. *Paul*'s portrait performance in the presence of the public, which are the models for his drawings, unites the two components of the project – the robot and the drawings produced by it – into a single artistic whole. His hybrid order stems largely from the dialogue between art and science on which it is based and which is constitutive of the concepts of the French artist. Tresset's project takes place in the midst of art, computer science and robotics. As a result of this cooperation, *Paul*'s eye (perceptual apparatus) and hand (executive apparatus) are directly connected. *Paul* has reached the capacity of computer modelling and robotic technologies (Kluszczyński, 2016). His artificially created brain processes the data provided by the eye detected by the cameras and then sends it to the robotic commands of the hand. Here, when the viewer interacts with *Paul*, he participates in a self-portrait created by an artificial intelligence that guides *Paul*'s creative processes, building a level of communication between the robot and the human, which aims to a kind of naturalization of the robot in the human world. In this case the self-portrait is material, physical, is *Paul*'s "creativity" which gives us back the drawing created by an algorithmic process and the self-portrait constructs the results of this encounter which preserves on the one hand the materiality of the sheet and the ink like the historical self-portraits and on the other hand gives us a hybrid artistic form more complex than the digital selfie. *Paul*'s meaning of his art also covers his scope and the seriousness of the aesthetic, philosophical and social problems he raises and makes evident, as well as the discussion he raises and the questions he asks, thus becoming an important part of contemporary artistic and scientific discourse.

Another complex and hybrid work by French artist Laurent Mignonneau, is *Portrait on a Fly*. It is an interactive installation consisting of a monitor showing a swarm of a few thousand flies. When a person stands in front of the monitor, the insects build the contour of the person. They begin to organize and reorganize themselves continuously, thus creating a recognizable resemblance of the individual. Posing in front of the monitor attracts flies. In a few seconds, they invade the face – but even the slightest movement of the head or parts of the face pushes them away (Kluszczyński, 2012). The portraits are therefore constantly changing, building and deconstructing. *Portrait on the Fly* is a commentary on our love of making images of ourselves (i.e. Selfie Culture), it concerns change, transience and impermanence. Mignonneau's work recovers the Kafkaesque "metamorphic" version of the fly. The portraits generated by the system are in a constant fluctuation between construction and deconstruction. In this celebration of the ephemeral moment of the self-portrait, in fact, each image exists only for a brief moment. This fragility makes us aware of how the symbolic use of the fly is the "pathological symptom" of a decadence in some way of the work of art itself trying to dissipate the distance between the virtuality of painting and the relevance of the real world. On the one hand, therefore, the obsession with representation and, on the other, the immediate fading of the same.

Another artistic project related to the concept of self-representation, this time, is approached to the topic about surveillance. The opportunity of this reflection is offered by the Australian artist with the project *Strange Visions*. Heather Dewey-Hagborg, through the DNA obtained from objects collected in the streets that belonged to unknown people, reconstructs their three-dimensional faces thanks to the collaboration of the Genspace biolaboratory in Brooklyn (New York). The most used places by the artist to collecting samples are the train stations, as well as the trains themselves, but also the bathrooms or the streets of the city. Heather Dewey-Hagborg's complex work could be another provocative response from genetic determinism and the widespread culture of Big Brother, but at the same time it could represent a metaphor for a continuous search for the self and one's own psychological identity. Curious (perhaps skeptical) we witness a continuous encounter between different languages and disciplines, where the artist and the scientist are the new alchemists of our time and the medium is no longer the message – as

Marshall McLuhan used to remind us – but it is life itself that acquires the dimension of medium (Savini: 2018), facing the new aesthetic practices (Detheridge: 2012).

The work of Lev Manovich with the project *Selfiecity* (http://selfiecity.net/) that investigates *selfies* using a mix of theoretic, artistic and quantitative methods, goes in a different direction. Since 2008, Software Studies Initiative (a research laboratory led by Manovich) has used data calculation and visualization methods to analyze a large number of Instagram photos. *Selfiecity.net* is a research project that analyzes about 3,200 photos shared via Instagram by five global cities: Bangkok, Berlin, Moscow, Moscow, New York and Sao Paulo. Manovich analyzes the construction of the dataset, the choice and application of computational methods of image analysis, as well as the results presented as visualizations and as an interactive web application. Manovich and his research center place the selfie in a broader context of the history of photography and argue that it is a new subgenre of photography that differs from the tradition of self-portraiture. Selfie is not just a photographic image that we recognize as self-portrait and that formally resembles numerous canonical photographic self-portraits of the 19th and 20th centuries. Instead, selfie is the product of a networked camera. Essential attributes of a selfie include its instantaneous distribution via Instagram or similar social networks (Rawlings 2013) as well as its metadata (automatically generated as geo-tags, added by the user as hashtags, or appearing later as comments, likes, and re-sharing by other users). The very raison d'être of a selfie is to be shared in social media. It is not made for personal consumption and producer contemplation. By sharing their self, Instagram users build their own identity and simultaneously express their belonging to a certain community. In this way the execution of the self is both a private act and a public and community activity. *Selfiecity* provides a starting point for further discussion on topics such as the functions of photography as probably the most democratic and accessible technology for creating images of the present moment, or the nature of visual communication and self-modelling in social media.

At this point, could the spontaneous question that arises be "who said that selfies are not an art form?" With *Arts Selfie,* the Google application that compares the faces of self-portraits with those of many more or less famous paintings. The idea of *Google Arts & Culture* uses facial recognition algorithms to search for similarities between the real faces of users and those in the database of paintings of the institution itself, which collects the works in over 1500 museums in 80 countries. In other words, Google Art is an online platform through which the public can access high-resolution images of works of art kept in the museums partners of the initiative. The project was launched on February 1, 2011 by Google through its Google Cultural Institute, in collaboration with 17 international museums, including the Tate Gallery in London, the Metropolitan Museum of Art in New York City and the Uffizi Gallery in Florence. The camera of our mobile phone takes our photo, selfie in the application through an algorithmic process and it is combined with faces, following some parameters, of portraits made by artists and preserved in different museums that participated in the project. The function became viral in January 2018. The function was initially created by Cyril Diagn.

The obsession with selfie has even generated a different way of making the museum an aesthetic experience, where the viewer does not enjoy the work of art in an almost "divine" way, but rather decides to occupy it, self-centering with his own image. The works of art are transformed into a self-service, radically changing the experience into narcissistic consumption. In 2018 in Glendale, County Los Angeles, the real work of art becomes selfie. An interactive experience explains the founders Tommy Honton and Tair Mamedov where the visitor can photograph himself with different imitations (even) of the most important works of art in history. New York's MoMA with *Art in Translation: Selfie* (2013) was the first to offer visitors the opportunity to photograph themselves in a large mirror. Art in Island of Manila

(Philippines) is another museum designed to allow visitors to physically enter the 3D reproductions of the most famous works, taking selfie of great impact. While on the one hand it was decided to limit the wild self-shots that have damaged works of inestimable value on several occasions, on the other hand some realities ride the success. The selfie then become impression management, attempts to control the impression on others, through a multitude of shots in series, in search of the pose, expression, light and the best shot, applying filters, graphic effects, retouching. We are constantly looking for a frozen time of like, approval of the other, sharing. The performance of selfie taking destabilizes the experience of being a body in a museum full of art. The body is tied to technology, holding the phone. The body bends and bends to get better angles, find a more flattering light, more favorable positions. The body becomes an object to be photographed together with art. In a sense, the body is guided through the museum by a project that is more overwhelming than just seeing art in the gallery: the identity project of representing the self in the act of being in the gallery and the even more important one of stating in some way that the self is worthy of an artistic status such as art.

ONLIFE

The portrait of the 21st century represents a sort of black mirror where we project ourselves into a sort of blindness. Mask and face are melted by an omnipresent multividuality in which the shield reveals itself and reveals other possible worlds. One no one and a hundred thousand. In the infosphere (Floridi, 2014) we live our lives online as a combination of adaptation in digital environments, between our being physically-analogically (based on carbon and offline) and the ubiquitous and digital there (based on silicon and online). In this onlife experience (Ivi, p. 47) the risk is to behave and to represent oneself as anonymous mass exhibited products. It is our social self that is the main medium through which ICT exerts its impact on our personal identities. According to Floridi it is precisely this hyper-awareness of self that is shared through social networks (Ivi, p. 69) in the digital swarm (Han, 2015). The technology of the self (Foucault, 1992) imbued by nature with information where precisely the ICTs exchange our body with a new, hybridized body and the self is structured on a platform, as if it were an application. The self becomes an app. In the ubiquitous dimension the conditions of presence and absence are mixed, everything is bit (Wheeler, 1990) participating in the fourth revolution (after the Copernicus, Darwinian and Freudian one) that brings to light the intrinsic nature of information of human identity (Floridi, 2014, p. 109). In other words we are living beings, that is, understood as entities composed of information (inforg), ready to be sold or purchased. The digital revolution brings out a new "multiindividuality" (Canevacci, 2017, pp. 248-250), offering us a radical challenge and a "political" perspective by entering into the connections of representation, ubiquitous self-representation mixed in with pixels and egocentric interfaces. The growing obligation for digital presence threatens representation (Han, 2015, p. 31).

The era of representation determines the end of reality, hyper-reality does not represent anything but rather presents (Ivi, p. 82). Repositioning our gaze should be an invitation to see the world from another angle, learning to see it in a multidimensional way, but above all we should be able to change it so as not to get caught in the smooth opacity of a black screen where our liquid shadow is reflected. The history of faces encloses within the history of the gaze, its multiple positions, while self-representation reveals the desire for multiplication of the selves that dissolve within the cold surfaces of the "emotional" interfaces that we touch activating a technologically human experience.

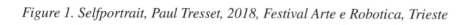

Figure 1. Selfportrait, Paul Tresset, 2018, Festival Arte e Robotica, Trieste

Figure 2. Portrait on a Fly, Laurent Mignonneau, 2019, Artists & Robots, Paris, 2018

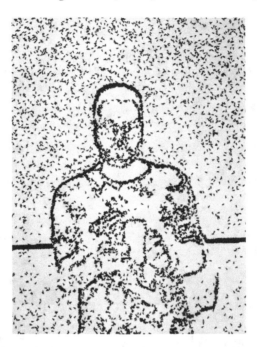

Figure 3. Heather Dewey-Hagborg, Adapted from [source of copyrighted image here
https://deweyhagborg.com/projects/stranger-visions]

Figure 4. Selfiecity (Adapted from [source of copyrighted image here http://selfiecity.net/]

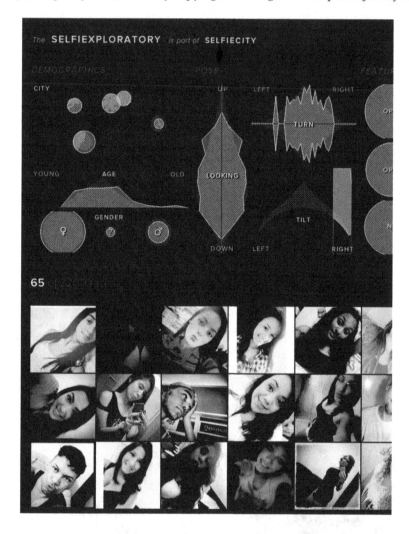

Figure 5. Selfportrait, Art Selfie, Google Arts & Culture

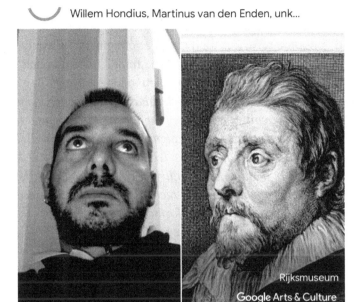

As we have seen, the increased self, the multiplied self, the fragmented self are the new conditions of existence of digital and ubiquity. The ubiquitous self becomes the driving self-portrait of the twenty-first century. The contemporary self-portrait is the digital portrait of an increasingly facial and "eXcessed" society. The self is hidden, collaborative, ambiguous, transvestite, fleeting. The self is the new performance of the contemporary always present, but difficult to define. The self is elusive and ubiquitous.

CONCLUSION

What is a selfie if no one in the photo is the real self? Of course the final product of a selfie is always only a representation of the real self, but that's not what's happening. In this case, it's as if you're taking a photo of yourself and calling it a selfie. Furthermore the question of what a 'selfie' is will actually bring with it a lot of other pertinent questions about the self in general. As it is increasingly happening, It provides us even more layers to hide behind and pretend that everything is okay, while we hide all real emotions behind two layers of abstraction (Gedeon: 2016). The selfie craze speaks volumes about the era in which we live, on how images race around the globe and can dominate public discourse, eliciting strong emotions and even blurring the lines of reality. It's the lines of reality that get confused by crossing virtual and augmented realities. The increased self is the natural and artificial consequence of other, plural, hybrid, mixed realities (MR). Selfie somehow represents our language and total control of our images. Currently there are many applications that allow us to recreate ourselves in space such as NASA Selfies (http://www.spitzer.caltech.edu/spitzer15/nasa-selfies) that allow you to take a photo in a virtual spacesuit in front of some of NASA's most captivating space images. Share these space selfies on social media, and learn about the science behind the pictures. This app was developed by the IPAC Communications & Education group and was released on the 15th anniversary of NASA's Spitzer Space

Telescope mission. Today the desire to immerse oneself in an image is satisfied by augmented (AR) and virtual reality (VR). It is in the ubiquitous self that we can reflect on the evolution of new realities. According to philosophers Michael Madary and Thomas Metzinger virtual reality is the representation of "possible worlds" and "possible selves" with the aim of creating a "sense of presence" in the user. The same phenomenon occurs in the best "theories of the mind", which create internal models of the world (neural virtual representations) and generate predictive hypotheses. They write about the human mind, *"we live in a "new world" trapped by technologies that aim to change human nature, an artificial world in which the perceptive and cognitive abilities of the human being would be enhanced by the use of devices that would give access to a richer reality (augmented, virtual, mixed), but whose risks are ignored. What is historically new in virtual reality is that it creates not only new risks, but also new ethical and legal dimensions due to the fact that a virtual reality (the human mind) is deeply incorporated into another virtual reality: the conscious human mind, which has evolved under certain specific conditions over millions of years, now becomes causally and informally intertwined with technical systems for the representation of possible realities"* (Madary, Metzinger: 2016).

REFERENCES

Argyle, M. (1975). *Bodily communication*. London, UK: Methuen Publishing Ltd.

Barbieri, G. L. (2016). Il selfie: pensieri nascosti, fantasie di autocreazione, tratti di personalità. In Rivista Internazionale di Filosofia e Psicologia, 7(3), 378-389.

Barthes, R. (1981). *Camera lucida: reflections on photography*. New York: Hill and Wang.

Baudrillard, J. (1988). The ecstasy of communication. New York: Semiotext(e).

Belpoliti, M. (2005). *Crolli*. Torino, Italy: Einaudi.

Belting, H. (2017). *Face and mask: a double history*. Princeton, NJ: Princeton University Press.

Benjamin, W. (1999). *Little history of photography in Selected writings*. Cambridge, MA: The Belknap Press of Harvard University Press.

Bollas, C. (2018). *Meaning and melancholia. Life in the age of bewilderment*. London, UK: Routledge. doi:10.4324/9781351018500

Bolter, J. D., & Grusin, B. (1999). *Remediation: Understanding new media*. Boston, MA: MIT Press.

Bonami, F. (2019). *Post. L'opera d'arte nell'epoca della sua riproducibilità sociale*. Milano, Italy: Feltrinelli.

Bredekamp, H. (2015). *The technical image: a history of styles in scientific imagery*. Chicago, IL: The University of Chicago Press. doi:10.7208/chicago/9780226258980.001.0001

Bright, S. (2010). *Autofocus. The self-portrait in contemporary photography*. London, UK: Thames & Hundson.

Canevacci, M. (2017). *Antropologia della comunicazione visuale*. Milano, Italy: Postmedia Books.

Cipolletta, G. (2014). *Passages metrocorporei. Per un'estetica della transizione.* Macerata, Italy: eum.

Codeluppi, V. (2015). *Mi metto in vetrina. Selfie, Facebook, Apple, Hello Kitty, Renzi e altre "vetrinizzazioni".* Milano, Italy: Mimesis.

Cousins, M. (2017). *The story of looking.* Edinburgh, UK: Canongate.

De Kerckhove, D. (2016). *La rete ci renderà stupidi?* Roma, Italy: Castelvecchi.

Debord. (1970). *Society of spectacle.* Detroit, MI: Black & Red.

Detheridge, A. (2012). *Scultori della speranza. L'arte nel contesto della globalizzazione.* Torino, Italy: Einaudi.

Eco, U. (1985). *Sugli specchi e altri saggi.* Milano, Italy: Bompiani.

Floridi, L. (2014). *The fourth revolution - How the infosphere is reshaping human reality.* Oxford, UK: Oxford University Press.

Flusser, V. (2000). *Towards a philosophy of photography.* London, UK: Reaktion Books.

Fontcuberta, J. (2018). La furia delle immagini. Torino, Italy: Einaudi.

Gedeon, C. (2015, Oct. 7). A selfie was taken in virtual reality and no one seems to be bothered. *Medium.* Retrieved from https://medium.com/@charlesgedeon/a-selfie-was-taken-in-virtual-reality-and-no-one-seems-to-be-bothered-bc9162a73571

Han, B.-C. (2015). *The transparency society.* Palo Alto, CA: Stanford UP.

Han, B.-C. (2017a). *In the swarm: digital prospects.* Boston, MA: MIT Press.

Han, B.-C. (2017b). *Saving beauty.* Cambridge, UK: Polity Press.

Hussain, Z., & Pearson, C. (2016). *Smartphone addiction and associated psychological factors.* Turkish Green Crescent Society.

Khanna, A., & Khanna, P. (2012). *Hybrid reality: thriving in the emerging human-technology civilization.* TED Books.

Kluszczyński, R. W. (Ed.). (2012). Wonderful life. Laurent Mignonneau & Christa Sommerer. LAZNIA Centre for Contemporary Art, Gdańsk.

Kluszczyński, R. W. (Ed.). (2016). Patrick Tresset: Human traits and the art of creative machines. LAZNIA Centre for Contemporary Art, Gdańsk.

Macho, T. (1996). Vision und visage. Überlegungen zur Faszinationsgeschichte der Medien. In W. Müller-Funk & H. U. Reck (Eds.), *Inszenierte imagination. Beiträge zu einer historischen Anthropologie der Medien* (pp. 87–108). Wien, Austria: Springer-Verlag.

Madary, M., & Metzinger, T. K. (2016). Real virtuality: A code of ethical conduct. Recommendations for good scientific practice and the consumers of vR-technology. *Robotics and AI 3,* 3. doi:10.3389/frobt.2016.00003

Magli, P. (1995). *Il volto e l'anima. Fisiognomica e passioni*. Milano, Italy: Bompiani.

Malik, S. (2015, March). Impact of Facebook addiction on narcissistic behavior and self-esteem among students. *JPMA. The Journal of the Pakistan Medical Association*, *65*(3), 260–263. PMID:25933557

Matisse, H. (1972). *Henri Matisse. Scritti e pensieri sull'arte*. Torino, Italy: Einaudi.

McLuhan, M. (1994). *McLuhan. Understanding media. The extensions of man*. Cambridge, MA: MIT Press.

Mehdizadeh, S. (2010, August). Self-presentation 2.0: Narcissism and self-esteem on Facebook. *Cyberpsychology, Behavior, and Social Networking*, *13*(4), 357–364. doi:10.1089/cyber.2009.0257 PMID:20712493

Mirzoeff, N. (2015). *How to see the world*. London, UK: Penguin Books.

Nadkarni, A., & Hoffman, S. (2012). Why do people use facebook? Amsterdam, The Netherlands: Elsevier. *Personality and individual differences*, *52*(3), 243–249. doi:10.1016/j.paid.2011.11.007 PMID:22544987

Nancy, J.-L. (2000). *Il ritratto e il suo sguardo*. Milano, Italy: Raffaello Cortina Editore.

Rawlings, C. (2013). Making the connection: social bonding in courtship situations. In The American Journal of Sociology, 118(6), 1596-1649.

Riassunto del libro. (2019, June 5) *La furia delle immagini*. Retrieved from https://www.docsity.com/it/la-furia-delle-immagini-2/4631013/

Savini, M. (2015, April 15). Selfie, la rappresentazione di se stessi è affermazione dell'essere hic et nunc. *Wired*. Retrieved from https://www.wired.it/gadget/foto-e-video/2015/04/17/selfie-rappresentazione-se-stessi-affermazione-dellessere-hic-et-nunc/

Savini, M. (2018). *Arte transgenica. La vita è un medium*. Pisa, Italy: Pisa University Press.

Vaccari, F. (2011). *Fotografia e inconscio tecnologico*. Torino, Italy: Einaudi.

KEY TERMS AND DEFINITIONS

Facial Society: This term was coined by Thomas Macho. The face-to-face contact is transferred to the Internet–Facebook where the mass media subtract its body presence from the face, changing one of the fundamental habits of our perception that involves the need to recognize faces.

Fourth Revolution: This term was coined by Luciano Floridi. In the ubiquitous dimension the conditions of presence and absence are mixed, participating in the fourth revolution (after the Copernicus, Darwinian and Freudian one) that brings to light the intrinsic nature of information of human identity, in other words we are living beings, that is, understood as entities composed of information (inforg) ready to be sold or purchased.

Infosphere: This term was coined by Professor of Philosophy and Ethics of Information and Director of the Digital Ethics Lab, at the University of Oxford. This neologism describes our lives online as a combination of adaptation in digital environments, between our being physically-analogically (based on carbon and offline) and the ubiquitous and digital there (based on silicon and online).

Metrobody: It is a neologism for representing the idea of a new metrics of the body, conceived both as a mutant parameter and a transitive variable. It does not measure, it is not measure, but is measured in relation to the physical and digital environment at the same time, losing even the limits of reality.

Post-Photography: It refers to photography that flows into the hybrid space of digital sociality and is a consequence of visual overabundance.

Selfie: A Present since 2009 in *Wiktionary*, it was recently registered as a neologism (August 2013) and elected "word of the year" by the *Oxford Dictionaries*. Selfie is not a perfect synonym of selfie (in neither of its two senses of "device for late shooting of a camera" and "photography in which the shooter is also the subject"), as it is not in English of automatic shutter release or self-shot or self-portrait: as suggested by the Oxford Dictionaries Online, the term means a photograph taken to oneself and typically one taken with a smartphone or webcam and uploaded to a social media website, typically without the aid of time, with a smartphone or webcam, destined to be shared on social networks (*a photograph that one has taken of oneself, typically one taken with a smartphone or webcam and uploaded to a social media website*). It is no coincidence, in fact, that the practice of selfie has had a boom in popularity at the same time as the introduction of the front camera in smartphones.

"Touch-Screen" Aesthetic: The diffusion of new digital trends involves all disciplines and influences the status of the body at various levels, both psychological and physical, cultural and biological. This digital experiential contamination is born a new subjectivity based on the possibility of being connected and of "touching" us virtually. It develops, what I call a "touch-screen" aesthetic.

ENDNOTE

[1] The word "face" replaced Old English words derived from the verb "to see, look", just like in Indo-European where words for "face" are commonly based on the notion of "appearance, look", and mostly derive from verbs for "to see, look". Also, in some cases, the word for "face2 means "form, shape": from Latin 'visus' we have French 'visage', Italian 'viso', ned English 'visage'. https://www.etymonline.com/search?q=face

Section 2
Virtual and Augmented Reality in Art and Museums

Chapter 7

Reinventing Museums in 21st Century:
Implementing Augmented Reality and Virtual Reality Technologies Alongside Social Media's Logics

Antonios Kargas

(iD) https://orcid.org/0000-0001-6157-1761

National and Kapodistrian University of Athens, Greece

Nikoletta Karitsioti

Department of Political Sciences and International Relations, University of Peloponnese, Greece

Georgios Loumos

COMIC, Greece

ABSTRACT

The forthcoming Industry 4.0 is expected to change not only manufacturing and industrial services, but will rearrange how services are offered in a variety of sectors, including museum's services. Museums will inevitably be led to more digital (VR & AR) and promoting (Social Media) paths. A forthcoming "digital convergence" between VR & AR technologies and social media's promoting logic could enlarge museums' potentialities in attracting more visitors, younger visitors, while new patterns for connecting learning effects and amusement should be established. This chapter contributes to the following:
• Presenting existing theoretical and empirical research on Virtual Reality and Augmented Reality technological implementation in Museums. • Presenting current tensions on social media's usage from cultural organizations. • Exploring how VR & AR applications can incorporate various elements coming from social media operational logic.

DOI: 10.4018/978-1-7998-1796-3.ch007

Copyright © 2020, IGI Global. Copying or distributing in print or electronic forms without written permission of IGI Global is prohibited.

INTRODUCTION

Since mid-90s, museums face an ongoing need to implement new technologies and to answer visitors changing needs. The first steps to the digital world came World Wide Web and the development of Web Pages, which open a window to global public, arising questions about the relationship between "increased accessibility" (via internet) and "attractiveness" (from digital) to the real museum place. Even form these first digital steps, where content and context were delivered via web pages, many researchers and professionals started to visualize what Marlaux (Malraux, 1996) introduced in 1947 as "imaginary museum"

(. . .) a logically related collection of digital objects composed in a variety of media, and, because of its capacity to provide connectedness and various points of access, it lends itself to transcending traditional methods of communicating and interacting with the visitors being flexible toward their needs and interests; it has no real place or space, its objects and the related information can be disseminated all over the world. (Schweibenz, 1998).

A bit later, social media become part of everyday life and most of the museums worldwide created their own accounts in order to stay "connected" with visitors, world's audience and social stakeholders. Social media was an alternative, faster, low cost and direct (user friendly) way (Sylaiou, Liarokapis, Kotsakis, & Patias, 2009) to share content, to announce events and to extend "potential" visitors' pool. This kind of communication was radically facilitated by mobile devices (phones and tablets), enabling a series of dynamic and interactive applications (Hin, Subramaniam, & Aggarwal, 2003). Smartphones are nowadays reshaping the environment, permitting new applications in emerging eras (Kim et al., 2014), such as Virtual Reality (VR) and Augmented Reality (AR) platforms and applications.

These two technologies have already gained interest from both methodologically and empirically research. For example, Sparacino et al. (Sparacino, Davenport, & Pentland, 2000) and Grinter et al. (Grinter et al., 2002) studied interactive technologies in museums, while Brown et al. (Brown, Maccoll, Chalmers, & Galani, 2003) and Bowers et al. (Bowers et al., 2007) explored interactive exhibits using ubiquitous displays with augmented reality. More recent studies concentrated on comparisons of VR, AR and Web3D in virtual museums / exhibitions (Sylaiou et al., 2009), in implementing AR on archaeological site (Angelopoulou et al., 2012; Gutierrez, Molinero, Soto-Martín, & Medina, 2015), in evaluating VR and AR experience in cultural places (Higgett, Chen, & Tatham, 2016; Izzo, 2017).

Current research on VR & AR mainly targets aspects related with their operational strengths and weakness (Loumos, Kargas, & Varoutas, 2018), while social media literature has its own goals related mainly with distribution and promotion. Authors will use their experience from creating a VR & AR application for cultural organizations (named VAREAL and being prepared for market release in late 2019) to explore the technological and business opportunities / limitations of incorporating social media elements in VR & AR apps (such as emoticons, comments, like-dislike, chatting, social networking etc.). Authors aim to reveal that the ongoing technological development made feasible to re-examine digital technologies' s usages and potentialities, by incorporating tools and techniques from different digital fields, such as social media.

A strong motive to this direction has been given from a growing tension between museums to re-invent themselves following a more alternative perception. "Instagramization" is a tension describing the creation of immersive exhibits or even museums themselves in order to provoke visitors to get part of the exhibition, to create their own "photograph" art and to use Instagram (and other social media) to promote their visit / participation / creation. Such an approach has been used by well-known museums such as Smithsonian American Art Museum ("Wonder" exhibition available at: https://americanart.si.edu/exhibitions/wonder), the Getty Museum rearranged mirrors in its decorative arts gallery to make selfies easier, while San Francisco's Museum of Modern Art designed selfie spots. At the same time, exhibition places, such as "Color Factory" (https://www.colorfactory.co/), "Museum of Ice Cream" (https://www.museumoficecream.com/) and moreover "29Rooms" (https://www.refinery29.com/en-us/29rooms) offer interactive experiences with a direct link to social media tools. Visitors choose their exhibitions targeting on promoting their visit in social media and exhibitors create places exactly to inspire and facilitate them.

A forthcoming "digital convergence" between VR & AR technologies and social media's promoting logic, could enlarge museums potentialities in attracting more visitors, younger visitors, while new patterns for connecting learning effects and amusement should be established. The forthcoming Industry 4.0 is expected to change not only manufacturing and industrial services, but moreover will rearrange how services are offered in a variety of sectors, including museum's services. Museums will inventible be led to more digital (VR & AR) and promoting (Social Media) paths. These paths will be explored in our research.

The book chapter aim to contribute to the following:

- Presenting existing theoretical and empirical research on **Virtual Reality and Augmented Reality technological implementation** in Museums.
- Presenting current tensions on **social media's usage** from cultural organizations.
- Exploring how VR & AR applications can incorporate various **elements** (such as emoticons, comments, like-dislike, chatting, social networking etc.) coming from **social media operational logic**.

BACKGROUND INFORMATION ON VR – AR TECHNOLOGIES AND SOCIAL MEDIA FOR MUSEUMS

Museums are facing one of the most important challenges of their modern history. In order to adopt new technologies and follow the overall technological pace of the Industry 4.0, museums should reinvent themselves by developing new ways to provide content to their audience or even use technological aspects to create new content. Technologies used nowadays can be divided according to their "position" in the Virtuality Continuum, presented in Figure 1.

From the one side there is physical world and the real environments. In real environments (e.g. the museums' physical place or their exhibitions), a series of technologies can be applied. First of all, there are technologies that can only re – present the physical world to the digital era. Such technologies are **Video 360 and VR Videos**. Moreover, in real environment can be classified the **social media's technologies**. Their difference from the above-mentioned technologies lies on the fact that social medias' technologies aim to develop a more artistic view of reality, creating new forms of public art. The former technologies target on "representing accuracy", while the later technologies target on gaining public's approval (via "likes", re-posts, re-tweets, etc.) putting less emphasis on accuracy and more on artistic representation.

Leaving real environment, a user can be involved to more complex levels of virtuality. **Augmented reality** aim to provide user with rich content, which should be directly linked to the physical world. By using mobile devices (e.g. tablets and smartphones) users can enrich their experience during a museum's visit by augmenting reality (e.g. putting authentic colors to an ancient statue or visualizing how

Figure 1. Virtuality continuum (Muikku & Kalli, 2017)

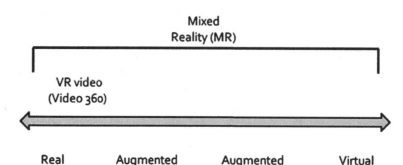

a partly – destructed statue would look like if restored). A more complex situation comes when **augmented virtuality** is implemented. Under its environment, augmented virtuality mainly aim to enrich virtual worlds with content coming from real world (e.g. with an appropriate digitization). The borders between virtual – real are usually clear and well set, while the reasons for bringing digitized real items in a virtual world lies on the willingness to bring historical elements in a fantastic world or situation. Finally, virtual reality can be defined as a pure artificially created environment targeting on embodying users and to deepen their experiences, leading them in the borders of forgetting the real world. All the above – mentioned reshape museums environment bringing them from solely or merely real environment to a **mixed reality** world.

Museums have already proved willing to adopt these technologies, even though their adjustment could be faster and more decisive. Museums can realize digital technologies potentialities on reaching a wide public and increase their attractiveness, but it is obvious that they face lack of critical resources (e.g. financial and specialized human resources) leading to just "following" Industry's 4.0 changes. Their willingness to keep up with technological changes is based on the potentialities proposed that can be summarized on (Loumos et al., 2018): (a) reusing exclusive digital content for conventional (e.g. artistic or historical purposes) and alternative uses (e.g. online gaming or cinema purposes), (b) exploiting content to reach mass markets at a global level and (c) enriching users' and visitors' s experiences.

The most widespread technologies among museums are coming mainly from social media technologies. These technologies become popular in recent years coming to give answers to museums' promotion and communication agonies. More specifically, social media's technologies are used as part of museums' communication and public relation techniques (Capriotti, Carretón, & Castillo, 2016). The role of "photography" in the everyday museums' operation and their communication strategy has been upgraded. Photographs are used in social media as ephemeral moments of communication and also in order to share experiences (Budge & Burness, 2018). Social media have been based on photographs and have evolved the digital photography on the central elements of social networks.

Jyri Engeström (2005) explains "social networks consist of people who are connected by a shared object" and the type of object determines the types of people and the reasons why they connect (Engeström, 2005). In most well-known social platforms, such as Facebook and Instagram, photographs and videos are used as a point of reference, while the tension appears the users to be more positive on photographs rather than text. The above-mentioned facts regarding social media usage are common both inside and outside the museum sector.

Talking about the cultural sector and in particular the museums, social media aim to bring together the user with the museum aiming to create engagement. Up to the digital era, the engagement was cultivated in the physical place of the museum. Through social media, the engagement may increase or be developed after the visit, when the visitor has returned home and would like to see again something or get informed for something new. O'Brien and Toms defined engagement as 'a quality of user experience characterized by attributes of challenge, positive affect, endurability, aesthetic and sensory appeal, attention, feedback, variety/novelty, interactivity, and perceived user control' (O'Brien & Toms, 2008).

Moreover, the wide use of Internet has modified the traditional ways in which the organizations contacted their audiences and has inserted modern ways in order to reach its audiences and disseminate its arts and information, so the cultural section and more specifically the museums could not consist an exception on this trend (Padilla-Meléndez & del Águila-Obra, 2013).

As a result, the IT developments drive in rapid developments in the cultural communication and the communication strategies for museums are designed based on the online tools, such as the web and social media. However, the case of museums is not a common one. Both the audiences the museums address and the information the museums share, consist a peculiarity (Padilla-Meléndez & del Águila-Obra, 2013). For this reason, it is important to take into consideration these characteristics before identifying the most effective ways in order to address the audiences and present the museum's information, through social media.

It is important to consider that the promotion subject of a museum is an exhibit, with which the visitor has eye contact when in live visit. Thus, this will be the base to build the digital communication strategy. In particular, through social media the visitor should be able to live the experience and feel anyhow the interaction with the exhibit. Among the most well-known social media, the most popular in museums is Instagram. Instagram looks like an online gallery, presenting information through pictures or short videos, accompanied with short text and smart taglines and hashtags. Museums with online presence seem to prefer this online media, as the most artistic and suitable in the cultural sector among the massive social media. Current chapter aims to contribute on understanding the relationship between Instagram and museums, while specific examples of museums using Instagram will be presented, in order to enlighten this topic.

DIGITAL MUSEUMS' PROJECTS WITH VR AND AR TECHNOLOGIES

Virtual Reality and Augmented Reality technologies are not something for museums. Starting back to earlies 2000 a series of researchers developed their frameworks and studied how interactive technologies could be implemented in museums (Grinter et al., 2002; Sparacino et al., 2000), or how interactive exhibits could become reality (Bowers et al., 2007; Brown et al., 2003). The whole research was facilitated by European Union that funded a series of research projects on the field of interactive technologies in cultural industries. SHAPE (Hall et al., 2002) was one of the first projects, alongside with 3DMURALE (Cosmas et al., 2001), Ename974 (Pletinckx, Callebaut, Killebrew, & Silberman, 2000) and the AR-CHEOGUIDE project (Augmented Reality-based Cultural Heritage On-site GUIDE) (Stricker, Stricker, Dähne, Seibert, & al., 2001).

Each one of these projects, had its one purpose, while the final deliverable came to serve a unique goal. From serving educational goals to creating 3D multimedia tools, each project had a uniqueness, while at this stage there was not a wide accepted and common vision about how Virtual Reality technologies should be implemented in cultural industries. Soon enough more and more applications where presented incorporating aspects such as:

- Recreating Ancient Rome (Dylla, Muller, Ulmer, Haegler, & Frischer, 2009),
- Presenting Minoan civilization and culture via the Archeomatica Project (Sangregorio, Stanco, & Tanasi, 2008),
- Developing versions of archaeological artifacts from Syracuse, Italy and testing on mobile devices via augmented reality's application (Stanco, Tanasi, Gallo, Buffa, & Basile, 2012),
- Augmenting historical places in Iraq (Mohammed-Amin, Levy, & Boyd, 2012), United Kingdom (Angelopoulou et al., 2012), Greece (Galatis, Gavalas, Kasapakis, Pantziou, & Zaroliagis, 2016) and other historical places,
- Creating 3D models for cities such as Prague (Prague (City of), 2018), Hamburg (Kersten, Keller, Saenger, & Schiewe, 2012) and Marsal, Aire sur la Lys and Saint-Omer (Chevrier, 2016).

All these are part of a large bibliography on VR technologies and AR technologies targeting directly cultural industries. Their results indicate that both technologies aim to deliver different experience and result to its end – users. Moreover, museums can exploit its technology's unique characteristics (Loumos et al., 2018) to achieve different goals. For example Augmented Reality technology has been proved to deliver high added – value (D'Auria, Mauro, Calandra, & Cutugno, 2015; Damala, Hornecker, Van Der Vaart, Van Dijk, & Ruthven, 2016) in cases involving: user's experience enrichment, providing information and content via alternative ways and reconstructing item / artifact / building that have face damages. From the other hand Virtual Reality technology is ideal to create virtual environments and museums, to support empirical learning or other educational purposes and of course to amuse users (Gonizzi Barsanti, Caruso, Micoli, Covarrubias Rodriguez, & Guidi, 2015; Pietroni, Pagano, & Rufa, 2013).

Authors confirmed these findings (Kargas, Loumos, & Varoutas, 2019; Loumos et al., 2018) from their own project that took place in 2015 and aimed on creating a 3D representation of Nafplio city (Greece) as it was in 19th Century. The principles of diachronic reconstruction were used (Guidi & Russo, 2011; Micoli, Guidi, Angheleddu, & Russo, 2013) in order to configure how the city's historical monuments:

- Are now (current state of existing versus not any – more existing monuments),
- Have faced interventions coming from past ages and the cultural variety of its rulers (Venetian, Ottoman and Greek rules) and
- Have been described in historical resources (historical research).

The developed application is property of a local museum (the "V. Papantoniou" Peloponnesian Folklore Foundation), which uses is to attract visitors and for educational purposes via an online, 3D, quiz game. A small part of the material used and the 3D model of a significant building in Nafplio, is presented in Figure 2. Gamifying cultural heritage and cultural artifacts is another growing tension that is gaining researchers interest (Vayanou, Ioannidis, Loumos, & Kargas, 2019; Vayanou, Ioannidis, Loumos, Sidiropoulou, & Kargas, 2019). This tension is expected to gain more interest the next years as a result of the existing and forthcoming large – scale digitization of cultural artifacts (Sotirova, Peneva, Ivanov,

Doneva, & Dobreva, 2012), as well as by technological evolution and the facilitation in implementing new forms of technological applications (Bontchev, 2012).

MUSEUM'S INSTAGRAMIZATION

Recent surveys have proved that the social platform, Instagram, is the most appropriate to disseminate museums as it combines visualization and a sense of aesthetic. Instagram is now considered as the most popular and widespread social platform for museums. Due to its aesthetic power, user-friendly design and popularity, museums are increasingly using Instagram to disseminate their exhibits and experiences too (Suess, 2014). The extent use of social media as well as the technological developments have pointed the interest at the online strategy. The picture's power has transformed the role of photography and has produced new communication channels. This new development is taken into consideration while designing the online strategy as the main point of the latest developments. The digital era has affected the museums as well as the strategy to be followed.

The first point that should be examined is the aim of the museums' online strategy. In particular, it should be clear if the museum uses social media in order to promote itself or disseminate its exhibits or to develop visitor learning. The primary concern of this strategy should be clear before starting to design the online strategy.

Figure 2. Fragkoklissia church (Kargas et al., 2019)

The museums' online strategy is designed while first identifying the messages as well as the target audiences they aim to reach. In particular, specific messages per target audience are designed so as to effectively promote the museum or its exhibits online. Commonly the online audiences are younger and familiar with new technologies. This means that the audiences in the online communication strategy may differ from the total communication strategy, thus the messages too. The most common is to use social media so as to facilitate participation with users and insert new types of participation.

In addition, through social media have begun to offer to visitors a variety of capabilities. A decision that should be taken within the online strategy configuration is the capabilities that will be used. For instance, in the case of photography's' use, what should be taken into consideration while designing the online strategy, is the scope of the photographic communication. Communication based on photos may be reminiscing or storytelling. In the first option, people are looking photos of events or visits they have made and recall in their memory the visit as well as their feelings during the visit. On the other hand, in the storytelling option, people narrate a story to other people that were not present in the event or the visit, trying to carry them forward (Weilenmann, Hillman, & Jungselius, 2013).

Another way to involve users while designing the online strategy is to include others in museum's experience through tags, comments and opening online conversations. In addition, a museum should have effective and powerful hashtags so as to increase its followers and attract people interested in the cultural sector. All the above, reflect the call for museums to be more responsive, democratic and reflective and to reach broader audiences outside the museums' buildings (Weilenmann et al., 2013).

While talking for museums using Instagram, a new trend has appeared, evolving this tension, the Instagram Museums. These Museums have been designed taking into consideration the Instagram widespread and are based on the trend of Instagram posts and stories. This kind of museums aims to attract visitors in order to create Instagram posts and stories. In the following section museums using Instagram will be presented, as well as Instagram Museums.

Museums Using Instagram

In the current sub-section, a series of case studies will be presented aiming on revealing how each one of the presented museums uses its social media and more specifically its Instagram account.

The Louvre Museum

The Louvre Museum originates to 1793 during the French Revolution. Its collections are displayed on five levels, in 3 interconnecting wings named from three prominent personalities from French History: Richelieu (1585-1642), chief minister of King Louis XIII, Sully (1559-1641), chief minister of King Henri IV and Denon (1747-1825), first director of the Louvre Museum. The Louvre Museum maintains an Instagram account here.

The Louvre Museum account is followed by 3.2 million followers. The account has about 1850 posts mainly providing exhibits or pictures from the museum premises. The posts are concentrated on the tool of picture and no video is provided from the museum's internal. However, there are only short clip, promoting the museum's exterior. The interaction with the Instagram visitors is worthy mentioned, as each post collects an average of 300 comments.

Figure 3.

The Acropolis Museum

The Acropolis Museum, is among the most famous and modern museums in Greece, attracting a large number of visitors. It is available on Instagram here since 2015 and is followed by almost 9000 people.

This account has 123 posts, presenting the museum, its activities, the Acropolis monument, as well as exhibitions taking place in the museum. This account is not concentrated on the museum's exhibits, its character is more general. In addition, it seems to be used indirectly as a marketing tool, since it promotes gift ideas to be sold in the museum.

The Van Gogh Museum

The Van Gogh Museum in Amsterdam holds an Instagram account too, available here. The Van Gogh Museum has about 1.3 million followers. This museum aiming to increase the interaction with visitors is using one additional Instagram tool, the #hashtag. In particular, the museum invites the visitors to share their photos and inspirations using the specific hashtag #vangogmuseum in order to increase involvement and create the sense of a community.

This account, with almost 1670 posts, is concentrated on the Van Gogh paintings, providing more information about each exhibit as well the techniques used by the famous painter. The Van Gogh's Instagram account works as an online exhibition, aiming to attract more visitors in the Van Gogh painting as well as to increase the popularity of the painter and his work.

Figure 4.

Figure 5.

Figure 6.

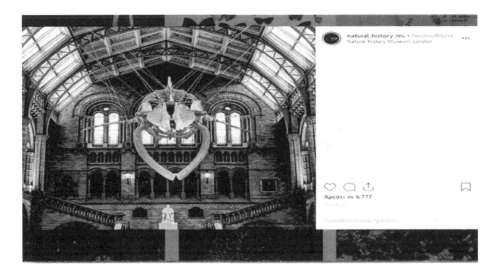

In contrast to other museums, Van Gogh Museum is using Instagram as an additional tool to promote specifically its exhibits and provide an online gallery available to more visitors than the physical one. The number of comments in the posts, in average 80 per picture, confirm that this mean is directed to experts as well as to serious people admiring the culture who usually avoid commenting with hearts, happy faces, etc.

The Natural History Museum

The Natural History Museum in London has 469k followers on its Instagram account here. This account is an average account, with about 2.000 posts and a mix character. Its posts are about its exhibits, festivals and other activities, researches, etc.

The innovation on Instagram use for the Natural History Museum is that it invites people to an Instagram Live, where the museum's team will be able to chat and discuss with visitors and answer their questions.

This use is included among the best practices of Instagram use in Museums, increasing the visitors involvement and enhancing the museum's fame in various age groups with real interest on the museum's content.

The Guggenheim Museum

Guggenheim Museum is available on Instagram here attracting about 2.3 million followers. This account has about 3.400 posts emitting the modern character of the museum. The account's administrators are using the #hashtag tool to encourage more visitors share their experiences in Guggenheim and indirectly promote the museum.

The posts are concentrated on the picture accompanied with text and mostly explanation of what is illustrated. The comments coming from the followers are about 50 in average per picture, which confirms that the Guggenheim Museum is directed in a more specific audience.

Figure 7.

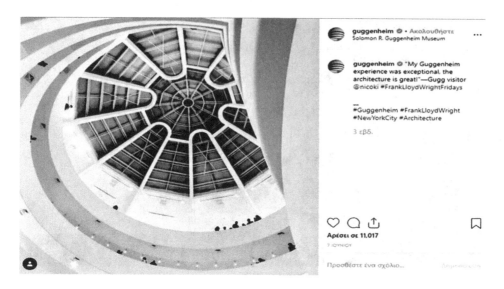

Figure 8.

The Victoria and Albert Museum

Victoria and Albert Museum is presented on Instagram here as the world's leading museum of art, design and performance. On its Instagram account has about 1.2 million followers.

This Museum is very active on Instagram having 2,589 posts. The most impressive on this account is the very high number of likes in pictures and videos. For instance, there are pictures with about 20.000 like as well as videos with 30.000 like. This confirms that the Victoria and Albert Museum has a wide audience actively involved on its Instagram account.

The 'Instagram" Museums

Recently, a grate development in museum's sector took place, the 'Instagram Museums'. This development was more than unexpected, especially for the traditional cultural sector. However, nobody can dispute that this is the new trend on museums which will strongly affect the new culture's configuration.

As we mentioned above, Instagram tends to be a popular online tool to communicate and disseminate the museums and its exhibits. In addition, we have seen the wide use of new technologies, such as VR and AR technologies in Museums, but still an Instagram Museum seems to be something innovative and completely strange and will definitely change both the museum and Instagram world. In this chapter, we will provide some examples of 'Instagram Museums' in order to explain this new trend.

Museum of Ice-Cream

The Museum of ice-cream was the first Instagram Museum that opened on 2016. Since then, has inspired a variety of concepts to come to life. The idea behind this museum is to provide miniature sweet objects, inspired by the happy childhood, where visitors can take pictures and live the experience of being a child, licking an ice-cream or a lollipop, make snow angels, etc. The cost for this experience is about $38, while there is a limited quantity of tickets (Goldstein, 2018).

The Museum of ice-cream idea is based on the user experience, aiming to create an experience inspired by ice-cream. This experience is located in San Francisco and New York. In the physical premises the user enters to a museum where he is able to taste ice-cream and also play and interact in cookie carousels, swimming in a pool filled with rainbow sprinkles, etc.

This museum holds an Instagram account, available here with more than 2.000 posts and about 394,000 followers. Its ultimate goal is the users to experience its environment in order to take funny pictures, based on the power of Instagram. This is the reason it keeps only an Instagram account instead of other popular social media.

29ROOMS by REFINERY29

This museum opened its doors on 2015 and consists of 29 rooms with different artistic decorations. As its name betrays this "museum" contains 29 rooms under one roof. Through these rooms are taking place performances, workshops and other artistic experiences so as to connect the users with culture and creativity and also create a kind of community. In parallel, the 29 rooms are travelling and changing places so as to attract new artists and partners, bring out new ideas and experiences for their audiences.

29Rooms holds an Instagram account which is available here and is followed by almost 146.000 people. Its 1.000 posts are mainly videos coming from the 29Rooms experience, while some of them have reached the 42.000 likes.

Color Factory

The Color factory was launched in San Francisco, in 2017. The owner was a blogger who collaborated for this idea with an artist and a designer to create a rainbow decorated place. It started as a color celebration which would last for only one month. Finally lasted for other eight sold-out months. Now it is hosted in New York City while in parallel is organizing experiential exhibits so as to engage wider audiences in other places, such as Houston in summer 2019. In New York the premises cover about 20.000 square feet and all experience is based on color. Artists, designers etc. participate telling their own color stories and engage the visitors.

The Color factory is based on user experience too. Besides its physical place, maintains an Instagram as well as a Facebook account. In Instagram is followed by 237.000 people and its posts are basically colorful pictures taken from the user experience.

Candytopia

Candytopia is one more Instagram museum, which is based on the idea of user experience. Its purpose is not to be a museum or retail location or amusement park, but places configured to offer experience.

In particular, the concept behind Candytopia is to provide an ideal and fairytale scenery in order to take a pose and share the best pictures with your friends and followers. The scenery is organized around a series of rooms, with different decorations, focused on sweets. Sculptures of animals made from gummy bears and jellybeans are only some of the exhibits the visitor may see. At this moment, Candytopia is located on three different locations: Dallas, Houston and Philadelphia.

Regarding its social media, Candytopia maintains an Instagram as well as a Facebook account. Its Instagram account available here, follows the Candytopia rationale full of happy colors and sweets.The account which is followed by 223.000 people provides mainly posts -both videos and photos - showing the user experience in the Candytopia premises.

The Beach on Snarkitecture

The Beach initially launched in 2015 in Washington. Since then, has traveled to Florida, Sydney, Paris, Thailand and many other places overworld. The idea behind the beach, was to create an interactive installation that familiarizes a day at the beach, enjoying the see, the waves, creating bubbles, playing as a kid, using everyday materials. Beach deck chairs, umbrellas, lifeguards and other elements symbolizing the beach-going experience are spread all over the Beach consisting its scenery and offering the beach experience in participants.

This Instagram museum differentiates on the number of social media than the others. It maintains an Instagram, Tumblr, Facebook and Twitter account. On Instagram, has about 237.000 followers and is providing about 1400 posts mostly with professional pictures showing the Snarkitecture scenery in a more artistic way.

VR and AR Tours on Museums

360, VR and AR technologies have been incorporated into museums' narratives, offering new experiences to the visitors as well as the online users. Through the new technologies the user is able to visit online a museum while being at his home or at his work, digitally look the exhibits and visualize this experience through highlighting his points of interest.

National Museum of Natural History

The National Museum of Natural History has established an online virtual tour through a web VR Platform, which is available here. This means that the visitors are able to visit the museum through their desktop, laptop or mobile. During the tour the visitor is able to live the experience of a room-by-room visit, enter the rooms, navigate among the exhibits and look up at exhibits that are not still on display in the physical museum.

Renwick Gallery, Smithsonian American Art Museum

A 360 experience offers the Renwick Gallery, Smithsonian American Art Museum only by clicking here. The Web VR platform named as "WONDER 360" is free to download from Google Play and iTunes. Through the application the visitor is able to move in the Renwick Gallery exploring the place and the exhibits.

The Louvre Museum

An impressive experience is offering the Louvre Museum as it is expected from such a famous museum worldwide. Through YouVisit platform, available here, the visitor is able to make a tour in the museum, its exterior and interior as well. The visitor may select the hall he prefers to visit and enter this. He is also able to scroll and zoom in or out.

The British Museum

The British Museum prefers Boulevard, a platform based on Occulus Rift/gear, available free here. The only requirement is that the users must have an Oculus headset so as to be able to make the tour.

Metropolitan Museum of Art

The Metropolitan Museum of Art is providing a 360 tour in the museum in a simpler way and widely available. Through the YouTube 360 platform available here, the Metropolitan Museum offers the experience to the visitor to have access in the museum's premises.

Hintze Hall, NHM London

The 3D technology prefers the Hintze Hall, when offering the visitors the opportunity to walk on it and explore dozens of exhibits. The visitor is able to wander among meteorites, mammals, fish, birds, etc. and also hear the stories that shaped the museum. The 3D tour is available online here by any device.

CONCLUSION

AR and VR technologies are among the fastest growing technologies in the ICT sector, affecting in general many other sectors. An indicative example is the cultural sector, which has been strongly influenced from the aforementioned technologies. VR and AR as well as 360 were introduced the last 10-12 years in the cultural sector and have already been pervaded as a communications medium in museums, offering new tools to communicate with users (Hammady, Ma, & Temple, 2016). In parallel, the new social media and its increasing use have totally converted the traditional museums in modern museums following the trend of the season.

It is noteworthy to mention the museums' definition of the ICOM, the International Council of Museums. According to this, a museum is a non-profit making, permanent institution in the service of society and of its development, and open to the public, which acquires, conserves, researches, communicates and exhibits, for purposes of study, education and enjoyment, material evidence of people and their environment (ICOM, 2007). The online museums have nothing less, enjoy the same functions that are analyzed in the above-mentioned definition. However, they have the ability to act in a complementary manner as they can provide worldwide awareness.

The most critical difference among the physical and the online museum is the access. It is astonishing that audience can visit a museum without moving in the museum or in the country it is based. The only requirement is a personal computer or even a smartphone or any mobile device. In addition, online visitors don't need a ticket as in most cases this online service is free. This results on the cost reduction of a visit. If somebody considers that the most popular museums have a quite expensive ticket, this difference is noteworthy.

In addition, the easy access results on the museum's increasing awareness. The fact that it has no cost and it requires no move, means that it is not forbidden to anyone. Visitors that would never be able to visit the museum have the opportunity to make an online tour and find out information about the art pieces that would never had before. The museums following this technological trend are interested in digitalizing their collections so as to make more and more content accessible to a wider audience in an attractive way (Sylaiou et al., 2009).

One of the differences of the physical and the digital visit in a museum is the space and how it is used (Wagner, Schmalstieg, & Billinghurst, 2006). In the physical premises, the artifacts are exhibited on a specific physical place, in display cases and combined with limited information. In a digital museum, even if it is an AR, VR or an Instagram account, the artifacts are digitalized and visualized into an interactive environment. Through the technologies the user has the opportunity to interact, to move the exhibit, observe it from all angles, to find out more information, to like, express his feelings, offering the user a sense of freedom. In addition, through new technologies the user experience is more entertaining and interesting. The factor of amusement may be due to the visually appealing nature of new technologies interface, combining virtual imagery, sound, text, etc (Wagner et al., 2006). Thus, the online museums offer a more rewarding experience in comparison to strict artifacts closed on display cases.

Museums around the world are facing the need to reshape their structures and operational methodologies in order to keep pace with the ongoing technological changes. As a result of the now – taking – place procedure of the 4th Industrial Revolution, the extent and the depth of the required changes are not yet known. More traditional museums (e.g. archaeological museums) may affected more, while more alternative organizations (e.g. modern art museums) may face less difficulties as a result of their nature.

The procedure of museums' digitization and the implementation of VR and AR technologies should be further studied in order to develop the most appropriate business and operational models and to facilitate the museums' "transformation". Museums may be found themselves in a crossroad where critical decisions should be taken. "Do nothing" can always be an easy path, but choosing alternative paths seem more appropriate for a fast digitized and online – oriented world / audience.

Re – inventing museums role, may sound unfamiliar but it is an already started procedure. Museums spend more and more resources on their social media presence, they invest on digitize their content and to develop online services and applications. These actions are taken not only as part of their communication strategy, but moreover as a mean to widespread via alternative methods their content. Virtual museums are developed, operating supplementary to the physical ones, while soon enough audience may have the opportunity to visit private collections or not – for audience items in virtual reality's environments.

REFERENCES

Angelopoulou, A., Economou, D., Bouki, V., Psarrou, A., Jin, L., Pritchard, C., & Kolyda, F. (2012). Mobile augmented reality for cultural heritage. In *MOBILWARE 2011: Mobile wireless middleware, operating systems, and applications* (pp. 15–22). Berlin, Germany: Springer; doi:10.1007/978-3-642-30607-5_2

Bontchev, B. (2012). Evolving Europeana's Metadata: from ESE to EDM. In *Proc. of Digital Presentation and Preservation of Cultural and Scientific Heritage, (II)* (pp. 27–37). Retrieved from http://pro. europeana.eu/

Bowers, J., Bannon, L., Fraser, M., Hindmarsh, J., Benford, S., Heath, C., … Ciolfi, L. (2007). From the disappearing computer to living exhibitions: shaping interactivity in museum settings. In The disappearing computer (pp. 30–49). Berlin, Germany: Springer. doi:10.1007/978-3-540-72727-9_2

Brown, B., Maccoll, I., Chalmers, M., & Galani, A. (2003). Lessons from the lighthouse: Collaboration in a shared mixed reality system. In *SIGCHI Conference on Human Factors in Computing Systems* (pp. 577–584). New York: ACM; doi:10.1145/642611.642711

Budge, K., & Burness, A. (2018). Museum objects and Instagram: Agency and communication in digital engagement. *Continuum (Perth)*, *32*(2), 137–150. doi:10.1080/10304312.2017.1337079

Capriotti, P., Carretón, C., & Castillo, A. (2016). Testing the level of interactivity of institutional websites: From museums 1.0 to museums 2.0. *International Journal of Information Management*, *36*(1), 97–104. doi:10.1016/j.ijinfomgt.2015.10.003

Chevrier, C. (2016). *3D semantic modelling of scale models from 2D historical plans*. Retrieved from http://meurthe.crai.archi.fr/wordpressFr/wp-content/plugins/Lab_BD/media/pdf/Eurographics.pdf

Cosmas, J., Green, D., Grabczewski, E., Weimer, F., Leberl, F., & Grabner, M., … Kampel, M. (2001). 3D MURALE: A multimedia system for archaeology desi vanrintel, Eyetronics NV. In *Symposium on Virtual Reality, Archaeology, and Cultural Heritage*. ACM SIGGRAPH. Retrieved from https://www.inf.ethz.ch/personal/pomarc/pubs/CosmasVAST01.pdf

D'Auria, D., Di Mauro, D., Calandra, D. M., & Cutugno, F. (2015). A 3D audio augmented reality system for a cultural heritage management and fruition. *Journal of Digital Information Management, 13*(4), 203. Retrieved from https://www.semanticscholar.org/paper/A-3D-Audio-Augmented-Reality-System-for-a-Cultural-D'Auria-Mauro/40aad70c8e8337c2e02d3424179b586fa9e9a922

Damala, A., Hornecker, E., Van Der Vaart, M., Van Dijk, D., & Ruthven, I. (2016). The Loupe: Tangible augmented reality for learning to look at ancient Greek art. *Mediterranean Archaeology and Archaeometry, 16*(5), 73–85. doi:10.5281/zenodo.204970

Dylla, K., Muller, P., Ulmer, A., Haegler, S., & Frischer, B. (2009). Rome reborn 2.0: A framework for virtual city reconstruction using procedural modeling techniques. In Computer Applications and Quantitative Methods in Archaeology.

Engeström, J. (2005). Why some social network services work and others don't — Or: The case for object-centered sociality | locative lab. Retrieved from https://locativelab.wordpress.com/2006/11/08/why-some-social-network-services-work-and-others-dont-—-or-the-case-for-object-centered-sociality/

Galatis, P., Gavalas, D., Kasapakis, V., Pantziou, G., & Zaroliagis, C. (2016). Mobile augmented reality guides in cultural heritage. In *Proceedings of the 8th EAI International Conference on Mobile Computing* (pp. 11–19). Cambridge, UK: Applications and Services; doi:10.4108/eai.30-11-2016.2266954

Goldstein, C. (2018). 8 Instagram-ready art attractions that prove the museum of ice cream was just the beginning | Artnet News. Retrieved from https://news.artnet.com/art-world/the-children-of-the-museum-of-ice-cream-1258058

Gonizzi Barsanti, S., Caruso, G., Micoli, L. L., Covarrubias Rodriguez, M., & Guidi, G. (2015). 3D visualization of cultural heritage artefacts with virtual reality devices. *The International Archives of Photogrammetry, Remote Sensing, and Spatial Information Sciences, 40*(5), 165–172. doi:10.5194/isprsarchives-XL-5-W7-165-2015

Grinter, R. E., Aoki, P. M., Szymanski, M. H., Thornton, J. D., Woodruff, A., & Hurst, A. (2002). Revisiting the visit: In *Proceedings of the 2002 ACM Conference on Computer Supported Cooperative Work - CSCW '02* (p. 146). New York, NY: ACM Press. doi:10.1145/587078.587100

Guidi, G., & Russo, M. (2011). Diachronic 3D Reconstruction for Lost Cultural Heritage. In 3D Virtual Reconstruction and Visualization of Complex Architectures (3D ARCH) (pp. 371–376). Trento, Italy. doi:10.5194/isprsarchives-XXXVIII-5-W16-371-2011

Gutierrez, J. M., Molinero, M. A., Soto-Martín, O., & Medina, C. R. (2015). Augmented reality technology spreads information about historical graffiti in Temple of Debod. *Procedia Computer Science, 75*, 390–397. doi:10.1016/j.procs.2015.12.262

Hall, T., Ciolfi, L., Bannon, L., Fraser, M., Benford, S., & Bowers, J., … Flintham, M. (2002). The visitor as virtual archaeologist: Explorations in mixed reality technology to enhance educational and social interaction in the museum. In *Virtual Reality, Archaeology, and Cultural Heritage*. Glyfada, Greece: ACM SIGGRAPH. Retrieved from http://www.disappearing-computer.net/

Hammady, R., Ma, M., & Temple, N. (2016). Augmented reality and gamification in heritage museums live brain-computer cinema performance view project automatic conversion of natural language to 3D animation view project. In *International Conference on Serious Games* (pp. 181–190). Brisbane, Australia. Berlin, Germany: Springer-Verlag. 10.1007/978-3-319-45841-0_17

Higgett, N., Chen, Y., & Tatham, E. (2016). A user experience evaluation of the use of augmented and virtual reality in visualising and interpreting Roman Leicester 210AD (Ratae Corieltavorum). *Athens Journal of History*, 2(1), 1–7. doi:10.30958/ajhis.2-1-1

Hin, L. T. W., Subramaniam, R., & Aggarwal, A. K. (2003). Virtual science centers: a new genre of learning in Web-based promotion of science education. In *36th Annual Hawaii International Conference on System Sciences* (p. 10). Big Island, HI: IEEE. doi:10.1109/HICSS.2003.1174346

ICOM. (2007). Development of the museum definition according to ICOM statutes (1946 - 2001). Retrieved from http://archives.icom.museum/hist_def_eng.html

Izzo, F. (2017). Museum customer experience and virtual reality: H. Bosch Exhibition case study. *Modern Economy*, 08(04), 531–536. doi:10.4236/me.2017.84040

Kargas, A., Loumos, G., & Varoutas, D. (2019). Using different ways of 3D reconstruction of historical cities for gaming purposes: The case study of Nafplio. *Heritage*, 2(3), 1799–1811. doi:10.3390/heritage2030110

Kersten, T. P., Keller, F., Saenger, J., & Schiewe, J. (2012). *Automated generation of an historic 4D city model of Hamburg and its visualisation with the GE engine* (pp. 55–65). Berlin, Germany: Springer; doi:10.1007/978-3-642-34234-9_6

Kim, S. L., Suk, H. J., Kang, J. H., Jung, J. M., Laine, T. H., & Westlin, J. (2014). Using unity 3D to facilitate mobile augmented reality game development. In *2014 IEEE World Forum on Internet of Things (WF-IoT)* (pp. 21–26). IEEE. doi:10.1109/WF-IoT.2014.6803110

Loumos, G., Kargas, A., & Varoutas, D. (2018). Augmented and virtual reality technologies in cultural sector: exploring their usefulness and the perceived ease of use. *Journal of Media Critiques*, 4(14). doi:10.17349/jmc118223

Malraux, A. (1996). *Le musée imaginaire* [orig. 1947]. Paris, France: Gallimard; Retrieved from http://www.gallimard.fr/Catalogue/GALLIMARD/Folio/Folio-essais/Le-Musee-Imaginaire

Micoli, L., Guidi, G., Angheleddu, D., & Russo, M. (2013). A multidisciplinary approach to 3D survey and reconstruction of historical buildings. In *2013 Digital Heritage International Congress (Digital-Heritage)* (pp. 241–248). IEEE. 10.1109/DigitalHeritage.2013.6744760

Mohammed-Amin, R. K., Levy, R. M., & Boyd, J. E. (2012). Mobile augmented reality for interpretation of archaeological sites. In *Proceedings of the second international ACM workshop on personalized access to cultural heritage - PATCH '12* (p. 11). New York, NY: ACM Press. 10.1145/2390867.2390871

Muikku, J., & Kalli, S. (2017). *The IMD project VR/AR market report.* Retrieved from http://www.digitalmedia.fi/wp-content/uploads/2018/02/DMF_VR_report_edit_180124.pdf

O'Brien, H. L., & Toms, E. G. (2008). What is user engagement? A conceptual framework for defining user engagement with technology. *Journal of the American Society for Information Science and Technology, 59*(6), 938–955. doi:10.1002/asi.20801

Padilla-Meléndez, A., & del Águila-Obra, A. R. (2013). Web and social media usage by museums: Online value creation. *International Journal of Information Management, 33*(5), 892–898. doi:10.1016/j.ijinfomgt.2013.07.004

Pietroni, E., Pagano, A., & Rufa, C. (2013). The Etruscanning project: Gesture-based interaction and user experience in the virtual reconstruction of the Regolini-Galassi tomb. In *2013 Digital Heritage International Congress (DigitalHeritage)* (pp. 653–660). IEEE. 10.1109/DigitalHeritage.2013.6744832

Pletinckx, D., Callebaut, D., Killebrew, A. E., & Silberman, N. A. (2000). Virtual-reality heritage presentation at Ename. *IEEE MultiMedia, 7*(2), 45–48. doi:10.1109/93.848427

Prague (City of). (2018). Scale model of Pragues. Retrieved from http://www.langweil.cz/index_en.php

Sangregorio, E., Stanco, F., & Tanasi, D. (2008). The Archeomatica Project: Towards a new application of the computer graphics in archaeology. In *Eurographics Italian Chapter Conference* (pp. 1–5). Postfach 8043, 38621. Goslar, Germany: The Eurographics Association. doi:10.2312/LocalChapterEvents/ItalChap/ItalianChapConf2008/001-005

Schweibenz, W. (1998). The "virtual museum": new perspectives for museums to present objects and information using the internet as a knowledge base and communication system. In H. Zimmermann, & H. Schramm (Eds.), *6th ISI, 34,* 185-200. Retrieved from https://www.semanticscholar.org/paper/The-%22Virtual-Museum%22%3A-New-Perspectives-For-Museums-Schweibenz/9e33a47afcc9ce8f64c71e85cfd9c28e1ade502a

Sotirova, K., Peneva, J., Ivanov, S., Doneva, R., & Dobreva, M. (2012). Digitization of cultural heritage-standards, institutions, initiatives. In *Access to digital cultural heritage: innovative applications of automated metadata generation* (pp. 23–68). Plovdiv, Bulgaria: Plovdiv University; Retrieved from http://icom.museum/

Sparacino, F., Davenport, G., & Pentland, A. (2000). Media in performance: Interactive spaces for dance, theater, circus, and museum exhibits. *IBM Systems Journal, 39*(3.4), 479–510. doi:10.1147j.393.0479

Stanco, F., Tanasi, D., Gallo, G., Buffa, M., & Basile, B. (2012). Augmented perception of the past. the case of Hellenistic Syracuse. *Journal of Multimedia, 7*(2). doi:10.4304/jmm.7.2.211-216

Stricker, D., Dähne, P., Seibert, F., Christou, I., Almeida, L., Carlucci, R., & Ioannidis, N. (2001). Design and development issues for archeoguide: An augmented reality-based cultural heritage on-site guide. In *International Conference on Augmented, Virtual Environments, and Three-Dimensional Imaging* (pp. 1–5). IEEE Computer Society. Retrieved from http://publica.fraunhofer.de/documents/N-5833.html

Suess, A. (2014). *Art gallery visitors and Instagram*. University of Arts London. Retrieved from https://www.academia.edu/12086365/Art_Gallery_Visitors_and_Instagram

Sylaiou, S., Liarokapis, F., Kotsakis, K., & Patias, P. (2009). Virtual museums, a survey and some issues for consideration. *Journal of Cultural Heritage*, *10*(4), 520–528. doi:10.1016/j.culher.2009.03.003

Vayanou, M., Ioannidis, Y., Loumos, G., & Kargas, A. (2019). How to play storytelling games with masterpieces: From art galleries to hybrid board games. *Journal of Computers in Education*, *6*(1), 79–116. doi:10.100740692-018-0124-y

Vayanou, M., Ioannidis, Y., Loumos, G., Sidiropoulou, O., & Kargas, A. (2019). Designing performative, gamified cultural experiences for groups. *Extended Abstracts of the 2019 CHI Conference on Human Factors in Computing Systems - CHI EA '19*, 1–6. doi:10.1145/3290607.3312855

Wagner, D., Schmalstieg, D., & Billinghurst, M. (2006). *Handheld AR for collaborative edutainment* (pp. 85–96). Berlin, Germany: Springer; doi:10.1007/11941354_10

Weilenmann, A., Hillman, T., & Jungselius, B. (2013). Instagram at the museum: communicating the museum experience through social photo sharing. In *Proceedings of the SIGCHI Conference on Human Factors in Computing Systems - CHI '13* (p. 1843). New York, NY: ACM Press. 10.1145/2470654.2466243

KEY TERMS AND DEFINITIONS

Augmented Reality (AR): Augmented Reality (AR) is the technology that integrates digital information with the real world in a way that enhances graphics, sounds and 3D objects over the natural objects. AR technology focuses on the enriched experiences of the users, presenting visual information complementary of the natural environment through users' devices. The digital augmented content interacts with the user actions as most of the time the AR content is touchable and quite responsive on user's input.

Cultural Sector: A large variety of industries, also called under the term "cultural and creative industries". The term is used to describe a wide variety of organizations and private companies enabling in an even wider list of activities including (representatively): Museums, galleries and libraries, IT, software and computer services, Architecture, Advertising and marketing, Crafts, Design (product, graphic and fashion design), Film, TV, video, radio and photography, Publishing, Music, performing and visual arts.

Industry 4.0: a "marriage" between the physical world / sciences with digital technologies. Digital technologies offer new ways of interconnection with "physical", effective data collection and wise systems capable to interpret the gathered data for a more holistic, informed decision making (action back to physical world).

Instagram Museums: Museums / cultural places that have as main target the development of experiences for their visitors in order to make them create and reproduce Instagram posts. Through this procedure they can gain popularity indirectly, while their visitor gain a worth – to – mention – online experience. Artefacts, exhibitions and physical place is designed in such a manner that facilitates or even provoke "photoshoots", while visitors are expected to be part of the photo. More traditional museums forbid photographs and even when it is allowed it is expected to target the cultural artifacts only.

Mobile Devices: The term is used to describe devices that users usually have with them and can be used to deliver high added value content during a visit in a museum. Such devices can be smartphones and tablets, while technological evolution is constantly developing handsets capable to deliver VR or AR content.

Museums' Instagrammization: The new trend of widespread use of Instagram in Museums. Instagram is counted as one of the communication tools for museums. In particular there are museums using Instagram to showcase their art pieces or attract wider audiences or even carry on the user experience after the visit's end.

Social Media in Museums: More and more museums are using Social Media accounts so as to build awareness and interact with their audiences. The most popular social media for museums are Instagram, Facebook and afterwards follows twitter. The social media accounts are usually available in the museum's official website, in the Contact page.

Virtual Reality (VR): Virtual Reality (VR) is the technology that creates 3D scenes, places and worlds where users, through headset devices are connected and participating in. These environments are computer generated, capable to interact with users' actions and allow them to discover fantastic worlds by using most of their senses as living in the real world. VR experiences depends on system's capabilities, as the visual quality is directly related with the graphics rendering hardware and the simulation software.

Chapter 8
Employing Digital Reality Technologies in Art Exhibitions and Museums:
A Global Survey of Best Practices and Implications

Yowei Kang

https://orcid.org/0000-0002-7060-194X

National Taiwan Ocean University, Taiwan

Kenneth C. C. Yang

https://orcid.org/0000-0002-4176-6219

The University of Texas at El Paso, USA

ABSTRACT

The global AR, MR, and VR markets will reach USD\$40.6 billion in 2019. As a result, digital reality technologies have become a key component of promoting art exhibition and museum industries to the general public around the world. Emerging applications such as ARCHEOGUIDE, ARCO, and 3D-MURALE have allowed museum-goers to access archeological artefacts and sites remotely without physically visiting the museums. Digital reality technologies have therefore been perceived to have the great potential to promote (creative) cultural industry contents, because of the characteristics of these platforms (e.g., interactivity, realism, and visualization). This chapter employs a case study approach to discuss the current state of digital reality technology applications in museums and art exhibitions around the world. The study provides several best practice examples to demonstrate how digital reality technologies have fundamentally transformed the art exhibitions and museums.

DOI: 10.4018/978-1-7998-1796-3.ch008

Copyright © 2020, IGI Global. Copying or distributing in print or electronic forms without written permission of IGI Global is prohibited.

Figure 1. Digital reality technology market around the world
Note: in Billion
Source: Deloitte Consulting LLP & Consumer Technology Association (2018), https://www2.deloitte.com/insights/us/en/topics/emerging-technologies/digital-reality-technical-primer.html

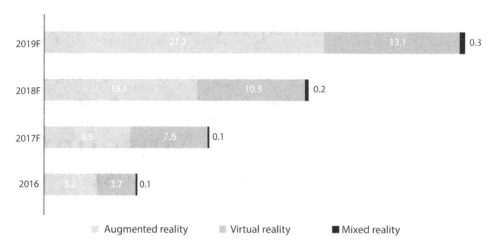

INTRODUCTION

According to Deloitte Consulting LLP & Consumer Technology Association (2018), the term, digital reality technology, refers to a cluster of technologies that are able to immerse partially or fully users in a computer-generated virtual environment. In general, these technologies include the following immersive technological platforms, ranging from augmented (AR), mixed (MR), virtual reality (VR), 360 degree video, etc (Deloitte Consulting LLP & Consumer Technology Association, 2018; Forbes, Kinnell, & Goh, 2018; eMarketer.com, 2018a, b, c, d, e, f).

Rosy economic outlook may justify recent surging interest in these digital reality technologies among art exhibition and museum professionals. According to a report by ResearchandMarkets.com (2018), global revenues for both augmented reality (henceforth, AR) and virtual reality (henceforth, VR) are expected to reach $94.4 billion by the year of 2023. The combined yearly growth of AR and VR is also expected to reach $143.3 billion in 2020 (IDC, 2017). Figure 1 offers a longitudinal prediction of the global AR, MR, and VR markets that are expected to grow USD$9 billion in 2016, to USD$25.6 billion in 2018, and to USD$40.6 in 2019 (Deloitte Consulting LLP & Consumer Technology Association, 2018). Thanks for the exponential growth of mobile devices (such as smartphones or tablets), AR technologies have exceeded VR in 2016 in terms of its market size of USD$5.2 billion vs. USD$3.7 billion in 2016 (Deloitte Consulting LLP & Consumer Technology Association, 2018). The augmented reality market has grown much faster than other digital reality platforms in 2019. In 2019, AR market is expected to grow to USD$27.2 billion, when compared with that of VR (USD$13.1 billion) and MR (USD$0.3 billion) (Deloitte Consulting LLP & Consumer Technology Association, 2018). Refer to Figure 1 below for more details of these different digital reality technologies.

Figure 2. Types of creative and cultural industries
Source: Mariani, 2018, n.p.

Art Exhibitions and Museums in the (Creative) Cultural Industry Ecosystem

Defining (Creative) Cultural Industry

Art exhibitions and museums have often been considered as part of (creative) cultural industry ecosystem, which can find its past foundation in the Frankfurtian school (Abruzzese & Borrelli, 2000; Colombo, 2018). On the basis of the original 1998 classification by U.K. Department for Culture, Media and Sport, the (creative) cultural industry is made of thirteen different industries that comprise the production and dissemination of a variety of cultural contents, ranging from "(1) advertising, (2) architecture, (3) art & antiques market, (4) crafts, (5) design, (6) designer fashion, (7) film & video, (8) interactive leisure software, (9) music, (10) performing arts, (11) publishing, (12) software and computer services, and (13) television and radio" (Yoshimoto, 2003, p. 1). In terms of their contents, these (creative) cultural industry sectors often include cultural contents from audiovisual, cinematographic productions, crafts and design, phonographic contents, printing and publication, multimedia, among others (Mariani, 2018) (Refer to Figure 2 below).

Like other industry sectors in the ecosystem the (creative) cultural industry, art exhibitions and museums are also influenced by the emergence of digital technologies as predicted by Dueze (2007). Colombo (2018) boldly states the phrase, platforms as cultural industries and argues that the arrival of digital platforms and their "revolutionary characteristics" have influenced the cultural production in a variety of cultural industry sectors (such as book publishing, music, cinema, and television) (p.141). Other challenges to the (creative) cultural industry include the increasingly active audience that demand participation in the communication processes, as well as the predictive power of (creative) cultural industry professionals to foresee how consumers will behave (Colombo, 2018).

One of the most significant attributes of these digital technologies will be their technical capabilities to allow the contents of (creative) cultural industry to be easily distributed to and shared among consumers (Dueze, 2007). Scholars have in general described these digital reality technology systems to be composed of 1) a graphic rendering system; 2) gloves, trackers, and user interface to sense and input users' movements; 3) output devices to enable aural, haptic, and visual interactions in a virtual environment; 4) a software to model virtual objectives and to construct databases; 5) a system to deliver sensory stimuli such as visual display technology to offer users interactive and immersive experiences (Claudio & Maddalena, 2014; Yang & Kang, 2018). For specific applications such as AR games, location-sensitive geo-information also becomes part of the technical system to overlap computer-generated images with those from the physical setting (de Gortari, 2018).

Impacts of Digital Reality Technologies on Art Exhibitions and Museums

Existing literature has reported that communication technologies have impacted on the production and dissemination of (creative) cultural industry sectors (Ryan & Hearn, 2010). For example, Ryan and Hearn (2010) reason that the convergence of multiple media platforms has empowered film makers to produce multi-media contents to let audience to consume film contents through multiple platforms (Ryan & Hearn, 2010). New digital reality technologies have the benefits of lowering of distribution cost through digital platforms many (creative) cultural industries, which is likely to have the same influences on art exhibitions and museums, as articulately described by Ryan and Hearn (2010, p. 135) below:

Digital distribution, the rapidly increasing availability of high-quality, low-cost digital video production and editing equipment, and the rise of online content aggregators, among other factors, are both lowering barriers to aspiring filmmakers and creating possibilities for screen production to bypass traditional distribution avenues.

Digital reality technologies have the great potential to generate new cultural contents that can contribute to users' interactions with (creative) cultural products (Ministry of Culture, 2017). In the context of art exhibition and museum sectors, VR refers to a computer-generated and simulated virtual world where users are immersed in a virtual environment to experience the presence of other objects or realities through interaction with them (Heim, 1998; Hsu, 2017; Kerrebroeck et al., 2017; Pan & Hamilton, 2018; Shin, 2017; Yang & Kang, 2018). For example, the Swiss company, VR-All-Art, claims to change "the way we present, discover, experience and trade art affects many players in the field" (https://vrallart.com/about). This VR gallery has included VR, mobile AR, MR, and classic website as its platforms to enable "artists, galleries and museums to overcome all boundaries of space and time and reach audiences around the world" (VR-All-Art, n.d., n.p.). Its mobile AR platform claims to empower "art-lovers to experience artworks they like at home, just with the camera on their smartphone and a mobile app" (VR-All-Art, n.d., n.p.).

Similar to museum curators (Ang, 2017; Baker, 2018), artists are among the fore-runners of employing new digital reality technologies to create an immersive experiential space for the general public (Farago, 2017). For example, Ian Cheng's art exhibition at MoMA PS1 in 2017 has employed the Oculus Rift device to immerse viewers to become a Brazilian rain forest (Farago, 2017). Similarly, Jordan Wolfson also developed a virtual reality project, Real Violence, in the biennial Whitney exhibitions that feature contemporary American arts (Farago, 2017; Whitney, 2017). In this virtual reality film, the artist focuses on the capacity of VR "to isolate the viewer" (Whitney, 2017, n.p.). In the annual Sundance Film Festival, over 20 submissions were entered into its newly-established New Frontier Experimental section (Robertson, 2018). These projects include mobile 360-degree videos to multi-person performance art installations (Robertson, 2018).

Museums around the world have taken advantage of the potential of these digital reality technologies (Farago, 2017). For example, Smithsonian American Art Museum (SAAM) (2017) employs VR technology to allow museum goers to experience Renwick Gallery's Wonder Exhibition through its downloaded app to provide a detailed 360 degree 3D panoramic views of the gallery. However, some critics have pointed out that technical limitations (such as smartphone resolution and lens) have failed to create an experience equivalent of actual museum visits (Farago, 2017). Ang (2017) also claims that both educational and art institutions have eagerly embraced the advent of digital reality technologies. For example, American Museum of Natural History has included AR to enable viewers to experience life-size dinosaur models virtually (Ang, 2017). Boston's Isabella Stewart Gardner Museum has also used AR to "place" the stolen painting on the wall they used to hang. An art exhibition in Laguna Beach, CA, called Moment in Time, visitors can point their Android or iOS devices to virtually stir up a image through its Aurasma app (Baker, 2012).

Digital reality technologies have played an important role for art exhibition and museum sectors in the (creative) cultural industry ecosystem (Ministry of Culture, 2017). Particularly, in the context of art exhibitions and museum that this book chapter aims to focus on, Ministry of Culture (2017) in Taiwan has encouraged and invested on the convergence of arts and technologies to enable digital and Internet technologies to be used in a variety of museum and art exhibitions. Applications such as ARCHEO-GUIDE, ARCO, and 3D-MURALE have allowed museum-goers to access archeological artefacts and sites remotely without visiting the museums (Bruno et al., 2010). Digital reality technologies (such as AR, MR, VR, and other immersive technologies) have the great potential to promote the production and dissemination of (creative) cultural industry contents, because of their interactivity, realism, and visualization (cited in Bruno et al., 2010).

Objectives of this Chapter

This book chapter offers a thorough description of AR, MR, and VR applications in art exhibitions and museums by reviewing best practice cases. This chapter provides definitions and examples of AR, MR, and VR and explains their importance for professionals in the art exhibitions and museums. Compared with more traditional communication platforms, digital reality technologies offer a great potential for artists, galleries, collectors, art-lovers, museums, curators, and the general public to interact with contents (Farago, 2017; Javornik 2016; Kang, 2019; Yang & Kang, 2018). According to Javornik (2016), these technologies are characterized with their interactivity, hypertextuality, modality, connectivity, and location-specificity.

These characteristics have made these technologies promising for many art exhibition and museum practitioners because they represent a "fundamental shift" as to how communication contents will be experienced and presented (Walker, 2017, n.p.). For example, Sommerauer and Müller (2014) describe the augmented reality technology as a platform "that dynamically blend real-world environments and context-based digital information" (p. 59). This book chapter reviews what has been argued in the existing literature and then concludes with several art exhibition and museum best practice applications that take advantage of AR, MR, and VR to better engage consumers of (creative) cultural products. The objectives of this book chapter intend to provide art exhibition and museum professionals to understand the emergence of AR, MR, and VR platforms by focusing on several key areas to affect the success of digital reality technologies in their applications in art exhibitions and museums. The authors conclude this chapter by examining several best practice applications in art exhibition and museum industry sectors to provide evidence to demonstrate how these digital reality technologies could enhance consumers' overall experiences with the cultural contents presented by art exhibitors and museum curators. This chapter employs a case study approach to discuss the current state of digital reality technology applications in art exhibitions and museums around the world. The study provides ample best practice examples to demonstrate how digital reality technologies can help. This study will answer the following questions:

RQ #1: What is the current state of augmented (AR), mixed (MR), or virtual reality (VR) applications among art exhibition and museum professionals?

RQ #2: What insights can be generated after analyzing best practice in AR, MR, and VR applications among art exhibition and museum professionals?

MAIN FOCUS OF THE CHAPTER

The Emergence of AR, MR, and VR Technologies in Art Exhibition and Museum Applications: Theoretical Foundations

AR, MR, and VR applications have revealed their most creative applications by art exhibitions, art galleries, and museums to deliver creative and cultural contents to promote art, crafts, literature, music, among others (Chang, Chang, Hou, Sung, Chao, & Lee, 2014; Kang, 2019; Iyer, 2015/2016; Yang, 2019). Art exhibitors and museum curators around the world are now increasingly offering new methods of engaging and educating their visitors by means of human–computer interaction (HCI) systems (Alelis, Bobrowicz, & Ang, 2015; Bruno et al., 2010; Chang et al., 2014; Chatzidimitris et al., 2013). For example, Bruno et al., (2010) employ a 3D reconstruction of archeological discoveries to convert a museum into a virtual institution and remotely available to any attentive visitors. Chang et al. (2014) and Chatzidimitris et al. (2013) both discover the potential of mobile or smartphone devices on enhancing visitors' engagement, learning effectiveness, and behavioral intention of cultural heritage, which is a critical part of creative and cultural industries.

Praised as a smart technology (Celtek, 2015), AR also lets consumers to interact with virtually-created digital graphics, imagery, and objects that are made up of both computer-generated virtual and real world data to make simultaneous interactions possible, with the illusion of co-existing in the same space (Rese et al., 2017; van Krevelen & Poleman, 2010; Williams, 2009; Yang & Kang, 2018; Yang, 2019). AR is a subdivision of VR because both integrate virtual digital information into a 3D real environment in real time (Chen et al., 2016; Yang & Kang, 2018). For example, Iyer (2015/2016) and nextplayground guardian (2015) describe the AR art gallery, Martell AiR Gallery (https://appadvice.com/app/martell-air-gallery/1048900688), in Singapore as the first of its kind in the world to mix augmented reality with contemporary art exhibition. The company website claims that its app will present the first AR contemporary art exhibition in Singapore and the AR project is created by cognac house Martell to celebrate the brand's anniversary in Singapore (AppAdvice LLC, 2019a). The virtual art exhibition, Zoe –The art of the Alchemist, was curated by Kelly Cheng from the Press House in Singapore to feature Singaporean artists (Shih Yun Yeo and Michael Lee) and can be viewed through Martell Air Gallery App. (Time Out, n.d.).

Many of these applications have the potentialities to change conventional cultural institutions (such as museums, art exhibit halls, performance arts centers, galleries, among others) to become virtual to allow visitors to stay at home to experience their huge amount of archeological, cultural, or artistic collections. Past academic research that observes the integration of digital reality technologies into art exhibitions and museums has often investigated the following research areas.

First, many scholars have explored the applications of art exhibitions and museums by focusing on the psychological impacts of these digital reality technologies. For example, Choi and Kim (2017) have argued that the implementation of digital technologies (such as head-mounted display devices and beacons) for museum exhibitors is likely to improve museum visitors' overall experiences by telling a captivating stories about artefacts. Related to the art education setting, Sommerauer and Müller (2014) also employ an pre-test and post-test experimental design to study 101 participants to examine the efficiency and effects of AR training module on students' cognitive abilities.

Secondly, Capuano, Gaeta, Guarino, Miranda, and Tomasiello (2016) have studied the effects of using narratives to overlay with artefacts to enrich and enhance museum visitors overall experiences. The study employs AR with semantic techniques to create digital stories tied to traditional museum artefacts (Capuano et al., 2016). The conventional static cultural artefacts are improved through AR to enhance their presentation and meaningful experiences to museum visitors. Sensory inputs, such as 3D animations, sound, video, and even haptic, have the benefits of enriching people's experiences with media contents (Capuano et al., 2016). These types of multi-platform descriptions and storytelling techniques in digital reality technology have been proven beneficial to the promotion and dissemination of oceanic creative and cultural contents as discussed above (Kang, 2019). Similarly, Collin-Lachaud and Passebois (2008) employ a qualitative interview to conduct about 25 in-depth inquiry with 21 participants and museum visitors. Several important aspects of visitors' experiential narratives have been identified in this study that may support the importance of overlaying narrative information with the static creative and cultural artefacts such as archeological finds (Bruno et al., 2010), artistic objects (Chang et al., 2014), and cultural heritage (Chatzidimitris et al., 2013). Immersive technologies such as AR, MR, VR, and 360-degree videos are conductive to enhancing museum visitors' cognitive, play, and functional values as manifested in the experiential narratives of 21 participants of this study (Kang, 2019).

Thirdly, following Colombo's stance in dealing with the technological platforms in the (creative) cultural industries, the effects of communication modality (such as those provided by digital reality technologies) on consumer emotional or cognitive responses have been extensively studied (Alelis, Bobrowicz, & Ang, 2015; Jarrier & Bourgeon-Renault, 2012). The diffusion of digital reality technologies not only poses challenges to the conventional manner of disseminating (creative) cultural contents, but also are likely to transform museums, music halls, art exhibitions, performance arts centers, as the physically present institutions to disseminate these contents. Other scholars of AR, MR, and VR applications in art exhibitions and museums have explored whether the (communication/media) modalities to interact with (creative) cultural contents in a museum could have any effects on visitors' overall experiences (Jarrier & Bourgeon-Renault, 2012). Chang et al.'s (2014) study of AR-guided, audio-guided, and no-guided devices in their art gallery study may offer some insights into the potential modality effects. Alelis et al. (2015) point out the wide availability of cutting-edge computer software and hardware is likely to allow cultural institutions such as museums to become digital and virtual to share and store their artefacts. A website, called Virtual Tours (http://www.virtualfreesites.com/museums.museums.html), claims to offer "over 300 Museums, Exhibits, Points of Special Interest and Real-Time journeys which offer online multimedia guided tours on the Web (Kang, 2019). Most of the following offer text and pictures, others in addition transmit sound and an occasional movie" around the clock (Kang, 2019; Virtual Tours, n.d., http://www.virtualfreesites.com/museums.museums.html)

Fourthly, scholars have employed a variety of research methods to study the effects of these emerging technologies on the applications among art exhibitors and museum curators. For example, Chang et al. (2014) employ a quasi-experiment design to examine the effects of an AR-guided, audio-guided, and non-guided device in an art appreciation context among 135 college participants. Their empirical results confirm the superiority of AR technology to positively improve exhibition visitors' overall learning effectiveness, result in better flow experience, produce higher engagement in their gallery experience, and increase the amount of time visitors spent on the paintings (Chang et al., 2014).

Adopting VR technologies to promote cultural heritage, Bruno, Bruno, De Sensi, Luchi, Mancuso, and Muzzupappa (2010) propose a VR-based Virtual Exhibition System that will enable archeological museums to transform their archeological finds into more immersive creative and cultural contents to lay persons. With the arrival of these digital reality technologies, many museums curators and art exhibitors have ventured to develop an immersive and virtual museum experiences for potential visitors. Other best practice examples discussed in this book chapter also demonstrate a similar trend of virtualization of these long-existing cultural institutions (Alelis et al., 2015).

Research Methodology: A Case Study Approach

Case study has been an extensively used research method in business and other social scientific disciplines to examine a phenomenon of significant interest to the researchers within a specific context (Kang, 2019; Mills & Duprepos, 2013; Research Methodology, n.d.). A case study method is able to provide "the intense focus on a single phenomenon" (Mills, Duprepos, & Wiebe, 2010, n.p.) by recording, analyzing, and interpreting facts and statistics related to the phenomenon (Kang, 2019).

Past literature has often identified two types of case study methods; that is, exploratory and descriptive case study (Kang, 2019; Mills et al., 2010; Research Methodology, n.d.). Using an explanatory case study method will involve the researchers to provide very meticulous explanation of facts, statistics, and other pertinent information about a phenomenon to provide a consistent explanation reliable with these factual materials (Kang, 2019; Mills et al., 2010). On the other hand, a descriptive case study aims to "assess a sample in detail and in depth" to generate a descriptive theory after "mining for abstract interpretations of data and theory development" (Kang, 2019; Mills et al., 2010).

The case study technique has been used in previous research in the study of (creative) cultural industries (Deuze, 2007; Kang, 2019). For example, Deuze (2007) offers a very detailed study of digital games, advertising, and other creative and cultural industries to examine the interactions between media companies and cultural convergence. Kang (2019) also offers detailed analyses of new technologies applications in the oceanic cultural industry. As an exploratory study, this book chapter likewise employs an explanatory case study to demonstrate what have been accomplished through the integration of AR, MR, and VR in the context of art exhibitions and museums of (creative) cultural contents.

Figure 3. The 5D Dinosaur Park, The National Museum of Natural Science, Taichung, Taiwan
Source: Su, 2017

Figure 4. Mobile AR App., The National Museum of Natural Science, Taichung, Taiwan

In the following sections, the authors would review and discuss several best practice applications of digital reality technologies in the context of art exhibitions and museums.

Best Practice Example #1: The National Museum of Natural Science in Taiwan

Museum curators have eagerly adopted these emerging digital reality technologies to attract more museum-goers (Kang, 2019). For example, in their study of AR museum guide in a gallery, Chang et al. (2014) observe that "AR not only retains the advantages of the digital guide, but also allows visitors to see the supplementary explication above a painting through a camera lens, bringing the guide information and the artwork together within the user's range of vision" (p. 186). The National Museum

Figure 5. 3D Animation of Peinan People
Source: National Museum of Prehistory, www.nmp.gov.twb

of Natural Science in Taichung, Taiwan is an exceptional instance of employing AR, VR, and other immersive technologies to permit museum visitors to experience running with dinosaurs in a virtually-created world (Ministry of Culture, 2017; Su, 2017) (Refer to Figure 3 below). A treasure hunt App is also developed to integrate mobile platforms to further involve visitors of the museum (Kang, 2019; Ministry of Culture, 2017; Su, 2017).

The National Museum of Natural Science in Taiwan also developed a mobile app to enable museum visitors to learn scientific facts through its AR application (Refer to Figure 4 below) (AppAdvice LLC, 2019b).

Best Practice Example #2: The National Museum of Prehistory (Taitung, Taiwan)

Digital reality technology is able to convert static and information-intensive museum exhibitions and their cultural artefacts to be more emotionally-charged and highly experiential to enhance visitors' overall experience (Kang, 2019). Chang et al. (2014) recapitulate previous studies in the area and conclude that past studies have found the benefits of AR in offering museum- and exhibition-goers "interesting, fun, and challenging experiences, as well as immersive sensations" (p. 185).

Figure 6. AR Application in Peinan archeological remains
Source: National Museum of Prehistory, www.nmp.gov.twb

The second-best practice example discusses The National Museum of Prehistory which is located in the eastern part of Taiwan has been an innovator in discovering how 3D animation and other digital reality technologies can alter visitors' overall experiences with the archeological artefacts (Chen, 2012). Its AR application developed by Next Animation Studio (2017) through its AR and 3D animation technologies is another best practice example to determine how the archeological remains at the Peinan Site can be turned into interactive and authentic experiences for museum visitors of Beinan Cultural Park, as part of National Museum of Prehistory (www.nmp.gov.tw).

Digital game has increasingly emerged as a platform for deliver digital reality experiences. An interactive digital game is also developed to allow visitors to virtually participate in the archeological excavation process, through virtually learning about the Peinan people resided in this region from 3,000 years ago, living inside the pre-historical settlement, and uncovering archeological cultural objects with the other explorers (Chen, 2012; Kang, 2019; Next Animation Studio, 2017). This best practice example demonstrates that digital reality technology has the abilities to enhance the value of (creative) cultural contents by engaging the general public with the archeological artefacts with more attractive storytelling and immersive experiences, as empirically tested by many scholars (Bruno et al., 2010; Chang et al., 2014; Kang, 2019). Figure 6 below has shown that museum visitors are now able to see what Peinan people look like and how they live their lives 3,000 years ago. The AR reconstruction of the Peinan Site lets users to overlap computer-generated image of this pre-historical settlement above the archeological remains to feel what it is like to walk around the settlement (Refer to Figure 6) (Kang, 2019).

Kang (2019) has also pointed out that digital reality technology has aided the development and implementation of the museum's promotion of (creative) cultural contents through its other on-going projects, such as The Digital Project for the Education and Promotion of Taiwan's Prehistory Cultures, The Peinan Site and Peinan Culture, to develop a virtual museum and exhibition hall of indigenous

Figure 7. Met 360 Degree VR Project
Source: https://www.metmuseum.org/art/online-features/met-360-project

peoples in Taiwan through "a virtual reality for interactive reconstruction of archaeological discoveries" (Chen, 2012, n.p.). The AR application has allowed this museum to integrate the physical archeological artefacts, or other (creative) cultural contents, with digitally-generated information have been empirically confirmed to activate inquisitiveness and inspire intention to explore the museum space (Chatzidimitris, Kavakli, Economou, & Gavalas, 2013; Kang, 2019).

Best Practice Example #3: Met 360 ° by The Metropolitan Museum of Art and The British Museum

This award-winning VR project, Ancient Egyptian Collections Project, by The Metropolitan Museum of Art includes six short VR videos and have been viewed by 11 million times to virtually explore the interior of the museum (The MET, n.d.). Included in the accolades of this project are 2017 Webby Award, Best Culture & Lifestyle Video, as well as 2017 Shorty Award, Best Cultural Institution (The MET, n.d.). The Metropolitan Museum of Art and The British Museum has collaborated to create a virtual exhibition to allow visitors to experience a virtual through either a Google Cardboard or any VR headset (such as Samsung Gear VR headset) (GearBrain, 2018; Kang, 2019). Labelled as Met 360° (https://www. youtube.com/watch?time_continue=20&v=h9OTCFAmbmA), this VR and 360 degree video project allows users to experience The Temple of Dendur that was built around 15 B.C. when Egypt was ruled by the Roman Emperor Augustus (The MET, 2017, https://youtu.be/h9OTCFAmbmA).

The Met 360° is designed to be multi-platforms to allow users to access the VR materials on their smartphone, desktop computer, Google Cardboard, or any VR headset (such as Samsung Gear VR headset) (GearBrain, 2018; Kang, 2019) (Refer to Figure 7).

Figure 8. The Greenway conservancy augmented reality exhibition
Source: https://www.rosekennedygreenway.org/public-art/currently-greenway/augmented-reality-art

Figure 9. The greenway conservancy augmented reality exhibition
Source: https://vrscout.com/news/rose-kennedy-greenway-ar-experience/#

The Met 360° VR project is among many digitalization initiatives that the Met has undertaken to create its digital presences (Kraus, 2018). As Dr. Miriam Posner points out, "Now that many people can access representations of museums and objects online, it's forced museums to really think about what aspect of artwork they think is really special……. Every museum has to decide what its priorities are" (Kraus, 2018, n.p.). For example, the Met has released 375,000 images of its collection to the public domain under Creative Commons Zero (CC0) license (Kraus, 2018). Similarly, a public Application Programming Interface, or API, has been used to allow all computers around the world to read and analyze changing information of its 200,000 open access cultural objects (Kraus, 2018).

Best Practice Example #4: Rose Fitzgerald Kennedy Greenway in Boston

The Greenway Conservancy's Augmented Reality (AR) exhibition (https://youtu.be/fnBmyumEJK0) is another good example to demonstrate the overlapping of physical surroundings from historical photos of downtown Boston with interactive digital elements is able to enhance consumers' overall experiences with these cultural artefacts through "engaging people in meaningful experiences, interactions, and dialogue with art and each other (The Green Way, 2019, n.p.). In collaboration with Boston's Cyberarts and Hoverlay as a public art project, three AR artists (e.g., Nancy Cahill Baker, Will Pappenheimer and John Craig Freeman and one local historian (i.e., Amy D. Finstein) are commissioned to superimpose the historical images of The Greenway area with their contemporary landscape (Carlton, 2019; The Green Way, 2019). Once the consumers download the free Hoverlay app to their mobile phone, they will be able to access 16 AR application access points to interact with digitally-enhanced contents to see what the area look like in the past (Carlton, 2019) (Refer to Figure 8 and Figure 9 below). For example, as seen in Figure 9, viewers will be able to see the historical image of the place in the 1950s and 1960s. Their experiences are enhanced by descriptive narratives to provide viewers multi-sensory and –platform experiences of these cultural artefacts.

Study Limitations

Despite the attempt to contain as many best practice examples as possible, this book chapter is limited by its length allowed by the publisher to fully explore the potentialities of AR, MR, VR, and other immersive technologies (such as 360 degree video) in promoting (creative) cultural contents in the context of art exhibitions and museums. Nevertheless, this study has provided an initial attempt to scrutinize the possible influences of emerging digital reality technologies on the consumption, production, dissemination, and sharing of (creative) cultural industry contents. Written as a case study for art exhibition and museum practitioners, future research directions are not the main focus of this book chapter. However, scholars of digital reality technologies are likely to follow issues related to the design of an AR, MR, and VR system in the context of museums and exhibitions, or broadly for (creative) cultural industry sectors. Issues related to system design, modality effects, consumer responses, and content development issues are likely to produce interesting insights into how these digital reality technologies will enhance the transformation of (creative) cultural industries and the promotion of cultural contents to a wide audience.

REFERENCES

Alelis, G., Bobrowicz, A., & Ang, C. S. (2015). Comparison of engagement and emotional responses of older and younger adults interacting with 3D cultural heritage artefacts on personal devices. Behaviour & Information Technology, 34(11), 1064–1078.

Ang, B. (2017, March 26). Augmented Reality in the classroom: Move over, Pokemon Go, it's time for science class; Augmented reality, the technology used in the mobile game, is now being used in education and design, among other things. *The Strait Times,* Retrieved from https://www.straitstimes.com/lifestyle/augmented-reality-in-the-classroom-move-over-pokemon-go-its-time-for-science-class

AppAdvice LLC. (2019a). Martell AiR Gallery. Retrieved from https://appadvice.com/app/martell-air-gallery/1048900688

AppAdvice LLC. (2019b). Martell AiR Gallery. Retrieved from https://appadvice.com/app/martell-air-gallery/1048900688

Baker, N. (2017, July 21). Augmented reality apps bring exhibits to life; Toronto Museum, Laguna Beach gallery incorporate untapped medium. *The Gazette (Montreal),* p. 8.

Bentkowska-Kafel, A., & MacDonald, L. (Eds.). (2018). Digital techniques for documenting and preserving cultural heritage. Kalamazoo, MI: Arc Humanities Press.

Bruno, F., Bruno, S., De Sensi, G., Luchi, M. L., Mancuso, S., & Muzzupappa, M. (2010). From 3D reconstruction to virtual reality: A complete methodology for digital archaeological exhibition. Journal of Cultural Heritage, 11(1), 42–49.

Capuano, N., Gaeta, A., Guarino, G., Miranda, S., & Tomasiello, S. (2016). Enhancing augmented reality with cognitive and knowledge perspectives: A case study in museum exhibitions. Behaviour & Information Technology, 35(11), 968–979.

Carlton, B. (2019, May 25). Boston's Rose Kennedy Greenway is now one of the largest AR exhibits in North America. Retrieved from https://vrscout.com/news/rose-kennedy-greenway-ar-experience/

Chang, K.-E., Chang, C.-T., Hou, H.-T., Sung, Y.-T., Chao, H.-L., & Lee, C.-M. (2014). Development and behavioral pattern analysis of a mobile guide system with augmented reality for painting appreciation instruction in an art museum. Computers & Education, 71, 185–197.

Chatzidimitris, T., Kavakli, E., Economou, M., & Gavalas, D. (2013). Mobile augmented reality edutainment applications for cultural institutions. In N. G. Bourbakis, G. A. Tsihrintzis, & M. Virvou (Eds.), *2013 Fourth International Conference on Information, Intelligence, Systems, and Applications (IISA)* (pp. 1-4). Piraeus, Greece: IEEE.

Choi, H.-S., & Kim, S.-H. (2017, February). A content service deployment plan for metaverse museum exhibitions-centering on the combination of beacons and HMDs. International Journal of Information Management, 37(1b), 1519–1527.

Claudio, P., & Maddalena, P. (2014, January). Overview: Virtual reality in medicine. Journal of Virtual Worlds Research, 7(1), 1–34.

Collin-Lachaud, I., & Passebois, J. (2008). Do immersive technologies add value to the museum-going experience? An exploratory study conducted at France's Paléosite. International Journal of Arts Management, 11(1), 60–71.

Colombo, F. (2018). Reviewing the cultural industry: From creative industries to digital platforms. Communicatio Socialis, 31(4), 135–146.

Craig, E. (2019, May 26). Boston the site of the largest AR art exhibit in America. Digital bodies: VR, AR, and the future of learning. Retrieved from https://www.digitalbodies.net/augmented-reality/boston-the-site-of-the-largest-ar-art-exhibit-in-america/

Deuze, M. (2007, June 1). Convergence culture in the creative industries. International Journal of Cultural Studies, 10(2), 243–263.

eMarketer.com. (2018a, April 9). Chart: Virtual and augmented reality device shipment and sales share worldwide, by device type, 2022 (% of total). eMarketer.com. Retrieved from http://totalaccess.emarketer.com/chart.aspx?r=219212

eMarketer.com. (2018b, April 24). Chart: UK smartphone users who prefer using smart glasses vs. Smartphone for select augmented reality activities (% of respondents). eMarketer.com. Retrieved from http://totalaccess.emarketer.com/chart.aspx?r=220210

eMarketer.com. (2018c, April 5). Industries in which augmented reality users in select countries in Western Europe have used AR, Nov. 2017 (% of respondents). eMarketer.com. Retrieved from http://totalaccess.emarketer.com/chart.aspx?r=219349

eMarketer.com. (2018d, Nov. 12). Ownership of VR headsets among US internet users, July 2014-Aug 2018 (% of respondents). eMarketer.com. Retrieved from http://totalaccess.emarketer.com/chart.aspx?r=224365

eMarketer.com. (2018e, Sept. 7). Executives in select countries whose companies are experimenting with vs. implementing AR & VR for industrial use, by country (% of respondents, June 2018). eMarketer.com, Retrieved from http://totalaccess.emarketer.com/chart.aspx?r=222816

eMarketer.com. (2018f, April 5). Usage and awareness of augmented reality among internet users in select countries in Western Europe, Nov 2017 (% of respondents). eMarketer.com. Retrieved from http://totalaccess.emarketer.com/chart.aspx?r=219347

Farago, J. (2017, Feb. 3). Virtual reality has arrived in the art world. Now what? *The New York Times,* Retrieved from https://www.nytimes.com/2017/2002/2003/arts/design/virtual-reality-has-arrived-in-the-art-world-now-what.html

Forbes, T., Kinnell, P., & Goh, M. (2018, Aug. 17). *A study into the influence of visual prototyping methods and immersive technologies on the perception of abstract product properties.* Paper presented at the NordDesign: Design in the era of digitalization, NordDesign 2018.

Freeman, J. P. (2018, April 26). Word wise: Augmented reality. InsideSources.com, Retrieved from https://www.insidesources.com/word-wise-augmented-reality/

GearBrain (GB). (2018, June 4). The 5 best museum AR/VR experiences this summer. GearBrain (GB). Retrieved from https://www.gearbrain.com/virtual-reality-museum-art-summer-2577767924.html

IDC. (2017, Feb. 27). Worldwide spending on augmented and virtual reality forecast to reach $13.9 billion in 2017, according to IDC. Retrieved from https://www.idc.com/getdoc.jsp?containerId=prUS42331217)

International Data Corporation (IDC). (2018, Sept. 20). AR/VR headset shipments worldwide, commercial vs. consumer, 2018 & 2022 (millions and CAGR). eMarketer.com. Retrieved from http://totalaccess.emarketer.com/chart.aspx?r=222930

Iyer, B. (2015, December/2016, January). Augmented-reality gallery enhances Singapore sights. *Campaign Asia-Pacific,* p. 31.

Jarrier, E., & Bourgeon-Renault, D. (2012, Fall). Impact of mediation devices on the museum visit experience and on visitors' behavioural intentions. International Journal of Arts Management, 15(1), 18–29.

Javornik, A. (2016). Augmented reality: Research agenda for studying the impact of its media characteristics on consumer behaviour. Journal of Retailing and Consumer Services, 30, 252–261.

Kang, Y. W. (2019). The applications of digital reality in creative and oceanic cultural industries: The case of Taiwan. In K. C. C. Yang (Ed.), Cases on immersive virtual reality techniques (pp. 269-296). Hershey, PA: IGI Global.

Kim, K., Hwang, J., Zo, H., & Lee, H. (2016). Understanding users' continuance intention toward smartphone augmented reality applications. Information Development, 32(2), 161–174.

Kraus, R. (2018, Oct. 25). A museum without walls: How the Met is bringing its ancient collection online. *Mashable.* Retrieved from https://mashable.com/article/the-met-museum-api/

Mariani, G. (2018). The cultural and creative industries. Guillaume Mariani. Retrieved from https://www.guillaume-mariani.com/creative-industries/

Mills, A. J., & Durepos, G. (2013). Case study methods in business research (1–4). Thousand Oaks, CA: Sage.

Mills, A. J., Durepos, G., & Wiebe, E. (2010). Explanatory case study. In Encyclopedia of case study research. Thousand Oaks, CA: Sage.

Ministry of Culture (Taiwan). (2017). 2017 Taiwan cultural & creative industries annual report. Taipei, Taiwan: Ministry of Culture. Retrieved from http://cci.culture.tw/upload/cht/attachment/b131e555e-c34a192be359838c9a4eb07.pdf

Next Animation Studio. (2017, March 5). Next Animation Studio partners with national museum of prehistory. Retrieved from https://eprnews.com/next-animation-studio-partners-with-national-museum-of-prehistory-87380/

Nextplayground guardian. (2015, Nov. 3). Martell Singapore: Experience Martell air gallery. Nextplayground guardian, Retrieved from https://nextplayground.net/campaigns/martell-singapore-experience-martell-air-gallery/

Pan, X., & Hamilton, A. F. C. (2018). Why and how to use virtual reality to study human social interaction: The challenges of exploring a new research landscape. British Journal of Psychology, 109, 395–417.

Rae, J., & Edwards, L. (2016, January). Virtual reality at the British Museum: What is the value of virtual reality environments for learning by children and young people, schools, and families? In *Proceedings of MW2016: The Annual Conference Museums and the Web,* Los Angeles, CA.

Research methodology. (n.d.). Case study. Research methodology. Retrieved from https://research-methodology.net/research-methods/qualitative-research/case-studies/

ResearchAndMarkets.com. (2018, July 30). Global augmented reality (AR) & virtual reality (VR) market outlook to 2023 by devices, component, application, and geography: ResearchAndMarkets.com. Retrieved from https://www.businesswire.com/news/home/20180730005663/en/

Robertson, A. (2018, Jan. 26). The best VR and AR from Sundance 2018, from haptic gloves to alien abduction. *The Verge,* Retrieved from https://www.theverge.com/2018/2011/2026/16919236/sundance-16912018-best-virtual-reality-augmented-vr-ar-new-frontier

Ryan, M. D., & Hearn, G. (2010, August). Next-generation "filmmaking": New markets, new methods and new business models. Media International Australia, 136, 133–145.

Shin, D. (2018). Empathy and embodied experience in virtual environment: To what extent can virtual reality stimulate empathy and embodied experience? Computers in Human Behavior, 78, 64–73.

Shin, D.-H. (2017). The role of affordance in the experience of virtual reality learning: Technological and affective affordances in virtual reality. Telematics and Informatics, 34, 1826–1836.

Smithsonian American Art Museum (SAAM). (2017). WONDER 360: Experience the Renwick Gallery Exhibition in Virtual Reality.

Smithsonian American Art Museum (SAAM). Retrieved from https://americanart.si.edu/wonder2360

Sommerauer, P., & Müller, O. (2014). Augmented reality in informal learning environments: A field experiment in a mathematics exhibition. Computer Education, 79, 59–68.

Su, M. J. (2017, Nov. 7). Engaging audience through VR and AR technology in the National Museum of Natural Science. *The Liberty Times,* Retrieved from http://news.ltn.com.tw/news/life/breaking-news/2246155

The Green Way. (2019). Past, present, and future meet on The Greenway! Retrieved from https://www.rosekennedygreenway.org/

The MET. (n.d.). The Met 360° Project. Retrieved from https://www.youtube.com/watch?time_continue=2020&v=h2019OTCFAmbmA

Time Out. (n.d.). Martell Air Gallery: Zoe – The art of the alchemist. Time Out, Retrieved from https://www.timeout.com/singapore/art/martell-air-gallery-zoe-the-art-of-the-alchemist

UK Creative Industry Council (CIC). (2018, November). UK creative industries-value. UK Creative Industry Council (CIC), Retrieved from http://www.thecreativeindustries.co.uk/resources/infographics

Whitney. (2017). Jordan Wolfson. Retrieved from https://whitney.org/exhibitions/2017-biennial#exhibition-about

Yang, K. C. C. (2019). Reality-creating technologies as a global phenomenon. In K. C. C. Yang (Ed.), *Cases on immersive virtual reality techniques* (pp. 1–18). Hershey, PA: IGI Global.

Yang, K. C. C., & Kang, Y. W. (2018). Integrating virtual reality and augmented reality into advertising campaigns: History, technology, and future trends. In N. Lee, X.-M. Wu, & A. El Rhalibi (Eds.), Encyclopedia of computer graphics and games. New York, NY: Springer. doi:10.1007/978-3-319-08234-9_132-1

Yang, K. C. C. (Ed.). (2018). Multi-platform advertising strategies in the global marketplace. In Advances in marketing, customer relationship management, and electronic services (AMCRMES) book series. Hershey, PA: IGI Global.

Yoshimoto, M. (2003, December). The status of creative industries in Japan and policy recommendations for their promotion. *NLI Research,* 1-9.

ADDITIONAL READING

Adval, R., & Wyer, R. Jr S. (1998). The role of narratives in consumer information processing. Journal of Consumer Psychology, 7(3), 207–245.

Barrettara, M. (2013). New methods for sharing and exhibiting 3D archaeology. The Posthole, 31, 8–13.

Baumgartner, J. (2016, January 23-30). Top VR adoption challenge: Cost. Broadcasting & Cable, p.12.

Bazilian, E. (April 23, 2017). Infographic: What consumers really think about VR. AdWeek, Retrieved on November 15, 2017 from http://www.adweek.com/digital/infographic-what-consumers-really-think-about-vr/

Bazilian, E. (May 1, 2017). Time Inc.'s VR guru is forging a new path through immersive storytelling. AdWeek, Retrieved on November 15, 2017 from http://www.adweek.com/digital/time-inc-s-vr-guru-is-forging-a-new-path-through-immersive-storytelling/

Bekele, M. K., Pierdicca, R., Frontoni, E., Malinverni, E. S., & Gain, J. (2018). A survey of augmented, virtual, and mixed reality for cultural heritage. [JOCCH]. Journal on Computing and Cultural Heritage, 11(2), 7.

Biggs, M., & Buchler, D. (2008). Eight criteria for practice-based research in the creative and cultural industries. Art. Design & Communication in Higher Education, 7(1), 5–18. doi:10.1386/adche.1387.1381.1385/1381

Bolter, J. D., & Grusin, R. (1998). Remediation: Understanding New Media. Cambridge, MA: MIT Press.

Bordnick, P. S., Carter, B. L., & Traylor, A. C. (2011, March). What virtual reality research in addictions can tell us about the future of obesity assessment and treatment. Journal of Diabetes Science and Technology, 5(2), 265–271.

Bulearca, M., & Tamarjan, D. (2012). Augmented reality: A sustainable marketing tool? Global Business and Management Research: An International Journal, 2(2 &3), 237–252.

Carmigniani, J., & Furth, B. (Eds.). (2011). Augmented reality: An overview. Heidelberg: Springer Verlag.

Cenfetelli, R. T. (2004). Inhibitors and enablers as dual factor concepts in technology usage. Journal of the Association for Information Systems, 5(11-12), 472–492.

Chahal, M. (2016, January 28). Bringing brands virtually to life. Marketing Week, 29-31.

Chen, Z.-H. (2018, May 10). Reflections on the development of creative cultural industries in South Korea, Thailand, France, and US: What went wrong for Taiwan? Chung, N., Lee, H., Kim, J.-Y., & Koo, C. (2017). The role of augmented reality for experience-influenced environments: The case of cultural heritage tourism in Korea. Journal of Travel Research, 1–17.

Claudio, P., & Maddalena, P. (2014, January). Overview: Virtual reality in medicine. Journal of Virtual Worlds Research, 7(1), 1–34.

Conway, R. (2017, April). The future of online advertising. NZB, 40-41.

Cox, A. M., Cromer, K. W., Guzman, I., & Bagui, S. (2017, May). Virtual worlds, virtual reality, and augmented reality: Differences in purchase intentions based on types, users, and sex. Journal of Virtual Worlds Research, 10(1), 1–21.

Dacko, S. G. (2017). Enabling smart retail settings via mobile augmented reality shopping apps. Technological Forecasting and Social Change, 124, 243–256.

Damala, A., Cubaud, P., Bationo, A., Houlier, P., & Marchal, I. (2008). Bridging the gap between the digital and the physical: design and evaluation of a mobile augmented reality guide for the museum visit. In Tsekeridou, S., Cheok, A. D., Giannakis, K., & Karigiannis, J. (Eds.), The Third International Conference on Digital Interactive Media in Entertainment and Arts (pp. 120–127). Athens: ACM.

De Souza e Silva, A. (2006). From cyber to hybrid: Mobile technologies as interfaces of hybrid spaces. Space and Culture, 9(3), 261–278. doi:10.1177/1206331206289022

Engberg, M., & Bolter, J. D. (2014). Cultural expression in augmented and mixed reality. Convergence (London), 20(1), 3–9.

Haenlein, M., & Kaplan, A. M. (2009). Flagship brand stores within virtual worlds: The impact of virtual store exposure on real-life attitude toward the brand and purchase intent. Recherche et Applications en Marketing, 24(3), 57–79.

Hofmann, S., & Mosemghvdlishvili, L. (2014). Perceiving spaces through digital augmentation: An exploratory study of navigational augmented reality apps. Mobile Media & Communication, 2(3), 265–280.

Jennett, C., Cox, A. L., Cairns, P., Dhoparee, S., Epps, A., Tijs, T., & Walton, A. (2008). Measuring and defining the experience of immersion in games. International Journal of Human-Computer Studies, 66, 641–661.

Jin, S.-A. A., & Sung, Y. (2010). The roles of spokes-avatars' personalities in brand communication in 3d virtual environments. Journal of Brand Management, 17, 317–327.

Jin, S.-A. A. (2009). Modality effects in second life: The mediating role of social presence and the moderating role of product involvement. Cyberpsychology & Behavior, 12(6), 717–721.

Kelly, L., & Groundwater-Smith, S. (2009). Revisioning the physical and on-line museum. Journal of Museum Education, 34(1), 55–68.

Liarokapis, F. (2006). December). An exploration from virtual to augmented reality gaming. Simulation & Gaming, 37(4), 507–533.

Mahony, S. O. (2015). A proposed model for the approach to augmented reality deployment in marketing communications. Procedia: Social and Behavioral Sciences, 175, 227–235.

Metz, R. (2015, March 18). Virtual reality advertisements get in your face. MIT Technology Review, Retrieved on November 13, 2017 from https://www.technologyreview.com/s/535556/virtual-reality-advertisements-get-in-your-face/

Olson, K. E., O'Brien, M. A., Rogers, W. A., & Charness, N. (2011). Diffusion of technology: Frequency of use for younger and older adults. Ageing International, 36(1), 123–145.

Pallud, J., & Monod, E. (2010). User experience of museum technologies: The phenomenological scales. European Journal of Information Systems, 19, 562–580.

Petridis, P., White, M., Mourkousis, N., Liarokapis, F., Sifniotis, M., Basu, A., & Gatzidis, C. (2005). Exploring and interacting with virtual museums. In A. Figueiredo & G. A. Velho (Eds.), Proceedings of Computer Applications and Quantitative Methods in Archaeology. Tomar: CAA.

Styliani, S., Fotis, L., Kostas, K., & Petros, P. (2009). Virtual museums, a survey and some issues for consideration. Journal of Cultural Heritage, 10(4), 520–528.

Sylaiou, S., Mania, K., Karoulis, A., & White, M. (2010). Exploring the relationship between presence and enjoyment in a virtual museum. International Journal of Human-Computer Studies, 68(5), 243–253.

Tallon, L., & Walker, K. (2008). Digital Technologies and the Museum Experience: Handheld Guides and Other Media. Maryland: AltaMira Press.

Tillon, A. B., Marchal, I., & Houlier, P. (2011, October 26-29). Mobile augmented reality in the museum: Can a lace-like Technology take you closer to works of art? In Proceedings of 10th IEEE International Symposium on Mixed and Augmented Reality (pp. 41–47). Basel, Switzerland.

Wojciechowski, R. (2012). Modeling interactive augmented reality environments. In Interactive 3D Multimedia Content (pp. 137–170). London: Springer.

KEY TERMS AND DEFINITIONS

Augmented Reality: Commonly abbreviated as AR, the term refer to a simulated, but enhanced, reality that combines both computer-generated virtual and real-world data to allow users to complete real-time interactions with computer-generated graphics, imagery, and objects, in a smooth way and with an illusion of these layers of information coexisting in the same space.

Best Practice: A term that refers to a method or a procedure that can generate the best outcome, when compared with other alternative solutions.

Case Study Approach: Refers to a social scientific research method that offers detailed and thorough description of an issue, an objective, a phenomenon, or a situation of interest as a case object.

(Creative) Cultural Industry: A term to refer to a set of knowledge-based and –generating economic sectors, ranging from advertising, broadcasting, crafts, film, graphic design, music, publishing, tourism, etc. This term is often used along with "creative". This concept originated from Marxist philosophy and was coined by Theodor Adorno and Max Horkheimer to describe the production and marketing of culture as a branch of the industry. It often covers a wide variety of industries, such as architecture, craft, film and television production, music, publication, etc.

Cultural Object: The term refers to human-made artefacts for a spiritual and/or practical purpose or activity that may have functional and/or artistic relevance to the general public.

Digital Reality Technology: A umbrella term to encompass a set of reality-creating technologies such as augmented reality, mixed reality, virtual reality, 360 degree video, and other emerging immersive technologies that are able to create a totally artificial virtual environment through computer-generated contents.

Ecosystem: A biological term that describes a community of living organisms and lifeless elements such as mineral, air, water, and soil. This term has been extended to study different operators/players in a specific industry. For example, the AR and VR ecosystem is made up for different industry sectors such as software development, 360 degree video developers, arcade, agency, education, network, university, accelerator, platform, corporate lab, tech vendor, among others.

Engagement: A term to describe the procedure or outcome to encourage a company's customers to interact and share their experiences with the communication contents, cultural contents, the advertised brand, or the company (i.e., advertiser).

Head/Helmet-Mounted Display: Also known as HMD, this term refers to the display device worn by users when they use digital reality applications to experience the virtual worlds through a small display in front of each eye. There are two types of HDM: monocular and binocular HDM, depending on if one or two displays are available to users.

Immersion: As a loosely-defined psychological term, this term has been used to define a unique experience when using a media or technology platform. Often affiliated with digital reality technologies, and other "immersive" technologies, this concept refers to users' perceptions to feel a sense of presence in a non-physical world. This term often refers to a fully surrounded experiences when using HMD in a virtual space.

Mixed Reality: Abbreviated as MR. This term sometimes refers to another term, hybrid reality. MR refers to the merger of both actual and virtual worlds to create an immersive virtual space where digital reality meets and coexists with physical objects to allow users to interact with reality-creating objects in real time.

Museum: Refers to an establishment that conserves, restores, and exhibits a collection of artistic, cultural, historical, scientific objects that are of importance to human experiences.

Virtual Reality: Commonly abbreviated as VR is the most well-known digital reality technologies and was studied as early as in the 1980s. VR is able to produce an interactive and computer-generated experience by engrossing users within an artificial environment where interacting with the virtual articles are accomplished through auditory, visual, and haptic inputs.

Chapter 9
Challenges of Mobile Augmented Reality in Museums and Art Galleries for Visitors Suffering From Vision, Speech, and Learning Disabilities

Ajinkya Rajendrakumar Kunjir

https://orcid.org/0000-0001-7634-4115

Lakehead Univeristy, Canada

Krutika Ravindra Patil

MES College of Engineering, Pune, India

ABSTRACT

In Today's digital world, AR is a tech which imposes layers of virtual segments on the real world. Research Practitioners and Designers in all applications seem to be more concerned about the learning facilities than keeping the visitors engaged in public art exhibitions, Museums, and holiday tourist locations. These ignored circumstances have provoked studies to emphasize more on the usability of Mobile Augmented Reality (M.A.R.) at Art galleries and Museums. According to the recent surveys, the current M.A.R. applications at target locations focus on healthy people without any disabilities, and not on those with disabilities. This chapter recommends major design elements of M.A.R. at museums and art galleries, and highlights all the challenges faced by visitors suffering from visual, speech, and Learning Disorders. The research discusses the 11 vital elements which include Usability, Design, Motivation, Interaction, Perceived control, Satisfaction, Attention, and others involving engagement of M.A.R. necessary for building an effective M.A.R. application for disabled people.

DOI: 10.4018/978-1-7998-1796-3.ch009

Copyright © 2020, IGI Global. Copying or distributing in print or electronic forms without written permission of IGI Global is prohibited.

INTRODUCTION

Augmented Reality, also called as A.R. is a subpart of the Virtual Reality (V.R.) technology. A.R. is a recreation of V.R. which imposes several intrinsic layers of virtual content on the physical objects in the real environment. By imposing virtual content, it provides a medium to describe the physical object on a screen of any smart mobile device by directly pointing the device towards the object. The pervasive devices possess ubiquity for the public to get accustomed to the A.R. applications existing in the digital market. The fundamental difference between V.R. and A.R. is that V.R. is all about placing the user in a virtual environment where the sensations such as smell, touch, and view can be created artificially. A.R. is in the form of an application where the user needs to use the G.P.S. (Global Positioning System) of the smartphone to pinpoint it to the user's location and view the scene on displays (Mandy Bing, 2017). The appeal for implementing A.R. in Museums and Art galleries is obvious and concise- The technology permits rich media such as videos and images to lay over the real environments and enhance the user experience. Moving forward, the research focuses on Mobile Augmented Reality and its challenges for the visitors suffering from vision disabilities and impaired learnings. In this section, we are going to shed light on A.R., real-time applications of A.R., and A.R. in Museums.

AR: A Creative and Powerful Tool of Information

Being a platform for endless layers of Information, AR tools has discovered the potential ability to offer the visitors an extra pack of Information on their pocket-sized smartphone displays. On comparing with Q.R. scanning applications which makes use of standard tracking features, A.R. tools emphasize more on Deep learning and Image recognition methods for scanning the real world objects and putting all its cards on the table. Museums mostly make use of location-based A.R. applications, which enables the visitors to inspect the details of the real entities. Similar parallel researches are being conducted to allow visitors to save the Information and insights of real objects in their local phone storage for making it work offline. Offering more features strengthens the connections between visitors and museums. A.R. apps don't only create a medium to suck knowledge, but also makes one dive deeper into details by engaging the users by a super friendly G.U.I. (Graphical User Interface). Therefore, AR is also depicted as a creative tool for education.

M.A.R. (Mobile Augmented Reality)

Like we discussed in the above section, Mobile Augmented Reality can ideally be defined as a carry-and-go Augmented Reality in your pockets via smart devices such as mobile phones, tablets, P.D.A.'s and wearable devices. Alan B. Craig states that smart device acts as hardware for your A.R. software application, simply put (Alan, 2013). There is significant confusion between the concepts' portable A.R.' and 'Mobile Augmented Reality (A.R.)'. Portable AR allows the users to move the technology flask from one place to another. It's just like the definition of 'Energy' – Can be exchanged and Transferred, but cannot be created nor can be destroyed. Desktops and chargeable laptops are a few common examples of portable A.R. devices, whereas a compact mobile device can suit mobile A.R. example. The newest A.R. devices available for public use include Microsoft Holo Lens, Magic Leap, Oculus Rift, Samsung Gear V.R., H.T.C. Vive and others to be made available shortly. The below-given figure enlists the latest portable and M.A.R. applications for A.R. apps.

Figure 1. Portable & M.A.R applications

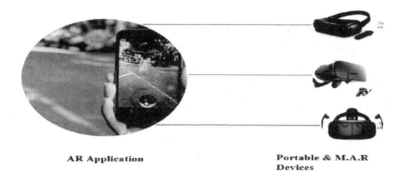

AR Application   Portable & M.A.R
                                  Devices

- **Advantages of M.A.R.:** The advantages related to M.A.R. are experiencing A.R. whenever and wherever wanted, Mobility, Easy Installation, and quick connectivity.
- **Disadvantages of M.A.R.:** The number of cons is equal as the number of pros, they say. M.A.R. also have many difficulties over their compatibility feature. The impactful ones include Environmental constraints, technology constraints, sophisticated user understanding, and complicated system architecture. One out of ten M.A.R. devices is non-repairable.

Despite having so many advantages in the applications of Museums and Art galleries, M.A.R. has disappointed and failed a lot of previous researches when being potentially tested and explored for increasing user experience and enhancing user engagement. The authors in their research mentioned that M.A.R. has unfortunately proven a failure for expanding the user experience for blind and hearing impaired (H.I.) people, especially the disabled people visiting museums and art galleries (J. Goss et.al, 2015). The reason for this drawback of M.A.R. is that there are technological constraints in the mobile devices which are not suitable to support the activities of people with H.I. and blind disorder. There are certain elements which are necessary to be embedded in M.A.R. devices for engaging disabled people including H.I. affected people at tourist locations such as Museums, Art exhibitions, Theatres and Artificial environments (7D, 8D Theatres). Section III focuses more on the designing elements for Mobile AR devices and explains how H.I. user engagement can be increased.

DESIGNING ELEMENTS FOR M.A.R. APPLICATION

The authors in their research study determined several major designing elements necessary for an A.R. application for accurate interaction and engagement of H.I. visitors in Museums and Art galleries (Esraa Jaffar Baker, 2017). The few critical elements of several stated were elaborated as Usability, Interaction, Motivation, Satisfaction, Perceived Control & Attention. The other components of interest which were defined but not emphasized much because of less credibility were Aesthetics, Curiosity, Self-efficacy, Enjoyment, and Interest. The elements are further discussed as follows:

Figure 2. M.A.R. Applications for engaging H.I. People

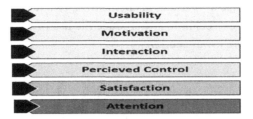

1. **Interaction:** These elements play a vital role as communication refers to the engagement of the user with the A.R. application. The application should be capable enough to dive the user for a secure connection flow with the application graphics. The nature of the form is directly dependent upon its interaction.

2. **Usability:** Usability is the element which is mostly related to 'Satisfiability' for the user with the application. There should be ease of use of the application to promote user engagement.

3. **Motivation:** The concept 'Motivation' refers to the ability of users to be willing to accompany the task. Once the user gets engaged with the app, he/she should thrive to achieve excellence and learn more about the application.

4. **Satisfaction:** The element creates delightful moments with the app, which is users fulfilling their application expectations. Research states that every user has an expected behavior from the application, the application fails satisfaction criteria if the expectation is not met to the point.

5. **Focused Attention:** Attention is just an element required to attract the user's awareness to engage funny conversations. Many previous studies (H.L O'Brien et al., 2010) & (Di Serio et al., 2013) found out that the application which attracted users attention was able to achieve engagement.

6. **Perceived Control:** The elements invites a feeling for users that the application is under their action control. The use creates an environment wherein the users feel influenced by the app and can bring out desired outcomes. This element itself involves other factors partially such as aesthetics, attention, enjoyment, and interest.

AR TECHNIQUES FOR MUSEUM ENVIRONMENTS

Art galleries and Museums typically display data in an indoor environment as the spaces are closed and objects are kept inside a boxed dome with walls enclosure. A.R. works pretty well in indoor or closed environments. Installing wireless sensors, location markers, surveillance cameras, and G.P.S. markers can enhance the favorable conditions for A.R. applications to function in the aspects of localization and network connectivity (Behzadan et al., 2008). The marker-based technique of A.R., which is generally intended for visual tracking, is proven to be beneficial for indoor experimental purposes. The only disadvantage of A.R. in indoors is invariances and inconsistencies in the light conditions, for visual tracking. Using visual markers is always a better hand option, but it keeps users from engaging with applications and indirectly leads to failure in user experience. It is suggested to hide the markers from users to avoid user distraction while displaying visual content (Ellsworth. J.J. et.al, 2016).

Previous studies have found out the new technologies use computer vision, deep learning, and a slight mixture of both to eliminate the use of markers in enclosures. To sound recent, Google Tango, now also upgraded to 'ARCore' is the newest technology to reduce the use of tags. We will discuss more Google Tango and its core concepts in the lower sections.

Google Tango

Google announced its Tango platform or 'The Tango project' in 2014. Tango was a real-time location & mapping A.R. platform which could efficiently resolve visual tracking issues. Tango was equipped to notify the real world about its device location using the principles of computer vision. The project Tango documentation mentioned that Google Tango was based on core features – Motion tracking, Area learning & depth perception to discard visual elements and markers (Retrieved from websource). We will discuss the three concepts in short and then proceed with the details of ARCore.

- **Motion Tracking:** Any smart device equipped with Motion tracking feature of Tango is capable of attaining localization in a 3D space. G.P.S. powered nodes can be detected outside the world, in outdoor environments. Tango preferably keeps a relative location to its origin, which corresponds to its location at the start of the service.
- **Area Learning:** These concepts allows the device to learn the previous area it has visited and stores the map information for future use and user convenience. A machine can improve its trajectory in the environment, also called as drift correction and re-localization. The relocalization data is stored in an A.D.F. file (A.D.F. also stands for Area Description File) which enables a Google Tango device to load and localize the previously visited areas.
- **Depth Perception:** Unlike Area Learning, Depth perception is not related to information learning. Depth Learning activates and enables a device with Google Tango to understand the distance between all the three axes.

ARCore

When Google Tango was launched in 2014, it was embedded into developer kits and required special sensors in the device to achieve the intended functionality. In no time, Google figured out the way of attaining A.R. in smart devices which has hardware on board. ARCore was deployed in Pixel devices at first and then followed by Pixel 2. The Tango project was shut down in late 2018 after Google's ARcore was a success for smart devices with no individual external sensors availability. Like Tango, even ARCore uses three key capabilities to integrate virtual content through your phone's camera (*ARcore also possess the critical concepts of Google Tango*) (Retrieved from web source):

Figure 3: ARCore concept of Environment Understanding

- **Environmental Understanding:** This feature of ARCore allows the device to detect the location and sizes of all types of surfaces like flat ground surface, edgy walls, or even disrupted coffee mug structures. ARcore detects these pointy features and makes them appear as planes to your applications. It can also acknowledge the boundaries and avail the Information on apps. One can place virtual objects resting on the planes.

- **Light Estimation:** ARCore is capable enough of detecting Information about the lightings in the environment and return, provide you with the average intensity and color correction of the captured image. To increase the sense of realism, the Information lets you light the virtual objects according to the environment around.

ARCore supports devices on Google play, China, and IoS. The other core features, such as User interaction, oriented points, Anchors, trackable, and Augmented Images, makes the involvement of ARCore with Unreal, Unity, and N.D.K. possible.

A PROTOTYPE SYSTEM ARCHITECTURE

The system architecture has been specifically designed to operate under closed environmental conditions such as in Museums, Art galleries, exhibitions, or any indoor environments. The process is divided into two stages, such as Object Modelling and Object refining. The steps have been discussed as follows:

Figure 4. 3D image modelling plan

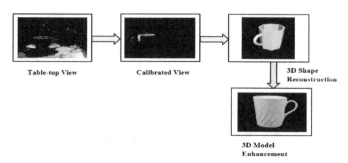

Object Modelling

In this very first stage, the broken or damaged objects are modeled accurately using Industry standard tools and photogrammetry techniques. The real artifacts are modeled using a few digital photographs and robust visualization techniques via A.R.'s marker-based methods. A combination of marker-based technology, along with with object visual tracking and A.R. Interface toolkit, can make partial or complete Augmentation possible.

Object Refining

In this stage, the 3D representation is refined using the modeling tools for 3D shape reconstruction and model enhancement. A variation of Complete Augmentation, also called as 'Realistic Augmentation' is achieved by incorporating computer graphics features, algorithms, and concepts into the Augmentation data. API's such as OpenGL and CUDA can be of extreme use for implementing realistic Augmentation. Content Acquisition and Content generation are two main steps to be undertaken in this particular stage of architecture. Object's shape reconstruction and model enhancements are conducted under these steps as well. For a content generation, the images of unbroken objects were captured by a high-quality camera(s) such as Canon E.O.S.- D30 at certain angles. For achieving photogrammetry, there are many inexpensive tools and techniques available in the digital market (S. Zheng, 2004), (E.P. Baltsavias, 2002), (P. Debevec, 2001). Thus the IMMR tool provides the base to generate 3D models from scratch and refine those using external systems. The 3D image modeling flow-plan along with the system architecture, is shown below in the form of figures and block diagram representation.

From figure 4, we understand the Image modeling pipeline in which the entire pipeline consists of 4 stages. Here, for example, we will consider a 'coffee mug.' In the first stage, a clear table-top view of the cup is captured using digital devices such as a high-resolution camera. The table view is converted into calibrated view to enhancing the image by resolving tiny defects caused by camera and fixing the daylight/night tuning. The object is isolated from the background and reconstructed into a model. The model enhancement is the last stage of the modeling pipeline, which is aided by 3D model enhancing tools and methods.

Figure 5. Prototype system architecture

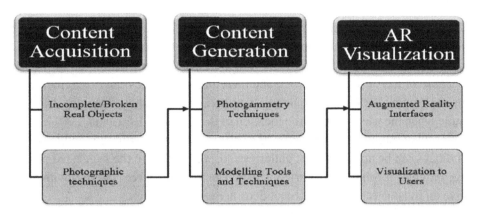

For the system architecture, in the content acquisition stage, the motive is to collect all the necessary data required for photographing and digitization of images. The digital images are captured when all the Information is gathered, and 3D model has generated then after. The later part of processing depends on the complexity of the object, such as center revolution factor analyzing complexity. Objects which are way too complicated would prefer using a photogrammetry method or a cheap laser scanning method. The photogenerated model is stored and used for creating visualizations in the graphical representation phase. In the last output stage, the modeled & stored image is given as an input to the A.R. interface toolkit, and the interface is visible to the users for interaction and engagement in an effective way.

AR VISUALIZATION TYPES

There is no indoor A.R. system as of yet, which complements the missing parts of missing objects with the virtual ones (M. White et al., 2004), (F. Liarokapis, 2002). Placing marker on objects does not sound a feasible method because it might be inappropriate for indoor exhibits such as museums or art galleries. The indoor exhibits can be sensitive and therefore, cannot be moved or touched. To applaud the missing objects, two simple visualization methods have been proposed, such as Partial Augmentation and Complete Augmentation.

Partial Augmentation

In a partial Augmentation scenario, a 3D broken object is placed in a scene fitting accurately into the real object. The Image registration algorithm is based on the toolkit and relies upon between the marker and camera distance. The experiment conducted by authors in their research stated that the gap between 1 to 2.5m is proportionally fit for increasing the registration error (P. Malbezin et al., 2002). To achieve partial Augmentation, the broken object is placed nearby the marker (approximately 20-30 cms) to minimize the registration error produced by A.R. toolkit and give out expected outcomes. Users can be provided with flexibility by placing the cameras anywhere in the line of sight of marker cards, offering the ability to move around the environments.

Complete Augmentation

Unlike Partial Augmentation, perfect Augmentation does not deal with rendering a small bit of Information to complete the circle of Augmentation. Full Augmentation is when the whole real object is represented in 3D in an exhibition Environment. For example, in a museum, you cannot show the live monuments because of the sensitivity factors, and therefore, the statues can be augmented for the users by using complete Augmentation techniques. In the previous researches, they have tried to represent a 3D Greek temple when the user points to the location of the temple (D. Stricker, 2001). Even though the temple is not present at that location currently, the users can view it using the mobile A.R. application. The same techniques can be applied to Art galleries and exhibitions. In the suggested prototype system, visual tracking provides a robust registration effect. The virtual objects overlap with the real objects marker and give an illusion that the real object does not exist in Reality.

The prototype system can be implemented in cases where the object is restricted from the user's physical interaction. Few of the disadvantages of complete Augmentation includes heavy rendering and modeling of the system. The more realistic the 3D augmented model is, the more are the possibilities for user engagement. User's smart devices should be capable enough to handle the heavy rendering caused by the A.R. application and not crash because of the shortage of processing speed and power.

DISCUSSION AND FUTURE WORK

In this paper, we highlight our research work with the proposed system architecture and a constructive pipeline for demonstrating the applications in Museums and Art galleries. We also covered the necessary elements required for constructing an efficient M.A.R. use for users suffering from disabilities such as learning disability, autism, Vision, and speech disability. The modeling phase explains and exposes all the objects in the scene and provide adaptable solutions for modeling tools. Customized tools can allow naïve users to generate fast 3D representations of real objects.

In indoor environments of Museums and Art galleries, real objects can be augmented with digital Information directly dependent on the environment. The section 'A.R. visualization types' discusses two cheap and efficient methods to generate partial and complete Augmentation for broken/damaged objects. Images and texts can also be superimposed onto the environment for increasing the realism and interaction with the users. The primary disadvantage of an A.R. system is the tracking algorithms effectiveness for great conditions or in bright conditions. To increase the interaction between disabled users and the A.R. environment, haptic devices, which are categorized into 'tactile' and 'kinesthetic' groups based on human sensing capabilities can be merged with the proposed system. The focus can be diverted on the wearable haptic devices for the excellent quality of interaction between the Augmentation of sensitive objects of museums and disabled people. Our current goal is to expand and extend the research across Museums and Art galleries for engaging disabled peoples interaction with the objects and get rid of the test data to start working on the real archaeological objects. Finally, we can promise that the proposed framework can be adopted by a variety of cultural organizations which require complete or partial Augmentation in indoor environments.

CONCLUSION

The research work presented in the previous researches is considered to be imperative in the realm and issues of augmented reality and museum studies when it comes to approaching a new application in the same areas for engaging disabled users. The significant elements necessary to engage disabled users suffering from learning, Vision, and speech impairment in a M.A.R. application is mentioned in this paper, along with the essential features and components. The prototype system has been described along with its architecture and Image modeling pipeline. Apart from the methodology, the A.R. visualization types such as partial and complete Augmentation have been explained in the lower sections, along with its advantages and disadvantages. The study also purposes the use of complete Augmentation in museums and Art galleries for engaging disabled people and enhancing their experience by adding suggestive remedies (haptic devices) for sensing human touch. The extension and expansion of this research have been deduced in the discussion and future work section above. All things considered, this study also provides a comprehensive background of the crossover of the museum and augmented technology and the establishment of museums through these exhibits.

ACKNOWLEDGMENT

We want to thank Dr. Sabah Mohammed for his expertise in this area of research and would also like to appreciate his significant contribution to this chapter. This research was much supported by Ms. Krutika Patil, who provided theories and comments that significantly improved the manuscript. We are immensely grateful to Dr. Vinaya Kunjir and the previous researchers for their comments on the script, although any errors identified are our own and should not hurt their reputations.

REFERENCES

Baker, S., Bakar, J., & Zulkifli, A. (2017). Elements of museum mobile augmented reality for engaging hearing-impaired visitors. *AIP Conference Proceedings*, 020033. doi:10.1063/1.5005366

Baltsavias, E. P. (2002). Object extraction and revision by image analysis using existing geospatial data and knowledge: State-of-the-art and steps towards operational systems, *International Archives of Photogammetry, part 2.*

Behzadan, A. H., Timm, B. W., & Kamat, V. R. (2008). General purpose modular hardware and software framework for mobile outdoor augmented reality applications in engineering. *Advanced Engineering Informatics*, 22(1), 90–105. doi:10.1016/j.aei.2007.08.005

Bing, M. (2017). *Augmented reality in museums*. Arts Management & Technology Laboratory.

Craig, A. (2013). *Understanding augmented reality*, Elsevier.

Debevec, P. (2001). Reconstructing and augmenting architecture with image-based modelling, rendering and lighting, *Proc. International Symposium on Virtual and Augmented Architecture*, Trinity College, Dublin. 10.1007/978-1-4471-0337-0_1

Ellsworth, J. J., Gossett, C. P., & Clements, K. (2016). *U.S. patent application No. 15/160, 996.*

Google ARcore. (n.d.). Retrieved from https://developers.google.com/ar/discover/

Goss, J., Kollmann, E., Reich, C., & Iacovelli, S. (2015). Understanding the multilingualism and communication of museum visitors who are deaf or hard of hearing, *Museums and Social Issues 10. Google Tango Documentation.* Retrieved from https://web.archive.org/web/20170714191228/https://developers.google.com/tango/apis/unity/

Liarokapis, F. (2002). *Augmented reality interfaces –architectures for visualising and interacting with virtual information.* (PhD thesis), University of Sussex, UK.

Malbezin, P., Piekarski, W., & Thomas, B. (2002). Measuring ARToolkit accuracy in long distance tracking experiments, *Poster session in 1ˢᵗ International Augmented Reality Toolkit Workshop*, Germany.

O'Brien, H. L., & Toms, E. G. (2010). The development and evaluation of a survey to measure user engagement. *Journal of the American Society for Information Science and Technology, 61*(1), 50–69. doi:10.1002/asi.21229

Serio, Di., Ibanez, M. B., & Kloos, C. D. (2013). *Impact of an augmented reality system on students motivation for a visual art course.* Computer and Education Society. doi:10.1016/j.compedu.2012.03.002

Stricker, D., & Daehne, P. (2001). Design and development issues for ARCHEOGUIDE: An augmented reality based cultural heritage on-site guide, *Proc. Of International Conference on Augmented Virtual Environments and three-dimensional imaging*, Mykonos, Greece.

White, W., & Liarokapis, F. (2004). *ARCOLite-an XML based system for building and presenting virtual museum exhibitions using Web3D and augmented reality. Proc. Theory and Practice of Computer Graphics* (pp. 94–101). Bournemouth, UK: IEEE Computer Society.

Zheng, S., Zhan, Z., & Zhang, Z. (2004). *A flexible and automatic 3D reconstruction method.* Istanbul, Turkey: ISPRS.

KEY TERMS AND DEFINITIONS

Calibration: In relations with measurement technology, calibration can be defined as a comparison of measurements obtained from a device for accuracy purposes.

GPS (Global Positioning System): A GPS is a global navigation satellite in general, but in terms of mobile devices, a G.P.S. chip is software encoded in a smart device which retrieves user's location via network technology.

Hearing Impaired (H.I.): Disabled people who are not able to hear partially or fully are classified as Hearing Impaired people.

Kinesthetic: Kinesthetic is a state in which there is a need of a physical touch or sense for the activity to happen. Say Kinesthetic Learning, is also called as tactile learning which takes place by the students carrying physical learning besides learning via audio or video.

Mobile Augmented Reality (M.A.R.): Unlike Portable AR, M.A.R. is an easy-to-go A.R. which one can carry in pockets and access remotely via a mobile device.

Perceived Control: Perceived control (P.C.) is a belief that one sees or he or she has control and power on their inner state of mind.

Photogrammetry: The process of transforming digital 2D photographs into a 3D mapping or a 3D model is defined as Photogammetry.

Relocalization: In technical terms, Relocalization is a repetitive process in which the localized Information is re-scaled and re-adjusted for backtracking purposes.

Visualization: Representation of textual content into patterns, pie charts, graphs, maps for ease of understanding is called as Visualization. Visualization can be Augmented, digital and also in form of videos.

Chapter 10
Role of Emotions in Interactive Museums:
How Art and Virtual Reality Affect Emotions

Giuliana Guazzaroni
Università Politecnica delle Marche, Italy

ABSTRACT

Virtual reality (VR), augmented reality (AR), and artificial intelligence (AI) are increasingly being used by educational institutions and museums worldwide. Visitors of museums and art galleries may live different layers of reality while enjoying works of art augmented with immersive VR. Research points out that this possibility may strongly affect human emotions. Digital technologies may allow forms of hybridization between flesh and technological objects within virtual or real spaces. They are interactive processes that may contribute to the redefinition of the relationship between identity and technology, between technology and body (Mainardi, 2013). Interactive museums and art galleries are real environments amplified, through information systems, which allow a shift between reality, and electronically manipulated immersive experiences. VR is emotionally engaging and a VR scenario may enhance emotional experience (Diemer et al., 2015) or induce an emotional change (Wu et al., 2016). The main purpose of this chapter is to verify how art and VR affect emotions.

INTRODUCTION

A new generation of mobile devices flanks the traditional media and the generation of desktop computers. The technologies, connected and wearable, submit humans to a multisensory perception where the real special dimension and the virtual one are mixed together extending and amplifying emotional stimuli (Griziotti, 2012). The bio-hypermedia is a neologism to highlight the fact that using these sophisticated devices there is a qualitative jump in the interaction. They are characterized by miniaturization and portability, and they can be worn. Nowadays, emotions are dominant and the interaction of five senses with

DOI: 10.4018/978-1-7998-1796-3.ch010

Copyright © 2020, IGI Global. Copying or distributing in print or electronic forms without written permission of IGI Global is prohibited.

the network is central. Handheld tools can augment reality by overlaying information, or they may become the hub of vital biological functions. In addition, anthropomorphic devices, like *Google Cardboard* (i.e. the VR platform developed by Google. Named for its fold-out cardboard viewer, a low-cost system to encourage interest in VR applications), increasingly flank screens. All these smart interfaces can augment human senses and impose extra attention or cognitive overload. The skilled user, after having overcome technological barriers, introduces settings, multimedia and applications in relation to the dynamics of his/her own life and aspirations. When mobile devices are constantly reshaped, their usage, content and performance evolve and transform themselves (Griziotti, 2012). Smart and wearable interfaces require the use of new habits, practices, rituals and gestures. The actions people enact using handheld devices or wearable technologies are repeated every day, each time a multisensory experience is required. Some people are dependent and need to perform these new gestures from when they wake up in the morning. All the actions people enact, each time they walk in a path superimposed with AR and VR, are repeated. The reiteration of new habits may represent a daily ritual. In a VR performance, the concept of ritual behavior of participants may become a contemporary social procedural. The ritual is the connection between the trials using AR and performance. The experience of 'Walking Eight' rebuilds the empathy of visitors with usual and homologated places, to protect those places, their uniqueness and complexity. Mobile device and VR facilities 'may represent access points to navigate the city, to observe different layers of reality, to redraw the urban geography and to explore the real environment. It is an emotional journey to observe also familiar places from different perspectives and angles: a continuous sliding between two worlds (real and virtual), an invitation to participation, reflection and rediscovery of public spaces' (Guazzaroni, 2013). In this context, 'Walking Eight' is an invite to dynamic reflection, an offer to walk usual places, of every city. An invite to re-collocate semantic fields relating to a city in unusual semantic fields, open to creative reflection and self-empowerment. It is a sort of performative city, a micro universe, characterized by the symbol of infinity ('eight'). It is also a stage; the stage of Leonardo Da Vinci renewed in a post-contemporary way to offer the vision of virtual tours and add information in museums and art galleries. The objective of this chapter is to explore how the combination of art and VR may affect human emotions. For this purpose, a real experience, regarding an art exhibit is described.

BACKGROUND

Brain research highlights the role of emotions in the fruition of art. Damasio (2000) uses the term emotion to refer to internal changes in the state of human body (e.g. chemical, visceral, muscular etc.) and the resulting changes in the nervous system. Emotions are not aware, and can be induced, for example by the sight of an object in a museum. They can create a specific emotional state, which can be a stimulus for the action. Emotions play a crucial role in an aesthetic experience. The visual act is not a passive recording of the physical environment, but an active construction that involves elaboration and analysis processes. Complex cognitive and affective psychic processes are involved when people visit an art gallery. Authors separate emotion from cognition, based on a differentiation of the cerebral hemispheres, placing the processing of emotions on the right hemisphere. When individuals live an aesthetic emotion, the action consists in the interest aroused by the artwork. The interest produces a mobilization of the whole organism based on the exclusive role of the perceived aesthetic object. The object is contemplated by the subject (e.g. visitor of a museum), if this occurs in an intense way the emotion can induce tears or other strong reactions (Mastandrea, 2011). The aesthetic emotion can generate enthusiasm and can lead to the social sharing of an emotional content (Frijda, 2007). The emotions human beings can experience in front of art are numerous, and like those experienced in everyday life. People can experience a ludic response (e.g. in front of a contemporary work of art), joyousness (e.g. in front of colors), or disgust (e.g. in front of cruel images). The emotions that a visitor of a museum can experience are analogous to everyday emotions. But they are different as they are induced by an artistic artefact (Mastandrea, 2011). The emotions similar to the 'utilitarian' ones are not true aesthetic emotion but they contribute to achieve it. First, the object of art should be perceived and recognized in its structural characteristics (e.g. lines, shapes, colors etc.). A physiological response will then be activated, followed by an expressive reaction, empathetically emotional. A contemplative reaction, more or less intense (e.g. admiration, amazement, fascination etc.) will result in a general benefit for the whole body (Mastandrea, 2011). Nathalie Bondil (2018), the director of Montreal Museum of Fine Arts (MMFA), believes that 'cultural experiences will soon be recognized, like physical activity currently, for their health benefits'. In fact, the 'neutral, beautiful, inspiring space' of a museum can improve mood, well-being, and offer depressed patients a chance to explore experiences and senses outside of their illness. Research suggests that the contact with art has a positive impact on people's health, especially in mental health treatment. As a result, doctors in Montreal, Canada, can prescribe museum visits to help both physical and mental ailments of patients. (BBC News, 2018). Emotion terms used for aesthetic generally embrace positive emotions. Several authors point out great beneficial effects of artworks for health. Menninghaus et al. (2018) affirm that 'aesthetic emotions are typically sought and savored for their own sake, with subjectively felt intensity and/or emotional arousal being rewards in their own right. The expression component of aesthetic emotions includes laughter, tears, and facial and bodily movements, along with applause or booing and words of praise or blame. Aesthetic emotions entail motivational approach and avoidance tendencies, specifically, tendencies toward prolonged, repeated, or interrupted exposure and wanting to possess aesthetically pleasing objects. They are experienced across a broad range of experiential domains and not coextensive with art-elicited emotions'. Aesthetic emotions represent a subgroup of the emotions paintings can provoke. They are indebted with specific aesthetic qualities, such as the power of an artwork to move, fascinate and surprise (Menninghaus et al., 2018). In immersive museums, VR and AR experiences boost the emotions guests can feel and attract younger people to visit heritage. In an authentic context, emotions play a relevant role in engaging students in a rich learning experience. Brain research has pointed out the role of emotions in learning and decision-making. In recent years, Damasio (2000) demonstrates that feelings are the results of the brain interpretation of emotions. He considers emotions as physical signals of the body reacting to external stimuli. Damasio (2000) is interested in the function emotions play in decision-making processes and in self-image (the personal view a person has of himself/herself). According to him, certain feelings are at the basis of human beings' survival. In fact, he argues that emotional regulatory processes preserve life and form cultural achievements. Damasio (2005) uses the term emotion to refer to internal changes in body state and resulting changes in the nervous system. Emotions are not conscious. On the other hand, emotions can be induced, for example by the sight of an object into a museum. They can create feelings, which supply the provocation for action. Learning in informal settings augments the range of emotions students can prove. In fact, they are immersed in a special context full of new inputs. Thus, a neurological base of how human brain reacts to artefacts or other interesting objects (e.g. archaeological finds) is important for educators and museums' staff to activate a proper mobile and ubiquitous environment (Guazzaroni, 2013). In a place of interest, augmented by technologies, the number of stimuli for users is elevate. Consequently, visitors activate complex neural responses in their brain. Neural responses will lead to specific actions, decision-making and learning. Another important neurological discovery is represented by mirror neurons. In fact, the human brain has multiple mirror neuron systems that specialize in executing and understanding the actions of others and their intentions, the social meaning of their behavior and their emotions. Rizzolatti and Fabbri-Destro (2008) think human beings' survival depends on 'understanding the actions, the intentions and emotions of others'. Mirror neurons allow people to interpret the minds of others not through logical thinking but through direct simulation, by feeling and not by thinking. This discovery has influenced numerous scientific disciplines. Mirror neurons unveil how students learn and why groups of people respond to body gesture, dance and artwork (Rizzolatti & Fabbri-Destro, 2008). When guests are in a museum and view, for example, the statue of a running athlete they experience, in their mind, the same thing: running. Thus, people can practice the same actions and emotions of others, observing their artworks as well. According to Freedberg and Gallese (2007), in fact, even artist's movements in producing artefacts let people experience a sort of 'empathetic engagement' by activating a correspondent simulation. Consequently, the mirror neuron research suggests that everything may happen in a museum or art gallery (interactive or not) is an important element to activate complex processes in the participants' brain. If a user observes an archaeological find (e.g. shin-guard) he/she can experience the action behind it and, consequently, learn how the object was effectively used. A student can be empathetic engaged by a find and he/she can amplify his/her own cultural experience of past heritage (Guazzaroni, 2013). Humans are social beings. They spend time observing others and trying to understand what they are doing and why. Mirror neurons were originally found in the monkey ventral premotor cortex, they are active both when a monkey does an action and when it observes another individual doing a similar action. The mirror mechanism appears to be a mechanism particularly well suited for imitation and learning. Classically, an individual observing an action done by another person not only understands what that individual is doing, but also why he/she is doing it (Rizzolatti & Craighero, 2005). Mirror neurons can be stimulated by work of arts. A team of neuroscientists led by Giacomo Rizzolatti is unraveling the mystery of mirror neurons and the relationship between human brain, art and positive behavior (Rizzolatti & Fabbri-Destro, 2008; Giannella & Cuoghi, 2013). During a research, original Greek statues activate the brain much more than electronically modified Greek ones, but the most interesting thing is that only the original sculptures activate those emotional areas where there are the mirror neurons of empathy (empathy is a Greek word that means: to feel inside). Therefore, the mechanism that these Greek sculptors 'invented' is not a bare activation of cerebral cortex and nervous circuits, but the power to hit emotional centers. Consequently, the good artist succeeds, with his/her work of art, to stimulate the emotional centers. Art may reinforce human empathy and imitation processes. Therefore, beauty generates additional beauty (Giannella & Cuoghi, 2013). Mirror neurons let people see the mind of others, through direct simulation, feeling and not thinking (Rizzolatti & Fabbri-Destro, 2008). If a user observes an archaeological find, he/she experiences the action behind the object and can be emphatically involved in an art exhibition. He/she can intensify his/her own cultural experience of heritage. Sophisticated technological tools are being distributed to more and more citizens. Mobile phones, tablets and other smart devices offer the possibility of interacting and staying fluidly connected to the mobile Internet (Alexander, 2004; Bruce, 2008). The consequence is that the mobile Internet may facilitate the development and the popularity of informal learning environments (Leone et al., 2010). Mobile and ubiquitous technologies may be effectively used to create learner-centered experiences in a museum (Guazzaroni & Leo, 2011). Users can enjoy artworks during a didactic experience. Moreover, museums are places for learning by exploration. Museums and other places of interest allow students to engage with authentic artefacts and create their own responses to the exhibition (Astic & Aunis, 2011). Museums are used as a resource by visitors and learners at all levels of formal education and by other users (e.g. groups of people, adult learners, communities etc.). Therefore, there are differences in the experiences and knowledge that people bring to and take away from a museum (Naismith & Smith, 2009). The challenge is providing flexible opportunities to appeal different visitors' interests. Learning is something active that engages students in a real experience. In fact, museums are suitable for exploration 'to make sense of the world'. Like other places of interest (e.g. historical towns), museums allow visitors to be attracted by artefacts. Users or students are generally encouraged to explore and discover exhibits to create meaning and build new knowledge and skills. According to the Italian philosopher Galimberti (2009), a sentimental dimension should be cultivated in young people. In fact, today's learners are subjected to many stimuli (e.g. school, television, sports, different baby-sitters etc. in the absence of an authentic communication with adults). When stimuli are excessive, compared to the capacity of elaborating them, the young person tends to suppress the sentimental dimension and consequently intelligence riskily evolves without the anchor of sense (Galimberti, 2009). Are the emergent projects, relating to urban experiences (augmented by smart technologies and aimed at exploring cities through an emotional lens) unconsciously trying to regain forgiven emotional and sentimental dimensions? Nold in *Emotional Cartography. Technologies of the Self* (2009) proposes a collection of essays centered on the profitable use of emotional maps. The declared objective is to 'explore the political, social and cultural implications of visualizing people's intimate biometric data and emotions using technology'. Over 2000 people have participated in bio mapping projects in over 25 towns all around the world. Participants re-explore local areas using a special device invented by Nold (2009) which indicates the emotional state of a person in conjunction with his/her geographical position. Thus, a map is created which visualizes interesting points based on users' emotions. Nold uses this methodology in different contexts (e.g. art, community development, science research, architectural, political consultations etc.). An emotional map can represent an interesting tool in an authentic experience. In fact, when users are immersed in a real environment, the emotional map can offer the possibility to better understand how different people have interpreted the location through their creations (e.g. stories, draws, recorded interviews etc.). This tool can be used for didactic purpose or for promoting cultural heritage (Guazzaroni, 2013). Walking the streets of a city is a way to discover points of interests and to create smart experiences. It is a sort of poetic rite and rhythm, a performance where each time participants raise their arms using a smartphone or other devices to detect synthetic objects. This concept may be related to a kind of contemporary oikos (in ancient Greek: οἶκος), which is the ancient Greek equivalent of household, house, or family. An oikos was the basic unit of society in Greek city-states. The term oikos may describe social groups. The contemporary oikos, includes citizens that share a sort of social interaction, be it through conversation or interaction. Consequently, the concept of oikos is often related to a specific location, even a virtual location can be included in this concept (e.g. daily interaction in the same virtual social media). Among the streets, within museums, or galleries, at each step a user may redraw the inner geography derived from the interaction of different visitors and from the geolocated information. The growing number of smartphones and smart wearable devices offers an instant interaction, and a very complex experience may arise from a real situation. For the sociologist Castells (1983) cities are an essential raw material in the production of human experience. For this reason, interactive art projects are increasingly used as a platform of expression. Museums' and art galleries' guests may enjoy different layers of reality while exploring works of art augmented with immersive VR experiences. Research points out that this possibility may strongly affect human emotions. Digital technologies may allow forms of hybridization between flesh and technological objects within

Figure 1. VR Experience in Palazzo Buonaccorsi, Macerata (Italy)

virtual and real spaces. They are interactive processes that may contribute to the redefinition of the relationship between identity and technology, between technology and body (Mainardi, 2013). The attention between visitors and museums shows that 'audiences want to feel connections between themselves and the environment they are experiencing. These connections take the form of both intellectual and emotional experiences. Emphasis is placed more heavily on positive emotions and emotional experiences' (Bedigan, 2016). Interactive museums and art galleries are real environments amplified, through information systems, which allow a shift between the experimentation of the reality, perceived through sensory organs, and the electronically manipulated reality to create immersive virtual experiences. VR, in this context, is emotionally engaging, and a VR scenario may enhance emotional experience (Diemer et al., 2015).

MAIN FOCUS OF THE CHAPTER

A Three-Dimensional First-Person Experience

Over the past few decades, VR has developed dramatically and is now employed in several fields, such as education, training, museum, industrial design, architecture, space exploration, medicine, rehabilitation, entertainment, model building and research in many fields of science. This technology can create a three-dimensional first-person experience by enveloping people in a virtual space (Torisu, 2016). VR represents a unique tool to simulate complex real situations and specific contexts in psychology. It offers researchers the opportunity to investigate human behavior in laboratory (e.g. mental disorders). Perception, fear, and exposure therapy reveal general aspects of the relation between perception and emotion. VR can induce emotional reactions, and is emotionally engaging (Diemer et al., 2015). Moreover, to tell a story, a narrative (i.e. storytelling), VR offers a proper scenario that may enhance experiential emotions. Research affirms that another VR phenomenon linked to emotions is presence. It is 'a dimensional construct and describes the extent to which a user feels present in a VR environment'

(Diemer et al., 2015). North and North (2018) emphasize that the sense of presence in VR can contribute to learning. This is because, the experience of high levels of presence is a key factor for learning and the user will be focused on the activity that occurs in the virtual environment. The association of presence and emotions in VR exposure therapy is a crucial issue for researchers. Presence is generally seen as a necessary mediator that allows real emotions to be activated by a virtual environment (Diemer et al., 2015). The sense of presence is considered a complex mental mechanism that is strongly related to humans' emotional reasoning abilities (Duarte et al., 2013; Diemer et al., 2015). More sophisticated technology is often thought to result in more presence. More emotional reactions are expected if the user wears a high-quality head-mounted display (HMD). Higher level of presence is experienced using more immersive VR systems. Research shows that the stronger the feelings involved (e.g. fear), the greater the correlation between presence and emotion (Diemer et al., 2015). VR may offer 'systematic human testing, training, and treatment environments that allow for the precise of complex, immersive, dynamic 3D stimulus presentations, within which sophisticated interaction, behavioral tracking, and performances recording is possible' (Rizzo & Kim, 2005). The association of presence and emotion in immersive VR has been studied in correlation with the exposure therapy. In these studies, the degree of presence of the immersive environment is commensurate with the fear it causes in patients (e.g. exposure to phobic stimuli, such as arachnophobia) (Rizzo et al., 2009). Through these exposures, individuals learn to confront the trauma and begin to think differently about it, leading to a marked decrease in levels of anxiety and other symptoms (Foa et al., 2007). To address this problem, researchers use VR to deliver exposure therapy by immersing patients in simulations of trauma-relevant environments that allow for precise control of stimulus conditions (Rizzo et al., 2009). More immersive, and isolated from real world, the VR environment, greater the sense of presence in the virtual scenario that will consequently produce more stimuli for the subject (Diemer et al., 2015). Participants feel a high level of presence when they are emotionally involved. Neutral stimuli do not inspire, while the involvement due to feelings of fear, or other, produce a greater sense of presence, compared to emotional states of calm and serenity (Diemer et al., 2015). An immersive environment can induce a change in people's emotional state, instigating different types of emotions (Wu et al., 2016). Moreover, presence in VR is commonly compared to the concept of immersion, or the perception of being physically present in a non-physical world, or a state of consciousness where the user experiences a virtual environment, which appears real and is perceived as real. Constant improvement in the ability to create presence will make someone genuinely believe he/she is experiencing another world. In fact, interacting is a powerful thing that greatly enhances the sense of presence. In addition to, letting users feel more present, it also keeps attention rooted in the virtual world. While the handlers are interacting, they are engaged and physically behaving like in a reality. The more the users behave like they are in reality, the more 'real' it potentially feels. Presence implies the implementation of a wide range of sensorial inputs and elements that can be controlled or manipulated by the user, and the improvement of the speed and fluidity with which the virtual environment responds to controls or manipulations (Hersko-Ronatas, 2017; Schwartz & Steptoe, 2018; Bonasio, 2019).

Empathetic Engagement to Digital Artefacts

Emotions are not conscious and a physical object (e.g. a work of art) in a street or a museum could stimulate them. They create effective feelings, which provide stimuli for human action. A protracted feeling state can represent a mood (Damasio, 2000). Learning or interacting in an informal environment augments the different range of emotions participants can experience as they are immersed in a specific

Figure 2. VR Experience in Pinacoteca P. Tacchi-Venturi, San Severino Marche (Italy)

context full of inputs. In a synthetic or augmented outdoor setting, the number of provocations is high. Neural consequences are consequently complex, as described by Damasio's theory. These responses can lead to peculiar single actions, learning and decision-making. Mirror neurons is a recent neurological discovery to see how the human brain interacts with objects, fine art and heritage. Mirror neuron systems are specialized in understanding the human actions, their intentions, as well as the social meaning of their behavior or emotions. An action is foreseeable when it activates, in the observer's brain, a correspondent representation. Even if the individual does not execute that action, the action is elicited and allows him/her to understand the meaning of what he saw (Rizzolatti & Craighero, 2005). When participants are in the streets, when they enjoy interactive performance, they naturally react to specific stimuli and to other people's movements. They may also activate a sort of empathetic engagement by starting a corresponding simulation to digital artefacts (Guazzaroni, 2013). Unobjectively live mapping does not indicate morphological features of a specific location, but the way people emotionally and digitally interact with the geography of a place. During performances, emotional content is collected, such as anecdotes, legends, stories, poetry, messages to be read in the future. In an open-air setting, performing bystanders are actively engaged in activating emotions and feelings through action and artefacts. In such a place, it is important to consider the decisive role mirror neuron plays in people's brains; visitors may experience action by observing objects (e.g. a digital picture suggesting a movement of the body). Historical, cultural and contextual aspects do not prevent the consideration of the importance of neural processes that result from the empathetic understanding of visual artworks (Freedberg & Gallese, 2007). At the same time, emotions are crucial to activate complex processes in humans' brains. Those important processes are at the basis of the action of museums' or art galleries' visitors. Virno (2004) said that 'each one of us is, and has always been, a virtuoso, a performing artist, at times mediocre or awkward, but, in any event, a virtuoso. In fact, the fundamental model of virtuosity, the experience that is the base of the concept, is the activity of the speaker. This is not the activity of a knowledgeable and erudite locutor, but of any locator. [...] Every utterance is a virtuosic performance. And this is so, also because, obviously, utterance

Figure 3. VR Experience in the Monastery of Santa Maria delle Rose, Sant'Angelo in Pontano (Italy)

is connected (directly or indirectly) to the presence of others'. According to Virno (2003), a speaking person becomes a phenomenon. For instance, there are some situations where humans communicate only what they say (e.g. phatic expressions, echolalia or religious words), in general each time the ritual characteristics of our language arise. These examples may be called 'performative absolute'. It appears during difficult situations. It is a sign of danger. For instance, an unpredictable output, or something not expected (e.g. an interrupted mobile phone call). In other words, it is a sort of 'cultural apocalypse', and during these events humans invent strategies or react using monologues to establish more predictable outputs during communication (Virno, 2003).

The Experience of 'Walking Eight', an Immersive Exhibition And Performance

'Walking Eight' is a micro universe, a kind of Indra's net to describe the non-dual basis of all existence. An Indra's net or a street poetry performance recreated into a museum to augment or to rebuild the empathy with homologated places, to protect those places, their uniqueness and complexity. 'Walking Eight' is an invite to dynamic reflection, an invite to walk usual places, of every city or land. An invite to re-collocate semantic fields relating to a place in unusual semantic fields, open to creative reflection and self-empowerment. 'Walking Eight' is a sort of performative interactive installation, a micro universe, characterized by the symbol of infinity ('eight'). This universe is based on an Italian town called Tolentino, situated in Marche Region. This town has been homologated in recent years and has lost lots of its traits. Nowadays, Tolentino looks like an anonymous town, like other towns after a homologation process, partly caused by a recent economic downturn. Moreover, in 2016 Tolentino was partially destroyed by different strong earthquakes. In the 'eight' of 'Walking Eight' are collocated different characters painted by the visual artist Tomas (Luca Tomassini). The characters are real people and they are taken from old photos of individuals living in Tolentino and performing their own life. The oil painted canvas is 13 meters long and partially wrapped in a pipe to represent time or a story that unfolds from an ancient papyrus. The second part of the space is a performative place where *Google Cardboards* and other Virtual reality visors (e.g. *Oculus Rift*) are offered to visitors. There are two mirrors to reflect performative people and the canvas. Using VR viewers participants may see a 360° performance where performers/actors reproduce gestures taken from the canvas (i.e. from the characters represented on canvas). The 360° performance takes place in Tolentino, in the same locations contained in the oil painting, actors use the same gestures, to strike the participant's 'mirror neurons' and to offer an unusual vision of the homologated Tolentino. A performativity 'eight', or an archive in progress, the 360° performance can be enriched with walking workshops. In fact, participants who visited 'Walking Eight' were invited to enter the 360° Virtual reality performance taking place in a walking workshop. The 'eight' is a performative stage, equipped with mirrors and systems to take photos of the visitors through 360° cameras, to gather information and performative acts. A record in progress to contrast, the tendency to homologation of the city, a boost to the creative and plural thinking to introduce new ideas, to ameliorate the real economy and to empower citizens and visitors. 'Walking Eight' was first showed in Tolentino during TOC Festival 2016 (on show from May 27 until June 13 at Palazzo Parisani-Bezzi – Museo Napoleonico, Tolentino, Italy). A compact edition of 'Walking Eight' was presented in Bologna, during Set Up+ Festival 2017). The installation was shown to the public at TOC Festival in Tolentino. TOC is an acronym for *Open Territorial Culture Festival*. The place where 'Walking Eight' was equipped is Palazzo Parisani-Bezzi. The palace hosts the Napoleonic Museum, and during the festival welcomed hundreds of visitors curious to discover the exhibition, the artists, and the spectacular halls of the noble floor where in 1797 Napoleon signed the Peace of Tolentino. During these days, a 'first performer' (Guazzaroni & Compagno, 2013) was placed in the room dedicated to 'Walking Eight' with the task of helping people using VR. A first performer is a kind of facilitator that helps the public to interact with the artistic work and the technologies available for fruition. Moreover, 33 selected participants were invited to complete a test and leave comments for the evaluation of the experience.

The participants had to decide:

1.   If the virtual reality (VR) experience was fun;
2.   If the virtual reality (VR) experience improved their inner emotional engagement with fine art;
3.   If they would promote virtual reality (VR) experiences to other visitors;
4.   If they had technological difficulties.

Most of the 33 users (78%) decided that the VR experience linked to the canvas was fun (26 out of 33; see graphic n.1). In fact, the first performer said that people, mostly children, were fascinated by the VR experience (Table 1).

The selected visitors had to decide if the VR experience improved their emotional bond with art, they chiefly thought (57%) that their engagement was enough improved (19 out of 33). While 11 out of 33 believed the experience was really engaging (33%), and they could improve their inner relationship with the artwork (Table 2).

Most (81%) of the interviewed would promote similar experiences to other visitors (27 out of 33) (Table 3).

Table 1.

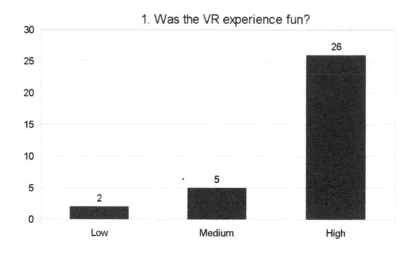

Table 2.

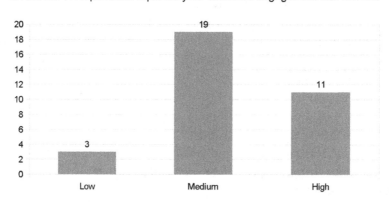

Table 3.

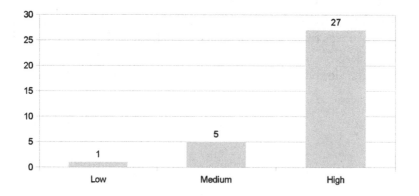

Figure 4. VR Experience of 'Walking Eight' in Palazzo Parisani Bezzi, Tolentino (Italy)

Most of the selected participants (84%) decided that they did not have any difficulty using VR facilities (e.g. a head mounted display) to enjoy the 'Walking Eight' experience. 'Walking Eight' is an invite to reflection, to cultivate inner and emotional life, an invite to walk usual places with different eyes. An invite to re-collocate semantic fields relating to a place in unusual semantic fields, open to creative reflection and self-empowerment. 'Walking Eight' is a performative and interactive installation, a micro universe, characterized by the symbol of infinity ('eight'). The 33 selected visitors were adults that accepted the invitation to enjoy the immersive VR experience relating to the canvas. For the most part, they decided that the experience was amusing. In fact, they could discover their town from different points of view and they really enjoyed the experience (78%). The interviewed believed that the VR experience had improved their emotional bond with art, they mainly thought that their engagement was plenty developed (57%). On the other hand, 33% thought 'Walking Eight' was really engaging and they could strongly ameliorate their interior relationship with the artwork. 81% of the participants were enthusiastic, and they would promote the VR experience and the emotional tour to other visitors. Most of the visitors did not have any difficulty using a VR headset (84%).

Issues, Controversies, Problems

'Walking Eight' was created to make visitors perform a unique experience in an art gallery. The public may dynamically live something special, while appreciating paintings and installations. The trial was carefully prepared to create a joyful performance, where technology is conceived as playful and pleasing. To achieve this goal, as VR is not a daily practice for most of the guests, a first performer was introduced to animate the art gallery showing how to play with art and technology. The outcomes of the experience, obtained using ex post questionnaires and direct observation, enlighten that individuals participating in vanguard experiences, enhanced by technologies, need clear explanation and modelling of what they are going to live before starting the real experience, to avoid confusion and lack of interest. The first phase regards the choice of technologies and content to create a positive experience for the exhibition event. The second phase is devoted to engaging guests in the performance and in activating their mirror neurons. This is the reason why a first performer was introduced to model the experience visitors could live interacting with VR and visual art. Most of the participants believed that it was engaging and exciting to experience 'Walking Eight'. It allowed them to deal with art in a different and touching way. Thanks to immersive VR facilities there was no longer a simple contemplation, but a real opportunity to experience the exhibition as a whole. Moreover, it becomes a real chance to share feelings with other spectators. A new way to enjoy contemporary art merged in a new surreal dimension, the dimension of creativity and art (Guazzaroni & Compagno, 2013). The evaluation has revealed that most of the visitors heartily enjoyed the exhibition. They could perform an active experience and abandon the apathy of the user's role in a traditional art gallery or museum. The best outcomes are relating to the playfulness of the performance. A kind of modern circus based on VR, on the mutable and unpredictable properties of the canvas that was enriched of synthetic elements, as well as on the involvement of the visitor invited by a first performer to enter a surreal world. The performance promoted an emotional bond with contemporary art. Moreover, most of the spectators would have recommended such experiences to other people. The whole experience originates a format for contemporary art galleries where a first performer engages visitors, modelling the experience to activate other people's mirror neurons. According to the philosophers Madary and Metzinger (2016) VR is the representation of 'possible worlds' and 'possible selves' with the aim of creating a 'sense of presence' in the user. The same phenomenon occurs in the best 'theories of mind', which create internal models of the world (i.e. virtual neural representations) and generate predictive hypotheses (Madary & Metzinger, 2016). As for the exhibition of 'Walking Eight', VR immersive technologies can help to facilitate empathy or destroy it. These methods are powerful tools for psychological manipulation. Consequently, it is important to establish ethical standards. Unlike physical environments, immersive VR environments can be modified rapidly and simply with the goal of influencing users' behavior. Actions while in the VR environment can have a lasting psychological impact after subjects return to the real physical world. (Madary & Metzinger, 2016). In VR, for instance, one might have the illusion of being embodied in a human avatar with specific characteristics. A user can have the illusion of being embodied in an avatar of a different size, age, or skin color. In all these cases, the illusory nature of virtual worlds is preserved after leaving the virtual environment. Accordingly, VR technology can induce illusions of embodiment and it may represent a new risk generated by using VR. Rosenberg et al. (2013) have people perform tasks in a virtual smart city. Avatars could fly through the smart city either using a helicopter or by their own body movements, like superheroes. They find out that subjects given the superpower are more likely to show altruistic behavior afterwards out the VR environment. What is historically new in an immersive VR environment is that it creates not only new risks, but also new ethical and legal dimensions. This is due to the fact that a virtual reality (i.e. human mind) is deeply embedded in another virtual reality: the conscious human mind, which evolved under certain specific conditions and in millions of years. Now the mind is informatively tangled with technical systems for the representation of possible realities (Madary & Metzinger, 2016).

SOLUTIONS AND RECOMMENDATIONS

Some risks may arise with the use of immersive VR and new ethical recommendations seems more and more necessary by different researchers (Madary & Metzinger, 2016). The trial experience of 'Walking Eight' represents a creative use of immersive VR worlds. In this artistic context VR is used to help the user to enhance his/her own experience of a homologated town with elements from the past and the future. The evaluation of the artistic performance reveals that most of the visitors emphatically enjoyed the exhibition. In fact, they could perform a creative and active experience. They abandoned the apathy of visitors in traditional galleries. The best outcomes of 'Walking Eight' are relating to the playfulness of the performance and to the developing of independent creative thinking. Visitors could see their town from a different perspective. They were offered an emotional map of it. They could enter the artistic canvas using VR viewers and live their place from a different point of view. At the end of the VR performance, they felt relieved from everyday routine and enjoyed an imaginative world. Like in Rosenberg et al. (2013) experience, the visitors of 'Walking Eight', after the immersion in the 360° VR performance, felt more empathetic with their real context (both inhabitants and places). In this case, an art exhibition supported the efforts to empower the local community. Museums and art gallery should use creatively VR and AR facilities to let visitors be aware of their real background, develop their creative thinking and ameliorate social and cultural context. Artists, on the other hand, may represent sort of facilitators helping to develop positive actions in smart cities of the future, or to educate visitors to active citizenship.

FUTURE RESEARCH DIRECTIONS

In coming years people will experience more of their bodies brought into VR in ever greater detail, and new and incredible opportunities to make worlds more interactive and reactive to various behaviors. Museums and art galleries will appear more and more virtual and smart. Interactive objects and complex technological experience will be implemented. AI will dominate as well, offering rich interactive experience. There will be no boundaries between visitors and artwork, visitors will be part of the artwork. There will be more and more interaction from people. The combination of exploration and participation in interactive museums will keep audiences engaged and able to create unique experiences. According to Teamlab a Tokyo-based art collective (2018), 'each visitor will have their own narrative'. Narratives will be different and adequate to different interests. In the very near future VR, AR, AI, mobile learning and ubiquitous facilities will play a more and more important role in digital and interactive heritage. Mobile strategies will include education and interpretation. Especially, edutainment will be an engaging way to learn in a gallery. Consequently, more and more museums or cities will adopt new interpreting strategies including mobile and ubiquitous learning, in addition with multisensory augmented experiences. 'Walking Eight' represents a joyful way to promote contemporary art while stimulating an emotional bond with the town or heritage. Audience appreciates the immersive creative experience. Local government have seen VR artistic experience as a way to be innovative and competitive. Nevertheless, VR to enhance art and museums needs more usable practical experience and people who currently use it are ahead of the curve. One of the main reasons is that it is not a usual practice for every mobile customer. Cities may offer visitors different narrations through AR, VR and AI. The smart city of the future should provide rich culture and educational facilities for many singular individuals who need a personalized and inclusive experience (Guazzaroni, 2012).

CONCLUSION

The study brings to light the positive influence that a VR exhibition arrangement has on the emotions of users and on their satisfaction. Summarizing the main points of the chapter, visitors are affected by heritage and art if their emotions are stimulated. Mirror neurons play an important role, as this neurological mechanism stimulate real empathy of the audience. VR immersive environments are powerful tools that can induce user's emotion change. In fact, VR technology may generate a simulated immersion that may relieve emotional stress (Wu et al., 2016). VR immersion is also used as exposure therapy for post-traumatic stress disorder (PTSD) (Rizzo et al., 2009). Art stimulates neural activity, and the contact with culture and art can really help patient's well-being. In fact, since 2018 a select group of physicians in Canada have been able to prescribe museum visits as treatment for an array of ailments (Solly, 2018). Moreover, using immersive technologies, audience of museums and art galleries may live different layers of reality while enjoying works of art augmented with immersive VR experiences. Research points out that this possibility may strongly affect human emotions. 'Walking Eight' is an artistic VR art experience. The result of this trial research draws attention to the fact that by designing an exhibit that meets with the interests of visitors, the museum can arouse their emotions. These results, seemingly of a small nature, can instead have an enormous impact for a museum in terms of reaching its cultural and economic goals. Therefore, to excite emotions and establish an empathetic relationship of communication with visitors is crucial to engage visitors and to promote active interaction. A number of different qualities are essential in an exhibit arrangement. In fact, it must be engaging and interactive, encourage active participation; provide a large quantity of stimuli for neurons, create a pleasant a joyful atmosphere, stimulate active citizenship, and creative mind (Gardner, 2006). The final goal must be to make art accessible and appealing to every kind of audience, offering different narratives. Summing up, exhibit arrangement, if designed in such a way as to interact with visitors and respond to their needs, influences their emotions to a significant degree. In the future, this topic could be investigated further by focusing attention on offering rich interactive experience, removing boundaries between visitors and artwork, promoting live interaction, exploration and participation in interactive museums, offering inclusive and personalized narratives and developing user's creative thinking.

REFERENCES

Alexander, B. (2004). Going nomadic: Mobile learning in higher education. *EDUCAUSE Review*, *39*(5), 28–35. Retrieved from http://www.educause.edu/EDUCAUSE+Review/EDUCAUSEReviewMagazineVolume39/GoingNomadicMobileLearninginHi/157921

Astic, I., & Aunis, C. (2011). A ubiquitous mobile edutainment application for learning science through play. *Proceedings of Museums and the Web 2011. Archives & Museum Informatics*, Toronto. Retrieved from: http://conference.archimuse.com/mw2011/papers/a_ubiquitous_mobile_edutainment_application_fo

Bedigan, K. M. (2016). Developing emotions: Perceptions of emotional responses in museums. *Mediterranean Archaeology and Archaeometry*, 16(5), 87–95. Retrieved from http://maajournal.com/Issues/2016/Vol16-5/Full9.pdf

Bonasio, A. (2019). *Scientists Use Yawning to Study Social Presence in VR*. Retrieved from: https://vrscout.com/news/yawning-social-presence-vr-study/

Bruce, B. C. (2008). Ubiquitous learning, ubiquitous computing, and lived experience. In C. Jones, M. Zenios & A. Jesmont (eds.). *Proceedings of the Sixth International Conference on Networked Learning*, Halkidiki, Greece. Retrieved from: http://www.networkedlearningconference.org.uk/past/nlc2008/abstracts/PDFs/Bruce_583-590.pdf

Castells, M. (1983). *The City and the Grassroots: A Cross-Cultural Theory of Urban Social Movements.* Berkeley, CA: University of California Press.

ChiuE. (2018). *The Future Museum.* Retrieved from https://www.jwtintelligence.com/2018/09/the-future-museum/

Damasio, A. R. (2000). *The Feeling of what Happens: Body, Emotion and the Making of Consciousness.* New York, USA: Harcourt Brace.

Damasio, A. R. (2005). Feeling our Emotions. *Scientific American.* Retrieved from http://www.scientificamerican.com/article.cfm?id=feeling-our-emotions

Diemer, J., Alpers, G. W., Peperkorn, H. M., Shiban, Y., & Mühlberger, A. (2015). The impact of perception and presence on emotional reaction: A review of research in virtual reality. *Frontiers in Psychology,* Retrieved from https://www.ncbi.nlm.nih.gov/pubmed/25688218

Duarte, E., Rebelo, F., Teixeira, L., Vilar, E., Teles, J., & Noriega, P. (2013). Sense of Presence in a VR-Based Study on Behavioral Compliance with Warnings. In A. Marcus (Ed.), *Design, User Experience, and Usability. User Experience in Novel Technological Environments. DUXU 2013. Lecture Notes in Computer Science* (Vol. 8014). Berlin, Heidelberg: Springer. doi:10.1007/978-3-642-39238-2_40

Foa, E. B., Hembree, E. A., & Rothbaum, B. O. (2007). *Treatments that Work. Prolonged Exposure Therapy for PTSD: Emotional Processing of Traumatic Experiences: Therapist Guide.* New York, NY, US: Oxford University Press; doi:10.1093/med:psych/9780195308501.001.0001

Freedberg, D., & Gallese, V. (2007). Motion, emotion and empathy in aesthetic experience. *Trends in Cognitive Sciences, 11*(5), 197–203. Retrieved from http://www.unipr.it/arpa/mirror/pubs/pdffiles/Gallese/Freedberg-Gallese%202007.pdf. doi:10.1016/j.tics.2007.02.003 PMID:17347026

Frijda, N. H. (2007). *The laws of emotion.* Mahwah, NJ, US: Lawrence Erlbaum Associates Publishers.

Galimberti, U. (2009). I miti del nostro tempo. Milano, IT: Feltrinelli.

Gardner, H. (2006). *Five Minds for the Future.* Boston, MA: Harvard Business School Press.

Giannella, S., & Cuoghi, M. (2013). *A Parma, studiando i neuroni, hanno capito perché il bello e il buono accendono il nostro cervello.* Retrieved from https://www.giannellachannel.info/neuroni-specchio-parma-perche-bello-e-buono-accendono-cervello/

Griziotti, G. (2012). Bring your own device. *Uninomade 2.0.* Retrieved from http://www.uninomade.org/bring-your-own-device

Griziotti, G. (2013). Sotto il regime della precarietà. Bring your own device. In G. Griziotti (Ed.), *Bioipermedia Moltitudini Connesse, Alfabeta2, 29(2).*

Guazzaroni, G. (2012). *Experiential Mapping of Museum Augmented Places – Using Mobile Devices for Learning.* Saarbrücken, D: LAP.

Guazzaroni, G. (2013). The ritual and the rhythm: Interacting with augmented reality, visual poetry and storytelling across the streets of scattered L'Aquila. *eLearning Papers on Design for Learning Spaces and Innovative Classrooms* (34).

Guazzaroni, G., & Compagno, M. (2013). AR moulded-objects performing Giuseppe Verdi's 200th birthday. In Archeomatica, 4, 38-41.

Guazzaroni, G., & Leo, T. (2011). *Emotional Mapping of a Place of Interest Using Mobile Devices for Learning*. In I. Arnedillo Sánchez, & P. Isaías (Eds.) *Proceedings of IADIS International Conference on Mobile Learning* (pp. 277-281) Avila, E.

Hersko-Ronatas, A. (2017). *Presence in Virtual Reality*. Retrieved from https://blogs.brown.edu/gaspee/presence-in-virtual-reality/

Lave, J., & Wenger, E. (1991). *Situated Learning: Legitimate Peripheral Participation*. Cambridge, UK: Cambridge University Press. doi:10.1017/CBO9780511815355

Leone, S., Guazzaroni, G., Carletti, L., & Leo, T. (2010). The increasing need of validation of non-formal and informal learning. The case of the community of practice "WEBM.ORG". *Proceeding of IADIS International Conference on Cognition and Exploratory Learning in Digital Age* CELDA 2010, Timisoara.

Madary, M., & Metzinger, T. K. (2016). Real virtuality: A code of ethical conduct. *Recommendations for Good Scientific Practice and the Consumers of VR-Technology. Front. Robot and AI*, 3(3). Retrieved from https://www.frontiersin.org/articles/10.3389/frobt.2016.00003/full

Mastandrea, S. (2011). Il ruolo delle emozioni nell'esperienza estetica. *Arte, Psicologia e Realismo*, 48.

Menninghaus, W., Wagner, V., Wassiliwizky, E., Schindler, I., Hanich, J., Jacobsen, T., & Koelsch, S. (2018). What are aesthetic emotions? *Psychological Review*, *126*, Retrieved from https://www.researchgate.net/publication/327779286_What_Are_Aesthetic_Emotions/link/5ba3e7c0a6fdccd3cb662478/download PMID:30802122

Naismith, L., & Smith, M. P. (2009). Using mobile technologies for multimedia tours in a traditional museum setting. In M. Ally (Ed.), *Mobile Learning. Transforming the Delivery of Education and Training. AU Press*. Edmonton: Athabasca University; Retrieved from http://www.aupress.ca/books/120155/ebook/12_Mohamed_Ally_2009-Article12.pdf

News, B. B. C. (2018). *Montreal museum partners with doctors to 'prescribe' art*. Retrieved from https://www.bbc.com/news/world-us-canada-45972348

Nold, C. (2009). *Emotional Cartography. Technologies of the Self*, Retrieved from http://emotionalcartography.net

North, M. M., & North, S. (2018). The sense of presence exploration in virtual reality therapy. *Journal of Universal Computer Science*, *24*, 72–84.

Rizzo, A., & Kim, G. J. (2005). A SWOT analysis of the field of virtual reality rehabilitation and therapy. *Presence (Cambridge, Mass.)*, *14*(2), 119–146. doi:10.1162/1054746053967094

Rizzo, A., Reger, G., Gahm, G., Difede, J., & Rothbaum, B. O. (2009). Virtual reality exposure therapy for combat-related PTSD. In P. J. Shiromani, T. M. Keane, & J. E. LeDoux (Eds.), *Post-traumatic stress disorder: Basic science and clinical practice* (pp. 375–399). Totowa, NJ, US: Humana Press; doi:10.1007/978-1-60327-329-9_18

Rizzolatti, G., & Craighero, L. (2005). Mirror neuron: a neurological approach to empathy. In J. P. Changeux, A. R. Damasio, W. Singer, & Y. Christen (Eds.), *Neurobiology of Human Values. Research and Perspectives in Neurosciences*. Berlin, Heidelberg: Springer; Retrieved from http://robotcub.org/misc/papers/06_Rizzolatti_Craighero.pdf doi:10.1007/3-540-29803-7_9

Rizzolatti, G., & Fabbri-Destro, M. (2008). The mirror system and its role in social cognition. *Current Opionion in Neurobiology*, Retrieved from http://cogsci.bme.hu/~gkovacs/letoltes/mirror.pdf

Rosenberg, R., Baughman, S., & Bailenson, J. (2013). Virtual superheroes: Using superpowers in virtual reality to encourage prosocial behavior. *PLoS One*, 8. PMID:23383029

Schwartz, R., & Steptoe, W. (2018). The Immersive VR self: Performance, embodiment and presence in immersive virtual reality environments. *A Networked Self and Human Augmentics, AI, Sentience*. Retrieved from https://research.fb.com/publications/the-immersive-vr-self-performance-embodiment-and-presence-in-immersive-virtual-reality-environments/

Solly, M. (2018). *Canadian Doctors Will Soon Be Able to Prescribe Museum Visits as Treatment*. Retrieved from https://www.smithsonianmag.com/smart-news/canadian-doctors-will-soon-be-able-prescribe-museum-visits-180970599

Torisu, T. (2016). *Sense of Presence in Social VR Experience*. Retrieved from http://www.interactivearchitecture.org/sense-of-presence-in-social-vr-experience.html

Virno, P. (2003). Quando il Verbo si fa Carne. Linguaggio e Natura Umana. Torino, IT: Bollati Boringhieri.

Virno, P. (2004). *A Grammar of the Multitude: For an Analysis of Contemporary Forms of Life*. Los Angeles, CA: Semiotext(e) Foreign Agents Series. Retrieved from http://www.generation-online.org/c/fcmultitude3.htm

Wu, D., Weng, D. & Xue, S. (2016). Virtual Reality System as an affective medium to induce specific emotion: A validation study. *Electronic Imaging*, 1(6).

ADDITIONAL READING

Ahn, S. J., Bailenson, J., & Park, D. (2014). Short- and long-term effects of embodied experiences in immersive virtual environments on environmental locus of control and behavior. *Computers in Human Behavior*, *39*, 235–245. doi:10.1016/j.chb.2014.07.025

Guazzaroni, G. (2013). Piegare la tecnologia alla creatività. Superfici specchianti, gesti, forme e linguaggi non scontati. La narrazione dell'Aquila in realtà aumentata. In G. Griziotti (Ed.), *Bioipermedia Moltitudini Connesse. Alfabeta2 (29), 4*.

Guazzaroni, G. (2019). *Virtual and Augmented Reality in Mental Health Treatment* (pp. 1–335). Hershey, PA: IGI Global. doi:10.4018/978-1-5225-7168-1

Guazzaroni, G., Aguzzi, E., Lautizi, C., & Settembri, A. (2015). Convinzioni ingenue sull'infinito e realtà aumentata nella scuola dell'infanzia. In L. Salvucci (Ed.) Strumenti per la Didattica della Matematica. Ricerche, esperienze, buone pratiche. Milano, IT: Franco Angeli.

Leo, T., Manganello, F., & Chen, N. S. (2010). From the learning work to the learning adventure. In *Proceedings of EDEN 2010*. Valencia, E. June, 2010.

Levine, L. J., & Pizarro, D. A. (2004). Emotion and memory research: A grumpy overview. *Social Cognition*, 22(5, Special issue), 530–554.

Maffesoli, M. (2009) Icone d'oggi. Le nostre idol@trie postmoderne. Palermo, IT: Sellerio.

O'Brolcháin, F., Jacquemard, T., Monaghan, D., O'Connor, N., Novitzky, P., & Gordijn, B. (2016). The convergence of virtual reality and social networks: Threats to privacy and autonomy. *Science and Engineering Ethics*, 22(1), 1–29. doi:10.100711948-014-9621-1 PMID:25552240

Riva, G., Waterworth, John A., Waterworth, Eva L. & Mantovani, F. (2009). From intention to action: The role of presence. *New Ideas in Psychology*, 1–14.

Rizzolatti, G., Fogassi, L., & Gallese, V. (2009). The mirror neuron system: A motor-based mechanism for action and intention understanding. In M. S. Gazzaniga (Ed.), The Cognitive Neurosciences (4 ed., pp. 625-640). Cambridge, MA: MIT Press.

Rizzolatti, G., Semi, A. A., & Fabbri-Destro, M. (2014). Linking psychoanalysis with neuroscience: The concept of ego. *Neuropsychologia*, *55*, 143–148. doi:10.1016/j.neuropsychologia.2013.10.003 PMID:24140952

Scherer, K. R. (2009). Emotions are emergent processes: They require a dynamic computational architecture. *Philosophical Transactions of the Royal Society of London. Series B, Biological Sciences*, *364*(1535), 3459–3474. doi:10.1098/rstb.2009.0141 PMID:19884141

Sedikides, C., Wildschut, T., Routledge, C., Arndt, J., Hepper, E. G., & Zhou, X. (2015). To nostalgize: Mixing memory with affect and desire. *Advances in Experimental Social Psychology*, *51*, 189–273. doi:10.1016/bs.aesp.2014.10.001

Shimizu, H., Yuasa, M., & Anderson, D. (2014). The significance of research on visitors' long-term memories with nostalgic responses in socio-cultural history museums. *Bulletin of Japan Museum Management Academy*, *18*, 19–25.

Vessel, E. A., Starr, G. G., & Rubin, N. (2012). The brain on art: Intense aesthetic experience activates the default mode network. *Frontiers in Human Neuroscience*, *6*(66). PMID:22529785

KEY TERMS AND DEFINITIONS

Augmented Reality: Augmented reality provides an overview of sensory integration with the perception that the user has of the environment in which he/she is located (in a real environment where the user interacts with objects). It is a superimposition of different levels of information integrated with real objects.

Emotional Mapping (or Bio Mapping): It is a methodology for visualizing people's reaction to the external world (Nold, 2009). It is a methodology and tool to get the participants involved in the experience. It does not indicate the socio-political or morphological characteristics of a location, but the way citizens or students emotionally interact with it.

Immersion: It is the perception of being physically present in a non-physical world, or a state of consciousness where the user experiences a virtual environment, which appears real and is perceived as real.

Immersive Learning Environment: A virtual environment where students can connect, interact, find 360-degree learning objects and complete educational tasks wearing a special head-mounted display. **Informal learning**: Informal learning allows people to learn from daily experience, within the individual's environment (e.g. family, friends, other students etc.) and outside the formal established organization. Consequently, learning does not happen in traditional spaces and it is not centred on the teacher. Today's learners can create and share content and aggregate themselves in informal social networks (Leone, Guazzaroni, Carletti & Leo, 2010). Here the boundaries between learning, gaming, being a citizen, being a tourist are not well-defined.

Mobile and Ubiquitous Learning: Learning is not the transmission of abstract and decontextualized knowledge, but a complex social process where knowledge is co-constructed by a community of learners. Such learning is situated in a real context and embedded within a social and physical environment. During Mobile and Ubiquitous Learning experiences participants are immersed in a place of interest and they learn through the interaction with real objects. Learning is a process of continuous interaction with the real-world where students continually reanalyse and reinterpret new information and its relations to reality (Lave & Wenger, 1991).

Smart City: The concept of a smart city or intelligent city describes a developed urban area that creates sustainable economic development and high-quality life by excelling in multiple key areas: economy, mobility, environment, people, living, education and government. Excelling in these key areas may be achieved through human capital, social capital, relational capital, education and ICT infrastructure as important drivers of urban growth.

Virtual Reality (VR): The possibility to immerse in a completely virtual world using special goggles to visualize computer graphics or computer sound.

Virtual and Augmented Reality Performance: An experience of mixed reality through the layering of real and virtual elements. Virtual objects are synthetic artworks created by artists, which can be detected using mobile devices and augmented reality facilities or immersive 360° experiences.

Chapter 11
Digit(al)isation in Museums:
Civitas Project – AR, VR, Multisensorial and Multiuser Experiences at the Urbino's Ducal Palace

Paolo Clini
Università Politecnica delle Marche, Italy

Ramona Quattrini
https://orcid.org/0000-0001-5637-6582
Università Politecnica delle Marche, Italy

Paolo Bonvini
Università Politecnica delle Marche, Italy

Romina Nespeca
Università Politecnica delle Marche, Italy

Renato Angeloni
Università Politecnica delle Marche, Italy

Raissa Mammoli
Università Politecnica delle Marche, Italy

Aldo Franco Dragoni
https://orcid.org/0000-0002-3013-3424
Università Politecnica delle Marche, Italy

Christian Morbidoni
Università Politecnica delle Marche, Italy

Paolo Sernani
Università Politecnica delle Marche, Italy

Maura Mengoni
https://orcid.org/0000-0003-2826-7455
Università Politecnica delle Marche, Italy

Alma Leopardi
https://orcid.org/0000-0002-1157-3803
Università Politecnica delle Marche, Italy

Mauro Silvestrini
Università Politecnica delle Marche, Italy

Danilo Gambelli
https://orcid.org/0000-0002-1399-8303
Università Politecnica delle Marche, Italy

Enrico Cori
Università Politecnica delle Marche, Italy

Marco Gallegati
Università Politecnica delle Marche, Italy

Massimo Tamberi
Università Politecnica delle Marche, Italy

Fabio Fraticelli
Università Politecnica delle Marche, Italy

Maria Cristina Acciarri
Università Politecnica delle Marche, Italy

DOI: 10.4018/978-1-7998-1796-3.ch011

Copyright © 2020, IGI Global. Copying or distributing in print or electronic forms without written permission of IGI Global is prohibited.

Serena Mandolesi

iD https://orcid.org/0000-0001-5565-6902
Università Politecnica delle Marche, Italy

ABSTRACT

Digit(al)isation of Cultural Heritage is a multidimensional process that helps in the rescue of European Cultural Identity, and the paradigm of Digital Cultural Heritage (DCH) is a valid instrument for social and cognitive inclusion of museum visitors. In light of disseminating and validating new paradigms for the enjoyment and exploitation of Cultural Heritage (CH) artifacts, this chapter shows main first results from CIVITAS (ChaIn for excellence of reflectiVe societies to exploit dIgital culTural heritAge and museumS). The project develops virtual/augmented environments, through the multisensorial interaction with virtual artworks, to satisfy needs and overcome limitations in a larger CH scenario, applying a bottom-up approach. The research presented show a robust and interdisciplinary approach applied to Ducal Pace at Urbino: key activities and faced challenges demonstrated to test cross-fertilization strategies, involving multilayered issues.

INTRODUCTION

Digit(al)isation of Cultural Heritage is here intended as the merging of two terms (Digitalisation and Digitization) with the aim to highlight the complexity of a multidimensional process that helps in the rescue of European Cultural Identity and increases awareness of values and memories. The differences between the two terms are better defined in the key terms section: the coinage in the title stresses the role of digital contents and virtual facsimiles, referring to digitization, as engine of digital innovation in museum life, that is the digitalization. Making sense of Europe's Cultural Heritage (CH) means to shape the new reflective societies starting from Digital Cultural Heritage (DCH) and diffusing adaptive methods for conservation, fruition and social inclusion. The theme of CH fruition is strongly correlated to the way that information is transmitted and to different types of visitors. For these reasons, the paradigm of DCH is a valid instrument for social and cognitive inclusion of the people visiting the museum. In this context, museums should be more than just places where collections of artworks are preserved and exposed: they should witness identities and cultures. They make culture accessible to the mass audience. The CH collection, conservation and access in the original, accessible and attractive ways demand for digitizing museums and archaeological/historical sites, as well as for designing methodologies to represent, manage and exploit CH data at different levels, ranging from 3D/4D models to domain-specific (e.g., architectural, historical, etc.). The use of virtual "facsimile" of artworks, monuments and architectures can unify the scattered elements of them, allow public access to inaccessible places, allow the visitor to interact with perishable objects, promote the preservation of fragile sites and simulate damaged or lost objects. The availability of semantically reach data enables smart applications for fruition, preservation and study of DCH collections.

The development of digital tools and researches for museums has the potential both to collect and disseminate the CH in an effectively and low-cost mode and to implement a key strategy to interact with virtual "facsimile" in order to engage users, to increase capabilities thanks to the application of the "learning by interacting" paradigm, to diversify museum's cultural proposals, etc. In the light of disseminating and validating new paradigms for the enjoyment and exploitation of Cultural Heritage (CH) artifacts, the present chapter shows main first results from CIVITAS (ChaIn for excellence of reflectiVe Societies to exploit dIgital culTural heritAge and museumS). The project, founded by Univpm as a strategic research project, is driven by the motivations to make significant progress in design methodologies and reference architectures about the remote sensing survey/processing/management and communication of architectural and cultural heritage objects. CIVITAS expects to give answers and significant advancements in the DCH domain, also introducing innovative approaches, for example having in mind unusual target groups, such as cognitively impaired people.

A longer life expectancy, especially in developed societies, has resulted in an increasing number of subjects with cognitive impairment. The reduction of cognitive performance can induce social isolation also through a decreased possibility to attend and use places of public interest, including the fruition of cultural heritages. On the other hand, the possibility of accessing and interacting with cultural areas for cognitively impaired subjects is considered a positive personal relationship modality and could result in considerable advantages from an economic and social point of view as well as from a health prospective. In this respect, cognitive stimulation and promotion of activities may represent an effective approach to contrast the negative evolution of cognitive impairment. However, the presence of reduced cognitive performances, particularly in some specific domains, requires facilities for a full access to areas of cultural interest. An improved offer, obtainable by adapting the use of artistic heritage in relation to the characteristics of the remaining cognitive abilities, could result in an increased number of potential users which may positively benefit from cultural heritage.

The project develops virtual/augmented environments, through the multisensorial interaction with virtual artworks, in order to satisfy needs and overcome limitations in a larger CH scenario, applying a bottom-up approach.

Moreover, a primary goal is to identify the best technological set-up to achieve a multisensory experience of the digital artifact, to increase the level of engagement and interest, to improve learning and finally push coming back to the museum.

To guarantee a solid and actual method, some parts of the project CIVITAS deal with a complete analysis of a Museum, the National Gallery of Marche, and the historical building hosting it, the Ducal Palace at Urbino. Other tasks are more focused on single parts previously identified in agreement with National Gallery of Marche and its director. Therefore, a complete technological framework is defined and established on a set of integrated and interconnected Spatial Augmented Reality (SAR) technologies. The imagined use scenario, for more detailed and finalized applications, concerns the Studiolo[1] del Duca's: an AR application, a full-scale physical reconstruction of the space and the dynamic projection of digital elements to animate the wood marquetry of such space, according to the user behavior and characteristics (e.g. age, gender, etc.) and analysis of heat map from different set of users.

BACKGROUND

In CH digitization, with particular regard to 3D models and high-quality textures and pictures, is well recognized the need of a heterogeneous and multi-purpose documentation for studies, restoration, and valorization purposes. In the majority of successful case studies, multiple and integrated techniques as Terrestrial Laser Scanning (TLS) and Digital Photogrammetry (DP) are applied (Remondino, 2011). As in (Liang et al., 2018) the integration of multi-source data acquired allows to obtain a "virtual twin" that can describe all the physical features of the surveyed item. Unfortunately, CH artifacts can be problematic for digital acquisition due to unstructured, monochrome, translucent, reflective, and/or self-resembling surface (Schaich, 2013). Considering previous studies as (Nicolae, Nocerino, Menna, & Remondino, 2014) and (Noya, García, & Ramírez, 2015) an integrated winning methodology for the acquisition of high reflective items should be developed.

More in general advances in digitization tools and methods lead to a huge amount of 3D models and high-quality contents, useful for knowledge-based architecture dissemination and archaeological heritage exploitation and communication. High-quality contents are more easily accessible, the most innovative projects embrace the Linked Open Data paradigm for Libraries, Archives and Museums (Museum and The Web, 2015). A big challenge is still the sustainability of digital contents: recent works faced it with robust technical knowledge and strategies (DCH-RP, 2014). These strategies outline the principles of preservation; implementing a shared archival lifecycle and merging different services. To guarantee and perform the sustainability of digital contents, a global approach is needed thanks to their dissemination and democratization, moreover, using social & gaming interactive applications. A winning strategy is explained in (Clini, Quattrini, Frontoni, Pierdicca, & Nespeca, 2016). In fact, digitizing cultural heritage and supporting its economic exploitation are activities promoted by the Digital Agenda for Europe. Other directives lay down the general principle that documents from libraries, museums and archives shall be re-usable for commercial and non-commercial purposes, and promotes availability in open, machine-readable format together with metadata and the use of open standards (Interreg Europe Policy Learning Platform on Environment and resource efficiency, 2018).

A quite recent topic, showing high speed of development, is HBIM. A review of the existing approaches on HBIM and its effective implementation in the cultural heritage sector, exploring the effectiveness and the usefulness of the different methodologies that were developed to model families of elements of interest (López, Lerones, Llamas, Gómez-García-Bermejo, & Zalama, 2018). It should be noted, moreover, that the semi-automatic construction of HBIM models is a current topic in Research & Development projects. This is demonstrated in the context of the EU H2020 research framework program under two leading projects: DURAARK (Durable Architectural knowledge: http://duraark.eu/) and INCEPTION (Inclusive cultural heritage in Europe through 3D semantic modeling: www.inception-project.eu).

While the process of producing a meaningful digital representation of a historical building surely needs knowledge and work from domain experts, it is a time-consuming task and demands for automatization of particular steps to increase speed. A semi-automatic modeling workflow using Revit was proposed in (José López, Martin Lerones, Llamas, Gómez-García-Bermejo, & Zalama, 2018) as an outcome of the INCEPTION project, while the automatic surfaces segmentation in indoor environment is addressed in (Tamke et al., 2016) (outcome of the DURAARK project) and more recently in (Ochmann, Vock, & Klein, 2019).

While these studies provide interesting results that can be applied to the built heritage domain, the accurate 3D modeling of a historical building demands for recognition and fine-grained segmentation of possibly complex architectural elements.

In the last years, following the considerable success of Deep Learning-based methods on images and text, the application of Deep Neural Networks to 3D data, and point clouds, was widely explored. The two main tasks addressed in literature are classification and semantic segmentation of 3D scenes. Since the seminal work in this research strand, PointNet (Qi, Su, Mo, & Guibas, 2017), a number of improvements to the original model and of alternative deep learning methods have been proposed, as in

(Qi, Yi, Su, & Guibas, 2017) and (Wang et al., 2018), achieving good results in identify different kind of objects in outdoor and indoor scenes.

Accurate automatic segmentation of point clouds has many applications in the Historical Building domain (Grilli, Dininno, Petrucci, & Remondino, 2018), however, no attempts were made to asses deep learning methods in the historical building domain. This is partially due to the high demand of data for deep learning methods to succeed and the lack of consolidated annotated datasets.

Another relevant research strand is related to the enrichment of 3D HBIM model with semantic information for supporting the creation, the management and the visualization of built heritage (Cursi, Simeone, & Toldo, 2015) (Apollonio, Gaiani, & Sun, 2013) (Quattrini, Pierdicca, & Morbidoni, 2017-a). The recognized need for incorporating into BIM models additional information, including metadata, media files and point-based representation of 3D objects, lead to extension proposals of the IFC standards in this direction, as described in (DURAARK, 2015).

Several studies have already produced significant results in studying the influences between CH interaction and cognitive and behavioral positive response. Art museum-based interventions in patients with dementia, seem to be able to improve the subjective well-being, mood and quality of life (Schall, Tesky, Adams, & Pantel, 2018). However, it has been demonstrated that patients with more severe cognitive impairment have minor benefits than those with mild cognitive problems (Hendriks et al., 2018).

Further, in early stage cognitive deterioration, handling museum objects increases the subjective quality of life and cultural learning and visiting museums regularly is associated with a lower incidence rate of dementia (Camic, Tischler, & Pearman, 2014). Some studies showed that patients who physically visit a museum, compared to those who only view artworks photos, are able to better remember what they have seen using spatial layout cues for recovery and empowering long-term memory (Johnson, Culverwell, Hulbert, Robertson, & Camic, 2017). Furthermore, arts and museum programs can provide a means of communication with people who have language failure. In this respect, participants with dementia demonstrated significantly more interest, sustained attention, pleasure and self-esteem compared to subjects participating in more traditional adult day care activities (Kinney & Rentz, 2005). A survey performed after a visit to the Museum of Modern Art in New York demonstrated mood improvement in both dementia patients and their caregivers (Mittelman & Epstein, n.d.).

The evoked reactions and positive impacts of art programs are influenced by different conditions, such as the severity of dementia, the specific cognitive domain impairments and the type of artwork shown. Accordingly, different types of visual art, such as representational, abstract, or conceptual art, may impact the effectiveness of a cultural program. Many studies, concerning the reproduction of artworks and art labs, have shown that creativity remains preserved or can emerge during the evolution of cognitive impairment (MacPherson, Bird, Anderson, Davis, & Blair, 2009). Recently, some studies have described different neural systems that are thought to contribute to the aesthetic experience: the sensory-motor system, the emotional valuation system, and the knowledge meaning system. It can be speculated that some attributes of art, such as color, shapes, natural elements, or complexity of the artwork, may impact the reactivity for particular types or severity of dementia. Moreover, even the type of the prevalent compromised cognitive function can require different access to cultural heritage and consequently a different response to stimulation (Chancellor, Duncan, & Chatterjee, 2014). In this respect, Alzheimer's Disease patients are characterized by a prevalent memory impairment while in Vascular Dementia attention and executive functions are specifically compromised.

For this reason, especially during the early stages of cognitive deterioration, patients with different forms of dementia are expected to show an individualized response to cultural and artistic interventions according to a particular modality of presentation.

In this context, the development of virtual museums has the potential to collect the cultural heritage and to implement its capabilities thanks to the application of the "learning by interacting" paradigm. The project CIVITAS aims to develop and test new paradigms of digitisation and multisensory (visual, haptic, sound) fruition for cultural heritage in the setting of the Ducal Palace at Urbino. The application of a digitized access with differentiated and augmentative learning modalities could thus allow for better interaction with the cultural material in patients with cognitive impairment; this, in turn, would allow enhancing the visitor experience and social inclusion and could represent a positive stimulus for patients' cognitive ability.

For this reason, some museums (MoMa Museum in New York, Marino Marini's Museum in Florence, Butler Gallery in Ireland, Lehmbruck Museum in Duisburg, and many others), have already successfully applied increased and interactive communication strategies and art labs to facilitate the access of people with cognitive impairment. These projects have shown that the visits, the vision of the historical objects, the location of the museum and the multimodal presentation modalities of the artworks could have a positive impact on the long term and autobiographical memory and on the attention ability; they could also indirectly help communication and spontaneous conversation, with possible positive implications on careers and family members too. The art thus becomes a "relational device", with positive effects on both the patients and relatives.

Despite the primary role of museums, as custodians of heritage and culture, is to engage and educate people, visiting museums can also become a meaningful experience that contributes in developing the personal mind and enhancing social relationships.

Novel applications based on virtual reality (VR) and augmented reality (AR) technology are becoming more and more appreciated tools for the fruition of art encouraging the dissemination of cultural heritage and allowing to reach a larger number of visitors.

Both virtual reality (VR) and augmented reality (AR) technologies, thanks to the continuous improvements, are used in different fields such as retail (Pizzi, Scarpi, Pichierri, & Vannucci, 2019), tourism (Guttentag, 2010), healthcare (McCarthy & Uppot, 2019), research (Farshid, Paschen, Eriksson, & Kietzmann, 2018) and more.

In relation to art, several studies reported the application of both technologies (VR and AR) that can facilitate the presentation of cultural artifacts from museums' collections (Jones & Christal, 2002) (Sylaiou, Mania, Karoulis, & White, 2010) (Carrozzino & Bergamasco, 2010) (Cianciarulo, 2015) (Jung, tom Dieck, Lee, & Chung, 2016) (Gimeno, Portalés, Coma, Fernández, & Martínez, 2017) (He, Wu, & Li, 2018).

AR-based applications emerged in recent years to enrich the visit quality of CH sites. In most cases, the aim is to overcome the issues related to the communication of the information hidden in a work of art: the risk might be overwhelming the visitors, especially the youngest, losing their attention. In this context, AR has been applied to gamify visits, encouraging users to move towards specific POI or providing additional content (Mortara et al., 2014) (Hammady, Ma, & Temple, 2016). AR has been proven useful also in the visualization of lost or hidden artifacts in archeological sites (Canciani, Conigliaro, Del Grasso, Papalini, & Saccone, 2016) (Empler, 2015). In AR-based mobile applications, AR usually relies on the recognition of an image target which acts as a reference for computer graphics to be overlaid (Amin & Govilkar, 2015). However, image target recognition is not enough to achieve a stable AR, allowing the user to realistically move around superimposed 3D models (Dragoni, Quattrini, Sernani, & Ruggeri, 2019). To overcome the limits of image target recognition, other techniques are used to superimpose computer graphics artifacts to real elements on the screen of mobile devices. Among those, SLAM, usually applied in robotics to map unknown environments (Durrant-Whyte & Bailey, 2006) (Bailey & Durrant-Whyte, 2006), can be used to perform the tracking of objects for AR purposes (Gao, Wan, Tang, & Chen, 2017).

Through the x-reality technologies and the storytelling techniques (Mortara et al., 2014), it's possible to increase the level of engagement and interest of the museum's visitor (Sylaiou et al., 2010) (Barbieri, Bruno, & Muzzupappa, 2017).

Virtual/Augmented reality technologies cover an important role in the human-machine interaction (Mengoni, Germani & Bordegoni, 2009); for this reason, the choice of technologies to be implemented, is fundamental and it is different for each single case study. The creation of new technological application requires a deepen preliminary study, benchmarking of x-reality technologies based on Quality Function Deployment (QFD) method (Govers, 1996),(Mengoni & Leopardi, 2019). This method correlates all together user needs, technical requirements and technology functionalities. Through QFD method, the best technological setup has been identified for the specific environment contest (museum, "Studiolo del Duca", different users, etc.).

Today, visualization technologies are very numerous; for this reason, a comparative study is important to not omit some technology. To support benchmarking, there are also studies based on the evaluation of users who compare the different display technologies in the museum environment; these studies are based on the concept of presence, user perception, visitor experience, etc. (Loizides, El Kater, Terlikas, Lanitis, & Michael, 2014), (Jung et al., 2016), (Sooai, Sumpeno, & Purnomo, 2016).

Considering the peculiarities of the Studiolo del Duca's space, the study was directed in the field of Spatial visualization technologies. In literature, some applications have been developed in the context of the museum and cultural heritage, that employ the SAR paradigm (Lee et al., 2015), (Basballe & Halskov, 2010), (Ridel et al., 2014).

Once the setup has been implemented, the question that arises is: how can I evaluate the effectiveness of DH strategies applied to use? For monitoring the visitor's emotional and cognitive response, the methods can be divided in two measurement classes:

- Implicit measurement, with emotional detection (Ceccacci, Generosi, Giraldi, & Mengoni, 2018), questionnaire (Witmer & Singer, 1998)
- Invasive measurement, with biofeedback signal (Tröndle, Greenwood, Kirchberg, & Tschacher, 2014), (Sparrow, 2016)

As regards market strategies, as in (Bakhshi & Throsby, 2012), built on (Kevin F. McCarthy, 2001), we distinguish between audience broadening, diversifying, or deepening; where the first refers to the "capturing a larger share of the population already known to be audiences", the second to the attraction of "new groups of consumers that do not currently attend", and the third to the "increasing and/or intensifying the engagement of audiences" (Bakhshi & Throsby, 2012).

As far as digital technologies are concerned, we see as relevant the taxonomy proposed in (Styliani, Fotis, Kostas, & Petros, 2009), and the distinction by (Bonacini, 2011) between remote fruition technologies (e.g.: website, social networks) and on-site fruition technologies (e.g.: info-points, touch-screens, VR/AR devices, etc.).

Lastly, as regards digital skills, following the (Aica, Assinform, Assintel, 2017) taxonomy, we distinguish between applied and technical skills; where the applied digital skills refer to the ability to use software and devices by the decision makers and the employees involved in routine tasks, while technical skills are referred to knowledge and capabilities to intervene on solutions, platforms, programming languages.

THE CIVITAS PROJECT AS A REFERENCE FRAMEWORK IN DIGITAL CULTURAL HERITAGE

Starting from weak and strong points in the DCH scenario, CIVITAS proposes five strong Challenges:

- Digitisation of Cultural Heritage at different scales (CH1),
- Digital Content Management for 3D/4D semantic-aware models (CH2),
- Enhancement of Visitor Experience and Social Inclusion (CH3),
- Fruition by multisensory (visual, haptic, sound) Interaction paradigms (CH4),
- Business models based on Digital Heritage for Culture, Research, Tourism, Reflective Society promotion (CH5).

This chapter, in particular the following five paragraphs, is organized according to the CIVITAS challenges: the key activities and their responsible are, in this way, each other's connected, and a work break down the structure of the project helps in the follow-up and management of researchers' sub-groups. The project, as a whole, aims to develop and test new paradigms of digitisation and fruition for CH, the main museum and historical complex of the region was selected as a case study: the Ducal Palace at Urbino. Some key activities involve the whole building, whereas some are more focused on single artifacts or part of the building or the museum visit path.

In order to promote easy and sustainable creation of DCH contents (CH1) and to help the diffusion of Linked Open Data management in DCH and semantic content retrieval (CH2), experts from all relevant domains are involved in the project for establishing a generic architecture framework. These experts cooperate with test and verification drivers to develop new methodologies and tools for assessing systems with respect to safety and functional correctness.

To achieve the goal of Digital Heritage for cultures' promotion and social inclusion (CH3- CH4) in DCH exploitation, a scientific approach is carried out. In order to create different profiles of cognitive abilities that can target towards a particular and more profitable mode of interaction and usability and complete understanding and enjoyment of cultural heritage, a population of older subjects is undergo exhaustive neuro-psychological evaluation. An expected result would be to distinguish a subject with preserved visuospatial skills, compared to another evaluation, or, moreover, compared to another more skillful in language functions. The main focus of this part of the study is to increase the engagement of people with different abilities, skills, background, etc. visiting the museum. Today, there are some examples of applications (Sooai et al., 2016), but the major limits are the intrusiveness of visitor's space by technologies or the sensation that it isn't a really digital experience. From this first objective, it arises the second focus of the study: fusion of the digital installation with a physical museum, with the aim to create an integrated space where digital and real coexist.

Figure 1. Portion of the point cloud that includes hanging garden, Duca's apartment and conference hall. The plan shows a combination of different survey methods

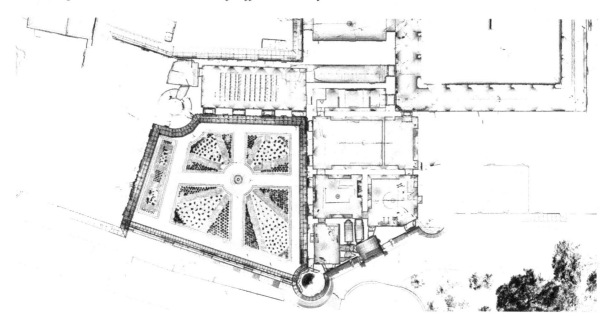

The SAR's paradigm and the multisensorial interaction, with the DCH, help the people to perceive the digital application englobed in the real space, so allowing visitors to play with the cultural clues in a very engaging way and to live an inclusive experience.

For the last challenge (CH5), the excellence chain of digitisation and exploitation arising from CIVITAS project is trying to provide a methodology tailored for the specific application case of Ducal Palace, as a principal and more challenging test bench. Another goal is to enlarge the knowledge, appreciation and exploitation of Ducal Palace as cultural-historical site, starting from existing databases and experiences.

The partnership shows a mix of skills: the backgrounds are complementary in order to work together and co-create technologies and methodologies in a new value-chain. CIVITAS is an interdisciplinary project that aims at developing a strategy that crosses disciplines' boundaries to create a holistic approach and merges the competences from Engineering, Economics, and Medicine.

The chapter aims to present a theoretical framework for public museum digitalization dealing with sustainable technologies and applications. The contribution introduces first research findings came from the CIVITAS project: a complete digital 3D model for the Ducal Palace, innovative uses of Artificial Intelligence in semantic classification of point clouds and its exploitation in Heritage Building Information Model (HBIM) domain, setting up of test users with some frailties, as well as validation of innovative Augmented/Virtual Reality (AR/VR) applications exploiting SLAM technologies and natural language understanding.

Digitisation of Cultural Heritage at Different Scales

The first challenging aim (CH1) regards the digitisation workflow and the combination of the related 3D sensor technologies to acquire and merge shapes at different scales (geospatial, architectural, sculptural,

Figure 2. Slice of the point cloud: section shows the survey accuracy in one of Duca's apartment room with a coffin

pictorial and archaeological) and with different levels of accuracy. A really innovative technique based on the combination and matching of the various datasets with different levels of detail (LOD) (UNI 11337-4, 2017), captured by photogrammetry (SfM), terrestrial laser scanner (TLS) static and mobile (Figure 1), based on time of flight and fringe projection-based scanner were developed and assessed. The 3D model also includes HD pictures, to obtain a high-quality realistic representation.

In this research line, innovation is represented by the stress of non-invasive acquisition systems to digitize paintings, frames, frescos, tapestries, etc. (Figure 2). The aim is to obtain a points cloud of the artwork characterized by high resolution and accuracy and to match it with the captured HD images in order to use the model both for digital collections and fruition, as well as for conservation and restoration purposes. The workflow and the LOD specification are applied for the digitisation of the Ducal Palace at Urbino and its art collections: a real multi-scale experience. As in deep described in (Nespeca, 2018), a complete 3D digitization of the Ducal Palace was carried out, mainly exploiting TLS equipment and allowing for the first time a comprehensive model for this large-complex building: the main reference data set was also provided by the Leica Backpack acquisition[2]. The documentary inputs and survey data will furthermore allow a diachronic description of the palace and its building phases.

Therefore, the support of multidimensional documents (4D, 5D, etc.) was immediately necessary for understanding the current state of the building, its original structure and changes during the time. This kind of data collection, corroborated by the 3D survey, opens up to new knowledge-based view and applications in order to narrate the long life of the Palace. The methodology respects, in fact, the

Figure 3. View of Laurana's honor courtyard in Autodesk Revit software

principles of the London Charter: for a CH computer-based visualization to match the rigour of conventional research, its rigour must be visible (www.londoncharter.org).

Digitisation of such a complex architectural object required the integration of different techniques and was the test field for the use of an innovative wearable instrument. From the first data mining, the chosen settings prove to be sufficiently rich in terms of geometry and colours to allow global and local analyses. In additional, to achieve the high levels of detail necessary for a complete and satisfactory 3D model, a dense acquisition campaign using a static terrestrial laser scanner is realized. Moreover, for the splendid inlaid study located between the two turrets, an accurate survey is achieved by the photogrammetric technique with polarized light, in order to remove the reflections of the wooden surface. The Studiolo was chosen as a particularly challenging acquisition: the wood marqueteries covering the walls were restored many times, and the application of a transparent protective varnish made them high reflective. Moreover, the expected 3D model with high-quality textures considering the different aims of this survey, both documentation and fruition, lead us to the choice of the integration of TLS and DP using polarized light photography. TLS was used to accurately document the geometry, on the other hand, DP implemented the high-resolution texture necessary to generate the image targets for the AR app. The use of polarized light has been adopted to eliminate the external reflectance generated by the light on the surface, enhancing the final image quality.

Digital Content Management for 3D/4D Semantic-Aware Models

The second challenge regards the DH collection archiving and management with a particular focus on HBIM representation of the DCH collections. In this context, the application of Linked Data and Semantic Web technologies is investigated and a methodology is implemented to provide accurate, semantically reach representations of the HBIM models.

Addressing this challenge, CIVITAS project enables advanced intelligent exploration by building on top of emerging specifications and by enriching the data model with domain knowledge and links to the Web of Data. In order to verify the robustness of the automatic classification, an HBIM of the Ducal Palace is under development as a benchmark or alternative data collector. A first nucleus of the Laurana's Courtyard has been modeled in Revit environment, implementing three different LODs according to literature and developing parametric reality-based families.

HBIM is conceived as a "reverse engineering" process of existing buildings in which modeling allows to acquire information that will be used to improve the subsequent modeling phase in an increasingly accurate iterative procedure. The modeling starts from a survey phase, as shown in the previous challenge, from which we obtain point clouds. From these, it is possible to generate an intelligent and parametric model that contains the highest possible degree of knowledge related to the building. The process takes a long time to complete because the BIM tools were not designed to shape the existing one. The step of the survey is therefore necessary in order to obtain a reality-based model. The intelligent elements created contain information of any kind that can be updated, replaced and added, and furthermore these parametric objects, although the modeled building is unique, could be used for similar cases. There is an increasing need to develop the digital database of information related to historical architecture and more generally to existing buildings, to protect them and to make this data usable for other professionals in the sector or for anyone who wants to use it.

To verify the strength of the automatic classification, an HBIM of the Ducal Palace of Urbino is under development in the DICEA unit as a benchmark or alternative data collector.

A first study is carried out in Laurana's honor courtyard (Figure 3). This architectural masterpiece is a rectangular space characterized by a perfect geometric strictness. Corinthian columns support round arches and define a rhythm that corresponds to the upper level, with pilasters, windows, and architraves. The courtyard is an example of a modular architecture for the rhythmic scanning: full and empty alternate parts and function of keystone regards to the various parts of the building. A different element placed on different levels according to an irregular pattern are reunited in this central space according to a purely mathematical and rational criterion.

A first semantic division of architecture has already been carried out in the model phase. The specificity and complexity of the surveyed geometry made it necessary to model and parameterize different architectural elements, such as system families, loadable and local, in a Revit environment[3].

The architectural elements modeled as families are Corinthian columns, vaults, windows, doors and main door. In addition to the TLS survey, their reconstruction referred in particular to texts of classical literature and contemporary scientific references that provided interpretative and operational tools for the correct modeling of each classical element.

The Corinthian column was a complex element to model due to the geometry of its moldings and the decorative elements of the capital. The column diameter was measured, at the base of the shaft, from the point cloud and consequently, all the column moldings were sized. As already said, in addition to the geometric survey, the modeling phase needed rules suggested by classical treatises, specifically those suggested in "The rules of the five Orders of Civil Architecture" (Barrozio da Vignola, 1562) and by contemporary background as in (Aubin, 2013).

Figure 4. Parameterization of the column

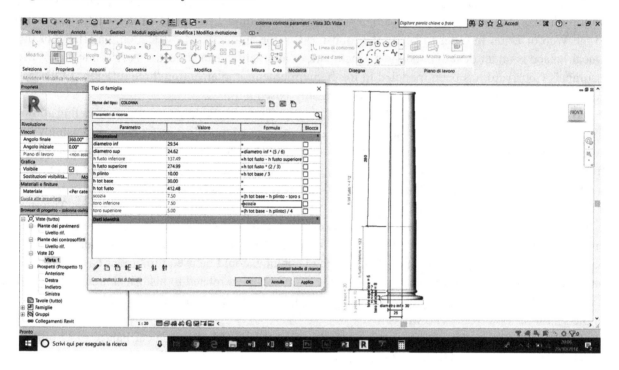

The Attic base, the shaft and the capital have been modeled with operations of revolution and extrusion on the path. The Corinthian capital is the most elaborate of the orders and because of its geometric complexity and decorative richness, it has been broken down and modeled by simplifying its component parts (bell, abacus, acanthus leaves, volutes and helix). Loadable families creation of other architectural elements of the courtyard, as for the Corinthian column, occurred through revolutions, extrusions, merged volumes and constraining curves.

Once the geometric models were completed, they were parameterized (Figure 4). The parameterization represents a very important step because it allowed to express measurements in terms of others by assigning type parameters and instance parameters to the elements. In this way, it will be possible to reuse the models created in other projects just working on parameters.

The application of different detail levels (LOD) was another important phase of these informed models. The 1:200 scale has been associated with the low level of detail, the 1:100 scale with the medium detail level and the 1:20 scale with the high one (Figure 5). To realize the LOD of the Corinthian column "Renaissance Revit: creating classical architecture with modern software" was used as a reference. Three profiles were modeled within the column family, each corresponding to a level of detail. For the high LOD, the profile is complex and elaborate, all the details of the capital and the shape of the moldings in the base will be visible. In the middle level, the components of the capital and the moldings are reduced to simpler geometric shapes that will become even more approximate in the low level (Figure 6).

Figure 5. The elevation represents the medium LOD of the courtyard that corresponds to a scale 1:100

Enhancement of Visitor Experience and Social Inclusion

The CH3 is trying to answer the following question: "How can research provide tools and methods to enhance the visitor experience, improve cultural contents' learning and create enjoyment into the museum?" Finding a structured answer implies the application of Customer Experience-oriented methodologies to define visitor journeys' requirements and the specifications of interactions with the digital contents and virtual facsimiles.

Another challenging issue of CH3 is how to foster social inclusion in public spaces as museums. The patients with a cognitive impairment population tend to social isolation and to the loss of important opportunities, including the fruition of cultural heritage. The increase in potential users but especially the positive stimulus linked to the use of cultural heritage may significantly receive development in relation to the characteristics of cognitive remaining assets. Cognitive performances will be measured with a neuropsychological battery, which is currently indicated from International Guidelines for the diagnosis of patients with mild cognitive impairment.

This research activity aims to create different profiles of cognitive skills that can target towards a particular and more profitable mode of interaction, complete understanding and enjoyment of a cultural site. Cognitive performances will be assessed in a population of people over the age of 65 in the Neurological Clinic of Ancona by means of an exhaustive neuropsychological battery, which is currently

Figure 6. Corinthian column level of detail (LOD): low, medium and high

indicated from International Guidelines for the diagnosis of mild cognitive impairment and able to investigate main cognitive domains. Specifically, the study will include 100 subjects suffering from initial forms of cognitive impairment and with an early stage of physical, learning, emotional, behavioral, or developmental disabilities. In these patients, we will try to identify, based on their specific cognitive aspect, the individual potentialities that allow them to interact and better understand the stimuli linked to the presentation of a cultural offer. It is foreseeable that with this modality it will be possible to discriminate different types of subjects with greater predisposition to assimilate information presented in different sensory modalities, for example visual, auditory, proprioceptive.

Accordingly, it will be possible to distinguish subjects with preserved visuospatial skills from those who are more skillful in language functions. The use of a complex interactive modality is expected to perform better in the former, while in the latter an offer based on an oral exchange of information would be probably more appropriate.

Another aim of the CH3 task is to obtain and analyze data using eye-tracking technique that can provide useful information to understand if an individual is involved or not in what is looking at (Shi & Wedel, 2013) and where the participant's visual attention is, without bringing them physically at the museum.

An eye-tracker allows to record eye-movements ("gaze directions") in terms of eye fixations and saccades. Fixations are brief moments when our eyes essentially stop scanning about the scene and giving

Figure 7. Eye tracking: heat map 1

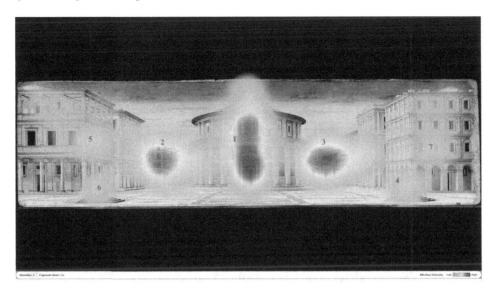

time to our visual system to take detailed information about what is looking. Saccades are rapid jumps of the eye between fixations to redirect the line of sight to a new point.

So far, this task team has identified the VR-eye tracking hardware and software, starting the analysis of the potential outcomes from the integration between the eye tracking in a VR environment.

The relation between eye-movements and internal brain processes is known for a long time and for this reason, eye gaze data have been used in many fields for analyzing user behavior: market research (Wedel & Pieters, 2008), human-computer interaction (Poole & Ball, 2006) and visualization research (Gegenfurtner, Lehtinen, & Säljö, 2011).

An example of how making museum spaces more interactive is proposed by (Naspetti et al., 2016) who used the eye-tracking technology to analyze the visual behavior of forty Italian students and employees at Università Politecnica delle Marche. The study defined a protocol for optimizing an existing AR application that allows the visualization of digital contents through a display. The study focused on the analysis of the eye-tracking data (collected using the Tobii Eye-Tracker X2-60 and the Imotions® Attention Tool software) of a group of respondents subjected to the visualisation of three digital paintings. The aim of the study was to provide a deeper analysis of data in the relation of the visitors' experience of the "The Ideal City" painting (1480-1490, National Gallery of Marche, Urbino). Data collected from this type of analysis considers two principal metrics: the TTFF-F metric that indicates the time to the first fixation, and the Time spent-F that provides the time spent in a specific area of interest (AOI). The quantitative analysis of these metrics allows to identify the visual behaviour of respondents when changing the visual stimulus of artworks. In particular, eye tracking records may be used to compare visual attention paid by respondents to the free-screening of the artworks with subsequent exposures of the same artwork in which respondents can be asked to pay attention to specific zones (Naspetti et al., 2016) (Pierdicca et al., 2018).

Available studies in this field may provide a basis for comparing results from eye tracking sessions. For instance, some studies show that during the free-screening phase, participants looked in the center at first (Quiroga & Pedreira, 2011) (Massaro et al., 2012). The study from (Naspetti et al., 2016) shows

Figure 8. Eye tracking: heat map 2

that, probably due to the lack of a human figure, participant visual attention was attracted by a central "vertical line" in the middle of the painting (Figure 7). This line suggested that two new AOIs needed to be included in the AR application for this painting: the window above the central door of the Baptistery and the cross of the Baptistery. As in Rothkopf (2007), during the free-screening respondents' eyes were likely to look more in the central zone, while for the second exposure the attention was more distributed between the six AOIs increasing both the number of fixations and the time spent increased for all AOIs (Figure 8).

Data from eye-tracking sessions collected across a set of trials and respondents may provide the basis for statistical models of attention. Integration with biometrical data collected in AR sessions may add relevant information for a more complete definition of the experience of museums and artworks visitors. Bayesian Networks BN may be effectively used to provide a classification of individuals and predictive or interpretative models for attention paid to AOIs. A BN is a compact probabilistic model based on Bayes theorem of conditional probabilities and aimed for the handling of uncertainty in expert systems (Horvitz, Breese, & Henrion, 1988) and can be interpreted as a graphical model of the interactions among a set of variables (nodes), and a set of directed edges between variables (arcs), where each variable has a finite set of mutually exclusive states. BN can be learned from collected eye-tracking data using unsupervised or supervised approaches. Learned models may be used to classify individuals according to measured visiting experience and to predict patterns of visual behavior according to a group of individuals according to their behavior when exposed to different visual experiences of artworks. Node force analysis may be performed to understand factors that may enhance visiting experience under different conditions. Simulations from learned probabilistic models may be of help for the identification of conditions for the visiting experience.

Figure 9. POI in the lower order of the Studiolo

Fruition by Multisensory (Visual, Haptic, Sound) Interaction Paradigams

CIVITAS project is a hive of challenging ideas to develop innovative human-machine interfaces to enhance the visitor experience and finally to facilitate the use of DCH (CH4). Experimentations are focus on the interaction with both virtual and physical facsimiles: advanced visualization displays (e.g. adaptive AR-glasses, Head-Mounted Displays), tactile stimulation technologies (e.g. force feedback displays) integrated with volumetric sound displays. In parallel, Rapid Prototyping techniques are exploited to create a physical reproduction of the digitized, reconstructed or reassembled artwork, frescos, sculptures, frames, plasters, etc.

Advanced Virtual/Augmented/Mixed Reality technologies can be combined and adopted, suited and adaptive to different user profiles (e.g., children, average users, professional users, etc.). Although these technologies are mature enough, they do not represent a mass phenomenon, especially in DCH. This is due to several factors (costs of equipment, systems accessibility and usability, IT acceptance, quality of the sensorial experience); therefore, provide effective solutions enhancing visitor's experience with artworks remains a challenge for research.

Most researches focus on the exploiting of ubiquitous and mobile AR displays (smartphones). However, only a few of them investigate the use of challenging installations for current state-of-art that (e.g. adaptive AR glasses into immersive VR or with haptic displays). Specifically, concerning visual interaction, inside the Studiolo in the Palazzo Ducale of Urbino has the potential to achieve such goal, by superimposing screen information about specific Points of Interest (POI) framed with a mobile device in an AR app. In this regard, changes in the lighting conditions affecting the Studiolo limit the accuracy in the recognition of POIs. Building on the findings of scientific literature, Simultaneous Localization And Mapping (SLAM) have been identified as an enhancement of the AR app for the Studiolo, in order to overcome the limitations due to lighting and achieve a stable AR.

To this end, SLAM can be used to virtually anchor to the Studiolo walls suggestions about additional POIs to guide users' attention. The Studiolo is a case study which is general and might be applied to different use cases.

Figure 10. The mobile app for the Studiolo. Once POIs are acquired, SLAM and image target recognition are combined to superimpose virtual elements (audio/video, 3D models, and text) on the walls of the lower order of the Studiolo

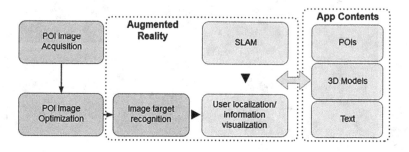

Figure 11. Structure of the application reconstructs in a laboratory

In this context, CIVITAS started studying new pervasive and effective solutions, which enable the development of a virtual/augmented environment, through the multisensorial interaction with virtual artworks. Specifically, concerning AR inside the Studiolo, image target recognition could be implemented to superimpose screen information about specific POIs framed with a mobile device in an AR app. In this regard, also changes in the lighting conditions affecting the Studiolo need to be tested, to assess the accuracy in the recognition of POIs. To overcome the limitations due to lighting and achieve a stable AR, SLAM has been identified as a possible enhancement of the AR app for the Studiolo. SLAM might be used to virtually anchor to the Studiolo walls suggestions about additional POIs to guide users' attention. However, even if SLAM has been already proven useful for Real Scale AR, its applicability inside a small space for the AR app needs to be tested.

The main goal of the AR mobile app for the Studiolo is the creation of a storytelling connecting some POI in the lower order of the Studiolo, specifically: the sword, the sandglass, the representation of the Duke, a landscape, the lectern and some books (Figure 9). However, to achieve a powerful storytelling, we need the support of technology, implementing a stable and reliable AR as described in the background section. Therefore, we propose to combine both image target recognition and SLAM into the mobile app. The goals of the app are:

- Providing specific information about the POI, once these are automatically recognized by the app (image target recognition);
- Suggesting other interesting POI inside the Studiolo interpreting the user relative position in the room, with the SLAM.

Figure 10 summarizes the mode of operation of the proposed AR mobile app. The images of POI are the targets to be recognized, i.e. the references for computer graphics to be overlaid. In addition to image target recognition, SLAM is used to locate the user's orientation inside the room and apply 2D images such as arrows and icons superimposed on the mobile device screen to direct the user's attention to other POI. Exploiting such features, the proposed app consists of a main scene presenting the app. There, the user activates the AR: when one of the POIs is framed and recognized by the app, a descriptive text, a video, an audio file or a 3D model about the POI popups. Moreover, after the acquisition of the image target, i.e. after the POI is recognized, the app automatically switches to SLAM mode, assigning the visual elements related to the suggestion of other POIs to a virtual ground plane. Therefore, the user of the app can move around, even framing different POIs, but the suggestions will maintain their original superimposed position even when the triggering POI is out of the field of view, preventing the need to recognize them again.

Another research team has carried out the benchmarking of x-Reality technologies based on Quality Functional Deployment method that correlates user needs, technical requirements and technology functionalities. The aim is to identify the best technological set-up to achieve a multisensory experience of digital artifact, increase the level of engagement and interest, improve learning and finally push coming back to the museum. Therefore, a complete technological framework is defined and is based on a set of integrated and interconnected Mixed Reality technologies that will be implemented in the next phase. The imagined use scenario concerns the full-scale physical reconstruction of the Studiolo (north and east wall) and the dynamic projection of one or more digital elements to animate the portraits of the famous men and the wood marquetry according to the user behavior and characteristics (e.g. age, gender).

The squirrel, allegorically representing the Duca, is shown in the east wall. The squirrel, selected as the subject of the story, helps the visitors to explore the other walls of the Studiolo. The reconstruction is made by wooden panels where some high definition photo of the "Tarsie" are paste. An animation is projected on these panels guiding the attention of the visitors along with the space.

The structure of the application is composed by: a projector mounted on a mirror head posed in front of the panels, a kinect that track the visitor in the corner area and some speakers (Figure 11).

Table 1. The sample investigated

	Museum	Place	Opening	Ownership	Visitors (2017)	Type of heritage
1	"Galleria Nazionale delle Marche" at Palazzo Ducale	Urbino	1912	Public (Government)	164.000	Renaissance painting
2	Museums at Palazzo Ducale	Mantova	1881	Public (Government)	323.000	Thematic exhibitions
3	Museum at La Venaria Reale	Torino	2008	Public-private network	1.049.000	Paintings and sculptures from the 15th to the 17th century. Thematic exhibitions
4	Museums at Castello Sforzesco	Milano	late 1800s	Public (Municipality)	450.000	Museums of archaeological finds, wooden sculptures, ancient art, decorative arts, musical instruments. Renaissance sculptures and paintings
5	San Domenico & Palazzo Romagnoli Museums	Forlì	2005	Public (Municipality)	20.000	Frescoes and paintings from the Middle Ages. Archaeological museum (forthcoming opening)
6	Pontifical Museum "Santa Casa"	Loreto (AN)	late 1800s	Public (Government)	20.000	Paintings and tapestries from the 15th to the 19th century.
7	Museums at Castello Scaligero	Malcesine (VR)	1960	Public (Municipality)	150.000	Natural history museum & museum of the Venetian galleys
8	Museo del Balì	Colli al Metauro (PU)	2004	Private	50.000	Science museum

The visitor's emotional state and cognitive response are monitored during the interaction with the developed digital contents and scenario, through two types of measurement method: implicit and invasive. For implicit measurement EMOJ (Emotional Analytics) technology is used to monitor the visitor emotional state. EMOJ technology is an innovative software to detect the emotional states from facial expression recognition, the technology uses a 4k camera (Ceccacci et al., 2018).

Instead for invasive measurement, two technologies have been selected:

- The Nesus 10 MKII with Biotrace software that is a wearable device to measure some biofeedback parameters (e.g. ECG, HR, temperature, etc.);
- The Tobii Pro VR Integration - based on HTC Vive that is able to measure heatmaps and gaze during the Studiolo virtual tour and identify the levels of interest and engagement.

The emotions monitoring has been made in both the reconstructions, to compare the visitor's reaction to understand the best technologies for this particular case study.

Digital Technologies and Skills for Cultural Heritage and Tourism Strategies

A final challenging issue of the project consists in the business and social innovation in DCH (CH5). Within the CIVITAS project, this challenge has been declined with reference to the relationships existing between market strategies, adoption of digital technologies, and development of (or access to) digital skills.

Starting from the experience of the "Galleria Nazionale delle Marche" at Ducal Palace at Urbino, this chapter collects reflections on the relationship between the museums' market strategies and the process of adoption of digital technologies. It is also addressed to understand how digital skills, held by museums, affect the organization's capability to match technological innovation and strategy. This study benefits from the integration of knowledge relating to the economy of tourism and the economy of cultural organizations, with reference to the issue of alignment between strategy, technology, and organization structure (skills).

The analysis is conducted on two distinct levels: the first one concerns the comparison between current and feasible strategies, in the light of some recent trends in tourism demand; the second level is aimed at assessing the adequacy of the technologies in use with respect to the market strategy, and of digital skills with respect to the adopted digital devices.

The analysis is supported by previous studies on the evolution of tourism demand and the associated opportunities for the Marche region, as well as by a qualitative survey conducted on a sample of Italian museums, currently interested in the adoption of digital technologies to support the usage of their collections. The sample has been built by considering the historical-architectural importance of the site and the collections housed in it. This choice is linked to the belief that combining the importance of the site and the hosted collections enhances the opportunities inherent in digital technologies, such as virtual or augmented reality devices. The main data relating to each museum are summed up in Table 1, below.

Current and Feasible Market Strategies

It seems appropriate to point out that the evolution of the structure of tourism demand can have a significant impact on the strategies pursued by cultural heritage organizations. Among the evolutionary trends affecting the tourism sector, one seems to have a significant impact on the market strategies of cultural heritage institutions. We refer to the so-called "slow tourism", that is, a type of tourism in which travel is an integral part of the holiday. The emergence of this segment of tourist demand is combined with a growing weight of "cultural tourism"; this, however, is declined in various ways (food and wine tourism, religious tourism, etc.); the corresponding tourist market niches, perhaps small if taken one by one, may become the subject of specific market strategies and government policies if they are considered as a whole (Cerquetti & Montella, 2015)

A particular version of slow tourism, the "outdoor cultural tourism", is experiencing an interesting development. The Marche seems to offer many opportunities for this type of tourism, which integrates the preference for a vacation characterized by sporting activity, however eco-sustainable, with an offer in which both the tourist attractions and the accommodation facilities are distributed throughout the territory. A tourism product that matches such needs and characteristics requires the development of a regional network based on the so-called "soft mobility", whose nodes are represented by the reception facilities and whose branches are represented by paths that can be traveled by bicycle, on foot or on horseback (Gallegati, 2014).

The evolution of tourism demand, including cultural demand, highlights the possibility (which sometimes seems to represent a real necessity) to implement market strategies focused at diversifying the type of audience by museums and, in general, by cultural institutions.

Besides this evidence on the tourism market evolution and on the root for the development of its current strategy, the "Galleria Nazionale delle Marche" at Palazzo Ducale shows a clear orientation at audience broadening, according to data gathered from key informants through semi-structured interviews. The management is strongly committed in finding new ways to reach more visitors in the market segments that are currently addressed (schools, tourist groups, etc.), while less pronounced is the orientation to audience deepening, which is going to be applied especially to school groups.

In perspective, therefore, there seem to be the ideal conditions to complete the range of strategies pursued, so as to better intercept the segment of the "outdoor cultural tourism", where the cultural term refers not only to the historical-artistic heritage but to all the traditions of a territory.

Technologies in Use and Digital Skills: Link With Strategy Issues

By shifting attention to the choices of adopting digital technologies, we consider it appropriate to emphasize the need for these to be consistent with the corporate strategy. Moreover, we believe that the organization must develop skills that are adequate to overcome any issues of "technology acceptance" and to allow the effective management of digital devices in use.

The "Galleria Nazionale delle Marche" is currently adopting only technologies for remote fruition, while a digital archive is under construction. No digital initiative for the implementation of technologies for on-site fruition was planned before the CIVITAS project. The museum's director became aware of the importance of this solution by interacting with the academic partner, as well as looking at the example of other museums. Considering the starting situation, the CIVITAS project focused on the experimentation of digital devices aimed primarily at enriching the visiting experience at Palazzo Ducale. In perspective, therefore, the museum in Urbino should be characterized by a massive use of technologies for on-site fruition.

This type of technology seems to be consistent with an audience deepening approach, that is aimed at intensifying the engagement of audiences; at present, this type of approach is primarily thought for the school audience. On the other hand, it is not perfectly clear to what extent an augmented or virtual reality device - per se - is able to attract new groups of consumers that do not currently attend (audience diversifying) or capturing (audience broadening). Indeed, the effectiveness of these digital solutions seems to depend on the extent to which the various audience targets are made aware of their existence.

If the alignment between museum strategy and digital technologies is not always easy to evaluate, the experience of the other museums under analysis highlights how the possession of (or access to) digital skills play a key-role in selecting digital technologies consistent with the market strategy of the museum and - ultimately - with its business model.

Digital skills currently held by the manager and operating roles at Palazzo Ducale mainly refer to software programs in use to update the website and the official social media channels (applied digital skills). Only a few roles hold those skills. Technical skills are accessible through the partnership with academic researchers. Several factors (budget constraints, university training offer, etc.) have slowed down the inclusion of these skills in museum staff over the past few years. No development has been planned to date. So, the museum plans to fully rely on external expertise for the coming years too. Yet, the experience of the museums that have been studied shows that the systematic lack of this type of skills influences the ability to develop market strategies that take into account the opportunities offered by digital technologies; besides, it makes the systematic and continuous use of these technologies uncertain over time.

FUTURE RESEARCH DIRECTIONS

Considering the project in the middle of its timeline, each challenge shows some weak points and will have the chance to go ahead with interesting research developments.

Regarding the digitization issues, to which the CIVITAS project deals with, additional development is expected throughout the collaboration with MAP CNRS (Marseille) exploiting and testing the of Aioli tool, In particular selected case studies, such as historical furniture and frames of paintings, will be able to test and compare the portability and, overall, a large amount of data acquired has generated the big files that require careful management.

The main achievement of the CH1 is already to have carried out an integrated survey of an important historical building, with a large amount and a multilevel detail of data to process: it implies currently the creation of the information system for management and scalability of these data. The quantity and the quality of the expected information required the optimized setup of best practices for the acquisition, processing and management of these big data. A validated and high accurate model guarantees the success of the next applications, in particular regarding the CH3 and CH4.

Both the point cloud representation, output of CH1 and the BIM model produced within CH2 allowed the consolidation of a first annotated 3D dataset that will drive experiments in assessing Deep Learning methods in the built heritage domain. The initial dataset has been enriched with data coming from other context and projects and is composed of 12 different annotated point clouds representing different historical buildings.

4 out of the 8 scenes have been manually annotated to segment 8 classes of architectural elements: columns, doors, windows, stairs, arcs, vaults, roofs and floors. The remaining 8 were synthetically created from the BIM models. Each element was sampled using he CloudCompare tool to create dense annotated point clouds. Synthetic data, even if different from real scans, e.g. more regular, generally easier to classify or automatically segment, can be valuable in training machine learning and deep models.

Future work will go in the direction of enriching the dataset in the attempt to create a first machine learning benchmark in the area of built cultural heritage architecture.

The literature review indicated different promising deep learning approaches to be evaluated, the first of which PointNet++ and its subsequent improvements. All these models have achieved good results in Big Data standard benchmarks, as the ScanNet dataset. The challenge is that of adapting those methods to succeed in cases where the amount of available data is significantly lower, as in the case of historical buildings. At the time of writing this chapter, promising preliminary results were already achieved applying PointNet++ on an historical building point cloud data set to automatically segment basic architectural elements (Malinverni et al., 2019).

In our experiments, we plan to augment the synthetic dataset by introducing noise and occlusions in an attempt to reach a critical mass of data to effectively train the neural networks.

Another research strand related to HBIM goes in the direction of fostering sharing and exploration of HBIM models in a Web environment (Quattrini et al. 2017-b). The goal is that of enabling both fruition and semantic enrichment of historical 3D models outside the boundaries of specific, and often proprietary, software, by leveraging Semantic Web annotation technologies already successfully applied, in the context of Digital Humanities and Cultural Heritage, to other kinds of media, e.g. text and images (Grassi et al. 2013). Extending Semantic Web annotation to 3D models poses interesting challenges in visualization and user interaction, and demands for the development of appropriate annotation ontologies.

Regarding the neurological researches in the CH3, on the basis of the obtained results, with the collaboration of the whole research groups, virtual platforms will be created for the presentation of information and materials of cultural value with different perceptive methods in order to verify the satisfaction of the patient in relation to his particular cognitive profile.

At the current stage, 55 subjects have been investigated in which the neuropsychological characterization allows to identify particular deficit specificities or vice versa, still conserved cognitive performances. Starting from the latter, we will try, at a later stage, to create an individualized path of presentation of cultural material, able to be received and processed in an optimal manner.

Regarding the fourth Challenge, future research originated by the combination of image target recognition and SLAM goes towards multiple directions:

- In the short term, the limitation of the proposed app needs to be addressed. In fact, SLAM stresses the mobile device on a computation point of view, potentially causing overheating. Hence, SLAM usage needs to be optimized.
- In the midterm, the visual interaction can be combined with Vocal Interaction (VI), for example building in-app dialogs with virtual avatars or works of art which becomes "alive" thanks to animation.
- In the long term, the proposed combination of technologies can be applied and validated on other use cases, different from the Studiolo.

The future research directions of the SAR and Dynamic Projection are:

- Implement the application in the real "Studiolo del Duca" and extend the projection in all of the four walls with the wood marquetry; in order to effectively evaluate the real fruition improvement with the SAR's implementation.
- Interact with the system, allowing the visitor to choose the details that he wants to know about the "Studiolo del Duca", through gesture tracking and the position of the visitor in the space.

CONCLUSION

The researches presented in the chapter show a robust and interdisciplinary approach in DCH, above all key activities and faced challenges demonstrated to test cross-fertilization strategies, involving multilayered issues.

The CIVITAS project is already tested as a favorable arena and a reference framework enabling digit(al)isation strategies for a museum. A first main achievement occurs as a container able to propose involvements and interactions at different scales, satisfying different levels of multisensory use. The 3D reality-based obtained models and the connected databases are configured as a fundamental starting point for the digitalization process at various scales and on different fields of application. The well-known limitations linked to the CH fruition are overcome in favor of a multidisciplinary scenario. In addition, transdisciplinary outputs a technology transfer from the research field to current applications are expected.

The positive stimulus linked to the use of cultural heritage in patients with cognitive impairment may significantly receive an improvement in relation to the characteristics of cognitive remaining assets. Digitisation and using virtual and augmented reality, with specific characteristics in relation to the best performing skills in patients with cognitive impairment could potentiate the possibility to interact and take advantage from the cultural offer so reducing the frailties that limit personal experience by enhancing the remaining skills, facilitating visitor emotional state and cognitive and behavioral positive response.

The previously carried out evaluations and the possible applications could contribute to breaking down barriers regarding the accessibility of museum assets for people with cognitive impairment, favoring a museum path tailored for a patient with certain cognitive abilities preservation, also with the help of the digitization of cultural material.

The combination of image target recognition and SLAM has been presented as a way of building AR mobile apps to support and guide a visitor during the fruition of the Studiolo inside the Palazzo Ducale of Urbino. The presented workflow has the potential to bring AR to the next level, mixing different mapping technologies to visualize information superimposed to artworks in a stable and reliable manner. Moreover, such an approach can be followed in other case studies in Cultural Heritage.

A challenging result is the introduction of SAR paradigm in DCH sector and the combined use of biofeedback, emotion detection and eye tracking to monitor user engagement, satisfaction and learning capabilities. The Studiolo del Duca's space is rich of elements with a hidden meaning, that through this application can be enjoyed in a simpler way by a different type of visitors. The visitor feels involved in the environment and he can live a very inclusive experience, increasing the level of interest in the historical space.

With regard to needs and strategies in DCH management, the analyzed cases stress the importance of having available digital technical skills, with which to structure digital transformation paths functional to relate to one's own reference market. The benefits connected to the development of this type of skills have already been tested by other Italian museums. These benefits are partly already visible in some museum management experiences. On the one hand, the spread of digital skills among museum roles can help reduce dependence on external suppliers, especially in cases where the relationship with the supplier is not structured in the form of long-term partnerships. On the other hand, it can facilitate the evaluation of proposals coming from technological partners (universities, consulting firms, etc.), in terms of adequacy with respect to the habits and needs of habitual and potential visitors. The scarcity of internal technical skills may also affect the capability of the organization of exploring and reaching different audience targets. In fact, we believe that a widespread awareness of the of the potential and the possible improvements of technologies in use could help cultural heritage's organizations to define a correct correspondence between technological choices and the type of audience with whom to activate or improve the relationship. In this regard, a facilitating condition could be represented by the fact that the Palazzo Ducale museum participate in the so-called "Polo Museale delle Marche"; in fact, being part of an integrated network offers the possibility of developing at central level some technical skills, without the need to develop them internally in each museum, as evidenced by some cases.

In conclusion, a high effectiveness of a museum's digitalisation path depends on the pursuit and constant monitoring of two levels of coherence: on the one hand that between the choices of technology adoption and the acquisition objectives of emerging and growing tourism segments; on the other, between the digital skills possessed by (or accessible to) the museum and the functionalities of digital devices in use.

ACKNOWLEDGMENT

The researches presented here are founded by Univpm in the framework of Strategic University projects. The project CIVITAS (ChaIn for excellence of reflectiVe Societies to exploit dIgital culTural heritAge and museumS) involves seven departments and several researchers of the Polytechnic University of Marche.

The group of researchers would like to thank the Galleria Nazionale delle Marche of Urbino and its director dr. Peter Aufreiter for the interest and the support in the CIVITAS implementation. Thanks to Leica Geosystems for the participation of some survey phases, making available the Leica Pegasus backpack.

REFERENCES

Aica, Assinform, Assintel, A. (2017). *Osservatorio delle competenze digitali 2017: scenari, gap, nuovi profili professionali e percorsi formativi.*

Amin, D., & Govilkar, S. (2015). Comparative study of augmented reality Sdk's. *International Journal on Computational Science & Applications*. doi:10.5121/ijcsa.2015.5102

Apollonio, F. I., Gaiani, M., & Sun, Z. (2013). 3D modeling and data enrichment in digital reconstruction of architectural heritage. *ISPRS Archives, 5*, W2–W2.

Aubin, P. (2013). *Renaissance revit: Creating classical architecture with modern software.* (G3B Press, Ed.).

Bailey, T., & Durrant-Whyte, H. (2006). Simultaneous localization and mapping (SLAM): Part II. *IEEE Robotics & Automation Magazine, 13*(3), 108–117. doi:10.1109/MRA.2006.1678144

Bakhshi, H., & Throsby, D. (2012). New technologies in cultural institutions: Theory, evidence and policy implications. *International Journal of Cultural Policy, 18*(2), 205–222. doi:10.1080/10286632.2011.587878

Barbieri, L., Bruno, F., & Muzzupappa, M. (2017). Virtual museum system evaluation through user studies. *Journal of Cultural Heritage, 26*, 101–108. doi:10.1016/j.culher.2017.02.005

Barrozio da Vignola, M. I. (1562). *La regola delli cinque ordini d'architettura.*

Basballe, D. A., & Halskov, K. (2010). Projections on museum exhibits: engaging visitors in the museum setting. *Proceedings of the 22nd Conference of the Computer-Human Interaction Special Interest Group of Australia on Computer-Human Interaction*, 80–87. 10.1145/1952222.1952240

Bonacini, E. (2011). Nuove tecnologie per la fruizione e valorizzazione del patrimonio culturale. (Aracne, Ed.). Roma, Italy.

Camic, P. M., Tischler, V., & Pearman, C. H. (2014). Viewing and making art together: A multi-session art-gallery-based intervention for people with dementia and their carers. *Aging & Mental Health, 18*(2), 161–168. doi:10.1080/13607863.2013.818101 PMID:23869748

Canciani, M., Conigliaro, E., Del Grasso, M., Papalini, P., & Saccone, M. (2016). 3D Survey and augmented reality for cultural heritage. The case study of Aurelian Wall at Castra Praetoria in Rome. In *International Archives of the Photogrammetry*. Remote Sensing and Spatial Information Sciences - ISPRS Archives; doi:10.5194/isprsarchives-XLI-B5-931-2016

Carrozzino, M., & Bergamasco, M. (2010). Beyond virtual museums: Experiencing immersive virtual reality in real museums. *Journal of Cultural Heritage, 11*(4), 452–458. doi:10.1016/j.culher.2010.04.001

Ceccacci, S., Generosi, A., Giraldi, L., & Mengoni, M. (2018). Tool to make shopping experience responsive to customer emotions. *International Journal of Automation Technology*. doi:10.20965/ijat.2018.p0319

Cerquetti, M., & Montella, M. M. (2015). Museum networks and sustainable tourism management. The case study of Marche region's museums. *Enlightening Tourism. A Pathmaking Journal, 5*(1), 100–125.

Chancellor, B., Duncan, A., & Chatterjee, A. (2014). Art therapy for Alzheimer's disease and other dementias. *Journal of Alzheimer's Disease, 39*(1), 1–11. doi:10.3233/JAD-131295 PMID:24121964

Cianciarulo, D. (2015). From local traditions to "Augmented Reality". The MUVIG Museum of Viggiano (Italy). *Procedia: Social and Behavioral Sciences, 188*, 138–143. doi:10.1016/j.sbspro.2015.03.349

Clini, P., Quattrini, R., Frontoni, E., Pierdicca, R., & Nespeca, R. (2016). Real/not real: Pseudo-holography and augmented reality applications for cultural heritage. In Handbook of research on emerging technologies for digital preservation and information modeling. doi:10.4018/978-1-5225-0680-5.ch009

COMMITTE, U. (2017). UNI 11337-4:2017 Edilizia e opere di ingegneria civile - Gestione digitale dei processi informativi delle costruzioni - Parte 4: Evoluzione e sviluppo informativo di modelli, elaborati e oggetti.

Cursi, S., Simeone, D., & Toldo, I. (2015). A semantic web approach for built heritage representation. In Communications in Computer and Information Science. doi:10.1007/978-3-662-47386-3_21

DCH-RP. (2014). *A roadmap for preservation of digital cultural heritage content*. Retrieved from http://www.dch-rp.eu/index.php?en/115/roadmap-for-preservation

Dragoni, A. F., Quattrini, R., Sernani, P., & Ruggeri, L. (2019). Real scale augmented reality. A novel paradigm for archaeological heritage fruition. doi:10.1007/978-3-030-12240-9_68

DURAARK. (2015). *D3.5 Point cloud schema extension for the IFC model.*

Durrant-Whyte, H., & Bailey, T. (2006). Simultaneous localization and mapping: Part I. *IEEE Robotics & Automation Magazine, 13*(2), 99–110. doi:10.1109/MRA.2006.1638022

Empler, T. (2015). Cultural heritage: Displaying the Forum of Nerva with new technologies. In *2015 Digital Heritage International Congress, Digital Heritage 2015*. 10.1109/DigitalHeritage.2015.7419576

Farshid, M., Paschen, J., Eriksson, T., & Kietzmann, J. (2018). Go boldly!: Explore augmented reality (AR), virtual reality (VR), and mixed reality (MR) for business. *Business Horizons, 61*(5), 657–663. doi:10.1016/j.bushor.2018.05.009

Gallegati, M. (2014). Il turismo culturale nelle Marche: dalle città d'arte ai centri culturali minori. In P. Alessandrini (Ed.), *RAPPORTO MARCHE +20 SVILUPPO NUOVO SENZA FRATTURE. Regione Marche*.

Gao, Q. H., Wan, T. R., Tang, W., & Chen, L. (2017). A stable and accurate marker-less augmented reality registration method. In *Proceedings - 2017 International Conference on Cyberworlds, CW 2017 - in cooperation with: Eurographics Association International Federation for Information Processing ACM SIGGRAPH*. 10.1109/CW.2017.44

Gegenfurtner, A., Lehtinen, E., & Säljö, R. (2011). Expertise differences in the comprehension of visualizations: A meta-analysis of eye-tracking research in professional domains. *Educational Psychology Review, 23*(4), 523–552. doi:10.100710648-011-9174-7

Gimeno, J. J., Portalés, C., Coma, I., Fernández, M., & Martínez, B. (2017). *Combining traditional and indirect augmented reality for indoor crowded environments. A case study on the Casa Batlló museum. Computers and Graphics*. Pergamon; doi:10.1016/j.cag.2017.09.001

Govers, C. P. M. (1996). What and how about quality function deployment (QFD). *International Journal of Production Economics, 46-47*, 575–585. doi:10.1016/0925-5273(95)00113-1

Grassi, M., Morbidoni, C., Nucci, M., Fonda, S., Piazza, F. (2013). Pundit: Augmenting web contents with semantics. *Literary and Linguistic Computing, 28*(4), art. no. fqt060, pp. 640-659.

Grilli, E., Dininno, D., Petrucci, G., & Remondinoa, F. (2018). From 2D to 3D supervised segmentation and classification for cultural heritage applications. In International Archives of the Photogrammetry, Remote Sensing and Spatial Information Sciences - ISPRS Archives. doi:10.5194/isprs-archives-XLII-2-399-2018

Guttentag, D. A. (2010). Virtual reality: Applications and implications for tourism. *Tourism Management, 31*(5), 637–651. doi:10.1016/j.tourman.2009.07.003

Hammady, R., Ma, M., & Temple, N. (2016). Augmented reality and gamification in heritage museums. In Lecture Notes in Computer Science (including subseries Lecture Notes in Artificial Intelligence and Lecture Notes in Bioinformatics). doi:10.1007/978-3-319-45841-0_17

He, Z., Wu, L., & Li, X. (2018). When art meets tech: The role of augmented reality in enhancing museum experiences and purchase intentions. *Tourism Management*. doi:10.1016/j.tourman.2018.03.003

Hendriks, I., Meiland, F. J. M., Slotwinska, K., Kroeze, R., Weinstein, H., Gerritsen, D. L., & Dröes, R. M. (2018). How do people with dementia respond to different types of art? An explorative study into interactive museum programs. *International Psychogeriatrics*. doi:10.10171041610218001266 PMID:30560737

Horvitz, E. J., Breese, J. S., & Henrion, M. (1988). Decision theory in expert systems and artificial intelligence. *International Journal of Approximate Reasoning, 2*(3), 247–302. doi:10.1016/0888-613X(88)90120-X

Interreg Europe Policy Learning Platform on Environment and resource efficiency. (2018). Digital solutions in the field of cultural heritage. A Policy Brief from the Policy Learning Platform on Environment and resource efficiency, (August), 12.

Johnson, J., Culverwell, A., Hulbert, S., Robertson, M., & Camic, P. M. (2017). Museum activities in dementia care: Using visual analog scales to measure subjective wellbeing. *Dementia (London), 16*(5), 591–610. doi:10.1177/1471301215611763 PMID:26468054

Jones, J., & Christal, M. (2002). *The future of virtual museums: On-line, immersive, 3D environments.* Created Realities Group.

José López, F., Martin Lerones, P., Llamas, J., Gómez-García-Bermejo, J., & Zalama, E. (2018). Semi-automatic generation of bim models for cultural heritage. *International Journal of Heritage Architecture: Studies, Repairs, and Maintenance.* doi:10.2495/ha-v2-n2-293-302

Jung, T., Dieck, M. C., Lee, H., & Chung, N. (2016). Effects of virtual reality and augmented reality on visitor experiences in museum. In Information and Communication Technologies in Tourism 2016. doi:10.1007/978-3-319-28231-2_45

Kevin, F., & McCarthy, K. J. (2001). *A new framework for building participation in the arts.* Rand; doi:10.3102/0013189X030007010

Kinney, J. M., & Rentz, C. A. (2005). Observed well-being among individuals with dementia: Memories in the Making©, an art program, versus other structured activity. *American Journal of Alzheimer's Disease and Other Dementias, 20*(4), 220–227. doi:10.1177/153331750502000406 PMID:16136845

Lee, Y. Y., Choi, J., Ahmed, B., Kim, Y. H., Lee, J. H., & Son, M. G., … Lee, K. H. (2015). A SAR-based interactive digital exhibition of Korean cultural artifacts. In *2015 Digital Heritage International Congress, Digital Heritage 2015.* 10.1109/DigitalHeritage.2015.7419591

Liang, H., Li, W., Lai, S., Zhu, L., Jiang, W., & Zhang, Q. (2018). The integration of terrestrial laser scanning and terrestrial and unmanned aerial vehicle digital photogrammetry for the documentation of Chinese classical gardens – A case study of Huanxiu Shanzhuang, Suzhou, China. *Journal of Cultural Heritage, 33*, 222–230. doi:10.1016/j.culher.2018.03.004

Loizides, F., El Kater, A., Terlikas, C., Lanitis, A., & Michael, D. (2014). *Presenting cypriot cultural heritage in virtual reality: A user evaluation.* Lecture Notes in Computer Science Including Subseries Lecture Notes in Artificial Intelligence and Lecture Notes in Bioinformatics; doi:10.1007/978-3-319-13695-0

López, F., Lerones, P., Llamas, J., Gómez-García-Bermejo, J., & Zalama, E. (2018). A review of heritage building information modeling (H-BIM). *Multimodal Technologies and Interaction, 2*(2), 21. doi:10.3390/mti2020021

MacPherson, S., Bird, M., Anderson, K., Davis, T., & Blair, A. (2009). An art gallery access programme for people with dementia: You do it for the moment. *Aging & Mental Health, 13*(5), 744–752. doi:10.1080/13607860902918207 PMID:19882413

Malinverni, E. S., Pierdicca, R., Paolanti, M., Martini, M., Morbidoni, C., Matrone, F., & Lingua, A. (2019). Deep learning for semantic segmentation of 3D point cloud. *International Committee of Architectural Photogrammetry, CIPA 27*th *International Symposium,* Avila, Spain.

Massaro, D., Savazzi, F., Di Dio, C., Freedberg, D., Gallese, V., Gilli, G., & Marchetti, A. (2012). When art moves the eyes: A behavioral and eye-tracking study. *PLoS One, 7*(5). doi:10.1371/journal.pone.0037285 PMID:22624007

McCarthy, C. J., & Uppot, R. N. (2019). Advances in virtual and augmented reality—exploring the role in health-care education. *Journal of Radiology Nursing, 38*(2), 104–105. doi:10.1016/j.jradnu.2019.01.008

Mengoni, M., Germani, M., & Bordegoni, M. (2009). Virtual reality systems: a method to evaluate the applicability based on the design context. doi:10.1115/detc2007-35028

Mengoni, M., & Leopardi, A. (2019). An exploratory study on the application of reverse engineering in the field of small archaeological artefacts. *Computer-Aided Design and Applications, 16*(6), 1209–1226. doi:10.14733/cadaps.2019.1209-1226

Mittelman, M., & Epstein, C. (n.d.). Meet me at MoMA - MoMA Alzheimer's Project. *MoMA.*

Mortara, M., Catalano, C. E., Bellotti, F., Fiucci, G., Houry-Panchetti, M., & Petridis, P. (2014). Learning cultural heritage by serious games. *Journal of Cultural Heritage, 15*(3), 318–325. doi:10.1016/j.culher.2013.04.004

Museum and The Web. (2015). Open cultural heritage data on the web. Retrieved from http://www.museumsandtheweb.com/mw2012/papers/radically_open_cultural_heritage_data_on_the_w

Naspetti, S., Pierdicca, R., Mandolesi, S., Paolanti, M., Frontoni, E., & Zanoli, R. (2016). Automatic analysis of eye-tracking data for augmented reality applications: A prospective outlook. In Lecture Notes in Computer Science (including subseries Lecture Notes in Artificial Intelligence and Lecture Notes in Bioinformatics). doi:10.1007/978-3-319-40651-0_17

Nespeca, R. (2018). Towards a 3D digital model for management and fruition of Ducal Palace at Urbino. An integrated survey with mobile mapping. *SCIRES-IT - SCIentific RESearch and Information Technology.* doi:10.2423/I22394303V8N2P1

Nicolae, C., Nocerino, E., Menna, F., & Remondino, F. (2014). Photogrammetry applied to problematic artefacts. In *International Archives of the Photogrammetry.* Remote Sensing and Spatial Information Sciences - ISPRS Archives; doi:10.5194/isprsarchives-XL-5-451-2014

Noya, N. C., García, Á. L., & Ramírez, F. C. (2015). Combining photogrammetry and photographic enhancement techniques for the recording of megalithic art in north-west Iberia. *Digital Applications in Archaeology and Cultural Heritage, 2*(2-3), 89–101. doi:10.1016/j.daach.2015.02.004

Ochmann, S., Vock, R., & Klein, R. (2019). Automatic reconstruction of fully volumetric 3D building models from oriented point clouds. *ISPRS Journal of Photogrammetry and Remote Sensing, 151,* 251–262. doi:10.1016/j.isprsjprs.2019.03.017

Pierdicca, R., Paolanti, M., Naspetti, S., Mandolesi, S., Zanoli, R., & Frontoni, E. (2018). User-centered predictive model for improving cultural heritage augmented reality applications: An HMM-based approach for eye-tracking data. *Journal of Imaging.* doi:10.3390/jimaging4080101

Pizzi, G., Scarpi, D., Pichierri, M., & Vannucci, V. (2019). Virtual reality, real reactions?: Comparing consumers' perceptions and shopping orientation across physical and virtual-reality retail stores. *Computers in Human Behavior, 96,* 1–12. doi:10.1016/j.chb.2019.02.008

Poole, A., & Ball, L. J. (2006). Eye tracking in HCI and usability research. In Encyclopedia of Human Computer Interaction. doi:10.4018/978-1-59140-562-7.ch034

Qi, C. R., Su, H., Mo, K., & Guibas, L. J. (2017). PointNet: Deep learning on point sets for 3D classification and segmentation. In *Proceedings - 30th IEEE Conference on Computer Vision and Pattern Recognition, CVPR 2017.* doi:10.1109/CVPR.2017.16

Qi, C. R., Yi, L., Su, H., & Guibas, L. J. (2017). PointNet++: Deep hierarchical feature learning on point sets in a metric space. Retrieved from http://arxiv.org/abs/1706.02413

Quattrini, R., Pierdicca, R., & Morbidoni, C. (2017-a). Knowledge-based data enrichment for HBIM: Exploring high-quality models using the semantic-web. *Journal of Cultural Heritage.* doi:10.1016/j.culher.2017.05.004

Quattrini, R., Pierdicca, R., Morbidoni, C., Malinverni, E. S. (2017-b). Conservation-oriented hbim. The bimexplorer web tool. *International Archives of the Photogrammetry, Remote Sensing and Spatial Information Sciences - ISPRS Archives, 42* (5W1), pp. 275-281.

Quiroga, R. Q., & Pedreira, C. (2011). How do we see art: an eye-tracker study. *Frontiers in Human Neuroscience, 5.* doi:10.3389/fnhum.2011.00098 PMID:21941476

Remondino, F. (2011). Heritage recording and 3D modeling with photogrammetry and 3D scanning. *Remote Sensing, 3*(6), 1104–1138. doi:10.3390/rs3061104

Ridel, B., Reuter, P., Laviole, J., Mellado, N., Couture, N., & Granier, X. (2014). The revealing flashlight: interactive spatial augmented reality for detail exploration of cultural heritage artifacts. *Journal on Computing and Cultural Heritage.* doi:10.1145/2611376

Schaich, M. (2013). Combined 3D scanning and photogrammetry surveys with 3D database support for archaeology & cultural heritage. A practice report on ArcTron's Information System aSPECT 3D. In Photogrammetric Week '13.

Schall, A., Tesky, V. A., Adams, A. K., & Pantel, J. (2018). Art museum-based intervention to promote emotional well-being and improve quality of life in people with dementia: The ARTEMIS project. *Dementia (London)*, *17*(6), 728–743. doi:10.1177/1471301217730451 PMID:28914089

Shi, S. W., Wedel, M., & Pieters, F. G. M. R. (2013). Decision making : A model-based exploration using eye-tracking data. *Management Science*, *59*(5), 1009–1026. doi:10.1287/mnsc.1120.1625

Sooai, A. G., Sumpeno, S., & Purnomo, M. H. (2016). User perception on 3D stereoscopic cultural heritage ancient collection. doi:10.1145/2898459.2898476

Sparrow, L. (2016). Variations in visual exploration and physiological reactions during art perception when children visit the museum with a mobile electronic guide. In *Aesthetics and Neuroscience*. Scientific and Artistic Perspectives; doi:10.1007/978-3-319-46233-2_9

Styliani, S., Fotis, L., Kostas, K., & Petros, P. (2009). Virtual museums, a survey and some issues for consideration. *Journal of Cultural Heritage*, *10*(4), 520–528. doi:10.1016/j.culher.2009.03.003

Sylaiou, S., Mania, K., Karoulis, A., & White, M. (2010). Exploring the relationship between presence and enjoyment in a virtual museum. *International Journal of Human-Computer Studies*, *68*(5), 243–253. doi:10.1016/j.ijhcs.2009.11.002

Tamke, M., Evers, H. L., Zwierzycki, M., Wessel, R., Ochmann, S., Vock, R., & Klein, R. (2016). An automated approach to the generation of structured building information models from unstructured 3D point cloud scans. Retrieved from http://www.re-ad.dk/ws/files/60642021/IASS2016_1248_An_automated_approach_to...pdf

Tröndle, M., Greenwood, S., Kirchberg, V., & Tschacher, W. (2014). An integrative and comprehensive methodology for studying aesthetic experience in the field: Merging movement tracking, physiology, and psychological data. *Environment and Behavior*, *46*(1), 102–135. doi:10.1177/0013916512453839

Wang, Y., Sun, Y., Liu, Z., Sarma, S. E., Bronstein, M. M., & Solomon, J. M. (2018). Dynamic graph CNN for learning on point clouds. Retrieved from http://arxiv.org/abs/1801.07829

Wedel, M., & Pieters, R. (2008). A review of eye-tracking research in marketing. *Review of Marketing Research*. doi:10.1108/S1548-6435(2008)0000004009

Witmer, B. G., & Singer, M. J. (1998). Measuring presence in virtual environments: A presence questionnaire. *Presence (Cambridge, Mass.)*, *7*(3), 225–240. doi:10.1162/105474698565686

ADDITIONAL READING

Archives Libraries Museums, A. X. I. E. L. L. (2016). Digital Transformation in the Museum Industry. *Exhibition on the South Liverpool Archives Show*, 15. Retrieved from http://alm.axiell.com/wp-content/uploads/2016/07/Axiell-ALM-Digitise-Museums-Report.pdf

Clini, P., Frontoni, E., Martini, B., Quattrini, R., & Pierdicca, R. (2017). New Augmented Reality applications for learning by interacting. *Archeomatica*, *8*(1), 28–33.

Generosi, A., Ceccacci, S., & Mengoni, M. (2018). A deep learning-based system to track and analyze customer behavior in retail store. In *IEEE International Conference on Consumer Electronics - Berlin, ICCE-Berlin*. 10.1109/ICCE-Berlin.2018.8576169

Giannini, T., & Bowen, J. (2019). *Museums and Digital Culture.*

Haugstvedt, A. C., & Krogstie, J. (2012). Mobile augmented reality for cultural heritage: A technology acceptance study. In *ISMAR 2012 - 11th IEEE International Symposium on Mixed and Augmented Reality 2012, Science and Technology Papers*. 10.1109/ISMAR.2012.6402563

Ioannidou, A., Chatzilari, E., Nikolopoulos, S., & Kompatsiaris, I. (2017). Deep Learning Advances in Computer Vision with 3D Data. *ACM Computing Surveys*, *50*(2), 1–38. doi:10.1145/3042064

Meroño-Peñuela, A., Ashkpour, A., Van Erp, M., Mandemakers, K., Breure, L., & Scharnhorst, A. … Van Harmelen, F. (2014). Semantic technologies for historical research: A survey. *Semantic Web*. doi:10.3233/SW-140158

Schall, A., & Romano Bergstrom, J. (2014). *Eye Tracking in User Experience Design*. Eye Tracking in User Experience Design; doi:10.1016/C2012-0-06867-6

Sciacchitano, E. (2019). Editorial. European year of Cultural-Heritage. A laboratory for heritage-based innovation. *SCIRES-IT - SCIentific RESearch and Information Technology, 9*(1), 1–14. doi:10.2423/I22394303V9N1P1

Sernani, P., Angeloni, R., Dragoni, A. F., Quattrini, R., & Clini, P. (2019). *Combining image targets and SLAM for AR-based cultural heritage fruition*. Augmented Reality, Virtual Reality, and Computer Graphics. doi:10.1007/978-3-030-25999-0_17

KEY TERMS AND DEFINITIONS

Artificial Neural Network: Artificial Neural Networks (ANN) are computational models, originally inspired by biological neural networks. An ANN is a nonlinear statistical data modeling tool composed by a set of units (usually arranged in layers) connected to each other via weighted edges. They are used to solve specific tasks by incrementally learning an unknown function of the input data and are usually trained with a number of known input-output pairs.

Digitalisation/Digitisation: Digitalisation is the adoption process of digital technologies for the public engagement and for back-office management. Digitization indicates procedures of data capturing and remote sensing in order to generate virtual facsimile, transforming tangible CH into digital contents. In some literature point of views, it also includes native digital contents.

Enhancing the Remaining Skills: The possibility to correctly characterize different profiles of cognitive performance in subjects with cognitive impairment is essential to individuate a profitable mode of interaction and enjoyment of a cultural site.

Level of Detail/Development: The level of detail and stability of the data and information of the digital objects that make up the models. It combines both the graphical and non-graphical attributes. It defines the quantity and quality of their information content and serves to achieve the goals of the process phases (and stages) and the model uses and goals to which they refer.

Market Strategy: Market Strategy: how an organization intends to serve the markets it chooses. Market strategies are statements through which an organization defines which customer segments wants to target, how it expects to differentiate from its competitors, how it wants to communicate its value proposition, and which activities intends to perform in order to reach these goals.

Outdoor Cultural Tourism: Sustainable touristic product that allows integrating the demands for cultural tourism and that for sustainable outdoor activities. It may be developed by creating short- to medium-distance routes which connect territorial areas characterized by ancient ruins, monuments, and archaeological sites through the use of intermodal mobility systems with low environmental impact (fast mobility: train and ship; slow mobility: bicycle, horses).

SLAM: Simultaneous Localization and Mapping.

Spatial Augmented Reality: is a technology that augments real world objects and scenes without the use of special displays such as head mounted displays or hand-held devices. SAR makes use of digital projectors to display graphical information onto the space.

Stable Augmented Reality: Combination of SLAM and Image Target Recognition which allows virtual objects to scale and rotate according to users' actions.

User Experience Design: is a process of enhancing user satisfaction with a product, service, process, and environment by improving the usability, accessibility, and desirability provided in the interaction. It is the practice with a focus placed on the quality of the user experience and culturally relevant solutions.

ENDNOTES

[1]   The Studiolo was the private study of the Duke Federico da Montefeltro, and it is the only internal space of Palazzo Ducale that keept its original design. The Studiolo is a small room with an almost rectangular plan: the perimeter of the room is about 3.60x3.35m and 5m high. All four walls are covered up to about 2.22m by inlaid wooden panels called "Tarsie". Various objects are represented on the panels (books, musical instruments, animals, characters, etc.), all with a strong symbolism that leads back to the deeds and power of the Duca Federico da Montefeltro

[2]   Leica Pegasus backpack is a wearable mobile mapping device.

[3]   Revit model has been carried out in Building Engineering Thesis Degree by Marianna Pistolesi and Marica Calvaresi, supervisor: Prof. Ramona Quattrini, co-supervisor: Romina Nespeca.

Chapter 12
Evaluating Augmented and Virtual Reality in Education Through a User–Centered Comparative Study:
SmartMarca Project

Roberto Pierdicca
Università Politecnica delle Marche, Italy

Emanuele Frontoni
Università Politecnica delle Marche, Italy

Maria Paola Puggioni
Università Politecnica delle Marche, Italy

Eva Savina Malinverni
ⓘD https://orcid.org/0000-0001-6582-2943
Università Politecnica delle Marche, Italy

Marina Paolanti
Università Politecnica delle Marche, Italy

ABSTRACT

Augmented and virtual reality proved to be valuable solutions to convey contents in a more appealing and interactive way. Given the improvement of mobile and smart devices in terms of both usability and computational power, contents can be easily conveyed with a realism level never reached in the past. Despite the tremendous number of researches related with the presentation of new fascinating applications of ancient goods and artifacts augmentation, few papers are focusing on the real effect these tools have on learning. Within the framework of SmartMarca project, this chapter focuses on assessing the potential of AR/VR applications specifically designed for cultural heritage. Tests have been conducted on classrooms of teenagers to whom different learning approaches served as an evaluation method about the effectiveness of using these technologies for the education process. The chapter argues on the necessity of developing new tools to enable users to become producers of contents of AR/VR experiences.

DOI: 10.4018/978-1-7998-1796-3.ch012

Copyright © 2020, IGI Global. Copying or distributing in print or electronic forms without written permission of IGI Global is prohibited.

INTRODUCTION

In classical education systems imperfections and challenges induce teachers to use new methods to improve the level of learning (Teferra & Altbachl, 2004; Luna Scott, 2005; Frey & Osborne, 2017). For this purpose, technology is a helpful aid in education, which allows to ease the learning methods, increasing the performances by introducing suitable technological materials (Richey, Silber, & Ely, 2008). Mainly, in the Primary school thanks to the didactic paths that are closer to the learning transmitted through the game, the preferential model of Virtual Reality (VR) and Augmented Reality (AR) applications, a great development of this disciplines has taken place. Some disciplines are more suitable for using these novel didactic forms, as for example sciences (Chen, Liu, Cheng, & Huang, 2017). The scientific disciplines have a major field of application in this innovative learning methodology and moreover, since these mobile devices are easily used by the younger generations, is established a greater familiarity and confidence during the learning process (Pierdicca, Frontoni, Pollini, Trani, & Verdini, 2017), and they take on the form of play or enjoyable quiz. Novel terms are coined as "learning by searching" and "Inquiry based science education" (Yin, Han-Yu, Hwang, Hirokawa, Hui-Chun, Flanagan, & Tabata, 2013), that are able to translate the different implemented processes through the creation of a knowledge based on researches, surveys and modelling construction. Taking into account different disciplines, the possibility of being completely immersed in monuments, or deepening in real time the contents of paintings or sculptures, without losing contact with the surrounding environment, is essential to enjoy an immersive and interactive experience of the work itself (Di Serio, Ibáñez, & Kloos, 2013; Naspetti, Pierdicca, Mandolesi, Paolanti, Frontoni & Zanoli, 2016).

For the students the process of learning requires, beyond the immediate response to the content proposal, even their permanence in time. The competences must generate an ability to understand and re-elaborate the information acquired to produce transversal and multidisciplinary skills. So an essential aspect is to use the technologies without weakening the ability of the students to create their own heritage of skills, refining cognitive techniques through their study and personal reworking. During the didactic activity, modulated on the class and on the single students, the use of technologies could lead to a method of work that is not flexible and can be modelled on the variable context of the students. The learning experience is modified with technological means (Dede, 1996) so it is important to study the effects of these technologies on learning, in particular on the student's ability to reuse the learned lessons in different fields. A certain effect is that the students, through their technological skills, can build paths that are more familiar to them. A real learning requires a more careful path to the relapse over time of the educational activities carried out by AR/VR technologies.

The aim of this work is to evaluate the real performances of AR/VR technologies for didactic purposes, considering their effect on the cultural and personal training of the students through the use of digital tools that involve all the aspects related to teaching and learning. The evaluation must also consider the ability to re-elaborate the learned knowledge. The work carried out with this research intends to be a contribution to the studies on the AR and VR applications in the educational field, evaluating as the contents and methods of these new educational paths can improve the real learning and how through a long-term educational path it is possible to direct the student towards a cognitive process and re-elaborate the learned knowledge. The test was executed inside the SmartMarca project, briefly described in Section 3. The platform underlying the project was specially created to handle AR/VR contents for cultural heritage located in the south part of the Marche region, in Italy. Since the students are oriented towards this kind of technologies, several experiments were produced exploiting and testing these users, with particular attention to the evaluation of AR/VR potential for learning in the field of Cultural Heritage (CH) and obtaining meaningful results in terms of the multimedia experience.

BACKGROUND

Studies revealed that AR and VR have a great potential to help students to improve their knowledge and skills. In fact the connection between AR/VR and education makes the teaching and learning experience more efficient and appealing (El Sayed, 2010; Crosier, 2002; Kaufmann, Schmalstieg, & Wagner, 2000). In this way, students not only better learn, but also the learning processes reach a more accurate knowledge (Christou, 2010; Sotiriou and Bogner, 2008). The work of Gargalakos, Giallouri, Lazoudis, Sotiriou and Bogner (2011) has demonstrated that the technology has much enhanced the learning results increasing the curiosity of the students and their willingness to communicate and share their enlightening experiences with other students, their anxiety to use new technologies and acquire knowledge having fun and living virtual and current realities. However, there are challenges and disadvantages in the use of AR/VR as educational tool in most classes of the world (Ardiny & Khanmirza, 2018). The first problem is that implementing AR/VR systems is expensive. The second problem is the lack of realism for VR or AR simulations. The third problem concerns health problems and physical effects on students. The head-mounted-displays (HMD) are relatively heavy and can cause fatigue to users after a long period. Lenses in an HMD may obstruct the view. Another side effect that is not limited to HMD is the disease of the simulator and seems especially in virtual reality experiences. The fourth challenge is related to the limitations of the hardware. Although recent hardware developments have improved AR and VR demonstrations, the limitations could reduce a high level of user experience.

AR Applications

AR can be defined as an interactive experience in the real world where computer-generated objects and elements of the real world are linked together (Ardiny & Khanmirza, 2018). Initially, AR was born for scientific and research purposes. Since the eighties, AR has been applied for the first time in the military field in head-up displays, devices installed on the control panel of combat aircraft, which has allowed the pilot to test some parameters and flight data without looking away from the dashboard of the aircraft. Then the usefulness of this system has led to its spread even on civil aircraft. These are the years in which, also in the scientific and medical fields, analysis and study techniques are developed which involve the use of AR. AR is a technology available on different devices: 1) PC: it uses stylized black and white markers (ARtags) which are created ad hoc to be captured by the webcam and recognized by the PC, which superimposes the multimedia contents. 2) Mobile devices: such as smartphones and tablets. In this case we also speak about Mobile augmented reality (MAR): the device must be equipped with GPS, compass and Internet connection. Through the framing of the surrounding world, the webcam is able to detect "points of interest" (POI) to which other 3D multimedia contents are superimposed. 3) Dedicated devices: viewers with transparent or semi-transparent lenses, gloves and others.

In their work, M. Akçayır and G. Akçayır (2017) propose an interesting review where the different aspects of the use of AR in education have been highlighted. Studies have shown that AR technology offers many advantages when used in education (Cheng and Tsai, 2013). For example, AR helps students to begin authentic explorations in the real world (Dede, 2009). By displaying virtual elements next to real objects, AR makes easy how events that cannot be otherwise observed with the naked eye, are observed (Wu, Lee, Chang & Liang, 2013). Saidin, Halim, and Yahaya (2015), focusing on the positive impact that these technologies have had on the community, affirm that AR can be defined as the new, extraordinary, way where it is possible to make concrete the abstract. Students can interact with a multimedia support animated and subject to changes: the possibility to interact with contents, facilitates the study above all of those who must analyse microscopic components of reality. According to Mark Billinghurst (Billinghurst, 2002), AR has the advantage of promoting collaboration among students, thanks to the possibility of recreating a real and common environment in which everyone can work. It creates involvement because it leads authentic materials and objects within the reach of the sensory experience of all learners. However, although many AR studies have been published, the educational advantages and related utilities of AR only recently have been explored (Chen & Tsai, 2012). To date there is not a comprehensive explanation of the educational effects and implications of AR (Radu, 2012). It is very important for a teacher to be able to assess the appropriateness of the applications to use in the classroom, especially in the case of AR, since most of these have not been born specifically for educational use. The first and fundamental criterion to deal with is the usability. In fact, the application that shall be used has the aim to satisfy the learning needs of the students, thanks to the intuitive access and use of the tools and ensuring the ease of understanding both the processes and the contents.

During his research, Nielsen (1994) established five fundamental requirements on which the concept of usability is based: ease of learning, efficiency of use, ease of understanding, reversibility of errors and satisfaction in use. Therefore, we can affirm that even if AR is not born for tutorial purposes, it has a huge exploitable potential in this field. For example, the AR interfaces are used in the medical field as a training tool that allows the students to visualize the inside of the human body and the various organs in 3D. In the chemical field, the AR has made the study of the elements interactive and attractive thanks to the 3D representation of their physical properties and of the reactions deriving from their combination. The possibility of scanning the most famous paintings to obtain real-time information has important implications in the teaching of art.

One of the most used apps on AR is the Aurasma app[1]. The software is free for both IOS and Android and is developed by the Autonomy company. Through this application, it is enough to frame a photo, a newspaper, and an image with a smartphone or tablet that immediately appears on the screen an additional related content. The added content could simply be a video, a link to a web page or more complex like a 3D animation. From the e-learning point of view, MAR has proven to be a winning solution (Etxeberria, Asensio, Vicent & Cuenca, 2012). In Garau and Ilardi, such as, a specific application was designed that allows people to download the contents related to the area of cultural heritage (CH) they were discovering. Given the enormous disposal of CH-related artifacts produced in recent years, contents such as building paintings have been increased, especially in the archaeological site. A good example can be found in (Garau & Ilardi, 2014).

In 2006, Wagner, Schmalstieg and Billinghurst developed a collaborative video game based on the educational game called Virtuoso. The purpose of this game is to order a collection of works of art based on their date of creation along a timeline with three different conditions: a paper, a PC and a PDA. The results showed that although the players were tested with three different game conditions, no significant differences were found in the educational results. It is interesting to note that the players preferred the paper and PDA version because it allows them to collaborate more effectively than the PC version. Furthermore, they chose the PDA interface as the most pleasant of the three conditions (Wagner, Schmalstieg & Billinghurst, 2006).

In 2009, Dunleavy, Dede and Mitchell designed Alien Contact!, a MAR game that focuses on teaching mathematics, language arts and scientific literacy to middle and high school students. The concept of the game is based on the scenario where the aliens landed on earth and work in teams. Students can interview virtual characters, collect digital objects and solve science, math and language problems to answer the question and find why the aliens have landed on earth. The results obtained from the study have documented the high involvement of students in the different case studies (Dunleavy, Dede, & Mitchell, 2009).

In 2009, Ardito and others presented a MAR game called Explore! with the aim of supporting during a visit and explorations of middle school students to archaeological sites in Italy. This game was played by groups of 3-5 middle school students in which each group was given 2 mobile phones and the site map on a sheet. The concept of the game required the students to explore important places on the sites supported by some tips provided on the phone by the game application. From the results of the study, it was shown that the students had fun playing with Explore! but in terms of learning, there were no significant differences (Ardito, Buono, Costabile, Lanzilotti & Piccinno, 2009).

Martín and others proposed an educational application called EnredaMadrid to make it easier for students to learn history. The goal of EnredaMadrid is to teach the history of the city in the 17_{th} century through previous online training and a later physical technological gymkhana. For the realization of this application, mobile devices based on geolocation and AR technology were used. The evaluation session was carried out through a questionnaire, and the results showed that AR certainly contributes to making learning more fun and motivating and that AR is the most proper tool for learning the history of the city (Martín, Díaz, Cáceres, Gago & Gibert, 2012).

VR Applications

Virtual Reality, unlike AR, is more widespread and known in the field of videogames and therefore young people are more familiar with the use of different devices that allow a VR vision in the various fields of application, not directly linked to the purely playful aspect. This familiarity constitutes an element in favor of the introduction of VR technology in a school educational path. Through the dissemination of video games, it is easy to offer students the use of devices such as visors and cardboard.

HMD used in combination with earphones and gloves produce an interesting immersive effect, not only in video games but also in educational applications. The user can be placed in an environment that reproduces simulation situations that facilitate emotional and sensorial involvement. An interesting example of the application of VR in training is the simulation of the risks in the construction site works. Living the fall from above in a simulated way allows the experience of the fall to be perceived in a realistic way and leaves the feeling of emptiness in the unconscious memory. The transmission of knowledge therefore passes through an experiential dynamic that allows us to broaden the aspect of student involvement in teaching practice. As result there will be not only a more correct behavior in the front of a risk situation, but also a more conscious ability to outline a work procedure that better complies with the normative requirements, as enriched by a direct practice that constitutes a heritage, the result of a training process developed in the field. There are different working sectors in which the application of VR performs the function of simulating dangerous situations for a correct and complete professional training. Rahimian, Arciszewski & Goulding (2014) describe the use of VR for the professional training of architectural engineering construction specialists. The direct vision of what is transmitted and its involvement amplify the learning process. In particular, according to Classen: "the sense of seeing is the most important sense and it is most closely linked to reason" (Classen, 1997).

Introducing therefore the technology of VR in specific didactic sectors facilitates the action of learning, thanks to the direct involvement of the student who becomes active subject in the transmission of knowledge. The educational areas that are most suited to being VR systems application scenarios are technical and scientific. In fact, these sectors have aspects that can be easily reproduced in simplified and operational situations. They allow the student to reproduce in a concrete and visible way the application of formulas or theories that, relegated to the textbook, would be dry and not very comparable. The risk may be that this activity is interpreted only as a game and therefore detached from the learning process, which although experiential, must lead students to increase their theoretical and conceptual knowledge. The application of VR in the field of visual arts and architecture and in any case in all cultural heritage is particularly interesting (Bekele, Pierdicca, Frontoni, Malinverni, & Gain, 2018). Reconstruction of monuments, archaeological sites or works of art through viewers that allow you to immerse yourself in the building are engaging experiences, especially for a young audience that uses digital devices with familiarity. Technologies can serve a function similar to X-rays to show what is hidden underground or to increase an environment with virtual reconstructions of lost heritage (Clini, Quattrini, Frontoni, Pierdicca, & Nespeca, 2017).

Virtual reconstructions of lost heritage can promote, not only the rediscovery of otherwise unknowable places, but also spread a culture of protection of what is present and tangible. In using a VR device to move to a place rich in history, a boy can be attracted to discovering aspects and details that he would not otherwise read only through a direct vision. Therefore, in the technological approach the added value of the digital methodological language brought to the didactic action is enclosed.

In (Martín, Díaz, Cáceres, Gago & Gibert, 2012) the authors indicate three key aspects linked to any VR system: immersion, interaction and visual realism. The action to surrounding the user with virtual technologies and devices creates the immersion. (Wu, Liu, Wang & Zhao, 2015), e.g. virtual glasses, gloves with movement sensors, HMDs, surround sound, and any element that creates sensorial stimuli, or sensors that allows the user to interact with a virtual environment as in a real environment. So that VR simulates the real presence of the user in a virtual environment, which is classified as sensory-motoric, cognitive, and emotional (Holopainen & Björk, 2004). Moreover VR also creates an immersive 3D spatial experience when the users feel of belonging to a virtual world, which is affected by his perceived feeling (Benford, Greenhalgh, Reynard, Brown, & Koleva, 1998). To seem real, this perception requires real-time interaction, in order that the user requires instant feedback of his movements, position, and sensations. This feedback allows the user to react and send commands to a computer by using trackers, gloves, keyboards, or any other input device simulating real-world user's reactions.

Traditionally, the invention VR is traced back to a device designed and patented by the American director Morton Heilig (Mihelj, Novak & Beguš, 2014) and named Sensorama. Heilig, already at the end of the 1950s, had designed a television that allowed for a 3D viewing experience. In fact it was a cabin equipped with stereoscopic screens, stereo speakers, as well as a movable seat.

But it was not until the 1990s that we started talking about VR again, when the videogame industry was finally able to have functional technological equipment for mass production, and therefore products capable of combining high-profile performance and low costs.

In the primary classes of the Unified School of San Francisco and of the Polk County Public Schools complex in Florida, through the Nearpod educational platform[2], virtual tours of Easter Island, in Ancient Egypt, along the coral reef and even on Mars are offered to children. While, in California, at the Marin

School of the Arts in Novato, many of the classrooms have been reorganized to be more in line with the spatial needs required by the VR systems in use. In these classes, a wall was occupied by ultra-flat monitors on which the children create and manipulate scenes at 360°; on the opposite side, now without desks and chairs, a protected area was created in which students can use an optical device: HTC Vive headset.

On this side of the Atlantic, the Mendel High School in Opava, in the Czech Republic was the first European high school to create integrated courses with the latest generation of VR technology. In the current school year, the Czech high school offers science and history teaching units through the optical device, Oculus Rift headset, and the Leap Motion controller, a technology that, connected to the hardware, allows, through simple hand movements, rather precise human-machine interactions.

The virtual application, Google Expeditions[3] allows taking part in hundreds of virtual visits to the most evocative locations around the world (like the Great Wall of China, Mars, and more) but also in the depths of the oceans or in the most extreme space. It is a product specifically designed for classroom work. The dedicated site, in fact, has instructions and advice on how to best organize a virtual lesson addressed directly to teachers. The test may be produced with a mobile phone and a Google Cardboard headset[4]. A VR tour requires 360° viewing so that the participant overall observes the scene they are viewing. The user can look to the right, and they can look up or down, or they can go towards an object.

In the InCell VR app[5], the user is miniaturized inside a human cell and has the task of reaching, before the virus does, the nucleus of the cell, so that it can thus defend itself from any attack. To be successful, the user will have to move between mitochondria, cytoplasm and centrioles, closely observing their forms and functions.

The app Vatican[6] is an application that provides tours and information about the Vatican in Rome. Students can enter each room with High Definition pictures. This application is only available for 360 views and not Google Cardboard.

Cave Automatic Virtual Environments (CAVE) (Christou, 2010) is a tool supporting immersive VR approach there are, where the user is in a room where all the walls and the floor, are projection screens. The user can wear 3D glasses, feels floating in the projected world where he can move around freely. CAVE environments are still rather expensive, they need to have a specific space dedicated to them and they cannot be moved easily. All these characteristics make it difficult a widely spread use in education and didactic. However, CAVE technology is particularly used in cultural heritage education (Ott & Pozzi, 2008).

DESCRIPTION OF SMARTMARCA APPLICATION

The cultural and tourist heritage of the territories is one of the constantly argued issues in the national and European panorama. Within this scenario, the innovative and digital systems supporting managers and users are still under-utilized and require a cultural leap with respect to the issues of digitization of cultural heritage and tourism in general. The SmartMarca project[7] is positioned within this scenario with the main objective of bringing the Fermano within the main national trends. The objectives of the project concern the numerous benefits and added value for all the actors involved in cultural tourism deriving from the digitisation of CH, from its publication on the net and from its re-use, that is:

- The possibility for cultural institutions to promote itself, enhance the known and less known, tangible and intangible heritage, increase the flow of visitors, tourists and users on the internet, and diversify the offer according to the recipients;
- The possibility for creative industries to exploit the potential of digital cultural heritage to create innovative services for tourism using professional figures with specialized skills and competences.
- The possibility for territories and territorial aggregators: to improve the quality of information on digital cultural heritage held by cultural institutions, respond to the needs of the tourism sector, build and strengthen contacts and links with the chain of actors involved and have more elements to promote digital cultural heritage as a driving force for strategies in the tourism market.
- The possibility for small and medium enterprises in the tourism sector (hotels, restaurants, tour operators, service cooperatives) to have cultural content available and offer more effectively on the market.
- The possibility for the tourist to benefit from additional tools of knowledge in order to be able to virtually visit less known or more peripheral places of cultural interest, live or plan and personalize their own travel experience through the opportunities offered by the technology, particularly mobile.

The project intends to propose the implementation of targeted strategies for each main territorial characteristic through the use of innovative technologies that can be inserted in paths for the enhancement and dissemination of the landscape/cultural heritage in order to expand the proposed offers, promote them on a scale worldwide and to finally generate an added economic value. Since the territory of Fermano is very heterogeneous, five main characteristics have been identified:

1. architecture, civil and religious monuments;
2. archaeological sites;
3. little villages and enogastronomy;
4. hills, mountains and hiking trails following the concept of sustainable mobility;
5. picture galleries and pictorial cultural heritage.

Through the use of 360° panoramic photos it is possible to recreate an exciting experience in the territories of the Fermano, going to emphasize the small villages and for example, through the virtual reality and Google Cardboard it is possible to live the Fermano, going to interact with points of interests to obtain contents of various types (texts, images, audio and video) and exciting the end user.

The Fermano territory is rich in itinerant routes and it is important that all citizens have exhaustive information that better allows them to discover and exploit. To achieve this scope, it is necessary that through the use of technologies such as Beacons, it is the territory itself that communicates to the user the relevant aspects of the surrounding environment. The result is that the key points of the territory are transformed into sensitive areas.

Furthermore by applying AR to the main Fermano paintings, an innovative method is obtained that provides information and interactive contents, favoring the accessibility and learning.

Then, SmartMarca aims to improve the quality of the territorial cultural offer by using the advanced technologies such as AR and VR, beacons and geolocalization systems this in order to provide users contextual services when traveling in the territory. The main innovative aspect is the management platform, which is able to manage several contents and output through a single cloud based service. The structure consisted of micro-services allows the managers of the platform to use different contents with different output. The common denominator of the project is the Senseable Space concept that defines a novel scenario where the user can use contextual services, but is simultaneously able to measure, analyze and reply accordingly actions, establishing a seamless information exchange (Osaba, Pierdicca, Malinverni, Khromova, Álvarez, & Bahillo, 2018).

For the question of this chapter, AR and VR application have been used to test multimedia for learning purposes and for these goals, contents can be used by the users through a mobile application, designed both for iOS and Android.

For the case of this paper, AR services are specifically designed to augment two of the most important paintings of the "Fermano", to increase accessibility and learn the painting itself. By using AR it is possible to identify a painting by framing it with the camera of a mobile phone to access augmented contents: emphasizing selected areas of the painting to give precise information on a specific feature, reproducing a video superimposed to the painting and visualizing appropriate images and texts in overlay. Concerning VR application, the image of Falerone amphitheatre 3D model is viewed. The users can interact with the image using VR headsets.

METHODOLOGY

The work described in this chapter was conducted following a rigorous methodology of study, divided into three main steps, described in the following: at a first stage, AR and VR have been studied separately, and then a comparison among the two technologies was carried out. The following sections follow this methodological approach.

AR Application: Rubens and Licini Paintings

An AR experience has been developed inside the SmartMarca project and it is related to the analysis of artworks belonging to the territory of Fermo: the "Adorazione dei pastori" by P.P. Rubens preserved in Palazzo dei Priori in Fermo and "Paesaggio" by Osvaldo Licini, present in the artist's house (museum in Monte Vidon Corrado). The app permits the augmentation of the artwork through tags that, deepening the critical contents of the paintings, propose a more attractive view both the details and the complete work. This project is mainly targeted for tourists, but with the aim to also use for didactic use that allows starting a first suggestion of knowledge of artworks in its fundamental contents. These tools have been employed to undertake an educational authentication path of AR. Some screenshots of the application running can be found in Figure 1. The research activity has been structured in different steps that can be summarized in the Table 1.

Didactic Methodology

In the secondary school curriculum, there is a first approach to the history of art through links that relates different disciplines and so students make a comparative reading of different including a synchronic and diachronic method of study. To the students, coming from the two-year period and the three-year period of a technical institute and a high school, were proposed the reading of the artworks using different methods, which provided a thorough introduction by the guide and/or the teacher. After the description,

Figure 1. AR application in front of the paintings
(a) "Adorazione dei pastori" by Rubens (b) "Paesaggio" by Licini

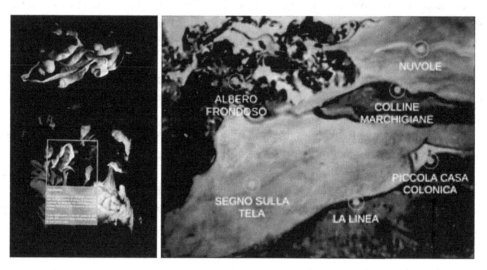

Table 1. First phase of the research path: description of the methodology used in the learning-teaching process, using AR application from SmartMarca project

First experimental phase				
With device	Explanation of the artwork by the teacher	Check online with the *Socrative* support	Data collection and statistical definition	Analysis, data comparison and conclusions
	Without explanation of the artwork			
Without device	Explanation of the artwork by the teacher			

the students using their smartphones had the access to the dedicated sector inside SmartMarca application. Through the painting they had access to AR content through overlay texts and the visualization of details, to which the markers were associated.

This information was subsequently verified through a series of multiple-choice questions included in Socrative application, an online application that allows verification and collection of results, data and statistics related to student learning. The questions included in the Socrative program and described also using images, were presented in table 3 and 4, found in the Appendix section of this manuscript. Questions have been organized with keywords that match with the overlap contents of the AR application, this in order to facilitate the link between the images and its related comments. Observing tables the questions had multiple choice (four options with only one correct) in order to have consistent data with a statistical meaning. Questions Q5, Q6, Q7, Q21 in table 3 are linked to the principal theme, chosen for its evocative value. Students have been asked to re-elaborate what was visualized in the app, to stress test their meta-cognitive learning. In the questionnaire related to table 4 questions to check the ability to re-elaborate contents and concepts are Q8, Q9, Q10, Q11, since they attempt to deepen some details of the painting like tree and house, the main theme of the whole painting. Figures 2 and 3 show the questionnaire results such as in the Socrative application used for this test.

Figure 2. Questionnaire data report "Adorazione dei pastori" of Socrative program

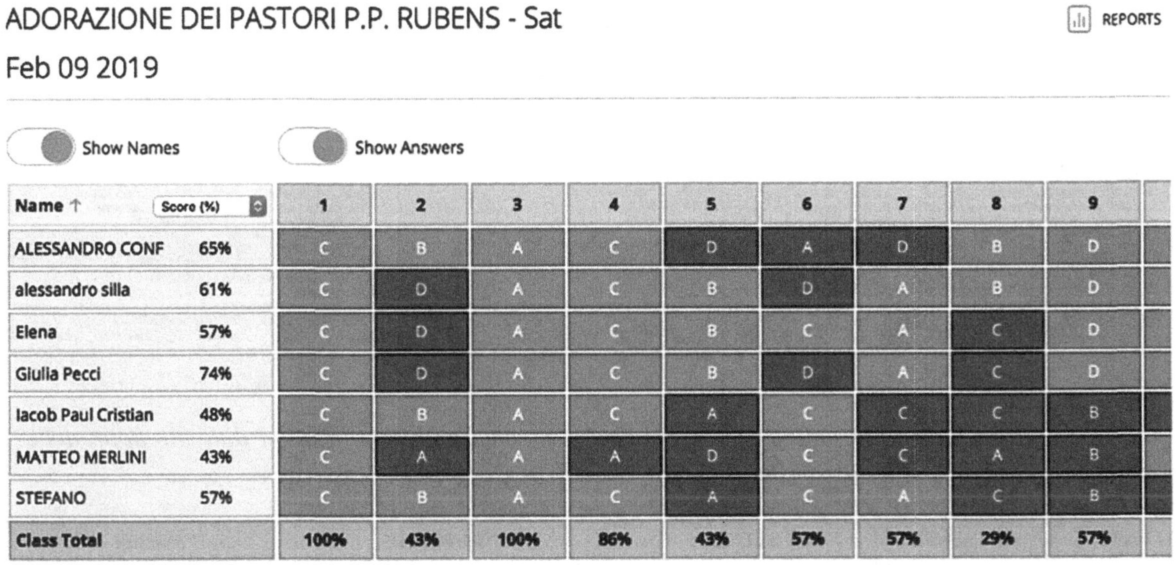

ADORAZIONE DEI PASTORI P.P. RUBENS - Sat

Feb 09 2019

REPORTS

Show Names   Show Answers

Name ↑	Score (%)	1	2	3	4	5	6	7	8	9
ALESSANDRO CONF	65%	C	B	A	C	D	A	D	B	D
alessandro silla	61%	C	D	A	C	B	D	A	B	D
Elena	57%	C	D	A	C	B	C	A	C	D
Giulia Pecci	74%	C	D	A	C	B	D	A	C	D
Iacob Paul Cristian	48%	C	B	A	C	A	C	C	C	B
MATTEO MERLINI	43%	C	A	A	A	D	C	C	A	B
STEFANO	57%	C	B	A	C	A	C	A	C	B
Class Total		100%	43%	100%	86%	43%	57%	57%	29%	57%

Figure 3. Questionnaire data report "Paesaggio" of Socrative program

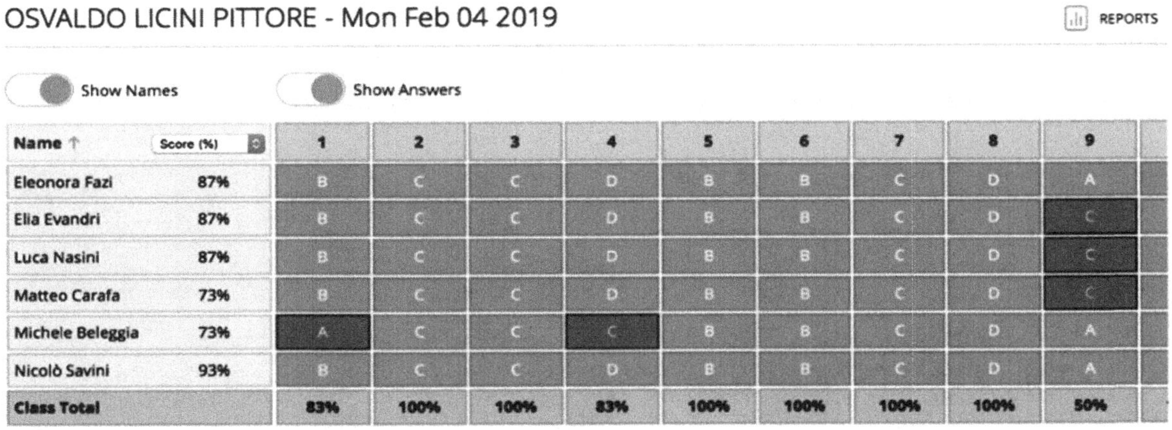

OSVALDO LICINI PITTORE - Mon Feb 04 2019

REPORTS

Show Names   Show Answers

Name ↑	Score (%)	1	2	3	4	5	6	7	8	9
Eleonora Fazi	87%	B	C	C	D	B	B	C	D	A
Elia Evandri	87%	B	C	C	D	B	B	C	D	C
Luca Nasini	87%	B	C	C	D	B	B	C	D	C
Matteo Carafa	73%	B	C	C	D	B	B	C	D	C
Michele Beleggia	73%	A	C	C	C	B	B	C	D	A
Nicolò Savini	93%	B	C	C	D	B	B	C	D	A
Class Total		83%	100%	100%	83%	100%	100%	100%	100%	50%

DATA ANALYSIS AND DISCUSSION

Figure 4 compares the results obtained making different testing method. The differences concern the rates of learning process by the students with or without the support of AR technology. Interesting is that Q8, Q9, Q10, Q11 questions have a higher percentage of positive answers combining lesson with AR (85.25%). Using only the app is not sufficient to reach a higher degree of in depth knowledge; hence the student is not able to elaborate meta-cognitive processes (less that 50%). The classical lecture confirms an average of 65% of right answers. These results demonstrate that adding AR increases the learning process, but its alone application is not enough. The overall statistics collected during the tests can be found in Table 2 and Figure 5.

Figure 4. Comparison of different learning methods. Left chart reports the number of right answers after the combination of classical lecture and AR. Central charts are the answers after the sole use of AR. Right chart the correct answer after the lecture without AR.

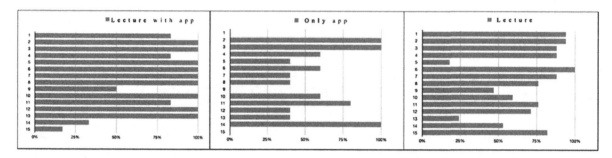

Table 2. Data final report. Comparison of all data collected with the different didactic approaches: classical lecture, only app and app plus lecture

	LICINI	RUBENS	Average
Lectures	70.11%	46.25%	58.18%
App	50.82%	57.33%	54.07%
Lectures+App	83.33%	57.85%	70.59%

Figure 5. Data final report

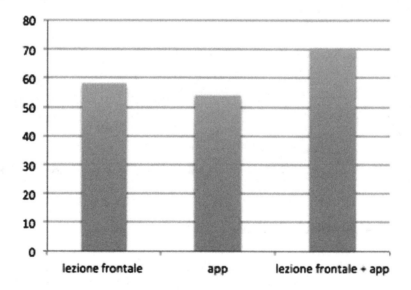

Summarizing the results obtained during the first step of experimental phase provided the following evaluations: the only frontal lesson is still a good means of transmitting contents and skills, valid for a satisfactory average learning response with a rate of 58.18%. The only use of the app is not a valid means of learning even if it is attractive and innovative with a rate of 54.07%. The combination of the frontal lesson and the app is a valid tool for learning, obtaining a rate of 70.59%.

Figure 6. Virtual Reality applied to the 3D reconstruction of the Roman theatre of Falerone: visualization of the informative tags inserted inside the reconstruction

The classical lecture still preserves its own value to spread and share the knowledge, since involves a bidirectional immersion among students and teacher. It is important the relation teaching-learning since involves several factors: emotional, experiential, relational, didactic, communicative, and psychological. Concerning the art being able to visit a museum, to know an archaeological site, to admire a monument constitutes an added value to the knowledge of the work, the technology helps this type of process by providing tools that involve the user, increasing the ability to obtain information, details, that would be difficult to find and consult in real time. The teaching experience and AR app increase the effectiveness of the learning process by giving scenarios increased with content that can be easily found in flexible and interconnected ways. The information that a teacher provides is then enhanced through a psychological and gestural involvement that cannot be transmitted by technology. On the other hand, the richness of connected information is mediated by versatile devices that create experiences in which the students find a response to methods that they are familiar with. The first data provided by this research leads to the conclusion of a mediated use between new technologies and traditional education. One cannot undertake innovative learning programs without validating their long-term efficiency. Analysing data it is clear that the didactic action has better value through the intervention of the teacher who succeeds in transmitting the contents in a more useful manner. The contribution of AR is enriching for a greater involvement of the students in the training activity, and demonstrates that increases the ability to learn, as shown by the increasing number of correct answers.

VR APPLICATION: THE ROMAN THEATRE OF FALERONE

The experience of reading the Roman theatre of Falerone reconstructed in 3D within the SmartMarca (Figure 6) application was proposed. The theatre contains not only charm as a place of entertainment, but also a direct testimony of Roman building capacity. The reconstruction represents both the unitary image of the entire artifact, and the descriptions of the various components of the monument and the relative precise definitions, in order to also provide concepts that can be used in the knowledge of similar architectural typologies.

All the Municipalities belonging to the District of Fermo (Provincial Capital in the Marche Region) have been the object of development of VR applications within the SmartMarca project. These applications are mainly aimed at reading the most significant urban and monumental places in the individual territories, to spread their knowledge. Among the various Municipalities in the area, the city of Falerone symbolically represents the added value that characterizes all the small and large towns of the Fermo area: keeping traces of the past that marks the historical and cultural value not only of the Marche but of the whole Italian territory. The Roman remains of the ancient city of Falerio Picenum date back to the 1st century A.C. when it was founded following an Augustan centuriation of the Tenna Valley.

This important testimony of the historical value of the territory has been the subject of a 3D VR reconstruction, inserted within the SmartMarca application.

The added value of the reconstructive hypothesis consists in having inserted the reading tags of the monument in its constitutive parts: architectural, structural and decorative. Therefore, the user, who can be any student or tourist, can know in detail the whole scenario of the theatre and learn about the functions of each single element: from the entrances (called vomitoria) to the subdivision of the seats for spectators, divided by census and political value. Figure 7 shows the view of the frontal scene and the lateral doors.

This detailed description also makes it possible to understand the functions and organization of the theatre's stage set-up, enriched by statues and decorations, which make the distinctive character of the theatre of Falerone. The statues dedicated to the goddess Ceres or Demeter, goddess of fertility and agriculture, declare the cultural nature of the territory mainly based on the cultivation of the fields and therefore linked to an agricultural tradition.

Figure 7. Visualization in Virtual Reality of the 3D model of the Theatre of Falerone: view of the front scene and side door

Figure 8. Students on a guided tour of the Roman remains of Urbisaglia (MC). Development of the second step of the educational research work: Visit to the remains of the temple, the amphitheatre and the theatre

Being able to observe these elements in detail through Virtual Reality also means having the time necessary to study carefully what is in front of you. Students can reflect and learn the elements necessary to implement the knowledge acquired with previous preparatory lessons for the virtual visit of the monument. So the advantage of the virtual visit to the monument is the time factor that allows the student to take advantage of the complete vision of the building in a more extended time frame and with a greater wealth of details. The information provided by the tags, directly related to the described element, help the student to visually focus the architectural part in question.

Didactic Methodology

Regarding the methodological analysis, the students of two first classes of upper secondary education were involved, respectively attending the Graphics and Communication Course (1AGR) and the Construction Environment and Territory Course (1ACAT). The school program of the discipline technologies and techniques of graphic representation involves the introduction of the History of architecture and art from the period from its origins to the late Roman period. Within the topics regarding Roman architecture, students are shown the major public buildings expressing classical Greek and Roman culture. Among these, is the theatre that represents, for its functions and its architectural typology, the expression of excellence of these civilizations founding the Mediterranean culture.

The first step of the didactic work concerned the traditional lesson in class in which the students learned the fundamental elements of the architectural and constructive culture of the Romans and the distributive and functional characteristics of the Roman theatre. The explanations have been enriched not only by the content of the textbook, but also by projections of images of remains of Roman theatres, taken from websites.

The second step has developed through a direct experience of visiting the archaeological park of Urbisaglia, in the province of Macerata. The area still shows evident and therefore easily legible traces of the ancient Roman settlement, of which the remains of the theatre, the amphitheatre and a temple remain well preserved in their characteristics. The site contains the most important peculiarities of a Roman urban intervention, for which it represents a valid instrument of knowledge of this historical and architectural testimony. As shown in Figure 8, during the visit, the students were invited to carefully read the architectural and distribution elements of the building.

Figure 9. Teaching content developed by the teacher, inserted in the tags of the SmartMarca application, related to the theatre of Falerone

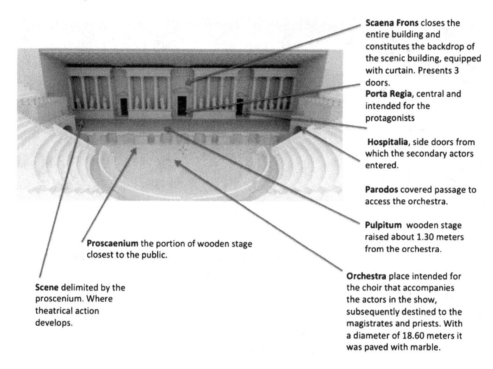

Scaena Frons closes the entire building and constitutes the backdrop of the scenic building, equipped with curtain. Presents 3 doors.

Porta Regia, central and intended for the protagonists

Hospitalia, side doors from which the secondary actors entered.

Parodos covered passage to access the orchestra.

Pulpitum wooden stage raised about 1.30 meters from the orchestra.

Proscaenium the portion of wooden stage closest to the public.

Scene delimited by the proscenium. Where theatrical action develops.

Orchestra place intended for the choir that accompanies the actors in the show, subsequently destined to the magistrates and priests. With a diameter of 18.60 meters it was paved with marble.

The third step took place again in the classroom through the use of the SmartMarca application that contains the 3D reconstruction of the Roman theatre of Falerone, coeval with the Urbisaglia theatre. The contents of the tags have been developed by the teacher and highlighted in figure 9. Each text contains descriptive elements useful for reading a Roman theatre in its distinctive features, so the educational validity of the application is guaranteed by the formative correspondence of the information to be transmitted.

A check was therefore proposed aimed at collecting data about the knowledge acquired from the educational path developed up to now, concluding the activity with the study of the contents inserted in the SmartMarca application.

The two class groups, up to this stage, carried out the work in a homogeneous and equivalent way, while in the next step they were divided: the first group of students was asked to prepare the verification by studying the contents of the application in advance at home, the second group was shown the content only shortly before the verification.

Figure 10 describes the work steps of the two class groups. First step: frontal lecture in class both 1ACAT and 1AGR. Second step: guided tour of archaeological park in Urbisaglia, both 1ACAT and 1AGR. Third step: use of the app with VR of the Teatro di Falerone, the 1ACAT class assigned study at home while the 1AGR class study in the classroom before verification. Fourth step: online verification with the Socrative program.

In the fourth step the students were engaged in the final verification of the course (Figure 11). The verification, administered to students through the Socrative web-based platform, contains multiple-choice questions. The requests contained in the questionnaire are substantially of 2 types: on the nomenclature

Figure 10. Description of the work steps of the two class groups

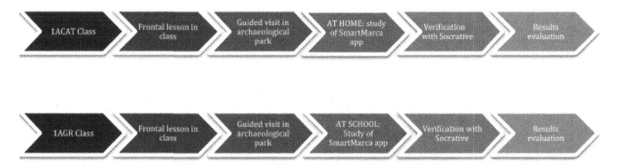

Figure 11. Students engaged in class in Socrative web-based verification

of the parts of the Roman theater (applicable to any theater in general) and on the historical, architectural and decorative features of the theater of Falerone, as Table 5 shows.

The answers collected highlighted the following information:

- definitions of the constituent parts of the theater have been acquired;
- the functions of the elements of the theater have been understood;
- the materials and construction techniques of the theater are known.

Data Analysis and Discussion

The results achieved in overall terms by the two groups are substantially and globally homogeneous, with a slight positive deviation for the class 1AGR group, as shown in figure 12.

From the analysis of the single questions it results that the 1AGR group correctly answered in greater percentage to the requests related to the information provided by the app regarding dates and numerical values that are easily memorized, if the information source has been recently consulted.

The 1ACAT group, which did not consult the app before the test but studied the content at home, instead memorized the technical aspect of the division of the rooms and the materials used and then responded correctly to the related questions.

Figure 12. Rate of correct answers for each class group

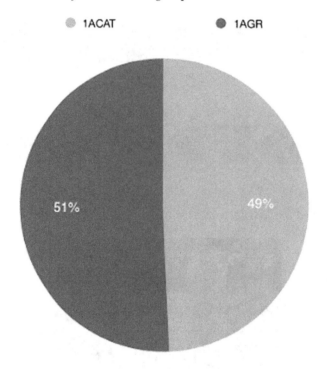

Looking at figure 13, the 1AGR class has a higher percentage of correct answers to notional questions, the 1ACAT class has a higher percentage of correct answers to technical questions

It should be emphasized that the first group belongs to the Graphics and Communication Course, therefore the students are particularly predisposed for training and aptitude to use multimedia means and to grasp the fundamental elements under the digital profile.

The second group belongs to the Course Construction Environment Territory, therefore particularly sensitive to the technological and structural aspect proposed in the analysis of the monumental artifact.

However, the average obtained by the two groups, 66.48% the first and 68.48% the second, confirm the effectiveness of the use of VR combined with traditional teaching systems, in the didactic field . These value can be extracted by Figure 14.

The following elements of validation of the analysis are noted:

- Having carried out a common path of acquisition of elements preparatory to the reading of the architectural artefact of the theater constituted a suitable element to validate the possession of the skills necessary for the didactically profitable use of the digital instrument;
- Both groups have demonstrated that they have reached more than sufficient knowledge of the subject in question;
- THE app proved to be a useful compendium of theoretical and practical knowledge;
- the consultation of the information provided by the app has highlighted the particular peculiarities of the two class groups, through the diversification of the correct answers provided.

Figure 13. Comparative table of the correct answers provided by the two class groups

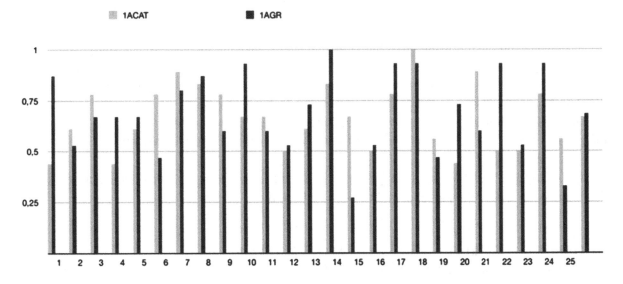

Figure 14. The results achieved by both class groups averaging stand at over 50%, confirming the more than sufficient acquisition of the proposed contents

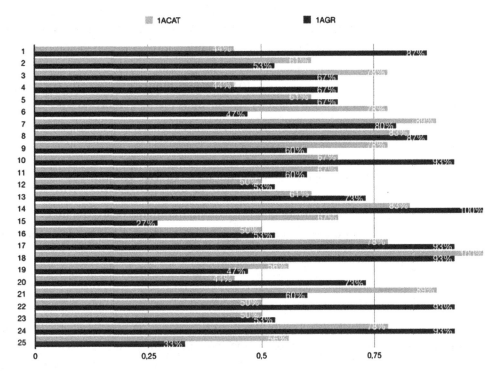

To add the particular interest shown by the students, through the active involvement shown during the entire educational path proposed. The diversification of the methodologies adopted, from the traditional frontal lesson accompanied by the direct visit of the site, followed by learning with the use of digital technology, has produced an interesting didactic result, which will now be verified in the long term.

For the teacher the development of the content of the app, its use within the training course offered to the students and the following proof has constituted an interesting methodological study.

In tracing the founding points of the subject matter, to carry out the insertion in the various tags, the teacher has identified the so-called minimum disciplinary objectives necessary for the students to develop the skills and knowledge that can be spent in a transversal way.

The verification methodology allowed a comparison of results between the two classes, highlighting the peculiarities of each one as evidence of the value of teaching based on students and therefore on individual skills.

It remains to be seen how, in the long term, it is possible to create similar methodological situations declined on the different topics and on the different disciplines.

AUGMENTED REALITY AND VIRTUAL REALITY: A COMPARISON IN THE DIDACTIC FIELD

The learning experiences conducted using AR and VR have highlighted the potential and limitations of individual technologies. Despite having peculiarities and different methods of presentation and use, the two technologies have been tested in the educational field to verify benefits, using the content of the applications related to the SmartMarca Project. In particular, the application of reading the "Adorazione dei Pastori" painting by Rubens, was used to test the AR, while for the VR, the vision of the Piazza del Popolo of Fermo was proposed.

The study carried out in this research phase, aims to verify and compare the greater correspondence of the two tools in terms of ease of use, the real capacity of transmission of content and student involvement.

Methodology

The activity carried out was organized with the following methodology (Figure 15):

- use of AR or VR system and reading the real image with the image proposed by the device;
- use of the device and immersion in the content proposed in AR and VR mode to understand the data to be tested;
- filling out the questionnaire prepared to gather information and elements for evaluation and comparison of the two technologies.

The students, after viewing the Rubens painting, used their smartphones to access the contents of the app in AR mode (Figure 16). The reading of the tags present in the painting was carried out in total autonomy by the students. Once this first phase was completed, the questionnaire was completed.

In reading Piazza del Popolo, the students wore Oculos visors where they had already inserted their smartphones (Figure 17). After selecting the section relating to the city of Fermo, they visited the Piazza in VR. At the end of the 360° view of the entire urban system, they completed the online questionnaire.

Figure 15. Methodology of study for the comparison of the two digital systems: vision of the real image, use of the device, compilation of questionnaire, data collection and analysis

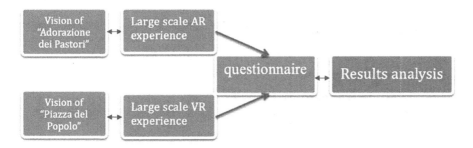

Figure 16. Use of Augmented Reality in front of the "Adorazione dei Pastori" of P.P. Rubens

Figure 17. Students while are testing VR applied to the 360° view of the "Piazza del popolo" in Fermo

Data Analysis

At the end of the experience of using devices with AR and VR applications, the online questionnaire proposed to the students was structured in two sections: one aimed at data collection related to the AR application on the painting by Rubens, the other to the collection data concerning the 360° visit applica-

Figure 18. Comparative histogram of the answers relating to table 7

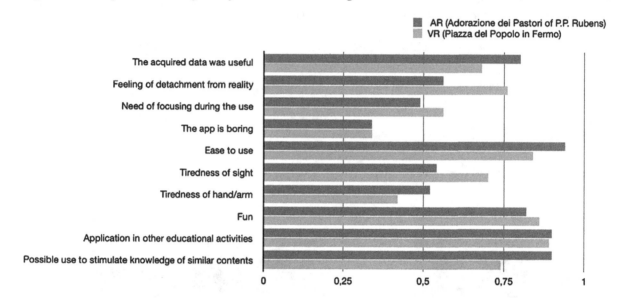

tion of the Piazza del Popolo. The questions tested different areas, as Table 6 in appendix 1, shows. The five-level Likert scale was used (1- not at all in agreement, 5- very much in agreement).

To facilitate the reading of the data the questions have been grouped by type, so as to allow a comparative view of the results. The percentages (Table 7, in appendix 1) represent the favorable answers. In figure 18, it is possible to verify the results compared, relating to the use of AR and VR.

CONCLUSION AND FUTURE RESEARCH DIRECTIONS

Within the framework of Smart Marca project, this chapter focuses on assessing the potential of AR/VR applications specifically designed for Cultural Heritage. More specifically, tests have been conducted on AR experience upon different paintings, while VR was developed on an ancient amphitheatre. Tests were made on two classrooms of teenagers to whom different learning approaches served as an evaluation method about the effectiveness of using these technologies for the education process. Analyzing the results obtained comparing AR and VR technologies and presented in Table 7 (in appendix 1), the following conclusions can be drawn:

- the AR system:
  - has greater ability to transmit information and content and their relative acquisition;
  - determines less sensation of detachment from reality;
  - needs less concentration during use;
  - it is easier to use and less tiring to look at;
  - is recommended for use in other areas and not only for teaching purposes.
- The VR system:
  - less fatigue in the hand / arm system;
  - creates more fun;
  - can be proposed for further educational uses.

Figure 19. A screenshot of SchoolAR application

However, both systems and their applications are not bored during their use.

It can be deduced that VR, despite being more widespread and known in the field of video games and non-didactic applications, has less potential for continuous use as it greatly strains the eyes and creates a greater detachment from reality. The use of the viewer also reduces its ease of use and in any case requires greater concentration on the part of the student. The AR in this case is easier to use, since it does not require any particular use devices. The constant relationship with reality facilitates concentration during use. The view is in fact stimulated by reading the data superimposed, creating a greater involvement of the student in understanding them. Overall, it therefore constitutes a methodology that is potentially more appropriate for application in the didactic and informative field, thanks to its characteristics of use of the device and transmission of content. What finally emerged from the study is that, despite technology is able to convey "disposable" information, it is far from stimulating the self reworking by the students, which still remains entrusted on the teacher role.

In the future, our proposal will be to create a platform called schoolAR for the creation of an educational content. In fact, it is well known that there is the necessity of developing new tools to enable users to become producers of contents of AR/VR experiences, since up to now there no exists a platform specifically designed for an agile creation, even for not skilled programmers. The intent is to propose a cooperative platform between teachers and students, which allows the use of innovative technologies (AR and VR) to stimulate student learning. After access, the user will be able to access a series of sections that will give the opportunity to continue the projects started, create new projects or consult the catalog of available content. Figure 19 shows the home screenshot of SchoolAR, an on-going project upon which our research group will concentrate the efforts. Another important aspect that will be investigated in the upcoming future is the long term effects of AR/VR in education. By submitting further test to the students, it will be interesting to uncover how, and if, technologies have real effects on knowledge retention.

ACKNOWLEDGMENT

This work was funded by the PSR 2014/2020 - M19.2.A.16.2 program, Action 19.2.16.2 - Sostegno a progetti pilota per la fruizione del patrimonio culturale.

REFERENCES

Akçayır, M., & Akçayır, G. (2017). Advantages and challenges associated with augmented reality for education: A systematic review of the literature. *Educational Research Review*, *20*, 1–11. doi:10.1016/j.edurev.2016.11.002

Ardiny, H., & Khanmirza, E. (2018, October). The role of AR and VR technologies in education developments: opportunities and challenges. In *2018 6th RSI International Conference on Robotics and Mechatronics (IcRoM)* (pp. 482-487). IEEE.

Ardito, C., Buono, P., Costabile, M. F., Lanzilotti, R., & Piccinno, A. (2009). Enabling interactive exploration of cultural heritage: An experience of designing systems for mobile devices. *Knowledge, Technology & Policy*, *22*(1), 79–86. doi:10.100712130-009-9079-7

Bekele, M. K., Pierdicca, R., Frontoni, E., Malinverni, E. S., & Gain, J. (2018). A survey of augmented, virtual, and mixed reality for cultural heritage. [JOCCH]. *Journal on Computing and Cultural Heritage*, *11*(2), 7. doi:10.1145/3145534

Benford, S., Greenhalgh, C., Reynard, G., Brown, C., & Koleva, B. (1998). Understanding and constructing shared spaces with mixed-reality boundaries. *ACM Transactions on computer-human interaction (TOCHI)*, *5*(3), 185-223.

Billinghurst, M. (2002). Augmented reality in education. *New horizons for learning*, *12*(5), 1-5.

Chen, C. M., & Tsai, Y. N. (2012). Interactive augmented reality system for enhancing library instruction in elementary schools. *Computers & Education*, *59*(2), 638–652. doi:10.1016/j.compedu.2012.03.001

Chen, P., Liu, X., Cheng, W., & Huang, R. (2017). A review of using augmented reality in education from 2011 to 2016. In *Innovations in smart learning* (pp. 13–18). Singapore: Springer. doi:10.1007/978-981-10-2419-1_2

Cheng, K. H., & Tsai, C. C. (2013). Affordances of augmented reality in science learning: Suggestions for future research. *Journal of Science Education and Technology*, *22*(4), 449–462. doi:10.100710956-012-9405-9

Christou, C. (2010). Virtual reality in education. In Affective, interactive and cognitive methods for e-learning design: creating an optimal education experience (pp. 228–243). Hershey, PA: IGI Global. doi:10.4018/978-1-60566-940-3.ch012

Classen, C. (1997). Foundations for an anthropology of the senses. *International Social Science Journal, 49*(153), 401–412. doi:10.1111/j.1468-2451.1997.tb00032.x

Clini, P., Quattrini, R., Frontoni, E., Pierdicca, R., & Nespeca, R. (2017). Real/not real: pseudo-holography and augmented reality applications for cultural heritage. In Handbook of research on emerging technologies for digital preservation and information modeling (pp. 201–227). Hershey, PA: IGI Global. doi:10.4018/978-1-5225-0680-5.ch009

Crosier, J. K., Cobb, S., & Wilson, J. R. (2002). Key lessons for the design and integration of virtual environments in secondary science. *Computers & Education, 38*(1-3), 77–94. doi:10.1016/S0360-1315(01)00075-6

Dede, C. (1996). The evolution of distance education: Emerging technologies and distributed learning. *American Journal of Distance Education, 10*(2), 4–36. doi:10.1080/08923649609526919

Dede, C. (2009). Immersive interfaces for engagement and learning. *Science, 323*(5910), 66-69.

Di Serio, Á., Ibáñez, M. B., & Kloos, C. D. (2013). Impact of an augmented reality system on students' motivation for a visual art course. *Computers & Education, 68*, 586–596. doi:10.1016/j.compedu.2012.03.002

Dunleavy, M., Dede, C., & Mitchell, R. (2009). Affordances and limitations of immersive participatory augmented reality simulations for teaching and learning. *Journal of Science Education and Technology, 18*(1), 7–22. doi:10.100710956-008-9119-1

El Sayed, N. A., Zayed, H. H., & Sharawy, M. I. (2010, December). ARSC: Augmented reality student card. In *2010 International Computer Engineering Conference (ICENCO)* (pp. 113-120). IEEE. 10.1109/ICENCO.2010.5720437

Etxeberria, A. I., Asensio, M., Vicent, N., & Cuenca, J. M. (2012). Mobile devices: A tool for tourism and learning at archaeological sites. *International Journal of Web Based Communities, 8*(1), 57–72. doi:10.1504/IJWBC.2012.044682

Frey, C. B., & Osborne, M. A. (2017). The future of employment: How susceptible are jobs to computerisation? *Technological Forecasting and Social Change, 114*, 254–280. doi:10.1016/j.techfore.2016.08.019

Garau, C., & Ilardi, E. (2014). The "non-places" meet the "places:" Virtual tours on smartphones for the enhancement of cultural heritage. *Journal of Urban Technology, 21*(1), 79–91. doi:10.1080/10630732.2014.884384

Gargalakos, M., Giallouri, E., Lazoudis, A., Sotiriou, S., & Bogner, F. X. (2011). Assessing the impact of technology-enhanced field trips in science centers and museums. *Advanced Science Letters*, *4*(11-12), 3332–3341. doi:10.1166/asl.2011.2043

Holopainen, J., & Björk, S. (2003). *Game design patterns*. Lecture Notes for GDC.

Kaufmann, H., Schmalstieg, D., & Wagner, M. (2000). Construct3D: A virtual reality application for mathematics and geometry education. *Education and Information Technologies*, *5*(4), 263–276. doi:10.1023/A:1012049406877

Luna Scott, C. (2015). *The futures of learning 3: What kind of pedagogies for the 21st century?*.

Martín, S., Díaz, G., Cáceres, M., Gago, D., & Gibert, M. (2012, October). A mobile augmented reality gymkhana for improving technological skills and history learning: Outcomes and some determining factors. In *E-learn: World conference on e-learning in corporate, government, healthcare, and higher education* (pp. 260-265). Association for the Advancement of Computing in Education (AACE).

Mihelj, M., Novak, D., & Beguš, S. (2014). Virtual reality technology and applications.

Naspetti, S., Pierdicca, R., Mandolesi, S., Paolanti, M., Frontoni, E., & Zanoli, R. (2016, June). Automatic analysis of eye-tracking data for augmented reality applications: A prospective outlook. In *International Conference on Augmented Reality, Virtual Reality and Computer Graphics* (pp. 217-230). Cham, Switzerland: Springer. 10.1007/978-3-319-40651-0_17

Nielsen, J. (1994). *Usability engineering*. Elsevier.

Osaba, E., Pierdicca, R., Malinverni, E., Khromova, A., Álvarez, F., & Bahillo, A. (2018). A smartphone-based system for outdoor data gathering using a wireless beacon network and GPS data: from cyber spaces to senseable spaces. *ISPRS International Journal of Geo-Information*, *7*(5), 190. doi:10.3390/ijgi7050190

Ott, M., & Pozzi, F. (2008, September). ICT and cultural heritage education: Which added value? In World summit on knowledge society (pp. 131-138). Berlin, Germany: Springer.

Pierdicca, R., Frontoni, E., Pollini, R., Trani, M., & Verdini, L. (2017, June). The use of augmented reality glasses for the application in industry 4.0. In *Proceedings International Conference on Augmented Reality, Virtual Reality and Computer Graphics* (pp. 389-401). Cham, Switzerland: Springer. 10.1007/978-3-319-60922-5_30

Radu, I. (2012, November). Why should my students use AR? A comparative review of the educational impacts of augmented-reality. In *2012 IEEE International Symposium on Mixed and Augmented Reality (ISMAR)* (pp. 313-314). IEEE. 10.1109/ISMAR.2012.6402590

Rahimian, F. P., Arciszewski, T., & Goulding, J. S. (2014). Successful education for AEC professionals: Case study of applying immersive game-like virtual reality interfaces. *Visualization in Engineering*, *2*(1), 4. doi:10.1186/2213-7459-2-4

Richey, R. C., Silber, K. H., & Ely, D. P. (2008). Reflections on the 2008 AECT definitions of the field. *TechTrends*, *52*(1), 24–25. doi:10.100711528-008-0108-2

Saidin, N. F., Halim, N. D. A., & Yahaya, N. (2015). A review of research on augmented reality in education: Advantages and applications. *International Education Studies*, *8*(13), 1–8. doi:10.5539/ies.v8n13p1

Sotiriou, S., & Bogner, F. X. (2008). Visualizing the invisible: Augmented reality as an innovative science education scheme. *Advanced Science Letters*, *1*(1), 114–122. doi:10.1166/asl.2008.012

Teferra, D., & Altbachl, P. G. (2004). African higher education: Challenges for the 21st century. *Higher Education*, *47*(1), 21–50. doi:10.1023/B:HIGH.0000009822.49980.30

Wagner, D., Schmalstieg, D., & Billinghurst, M. (2006, November). Handheld AR for collaborative edutainment. In *International Conference on Artificial Reality and Telexistence* (pp. 85-96). Berlin, Germany: Springer.

Wu, F., Liu, Z., Wang, J., & Zhao, Y. (2015, March). Establishment virtual maintenance environment based on VIRTOOLS to effectively enhance the sense of immersion of teaching equipment. In *2015 International Conference on Education Technology, Management and Humanities Science (ETMHS 2015)*. Atlantis Press. 10.2991/etmhs-15.2015.93

Wu, H. K., Lee, S. W. Y., Chang, H. Y., & Liang, J. C. (2013). Current status, opportunities and challenges of augmented reality in education. *Computers & Education*, *62*, 41–49. doi:10.1016/j.compedu.2012.10.024

Yin, C., Han-Yu, S., Hwang, G. J., Hirokawa, S., Hui-Chun, C., Flanagan, B., & Tabata, Y. (2013). Learning by searching: A learning environment that provides searching and analysis facilities for supporting trend analysis activities. *Journal of Educational Technology & Society*, *16*(3), 286.

KEY TERMS AND DEFINITIONS

Depth knowledge: Gaining information and data that become the own heritage of a student.

Learning by searching: The capability of a student to learn directly with a close research experience.

Learning needs: The necessity that every student might have during a learning experience.

Long term effects: Capability of using the gained competences over time.

Minimum disciplinary objectives: Knowledge of basics arguments of a discipline, compulsory for understand the fundamentals.

Training activity: The process of transmitting knowledge, through didactic strategies.

Transversal skills: The capability of a student to interpret information and rework it by using competences gained in other fields.

ENDNOTES

[1] https://www.aurasma.com/

[2] https://nearpod.com/

[3] https://edu.google.com/products/vr-ar/expeditions/?modal_active=none

[4]   https://vr.google.com/cardboard/
[5]   https://luden.io/incell/
[6]   http://w2.vatican.va/
[7]   http://www.marcafermana.it/it/Smart-Marca/

APPENDIX 1

Table 3. Survey administered to students upon completion of the teaching experience on "Adorazione dei Pastori'" di P.P. Rubens

ADORAZIONE DEI PASTORI		
CODE	QUESTION	ANSWERS
Q1	What are the elements present in the mantle of the Madonna that recall the late-ancient Christian tradition?	4 OPTIONS 1 RIGHT
Q2	In representing the face of the Madonna, Rubens was inspired by ...	4 OPTIONS 1 RIGHT
Q3	The sense of vitality of the Madonna's face comes ...	4 OPTIONS 1 RIGHT
Q4	The open mouth of the Madonna alludes	4 OPTIONS 1 RIGHT
Q5	The hands of the Virgin are ...	4 OPTIONS 1 RIGHT
Q6	The hands of the Virgin move for ...	4 OPTIONS 1 RIGHT
Q7	The hands of the Madonna ...	4 OPTIONS 1 RIGHT
Q8	The Child is the protagonist of the painting. The painter paints him ...	4 OPTIONS 1 RIGHT
Q9	The light that comes from the Baby Jesus illuminates the face of the Virgin and of the other characters ...	4 OPTIONS 1 RIGHT
Q10	The straw on which the Baby Jesus is laid, full of light, seems to be burning while ...	4 OPTIONS 1 RIGHT
Q11	The figure of St. Joseph is confused with the colors of the background of the painting, because ...	4 OPTIONS 1 RIGHT
Q12	The landscape on the background of the painting and the figure of Saint Joseph ...	4 OPTIONS 1 RIGHT
Q13	The shepherd with sheepskin is poorly dressed, leaning on a stick and has the face of an old man. It is confused with the bottom of the painting and is placed in the extreme part of the painting. The Rubens wanted ...	4 OPTIONS 1 RIGHT
Q14	The elderly pastor puts his hand on his forehead ...	4 OPTIONS 1 RIGHT
Q15	The red of the young kneeling shepherd's tunic represents ...	4 OPTIONS 1 RIGHT
Q16	The pose of the kneeling shepherd recalls for the Rubens ...	4 OPTIONS 1 RIGHT
Q17	The old woman with raised hands represents ...	4 OPTIONS 1 RIGHT
Q18	In realizing the character of the old woman, Rubens imitates a great master of painting ...	4 OPTIONS 1 RIGHT
Q19	The four angels that accompany the shepherds are positioned high up in the canvas and dominate the scene. The composition allows to appreciate ...	4 OPTIONS 1 RIGHT
Q20	The composition of the angels made by Rubens testifies to the passion of Rubens for ...	4 OPTIONS 1 RIGHT
Q21	The hands of the different characters in the painting represent ...	4 OPTIONS 1 RIGHT
Q22	Among the different characters which seems to be a stranger to the composition ...	4 OPTIONS 1 RIGHT
Q23	The painting was intended for the Oratory of the Church of ...	4 OPTIONS 1 RIGHT

Table 4. Survey administered to students upon completion of the teaching experience on Osvaldo Licini

	PAESAGGIO	
CODE	QUESTION	ANSWERS
Q1	The "Paesaggio'" by Osvaldo Licini is donated to the Municipality of Monte Vidon Corrado in 2015 in memory ...	4 OPTIONS 1 RIGHT
Q2	The painting the "Paesaggio" represents a view ...	4 OPTIONS 1 RIGHT
Q3	The birthplace of Osvaldo Licini is ...	4 OPTIONS 1 RIGHT
Q4	The artist usually paints "en plein air", that is ...	4 OPTIONS 1 RIGHT
Q5	The rich colors of the painting recalls the works of ...	4 OPTIONS 1 RIGHT
Q6	The clouds seem to transform ...	4 OPTIONS 1 RIGHT
Q7	The hills and the sky converse with each other ...	4 OPTIONS 1 RIGHT
Q8	The leafy tree in the foreground ...	4 OPTIONS 1 RIGHT
Q9	The small farmhouse ...	4 OPTIONS 1 RIGHT
Q10	The sign on the canvas ...	4 OPTIONS 1 RIGHT
Q11	The line has the purpose ...	4 OPTIONS 1 RIGHT
Q12	The painting the "Paesaggio" is made by the artist ...	4 OPTIONS 1 RIGHT

Table 5. Survey questions given to students at the end of the didactic experience on the Theatre of Falerone

	ROMAN THEATER OF FALERONE	
CODE	QUESTION	ANSWERS
Q1	Which was the name of the ancient Roman city of Falerone	4 OPTIONS 1 RIGHT
Q2	Unlike the Greek theater, the Roman theater ...	4 OPTIONS 1 RIGHT
Q3	The construction technique is that ...	4 OPTIONS 1 RIGHT
Q4	The place destined to the choir and subsequently destined to the magistrates and priests takes the name of ...	4 OPTIONS 1 RIGHT
Q5	The main place for spectators is called ...	4 OPTIONS 1 RIGHT
Q6	The service areas under the Cavea also have the function ...	4 OPTIONS 1 RIGHT
Q7	How many spectators could hold the theater of Falerone	4 OPTIONS 1 RIGHT
Q8	The Parados in the Roman theater is ...	4 OPTIONS 1 RIGHT
Q9	Secondary actors could enter the stage ...	4 OPTIONS 1 RIGHT
Q10	During the II century D.C., in the period of Antonino Pio, the theater of Falerone	4 OPTIONS 1 RIGHT
Q11	The Porta Regia is the entrance ...	4 OPTIONS 1 RIGHT
Q12	The stage housed dedicated statues ...	4 OPTIONS 1 RIGHT
Q13	The steps that hosted the audience and the orchestra were covered ...	4 OPTIONS 1 RIGHT
Q14	How high is the Pulpitum compared to the Orchestra ...	4 OPTIONS 1 RIGHT
Q15	With what material the Pulpitum is made	4 OPTIONS 1 RIGHT
Q16	The Roman city of Falerone was born ...	4 OPTIONS 1 RIGHT
Q17	The Vomitoria are...	4 OPTIONS 1 RIGHT
Q18	The theater has a semicircular shape ...	4 OPTIONS 1 RIGHT
Q19	The Roman theater has an external portico ...	TRUE/FALSE
Q20	The summa cavea was intended for magistrates and officials	TRUE/FALSE
Q21	The ima cavea was intended for women and the plebs	TRUE/FALSE
Q22	The backdrop of the theater scene has three doors	TRUE/FALSE
Q23	The velarium in the theater was used ...	4 OPTIONS 1 RIGHT
Q24	The actors in ancient Rome were only men	TRUE/FALSE
Q25	Actors in the Roman period used the buskins ...	4 OPTIONS 1 RIGHT

Table 6. Questions included in the online questionnaire to the students at the end of the experiences in AR and VR mode

"ADORAZIONE DEI PASTORI" – AR EXPERIENCE	
CODE	QUESTION
A1	Have you understood the explanation of the individual parts of the picture
A2	Do you think this method is useful for explaining a painting
A3	After using this app do you think you better know the Rubens painting
A4	Do you feel detached from reality when you use the app
A5	Do you feel immersed in the painting
A6	Are the explanations in the tags ease to read
A7	Do you think the use of this application requires a lot of concentration
A8	Do you think the app is boring
A9	Do you think the app is ease to use
A10	Your arm or hand got tired while you were using the app
A11	Do your sight get tired while using the app
A12	Do you enjoy using the app
A13	Would you like to read another picture with this system
A14	Would you like to read pictures of school books with this system
A15	Did you already know AR
"PIAZZA DEL POPOLO"- VR EXPERIENCE	
B1	Did you think this method helps you to learn more about place
B2	Did images help you see details
B3	Do you feel detached from reality when you use the app
B4	In your opinion, does using this application require a lot of concentration
B5	Do you think the app is boring
B6	Do you think the app is ease to use
B7	Your arm or hand got tired while you were using the app
B8	Do your sight get tired while using the app
B9	Is using cardboard/oculos uncomfortable
B10	In your opinion, can Virtual Reality be applied in educational activities
B11	Did you already know VR
B12	Do you enjoy using the app
B13	Do you prefer visit a place with the app rather than travel
B14	Do you think that using the app encourages the desire to visit a place

Table 7. Percentages of favorable answers to the questions asked in the online questionnaire, grouped together by typological classes

QUESTION	AR use: "Adorazione dei Pastori" by P.P. Rubens	VR use: "Piazza del Popolo" in Fermo
The acquired data was useful	80%	68%
Feeling of detachment from reality	56%	76%
Need of focusing during the use	49%	56%
The app is boring	34%	34%
Ease to use	94%	84%
Tiredness of sight	54%	70%
Tiredness of hand/arm	52%	42%
Fun	82%	86%
Application in other educational activities	90%	89%
Possible use to stimulate knowledge of similar contents	90%	74%

Section 3
Virtual and Augmented Reality in Education, Art, and Museums: Case Studies

Chapter 13
Employing Real–Time Game Technology for Immersive Experience (VR and Videogames) for all at MAIO Museum:
Museum of WWII Stolen Artworks

Giuliana Geronimo
Streamcolors srl, Italy

Salvatore Giannella
Independent Researcher, Italy

ABSTRACT

3D real time game technologies create an opportunity to design interactive immersive experiences developing affordable, easy-to-use, and incredible virtual worlds for Museums. This chapter presents the potential of these technologies for the development of edutainment content for their visitors at MAIO - Museum of Art Taken Hostage in Cassina de' Pecchi (Milan). The Museum presents the story of 1,623 masterpieces such as Michelangelo, Tiziano, Raffaello, and Canaletto that were stolen in Italy during World War II and never found again. Visitors can explore the artworks through 2 installations: MAIO Virtual Museum, through VR inside an oniric 3D environment, and MAIO Play, a multiplayer video game.

METHODOLOGY

Between 2016 and 2018, in order to identify the number of works still prisoners of war (1,622), the authors, commissioned by the MAIO Museum, carried out enormous research work to update the list drawn up by Rodolfo Siviero[1], on commission from the Italian government in the first post-war period.

DOI: 10.4018/978-1-7998-1796-3.ch013

Copyright © 2020, IGI Global. Copying or distributing in print or electronic forms without written permission of IGI Global is prohibited.

Works of art already identified by Siviero as having been returned to Italy immediately after the war or illegally exhibited abroad were excluded. The Carabinieri Headquarters for the Protection of Cultural Heritage (TPC), is the most efficient military police force in the world for the protection of works of art, have been contacted for an updated list of recently found works of art. Museums, ecclesiastical institutes and the common owners of the missing masterpieces have been contacted, asking for confirmation of the theft. Books and newspaper articles on the subject were read. In this way, the list of 1649 prisoner-of-war works from Siviero has been updated to 1622, excluding the 27 known masterpieces (*Tables 1-4*).

After updating the list, the authors identified the most emblematic works among those still prisoners of war and those found and asked the owners for permission to use the high-resolution images of the works for educational purposes, especially thinking of applications for the new generations.

Thus was born the gallery of 33 images of the works of art visible at MAIO:

27 images in black and white (masterpieces still prisoners of war) and 5 in color (masterpieces found).

To tell this page of history to the new generations, so that they could become aware of the theme, we chose a strategy that, at the same time, could allow you to discover and reinvent in a fun way the initial content.

In fact, the innovative use of technology and the fun component stimulates curiosity and users' interest (...). However, the goal is not only for fun, but to improve the learning experience of the users[2].

An artistic and technical challenge[3] entrusted to the digital art studio Streamcolors chosen for its aesthetic signature and for its experience in finding creative, unconventional, simple and attractive solutions thanks to its long experience in the gaming industry, in 3D modelling and in the pioneer use of the Unreal engine of Epic Games (a software framework with a rendering engine to display textured 3D models and a physical engine for the interaction of objects[4]) in cultural sector.

In order to involve the public, especially thinking about the needs of today's public, we have chosen not to create a virtual museum application, but to create a set of engaging, educational and immersive experiences by developing a tool for creative reworking of images (*Stream Machine* software developed by Streamcolors) for the creation of personalized postcards, a Virtual Reality application and a multi-player video game available on site:

active experiences drive the individual's intention to continue participating actively after the visit, seeking information and revisiting the museum, following it on social networks and making recommendations on opinion pages[5].

BACKGROUND

The tools and experiences, developed for the MAIO Museum, to help visitors to become an active explorer, reflect 3 of the main trends of study of the theme Digital Heritage: co-creation to unleash creativity, Virtual Reality and videogames.

Co-Creation to Unleash Creativity

In recent years, the way in which visitors, inside and outside the museum, make use of images from museum collections has completely changed. Studies on some applications developed to allow visitors to manipulate images from the collections have shown that these applications greatly stimulate learning[6] and affiliation with the contents of a museum, making them relevant also for the new generations.

One of the most successful cases in this field is the experience of the Rijksmuseum's new Rijkstudio, a digital application that allows users to manipulate high-resolution images of works in the collection

The purpose, in the words of Martijn Pronk, head of publications at the museum, is to encourage virtual visitors to get creative and become artists in their own right by using the downloaded images to make something new[7].

A truly inspiring example that is, together with the artistic research of Streamcolors studio, the basis of the development of *Stream Machine*, a platform designed to create experiences that can bring people closer to the content in an unexpected and creative way and that allows you to rework the images of the collections for digital postcards, immersive room or to customize merchandising.

Before the MAIO Museum, *Stream Machine* was used in various locations including: the North Carolina Museum of Art (2018). For the North Carolina Museum of Art *(NCMA)* in Raleigh, the kiosk interpretation *Create your Own Immersive Room* was created first for the temporary exhibition *You are here* (with numerous feedback from visitors who indicated it as a new way to experience art that allowed them to discover details of the work never before noticed) and then for the interactive *Threads of Experience* hands-on learning space of the newly reinstalled *African Gallery*, winner of the American Alliance of Museums Awards 2018 in the Excellence in Exhibition competition[8]:

Virtual Reality

In the last years, as the quality of the hardware, related accessories, and software experiences has improved[9] the use of virtual reality in the cultural sector, demonstrating enormous potential to encourage and to support younger audiences and visitors in general to learn about the history because it makes the experience lively and memorable[10].

At the heart of innovative techniques for virtual reality, are the corporeal experience and the evolution of a heterogeneous range of interactive relationships that come together to constitute co-active, co-creative and emergent modalities of viewer incorporation in the data sphere. Embodiment explodes traditional narrative strategies and signals a shift from isolated individual experience to interpersonal theaters of exchange and social engagement. In addition, the opportunities offered by interactive and 3D technologies for enhanced cognitive exploration and interrogation of high dimensional data are rich fields of experimentation that need to be realized within the domain of both humanities and sciences[11].

The MAIO VR experience, encouraging integrated multisensory and open-ended exploration[12], intended to contribute to these existing experiments with virtual reality technology in the heritage sector, by creating a interactive VR experience that presented some of the most important masterpieces stolen from Italian cultural institutions by the Nazis during the Second World War and some of the main masterpieces found.

Videogames

Recently video games becoming more powerful and sophisticated than they themselves were two or three years earlier[13] and have greatly increased their market especially because they respond, more than other media, to the need of people to be active protagonists of an experience.

According to the annual report on the video game industry in Italy in 2018 published by AESVI, the association that represents the video game industry in Italy, in Italy, in 2018, the turnover of this sector (102 million euros) has grown by 8.1% compared to the previous year:

The people who have played video games in Italy in the last 12 months are 16.3 million, or 37% of the entire Italian population aged between 6 and 64 years. Of these, 54% are men and 46% are women. The age groups in which the most people play, both men and women, are those between 15-34 years and between 45-64 years, concrete evidence of how today video games are a transversal phenomenon, with a greater cultural weight than in the past[14].

There is a variety of types of video games and those with educational purposes are called Serious Games (SGs):

The main feature of a SG is its objective of supporting the player to achieve learning targets through a fun experience. The fun aspect of a SG provides engagement and can be determined by several factors like storyboard, graphics, usability, collaboration/competition mechanisms and interaction devices[15].

The SGs vary a lot not only in terms of learning objectives, but also of genre and application context (e.g. virtual visit):

SGs in this domain appear in a wide variety of forms, spanning from trivia, puzzles and mini-games to engage in interactive exhibitions (e.g. History of a place, Multi touch Rocks) to mobile applications for museum or touristic site visits motivated by some reward/engagement mechanism (e.g. Muse-US, Tidy City), to simulations of past events (The battle of Waterloo) to adventures and role playing games stein faithful reconstructions or digital counterparts of real sites (e.g. the Priory Undercroft, Revolution), and action games (the least represented category)[16].

MAIO PLAY is a multiplayer exploratory video game (platform adventure) that can be played inside an arcade cabin in the museum before starting the following real visit to help visitors understanding and engaging the MAIO Museum mission and history.

THE ITALIAN MONUMENTS MEN

During the Second World War, Italy also had its "Monuments men", as in the famous film of the same name with George Clooney. With cunning and courage, seventy Superintendents saved most of Italy's artistic heritage. The symbol of this team of unknown heroes is Pasquale Rotondi, who was entrusted in the Montefeltro Marche, between Pesaro and Urbino, as many as 7,821 works of art, including *The Tempest of Giorgione* and the Treasure of St. Mark from Venice, all works then returned unharmed in their cities of departure (Milan, Bergamo, Venice, the Marches, Rome, Tarquinia). Women also played a decisive role: for example, Palma Bucarelli travelled by truck at night to secure many of Rome's treasures. They are the Schindlers of Italian art of whom the journalist Salvatore Giannella recounts the heroic deeds, together with those of the heroes of the world, in the book ***Operation Rescue***[17].

But after the war, 1,622 pieces of art taken from museums and private collections by the Nazis never returned to Italy, including 800 paintings, dozens of sculptures, tapestries, carpets, furniture, musical instruments, including Stradivari violins, and hundreds of manuscripts. Symbol of these works still "prisoners of war" is *The laughing Faun*, the first sculpture by Michelangelo stolen from the Castle of Poppi (Arezzo), in the night between 22 and 23 August 1944 by the Nazis of the 305th infantry division and never returned to the original headquarters of the Bargello Museum in Florence. According to Giorgio Vasari, the biographer of the artists of the Italian Renaissance, Lorenzo dei Medici, lord of Florence, wanted to create an art school. When in a garden he saw this sculpture made by the young Michelangelo, Lorenzo wanted it in the palace, giving the artist a salary, and also offered a job to Michelangelo's father.

The MAIO Museum was founded in May 2015, on the idea of the journalist Salvatore Giannella (already author of the books *The Ark of Art*[18] and *Operation Rescue*, coordinator of the jury of the Rotondi Prize for the Saviours of Art in Sassocorvaro), in the Montefeltro region of Marche and scriptwriter for *Rai Educational - La storia siamo noi (The story is us)* of the documentary film *La lista di Pasquale Rotondi (The Rotondi's list)*[19] which won the prize of the Presidency of the Italian Republic at the Art Doc Film Festival of Rome 2005 as "best film dedicated to Italian art"), and at the behest of the Municipality of Cassina de' Pecchi. Its mission is to raise awareness among Italians on the issue of the subtraction of artistic heritage and the need to recover it.

In a restored seventeenth-century tower, in the square named after Pasquale Rotondi and Guglielmo Pacchioni "saviors of art", visitors can meet the 1,622 works still "hostage". The titles, authors and places of origin are also told in a volume, now unobtainable, and published by the Ministry of Foreign Affairs and the Ministry for Cultural and Environmental Heritage, *L'opera da ritrovare*[20] *(The work to be found)* that is based on research carried out by Rodolfo Siviero, the 007 art commissioned by the Italian government in the first post-war period for the recovery of these artistic treasures disappeared.

UNIQUENESS IN ITALY

MAIO is a unique project in Italy, both for its theme and for its three souls, and with very few similar examples in the world: the MOSA - Museum of Stolen Art in New York (it is a virtual space for art that has been stolen or looted, lost to greed or conflict. It is a VR Cardboard experience where one can enjoy artwork that is otherwise hidden. Link: http://mosa.ziv.bz/) and The Museum of Stolen Art in Holland in Hertogenbosch 92 km south of Amsterdam (The Museum of Stolen Art offers, through augmented reality, the opportunity to experience famous works of art that have disappeared. Link: https://museu-mofstolenart.com/collectie).

The uniqueness of MAIO is mainly due to three reasons:

1. is a civic project, linked to the denied concept of "right to beauty" that aims to spread among citizens the need for a collective civil commitment to recover the lost heritage;
2. is a cultural project, which aims to give life to an experience of meeting and deepening of the Italian artistic heritage in its (the works told here range from ancient Rome to the early twentieth century);
3. is an exhibition project, which through an innovative and engaging use of video game technologies allows the visitor to live in real time immersive experiences (VR and video games) and invites the visitor to himself to emotionally meet the "fragments of memory" of the stolen masterpieces and, thanks to the software installed on the touch screen totem, to express his creativity to transform the beauty stolen in new visionary graphics.

GAME TECHNOLOGY: INSTALLATIONS REALIZED ALL OVER THE WORLD

The multimedia part and the installation have been designed and edited by the digital art studio Stream-colors (www.streamcolors.com), formed by a team of experts in the cultural sector and veterans of the gaming industry. It was founded in 2014 by Giacomo Giannella (videogames art director and professor of Digital Art at the European Institution of Design – IED Milano) and Giuliana Geronimo (cultural manager with a PhD in History and New Technology).

Streamcolors is one of the first companies to bring the Unreal graphics engine of Epic Games, the most advanced platform for the creation of video games, out of the gaming industry, allowing a wide audience to live immersive experiences through installations, videos, virtual reality and videogames. The uniqueness of Streamcolors lies in the programming the Unreal blueprints to adapt them to the needs of museums and cultural institutions to create a new visual language. In this way it offers enormous advantages in terms of time of realization, final aesthetic result and design development simultaneously on different platforms (PC, mobile, VR).

Streamcolors is specialized in the development of real-time software and in the production of interactive solutions for customers around the world: cultural institutions (North Carolina Museum of Art in the United States, Leonardo's Science Museum and Poldi Pezzoli Museum in Milan, Maxxi Museum in Rome, Scriabin Theatre in Moscow, MEET - Milan Cultural Center), companies, design and fashion brands (Etro, Martini, Fuksas Architecture, Ubisoft Italia, Milan and Ontario Chamber of Commerce, Toronto George Brown University).

Table 1. List of stolen artworks that Rodolfo Siviero indicates as returned to Italy after the end of the war

Author / Type	Title	Date of return	Today
Tapestry	*The Faith*	1950	Dublin
Tapestry	*The Law*	1950	Dublin
Lavinia Fontana	*The Sower*	1952	Rome
Sebastiano Ricci	*Ceiling of Palazzo Mocenigo in Venice*	1952	Berlin

Table 2. List of stolen artworks restored and today exhibited in Italy

Author	Title	Date of return	Today
Jan van Huysum	*Vase of Flowers*	2019	Florence
Matteo Civitali	*Bust of Christ*	2018	Lucca
Alessio Baldovinetti	*Trinità*	2016	Milan
Cima da Conegliano	*Virgin Mary with child*	2016	Milan
Girolamo Dai Libri	*Presentation of Jesus in the Temple*	2016	Milan
Andrea di Bartolo	*Dormitio Virginis*	2014	Assisi
Michele Cammarano	*The charge of the Bersaglieri*	2014	Caserta
Justus Sustermans	*Female figure*	2009	Assisi
Jacopo Bassano	*Parable of the Sower*	1995	Florence
Defendant Ferrari	*Presentation of Jesus in the Temple*		Baveno (VB)

Table 3. List of stolen artworks restored and today lawfully exhibited abroad

Author	Title	Date of return	Today
Amedeo Bocchi	*Malaria*	1995	America
	Statue of *Capitoline Venus*	1999	Tripoli
Giuseppe Angeli	*Elijah on the Fire Tank*	1951	Washington
Bernardino Strozzi	*Saint Catherine of Alexandria*	2009	Los Angeles

Table 4. List of stolen artworks illicitly displayed in foreign sites

Author	Title	Date of return	Today
Paul of John Fei	*Triptych*	1967	Belgrade
Jacopo Tintoretto	*Virgin Mary with child and donor*	1967	Belgrade
Paolo Veneziano	*Virgin Mary with child*	1967	Belgrade
Spinello Aretino	*Virgin Mary with child*	1967	Belgrade
Parmigianino	*Portrait of Pier Maria Rossi Count of St Secondo*	1939	Hannover
Roman IV century B.C.	*Torso of Niobide*	identified by Siviero in foreign sites	It results in a private collection in Bonn
	Bench church (sixteenth century)	identified by Siviero in foreign sites	It results in Vienna
	Cassone (fifteenth century)	identified by Siviero in foreign sites	It results in Vienna
Peter Berrettini	*Sacrifice of senophon Diana*	identified by Siviero in foreign sites	Illicitly exposed in Germany

FRAGMENTS OF MEMORY

The multimedia part consists of two exhibition areas and has as its common element, which connects the entire route, the active participation of the visitor inside the museum:

- Fragments of Memory (1 video, 8 panels and a touch screen);
- MAIO Virtual Museum (MAIO VR and MAIO Play).

The exhibition *Fragments of Memory* is composed of eight large suspended canvases with the names of the stolen artworks printed, divided by region inside a deliberately dark room so as to ideally represent the darkness in which the works are kept in unknown places. The visitor is invited to take a torch (to illuminate these works with his gesture) as it moves through the labyrinth created by the panels.

The list of stolen artworks is constantly updated, highlighting on the sheets those that are found thanks to the constant work of the Carabinieri Nucleus Cultural Heritage Protection.

In the Tables below (updated until September 2019) are presented the list of stolen artworks that Rodolfo Siviero indicates as returned to Italy after the end of the war[21] (*Table 1*), the list of artworks restored and today exhibited in Italy (*Table 2*), the list of artworks restored and today lawfully exhibited abroad (*Table 3*) and the list of stolen artworks illicitly displayed in foreign sites (*Table 4*):

A video and a touch screen enrich the path in MAIO, where you can create your own visionary graphics by reworking one of the works to take home a souvenir postcard.

The video *Fragments of Memory*, which can be found along the way, was created by breaking down the only black and white images we have of stolen masterpieces of art into different three-dimensional planes. Sometimes the image is reduced and replicated. Other times, however, it is not recognizable.

So we wanted to emphasize the idea that what we have left today are just fragments of memory. The fragments of a collective artistic memory of which we have been deprived.

The video, lasting 6:35 minutes, is in black and white and inside there are some of the main masterpieces not yet found: Guido Reni, *Holy Cecilia*; Bronzino, *Crucified Christ*; Michelangelo, *The laughing Faun*; Antonio Stradivari, *Violet*; Tiziano, *Portrait of Ludovico Ariosto*; Raffaello, *Virgin Mary of the veil*; Tiziano Vecellio (Scuola), *Venus*; Canaletto, *View of the slave bank to the East*.

The touch screen station has an interactive installation inside that allows visitors, thanks to the technology and artistic research of the creative and cultural company Streamcolors, to rotate the image, enlarge some details, to rework the image creating new, unpublished and personal fragments of memory. It is art that generates art.

The treasures still hostage are presented in black and white and can be explored and modified to create your own postcard. The works found, on the other hand, are in colours.

The info boxes present, tell the story of the main masterpieces:

1. Michelangelo Buonarroti, *The laughing Faun (Head of Faun)*
    Historical period: 1475 - 1564
    Features: sculpture, carved marble, h 26
    Origin: Florence, Bargello National Museum
    The Faun's Head, the first of the sculptures made by Michelangelo, is considered the symbolic work of the masterpieces still prisoners of war.
    The historian Giorgio Vasari tells us that around 1489 Lorenzo de' Medici, walking in the garden of Sant Marco, saw Michelangelo, then fifteen years old, sculpting the head of a faun "old and ancient wrinkle, which was broken in the nose and mouth laughed. The Magnificent noted that the Faun had all his teeth and pricked the young artist: "You should know that old people never have all their teeth and always someone lacks them. As an answer Michelangelo "immediately broke a tooth and drilled his gum so that it seemed that it fell".
    The Head of Faun until 1943 was exhibited in a room of the National Museum of Bargello in Florence, was one of the treasures transferred and hidden in the Castle of Poppi of the Counts Guidi in the province of Arezzo, Tuscany, to be saved from the bombing. From here it was stolen in the night between 22 and 23 August 1944 by the Nazi soldiers of the 305th infantry division. After a stop in Forlì on 31 August it continued northwards with other works, on trucks of the tenth army.
2. Raffaello Sanzio, *Virgin Mary with child and saint John the Baptist (Virgin Mary of the veil)*
    Historical period: 1483 - 1520
    Features: black pencil and chalk on yellow paper, mm 770x730
    Origin: Florence, Uffizi, Prints and Drawings Department
    During the Second World War, the work was transferred from the Uffizi to the Barberino di Mugello depot on the outskirts of Florence, where it was stolen in 1944 by the Fallschirm-Jeäger parachutist department.
3. Tiziano Vecellio (school), *Venus*
    Historical period: 1489 - 1576
    Features: oil on canvas, 40x60
    Origin: Trieste, Gino Pincherle Collection
    Stolen by Nazi troops in the Villa of the lawyer Gino Pincherle in via Giulia n. 55 in Trieste, in 1943.
4. Unknown Venetian painter, *Portrait of Ludovico Ariosto*
    Historical period: first half of the 16th century

Features: oil on canvas, 60x50

Origin: Casola Valsenio (Ravenna), Villa Cardella, Oriani Collection

The painting is traditionally considered to be the only true portrait of Ariosto. It was attributed to Titian and Dosso Dossi but today it is considered a canvas of the Venetian school.

Stolen by Nazi troops between September 1944 and April 1945 from Villa Cardella in Casola Valsenio (Ravenna).

5. Bronzino, *Crucified Christ*

Historical period: 1503-1572

Features: oil (?) on board, 28x18

Origin: Florence, Palazzo Pitti, Galleria Palatina

Typical example of Counter-Reformation painting, inspired by a late drawing by Michelangelo.

Stolen by Nazi troops from the deposit of Montagnana (Florence) in 1944.

6. Guido Reni, *Holy Cecilia*

Historical period: 1575-1642

Features: oil on canvas, 40x40

Origin: Rome, Church of Saint Cecilia in Trastevere

It is part of the large painting by Guido Reni still existing in Rome in the Church of Saint Cecilia on the altar of the Chapel of the Bath, depicting the martyrdom of the saint.

Stolen after the war emergency.

7. Antonio Stradivari, *Violet*

Historical period: 1663

Characteristics: bottom length 36,15

Origin: Cantone (Cotignola, Ravenna), Villa Strocchi, Strocchi Collection

"...Red dragon blood on a yellowish base, narrow, slender, classical shape, similar to the violin of Jerome I (from the Strocchi Collection) of which he was a pupil...Violins that are very rare because they are confused for their erroneous interpretation with those of his nephew Hyacinth".

Label: "Gio Battista Ruggier, known as Per fecit Cremona anno 1663".

Stolen from Villa Strocchi in Cantone in the province of Ravenna in Emilia Romagna, at the end of January 1945 by the Nazi department marked with the initials V.E.I.T.R.Z.

8. Canaletto (Giovanni Antonio Canal), *View of the slave bank to the East*

Historical period: 1735 approx.

Features: oil on canvas, 80x58

Origin: Camaiore (Lucca), Villa delle Pianore, Bourbon Parma Collection.

It is a variant of the view of the same subject preserved in the Albertini Collection in Rome. Stolen by the Nazi troops of the sixteenth armoured division (SS) from the Villa della Pianore (Camaiore, Lucca) in the spring of 1944.

9. Michele Cammarano, *The charge of the Bersaglieri*

Historical period: 1835 - 1920

Features: oil on canvas, cm 300 x 200

Origin: "Catena" Barracks of Verona

The Carabinieri of the Cultural heritage protection unit of Venice have recovered and seized a valuable pictorial work, an oil on canvas that is part of the larger composition of the painting entitled *The charge of the Bersaglieri* made by the painter Michele Cammarano (Naples 1835 - 1920), an established interpreter of the pictorial season of the Risorgimento. The painting was stolen by troops from the "Catena" Barracks of Verona, during the tragic days that followed September 8, 1943. The military traced the painting, a section cut out of the original work, to an auction house in Naples, thanks to the precious information contained in the Database of Cultural Assets illicitly stolen, the largest database in the world managed by the special department of the Carabinieri Corps, which made it possible to verify and recognize the painting.

10. Jacopo Bassano, *The sower*
    Historical period: 1566 - 1568
    Features: oil on canvas, 51 x 60 cm
    Origin: Uffizi Gallery of Florence
    The sower, also known as the Parable of the sower, is a painting, painted between 1566 - 1568 by Jacopo da Ponte, known as Jacopo Bassano (1510 ca. - 1592), in collaboration with his son and Francesco, now in the Uffizi Gallery in Florence.
    The work, which was owned by the Florentine state collections, was placed in March 1935 in Palazzo Szlenkier, the seat of the Italian embassy in Warsaw. During the Nazi occupation of Poland, the painting was stolen, and reappeared in 1955 on the American antiques market, where it was purchased by the Museum of Fine Arts in Springfield (Massachusetts, United States).
    In 2001, the painting was returned to Italy and exhibited in the Uffizi Gallery in Florence.

MAIO VIRTUAL MUSEUM

Since June 2018 the exhibition has been enriched with a new section, developed and conceived by the Milan based digital art studio Streamcolors and financed by the Cariplo Foundation, named MAIO Virtual Museum and composed of:

- MAIO VR, two installations in virtual reality that, with the use of the VR helmet, allows the user to undertake an interactive or guided journey in a 360° video, within a three-dimensional dream-like environment. In the interactive version of this installation, the user can decide to move virtually within the environment to deepen content (photos and texts) that most intrigue him in a totally immersive form. At the beginning of the experience, the environment is empty and some black and white fragments of masterpieces of art float in space: these are fragments of the memory of works created by artists such as Michelangelo, Raffaello, Botticelli, Luini, Canaletto, Bronzino, Tintoretto. If one of these fragments is pointed with the eyes, the corresponding work is composed and the caption of the work appears.

- MAIO PLAY, a multiplayer exploratory video game (platform adventure) that can be played inside an arcade cabin in the museum. The visitor is a ball that moves along suspended bridges in order to collect, in the shortest time possible but reading as much content as possible to earn more points, fragments of memory of the main masterpieces stolen. The aim is to collect more fragments in as little time as possible to get the stolen works out of the darkness and continue towards the light of those recovered to look for them and make them visible in the beauty of their colors (among the rediscovered, even those already returned in their museums, abroad, admirable by all through the video game).

MAIO VR and MAIO PLAY have a 3d dreamlike environment developed on the Unreal platform of Epic Games, characterized by the green color of the museum's logo. It starts from dark spaces (symbol of cultural emptiness) with the stolen works, and arrives in illuminated spaces (symbol of the right to beauty) with the works found. At the beginning, the works are fragmented, absent or dark, and only through interaction do they recompose themselves, showing themselves in a complete way.

They accompany the experience with ambient music, with the sounds of war, and the voice of the creator Salvatore Giannella that accompanies the user to the discovery of some works (images and info in Italian and English) with these words:

Imagine getting on a time machine with me and getting on the road.

It's eight o'clock in the evening on August 22, 1944. In Europe, the Second World War sowed mourning and chain pain. That day, in the Tuscan Casentino, there was a theft with dexterity. Three German officers came to the castle of Poppi to verify (as they say) whether weapons and ammunition were kept in the building.

Seven doors are locked with a double key. And after the seven doors, a wall. Iron, wood and stones do not stop the Nazi officers of the 305th infantry division. Once they get to the art depots, they pull out their guns. They block the municipal guard and take possession of cash no. 8. They escape, shooting, with a car that they have hidden near the castle. It is an armed robbery, repeated in the night: they return with a truck. They take possession of a good number of crates full of works of art. They contain sculptures, paintings and furnishings from Florentine museums. They had been transferred to Casentino to save them from bombing.

On the morning of August 23rd, the Germans pass through, the signs remain: crates gutted, the label of stolen paintings...

This is how the Head of Faun "ancient old face and grit", Michelangelo's first marble work exhibited until 1943 at the Bargello Museum in Florence, disappeared: a work that, according to Vasari, enchanted Lorenzo de' Medici and triggered the artistic fortune of that genius, a work that we like to identify as the symbol of all the thefts of art and of the 1,623 Italian cultural treasures still held hostage.

Perhaps the Faun is in the vault of a bank, in Switzerland or Germany, the result of an illegal purchase, or more likely is among the works that were seized by the Red Army in Berlin, withheld as payment for war damages.

These are the paths indicated by the investigations carried out by Rodolfo Siviero, the 007 of the art that, until his death in 1983, followed the stolen works.

Many were recovered but the list of goods still prisoners of war is long. At least 1622 pieces have never returned to Italy: 800 paintings, sculptures, tapestries, furniture, violins made by Stradivari, hundreds of manuscripts. This is also told in a rare catalogue, L'opera da ritrovare (The work to be found), published in 1995 by the will of the ministers of the time, Antonio Paolucci and Susanna Agnelli.

Figure 1. People playing MAIO VR

It is a real hostage museum that includes paintings: by Raphael, such as the Virgin Mary and Child and St. John, black pencil and chalk from the collection of the Uffizi, taken by German paratroopers from the deposit of Barberino del Mugello; by Canaletto are Venetian landscapes such as the View from the bank of the slave towards the east, stolen by SS from the villa of Pianore (Lucca); by Guido Reni is the Saint Cecilia stolen from the church of the same name in Rome; by Bronzino is the Crucified Christ, oil on wood requisitioned by the Nazi troops in the deposit of Montagnana (Florence), came from Palazzo Pitti; by Luca della Robbia is the Virgin Mary with child, a glazed terracotta stolen after the bombing of the church in Impruneta (Florence); attributed to Titian is the Portrait of Ludovico Ariosto stolen from the Oriani collection in Casola Valsenio (Ravenna) and of the school of Titian is Venus, an oil on canvas that was in the villa of the lawyer Gino Pincherle, in Via Giulia 55 in Trieste; by Antonio Stradivari, three violins from the Strocchi collection, stolen from the department marked with the initials Veitrz; and also works by Bellotto, Veronese, Tintoretto, Sebastiano del Piombo, Lorenzo di Credi, Cima da Conegliano...

Something has certainly been destroyed by the bombing, but many works have come out unscathed from the conflict and travel clandestinely. To get these works back, our "last prisoners of war, it is necessary a hard diplomatic work and not only the investigative one entrusted to the effective and tenacious Cara-

Figure 2. People playing MAIO PLAY

Figure 3. MAIO VR Screenshot MAiO VR developed by Streamcolors

binieri of the nucleus for the protection of the artistic patrimony that, of that list, have traced paintings like The Sower of Jacopo Bassano (he was in the United States, illegally bought at an auction) or The Charge of the Bersaglieri, of Michele Cammarano, stolen in Pordenone and traced a year ago in an auction house in Naples. And that's what it takes to avoid extinguishing the hope of recovering the Faun and his companions, who seem forgotten.

Table 5. Stolen artworks in the virtual reality helmets

Author	Period	Title	Property
Hans Memling	1433-1494	*Portrait of a Young Person*	Florence, Uffizi
Perugino	1450-1524	*Penitent Saint Jerome*	Bourbon Parma Collection
Michelangelo	1475-1564	*The laughing Faun (Head of Faun)*	Florence, National Museum of Bargello
Canaletto	1697-1768	*View of the slave bank to the East*	Bourbon Parma Collection
Bronzino	1503-1572	*Christ Crucified*	Florence, Palazzo Pitti, Galleria Palatina
Pietro Rotari		*Portrait of a Girl*	Florence, Contini Bonacossi Collection
Raffaello	1483-1520	*Virgin Mary of the veil*	Florence, Uffizi, Cabinet of Drawings and Prints
El Greco	1541-1614	*Copy of the Correction Night*	Florence, Contini Bonacossi Collection
Bernardo Bellotto	1721-1780	*View of the Grand Canal in Venice*	Bourbon Parma Collection
Jacopo Tintoretto	1519-1594	*Dead Christ supported by two angels*	Florence, Uffizi, Cabinet of Drawings and Prints
Sandro Botticelli	1447-1510	*Portrait of an unknown young man*	Filangeri Museum of Naples
Bernardino Luini	1485-1532	*Virgin Mary and Child with Sister Alessandra Bentivoglio*	Filangeri Museum of Naples
Guido Reni	1575-1642	*Saint Cecilia*	Church of Saint Cecilia in Trastevere, Rome
Peter Paul Rubens	1577-1640	*The three theological virtues*	Private collection, Rome
Giampietrino	1520-1540	*Virgin Mary and Child*	Naples, Anna Maria Acton Caracciolo Collection
Mabuse	1478-1533/36	*Virgin Mary and Child*	National Museum, Messina
Willem Key	1560-1627	*Christ mocked*	Van Marle Collection
Francesco Antonio Grue	1686-1746	*Majolica painted with St. Joseph with the Child Jesus*	Acerbic Collection
Biagio d'Antonio	1446-1508	*Saint Sebastian and Saint John the Baptist*	Faenza (RA), Civic Art Gallery
Antonio Stradivari	1649-1737	*Violin*	Strocchi Collection
Serafino de Tivoli	1826-1892	*Landscape (plateau)*	Strologo Collection, Milan
Giovanni Fattori	1825-1908	*Patrol along the sea*	Strologo Collection, Milan
Unknown author	II century	*Patera with handle decorated with Hermes, animals and plant elements*	Turin, Archaeological Museum
Unknown sculptor	XIX century	*Polychrome relief with allegorical representation*	Ernestina Guichardaz Collection
Spiridione Zerbini	18th century	*Magazine in Saint Maura*	Querini Stampalia Venezia Collection
Titian Vecellio (School)		*Venus*	Gino Pincherle Collection

Table 6. Rediscovered artworks in the virtual reality helmets

Author	Title	Find	Today
Defendente Ferrari	*Presentation of Jesus in the Temple*		Church of Saints Gervaso and Protaso in Baveno (VB)
Matteo Civitali	*Bust of Christ*	2018, Lucca	Museum of the Cathedral of Lucca
Bernardino Strozzi	*Saint Catherine of Alexandria*	2009, Sotheby's auction house in Milan	Los Angeles, County Museum of Arts
Giuseppe Angeli	*Elijah on the fire cart*		Washington, National Gallery of Art
Jacopo Bassano	*Parabola of the sower*	1995, Museum of Fine Arts Springfield	Uffizi, Florence

The southerner Giustino Fortunato often loved to tell this episode: the story of the archaeologist who discovered in an Egyptian tomb a handful of wheat left 5,000 years next to the mummy, without ever seeing the sun again, is well known. Could the germs of those withered grains give back the ears of corn to the winds? It seemed not. But the pharaoh's wheat scattered in the clods and fertilized by the waters of the Nile, returned to bloom the tender stems to the caress of the native air. Who can say that from the inexhaustible breast of this ancient mother, the sweet land of Italy, should not erupt one day, fruits of new life and youth?

This is the same emotional hope that has moved us, 70 years after the Liberation of Italy from Nazi-Fascism, to give birth to the MAIO convinced that it will grow that knowledge and that active defense of the cultural heritage born in Italy and that Italy must preserve for the world.

In the virtual reality helmets have been inserted 32 works in total:

1. 26 stolen artworks (*Table 5*), black and white photos, divided by region as on the hanging sheets. The information on each work was taken from the catalogue *L'opera da ritrovare*[22] (*The work to be found*) and is divided by region;
2. 5 rediscovered artworks (*Table 6*), in colour, for which MAiO has acquired the rights of use.

The interactive experience proposed at MAIO through these installations is designed to be easily replicated in other places thanks to *The Itinerant MAIO* package, a travelling copy of MAIO itself consisting of 5 parts: eight (8) double-sided sheets suspended with the names of the stolen works divided by region; the video file mp4 (duration 6:35 minutes) *Fragments of Memory*, the applications MAIO VR, the video game MAIO PLAY in a cabin eighties.

In fact, with the aim of promoting the cultural and civil project of MAIO within different places of Italian culture, *The Itinerant MAIO* package has been designed by Streamcolors to be easily transported, stored, set up and installed.

CONCLUSION

Starting from the black and with images of the book *L'opera da ritrovare*[23] *(The work to be found)*, the use of new technologies, with the original contents designed and developed by Streamcolors for the *Stream Machine* touch screen application, the Virtual Reality stations and the videogame, has served to involve audience to MAIO Museum leveraging the aspects of co-creation and immersion to create a new emotional bond between visitors and Stolen Art.

Showing some of the most important Italian masterpieces stolen during the Second War Word and some of the recovered artworks in a new, active and engaging way has also helped to create a civic awareness sensitive to the values of culture and art. A very actual and important theme, especially for the new generations. For this reason the authors hope that in the future, thanks to the package *The Itinerant MAIO*, stolen art could returned to show itself to the eyes of more people all around the world.

REFERENCES

AESVI. (2019). AESVI presents the annual report on the video game industry in Italy in 2018. Retrieved from http://www.aesvi.it/cms/view.php?dir_pk=902&cms_pk=3002

Anderson, E. F., McLoughlin, L., Liarokapis, F., Peters, C., Petridis, P., & Freitas, S. (2010). Developing serious games for cultural heritage: A state-of-the-art review. *Virtual Reality (Waltham Cross)*, *14*(4), 255–275. doi:10.100710055-010-0177-3

Antón, C., Camarero, C., & Garrido, M. J. (2018). Exploring the experience value of museum visitors as a co-creation process. *Current Issues in Tourism*, *21*(12), 1406–1425. doi:10.1080/13683500.2017.1373753

Economou, M., & Pujol Tost, L. (2011) Evaluating the use of virtual reality and multimedia applications for presenting the past. In F. Lazarinis, G. Styliaras, & D. Koukopoulos (Eds.), Handbook of research on technologies and cultural heritage: applications and environments, (pp. 223-239). Hershey, PA: IGI Global. doi:10.4018/978-1-60960-044-0.ch011

Giannella, S. (2014). *Operazione Salvataggio. Gli eroi sconosciuti che hanno salvato l'arte dalle guerre*. Milano, Italy: Chiarelettere.

Giannella, S., & Mandelli, P. D. (1999). *L'Arca dell'Arte, Cassina de' Pecchi (Milano)*. Italia: Editoriale Delfi.

Ioannides, M., Fink, E., Brumana, R., Patias, P., Doulamis, A., Martins, J., & Wallace, M. (2018). Digital heritage. In *Proceedings Progress in Cultural Heritage: Documentation, Preservation, and Protection 7th International Conference,* EuroMed 2018, Nicosia, Cyprus, Oct. 29–Nov. 3, 2018, Part II.

Jones-Garmil, K. (1997). *The wired museum: emerging technology and changing paradigms, (1997)*. Washington, DC: American Association of Museums.

Kenderdine, S. (2013). *How will museums of the future look?* TEDx Talks. Retrieved from https://www.youtube.com/watch?v=VXhtwFCA_Kc

Kenderdine, S., Schreibman, S., Siemens, R., & Unsworth, J. (2015). Embodiment, entanglement, and immersion in digital cultural heritage. In S. Schreibman, R. Simens, & J. Unsworth (Eds.), A new companion to digital humanities, Chichester, UK.

Marty, P. F., & Jones, K. B. (2009). *Museum informatics: people, information, and technology in museums*. New York: Routledge.

Minoli, G. (2014). *La Lista di Pasquale Rotondi, La storia siamo noi* – RAI. Retrieved from: https://www.youtube.com/watch?v=I5POv01SgBI

Morozzi, L., & Paris, R. (1995). *L'opera da ritrovare. Repertorio del patrimonio artistico italiano disperso all'epoca della seconda guerra mondiale*. Italia: Istituto Poligrafico dello Stato.

Mortara, M., Catalano, C. E., Bellotti, F., Fiucci, G., Houry Panchetti, M., & Petridis, P. (2014). Learning cultural heritage by serious games. Elsevier. *Journal of Cultural Heritage*, *15*(3), 318–325. doi:10.1016/j.culher.2013.04.004

Norris, L., & Tisdale, R. (2013). *Creativity in museum practice*. Left Coast Press.

Pantano, E., & Tavernise, A. (2009). Learning cultural heritage through information and communication technologies: a case study. [IJICTHD]. *International Journal of Information Communication Technologies and Human Development*, *1*(3), 68–87. doi:10.4018/jicthd.2009070104

Rae, J., & Edwards, L. (2016) Virtual reality at the British Museum: What is the value of virtual reality environments for learning by children and young people, schools, and families? *MW2016: Museums and the Web 2016*. Retrieved from https://mw2016.museumsandtheweb.com/paper/virtual-reality-at-the-british-museum-what-is-the-value-of-virtual-reality-environments-for-learning-by-children-and-young-people-schools-and-families/

Shaw, J., & Kenderdine, S. (2011) Future narrative, discovery engines and making meaning in VR. *IEEE International Symposium on VR Innovation* 10.1109/ISVRI.2011.5759591

Wheeler, L. J. (2018) *North Carolina Museum of Art receives two American Alliance of Museums Awards*. Retrieved from https://ncartmuseum.org/images/uploads/blog/2018_AAM_Awards_release_FINAL.pdf

KEY TERMS AND DEFINITIONS

Audience Engagement: Practises and installations to augment the participation of visitors during a museum visit. In the case study of Museum MAIO to engage the new generations the digital art studio Streamcolors developed the MAIO PLAY and the MAIO VR.

Digital Heritage: Cultural heritage made available to the public through the use of technologies.

Italian masterpieces: Works by the most important Italian painters, sculptors or craftsmen.

Mirror neurons: Nerve cells that are activated by imitation. In this way, the neurons reflect, like a mirror, that which they see in the mind of another.

Monuments men: Heroes who saved the masterpieces of art during the wars risking their lives.

Siviero Rodolfo: The 007 art commissioned by the Italian government in the first post-war period for the recovery of these artistic treasures disappeared.

Stolen art: Art stolen during the Second World War in Italy by the Nazis and not yet found.

ENDNOTES

[1] Morozzi L., Paris R. (1995). L' opera da ritrovare. Repertorio del patrimonio artistico italiano disperso all'epoca della seconda guerra mondiale. Italia, Istituto Poligrafico dello Stato.

[2] Pantano E. & Tavernise A. (2009). Learning Cultural Heritage Through Information and Communication Technologies: A Case Study. *International Journal of Information Communication Technologies and Human Development (IJICTHD)* 1(3)

[3] Kenderdine S. (2013). *How will museums of the future look?* TEDx Talks Retrieved from: https://www.youtube.com/watch?v=VXhtwFCA_Kc

[4] Ioannides M., Fink E., Brumana R., Patias P., Doulamis A., Martins J. & Wallace M. (2018). *Digital Heritage. Progress in Cultural Heritage: Documentation, Preservation, and Protection* 7th International Conference, EuroMed 2018, Nicosia, Cyprus, October 29–November 3, 2018, Proceedings, Part II

[5] Antón C., Camarero C. & Garrido M. J. (2018). Exploring the experience value of museum visitors as a co-creation process. *Current Issues in Tourism* (Vol.21 No.12 pp.1406-1425)

[6] Marty P. F. & Jones K. B. (2009). Museum Informatics: People, Information, and Technology in Museums, New York, Routledge

[7] Norris L. & Tisdale R. (2013). *Creativity in Museum Practice.* Left Coast Press Inc

[8] Wheeler L. J. (2018). *North Carolina Museum of Art Receives Two American Alliance of Museums Awards.* Retrieved from https://ncartmuseum.org/images/uploads/blog/2018_AAM_Awards_release_FINAL.pdf

[9] Rae J. & Edwards L. (2016). Virtual reality at the British Museum: What is the value of virtual reality environments for learning by children and young people, schools, and families? *MW2016: Museums and the Web 2016.* Retrieved from https://mw2016.museumsandtheweb.com/paper/virtual-reality-at-the-british-museum-what-is-the-value-of-virtual-reality-environments-for-learning-by-children-and-young-people-schools-and-families/

[10] Economou M. & Pujol Tost L. (2011). Evaluating the Use of Virtual Reality and Multimedia Applications for Presenting the Past. In Lazarinis F., Styliaras G.& Koukopoulos D. *Handbook of Research on Technologies and Cultural Heritage: Applications and Environments,* (pages 223-239) IGI Global

[11] Shaw J. & Kenderdine S. (2011) Future narrative, discovery engines and making meaning in VR. *IEEE International Symposium on VR Innovation*

[12] Kenderdine S., Schreibman S., Siemens R. & Unsworth J. (2015) Embodiment, Entanglement, and Immersion in Digital Cultural Heritage in Schreibman S., Simens R. & Unsworth J. *A new companion to Digital Humanities*, UK, Chichester

[13] Anderson E. F., McLoughlin L., Liarokapis F., Peters C., Petridis P. & De Freitas S. (2010). Developing serious games for cultural heritage: a state-of-the-art review, *Virtual Reality* 14 (4)

[14] Aesvi (2019). *AESVI presents the annual report on the video game industry in Italy* in 2018 retrieved from http://www.aesvi.it/cms/view.php?dir_pk=902&cms_pk=3002

[15] Mortara M., Catalano C. E., Bellotti F., Fiucci G., Panchetti M. H. & Petridis P. (2014). Learning cultural heritage by serious games. *Journal of Cultural Heritage (vol 15, 318-325),* Elsevier

[16] Mortara M., Catalano C. E., Bellotti F., Fiucci G., Panchetti M. H. & P. Petridis (2014). Learning cultural heritage by serious games. *Journal of Cultural Heritage (vol 15, 318-325),* Elsevier

[17] Giannella S. (2014). Operazione Salvataggio. Gli eroi sconosciuti che hanno salvato l'arte dalle guerre, Chiarelettere, Milano

[18] Giannella S. & Mandelli P. D. (1999). *L'Arca dell'Arte.* Editoriale Delfi, Cassina de' Pecchi (Milano).

[19] Minoli G. (2014). *La Lista di Pasquale Rotondi, La storia siamo noi* – RAI. Retrieved from: https://www.youtube.com/watch?v=I5POv01SgBI

[20] Morozzi L. & Paris R. (1995). L' opera da ritrovare. Repertorio del patrimonio artistico italiano disperso all'epoca della seconda guerra mondiale, Italia: Istituto Poligrafico dello Stato

[21] Morozzi L. & Paris R. (1995). L' opera da ritrovare. Repertorio del patrimonio artistico italiano disperso all'epoca della seconda guerra mondiale, Italia: Istituto Poligrafico dello Stato

[22] Morozzi L. & Paris R. (1995). L' opera da ritrovare. Repertorio del patrimonio artistico italiano disperso all'epoca della seconda guerra mondiale, Italia: Istituto Poligrafico dello Stato

[23] Morozzi L. & Paris R. (1995). L' opera da ritrovare. Repertorio del patrimonio artistico italiano disperso all'epoca della seconda guerra mondiale, Italia: Istituto Poligrafico dello Stato

Chapter 14
Through Achille Castiglioni's Eyes:
Two Immersive Virtual Experiences

Cecilia Maria Bolognesi
Polytechnic University of Milan, Italy

Damiano Antonino Angelo Aiello
University of Catania, Italy

ABSTRACT

The experimentations described here concern the virtualization of the Studio Museo Achille Castiglioni, a small museum that hosts important artefacts designed by one of the most famous architects and designers of the 20th century, winner of 7 "Compasso d'oro" awards. The digitization process creates two virtual experiences to enjoy the place and the design objects to give visibility to the small context far from the big museum. The first (less complex and immersive) experimentation deals with the semantic implementation of 360° panoramic photographs, giving rise to a virtual tour of the museum available on the web with no interaction: it is the description of the state of the art of this place. The second one (a real VR simulation) derives from a more complex workflow based on digital surveying, digital modelling, and developing of virtual environments and interactions. The two proposed case studies demonstrate how new technologies can represent indispensable instruments for the safeguard, enhancement, and communication of Cultural Heritage.

INTRODUCTION

In recent years, the spread of digital technologies is gradually expanding the possibilities of fruition of places and collections, with favourable effects in economic terms (Ambrose & Paine, 2018). In the same period, cultural tourism is becoming a priority on the European agenda. This is the reason why one of the main challenges that European Union is facing deals with the 3D visualization and documentation

DOI: 10.4018/978-1-7998-1796-3.ch014

Copyright © 2020, IGI Global. Copying or distributing in print or electronic forms without written permission of IGI Global is prohibited.

of Cultural Heritage (CH) in order to preserve its memory and use it to increase cultural education and tourism.

In the past, the use of digital technologies in order to disseminate CH allowed to create basic case studies characterized by very simple interactive elements, often made up of links able to connect objects to explanatory digital contents. The creation of the first web sites as a museum "showcase" had not yet faced the potentialities offered by 3D modelling or virtual tours, Virtual Reality, etc. in terms of enriching the museum offers (W. Schweibenz, 1991); but soon cultural institutions would have begun to understand the potential of new technologies improving and using them more and more within their apparatus.

In the 1980s, the demand of digitization went hand in hand with the need to catalogue the collections in the form of simple bi-dimensional images. As a consequence, many museums have started using the possibilities offered by the Internet (such as web sites and home pages) in order to collect and disseminate information about their exhibitions (Encyclopaedia Britannica, 2017). Year after year, with the development of new surveying techniques (such as laser scanner and photogrammetry), 3D modelling and digitization, the possibility of strengthening the archives and collections with 3D objects (virtual replicas of the real ones) has been expanding, increasing researches on the digital model, its geometry and its texturisation (Remondino & Rizzi 2010).

Nowadays, the theme of the safeguard and enhancement of CH through digital surveying and 3D modelling techniques is becoming more and more topical. Every issue related to digitization is related to the search for new balances between the great amount of data (collected during the digital survey and the historical research) and the innovative ways of dissemination, connected to new technologies and virtual environments, such as Augmented Reality and Virtual Reality (Banfi, Brumana, & Stanga, 2019).

In this context, it is necessary to define three concepts to understand the relationships between the existing data and their necessary virtual presentation (Figure 1):

- **Virtual Reality (VR):** It is an interactive computer-generated experience that takes place within a simulated environment. VR mainly incorporates auditory and visual feedback but can also allow other types of sensory feedback. A person who uses a VR equipment is able to "look around" in the artificial world, move within it and interact with the context (manipulating objects or activating interactive elements).
- **Augmented Reality (AR):** It is an interactive experience of a tangible environment in which the objects of the real world are "augmented" by virtual information generated by the computer through multiple sensory modalities.
- **Mixed or Merged Reality (MR):** It is not limited to the overlapping of virtual information with the real world, but it anchors virtual objects to the real world, allowing the user to interact with them. Sometimes it is defined "hybrid reality": it is a fusion of real and virtual worlds where physical and digital objects coexist and interact in real time.

This chapter, in addition to demonstrate the effectiveness of VR in learning processes, on the one hand tries to contribute to that branch of research that deals with experiments in the field of new technologies, VR, 3D modelling and digitization of Cultural Heritage, on the other hand is configured as a guide for those who approach VR for the first time. The finished product aims at a large-scale audience because it has a character of immediacy, intuitiveness, ease of use and understanding; however, in the narration there are ideas for researchers who wish to undertake the experience

Figure 1. Difference between VR, AR and MR

 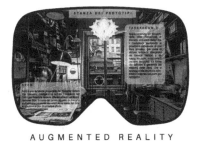 

VIRTUAL REALITY   AUGMENTED REALITY   MIXED REALITY

Specifically, the research presented focused on the concept of VR declined in two different ways. As will be seen, the first (simpler and more rudimentary) experimentation is the realization of a virtual tour through 360° panoramic photos, while the second one (more immersive and engaging) is the creation of a virtual environment entirely reconstructed with 3D modelling techniques and accompanied by very complex interactive elements.

BACKGROUND

In order to develop the present research, it is necessary to clarify some essential definitions. The first one is related to the concept of museum. According to the ICOM (International Council of Museums) Statutes (adopted by the 22nd General Assembly in Vienna, Austria, on 24 August, 2007), a museum "is a non-profit, permanent institution in the service of society and its development, open to the public, which acquires, conserves, researches, communicates and exhibits the tangible and intangible heritage of humanity and its environment for the purposes of education, study and enjoyment". On the basis of this definition, it is possible to say that the ultimate goal of a museum is to collect, safeguard, document, research, disseminate and teach.

In recent years, the places of art and culture have begun to understand the enormous potential offered by new technologies to enrich the museum experience for visitors, attracted by the possibility of being the new protagonists of the exhibition and no longer passive spectators. Museums thus open to new ways of describing the works of art, in order to get closer to a wider and heterogeneous audience.

With the development of new technologies, the classic definition of museum has been enriched with the debate on virtual museums, led by ViMM (Virtual Multimedial Museum). A virtual museum is described as "a digital entity that draws on the characteristics of a museum, in order to complement, enhance, or augment the museum through personalization, interactivity, user experience and richness of content" (Polycarpou, 2018).

This evolution in the concept of museum has been mainly characterized by the establishment of Virtual Reality, Augmented Reality and Artificial Intelligence; the introduction of these new visual and interactive technologies within cultural institutions leads to an enormous expansion of the activities allowed in a museum: now new technologies can be used to act directly on objects, observe them closely, study them and manipulate them, and can allow access to artefacts and collections not available in the real museum (for example all the assets stored in the deposits due to the lack of exhibition spaces).

The greatest strength of technologies such as VR, used within the museum institutions, is maybe connected to their extraordinary educational power. In the era of digital devices, knowledge and learning have become easily available and people have the opportunity to learn in a deeper and easier way. Nevertheless, the current approach to education has some significant problems:

- Traditional (and still predominant) methods of lecture-based education lead to disengaged students (Delialioglu, 2012), who consider them irrelevant, on the basis of a disconnection between content learned in textbooks and authentic practice in the 'real-world' (Gee, 2004).
- A lot of people have difficulties in gathering information.

In general, VR can offer an opportunity to solve these problems and increase students' engagement, providing them with:

- interactive and immersive experiences (Bricken, 1991; Lau, & Lee, 2015);
- a stronger sense of presence and immersion compared with traditional learning environments (Bailenson et al., 2008; Dalgarno, & Lee, 2010);
- an opportunity for constructivist learning, that allows students to construct their own knowledge facing authentic problems, exploring solutions and collaborating with others (Hu-Au, & Lee, 2018);
- the possibility to break down space and time barriers. This characteristic offers powerful learning opportunities for experiencing historical contexts, scientific environments, and meaningful moments.

An interesting concept, recently developed, which highlights the need for innovative ways to convey educational contents in the museum field, is that of edutainment (a term derived from the contraction of "education" and "entertainment") or playful learning. This idea is based on the need of a learning that takes place through pleasant teaching methods: the museum, in fact, has been competing with other cultural offers (cinema, theatre, concerts), often considered less demanding and therefore preferred by users. As a consequence, in the present historical period the museum can no longer carry out its educational function by addressing only the elite of the experts: it must develop strategies to arouse the interest of everyone. In this context, the edutainment takes the form of virtual simulations defined as serious games, digital games that do not exclusively have an entertainment purpose but contain educational elements. Serious games are characterized by a triple component: formative, simulative and playful. The formative component determines the fundamental purpose of the serious game, which is not entertainment for its own sake but learning; the simulative component makes it possible for the user to learn, with his/her senses, some notions that would otherwise be known only at a theoretical level; finally, the playful component allows for exciting experiences, which stimulate memory, curiosity and, consequently, facilitate the learning process. In a serious game, therefore, the playful element does not aim at bringing to life self-referential forms of entertainment, but it has an essentially pedagogical purpose, which is to transmit a message, to make people reflect on important issues, to question consciences (Kokkalia, Drigas, Economou, Roussos, & Choli, 2017; Camin, 2008; Pasek, Golinkoff, Berk, & Singer, 2009).

A final cause for reflection, essential for a complete definition of the contemporary museum (and for the development of the project idea proposed), concerns the concept of design. Specifically, the researchers have wondered whether the design object could be considered a work of art (and therefore part of the cultural heritage) and whether it was appropriate to introduce it within a process of virtual museification, with the goal to protect and disseminate the design pieces and the creative process that led to their conception.

According to the art critic Gillo Dorfles (2010), "there is nothing more burning than design. Our life is based on the problem of design: from the household object to the custom-built car, from cutlery to the artistic object, now design dominates our society. The questions that arise are always the same: is design only technical? Can it be considered art? The root of the problem lies in the distinction between pure art and utilitarian art: design and architecture are arts form with functionalities. Design is "partially" art, it is a form of art with an artistic quotient which a marketing quotient is added to. Consequently, it is correct to affirm that the design object can be characterized by a high aesthetic-artistic value, although it should not be realized with the sole purpose of becoming an art object and it should not satisfy the whim of being only artistic" (Dorfles, 2001).

In general, it is possible to say that both ancient and contemporary objects have their own unique and unrepeatable biography that is enriched with new meanings and new memories over time. Weather they are ancient artefacts or today's artistic creations, objects act as a bridge between those who designed and realized them and those who observe and interact with them.

Considering the object of design as an integral part of the vast world cultural heritage, it was decided to propose a virtualization project (which presents the characteristics of the serious game) of the works of Achille Castiglioni, one of the greatest designers in the world.

RELATED WORKS

There are several digital technologies and virtual experiences that have found a widespread use in the field of protection, enhancement and dissemination of CH: new technologies have given the opportunity to collect, analyse and disseminate information about CH sites. In this context, many projects have been developed with a view to give rise to innovative ways of communicating the legacy of the past and to get people into contact with distant or hardly accessible realities. Thanks to new technologies, in fact, it is possible to enrich the cognitive experience through an immersive and interactive virtual journey. In many cases, immersion is guaranteed by the use of spherical images which information is associated with, as happens in the project of valorisation of the Palazzo Geguti in Georgia (Ferrari & Medici, 2017) or in the project for the dissemination of the Building of Baths in Strasbourg (Koehl et al., 2013). Both virtual experiences are based on the use of 360° panoramic photos which textual and multimedia information is associated with, in order to obtain a virtual tour. This type of approach demonstrates that new technologies not only allow us to enrich the visit with information on history, architectural and decorative elements, but are configured as attractors for a vast and heterogeneous audience in terms of age, origin and education. Virtual tours reveal their effectiveness even when they are used for preliminary documentation and communication, as in the virtualization project of the Cuba's National School of Art where image galleries, hyperlinks to websites, videos, PDFs, and links to databases can be embedded within the scene and interacted with by a user. By using this information within the virtual tour, a user can better understand how the site was constructed as well as its current degraded conditions (Napolitano, Douglas, Garlock, & Glisic, 2017).

Other VR experimentations, more complex and immersive, have produced similar results by leveraging the ability to digitally preserve CH from particular risk factors and by promoting its dissemination, thus making it possible to cancel any constraint of distance or time (Liarokapis et al., 2017; Bruno et al., 2016; Bruno et al. 2018; Bruno et al., 2019). From this point of view, virtual models and simulations effectively guarantee that present and future generations can experience specific places, enjoy their beauty and learn important lessons from them. It is the principle which the project to enhance the Myin-pya-gu temple in Bagan (Dhanda et al., 2019) and the "Nefertari: Journey to Eternity" experience (Curiosity Steam, 2018) are based on. In the first case, the interaction is basic and characterized by the possibility of illuminating the detail elements through a torch, instead, in the second one the interactive component was developed with a higher level of complexity. The project consists in the virtual reconstruction of the tomb of the Egyptian queen, which is no longer accessible in order to preserve its precious and delicate pictorial cycle. This simulation allows the user, guided by a narrative voice, to explore each room and to use interactive elements to learn Egyptian history, art and mythology.

Similar characteristics and purposes can be traced in the virtualization project aimed at safeguarding Grotta dei Pipistrelli of Pantalica Nature Reserve in Sicily (Aiello et al., 2019): during the virtual exploration of the cave, the user has the possibility of coming into contact with an inaccessible environment, knowing its origin, its history, its evolution and the fauna that inhabits it.

With regard to the way digital technologies have become a privileged tool in the management of museum institutions, reference can be made to other experiments carried out in recent years. They aim at giving new life to visit experiences in the museums, making them more intense and engaging, capturing the interest of the users and transmitting their knowledge and teachings through captivating storytellings.

A well-known case is the temporary project "L'Ara com'Era" which, through three-dimensional reconstructions, allows to experience a cross-section of imperial Rome: visitors, accompanied by the narrative voice of Emperor Augustus, can fly over the original context (a large area surrounded by nature) where the Ara Pacis once stood and then witness a sacrificial rite at the foot of the altar (ETT SpA, Zètema Progetto Cultura, & Roma Capitale, Assessorato alla Crescita culturale - Sovrintendenza Capitolina ai Beni Culturali, 2016).

A further example of a perfect balance between museum tour and new technologies is represented by the interactive VR experience "Beyond the Castle", designed to be a preparation for the real visit of the Sforzesco Castle in Milan. Thanks to VR devices, visitors have the possibility of personally reliving the history and events linked to the Milanese fortress through a unique experience, designed to combine history and knowledge with a playful and interactive approach. During this experience the user is accompanied by a virtual narrator, Eva, who plays the role of guide alternating play sessions with historical tales, quizzes and curiosities about the castle collections (Beyond the Gate & Castello Sforzesco di Milano, 2018).

The analysis of these experiences was the basis of the design choices that led to the definition of the storytelling of the two experiments described in the following paragraphs.

CASE STUDY – STUDIO MUSEO ACHILLE CASTIGLIONI

As mentioned, this research focuses on Studio Museo Achille Castiglioni (Figure 2), the former studio of the architect and designer Achille Castiglioni, converted into a museum after his death. In 2006, the heirs of the designer signed a five-year agreement with "Triennale di Milano" so that the museum

Figure 2. Stanza dei Prototipi, Studio Museo Achille Castiglioni. (© 2018, Fondazione Achille Castiglioni. Used with permission)

could be opened to the public and continue its articulated archiving activity. For these reasons the Achille Castiglioni Foundation was born: it has the main purpose to catalogue, sort, archive and digitize projects, drawings, photos, models, films, conferences, objects, books, magazines: in a few words, the whole world which Achille worked in during more than 60 years of activity, first with his brother Pier Giacomo, then (since 1968) alone.

The museum hosts some of the most iconic works of the Milanese designer, exhibited in the place that served as a backdrop for his creative activity. The exhibition includes a visit to the four rooms of the studio: in the first one the prototypes and study models are hosted, in the second the drafting machines and many curiosities, in the third the anonymous objects that Achille Castiglioni collected during his life and that he used in his lessons at Politecnico of Turin and Milan (to teach, through them, important themes about design), in the fourth, the meeting room, some of the objects that have made the history of design.

In this way, visitors have the opportunity to closely understand the methodological approach behind the creative process of each design work (Fondazione Achille Castiglioni, 2014).

This place represents a small Milanese museum institution which is far from the great museum circuits (like other similar contexts); it has to independently face its own economic sustenance and the lack of visibility (due to the presence, in the same territory, of attractive and best known cultural proposals). In spite of everything, this place (like other small but important institutions in the Milanese and international scenario of Design) stays alive thanks to the passion of admirers and of various companies that support it.

One of the most important goals of the Achille Castiglioni Foundation is to raise awareness of the designer's creative genius and of his works outside the physical boundaries of the museum. For this

Figure 3. Flowchart of the steps for the creation of the 360 virtual tour

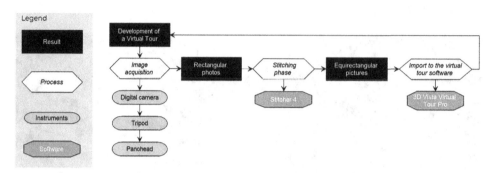

reason, the Foundation has warmly welcomed the proposal for the digitization and virtual fruition of the museum and the extraordinary heritage it hosts.

PROJECT WORKFLOW

The digitization of Studio Museo Achille Castiglioni aims to create two virtual projects that allow all categories of visitors to experience this place and the objects hosted inside it in order to give visibility to this small museum institution. This approach, inter alia, can offer a valid example applicable to other museums that are in the same difficult conditions: in fact, the proposed innovative ways of managing museums have proven to be effective tools to keep their memory alive and to facilitate the access of all categories of users.

After analysing the most used VR devices commercially available and describing in particular those chosen in this study, the two projects developed by the research group will be described in the following paragraphs. In detail, the first project consists in the creation of a virtual tour of the museum rooms, through 360° panoramic images. This virtual experience, designed to be performed on the web (through computers and smartphones) or, in VR mode (through a cardboard) was built following these steps: i) survey project and acquisition of the photographic dataset; ii) photo stitching; iii) design and implementation of the virtual tour (Figure 3).

The second experimentation led to a more articulated and immersive VR experience, developed for Oculus Rift. In this case, the workflow followed consists of four phases: i) digital survey of the rooms using laser scanning techniques; ii) point cloud's data processing; iii) 3D modelling of the architectural shell of the museum and of the design objects; iv) creation of the virtual experience within a game engine (Figure 4).

In order to realize both projects, as will be seen, two tools were used: a camera, associated with a tripod and a panohead, and a BLK 360 laser scanner (Figure 5).

Figure 4. Flowchart of the steps for the creation of the immersive virtual experience

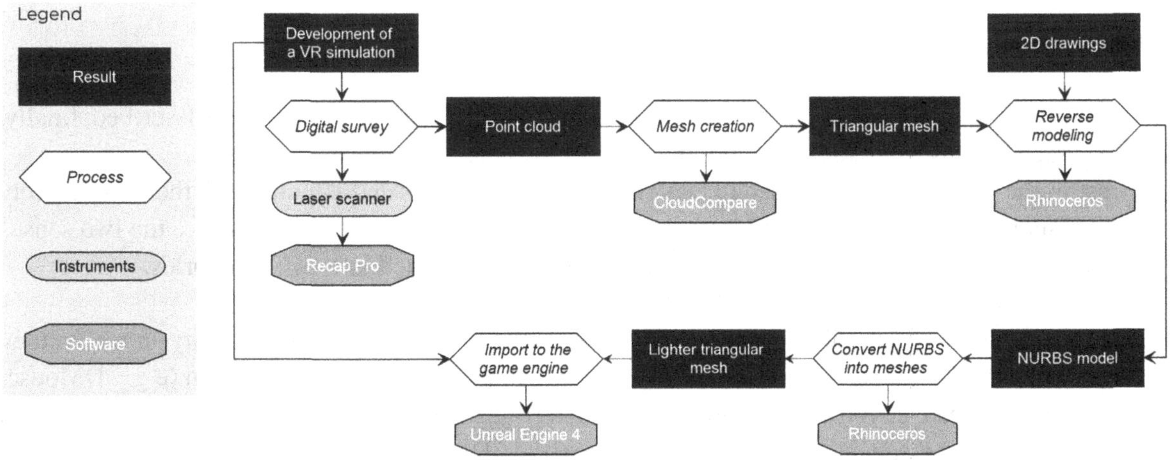

Figure 5. Instruments used: on the left, Canon EOS 70D camera mounted on a tripod with a panoramic head; on the right, laser scanner Leica BLK360

ADOPTED VR TECHNOLOGIES

Hardware

Here below the main devices used to allow the exploration of the VR environments are described; finally, the paragraph will focus on the tools chosen to experience the two projects developed.

Most of the devices currently used to "enter" virtual simulations and interact with them exclusively employ visual and auditory stimulation systems (considering that sight and hearing are the two senses most stressed within VR environments). These tools can be classified into two categories:

- **Input devices**, which allow users to influence and manipulate the virtual reality in which they are catapulted. This category traditionally includes tools for spatial manipulation (e.g. 3DMouse, gloves, gamepad, keyboard, etc.) and devices that record the position and orientation of the user's body. The most frequently used input devices are the 2D interaction devices like mouse, touchpad or basic game controller due to their cheapness and versatility.
- **Output devices**, which allow users to immerse themselves in the virtual dimension. This category includes all the equipment that returns visual and auditory stimuli, giving the user the feeling of being physically within the virtual world. The most common output devices are the head-mounted displays (HMDs). They are also called "fully immersive displays", as they completely block the view of the user and prevent any visual contact with the surrounding world. An HMD consists of a stereoscopic display that returns images to the user as they are perceived by the human eye: two images of the same scene with two slightly different points of view are projected into each eye to create the parallax effect, the phenomenon which allows the brain to perceive depth, based on the apparent position of objects. Between the display and the eyes, specialized lenses are juxtaposed: they allow to focus the image despite the proximity between the user's eyes and the images projected on the display. In general, the headset records the movements of the head and changes the images shown on the display. The phenomenon of recording the movements of the user's head, defined Rotational Tracking, is obtained through the IMU (Inertial Measuring Unit), an electric sensor located inside the HMD consisting of a gyroscope, an accelerometer and a magnetometer. The position and orientation of the Head-mounted Displays and of the input devices are traced by additional sensors, which are external to the HMD. There are two types of VR head-mounted displays:
  - Slide-on HMDs. They are the cheapest and the most accessible tools. The Slide-on HMDs use a smartphone for viewing, processing and rotational tracking and are suitable for the use of content in a mainly passive way. This means that the user does not have the possibility to interact directly with the content he observes. The most popular Slide-on HMDs are:
    - Google Cardboard
    - Samsung Gear VR
  - Discrete HMDs. These devices contain a display, lenses, rotational tracking systems, positional tracking systems and devices for auditory stimulation. In order to process, these headsets must be connected to a computer. Among the most popular HMDs are:
    - Oculus Rift
    - HTC Vive
    - PlayStation VR

In the context of the two experimentations described in these pages, it was decided to use a Slide-on HMD to visualize the virtual tour and an Oculus Rift device (developed by Oculus VR) for the VR simulation.

The equipment provided by Oculus consists of a fully immersive display, two sensors for the recognition of position, orientation and movement and two controllers (Oculus Touch), which allow the user to move and manipulate objects within the virtual world.

The Oculus Rift CV1 (Consumer Version-1) is a lightweight stereoscopic display with a wide field of view (FOV) of 110°, mounted on two low latency AMOLED flat screens with 1080×1200 resolution per eye. Of particular importance in this display is the use of highly specialized and free-form hybrid Fresnel lenses.

The position and orientation of the device are traced using the combination of an internal IMU and a series of infrared LEDs (incorporated in the display and in the support strap) which are detected by a separate IR camera. The system is designed for the use in an upright or sitting position and has an effective operating area measuring 5×11 feet. The position and orientation of the controllers are monitored using the Oculus Constellation tracking technology, consisting of an infrared camera that identifies the position of the LEDs arranged around each device. The inputs of the controllers, such as those that detect the position of the user's fingers, are sent via a wireless transmitter to a receiver in the HMD (Aukstakalnis, 2016).

Software

In this paragraph the software used for the creation of the two experimentations will be described:

- The software used for the creation of the virtual tour were Stitcher 4 and 3D Vista Virtual Tour Pro, both developed by 3D Vista. The first one automatically identifies homologous points between pictures to obtain panoramic images (sometimes it may be necessary to identify homologous points manually to ensure optimal alignment). It supports most popular cameras and lens types including standard, wide angle, Fisheye and One-shot lenses. It allows for full or partial, cubic, spherical and small-planet panoramas. The second software, instead, makes it possible to associate links between photos by adding hotspots. These links can direct you to a URL address, to an HTML page, to a digital document or can allow the user to move from one panoramic image to another.

- The software used for the design of the VR simulation was Unreal Engine 4. This choice is due to the software's versatility, the availability of a free version, the reliability of the results obtained and the possibility of drawing on vast libraries of materials and a substantial literature produced during the years in which the use of the software has been consolidated. One of the strengths of this tool is the visual scripting system Blueprint, constantly updated and so powerful that it can replace programming languages like C++ in very complex operations. Specifically, the Blueprints Visual Scripting system in Unreal Engine is a complete gameplay scripting system based on the concept of using a node-based interface to create gameplay elements from within Unreal Editor. As with many common scripting languages, it is used to define object-oriented (OO) classes or objects in the engine. In other words, Blueprints are visually scripted additions to the game. By connecting Nodes, Events, Functions and Variables with Wires, it is possible to create complex gameplay elements (object construction, individual functions and general gameplay events - that are specific to each instance of the Blueprint in order to implement behavior and other functionality).

The most commonly used Blueprint types are "Level Blueprints" and "Blueprint Classes".

The first type is specific to the level of the Unreal Editor in which Level Blueprints were developed, so they are especially suitable for creating unique actions that should not be repeated: start a movie when a certain object is touched or open a particular door after killing all the enemies.

On the other hand, Blueprint Classes are the best way to get a reusable behavior in the project: because of the self-contained nature of Blueprints, they can be constructed in such a way that they can be dropped into a level and they will simply work, with minimal setup required. This also means that editing a Blueprint that is in use throughout a project will update every instance of it. They are ideal for creating interactive assets such as doors, switches, playable sounds etc.

PROJECT 1: FROM 360° IMAGES TO an IMMERSIVE VIRTUAL TOUR

Purposes

The realization of the virtual tour of the museum through 180° x 360° panoramic images aims to create an immediate, accessible and user-friendly tool that allows anyone to come into contact with a part of the museum's contents as it is today. The suggestions provided by this type of virtual tour do not replace the real visit experiences but promote and encourage them. The acquisition of 360° images was preceded by a survey project aimed at capturing images (necessary to identify the best stations which to take the photos from) and by a virtual tour project.

Images Acquisition and Creation of 180° x 360° Panoramic Photos

7 acquisition stations were chosen, on the basis of the peculiarities of the surveyed spaces: the external atrium, the entrance area, the mirror room, the meeting room, the drawing room and the prototype room. In particular, the mirror and the prototype rooms have been captured from two different points of view to allow for a more in-depth visit (considering their size and the quantity of objects they contain). During the acquisition of the photographic dataset, a Canon EOS 70D camera (mounted on a tripod with a panoramic head) was used. In order to obtain a single 360° image for each acquisition point, a certain number of photos, organized on three bands (with a mutual distance to ensure an overlap of about 30% between contiguous images), was taken at eye-level (in this way, during the stitching phase, it is possible to identify homologous points between the photos, guaranteeing an optimal alignment). Specifically, for each acquisition point it was necessary to create a first circular band of images with an angle of 0° with respect to the horizontal, a second band with an angle of 45° upwards and a third one with an angle of 45° downward. To ensure that the images of each band had the right degree of overlap, 36 photos were taken for each station. The shots were acquired using a stable and aligned tripod and keeping the camera on a fixed rotation axis, to avoid a parallax error that would produce a misalignment with multiple problems in assembling photos. In order to eliminate the parallax effect, the camera must rotate around the nodal point (that is the perspective center of the optics), usually located at the diaphragm. The nodal point changes depending on the combination camera - lens and can be identified by taking snapshots to

Figure 6. Scheme of the shooting technique

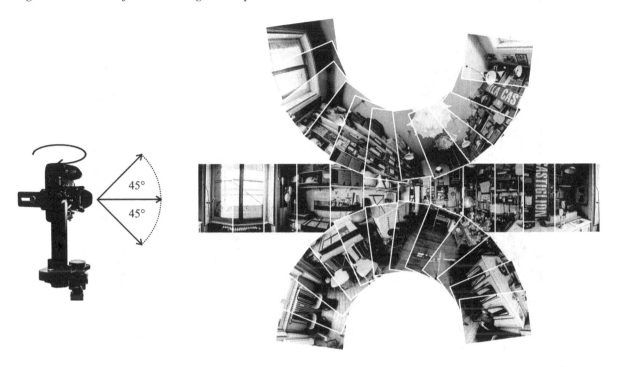

Figure 7. Panoramic image of "Stanza dei Prototipi"

empirically establish the centre of rotation: after identifying a scene with two vertical references (one near the camera and the other one towards the infinity) and framing them in such a way that they are perfectly overlapped, the camera is rotated through the joint at the base of the panoramic head, and it has to be verified whether the two references always appear in the same mutual position (Figure 6).

Figure 8. Virtual tour, view of the meeting room with interactive elements

After modifying the photos using Adobe Lightroom in order to optimize contrasts and exposures, the photos were combined on Stitcher 4. In this case study, automatic stitching was not always optimal due to the presence of a white plaster without macroscopic imperfections on many vertical surfaces and on the ceilings; it was necessary to manually associate common points between the photos and repeat the processing several times. Finally, the stitching software generated seven 180° x 360° panoramic images (of about 100 MB and with a resolution of 20000 x 8100 pixels), used for the virtual tour (Figure 7).

Project of the Virtual Tour

The tour, designed with 3D Vista Virtual Tour Pro, starts in the external atrium; from here the user can teleport at the museum entrance by clicking arrows, placed on the floor, that indicate the right direction. Once this new position is reached, it will be possible to move to the right or to the left (still following the arrows on the floor) to reach one of the adjacent station points. In this way the user is able to visit all the rooms one by one. During the visit, it will be possible to click on the main design objects exhibited in the museum to open an information panel that contains the essential information about the observed artifact (date of production, manufacturer, etc.). If the user wants to switch from one room to another without necessarily going through the intermediate stages, he/she can open a drop-down menu and directly select the desired panoramic photo (Figure 8).

PROJECT 2: FROM DIGITAL SURVEY TO an INTERACTIVE VR EXPERIENCE

Purposes

This digitization project aims at creating an immersive VR experience (developed for Oculus Rift) that allows to enjoy this place and the design objects in order to give visibility to the museum and to show how VR can be an effective tool for learning. This second experimentation derives from a more complex workflow based on digital surveying, digital modelling, developing of virtual environments and interactions.

Digital Survey

Data Acquisition

In order to obtain the data necessary for the reconstruction of the museum, a digital survey has been conducted using a laser scanner, a tool able to measure the distances between points in the real world by means of electromagnetic waves in the form of laser pulses. The information recorded by the laser scanner consists of a set of points that three Cartesian coordinates x, y, z are associated with; these coordinates allow to locate every point in the 3D space. This set of points constitutes the numerical model, defined point cloud.

The laser used to acquire the museum rooms is a Leica BLK 360, a scanner measuring 165 mm in height x 100 mm in diameter, chosen for its low cost, its lightness (the total weight is about 1 kg), its easy manageability and fast acquisition: within its field of view (360° wide horizontally and 300° vertically), BLK 360 is in fact able to acquire (choosing between high, standard and fast resolution) up to 360,000 pts / sec. Furthermore, it can carry out a complete circular scan (in standard resolution) in less than three minutes and can generate a spherical image at 150 MP.

Through the ReCap Pro mobile app, BLK360 can then transfer images and point cloud data to an iPad. The app filters and records the scan data in real time. After the acquisition, it is possible to use ReCap Pro to export the point clouds data to different CAD, BIM, VR and AR applications. The integration between BLK360 and Autodesk software considerably streamlines the process of acquiring reality.

The scanning range of this device is 0.6 - 60 meters with a scanning accuracy of 4 mm at 10 m and 7 mm at 20 m. The moderate level of precision did not represent a significant problem for the purposes of this experimentation, considering that the survey data were used only as a basis for reconstructing the museum rooms through a reverse modelling process.

BLK 360 was used to perform 21 scans in "high resolution" mode for this digitization project. During the survey, the laser camera was deactivated, considering that it was not necessary to have the chromatic data for modelling the architectural elements; in this way the registration has been facilitated and the acquisition time has been reduced. No less than two scans per room were performed, paying particular attention to the transition areas from one room to another, where more scans have been acquired in order to ensure the exact connection between the various portions.

At the end of this phase, 21 point clouds were generated and automatically aligned by the BLK360 with the Cloud to Cloud method. The final point cloud of the entire environment is made up approximately by 170 million points (Figure 9).

Figure 9. Detail of the point cloud (Recap)

Data Processing

The data obtained from the scans were directly transferred to the Recap Pro software via the iPad app. The point cloud was then cleaned of the noise generated by windows and other reflective surfaces (such as the mirror in one of the rooms and the materials of some design works). Considering the enormous amount of points, the numerical model has been divided into six smaller portions (each corresponding to one room) and imported into CloudCompare (a point cloud management software), where, through an algorithm, it was possible to convert the point cloud into a mesh, a three-dimensional object consisting of a network of polygonal faces.

Modelling

Reverse Modelling

The meshes obtained have been imported into the modelling software Rhinoceros, where the rooms have been reconstructed by performing a reverse modelling, a process which allows to deduce the rep-

Figure 10. Workflow for modelling the architectural components (Rhinoceros)

Figure 11. Workflow for modelling the design objects (Rhinoceros)

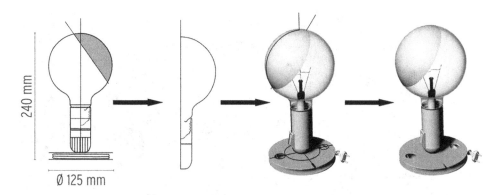

resentation of the morphology from the digital acquisition of the physical model. During this phase, the outline of the mesh was traced in order to reconstruct the entire model with a high degree of adherence in the form of "NURBS" (acronym which stands for "Non-Uniform Rational Basis-Splines"), easier to manage compared to the mesh. The reverse modelling has been performed by obtaining the generating curves of the various architectural elements (vaults, walls, doors, windows); these curves represented the guidelines used to realize all the NURBS surfaces (Figure 10).

Design Objects Modelling

Once the architectural elements were modelled in the form of NURBS, the most emblematic design objects were modelled on full scale. Each object was digitally built using an extensive photographic documentation and metric and geometric information, obtained from two-dimensional representations (provided by the Achille Castiglioni Foundation), always trying to make the reproduction as close as possible to the original. In this case, the models were created starting from the generating curves extrapolated from the images and from the 2D elaborations (Figure 11).

Virtualization of the Studio Museo Achille Castiglioni

After being modelled on Rhino, the mathematical model of the museum shell has been converted into mesh and exported in fbx format. The fbx file was finally imported into Unreal Engine for the creation of the virtual environment.

Within the game engine, materials have been applied to all the elements of the architectural model and the design objects (walls, floors, vaults, doors, windows).

A Material is an asset that can be applied to a mesh to control the visual look of the scene. Material literally defines the type of surface from which your object appears to be made. In Unreal Engine, materials are constructed via a network of visual scripting nodes (called Material Expressions) within the Material Editor. Each node contains a snippet of HLSL code, designated to perform a specific task.

Through the manipulation of the Material Editor parameters, it is possible to define a mesh color, its translucency, its transparency, etc. In more technical terms, when light from the scene hits the surface, materials are used to calculate how that light interacts with that surface. These calculations are done us-

Figure 12. Material Editor (Unreal Engine)

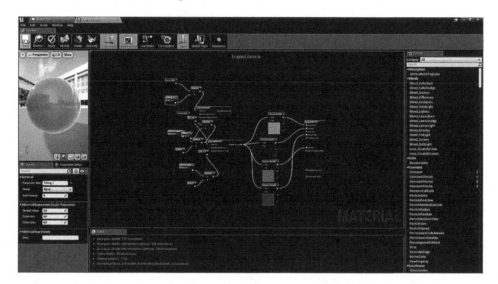

ing incoming data that is input to the material from a variety of images (textures) and math expressions, as well as from various property settings inherent to the material itself.

The textures used for this research try to recall the original materials and colors as much as possible, making the virtual reproduction extremely realistic (Figure 12).

The exhibition project was designed with the precious help of the Achille Castiglioni Foundation, which provided interesting causes for reflection, indicating the best way to interpret the meaning of each exhibited object and its relation with the context. On the basis of these considerations, it was decided to recreate the exhibition by generally respecting the objects location in the real world. Other objects, not physically present in the museum, have been included in the simulation because of their great value and the memories they contain: this is the case, for example, of the Sanluca armchair, which was placed in the mirror room (as detailed below), in the same position where an old photo provided by the Foundation portrays it.

The virtual museum exhibition thus takes place in the five rooms of the museum and starts from the entrance, which is centrally located along a corridor. From here, the visitor can choose whether to continue to the left or to the right, along two equivalent paths. Going to the right, the first environment the visitor comes across is a room that hosts a collection of original posters of important design exhibitions curated by Castiglioni himself. Approaching each of these, an information panel will appear, showing brief historical notes and anecdotes about the exhibition event (Figure 13).

Crossing two arches, the visitor reaches the mirror room, where he/she comes into contact with the first design objects created by Castiglioni: in the centre of the room there are the Leonardo table with the two Tric chairs and the large Sanluca armchair, flanked by the small Servomuto table, with the Noce floor lamp on it. The exhibition is completed by the Servomanto coat hanger, the Stylos floor lamp, the Mate coffee table and the iconic Arco lamp, which draws attention with its elegant curved profile. A mention should also be made to the large mirror (located behind the armchair) which is perhaps the hallmark of the room and gives it its name. During the exploration of this environment, the visitor has the opportunity to manipulate various objects: for example, he/she can rotate the mirror, remove the tray of the Mate table or pick up and closely observe the characteristic blue glasses with round lenses, placed on the Leonardo table, which belonged to Castiglioni (Figure 14). In the mirror room there are two closed interactive doors, designed to be opened by the visitor with the controllers, so as to allow him/her to pass into the next space. In this small room the user can find a great collection of objects (some of them designed by Achille Castiglioni in collaboration with his brother Pier Giacomo), including the Bramante table, four types of seating (Babela, Lierna, Sedile Mezzadro, Sella), two bookcases (Libreria Pensile, hanging on a wall, and Lungangolo), various lighting fixtures (Saliscendi lamp, Taccia table lamp, Snoopy, Lampadina, Parentesi Toio and Luminator floor lamp), two cabinets (Trio and Comodo), the Lapis vase and the Brionvega RR126 radio (Figure 15). As in the previous room, the user has the possibility of manipulating many objects, such as the Lapis vase or the sketches and the technical drawings scattered on a drawing board and realized by Castiglioni himself. In the same way, a page extracted from an original issue of Diabolik and placed on the Bramante table can be picked up: in this page, the two authors of the comic, the Giussani sisters, have drawn the Taccia lamp, in homage to the genius of the Milanese designer. A last interesting interactive element is represented by the buttons of the Brionvega RR126 radiograph: pushing them, it is possible to listen to five songs dear to Castiglioni (Maramao perchè sei morto, Nel blu dipinto di blu, Yellow submarine, Somewhere over the rainbow, Sing sing sing) (Figure 16).

Retracing his/her steps, the visitor can then reach the left wing of the museum, where it is possible to explore two other environments; the first one is the drawing room, characterized by the presence of two distinctive elements: some remains of Roman stilts and the shelves with the archives. Here the researchers tried to recreate the living room of Villa Olmo, designed by Achille and Pier Giacomo and characterized, inter alia, by the presence of a movable television. It can be turned on to watch the audiovisual excerpts of the documentary "Achille Castiglioni: tutto con un niente" (made by 3D Produzioni), that shows the designer telling anecdotes of his life and details of his works.

At this point, the visit ends in the last room, where the prototypes of important design objects are located, such as the lamps hanging from the ceiling (the Taraxacum '88, placed in a central position to emphasize its iconic profile, the Kd6, the Relemme, the Splugen Brau, the Taraxacum '60 and the Viscontea, the latter two flanked by two models of their structural frames), the floor lamps (Brera, Bibip), the Giovi wall lamp, the Gatto table lamp (flanked by its structural frame), the Allunaggio and Spluga chairs, the Cumano and Basello tables, the Phil oil and vinegar set. These objects are placed in an apparently chaotic way (just like in reality), as if to represent the freedom of the designer's creative genius, which expresses itself without limits in the experiments conducted within his laboratory (Figure 17).

The main interactive components are represented, once again, by the possibility of manipulating various objects, picking them up, moving them or opening them, such as in the case of the chests of the drawers (where it is possible to extract sketches, drawings, period photographs, etc.). Similar interactions are designed for the box marked with the phrase "prototipi Gibigiana", that reproduces Castiglioni's calligraphy (from which it is possible to extract the Gibigiana table lamp and a photo that shows the various stages of the prototype development), and for the Basello, which can be rotated so as to understand its operating system (Figure 18).

These interactive elements are implemented with other interactions placed in every room: this is the case, for example, of all the lighting fixtures, which can be switched on or off in order to understand their ignition mechanism and to study the way each cone of light illuminates the environment (Figure 19).

Figure 13. Virtual reconstruction of the entrance of the museum. In the background, view of the mirror room (Unreal Engine)

Figure 14. Detail of the characteristic blue glasses with round lenses belonged to Achille Castiglioni (Unreal Engine)

Figure 15. Virtual reconstruction of the meeting room (Unreal Engine)

Figure 16. Detail of the Brionvega RR126 radiograph (Unreal Engine)

Figure 17. Virtual reconstruction of Stanza dei Prototipi (Unreal Engine)

Figure 18. Virtual reconstruction of Stanza dei Prototipi. In the foreground, the interactive box (marked with the phrase "prototipi Gibigiana") and the openable drawers (Unreal Engine)

Figure 19. Detail of the lighting fixtures (Unreal Engine)

Figure 20. Example of Blueprint Classes (Unreal Engine)

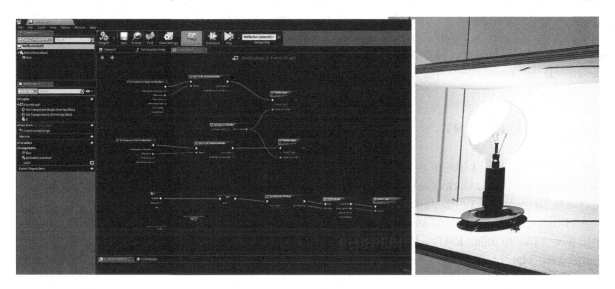

A final mention concerns some small details, which the most attentive visitor can notice during the virtual experience. It is the case, for example, of a peculiar whistle that can be heard from time to time during the visit. It is an original recording of Achille Castiglioni's voice, which echoes through the rooms almost as if he were the soul of the museum, which continues to live through his works. The presence of details like this is not casual and should not be considered as an end in itself. The researchers are aware that it is precisely the smallest details that give credibility to a VR experience; these elements (only apparently secondary) have been inserted in order to give life to the place, to have it accepted by the visitor and to make the emotional involvement more intense and profound.

All the interactions present in this VR experience (virtual doors, switchable lamps, pickable objects, movable drawers and design objects) were made using Blueprint Classes (Figure 20).

CONCLUSION

The two projects proposed show how the digitization of an important museum institution conducted with the most advanced technologies (from 360° panoramic images to Virtual Reality) represents now an indispensable tool of knowledge and protection of memory, but also an effective and immediate educational support, a vehicle for the promotion and communication of certain objects. The virtual tour and the virtual reality experiences are thus able to bring man closer to a priceless cultural heritage but often forgotten because it is little known and on the margins of the main tourist flows.

Specifically, the virtual tour consisting of panoramic photos (designed to be inserted into the web site of the Foundation, so as to increase its visibility), helped to guarantee a low-cost virtual experience that can be enjoyed easily and quickly from anywhere through the internet, without the aid of expensive tools.

As regards the virtual reality experience (available for Oculus Rift), it allows, thanks to the possibility of creating complex interactions (moving objects, manipulating them, disassembling them, opening them, turning on the lighting fixtures and studying their cone of light and their relationship with the surrounding space), to acquire an in-depth knowledge of the extraordinary heritage that the museum contains and to understand all the characteristics of complex, precious and delicate artefacts (such as design objects) even without coming into direct contact with them. Above all, this last experience is open to be implemented over time, in order to become a real database, a treasure chest that, if further developed, can permanently preserve the memory of all artefacts hosted in the museum.

ACKNOWLEDGMENT

The researchers would like to thank the members of the Achille Castiglioni Foundation (specifically Giovanna Castiglioni, Carlo Castiglioni, Antonella Gornati and Noemi Ceriani) for allowing the free access to all the rooms of the museum, for providing us with documents and images that are part of their collection and for helping and supporting us in the organization of the virtual museum exhibition. We also would like to thank RAD – Rete d'impresa per l'Artiginato Digitale (specifically Marco Cavalotto and Davide Manfredi) for truly believing in this project, supporting it professionally and economically.

REFERENCES

Aiello, D., Basso, A., Spena, M. T., D'Agostino, G., Montedoro, U., Galizia, M., ... Santagati, C. (2019). The virtual batcave: A project for the safeguard of a UNESCO WHL fragile ecosystem. *The International Archives of the Photogrammetry, Remote Sensing and Spatial Information Sciences, XLII-2*(W9), 17–24. doi:10.5194/isprs-archives-XLII-2-W9-17-2019

Ambrose, T., & Paine, C. (2018). *Museum basics: The international handbook.* London, UK: Routledge. doi:10.4324/9781315232898

Aukstakalnis, S. (2016). *Practical augmented reality: a guide to the technologies, applications, and human factors for AR and VR.* Boston, MA: Addison-Wesley.

Bailenson, J., Yee, N., Blascovich, J., Beall, A., Lundblad, N., & Jin, M. (2008). The use of immersive virtual reality in the learning sciences: Digital transformations of teachers, students and social context. *Journal of the Learning Sciences, 17*(1), 102–141. doi:10.1080/10508400701793141

Banfi, F., Brumana, R., & Stanga, C. (2019). A content-based immersive experience of basilica of Sant'Ambrogio in Milan: From 3D survey to virtual reality. *The International Archives of the Photogrammetry, Remote Sensing and Spatial Information Sciences, XLII-2*(W11), 159–166. doi:10.5194/isprs-archives-XLII-2-W11-159-2019

Beyond the Gate (Developer), & Castello Sforzesco di Milano (Client). (2018). *Beyond the Castle.* Retrieved from https://beyondthegate.io/castello-sforzesco/

Bricken, M. (1991). Virtual reality learning environments: Potentials and challenges. *Computer Graphics, 25*(3), 178–184. doi:10.1145/126640.126657

Bruno, F., Barbieri, L., Laudi, A., Cozza, M., Cozza, A., Peluso, R., & Muzzupappa, M. (2018). Virtual dives into the underwater archaeological treasures of South Italy. *Virtual Reality (Waltham Cross), 22*(2), 91–102. doi:10.100710055-017-0318-z

Bruno, F., Lagudi, A., Barbieri, L., Cozza, M., Cozza, A., Peluso, R., ... Skarlatos, D. (2019). Virtual tour in the sunken "villa con ingresso a protiro" within the underwater archaeological park of Baiae. *The International Archives of the Photogrammetry, Remote Sensing and Spatial Information Sciences, XLII-2*(W10), 45–51. doi:10.5194/isprs-archives-XLII-2-W10-45-2019

Bruno, F., Lagudi, A., Muzzupappa, M., Lupia, M., Cario, G., Barbieri, L., ... Saggiomo, R. (2016). Project VISAS - Virtual and augmented exploitation of Submerged Archaeological Sites: Overview and first results. *Marine Technology Society Journal, 50*(4), 119–129. doi:10.4031/MTSJ.50.4.4

Camin, G. (2008, June). Che cosa si intende per diletto? *Nuova Museologia, 18*, 28–29.

Curiosity Stream (Ed.), & Experius VR (Developer). (2018). *Nefertari: Journey to eternity.* Retrieved from https://www.oculus.com/experiences/rift/1491802884282318/

Da Rin De Lorenzo, F. (Interviewer), & Dorfles, G. (Interviewee). (2010, May 9). *Art crafts and industry* [Video interview]. Retrieved from https://venicedesignweek.com/gillo-dorfles-thanks/

Dalgarno, B., & Lee, M. J. W. (2010). What are the learning affordances of 3D virtual environments? *British Journal of Educational Technology, 41*(1), 10–32. doi:10.1111/j.1467-8535.2009.01038.x

Delialioglu, O. (2012). Student engagement in blended learning environments with lecture-based and problem-based instructional approaches. *Journal of Educational Technology and Society, 15*(3), 310–n/a.

Dhanda, A., Reina Ortiz, M., Weigert, A., Paladini, A., Min, A., Gyi, M., ... Santana Quintero, M. (2019). Recreating cultural heritage environments for VR using photogrammetry. *The International Archives of the Photogrammetry, Remote Sensing and Spatial Information Sciences, XLII-2*(W9), 305–310. doi:10.5194/isprs-archives-XLII-2-W9-305-2019

Dorfles, G. (2001). *Introduzione al disegno industriale*. Milano, Italy: Einaudi.

Encyclopaedia Britannica. (2017). *Virtual museum.* Retrieved from https://www.britannica.com/topic/virtual-museum

ETT SpA (developer), Zètema Progetto Cultura (organizer), & Roma Capitale, Assessorato alla Crescita culturale - Sovrintendenza Capitolina ai Beni Culturali (promoter) (2016). *L'Ara com'era.* Retrieved from http://www.arapacis.it/it/mostre_ed_eventi/eventi/l_ara_com_era

Ferrari, F., & Medici, M. (2017). The virtual experience for cultural heritage: methods and tools comparison for Geguti Palace in Kutaisi, Georgia. In *Proceedings of the International and Interdisciplinary Conference IMMAGINI? Image and Imagination between Representation, Communication, Education and Psychology, 1*, 932.

Fondazione Achille Castiglioni. (2014). *La fondazione.* Retrieved from http://fondazioneachillecastiglioni.it/la-fondazione/

Gee, J. P. (2004). *Situated language and learning: a critique of traditional schooling*. London, UK: Routledge.

Hu-Au, E., & Lee, J. (2018). Virtual reality in education: A tool for learning in the experience age. *International Journal of Innovation in Education, 4*(4), 215–226. doi:10.1504/IJIIE.2017.10012691

Koehl, M., Schneider, A., Fritsch, E., Fritsch, F., Rachedi, A., & Guillemin, S. (2013). Documentation of historical building via Virtual Tour: The complex building of baths in Strasbourg. *The International Archives of the Photogrammetry, Remote Sensing and Spatial Information Sciences, XL-5*(W2), 385–390. doi:10.5194/isprsarchives-XL-5-W2-385-2013

Kokkalia, G., Drigas, A., Economou, A., Roussos, P., & Choli, S. (2017). Paper-the use of serious games in preschool education the use of serious games in preschool education Spyridoula Choli. [IJET]. *International Journal of Emerging Technologies in Learning, 12*(11), 15–27. doi:10.3991/ijet.v12i11.6991

Lau, K., & Lee, P. (2015). The use of virtual reality for creating unusual environmental stimulation to motivate students to explore creative ideas. *Interactive Learning Environments, 23*(1), 3–18. doi:10.1080/10494820.2012.745426

Liarokapis, F., Kouril, P., Agrafiotis, P., Demesticha, S., Chmelık, J., & Skarlatos, D. (2017). 3D modelling and mapping for virtual exploitation of underwater archaeology assets. *The International Archives of the Photogrammetry, Remote Sensing and Spatial Information Sciences, XLII-2*(W3), 425–431. doi:10.5194/isprs-archives-XLII-2-W3-425-2017

Napolitano, R. K., Douglas, I. P., Garlock, M. E., & Glisic, B. (2017). Virtual tour environment of Cuba's National School of Art. *The International Archives of the Photogrammetry, Remote Sensing and Spatial Information Sciences, XLII-2*(W5), 547–551. doi:10.5194/isprs-archives-XLII-2-W5-547-2017

Pasek, K., Golinkoff, R. M., Berk, L. E., & Singer, D. G. (2009). *A mandate for playful learning in preschool: Presenting the evidence*. New York, NY: Oxford University Press.

Polycarpou, C. (2018, Jan. 10). *The ViMM definition of a virtual museum*. Retrieved from https://www.vi-mm.eu/2018/01/10/the-vimm-definition-of-a-virtual-museum/

Remondino, F., & Rizzi, A. (2010). Reality-based 3D documentation of natural and cultural heritage sites—Techniques, problems, and examples. *Applied Geomatics, 2*(3), 85–100. doi:10.100712518-010-0025-x

Schweibenz, W. (1991). The virtual museum: new perspectives for museums to present objects and information using the Internet as a knowledge base and communication system. In H. Zimmermann, & H. Schramm (Eds.), *Proceedings of the 6th ISI Conference* (pp. 185–200), Prague, Konstanz, UKV.

ADDITIONAL READING

Banfi, F., Brumana, R., Aljishi, A., Al Sayeh, N., Santana Quintero, M., Cuca, B., ... Midali, C. (2019). Generative modeling, Virtual Reality and HBIM interaction: immersive environment for built heritage: case study of Shaikh Isa Bin Ali House, Bahrain. *The International Archives of the Photogrammetry, Remote Sensing and Spatial Information Sciences, XLII-2*(W11), 149–157. doi:10.5194/isprs-archives-XLII-2-W11-149-2019

Eschenbrenner, B., Nah, F. F., & Siau, K. (2008). 3D virtual worlds in education: Applications, benefits, issues and opportunities. *Journal of Database Management, 19*(4), 91–110. doi:10.4018/jdm.2008100106

Ferrari, F., & Medici, M. (2017). The Virtual Experience for Cultural Heritage: Methods and Tools Comparison for Geguti Palace in Kutaisi, Georgia. In *Proceedings of the International and Interdisciplinary Conference IMMAGINI? Image and Imagination between Re-presentation, Communication, Education and Psychology, Brixen, Italy, 27–28 November 2017*, Firenze, Italy: DIDA Press, Dipartimento di Architettura Università degli Studi di Firenze. 10.3390/proceedings1090932

Hu-Au, Elliot, & Lee, Joey. (2018). Virtual reality in education: a tool for learning in the experience age. *International Journal of Innovation in Education.*

Johnson, L. F., & Levine, A. H. (2008). Virtual worlds: Inherently immersive, highly social learning spaces. *Theory into Practice, 47*(2), 161–170. doi:10.1080/00405840801992397

Paladini, A., Dhanda, A., Reina Ortiz, M., Weigert, A., Nofal, E., Min, A., ... Santana Quintero, M. (2019). Impact of Virtual Reality experience on accessibility of Cultural Heritage. *The International Archives of the Photogrammetry, Remote Sensing and Spatial Information Sciences, XLII-2*(W11), 929–936. doi:10.5194/isprs-archives-XLII-2-W11-929-2019

Palestini, C., & Basso, A. (2017). The photogrammetric survey methodologies applied to low cost 3D virtual exploration in multidisciplinary field. *The International Archives of the Photogrammetry, Remote Sensing and Spatial Information Sciences, XLII-2*(W8), 195–202. doi:10.5194/isprs-archives-XLII-2-W8-195-2017

Scandurra, S., Pulcrano, M., Cirillo, V., Campi, M., di Luggo, A., & Zerlenga, O. (2018). Integrated survey procedures for the virtual reading and fruition of historical buildings. *The International Archives of the Photogrammetry, Remote Sensing and Spatial Information Sciences, XLII-2*, 1037–1044. doi:10.5194/isprs-archives-XLII-2-1037-2018

Tousant, K. T. D., & Fai, S. (2019). The digital restitution of lot 3317: Using underwater image based modelling to generate value in virtual heritage experiences. *The International Archives of the Photogrammetry, Remote Sensing and Spatial Information Sciences, XLII-2*(W10), 189–195. doi:10.5194/isprs-archives-XLII-2-W10-189-2019

KEY TERMS AND DEFINITIONS

Achille Castiglioni: Castiglioni (Milan, 16 February 1918 - Milan, 2 December 2002) was one of the most famous Italian architect and designer of the twentieth century.

Edutainment: This term is a portmanteau given by the words "education" and "entertainment". It is a media with the aim of educating using a playful component.

Equirectangular Image: It is an unwrap of a spherical image onto a plane, the width is exactly twice its height.

NURBS geometry: NURBS is an acronym for "Non Uniform Rational Basis-Splines". It is a mathematical representation used to define curves and surfaces. A NURBS is defined by the degree, the control points, the knots and the evaluation rule.

Polygonal Mesh: It is a collection of vertices, edges and faces that defines the morphology of an object. **Reverse Modeling:** It is the process by which it is possible to reconstruct the shape of an object in the form of NURBS geometries starting from the data acquired through digital survey.

Serious Game: It is a digital game with educational purposes in addition to the playful ones.

Virtual Museum: It is a digital entity that shares some of the characteristics of the traditional museum, such as the accessibility, the educational purposes, etc. It aims at completing, improving, increasing the museum experience through forms of personalization, interaction and enrichment of the museum contents.

Chapter 15
Where Is Hanuman?
Hindu Mythology, Transmigration, and the Design Process of Immersive Experiences in Museums

Patrizia Schettino
Università della Svizzera italiana, Switzerland

ABSTRACT

The chapter presents the interpretative strategies used by designers of an immersive environment on Hindu mythology and Hampi, an archaeological site in India, and their own knowledge of Hindu deities and their attributes. The process of animating an Indian Hindu deity for a potentially international audience means not only mastering 3D computer graphics and producing high-quality panorama of the sacred and historical place, but also working carefully on the interpretation and representation. The chapter uses concepts and theories from different disciplines (iconology, hermeutics, design research, museums studies, etc.) with the aim to describe, deconstruct, and understand the design choices. The study uses as main method the grounded theory: data are interviews and observations and the patterns emerging from qualitative data are compared with previous theories, during the process of theoretical comparison.

INTRODUCTION

The paper has the following structure: in the first part, I will present the theoretical background of this paper. In the next section, I will present a specific case study on Hindu mythology and digital media. The following section provides a summary of the methodologies used to collect and analyse data regarding the case study and outlines the categories emerging from data.

DOI: 10.4018/978-1-7998-1796-3.ch015

Copyright © 2020, IGI Global. Copying or distributing in print or electronic forms without written permission of IGI Global is prohibited.

BACKGROUND

Migration of Images, Objects and Narratives, Cultural Appropriation and Hermeneutic Circle

Aby Warburg used the term migration of images to describe the process of using and transforming images from East to West and from the Middle Ages to the Renaissance (Cieri Via, 2018, p.56). Wittkover (1987) shows that images cannot migrate without human beings: "people move about and may transport objects across wide spaces. Such transmission may be accomplished in a great many ways: by migration of whole populations, by wars and conquests, as well as by wandering craftsmen, traders, travellers, embassies, pilgrims and missionaries". The artists and craftsmen adapted those images within their own context, in order to produce their own artefacts. The process of image migration implies a process of cultural appropriation, the adoption and translation by an artist or craftsman of an image from one context to another; Schneider (2006) studies how craftsmen in Argentina use symbols and images from ancient meso-American cultures to produce pottery and other artefacts and he calls this cultural appropriation. The Ashmolean Museum in Oxford, with its rich collection of ethnographic objects and works of art, is a good example of a museum re-built with the goal of showing these exchanges between cultures and image migration by appropriation. Image migration and cultural appropriation are complementary processes: there is no migration without an image and without an interpreter, who summarizes in one image or object different sources and symbols, including the attributes of Gods and Goddesses (mediated by other images or text descriptions), narratives (biography of saints, heroes, etc.), local elements and non-local elements (local and exotic animals, etc.), knowledge of astrology and the link between astrology and mythology, using the style of the time and local context or adapting a style from the other culture, etc. Wittkover also shows that, during the Renaissance, Italian artists and writers, when they wanted to use stories and images from Greek mythology, didn't always have classical sources available in their language and so they had to read texts from North Europe (x, p.51). Wittkover explains that, during the Middle Ages in Italy, some elements from classical mythology were adapted to represent Christian stories, for example using the dress styles from the Middle Ages and overlapping a completely different religious meaning (pp. 34-36).

The role of the iconologist is to deconstruct and reconstruct this creative process, using different sources but also the dialogue between elements within the images, comparing the whole and the details. The Atlas produced by Warburg is a visual tool, as proto-hypertext, with texts and images to deconstruct and reconstruct the artistic process of creating a new image from the migration of several images in different times and spaces. Interpretation is the key process analysed in the domain of iconology but also in hermeneutics. Panofsky (1955) wrote that iconology is based on synthesis, more than on analysis and Gadamer (1983) sees this synthesis, made by an interpreter, as a circle: the comparison between details and the whole are the key elements of the "hermeneutic circle". The importance of the detail is in understanding the whole expressed by Warburg's sentence: "God is inside the details" (Ceri Via, 2018). In the next paragraph, I will add more concepts on the interpretation process, from iconology and hermeneutics.

Interpretation, Representation, Interpretive Community, Interpretative Strategies and Memory

Wittkover (1987) wrote that the interpretation process by a viewer of a work of art is a complex one, because it entails re-making sense of a representation that is the result of an interpretation process followed by the artist and the author of the specific image. From the point of view of hermeneutics, the viewer and the artist are members of interpretive communities and the interpretive community is defined by the use of the same interpretative strategies to understand the same object, images, model, etc. (Fish1980, Hooper Green Hill, 2007) If the viewer, the artist and the iconologist share the same interpretative strategies, they are part of the same interpretive community. Warburg, Saxl, Panofsky, Wittkover, etc., discovered these interpretative strategies by looking into several sources and other art works in different times and spaces. The key issue and challenge for those iconologists is that they are not part of the same interpretive community as the artist and there is no common ground of knowledge to make all elements of the image understandable. Thanks to the research and the links reconstructed in time and space by those scholars using different visual and non-visual sources, we can now understand the meaning of some Renaissance paintings, for example Palazzo Schifanoia paintings in Ferrara, a mystery for the audience and also for experts before Warburg's study. Only by studying several texts (written by Abu Ma'shar, Manilio and Pellegrino Prisciani), was Warburg able to re-build the iconographic program and interpretative strategies used by the artist Francesco del Cossa, who produced the work for Borso D'Este (Ceri Via, 2018, pp. 56-57). In this paper, I want to describe the interpretative strategies used by Australian designers to construct immersive augmented panoramas and an immersive environment about Indian mythology and Hindu Gods and Goddesses: I had the opportunity to interview them and to compare their strategies with the visitors' interpretation. I want to show on one hand, using concepts from different disciples, how the designers constructed the images, with the cultural appropriation of Hindu symbols, and, on the other, how the images migrated from India to Europe and to Australia. I will describe the case more in depth in a specific paragraph.

MAIN FOCUS OF THE CHAPTER

Research Question

How do the designers of the PLACE Hampi immersive environment use the images of Hindu deities and the Ramayana in their project, how did they choose the attributes, and how were those images migrated from Indian to non- Indian contexts?

Case Study: What is PLACE-Hampi

Sarah Kenderdine (2011) describes PLACE-Hampi in this way: PLACE-Hampi is

*a vibrant theatre for embodied participation in the drama of Hindu mythology focused at the most signifi-
cant archaeological, historical and sacred locations of the World Heritage site Vijayanagara (Hampi),
South India. The installation's aesthetic and representational features constitute a new approach to the
rendering of cultural experience, and give the participants a dramatic appreciation of the many-layered*

significations of this site. In PLACE-Hampi, using a motorized platform, the user can rotate the projected image within an immersive 9-meter diameter 360-degree screen, and explore high-resolution augmented stereoscopic panoramas showing many of Hampi's most significant locations.

Place Hampi allows visitors to explore 360 degree digital panoramas in an interactive way. "The panorama of the nineteenth century could be described as a long circular set that surrounds the spectator and often includes props inserted between the viewer and the plane of the image, complete with dynamic (and natural) lighting effects (Kenderdine, 2006, p. 304).

The panorama made its debut in the late 1700s as the "first true mass medium" (Oettermann 1997, p. 7) It was invented in the United Kingdom during the Industrial Revolution. This technology lost popularity during the early twentieth century; however, the model can be found also after this period, used for military purposes, in electronic arts (e.g. experiments in the entertainment industry such as Disney's Circorama, 1958) and for research. Since the mid-80s artists such as Jeffrey Shaw have been working with panoramas and with augmented devices for panoramic images to extend narratives. Shaw's works, PLACE A User's Manual and PLACE-Ruhr, "reframed the traditional panorama within the new one of the virtual reality" (Kenderdine, 2006). As Oliver Grau (2003) wrote, "the platform (PLACE) is in the tradition of panoramas but innovates the way they can be explored, with a new interaction design paradigm".

The platform was re-designed for PLACE-Hampi, adding stereoscopic vision with 3D glasses and 3D computer graphic animation. As Sarah Kenderdine wrote, the panoramas are augmented (referring to the field of augmented reality) with 3D computer graphic animations.

The ambisonic sounds also improve the quality of immersion, giving the visitor full audio immersion in the experience. Kenderdine and Doornbusch (2004) say: "Particularly with photorealistic visual imagery, similarly realistic sonic elements are required to fully engage the observer, avoiding cognitive dissonance associated with sonic elements that mismatch the fidelity of the image".

The graphic design of PLACE-Hampi and the content design of the project is significantly influenced by the archaeological approach chosen by Sarah Kenderdine and her dialogue with the most important archaeologist of the site who she directly involved in the project and in the Ancient Hampi exhibition.

Manovich (2013, pp. 228-9) described PLACE-Hampi as a "metamedia", in which the "place" is "not only a virtual spatial scene but also a scene of media past and present where various technologies and languages simultaneously compete and cooperate, creating new media hybrids which remind us of their composite character".

PLACE-Hampi is now part of a permanent exhibition in India, in a purpose-built museum (the museum opened in October 2012). It is significant for the history and the future development of technology in museums and is a pioneering project in the history of immersive technology and for its future. The project received an award for innovation in 2013, at the Australian Arts in Asia Awards. PLACE-Hampi is a *revelatory case* because the researcher had the opportunity to analyze a phenomenon which was previously not accessible to scientific investigation.

Methodology

I analyzed my data (notes from observations and interviews) from the case study PLACE Hampi, using Grounded Theory Method: it is a systematic, inductive and comparative approach to conducting inquiry for the purpose of constructing a theory (Charmaz 2006). The method was developed by two scholars,

Glaser and Strauss, 40 years ago and was presented in their first work "Awareness of Dying" (1965). The main steps in the process are: data collection, initial coding, data collection, initial memo writing, focused coding, advanced memo writing, theoretical sampling, sorting memos by integrating the diagram concepts, writing the first draft. "Coding" is a key process of GTM: it means "categorizing segments of data with a short name that simultaneously summarizes and accounts for each piece of data". (Charmaz, 2006, p. 43). The GTM process is not linear: grounded theorists can stop and write whenever ideas occur to them. I will compare the categories emerging from data with concepts from the theoretical framework, during the process called "theoretical comparison".

Data Collection, Data Analysis, Coding and Theoretical Comparison

I collected data about PLACE-Hampi during three exhibitions in three museums (Martin Gropius Bau, ZKM Museum, Immigration Museums) in Germany and Australia. The first interview with the designers was conducted at the Martin Gropius Bau, Berlin, during the exhibition From Spark to Pixel. This paper is focused on qualitative analysis the designers' narrative about their own project.

An Australian software for qualitative data analysis, NVivo, was used for the initial coding, to store my data and memos, to keep a daily journal of my analyses. Using this software improved the reliability of my research. Focused coding, axial coding (intermediate) and theoretical coding (advanced coding) were then performed (Birks and Mills, 2011, p 95, p 116). I will present the analysis giving examples of the different steps, from the initial coding (key strategy in grounded theory) to the categorization. The categories are presented with:

- A quotation from the interview,
- My interpretation of the quotation, in which I will also compare what emerges from the text with some concepts from previous theories,
- My final definition of the category,

Interpreting

*S: So we chose the **most popular** and well understood epic. We did not use deities that are **specific to Hampi** only, that **can't be read by other people**.... There is the **local level of incarnations** of various gods.*

My interpretation:
Sarah Kenderdine is interpreting the different Indian deities: some are specific to Hampi but less well-known to a wider audience. The designers chose to animate the most popular deities such as Ganesha, Garuda, Shiva, Hanuman and Sita.

*S: **Hanuman**, the Monkey god, is used because Hampi is the home of the **monkeys** in **the Ramayana***

Sarah Kenderdine uses the Ramayana as an interpretative strategy to define Hampi as "the home of monkeys" and to explain why Hanuman is relevant in a project about Hampi. The Ramayana is a very important epic Hindu poem that tells the "journey of Rama", "avatar" or incarnation of the god Vishnu, and his wife Sita, "avatar" of the goddess Lakṣmī. The site is still full of "real" monkeys and Sarah documented their presence also in some photographs taken during the field work in Hampi, some of them included later in Ancient Hampi exhibtion.

My definition of the category:

Designers' interpretation and interpretative strategies for several possible aspects linked to their work, role, specific project, etc.

Theorizing

Designers are an "interpretative community" (Hooper-Greenhill 2007; Fish, 1980), in this case a couple, sharing interpretative strategies, negotiate a common interpretation before making design decisions. They are interpreters and, in this case, they describe their interpretation of cultural elements about India and the Hindu religion, their interpretation of other digital heritage works, their interpretation of their role as designer, their interpretation of the aim of the project, etc. In this case they are interpreters of culture, a place and a religion that is different from their own culture, home and religion, and this makes the project relevant in analyzing "intercultural" design thinking.

Representing

S: *It was a deliberate* **choice not to provide historical material, not to animate the Vijayanagara Empire**, *stuff like that, the history, the official history... we were much more interested in the abstract, intangible heritage... what is contemporary on that site, what is happening now... it is an historical site, but it is not only historical,* **it is a live** *place.*

My interpretation:

Sarah is describing two key decisions that were taken about how to represent Hampi: a living place, where Indian people live, and a destination for Hindu pilgrims.

Comparing this quote with what she said about Hampi in other papers, (Kenderdine 2007, p 66), Kenderdine defines Hampi as "an active pilgrims' site, not simply an historical place". She also wrote that pilgrims can experience the space with their entire body by repeating rituals which are part of the intangible heritage of the place (a spiritual place which is important for Hindu pilgrims). One of the most important aims of the project, for PLACE-Hampi designers, it is to represent both the tangible and intangible elements of the place.

The second key aspect of the representation was the decision not to animate the history of the people who built the temples, but the intangible heritage, such as the Ramayana.

J: *It is* **meant to create a kind of homage to the place**, *definitely, its* **beauty**, *its* **quality**...

My interpretation:

Jeffrey Shaw is describing one of his goals as a designer and one of his choices in the representation of Hampi; that is, to represent it as a beautiful place and to create a homage to this location, with emphasis on the aesthetical quality of the digital representation of the real place.

In her book, Kenderdine writes (2013, p 88) "The village of Hampi, the ruins of the Vijayanagara and the green, irrigated fields that surround it in a wilderness of extraordinary beauty (...)"

Thinking About the Visitors

S: *So, in terms of the Indian culture, it has to be read* **by Indians.** *If the animations move incorrectly, if they have the wrong attributes, they can be potentially offensive…*

My interpretation:

   Kenderdine is talking about the design of the animation of Indian deities and, thinking about Indian visitors, she shows her "cultural sensitivity" (Hammer, Bennett, Wiseman, 2003) towards a sacred topic and how this could be potentially offensive for Indian visitors. She points out that even just one wrong attribute or movement could be offensive.

J: And we also made the fundamental decision not to tell the whole story. There is just Ganesha there, it is not the whole story, it is just a piece of it…

S: …a vignette…

J: …of the Ramayana, it is just the presence… just Garuda flying in the sky… so it is just an intonation of the presence rather than telling the whole story… but again **we assume that the Indian audience** *will locate these indications of presence within the story as a whole…*

My interpretation:

   Jeffrey and Sarah are describing their design choice about the use of the epic poem Ramayana: they decided not to tell the full story, but just short sequences of it. They assume that the Ramayana forms part of the past knowledge of all Indian visitors, who will see just a short sequence of the story but make a connection with the full story.

J: the **DESIGN** *of the platform is meant to be very basic, very open.. it can be* **cross-culturally** *understood, the main difference may be between* **younger and older** *people and also between people that have* **experience in handling machines** *and those who do not… it is very basic… for some groups of people it may be mysterious… but it is very easy to learn how to use it…*

My interpretation:

   Jeffrey Shaw, thinking about visitors from different cultural backgrounds, calls the design of the platform *cross-cultural*. His intention is to design a single platform for a potentially diverse audience in cultural terms: he uses the expression "cross-culturally understood", to express the idea of an artifact that can be understood by different types of users, from different countries. Jeffrey also talks about future visitors of different ages and levels of computer literacy. The designers seem to have an idea of the future visitor in mind and, comparing this with other authors, we can say that they have a kind of "imagined reader" (Eco, 1984) or, better, several "visitor model" (Tota, 1999).
   My definition of the category "thinking about the visitors":
   Designers' strategies to take their future audience into consideration.

Triangulation with designers' publications

Sarah Kenderdine wrote (2007a, 2007b, 2007c) papers in which she presented some of the strategies to take audience diversity into account. The main strategies are: working with a multi-cultural team including several Indian members, studying and using Indian iconography, taking into consideration the concept of "seeing and being seen" by deities for Hindu visitors, choosing animated characters, and balancing between local ones and the more well-known ones outside India.

During this interview, Jeffrey Shaw added his own point of view about the platform, as the person who designed it in the 1990s. The platform was not originally designed following an intercultural design process, but some elements of the platform were later re-designed in collaboration with Kenderdine (Schettino and Kenderdine, 2011) and some other features of the platform, for example the software to manage the panorama, was designed by Shaw with other experts from ZKM, in Germany. For Jeffrey, "designing something basic" is a way of dealing with different cultural backgrounds. "Understood" means that visitors are able to understand how it works. This is one of the key challenges for any technology: even an iPhone is designed with the goal of being "cross culturally" understood. This does not mean that the artifact is neutral, because all artifacts are shaped by the cultures of their designers.

Jeffrey designed a platform that can create multiple performances based on "opera aperta" (Eco, 1964): the content can be different, but the platform is designed to encourage visitors to participate. Participation is a very important aspect of the project. In this, Shaw, who studied in Milan (and in other European cities) seems to have some affinity with Gruppo T, a group of artists based in Milan who designed several artifacts and events in the '60s with the aim to actively engaging visitors. "Our art is somatic and participatory", in this way Anceschi (2014), and Varisco (2014), two members of Gruppo T, highlighted the importance of "participation" by the visitors in their own works.

Thinking About the Context

Again, comparing quotes to define the next category:

*S: for **Indians** it is obvious… also for most **Westerns** it is obvious… for a person that doesn't know any-thing about Indian Gods …what we can add…and in fact will add when it is installed at **my museum, in Melbourne**, where it will remain for 1 year, at this highly didactical driven museum … where it will not be an art show ... will be a lot of contextual information…*

Sarah is describing the plans for Melbourne two years ahead. She is speaking about the Immigration Museum (she says "my museum", because the Immigration Museum is part of Museum Victoria for which she works) and is saying that in this specific context the immersive environment will be presented with didactic material. She is talking about the difference compared to the exhibition in Germany, in a museum dedicated to contemporary art where PLACE-Hampi was part of a collective exhibition on new media art.

My definition of the category:

designers' strategies linked to their interpretation of different possible contexts (in this case, Berlin, Melbourne, etc.).

Triangulation with designers' publications

Quoting Davis, Kenderdine (2007a) said "relocation and redisplay of an object will dramatically alter its significance for a new audience", thinking of PLACE-Hampi being installed in a different temporary exhibition in a different part of the world. She sees the analysis of what will happen, the possible new interpretations, as an area of future research.

Learning

S: The first time that the Ramayana **was animated, it was done by the Japanese**... *it was banned in India... It was five or six years ago... It was not long ago...*

My interpretation:
    Sarah has studied previous representations of Indian Gods. The mistakes made by other designers and the negative impact on users/visitors is a lesson for designers. The design phase began after an intense period of research on previous similar projects.

Triangulation and theorizing

Comparing what the designer said in this interview with what she wrote about animations in one of her papers (2007), Kenderdine explained that "an analysis of the current commercial animation industry offers a point of departure to imagine future Indian mythological imagery". In the same paper she points out that the PLACE-Hampi animations are based on religious Indian iconography.

In her book (2013, pp. 154-155) Kenderdine compared the animations produced by a Japanese company with an Indian filmmaker in 1984 with what her team did. The Japanese-Indian film, the first animated version of the Ramayana, had a "fusion style", influenced by the Indian and Japanese manga and was banned because "the Indian government feared that the epic might be trivialized by animations". Kenderdine and Shaw worked with Paprikaas Animation Studios in Bangalore, which usually works only on projects for the American and European market and not on Indian content. In her book Kenderdine also mentioned another project by Virgin Comics: an "East-West fusion version of the Ramayana" in 2007.

Studying these two projects which "animated Hindu deities" was an essential part of the learning process for Sarah and Jeffrey, to define their own method and strategies for the design of the animations for PLACE-Hampi and the learning process continued later, analyzing what emerged from the evaluation of the visitors' interpretation of the animations.

PLACE-Hampis was made by an international team: an archeologist and a video artist from New Zealand and Australia worked with Indian graphic designers, an Indian composers, Indian archeologists, French producers, engineers from Germany, Australia, etc., learning from each other's. This extends the categorization by Wittkover: images can also transmigrate during a complex design process (Norman, 2014), global and local at the time, involving experts with difference cultural background and different knowledge about the same images. They can meet in person or communicate using video calls, but they became part of the same interpretative community (Fish, 1980), sharing common interpretative strategies to interpret and digitally represent Hindu deities with their attributes.

My definition of the category:
Designer's reflections on their learning process during the design process.

FUTURE RESEARCH DIRECTIONS

This chapter is an attempt to apply hermeneutics and iconology theories to the analysis of immersive media. There is a potential to develop as new field "digital immersive media iconology and hermeneutics", to describe and understand new digital media design and art history. In this chapter, I analyzed the designer's point of view. The visitor's point of view is analyzed in other papers (Schettino, 2013a, Schettino 2013 b, Schettino 2013 c, Schettino and Kenderdine, 2011), constructing theories from 92 interviews and notes from observation (about 500 visitors). This is a possible future research direction, as new approach to rethink the designer's interpretation process, the visitor's interpretation process, to understand how designers can use mythologies to build new cultural heritage immersive experiences and how visitors can construct their own meaning from those narratives and their "homes" (Schettino, 2013 a). From the methodological perspective, more mix methods studies and longitudinal studies are needed in museums, to understand the impact of immersive media on different stakeholders, in including the museum staff members. In Italy, where the augmented and immersive media and gamification in museums are a growing trend, we need more visitor studies on immersive media, to understand how those media can be designed and how they can change the experience, before, during and after the visit.

CONCLUSION

This chapter, combining concepts from iconology, cultural anthropology, hermeneutics, design research, museum studies (transmigration, interpretative communities, interpretative strategies, cultural appropriation, etc.), expands the area of application for those theories to help us better understand digital media design process. The chapter shows how the designers of the PLACE Hampi immersive environment used the images of Hindu deities and the Ramayana in their project, how they chose the attributes, and how those images were migrated from Indian to non- Indian contexts. From data analysis and theoretical comparison, comparing the interpretative strategies with the list of possible transmigration by Wittkover, this paper extends those categories: images can transmigrate because designers can work on digital animation of mythologies as part of an international team, on travelling exhibitions and they can adopt an intercultural design approach. "Design is a cultural appropriation of technology"(Lunelfeld, cited in Laurel, 2004): animating an Indian Hindu deity for a potentially international audience means not only mastering 3D computer graphics but also working carefully on the interpretation and representation process, to avoid a representation that could be offensive or too romanticized. It means playing with the possible prior knowledge of future visitors and selecting the deities that are potentially better known to a wider audience. Cultural appropriation (Schneider, 2006) and transmigration of symbols (Wittkover, 1987) from one context to another is in general a challenge for museums because visitors have a hybrid identity and different level of knowledge. For the museum, the challenge is also to support and guide visitors with no prior knowledge of the Ramayana, Hindu deities or the history of Hampi to give them a key element to construct their own interpretation. The most effective way to deal with this diversity is to conduct visitor studies and to build, also after the first months of the exhibition, specific guided tours or tools or documents to support the visit. This was done by the Immigration Museum, balancing the possibility for visitors to explore PLACE Hampi by themselves or with the support provided by a customer service. As a result, the museum offered to visitors an enjoyable and inclusive experience and a way to build new knowledge, from their own specific identity and previous knowledge.

ACKNOWLEDGMENT

For this paper, I have to say thank you to Prof. Martina Corgnati for her teachings on iconology and iconography in 2018-2019. I learned a great deal from the books she recommended, from conversations with her about some key authors in this field and from her wonderful course on iconology and iconography held at the Accademia di Belle Arti, Brera, Milan.

This research is supported by: the Swiss National Science Foundation and ICOM (International Council of Museums) Switzerland.

REFERENCES

Anceschi, G., & Varisco, G. (2014) Participation, interactivity and somatic art. Re-programmed art seminar. Lugano, Switzerland.

Birks, M., & Mills, J. (2011). *Grounded theory, A pratical guide* (p. 95). London, UK: Sage.

Ceri Via, C. (2018). *Nel dettaglio nascosto Per una storia del pensiero iconologico.* Rome, Italy: Carocci.

Charmaz, K. (2006). *Constructing grounded theory, a practical guide through qualitative analysis.* London, UK: Sage.

Eco, U. (1962). *Opera Aperta*. Milano, Italy: Bompiani.

Fish, S. (1980). *Is there a text in this class? The authority of interpretive communities*. Cambridge, UK: Harvard University Press.

Gadamer, H. G. (1983). *Verità e Metodo*. Milano, Italy: Bompiani.

Glaser, B. G., & Strauss, A. L. (1965) Awareness of Dying, Chicago, Usa: Aldine Publishing Company

Grau, O. (2003). *From illusion to immersion*. Cambridge, MA: MIT Press.

Hammer, M. R., Bennett, M. J., & Wiseman, R. (2003). Measuring intercultural sensitivity: The intercultural development inventory. [Special Training Issue.]. *International Journal of Intercultural Relations*, *27*(4), 421–443. doi:10.1016/S0147-1767(03)00032-4

Hooper-Greenhill, E. (2007). Interpretative communities, strategies and repertoires. In S. Watson (Ed.), *Museum and their communities* (pp. 76–94). Abingdon, UK: Routledge.

Kenderdine, S. (2007a), Somatic solidarity, magical realism and animating popular gods: PLACE-Hampi where intensities are felt. In E. Banissi, & ... (Eds.), *Proceedings of 11th European Information Visualisation Conference, IV07*, July 3-7, Zurich, Switzerland: IEEE, 402-408. 10.1109/IV.2007.103

Kenderdine, S. (2007b). The irreducible ensemble: Place-Hampi. In *Selected Proceedings, 13th Annual Virtual System and Multimedia Conference*, Brisbane, Lecture Notes in Computer Science: Springer Berlin/Heidelberg, pp. 58-67.

Kenderdine, S. (2013). Theatre, archaeology and new media. In S. Kenderdine (Ed.), Place-Hampi, Inhabiting the panoramic imaginary of Vijayanagara. Berlin Heidelberg, Germany: Kehrer Verlag, 223.

Laurel, B. (2004). *Design research: methods and perspectives*. Cambridge, MA: MIT Press.

Manovich, K. (2013). Multimedia versus metamedia. In S. Kenderdine (Ed.), *Place-Hampi, Inhabiting the panoramic imaginary of Vijayanagara* (pp. 226–229). Berlin Heidelberg, Germany: Kehrer Verlag.

Norman, D. A. (2011). *Living with complexity*. Cambridge, MA: MIT Press.

Oettermann, S. (1997). The panorama. History of a mass medium. New York: Zone Book, 7.

Panofsky, E. (1955). *Meaning in visual art*. Chicago, IL: Chicago University Press.

Schettino, P. (2013a). Rethinking the digital media process in museum, Design Principles and Practices: An International Journal — Annual Review, 7. Champaign IL, University of Illinois Research Park: Common Ground Publisher. pp. 1-18.

Schettino, P. (2013b). Home, sense of place and visitors' interpretations of digital cultural immersive experiences in museums: An application of the "embodied constructivist GTM digital ethnography in situ" method, *Digital heritage international congress (DigitalHeritage)*, Marseille. Oct. 28-Nov. 1, 2013. IEEE Proceedings. 1. pp. 721-124.

Schettino, P. (2013c). Emotions, words and colors: strategies to visualize and analyze patterns from visitors narratives in museums. In *Proceedings 2013 17th International Conference Information Visualisation (IV)*, London, UK. July 16-18, 2013. IEEE. pp. 551-554.

Schettino, P., & Kenderdine, S. (2011). Place-Hampi. Narratives of inclusive cultural experience. *Journal of Inclusive Museums, 3*(3), Common Ground Publisher. 141-156.

Schneider, A. (2006). *Appropriation as practice. Art and identity in Argentina*. New York: Palgrave MacMillan.

Tota, A. (1999). *Sociologie dell'arte. Dal museo tradizionale all'arte multimediale*. Rome, Italy: Carocci.

Urry, J. (2001). *The tourist gaze. London* (2nd ed.). Thousand Oaks, CA: Sage.

Wittkover, R. (1987). Allegory and the migrations of symbols, New York: Thames and Hudon, 11.

ADDITIONAL READING

Corgnati, M. (2018). *L'ombra lunga degli Etruschi*. Monza, Italia: Johan&Levi.

Gombrich, E. J. (1970). *Aby Warburg, an Intellectual Biography*. London, UK: The Warburg Institute.

Hooper-Greenhill, E. (2000). *Museums and the Interpretation of visual culture*. London: Routledge.

Mirzoeff, N. (1999). *An introduction to visual culture*. London: Routledge.

Mussachio, A. L. (2009). *Storytelling in Organizations*. London: Palgrave. doi:10.1057/9780230271753

Schettino, P. (2008) From textile to texture. In F. Sudweeks, H. Hrachovec, & Ch. Ess eds. Catac, *6th International Conference Cultural Attitudes towards Technology and Communication 2008*. Nimes, France.

Schettino, P. (2014) Rethinking immersive cultural experiences in museums. A cross-cultural analysis of visitors' behaviors based on roles. Cultural Attitudes towards Technology and Communication (CaTac). University of Oslo, Oslo, 10-20 June 2014.

KEY TERMS AND DEFINITION

Immersion: It is a combination of flow (being very focused), sense of presence (the feeling of being in another place), embodiment (having all the senses involved), interactivity (moving and acting in a space and playing a role with other actors), transportation (the feeling of being inside a story).

Immersive Environment: A digital artifact designed with the intention, from the designer's point of view, to offer to visitor an immersive experience.

Interpretative Community: A community of interpreters sharing the same interpretative strategies.

Interpretative Strategy: A strategy used by an interpreter to construct an interpretation.

Theoretical Comparison: In grounded theory, it is a comparison between patterns emerging from data and previous theories.

Transmigration: The process of using and transforming images from one place to another, to one period to another, etc.

Triangulation: It is a process of comparing data, from different sources, different point of views, comparing data collected in different times, etc.

Chapter 16
An Augmented Reality (AR) Experience for Lorenzo Lotto

Biancamaria Mori
MenteZero, Italy

Carlo Gioventù
Macerata Academy of Fine Arts, Italy

ABSTRACT

Virtual interactive experience created for the Picture gallery of Jesi (Italy). Namely, three interactive works realized with Unreal Engine 4 to give the spectator a greater immersiveness on the immortal pictures of Lorenzo Lotto. The goal was achieved by creating three choreographies with audio supervised by a historian, recreation of the works with three-dimensional graphics and a specially composed soundtrack by Tecla Zorzi. The augmented reality (AR) application was realized specifically for Android tablets.

AR AND VR IN GAMIFICATION: NEW WAYS TO EXPERIENCE REALITY (MIXED REALITY, LAST FRONTIERS OF GAMIFICATION)

Thanks to new software and hardware technologies, the user can experience ever more immersive and tangible experiences from our senses.

Thanks to special viewers that isolate the user from the surrounding environment, Virtual Reality allows to enter an immaterial space, digitally created and to live it not through the perception of a luminous rectangle, like the screen, but through a spherical projection that develops around the user. Through these new devices, the user can turn his head and look at this world from the angle he prefers, moving inside thanks to joysticks or more advanced devices that allow the real movement of the body. Thanks to gesture technology and hand recognition, the experience becomes even more realistic and immersive, bringing the user to have a "tactile" relationship with virtual objects: although he cannot actually touch them, he is able to manipulate them with same gestures that he would carry out in reality. VR is used in entertainment and gaming, creating more and more engaging gaming experiences.

DOI: 10.4018/978-1-7998-1796-3.ch016

Copyright © 2020, IGI Global. Copying or distributing in print or electronic forms without written permission of IGI Global is prohibited.

Figure 1.

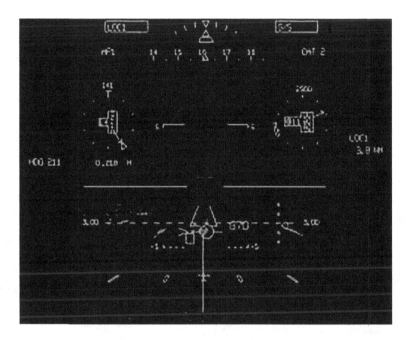

Initially used to build HUDs[1], the latest Augmented Reality technology is very different, allowing us to enrich the world around us with digital content. In this way, the user is not estranged from the real world, never losing visual contact with it, but rather enriching it with digital interactive content.

The fields of application of AR are manifold, from the simple display of useful information in places like stations and roads (let's think of Google Maps AR), up to the interaction between public and work in a museum.

Recent examples are the Google Street View AR, which recognizes buildings and streets and allows orientation through digital road signs, and Google Lens, a tool that allows the recognition of texts, their translation, the recognition of objects and products.

A Military Jet HUD

The Mixed Reality superimposes the virtual reality to the physical one observing the real world by drawing information in AR or allows to see and move virtual objects that interact with the analog world perfectly integrated with the environment.

The landing on the market is still far away but in recent years many experiments have been made, one of these is Microsoft's HoloLens: a device, similar to a helmet for VR technology, which includes transparent lenses that allow the visualization of one's field visual and information about it in AR. HoloLens can be adapted to different types of applications, from assistance in the construction and maintenance of any project to playful applications such as the visualization of the Minecraft world on one's home table, allowing for complete interaction.

Figure 2.

WHAT WE PRODUCED AND HOW

The project "APP: Open Palazzo Pianetti" was promoted by the Municipality of Jesi, Italy, in response to the *Call for Culture 2018* of the *Cariverona Foundation*.

The idea wants to equip the Civic Museums of Palazzo Pianetti with an instrument of inclusion and accessibility, strengthened by the desire to bring interactivity of the playful world closer to the museum environment, in order to facilitate the approach of a new target, like children, elderly, visually impaired and blind, to art and culture.

The project was developed in collaboration with other Italian excellences, such as *Marchingegno, Palazzo Pianetti and RossodiGrana*.

The inclusive application makes the museum's contents playful and accessible through three different thematic routes corresponding to the three exhibition areas: treasure hunts for children, narrative guides and augmented reality applications.

Figure 3.

MenteZero was involved in the creation of interactive applications in Augmented Reality, trying to combine modern technologies with a fruition of the works of Lorenzo Lotto, which gave an added value to the already present enormous historical value of the paintings, proposing an alternative vision to the analogue one and looking for to give emotions and perspectives alternative to the usual ones, so as to be lived as an experience.

SANTA LUCIA AR: A STORY FROM THE PAST

This painting by Lorenzo Lotto dated 1532, narrates in many episodes the entire story of Saint Lucia, always recognizable thanks to the symbolic choice of its yellow and red cloak. The artist, during the creation of the work, made a rather temporal rather than a symbolic narrative choice, where the chronology of events flows in a manner similar to a comic strip: the figure of Saint Lucia recurs simultaneously in several areas of the table below the picture telling us the whole series of events.

According to the *Legenda Aurea*[2], the Saint, after having taken her vows, given all her possessions to the most needy and refused a marriage proposal, is denounced as a Christian and accused of not worshiping pagan idols, then will be brought before the Roman consul Pascasio and found guilty, but none of the men present will be able to drag her away, thanks to the divine determination she has acquired.

The application created by MenteZero operates in such a way that by framing the protagonist of the picture with the tablet, she immediately perceives the presence of the visitor and, through a 3D animation, tells his story directly addressing the interlocutor.

The text, created and approved in collaboration with historians, tells the events in a pleasant and direct manner, using a language congruent with the age of the saint: a 16-year-old girl who naturally tells her story, resolving herself into a rebellion of a teenager in the face of arrogance, stripping it of the role of the saint and making her more human.

Figure 4.
Motion Capture phase Santa Lucia AR running

In another way, this narrative would have remained in high culture or in contexts not reserved for children, otherwise MenteZero has tried to use a more recognizable language to a young audience, trying to facilitate the learning of children through a precise choice of communication that facilitates empathy with S. Lucia.

This choice does not want to be servile or hypocritical, the intent instead was based on the opening to museum spaces to a type of use that seeks to combine culture with the possible astonishment with technological means, all done with the intention of provoking an emotional reaction of the viewer that results in an empathic connection with the protagonist of the picture, and that therefore transforms the experience into a long-term memory.

LA DEPOSIZIONE DI CRISTO: PARTICIPATING TO THE ARTWORK

In this second work, located in the same room as the first, the intent is to provide an emotional reading of the picture of the Deposition of the Lot through greater interactivity on the part of the visitor.

It is the first preparatory pencil of Lotto, in fact the artist paints this picture through a technique learned during his stay in Rome thanks to his first contact with Raffaello Sanzio, that is to say there are no other works by the artist who had a preliminary sketch before their creation.

Through augmented reality, the preparatory pencil drawing is revealed to the visitor, which superimposed on the final work allows him to personally notice the differences with the painting.

Once the pencil has been revealed, the construction lines of the picture appear which, once touched by the user, start an interactive reading of the image, which is enlarged to reveal details that are otherwise too small to be noticed with the naked eye, the figures come to life and recolour, explaining the meaning and emotion of the finished gesture, supported by a work of sound design that puts the accent on the dramatic silence of the scene, where no protagonist talks to the other, respecting the original visual choice of the painter: the ambient sounds amplify the silence, telling us about the emptiness left after the rise of Christ.

Figure 5.

To realize this part of the App MenteZero wanted to design an experience based on what was assumed to have been the original narrative choice of Lotto, the pain of the dumb and terrible characters, told through their incommunicability, or the reaction to the dismay of end of the Christ with the blind desperation of taking refuge in oneself, a multimedia narration was then carried out animating the parts of the picture and creating a soundtrack made only of deaf and compound laments, in order to create an emotional state able to involve the visitor in a participatory way to the picture he is observing.

Once the user has interacted with each construction line and the painting is completely re-colored, it will transform into a 3D object and the point of view will assume the place of Nicodemus, the one who holds the body of Christ in his very hands, and also here the intention of the multimedia work is to provide the visitor with an experience, giving it a point of view inside the picture, breaking the two-dimensional barrier of the painting always with the ultimate goal of creating a personal experience that goes beyond the simple vision.

ANNUNCIAZIONE: REVEALING THE LOST PIECE

The third work consists of two tablets that were part of a triptych whose central part, which represented a St. John in Patmos[3], was lost in the Napoleonic era. The archangel Gabriel is portrayed while he lands on the ground after his approaching flight, while the virgin, hit by the movement of air, immediately retracts her body backwards.

There is no trace of the missing table, but thanks to a rediscovered preparatory drawing (kept in Siena) and 3D graphics, framing the two tablets with the tablet, the median blade is revealed, emerging from behind the two tables that move to the sides, leaving space to the missing. In this way we transform the work into a spectacular and unpublished triptych, respecting the original idea of the artist.

An additional benefit that comes from this type of intervention is the fact that this work is rarely, or only by experts, perceived in its entirety as a triptych, as the two tables are always displayed or portrayed close together, going to be imprinted in the memory of those who see them just as a duo.

In this third work MenteZero has therefore chosen to operate what is not objectively possible to do in the analog world, to recreate and make accessible what has been lost, therefore, as is done in archeology or museography, we try to reconstruct, following reliable sources, the missing part of the work in order to provide the visitor with a more sincere and reliable view of the overall work or damaged, leaving clear what are the original and reconstructed parts, finally creating a complete experience, at least from the point of view of the missing parts.

ADDITIONAL READING

Barata, G., Gama, S., Jorge, J., & Goncalves, D. (2013). Engaging engineering students with gamification. In *Proceedings 5th International Conference on Games and Virtual Worlds for Serious Applications*, pp. 1-8.

Bergstrom, K., Fisher, S., & Jenson, J. (2016). Disavowing that guy: Identity construction and massively multiplayer online game players. *Convergence (London)*, 22(3), 233–249. doi:10.1177/1354856514560314

Dewey, J. (1938). *Experience and education*. New York: Macmillan.

Gardner, H., & Hatch, T. (1989). Multiple intelligences go to school: Educational implications of the theory of multiple intelligences. *Educational Researcher*, *18*(8), 4–9.

Humfrey. (1997). Lorenzo Lotto. Yale University Press.

Keeler, A. (2015). *Gamification: engaging the students with narrative* (pp. 1–3). Edutopia; Retrieved from www.edutopia.org/blog/gamification-engaging-students-with-narrative-alice-keeler

Kiang, D. (2014, Oct. 14). *"Edutopia", Using gaming principles to engage students.* Retrieved from **www.edutopia.org/blog/using-gaming-principles-engage-students-douglas-kiang**

Kim, A. J. (2014). Innovate with game thinking, Amy Jo Kim, Jan. 15. Retrieved from http://amyjokim.com/blog/2014/02/28/beyond-player-types-kims-social-action-matrix

Kingsley, T. L., & Grabner-Hagen, M. M. (2015). Gamification: Questing to integrate content, knowledge, literacy, and 21st-century learning. *Journal of Adolescent & Adult Literacy*, *59*(1), 51–61. doi:10.1002/jaal.426

Kumar, B., & Khurana, P. (2012). Gamification in education: Learn computer programming with fun. *International Journal of Computers and Distributed Systems*, *2*(1), 46–53.

Lotto, L., Gentili, A., & Washington National Gallery of Art. (1997). Lorenzo Lotto: rediscovered master of the Renaissance;[exhibition dates: National Gallery of Art, Washington, Nov. 2, 1997-March 1, 1998... Galeries Nationales du Grand Palais, Paris, Oct. 12, 1998-Jan. 11, 1999]. Yale University Press.

McGonigal, J. (2011). *Reality is broken: Why games make us better and how they can change the world.* New York, NY: Penguin Press.

Palazzo Pianetti. Retrieved from https://en.wikipedia.org/wiki/Palazzo_Pianetti

KEY TERMS AND DEFINITIONS

Augmented Reality: It is a superposition of digital data in the real world, providing the user with real-time contextual information in the surrounding environment, creating, as explained in the previous chapter, a useful interaction in the analogic world.

Gamification: Mix user interaction and user interface with the language and dynamics of the game, exploiting the new language used by video games together with the mechanics of the Game Design, combining the use of technological means and the learning of notions or procedures the entertainment of the game.

Lorenzo Lotto: He was one of the main exponents of the Venetian Renaissance of the early sixteenth century, although his original and unconventional nature soon led him to a sort of marginalization from the lagoon context, dominated by Titian. He then moved a lot, turning with his example the schools of areas considered peripheral to the great artistic centers, such as Bergamo and the Marche. His human story was sometimes marked by bitter failures and bitter disappointments - partly filled by the revaluation in modern criticism - which make his figure a suffered, introverted and humoral subject, of great modernity. https://it.wikipedia.org/wiki/Lorenzo_Lotto

Microsoft's HoloLens: A device, similar to a helmet for VR technology, which includes transparent lenses that allow the visualization of one's field visual and information about it in AR. HoloLens can be adapted to different types of applications, from assistance in the construction and maintenance of any project to playful applications such as the visualization of the Minecraft world on one's home table, allowing for complete interaction.

Mixed-Reality: It is the combination of Virtual Reality, Augmented Virtuality, Augmented Reality. **Palazzo Pianetti:** It is an ancient noble palace in the city of Jesi, in the Marche region. Today it is home to the Civic Art Gallery. It was the ancient city residence of the Marquis Pianetti, a noble and prestigious family aggregated to the Jesuit aristocracy since 1659. It represents the most significant of the buildings belonging to the rich local noble families, and the only example in Italy of Rococo style of Central European influence. https://it.wikipedia.org/wiki/Palazzo_Pianetti

Virtual Reality: It is the one in which the user finds himself in a world completely simulated by the stranger from physical Reality, completely immersing him in a simulated environment that replaces the senses of sight and hearing with the real ones created in an exclusive interaction with cyberspace.

ENDNOTES

[1] Head Up Display: military devices that allowed aircraft pilots and tanks to display useful information without shifting attention from the surrounding environment

[2] http://www.lorenzolottomarche.it/annuncia

Compilation of References

Aboumarzouk, O. M. (2019). *Blandy's urology*. Hoboken, NJ: John Wiley & Sons; Available at https://books.google.co.in/books?isbn=1118863372

Adams, E., (2004). Postmodernism and the three types of immersion. *Gamasutra: The art & business of making games, 9.*

AESVI. (2019). AESVI presents the annual report on the video game industry in Italy in 2018. Retrieved from http://www.aesvi.it/cms/view.php?dir_pk=902&cms_pk=3002

Ahmad, N. S. H. N., Wan, D. T. R., & Jiang, P. (2011). Health course module in virtual world. *Procedia Computer Science, 3,* 1454–1463. doi:10.1016/j.procs.2011.01.031

Aica, Assinform, Assintel, A. (2017). *Osservatorio delle competenze digitali 2017: scenari, gap, nuovi profili professionali e percorsi formativi.*

Aiello, D., Basso, A., Spena, M. T., D'Agostino, G., Montedoro, U., Galizia, M., ... Santagati, C. (2019). The virtual batcave: A project for the safeguard of a UNESCO WHL fragile ecosystem. *The International Archives of the Photogrammetry, Remote Sensing and Spatial Information Sciences, XLII-2*(W9), 17–24. doi:10.5194/isprs-archives-XLII-2-W9-17-2019

Akçayır, M., & Akçayır, G. (2017). Advantages and challenges associated with augmented reality for education: A systematic review of the literature. *Educational Research Review, 20,* 1–11. doi:10.1016/j.edurev.2016.11.002

Alelis, G., Bobrowicz, A., & Ang, C. S. (2015). Comparison of engagement and emotional responses of older and younger adults interacting with 3D cultural heritage artefacts on personal devices. Behaviour & Information Technology, 34(11), 1064–1078.

Alexander, B. (2004). Going nomadic: Mobile learning in higher education. *EDUCAUSE Review, 39*(5), 28–35. Retrieved from http://www.educause.edu/EDUCAUSE+Review/EDUCAUSEReviewMagazineVolume39/GoingNomadicMobileLearninginHi/157921

Ambrose, T., & Paine, C. (2018). *Museum basics: The international handbook*. London, UK: Routledge. doi:10.4324/9781315232898

Amin, D., & Govilkar, S. (2015). Comparative study of augmented reality Sdk's. *International Journal on Computational Science & Applications.* doi:10.5121/ijcsa.2015.5102

Anceschi, G., & Varisco, G. (2014) Participation, interactivity and somatic art. Re-programmed art seminar. Lugano, Switzerland.

Anderson, E. F., McLoughlin, L., Liarokapis, F., Peters, C., Petridis, P., & Freitas, S. (2010). Developing serious games for cultural heritage: A state-of-the-art review. *Virtual Reality (Waltham Cross), 14*(4), 255–275. doi:10.100710055-010-0177-3

Anderson, L. W. (2005). Objectives, evaluation, and the improvement of education. *Studies in Educational Evaluation*, *31*(2-3), 102–113. doi:10.1016/j.stueduc.2005.05.004

Ang, B. (2017, March 26). Augmented Reality in the classroom: Move over, Pokemon Go, it's time for science class; Augmented reality, the technology used in the mobile game, is now being used in education and design, among other things. *The Strait Times,* Retrieved from https://www.straitstimes.com/lifestyle/augmented-reality-in-the-classroom-move-over-pokemon-go-its-time-for-science-class

Angelopoulou, A., Economou, D., Bouki, V., Psarrou, A., Jin, L., Pritchard, C., & Kolyda, F. (2012). Mobile augmented reality for cultural heritage. In *MOBILWARE 2011: Mobile wireless middleware, operating systems, and applications* (pp. 15–22). Berlin, Germany: Springer; doi:10.1007/978-3-642-30607-5_2

Antin, J. (2012). Gamification is not a dirty word. *Interaction*, *19*(4), 14–16.

Antón, C., Camarero, C., & Garrido, M. J. (2018). Exploring the experience value of museum visitors as a co-creation process. *Current Issues in Tourism*, *21*(12), 1406–1425. doi:10.1080/13683500.2017.1373753

Apollonio, F. I., Gaiani, M., & Sun, Z. (2013). 3D modeling and data enrichment in digital reconstruction of architectural heritage. *ISPRS Archives*, *5*, W2–W2.

AppAdvice LLC. (2019a). Martell AiR Gallery. Retrieved from https://appadvice.com/app/martell-air-gallery/1048900688

AppAdvice LLC. (2019b). Martell AiR Gallery. Retrieved from https://appadvice.com/app/martell-air-gallery/1048900688

Appelman, R. (2005). Designing experiential modes: A key focus for immersive learning environments. *TechTrends*, *49*(3), 64–74. doi:10.1007/BF02763648

Appleton, J. J., Christenson, S. L., Kim, D., & Reschly, A. L. (2006). Measuring cognitive and psychological engagement: Validation of the student engagement instrument. *Journal of School Psychology*, *44*(5), 427–445. doi:10.1016/j.jsp.2006.04.002

Ardiny, H., & Khanmirza, E. (2018, October). The role of AR and VR technologies in education developments: opportunities and challenges. In *2018 6th RSI International Conference on Robotics and Mechatronics (IcRoM)* (pp. 482-487). IEEE.

Ardito, C., Buono, P., Costabile, M. F., Lanzilotti, R., & Piccinno, A. (2009). Enabling interactive exploration of cultural heritage: An experience of designing systems for mobile devices. *Knowledge, Technology & Policy*, *22*(1), 79–86. doi:10.100712130-009-9079-7

Argyle, M. (1975). *Bodily communication*. London, UK: Methuen Publishing Ltd.

ARpost. (2018, August). *3D tooth atlas 9: The virtual reality training system for dentists of the future.* Available at https://arpost.co/2018/08/14/3d-tooth-atlas-9-the-virtual-reality-training-system-for-dentists-of-the-future/

Astic, I., & Aunis, C. (2011). A ubiquitous mobile edutainment application for learning science through play. *Proceedings of Museums and the Web 2011. Archives & Museum Informatics*, Toronto. Retrieved from: http://conference.archimuse.com/mw2011/papers/a_ubiquitous_mobile_edutainment_application_fo

Aubin, P. (2013). *Renaissance revit: Creating classical architecture with modern software.* (G3B Press, Ed.).

Aukstakalnis, S. (2016). *Practical augmented reality: a guide to the technologies, applications, and human factors for AR and VR.* Boston, MA: Addison-Wesley.

Ausburn, L. J., & Ausburn, F. B. (2004). Desktop virtual reality: A powerful new technology for teaching and research in industrial teacher education. *Journal of Industrial Teacher Education*, *41*(4), 33–58.

Baard, P. P., Deci, E. L., & Ryan, R. M. (2004). Intrinsic need satisfaction: A motivational basis of performance and well-being in two work settings. *Journal of Applied Social Psychology*, *34*(10), 2045–2068. doi:10.1111/j.1559-1816.2004.tb02690.x

Bahar, A. (2015). Temel hemşirelik becerisi eğitiminde yenilik: Web tabanli eğitim (*An innovation in nursing basic skills education: web-based education*). [Journal of Anatolian Nursing and Health Sciences]. *Anadolu Hemşirelik ve Sağlık Bilimleri Dergisi*, *18*(4), 304–311.

Bailenson, J. N., Yee, N., Blascovich, J., Beall, A. C., Lundblad, N., & Jin, M. (2008). The use of immersive virtual reality in the learning sciences: Digital transformations of teachers, students, and social context. *Journal of the Learning Sciences*, *17*(1), 102–141. doi:10.1080/10508400701793141

Bailey, T., & Durrant-Whyte, H. (2006). Simultaneous localization and mapping (SLAM): Part II. *IEEE Robotics & Automation Magazine*, *13*(3), 108–117. doi:10.1109/MRA.2006.1678144

Baker, N. (2017, July 21). Augmented reality apps bring exhibits to life; Toronto Museum, Laguna Beach gallery incorporate untapped medium. *The Gazette (Montreal)*, p. 8.

Baker, S., Bakar, J., & Zulkifli, A. (2017). Elements of museum mobile augmented reality for engaging hearing-impaired visitors. *AIP Conference Proceedings*, 020033. doi:10.1063/1.5005366

Bakhshi, H., & Throsby, D. (2012). New technologies in cultural institutions: Theory, evidence and policy implications. *International Journal of Cultural Policy*, *18*(2), 205–222. doi:10.1080/10286632.2011.587878

Baltsavias, E. P. (2002). Object extraction and revision by image analysis using existing geospatial data and knowledge: State-of-the-art and steps towards operational systems, *International Archives of Photogammetry, part 2*.

Bamodu, O., & Xuming, Y. (2013). Virtual reality and virtual reality system components. In *Proceedings of the 2nd International Conference on Systems Engineering and Modeling (ICSEM-13)*. Paris, France: Atlantis Press.

Banfi, F., Brumana, R., & Stanga, C. (2019). A content-based immersive experience of basilica of Sant'Ambrogio in Milan: From 3D survey to virtual reality. *The International Archives of the Photogrammetry, Remote Sensing and Spatial Information Sciences*, *XLII-2*(W11), 159–166. doi:10.5194/isprs-archives-XLII-2-W11-159-2019

Barad, J. (2019). *Reality training for robotics-assisted surgery*. Available at https://healthiar.com/osso-vr-creates-first-virtual-reality-training-for-robotics-assisted-surgery

Barata, G., Gama, S., Jorge, J., & Goncalves, D. (2013). Engaging engineering students with gamification. In *Proceedings 5th International Conference on Games and Virtual Worlds for Serious Applications*, pp. 1-8. IEEE.

Barbieri, G. L. (2016). Il selfie: pensieri nascosti, fantasie di autocreazione, tratti di personalità. In Rivista Internazionale di Filosofia e Psicologia, 7(3), 378-389.

Barbieri, L., Bruno, F., & Muzzupappa, M. (2017). Virtual museum system evaluation through user studies. *Journal of Cultural Heritage*, *26*, 101–108. doi:10.1016/j.culher.2017.02.005

Barrozio da Vignola, M. I. (1562). *La regola delli cinque ordini d'architettura*.

Barsom, E. Z., Graafland, M., & Schijven, M. P. (2016). Systematic review on the effectiveness of augmented reality applications in medical training. *Surgical Endoscopy*, *30*, 4174. doi:10.100700464-016-4800-6

Barthes, R. (1981). *Camera lucida: reflections on photography*. New York: Hill and Wang.

Bartle, R. (1996). Hearts, clubs, diamonds, spades: Players who suit MUDS. Available at https://mud.co.uk/richard/hcds.htm

Basballe, D. A., & Halskov, K. (2010). Projections on museum exhibits: engaging visitors in the museum setting. *Proceedings of the 22nd Conference of the Computer-Human Interaction Special Interest Group of Australia on Computer-Human Interaction*, 80–87. 10.1145/1952222.1952240

Baudrillard, J. (1988). The ecstasy of communication. New York: Semiotext(e).

Baumann, S. L., Sharoff, L., & Penalo, L. (2018). Using simulation to enhance global nursing. *Nursing Science Quarterly*, *31*(4), 374–378. doi:10.1177/0894318418792877 PMID:30223748

Beaumont, C., Savin-Baden, M., Conradi, E., & Poulton, T. (2014). Evaluating a second life problem-based learning (PBL) demonstrator project: What can we learn? *Interactive Learning Environments*, *22*(1), 125–141. doi:10.1080/10 494820.2011.641681

Bedigan, K. M. (2016). Developing emotions: Perceptions of emotional responses in museums. *Mediterranean Archaeology and Archaeometry*, *16*(5), 87–95. Retrieved from http://maajournal.com/Issues/2016/Vol16-5/Full9.pdf

Behzadan, A. H., Timm, B. W., & Kamat, V. R. (2008). General purpose modular hardware and software framework for mobile outdoor augmented reality applications in engineering. *Advanced Engineering Informatics*, *22*(1), 90–105. doi:10.1016/j.aei.2007.08.005

Bekele, M. K., Pierdicca, R., Frontoni, E., Malinverni, E. S., & Gain, J. (2018). A survey of augmented, virtual, and mixed reality for cultural heritage. [JOCCH]. *Journal on Computing and Cultural Heritage*, *11*(2), 7. doi:10.1145/3145534

Belpoliti, M. (2005). *Crolli*. Torino, Italy: Einaudi.

Belting, H. (2017). *Face and mask: a double history*. Princeton, NJ: Princeton University Press.

Benford, S., Greenhalgh, C., Reynard, G., Brown, C., & Koleva, B. (1998). Understanding and constructing shared spaces with mixed-reality boundaries. *ACM Transactions on computer-human interaction (TOCHI)*, *5*(3), 185-223.

Benjamin, W. (1999). *Little history of photography in Selected writings*. Cambridge, MA: The Belknap Press of Harvard University Press.

Bentkowska-Kafel, A., & MacDonald, L. (Eds.). (2018). Digital techniques for documenting and preserving cultural heritage. Kalamazoo, MI: Arc Humanities Press.

Berger, M., Jucker, A. H., & Locher, M. A. (2016). Interaction and space in the virtual world of second life, *Journal of Pragmatics* 101, 83-100.

Bergstrom, K., Fisher, S., & Jenson, J. (2016). Disavowing that guy: Identity construction and massively multiplayer online game players. *Convergence (London)*, *22*(3), 233–249. doi:10.1177/1354856514560314

Bernhardt, S., Nicolau, S. A., Soler, L., & Doignon, C. (2017). *The status of augmented reality in laparoscopic surgery as of 2016*. Medical Image Analysis 37, 66–90. http://dx.doi.org/ 1361-8415/ doi:10.1016/j.media.2017.01.007

Beyond the Gate (Developer), & Castello Sforzesco di Milano (Client). (2018). *Beyond the Castle*. Retrieved from https://beyondthegate.io/castello-sforzesco/

Bifulco, P., Narducci, F., Vertucci, R., Ambruosi, P., Cesarelli, M., & Romano, M. (2014). Telemedicine supported by Augmented Reality: An interactive guide for untrained people in performing an ECG test. *Biomedical Engineering Online*, *13*(1), 153. doi:10.1186/1475-925X-13-153

Billinghurst, M. (2002). Augmented reality in education. *New horizons for learning, 12*(5), 1-5.

Bing, M. (2017). *Augmented reality in museums*. Arts Management & Technology Laboratory.

Birks, M., & Mills, J. (2011). *Grounded theory, A pratical guide* (p. 95). London, UK: Sage.

Blascovich, J., & Bailenson, J. (2005). Immersive virtual environments and education simulations. In P. Cohen & T. Rehberger (Eds.), *Virtual Decisions: Digital Simulations for Teaching Reasoning in the Social Sciences and Humanities.* Mahwah, New Jersey: Lawrence Earlbaum Associates, Inc.

Bogdan, C. M., Dinca, A. F., & Popovici, D. M. (2011). A brief survey of visuo-haptic simulators for dental procedures training. In *Proceedings of the 6th International Conference on Virtual Learning* (pp. 28-29).

Bollas, C. (2018). *Meaning and melancholia. Life in the age of bewilderment.* London, UK: Routledge. doi:10.4324/9781351018500

Bolter, J. D., & Grusin, B. (1999). *Remediation: Understanding new media.* Boston, MA: MIT Press.

Bonacini, E. (2011). Nuove tecnologie per la fruizione e valorizzazione del patrimonio culturale. (Aracne, Ed.). Roma, Italy.

Bonami, F. (2019). *Post. L'opera d'arte nell'epoca della sua riproducibilità sociale.* Milano, Italy: Feltrinelli.

Bonasio, A. (2019). *Scientists Use Yawning to Study Social Presence in VR.* Retrieved from: https://vrscout.com/news/yawning-social-presence-vr-study/

Bontchev, B. (2012). Evolving Europeana's Metadata: from ESE to EDM. In *Proc. of Digital Presentation and Preservation of Cultural and Scientific Heritage, (II)* (pp. 27–37). Retrieved from http://pro.europeana.eu/

Bowers, J., Bannon, L., Fraser, M., Hindmarsh, J., Benford, S., Heath, C., … Ciolfi, L. (2007). From the disappearing computer to living exhibitions: shaping interactivity in museum settings. In The disappearing computer (pp. 30–49). Berlin, Germany: Springer. doi:10.1007/978-3-540-72727-9_2

Bracq, M. S., Michinov, E., & Jannin, P. (2019). Virtual reality simulation in nontechnical skills training for healthcare professionals: A systematic review. *Simulation in Healthcare, 14*(3), 188–194. doi:10.1097/SIH.0000000000000347 PMID:30601464

Bradley, P. (2006). The history of simulation in medical education and possible future directions. *Medical Education, 40*(3), 254–262. doi:10.1111/j.1365-2929.2006.02394.x PMID:16483328

Brasil, I. S., Neto, F. M. M., Chagas, J. F. S., de Lima, R. M., Souza, D. F. L., Bonates, M. F., & Dantas, A. (2011). *An intelligent agent-based virtual game for oil drilling operators training.* Paper presented at the 2011 XIII Symposium on Virtual Reality (SVR).

Bredekamp, H. (2015). *The technical image: a history of styles in scientific imagery.* Chicago, IL: The University of Chicago Press. doi:10.7208/chicago/9780226258980.001.0001

Bricken, M. (1991). Virtual reality learning environments: Potentials and challenges. *Computer Graphics, 25*(3), 178–184. doi:10.1145/126640.126657

Bricken, M., & Byrne, C. M. (1994). Summer students in virtual reality: A pilot study on educational applications of virtual reality technology. In A. Wexelblat (Ed.), *Virtual reality: Applications and explorations* (pp. 199–218). Boston, MA: Academic Press.

Bright, S. (2010). *Autofocus. The self-portrait in contemporary photography.* London, UK: Thames & Hundson.

Brown, B., Maccoll, I., Chalmers, M., & Galani, A. (2003). Lessons from the lighthouse: Collaboration in a shared mixed reality system. In *SIGCHI Conference on Human Factors in Computing Systems* (pp. 577–584). New York: ACM; doi:10.1145/642611.642711

Brown, L. P. (2011). Revisiting our roots: Caring in nursing curriculum design. *Nurse Education in Practice*, *11*(6), 360–364. doi:10.1016/j.nepr.2011.03.007 PMID:21459042

Bruce, B. C. (2008). Ubiquitous learning, ubiquitous computing, and lived experience. In C. Jones, M. Zenios & A. Jesmont (eds.). *Proceedings of the Sixth International Conference on Networked Learning*, Halkidiki, Greece. Retrieved from: http://www.networkedlearningconference.org.uk/past/nlc2008/abstracts/PDFs/Bruce_583-590.pdf

Bruno, F., Bruno, S., De Sensi, G., Luchi, M. L., Mancuso, S., & Muzzupappa, M. (2010). From 3D reconstruction to virtual reality: A complete methodology for digital archaeological exhibition. Journal of Cultural Heritage, 11(1), 42–49.

Bruno, F., Barbieri, L., Laudi, A., Cozza, M., Cozza, A., Peluso, R., & Muzzupappa, M. (2018). Virtual dives into the underwater archaeological treasures of South Italy. *Virtual Reality (Waltham Cross)*, *22*(2), 91–102. doi:10.100710055-017-0318-z

Bruno, F., Lagudi, A., Barbieri, L., Cozza, M., Cozza, A., Peluso, R., ... Skarlatos, D. (2019). Virtual tour in the sunken "villa con ingresso a protiro" within the underwater archaeological park of Baiae. *The International Archives of the Photogrammetry, Remote Sensing and Spatial Information Sciences*, *XLII-2*(W10), 45–51. doi:10.5194/isprs-archives-XLII-2-W10-45-2019

Bruno, F., Lagudi, A., Muzzupappa, M., Lupia, M., Cario, G., Barbieri, L., ... Saggiomo, R. (2016). Project VISAS - Virtual and augmented exploitation of Submerged Archaeological Sites: Overview and first results. *Marine Technology Society Journal*, *50*(4), 119–129. doi:10.4031/MTSJ.50.4.4

Budge, K., & Burness, A. (2018). Museum objects and Instagram: Agency and communication in digital engagement. *Continuum (Perth)*, *32*(2), 137–150. doi:10.1080/10304312.2017.1337079

Bulu, S. T. (2012). Place presence, social presence, co-presence, and satisfaction in virtual worlds. *Computers & Education*, *58*(1), 154–161. doi:10.1016/j.compedu.2011.08.024

Butt, A. L. (2015). *Exploring the usability of game-based virtual reality for development of procedural skills, in undergraduate nursing students*. (Doctoral Dissertation), Boise State University, Idaho.

Butt, A. L., Kardong-Edgren, S., & Ellertson, A. (2018). Using game-based virtual reality with haptics for skill acquisition. *Clinical Simulation in Nursing*, *16*, 25–32. doi:10.1016/j.ecns.2017.09.010

CAE Healthcare announces first mixed reality ultrasound simulation solution with Microsoft HoloLens. CAE Healthcare Inc. Orlando, FL: CAE Healthcare; (2017). Available at https://www.cae.com/news-events/press-releases/cae-healthcare-announces-first-mixed-reality-ultrasound-simulation-solution/

Camic, P. M., Tischler, V., & Pearman, C. H. (2014). Viewing and making art together: A multi-session art-gallery-based intervention for people with dementia and their carers. *Aging & Mental Health*, *18*(2), 161–168. doi:10.1080/1360786 3.2013.818101 PMID:23869748

Camin, G. (2008, June). Che cosa si intende per diletto? *Nuova Museologia*, *18*, 28–29.

Canciani, M., Conigliaro, E., Del Grasso, M., Papalini, P., & Saccone, M. (2016). 3D Survey and augmented reality for cultural heritage. The case study of Aurelian Wall at Castra Praetoria in Rome. In *International Archives of the Photogrammetry*. Remote Sensing and Spatial Information Sciences - ISPRS Archives; doi:10.5194/isprsarchives-XLI-B5-931-2016

Canevacci, M. (2017). *Antropologia della comunicazione visuale*. Milano, Italy: Postmedia Books.

Cannon-Diehl, M. R. (2009). Simulation in healthcare and nursing: State of the science. *Critical Care Nursing Quarterly*, *32*(2), 128–136. doi:10.1097/CNQ.0b013e3181a27e0f PMID:19300077

Capriotti, P., Carretón, C., & Castillo, A. (2016). Testing the level of interactivity of institutional websites: From museums 1.0 to museums 2.0. *International Journal of Information Management, 36*(1), 97–104. doi:10.1016/j.ijinfomgt.2015.10.003

Capuano, N., Gaeta, A., Guarino, G., Miranda, S., & Tomasiello, S. (2016). Enhancing augmented reality with cognitive and knowledge perspectives: A case study in museum exhibitions. Behaviour & Information Technology, 35(11), 968–979.

Cardiff, E. (2018). *Response to local surgical challenges.* Available at https://eu.augmentedworldexpo.com/sessions/proximie-augmented-reality-providing-a-global-response-to-local-surgical-challenges/

Carlton, B. (2019, May 25). Boston's Rose Kennedy Greenway is now one of the largest AR exhibits in North America. Retrieved from https://vrscout.com/news/rose-kennedy-greenway-ar-experience/

Carrozzino, M., & Bergamasco, M. (2010). Beyond virtual museums: Experiencing immersive virtual reality in real museums. *Journal of Cultural Heritage, 11*(4), 452–458. doi:10.1016/j.culher.2010.04.001

Castells, M. (1983). *The City and the Grassroots: A Cross-Cultural Theory of Urban Social Movements.* Berkeley, CA: University of California Press.

Ceccacci, S., Generosi, A., Giraldi, L., & Mengoni, M. (2018). Tool to make shopping experience responsive to customer emotions. *International Journal of Automation Technology.* doi:10.20965/ijat.2018.p0319

Ceri Via, C. (2018). *Nel dettaglio nascosto Per una storia del pensiero iconologico.* Rome, Italy: Carocci.

Cerquetti, M., & Montella, M. M. (2015). Museum networks and sustainable tourism management. The case study of Marche region's museums. *Enlightening Tourism. A Pathmaking Journal, 5*(1), 100–125.

Chancellor, B., Duncan, A., & Chatterjee, A. (2014). Art therapy for Alzheimer's disease and other dementias. *Journal of Alzheimer's Disease, 39*(1), 1–11. doi:10.3233/JAD-131295 PMID:24121964

Chang, K.-E., Chang, C.-T., Hou, H.-T., Sung, Y.-T., Chao, H.-L., & Lee, C.-M. (2014). Development and behavioral pattern analysis of a mobile guide system with augmented reality for painting appreciation instruction in an art museum. Computers & Education, 71, 185–197.

Chang, K. K.-P., Chung, J. W.-Y., & Wong, T. K.-S. (2002). Learning intravenous cannulation: A comparison of the conventional method and the CathSim Intravenous Training System. *Journal of Clinical Nursing, 11*(1), 73–78. doi:10.1046/j.1365-2702.2002.00561.x PMID:11845758

Chan, K. Y. G., Tan, S. L., Hew, K. F. T., Koh, B. G., Lim, L. S., & Yong, J. C. (2017). Knowledge for games, games for knowledge: designing a digital roll-and-move board game for a law of torts class. *Research and Practice in Technology Enhanced Learning, 12*(1), 7. doi:10.118641039-016-0045-1 PMID:30613256

Charmaz, K. (2006). *Constructing grounded theory, a practical guide through qualitative analysis.* London, UK: Sage.

Chatzidimitris, T., Kavakli, E., Economou, M., & Gavalas, D. (2013). Mobile augmented reality edutainment applications for cultural institutions. In N. G. Bourbakis, G. A. Tsihrintzis, & M. Virvou (Eds.), *2013 Fourth International Conference on Information, Intelligence, Systems, and Applications (IISA)* (pp. 1-4). Piraeus, Greece: IEEE.

Chen, C. (2007). Formative research on the instructional design process of virtual reality-based learning environments. *ICT: Providing choices for learners and learning. Proceedings ascilite Singapore*, 149-156.

Chen, C. J., (2009). Theoretical bases for using virtual reality in education. *Themes in Science and Technology Education* (Special Issue), 71-90.

Chen, C. H., Yang, J. C., Shen, S., & Jeng, M. C. (2007). A desktop virtual reality earth motion system in astronomy education. *Journal of Educational Technology & Society, 10*(3), 289–304.

Chen, C. J., & Teh, C. S. (2013). Enhancing an instructional design model for virtual reality-based learning. *Australasian Journal of Educational Technology*, *29*(5), 699–716. doi:10.14742/ajet.247

Chen, C. J., Toh, S. C., & Fauzy, W. M. (2004). The theoretical framework for designing desktop, virtual reality-based learning environments. *Journal of Interactive Learning Research*, *15*(2), 147.

Chen, C. J., Toh, S. C., & Wan, M. F. (2004). The theoretical framework for designing desktop virtual reality-based learning environments. *Journal of Interactive Learning Research*, *15*(2), 147–167.

Chen, C. M., & Tsai, Y. N. (2012). Interactive augmented reality system for enhancing library instruction in elementary schools. *Computers & Education*, *59*(2), 638–652. doi:10.1016/j.compedu.2012.03.001

Cheng, K. H., & Tsai, C. C. (2013). Affordances of augmented reality in science learning: Suggestions for future research. *Journal of Science Education and Technology*, *22*(4), 449–462. doi:10.100710956-012-9405-9

Chen, P., Liu, X., Cheng, W., & Huang, R. (2017). A review of using augmented reality in education from 2011 to 2016. In *Innovations in smart learning* (pp. 13–18). Singapore: Springer. doi:10.1007/978-981-10-2419-1_2

Chevrier, C. (2016). *3D semantic modelling of scale models from 2D historical plans*. Retrieved from http://meurthe.crai.archi.fr/wordpressFr/wp-content/plugins/Lab_BD/media/pdf/Eurographics.pdf

Chia, P. (2013). Using a virtual game to enhance simulation-based learning in nursing education. *Singapore Nursing Journal*, *40*(3), 21–26.

Chittaro, L., & Ranon, R. (2007). Web3D technologies in learning, education, and training: Motivations, issues, opportunities. *Computers & Education*, *49*(1), 3–18. doi:10.1016/j.compedu.2005.06.002

ChiuE. (2018). *The Future Museum*. Retrieved from https://www.jwtintelligence.com/2018/09/the-future-museum/

Choi, H.-S., & Kim, S.-H. (2017, February). A content service deployment plan for metaverse museum exhibitions-centering on the combination of beacons and HMDs. International Journal of Information Management, 37(1b), 1519–1527.

Choi, K. S. (2017). Virtual reality in nursing: Nasogastric tube placement training simulator. *Studies in Health Technology and Informatics*, *245*, 1298. PMID:29295381

Chopin, A., Bediou, B., & Bavelier, D. (2019). Altering perception: The case of action video gaming. *Current Opinion in Psychology.*, *29*, 168–173. doi:10.1016/j.copsyc.2019.03.004 PMID:30978639

Chow, M. (2016). Determinants of presence in 3D virtual worlds: A structural equation modeling analysis. *Australasian Journal of Educational Technology*, *32*(1). doi:10.14742/ajet.1939

Christian, S. (2018, March 22). *Using virtual, augmented, and mixed realities for medical training*. Available at http://designinteractive.net/using-virtual-augmented-mixed-realities-medical-training/

Christou, C. (2010). Virtual reality in education. In Affective, interactive and cognitive methods for e-learning design: creating an optimal education experience (pp. 228–243). Hershey, PA: IGI Global. doi:10.4018/978-1-60566-940-3.ch012

Chuah, K.-M., Chen, C.-J., & Teh, C.-S. (2011). Designing a desktop virtual reality-based learning environment with emotional consideration. *Research & Practice in Technology Enhanced Learning, 6*(1).

Chuah, K.-M., Chen, C.-J., & Teh, C.-S. (2011). Designing a desktop virtual reality-based learning environment with emotional consideration. *Research and Practice in Technology Enhanced Learning*, *6*(1), 25–42.

Cianciarulo, D. (2015). From local traditions to "Augmented Reality". The MUVIG Museum of Viggiano (Italy). *Procedia: Social and Behavioral Sciences*, *188*, 138–143. doi:10.1016/j.sbspro.2015.03.349

Cipolletta, G. (2014). *Passages metrocorporei. Per un'estetica della transizione*. Macerata, Italy: eum.

Classen, C. (1997). Foundations for an anthropology of the senses. *International Social Science Journal, 49*(153), 401–412. doi:10.1111/j.1468-2451.1997.tb00032.x

Claudio, P., & Maddalena, P. (2014, January). Overview: Virtual reality in medicine. Journal of Virtual Worlds Research, 7(1), 1–34.

Clini, P., Quattrini, R., Frontoni, E., Pierdicca, R., & Nespeca, R. (2016). Real/not real: Pseudo-holography and augmented reality applications for cultural heritage. In Handbook of research on emerging technologies for digital preservation and information modeling. doi:10.4018/978-1-5225-0680-5.ch009

Codeluppi, V. (2015). *Mi metto in vetrina. Selfie, Facebook, Apple, Hello Kitty, Renzi e altre "vetrinizzazioni"*. Milano, Italy: Mimesis.

Collin-Lachaud, I., & Passebois, J. (2008). Do immersive technologies add value to the museum-going experience? An exploratory study conducted at France's Paléosite. International Journal of Arts Management, 11(1), 60–71.

Colombo, F. (2018). Reviewing the cultural industry: From creative industries to digital platforms. Communicatio Socialis, 31(4), 135–146.

COMMITTE, U. (2017). UNI 11337-4:2017 Edilizia e opere di ingegneria civile - Gestione digitale dei processi informativi delle costruzioni - Parte 4: Evoluzione e sviluppo informativo di modelli, elaborati e oggetti.

Cook, L. J. (2005). Inviting teaching behaviors of clinical faculty and nursing students' anxiety. *The Journal of Nursing Education, 44*(4), 156–161. PMID:15862048

Cosmas, J., Green, D., Grabczewski, E., Weimer, F., Leberl, F., & Grabner, M., … Kampel, M. (2001). 3D MURALE: A multimedia system for archaeology desi vanrintel, Eyetronics NV. In *Symposium on Virtual Reality, Archaeology, and Cultural Heritage*. ACM SIGGRAPH. Retrieved from https://www.inf.ethz.ch/personal/pomarc/pubs/CosmasVAST01.pdf

Cousins, M. (2017). *The story of looking*. Edinburgh, UK: Canongate.

Craig, A. (2013). *Understanding augmented reality*, Elsevier.

Craig, E. (2019, May 26). Boston the site of the largest AR art exhibit in America. Digital bodies: VR, AR, and the future of learning. Retrieved from https://www.digitalbodies.net/augmented-reality/boston-the-site-of-the-largest-ar-art-exhibit-in-america/

Craig, E., & Georgieva, M. (2017, Aug. 30). *VR and AR: Driving a revolution in medical education & patient care*. Available at https://er.educause.edu/.blogs/2017/8/vr-and-ar-driving-a-revolution-in-medical-education-and-patient-care

Crosier, J. K., Cobb, S., & Wilson, J. R. (2002). Key lessons for the design and integration of virtual environments in secondary science. *Computers & Education, 38*(1-3), 77–94. doi:10.1016/S0360-1315(01)00075-6

Curiosity Stream (Ed.), & Experius VR (Developer). (2018). *Nefertari: Journey to eternity*. Retrieved from https://www.oculus.com/experiences/rift/1491802884282318/

Cursi, S., Simeone, D., & Toldo, I. (2015). A semantic web approach for built heritage representation. In Communications in Computer and Information Science. doi:10.1007/978-3-662-47386-3_21

D'Auria, D., Di Mauro, D., Calandra, D. M., & Cutugno, F. (2015). A 3D audio augmented reality system for a cultural heritage management and fruition. *Journal of Digital Information Management, 13*(4), 203. Retrieved from https://www.semanticscholar.org/paper/A-3D-Audio-Augmented-Reality-System-for-a-Cultural-D'Auria-Mauro/40aad70c8e8337c2e02d3424179b586fa9e9a922

Da Rin De Lorenzo, F. (Interviewer), & Dorfles, G. (Interviewee). (2010, May 9). *Art crafts and industry* [Video interview]. Retrieved from https://venicedesignweek.com/gillo-dorfles-thanks/

Dalgarno, B., Hedberg, J., & Harper, B. (2002). The contribution of 3D environments to conceptual understanding. In 19th annual conference of the Australasian society for computers in learning in tertiary education, Winds of change in the sea of learning (pp. 1-10). Auckland, New Zealand: UNITEC Institute of Technology.

Dalgarno, B., & Lee, M. J. (2010). What are the learning affordances of 3-D virtual environments? *British Journal of Educational Technology*, *41*(1), 10–32. doi:10.1111/j.1467-8535.2009.01038.x

Damala, A., Hornecker, E., Van Der Vaart, M., Van Dijk, D., & Ruthven, I. (2016). The Loupe: Tangible augmented reality for learning to look at ancient Greek art. *Mediterranean Archaeology and Archaeometry*, *16*(5), 73–85. doi:10.5281/zenodo.204970

Damasio, A. R. (2005). Feeling our Emotions. *Scientific American*. Retrieved from http://www.scientificamerican.com/article.cfm?id=feeling-our-emotions

Damasio, A. R. (2000). *The Feeling of what Happens: Body, Emotion and the Making of Consciousness*. New York, USA: Harcourt Brace.

Davis, A. (2015). Virtual reality simulation: an innovative teaching tool for dietetics experiential education. *The Open Nutrition Journal*, *9*(1), 65–75. doi:10.2174/1876396001509010065

DCH-RP. (2014). *A roadmap for preservation of digital cultural heritage content*. Retrieved from http://www.dch-rp.eu/index.php?en/115/roadmap-for-preservation

De Kerckhove, D. (2016). *La rete ci renderà stupidi?* Roma, Italy: Castelvecchi.

Debevec, P. (2001). Reconstructing and augmenting architecture with image-based modelling, rendering and lighting, *Proc. International Symposium on Virtual and Augmented Architecture*, Trinity College, Dublin. 10.1007/978-1-4471-0337-0_1

Debord. (1970). *Society of spectacle*. Detroit, MI: Black & Red.

Decker, S., Sportsman, S., Puetz, L., & Billings, L. (2008). The evolution of simulation and its contribution to competency. *Journal of Continuing Education in Nursing*, *9*(2), 74–80. doi:10.3928/00220124-20080201-06 PMID:18323144

Dede, C. (2009). Immersive interfaces for engagement and learning. *Science, 323*(5910), 66-69.

Dede, C. (1995). The evolution of constructivist learning environments: immersion in distributed virtual worlds. *Educational Technology*, *35*, 46–52.

Dede, C. (1996). The evolution of distance education: Emerging technologies and distributed learning. *American Journal of Distance Education*, *10*(2), 4–36. doi:10.1080/08923649609526919

DeLeon, L. (2017, Oct. 26). *ForwardXP: XR Training for a F.A.S.T. Response*. Available at https://developer.qualcomm.com/blog/forwardxp-xr-training-fast-response

Delialioglu, O. (2012). Student engagement in blended learning environments with lecture-based and problem-based instructional approaches. *Journal of Educational Technology and Society, 15*(3), 310 – n/a.

Detheridge, A. (2012). *Scultori della speranza. L'arte nel contesto della globalizzazione*. Torino, Italy: Einaudi.

Deuze, M. (2007, June 1). Convergence culture in the creative industries. International Journal of Cultural Studies, 10(2), 243–263.

Dewey, J. (1938). *Experience and education*. New York: Macmillan.

Dhanda, A., Reina Ortiz, M., Weigert, A., Paladini, A., Min, A., Gyi, M., ... Santana Quintero, M. (2019). Recreating cultural heritage environments for VR using photogrammetry. *The International Archives of the Photogrammetry, Remote Sensing and Spatial Information Sciences, XLII-2*(W9), 305–310. doi:10.5194/isprs-archives-XLII-2-W9-305-2019

Diamandis, P. H. (2019). *5 breakthroughs coming soon in augmented and virtual reality.* Available at https://singularityhub.com/2019/05/10/5-breakthroughs-coming-soon-in-augmented-and-virtual-reality/

Dickey, M. D. (2005). Three-dimensional virtual worlds and distance learning: Two case studies of ActiveWorlds as a medium for distance education. *British Journal of Educational Technology, 36*(3), 439–451. doi:10.1111/j.1467-8535.2005.00477.x

Diemer, J., Alpers, G. W., Peperkorn, H. M., Shiban, Y., & Mühlberger, A. (2015). The impact of perception and presence on emotional reaction: A review of research in virtual reality. *Frontiers in Psychology*, Retrieved from https://www.ncbi.nlm.nih.gov/pubmed/25688218

Dorfles, G. (2001). *Introduzione al disegno industriale.* Milano, Italy: Einaudi.

Downey, S. (2011). i-MMOLE: Instructional framework for creating virtual world lessons. *TechTrends, 55*(6), 33–41. doi:10.100711528-011-0539-z

Dragoni, A. F., Quattrini, R., Sernani, P., & Ruggeri, L. (2019). Real scale augmented reality. A novel paradigm for archaeological heritage fruition. doi:10.1007/978-3-030-12240-9_68

Dreesmann, N. (2018). Virtual reality check, are you ready? *Journal of Gerontological Nursing, 44*(3), 3–4. doi:10.3928/00989134-20180213-01 PMID:29470583

Dreher, C., Reiners, T., Dreher, N., & Dreher, H. (2009). Virtual worlds as a context suited for information systems education: Discussion of pedagogical experience and curriculum design with reference to Second Life. *Journal of Information Systems Education, 20*(2), 211–224.

Duarte, E., Rebelo, F., Teixeira, L., Vilar, E., Teles, J., & Noriega, P. (2013). Sense of Presence in a VR-Based Study on Behavioral Compliance with Warnings. In A. Marcus (Ed.), *Design, User Experience, and Usability. User Experience in Novel Technological Environments. DUXU 2013. Lecture Notes in Computer Science* (Vol. 8014). Berlin, Heidelberg: Springer. doi:10.1007/978-3-642-39238-2_40

Duncan, I., Miller, A., & Jiang, S. (2012). A taxonomy of virtual worlds usage in education. *British Journal of Educational Technology, 43*(6), 949–964. doi:10.1111/j.1467-8535.2011.01263.x

Dunleavy, M., Dede, C., & Mitchell, R. (2009). Affordances and limitations of immersive participatory augmented reality simulations for teaching and learning. *Journal of Science Education and Technology, 18*(1), 7–22. doi:10.100710956-008-9119-1

DURAARK. (2015). *D3.5 Point cloud schema extension for the IFC model.*

Durrant-Whyte, H., & Bailey, T. (2006). Simultaneous localization and mapping: Part I. *IEEE Robotics & Automation Magazine, 13*(2), 99–110. doi:10.1109/MRA.2006.1638022

Dylla, K., Muller, P., Ulmer, A., Haegler, S., & Frischer, B. (2009). Rome reborn 2.0: A framework for virtual city reconstruction using procedural modeling techniques. In Computer Applications and Quantitative Methods in Archaeology.

Economou, M., & Pujol Tost, L. (2011) Evaluating the use of virtual reality and multimedia applications for presenting the past. In F. Lazarinis, G. Styliaras, & D. Koukopoulos (Eds.), Handbook of research on technologies and cultural heritage: applications and environments, (pp. 223-239). Hershey, PA: IGI Global. doi:10.4018/978-1-60960-044-0.ch011

Eco, U. (1962). *Opera Aperta*. Milano, Italy: Bompiani.

Eco, U. (1985). *Sugli specchi e altri saggi*. Milano, Italy: Bompiani.

Eker, F., Açıkgöz, F., & Karaca, A. (2014). Hemşirelik öğrencileri gözüyle mesleki beceri eğitimi (Occupational skill training through the eyes of nursing students). [Dokuz Eylul University Faculty of Nursing Electronic Journal]. *Dokuz Eylül Üniversitesi Hemşirelik Elektronik Dergisi, 7*(4), 291–294.

El Sayed, N. A., Zayed, H. H., & Sharawy, M. I. (2010, December). ARSC: Augmented reality student card. In *2010 International Computer Engineering Conference (ICENCO)* (pp. 113-120). IEEE. 10.1109/ICENCO.2010.5720437

Ellsworth, J. J., Gossett, C. P., & Clements, K. (2016). *U.S. patent application No. 15/160, 996*.

eMarketer.com. (2018a, April 9). Chart: Virtual and augmented reality device shipment and sales share worldwide, by device type, 2022 (% of total). eMarketer.com. Retrieved from http://totalaccess.emarketer.com/chart.aspx?r=219212

eMarketer.com. (2018b, April 24). Chart: UK smartphone users who prefer using smart glasses vs. Smartphone for select augmented reality activities (% of respondents). eMarketer.com. Retrieved from http://totalaccess.emarketer.com/chart.aspx?r=220210

eMarketer.com. (2018c, April 5). Industries in which augmented reality users in select countries in Western Europe have used AR, Nov. 2017 (% of respondents). eMarketer.com. Retrieved from http://totalaccess.emarketer.com/chart.aspx?r=219349

eMarketer.com. (2018d, Nov. 12). Ownership of VR headsets among US internet users, July 2014-Aug 2018 (% of respondents). eMarketer.com. Retrieved from http://totalaccess.emarketer.com/chart.aspx?r=224365

eMarketer.com. (2018e, Sept. 7). Executives in select countries whose companies are experimenting with vs. implementing AR & VR for industrial use, by country (% of respondents, June 2018). eMarketer.com, Retrieved from http://totalaccess.emarketer.com/chart.aspx?r=222816

eMarketer.com. (2018f, April 5). Usage and awareness of augmented reality among internet users in select countries in Western Europe, Nov 2017 (% of respondents). eMarketer.com. Retrieved from http://totalaccess.emarketer.com/chart.aspx?r=219347

Empler, T. (2015). Cultural heritage: Displaying the Forum of Nerva with new technologies. In *2015 Digital Heritage International Congress, Digital Heritage 2015*. 10.1109/DigitalHeritage.2015.7419576

Encyclopaedia Britannica. (2017). *Virtual museum*. Retrieved from https://www.britannica.com/topic/virtual-museum

Engeström, J. (2005). Why some social network services work and others don't — Or: The case for object-centered sociality | locative lab. Retrieved from https://locativelab.wordpress.com/2006/11/08/why-some-social-network-services-work-and-others-dont-—-or-the-case-for-object-centered-sociality/

Engum, S. A., Jeffries, P., & Fisher, L. (2003). Intravenous catheter training system: Computer-based education versus traditional learning methods. *American Journal of Surgery, 186*(1), 67–74. doi:10.1016/S0002-9610(03)00109-0 PMID:12842753

Ergül, Ş. (2011). Türkiye'de Yükseköğretimde Hemşirelik Eğitimi (Higher education of nursing education in Turkey). [Journal of Higher Education and Science]. *Yükseköğretim ve Bilim Dergisi, 1*(3), 152–155.

ETSI. (2018). *AR and VR at Glance*. Available at https://www.etsi.org/images/files/ETSITechnologyLeaflets/Augmented_VirtualReality.pdf

ETT SpA (developer), Zètema Progetto Cultura (organizer), & Roma Capitale, Assessorato alla Crescita culturale - Sovrintendenza Capitolina ai Beni Culturali (promoter) (2016). *L'Ara com'era*. Retrieved from http://www.arapacis.it/it/mostre_ed_eventi/eventi/l_ara_com_era

Etxeberria, A. I., Asensio, M., Vicent, N., & Cuenca, J. M. (2012). Mobile devices: A tool for tourism and learning at archaeological sites. *International Journal of Web Based Communities*, *8*(1), 57–72. doi:10.1504/IJWBC.2012.044682

Farago, J. (2017, Feb. 3). Virtual reality has arrived in the art world. Now what? *The New York Times,* Retrieved from https://www.nytimes.com/2017/2002/2003/arts/design/virtual-reality-has-arrived-in-the-art-world-now-what.html

Farshid, M., Paschen, J., Eriksson, T., & Kietzmann, J. (2018). Go boldly!: Explore augmented reality (AR), virtual reality (VR), and mixed reality (MR) for business. *Business Horizons*, *61*(5), 657–663. doi:10.1016/j.bushor.2018.05.009

Ferguson, C., Davidson, P. M., Scott, P. J., Jackson, D., & Hickman, L. (2015). Augmented reality, virtual reality and gaming: An integral part of nursing. *Contemporary Nurse*, *51*(1), 1–4. doi:10.1080/10376178.2015.1130360 PMID:26678947

Ferrari, F., & Medici, M. (2017). The virtual experience for cultural heritage: methods and tools comparison for Geguti Palace in Kutaisi, Georgia. In *Proceedings of the International and Interdisciplinary Conference IMMAGINI? Image and Imagination between Representation, Communication, Education and Psychology*, *1*, 932.

Fish, S. (1980). *Is there a text in this class? The authority of interpretive communities*. Cambridge, UK: Harvard University Press.

Floridi, L. (2014). *The fourth revolution - How the infosphere is reshaping human reality*. Oxford, UK: Oxford University Press.

Flusser, V. (2000). *Towards a philosophy of photography*. London, UK: Reaktion Books.

Foa, E. B., Hembree, E. A., & Rothbaum, B. O. (2007). *Treatments that Work. Prolonged Exposure Therapy for PTSD: Emotional Processing of Traumatic Experiences: Therapist Guide*. New York, NY, US: Oxford University Press; doi:10.1093/med:psych/9780195308501.001.0001

Fondazione Achille Castiglioni. (2014). *La fondazione*. Retrieved from http://fondazioneachillecastiglioni.it/la-fondazione/

Fontcuberta, J. (2018). La furia delle immagini. Torino, Italy: Einaudi.

Forbes, T., Kinnell, P., & Goh, M. (2018, Aug. 17). *A study into the influence of visual prototyping methods and immersive technologies on the perception of abstract product properties*. Paper presented at the NordDesign: Design in the era of digitalization, NordDesign 2018.

Foronda, C. L., Alfes, C. M., Dev, P., Kleinheksel, A. J., Nelson, D. A. Jr, O'Donnell, J. M., & Samosky, J. T. (2017). Virtually nursing: Emerging technologies in nursing education. *Nurse Educator*, *42*(1), 14–17. doi:10.1097/NNE.0000000000000295 PMID:27454054

Fowler, C. (2015). Virtual reality and learning: Where is the pedagogy? *British Journal of Educational Technology*, *46*(2), 412–422. doi:10.1111/bjet.12135

Freedberg, D., & Gallese, V. (2007). Motion, emotion and empathy in aesthetic experience. *Trends in Cognitive Sciences*, *11*(5), 197–203. Retrieved from http://www.unipr.it/arpa/mirror/pubs/pdffiles/Gallese/Freedberg-Gallese%202007.pdf. doi:10.1016/j.tics.2007.02.003 PMID:17347026

Freeman, J. P. (2018, April 26). Word wise: Augmented reality. InsideSources.com, Retrieved from https://www.insidesources.com/word-wise-augmented-reality/

Freina, L., & Ott, M. (2015). A literature review on immersive virtual reality in education: State of the art and perspectives. In I. Roceanu, F. Moldoveanu, S. Trausan-Matu, D. Barbieru, D. Beligan, & A. Ionita (Eds.), *Proceedings of the International Scientific Conference e-learning and Software for Education (eLSE 2015), Rethinking education by leveraging the eLearning pillar of the Digital Agenda for Europe!* (Vol. 1, pp. 133-141). "Carol I" National Defence University, Bucharest, Hungary.

Freina, L., & Ott, M. (2015). *A literature review on immersive virtual reality in education: state of the art and perspectives.* In The International Scientific Conference eLearning and Software for Education (Vol. 1, p. 133).

Freitas, S. d., Rebolledo-Mendez, G., Liarokapis, F., Magoulas, G., & Poulovassilis, A. (2009). Developing an evaluation methodology for immersive learning experiences in a virtual world. In *Proceedings of the Conference in Games and Virtual Worlds for Serious Applications*. 10.1109/VS-GAMES.2009.41

Frey, C. B., & Osborne, M. A. (2017). The future of employment: How susceptible are jobs to computerisation? *Technological Forecasting and Social Change, 114*, 254–280. doi:10.1016/j.techfore.2016.08.019

Frijda, N. H. (2007). *The laws of emotion.* Mahwah, NJ, US: Lawrence Erlbaum Associates Publishers.

Gaba, D. (2004). The future of simulation in healthcare. *Quality & Safety in Health Care, 13*(suppl_1), 2–10. doi:10.1136/qshc.2004.009878 PMID:14757786

Gadamer, H. G. (1983). *Verità e Metodo.* Milano, Italy: Bompiani.

Galatis, P., Gavalas, D., Kasapakis, V., Pantziou, G., & Zaroliagis, C. (2016). Mobile augmented reality guides in cultural heritage. In *Proceedings of the 8th EAI International Conference on Mobile Computing* (pp. 11–19). Cambridge, UK: Applications and Services; doi:10.4108/eai.30-11-2016.2266954

Galimberti, U. (2009). I miti del nostro tempo. Milano, IT: Feltrinelli.

Gallegati, M. (2014). Il turismo culturale nelle Marche: dalle città d'arte ai centri culturali minori. In P. Alessandrini (Ed.), *RAPPORTO MARCHE +20 SVILUPPO NUOVO SENZA FRATTURE. Regione Marche.*

Gao, Q. H., Wan, T. R., Tang, W., & Chen, L. (2017). A stable and accurate marker-less augmented reality registration method. In *Proceedings - 2017 International Conference on Cyberworlds, CW 2017 - in cooperation with: Eurographics Association International Federation for Information Processing ACM SIGGRAPH.* 10.1109/CW.2017.44

Garau, C., & Ilardi, E. (2014). The "non-places" meet the "places:" Virtual tours on smartphones for the enhancement of cultural heritage. *Journal of Urban Technology, 21*(1), 79–91. doi:10.1080/10630732.2014.884384

Gardner, H. (2006). *Five Minds for the Future.* Boston, MA: Harvard Business School Press.

Gardner, H., & Hatch, T. (1989). Multiple intelligences go to school: Educational implications of the theory of multiple intelligences. *Educational Researcher, 18*(8), 4–9.

Gargalakos, M., Giallouri, E., Lazoudis, A., Sotiriou, S., & Bogner, F. X. (2011). Assessing the impact of technology-enhanced field trips in science centers and museums. *Advanced Science Letters, 4*(11-12), 3332–3341. doi:10.1166/asl.2011.2043

Gazit, E., Yair, Y., & Chen, D. (2006). The gain and pain in taking the pilot seat: Learning dynamics in a non-immersive virtual solar system. *Virtual Reality (Waltham Cross), 10*(3-4), 271–282. doi:10.100710055-006-0053-3

GearBrain (GB). (2018, June 4). The 5 best museum AR/VR experiences this summer. GearBrain (GB). Retrieved from https://www.gearbrain.com/virtual-reality-museum-art-summer-2577767924.html

Gedeon, C. (2015, Oct. 7). A selfie was taken in virtual reality and no one seems to be bothered. *Medium*. Retrieved from https://medium.com/@charlesgedeon/a-selfie-was-taken-in-virtual-reality-and-no-one-seems-to-be-bothered-bc9162a73571

Gee, J. P. (2004). *Situated language and learning: a critique of traditional schooling*. London, UK: Routledge.

Gegenfurtner, A., Lehtinen, E., & Säljö, R. (2011). Expertise differences in the comprehension of visualizations: A meta-analysis of eye-tracking research in professional domains. *Educational Psychology Review*, *23*(4), 523–552. doi:10.100710648-011-9174-7

Giannella, S., & Cuoghi, M. (2013). *A Parma, studiando i neuroni, hanno capito perché il bello e il buono accendono il nostro cervello*. Retrieved from https://www.giannellachannel.info/neuroni-specchio-parma-perche-bello-e-buono-accendono-cervello/

Giannella, S. (2014). *Operazione Salvataggio. Gli eroi sconosciuti che hanno salvato l'arte dalle guerre*. Milano, Italy: Chiarelettere.

Giannella, S., & Mandelli, P. D. (1999). *L'Arca dell'Arte, Cassina de' Pecchi (Milano)*. Italia: Editoriale Delfi.

Gimeno, J. J., Portalés, C., Coma, I., Fernández, M., & Martínez, B. (2017). *Combining traditional and indirect augmented reality for indoor crowded environments. A case study on the Casa Batlló museum. Computers and Graphics*. Pergamon; doi:10.1016/j.cag.2017.09.001

Glaser, B. G., & Strauss, A. L. (1965) Awareness of Dying, Chicago, Usa: Aldine Publishing Company

Gökoğlu, S., & Çakıroğlu, Ü. (2019). Measurement of presence in virtual reality based learning environments: Adapting the presence scale to Turkish. *Education Technology: Theory and Practice*, *9*(1), 169–188.

Goldstein, C. (2018). 8 Instagram-ready art attractions that prove the museum of ice cream was just the beginning | Artnet News. Retrieved from https://news.artnet.com/art-world/the-children-of-the-museum-of-ice-cream-1258058

Gömleksiz, M. N., & Kan, A. Ü. (2012). Affective dimension in education and affective learning. Turkish Studies-International Periodical for the Languages. *Literature and History of Turkish or Turkic*, *7*(1), 1159–1177.

Gonizzi Barsanti, S., Caruso, G., Micoli, L. L., Covarrubias Rodriguez, M., & Guidi, G. (2015). 3D visualization of cultural heritage artefacts with virtual reality devices. *The International Archives of Photogrammetry, Remote Sensing, and Spatial Information Sciences*, *40*(5), 165–172. doi:10.5194/isprsarchives-XL-5-W7-165-2015

Goodwin, M. S., Wiltshire, T., & Fiore, S. M. (2015). Applying research in the cognitive sciences to the design and delivery of instruction in virtual reality learning environments. In *Proceedings of the International Conference on Virtual, Augmented and Mixed Reality*. 10.1007/978-3-319-21067-4_29

Google ARcore. (n.d.). Retrieved from https://developers.google.com/ar/discover/

Gore, T. N., & Loice, L. (2014). Creating effective simulation environments. In B. Ulric & B. Mancini (Eds.), *Mastering simulation: a handbook for success* (pp. 49–86). USA: Sigma Theta Tau International.

Gorman, L. M., & Sultan, D. F. (2007). *Psychosocial nursing for general patient care* (3rd ed.). Philadelphia, PA: F. A. Davis.

Goss, J., Kollmann, E., Reich, C., & Iacovelli, S. (2015). Understanding the multilingualism and communication of museum visitors who are deaf or hard of hearing, *Museums and Social Issues 10. Google Tango Documentation*. Retrieved from https://web.archive.org/web/20170714191228/https://developers.google.com/tango/apis/unity/

Govers, C. P. M. (1996). What and how about quality function deployment (QFD). *International Journal of Production Economics, 46-47*, 575–585. doi:10.1016/0925-5273(95)00113-1

Graafland, M., Schraagen, J., & Schijven, M. P. (2012). Systematic review of serious games for medical education and surgical skills training. *British Journal of Surgery, 99*(10), 1322–1330. doi:10.1002/bjs.8819 PMID:22961509

Grady, C., Danis, M., Soeken, K. L., O'Donnell, P., Taylor, C., Farrar, A., & Ulrich, C. M. (2008). Does ethics education influence the moral action of practicing nurses and social workers? *The American Journal of Bioethics, 8*(4), 4–11. doi:10.1080/15265160802166017 PMID:18576241

Grajewskia, D., Górskia, F., Hamrola, A., & Zawadzkia, P. (2015). Immersive and haptic educational simulations of assembly workplace conditions. *Procedia Computer Science, 75*, 359–368. doi:10.1016/j.procs.2015.12.258

Grassi, M., Morbidoni, C., Nucci, M., Fonda, S., Piazza, F. (2013). Pundit: Augmenting web contents with semantics. *Literary and Linguistic Computing, 28*(4), art. no. fqt060, pp. 640-659.

Grau, O. (2003). *From illusion to immersion*. Cambridge, MA: MIT Press.

Greenwald, W. (2018). *The best VR headsets of 2018*. Available at https://in.pcmag.com/consumer-electronics/101251/the-best-vr-virtual-reality-headsets

Grilli, E., Dininno, D., Petrucci, G., & Remondinoa, F. (2018). From 2D to 3D supervised segmentation and classification for cultural heritage applications. In International Archives of the Photogrammetry, Remote Sensing and Spatial Information Sciences - ISPRS Archives. doi:10.5194/isprs-archives-XLII-2-399-2018

Grinter, R. E., Aoki, P. M., Szymanski, M. H., Thornton, J. D., Woodruff, A., & Hurst, A. (2002). Revisiting the visit: In *Proceedings of the 2002 ACM Conference on Computer Supported Cooperative Work - CSCW '02* (p. 146). New York, NY: ACM Press. doi:10.1145/587078.587100

Griol, D., Sanchis, A., Molina, J. M., Callejas, Z. (2019). Developing enhanced conversational agents for social virtual worlds, *Neurocomputing, 354*, 27-40.

Griziotti, G. (2012). Bring your own device. *Uninomade 2.0*. Retrieved from http://www.uninomade.org/bring-your-own-device

Griziotti, G. (2013). Sotto il regime della precarietà. Bring your own device. In G. Griziotti (Ed.), *Bioipermedia Moltitudini Connesse, Alfabeta2, 29(2)*.

Groff, J., McCall, J., Darvasi, P., & Gilbert, Z. (2015). Using games in the classroom. in K. Schoenfield (Ed.), Learning, education and games Vol. 2: Bringing games into educational contexts (pp. 19-41). Pittsburgh, PA: ETC Press.

Groff, J., Howells, C., & Cranmer, S. (2010). *The impact of console games in the classroom: Evidence from schools in Scotland*. UK: Futurelab.

Guazzaroni, G. (2012). *Experiential Mapping of Museum Augmented Places – Using Mobile Devices for Learning*. Saarbrücken, D: LAP.

Guazzaroni, G. (2013). The ritual and the rhythm: Interacting with augmented reality, visual poetry and storytelling across the streets of scattered L'Aquila. *eLearning Papers on Design for Learning Spaces and Innovative Classrooms* (34).

Guazzaroni, G., & Compagno, M. (2013). AR moulded-objects performing Giuseppe Verdi's 200th birthday. In Archeomatica, 4, 38-41.

Guazzaroni, G., & Leo, T. (2011). *Emotional Mapping of a Place of Interest Using Mobile Devices for Learning.* In I. Arnedillo Sánchez, & P. Isaías (Eds.) *Proceedings of IADIS International Conference on Mobile Learning* (pp. 277-281) Avila, E.

Guidi, G., & Russo, M. (2011). Diachronic 3D Reconstruction for Lost Cultural Heritage. In 3D Virtual Reconstruction and Visualization of Complex Architectures (3D ARCH) (pp. 371–376). Trento, Italy. doi:10.5194/isprsarchives-XXXVIII-5-W16-371-2011

Guo, C., Deng, H., & Yang, J. (2014). Effect of virtual reality distraction on pain among patients with hand injury undergoing dressing change. *Journal of Clinical Nursing, 24*(1), 115–120. PMID:24899241

Gutierrez, J. M., Molinero, M. A., Soto-Martín, O., & Medina, C. R. (2015). Augmented reality technology spreads information about historical graffiti in Temple of Debod. *Procedia Computer Science, 75*, 390–397. doi:10.1016/j.procs.2015.12.262

Guttentag, D. A. (2010). Virtual reality: Applications and implications for tourism. *Tourism Management, 31*(5), 637–651. doi:10.1016/j.tourman.2009.07.003

Hacıalioğlu, N. (2011). Basic concepts of education and training. In N. Hacıalioğlu (Ed.), *Nursing teaching in learning and education* (pp. 10–17). Istanbul, Turkey: Nobel Medical Bookstores.

Hall, T., Ciolfi, L., Bannon, L., Fraser, M., Benford, S., & Bowers, J., … Flintham, M. (2002). The visitor as virtual archaeologist: Explorations in mixed reality technology to enhance educational and social interaction in the museum. In *Virtual Reality, Archaeology, and Cultural Heritage.* Glyfada, Greece: ACM SIGGRAPH. Retrieved from http://www.disappearing-computer.net/

Hamacher, A., Kim, S. J., Cho, S. T., Pardeshi, S., Lee, S. H., Eun, S. J., & Whangbo, T. K. (2016). Application of virtual, augmented, and mixed reality to urology. *International Neurourology Journal, 20*(3), 172.

Hammady, R., Ma, M., & Temple, N. (2016). Augmented reality and gamification in heritage museums live brain-computer cinema performance view project automatic conversion of natural language to 3D animation view project. In *International Conference on Serious Games* (pp. 181–190). Brisbane, Australia. Berlin, Germany: Springer-Verlag. 10.1007/978-3-319-45841-0_17

Hammer, M. R., Bennett, M. J., & Wiseman, R. (2003). Measuring intercultural sensitivity: The intercultural development inventory. [Special Training Issue.]. *International Journal of Intercultural Relations, 27*(4), 421–443. doi:10.1016/S0147-1767(03)00032-4

Han, B.-C. (2015). *The transparency society.* Palo Alto, CA: Stanford UP.

Han, B.-C. (2017a). *In the swarm: digital prospects.* Boston, MA: MIT Press.

Han, B.-C. (2017b). *Saving beauty.* Cambridge, UK: Polity Press.

Hanson, K., & Shelton, B. E. (2008). Design and development of virtual reality: analysis of challenges faced by educators. *Journal of Educational Technology & Society, 11*(1), 118–131.

Hanson, K., & Shelton, B. E. (2008). Design and development of virtual reality: Analysis of challenges faced by educators. *Journal of Educational Technology & Society, 11*(1), 118–131.

Haubruck, P., Nickel, F., Ober, J., Walker, T., Bergdolt, C., Friedrich, M., ... Tanner, M. C. (2018). Evaluation of app-based serious gaming as a training method in teaching chest tube insertion to medical students: Randomized controlled trial. *Journal of Medical Internet Research, 20*(5), e195. doi:10.2196/jmir.9956

Hendriks, I., Meiland, F. J. M., Slotwinska, K., Kroeze, R., Weinstein, H., Gerritsen, D. L., & Dröes, R. M. (2018). How do people with dementia respond to different types of art? An explorative study into interactive museum programs. *International Psychogeriatrics*. doi:10.10171041610218001266 PMID:30560737

Herron, J. (2016). Augmented reality in medical education and training. *Journal of Electronic Resources in Medical Libraries, 13*(2), 51–55. doi:10.1080/15424065.2016.1175987

Hersko-Ronatas, A. (2017). *Presence in Virtual Reality*. Retrieved from https://blogs.brown.edu/gaspee/presence-in-virtual-reality/

Hertz, A. M., George, E. I., Vaccaro, C. M., & Brand, T. C. (2018). Head-to-head comparison of three virtual-reality robotic surgery simulators. JSLS. *Journal of the Society of Laparoendoscopic Surgeons, 22*(1). doi:10.4293/JSLS.2017.00081

He, Z., Wu, L., & Li, X . (2018). When art meets tech: The role of augmented reality in enhancing museum experiences and purchase intentions. *Tourism Management*. doi:10.1016/j.tourman.2018.03.003

Higgett, N., Chen, Y., & Tatham, E. (2016). A user experience evaluation of the use of augmented and virtual reality in visualising and interpreting Roman Leicester 210AD (Ratae Corieltavorum). *Athens Journal of History, 2*(1), 1–7. doi:10.30958/ajhis.2-1-1

Hin, L. T. W., Subramaniam, R., & Aggarwal, A. K. (2003). Virtual science centers: a new genre of learning in Web-based promotion of science education. In *36th Annual Hawaii International Conference on System Sciences* (p. 10). Big Island, HI: IEEE. doi:10.1109/HICSS.2003.1174346

Hlova, M. (2018). *What does it take to develop a VR solution in healthcare*. Digital Health. Available at https://www.mddionline.com/what-does-it-take-develop-vr-solution-healthcare

Holopainen, J., & Björk, S. (2003). *Game design patterns*. Lecture Notes for GDC.

Hooper-Greenhill, E. (2007). Interpretative communities, strategies and repertoires. In S. Watson (Ed.), *Museum and their communities* (pp. 76–94). Abingdon, UK: Routledge.

Horvitz, E. J., Breese, J. S., & Henrion, M. (1988). Decision theory in expert systems and artificial intelligence. *International Journal of Approximate Reasoning, 2*(3), 247–302. doi:10.1016/0888-613X(88)90120-X

Hsu, C. Y., Tsai, M. J., Chang, Y. H., & Liang, J. C. (2017). Surveying in-service teachers' beliefs about game-based learning and perceptions of technological pedagogical and content knowledge of games. *Journal of Educational Technology & Society, 20*(1), 134–143.

Hu, H. Z., Feng, X. B., Shao, Z. W., Xie, M., Xu, S., Wu, X. H., & Ye, Z. W. (2019). Application and Prospect of Mixed Reality Technology in Medical Field. *Current medical science, 39*(1), 1-6. https://doi.org/ doi:10.100711596-019-1992-8

Huang, H.-M., Rauch, U., & Liaw, S.-S. (2010). Investigating learners' attitudes toward virtual reality learning environments: Based on a constructivist approach. *Computers & Education, 55*(3), 1171–1182. doi:10.1016/j.compedu.2010.05.014

Huang, T. K., Yang, C. H., Hsieh, Y. H., Wang, J. C., & Hung, C. C. (2018). Augmented reality (AR) and virtual reality (VR) applied in dentistry. *The Kaohsiung Journal of Medical Sciences, 34*(4), 243–248.

Hu-Au, E., & Lee, J. (2018). Virtual reality in education: A tool for learning in the experience age. *International Journal of Innovation in Education, 4*(4), 215–226. doi:10.1504/IJIIE.2017.10012691

Humfrey. (1997). Lorenzo Lotto. Yale University Press.

Hunter, A. (2015). *Vergence-accommodation conflict is a bitch — here's how to design around it*. Available from vrinflux-dot-com/vergence-accommodation-conflict-is-a-bitch-here-s-how-to-design-around-it.

Hussain, Z., & Pearson, C. (2016). *Smartphone addiction and associated psychological factors.* Turkish Green Crescent Society.

ICOM. (2007). Development of the museum definition according to ICOM statutes (1946 - 2001). Retrieved from http://archives.icom.museum/hist_def_eng.html

IDC. (2017, Feb. 27). Worldwide spending on augmented and virtual reality forecast to reach $13.9 billion in 2017, according to IDC. Retrieved from https://www.idc.com/getdoc.jsp?containerId=prUS42331217)

International Data Corporation (IDC). (2018, Sept. 20). AR/VR headset shipments worldwide, commercial vs. consumer, 2018 & 2022 (millions and CAGR). eMarketer.com. Retrieved from http://totalaccess.emarketer.com/chart.aspx?r=222930

Interreg Europe Policy Learning Platform on Environment and resource efficiency. (2018). Digital solutions in the field of cultural heritage. A Policy Brief from the Policy Learning Platform on Environment and resource efficiency, (August), 12.

Ioannides, M., Fink, E., Brumana, R., Patias, P., Doulamis, A., Martins, J., & Wallace, M. (2018). Digital heritage. In *Proceedings Progress in Cultural Heritage: Documentation, Preservation, and Protection 7th International Conference,* EuroMed 2018, Nicosia, Cyprus, Oct. 29–Nov. 3, 2018, Part II.

İsmailoğlu, E. G., & Zaybak, A. (2018). Comparison of the effectiveness of a virtual simulator with a plastic arm model in teaching intravenous catheter insertion skills. *Computers, Informatics, Nursing, 36*(2), 98–105. doi:10.1097/CIN.0000000000000405 PMID:29176359

Iyer, B. (2015, December/2016, January). Augmented-reality gallery enhances Singapore sights. *Campaign Asia-Pacific,* p. 31.

Izard, S. G., Juanes, J. A., García Peñalvo, F. J., Gonçalves Estella, J., Sánchez-Ledesma, M. J., & Ruisoto, P. (2018). Virtual reality as an educational and training tool for medicine. *Journal of Medical Systems, 50*(42), 50–54. doi:10.100710916-018-0900-2 PMID:29392522

Izzo, F. (2017). Museum customer experience and virtual reality: H. Bosch Exhibition case study. *Modern Economy, 08*(04), 531–536. doi:10.4236/me.2017.84040

Jamison, R. J., Hovancsek, M. T., & Clochesy, J. M. (2006). A pilot study assessing simulation using two simulation methods for teaching intravenous cannulation. *Clinical Simulation in Nursing, 2*(1), e9–e12. doi:10.1016/j.ecns.2009.05.007

Jarmon, L., Traphagan, T., Mayrath, M., & Trivedi, A. (2009). Virtual world teaching, experiential learning, and assessment: An interdisciplinary communication course in Second Life. *Computers & Education, 53*(1), 169–182. doi:10.1016/j.compedu.2009.01.010

Jarrier, E., & Bourgeon-Renault, D. (2012, Fall). Impact of mediation devices on the museum visit experience and on visitors' behavioural intentions. International Journal of Arts Management, 15(1), 18–29.

Javornik, A. (2016). Augmented reality: Research agenda for studying the impact of its media characteristics on consumer behaviour. Journal of Retailing and Consumer Services, 30, 252–261.

Jenson, C. E., & Forsyth, D. M. (2012). Virtual reality simulation: Using three-dimensional technology to teach nursing students. *CIN: Computers, Informatics, Nursing, 30*(6), 312–318. PMID:22411409

Jin, W., Birckhead, B., Perez, B., & Hoffe, S. (2017, December). *Augmented and virtual reality: Exploring a future role in radiation oncology education and training. applied radiation oncology.* Available at https://appliedradiationoncology.com/articles/augmented-and-virtual-reality-exploring-a-future-role-in-radiation-oncology-education-and-training

Johnson, J., Culverwell, A., Hulbert, S., Robertson, M., & Camic, P. M. (2017). Museum activities in dementia care: Using visual analog scales to measure subjective wellbeing. *Dementia (London)*, *16*(5), 591–610. doi:10.1177/1471301215611763 PMID:26468054

Johnson, L. F., & Levine, A. H. (2008). Virtual worlds: Inherently immersive, highly social learning spaces. *Theory into Practice*, *47*(2), 161–170. doi:10.1080/00405840801992397

Jonassen, D. H. (1999). Designing constructivist learning environments. In C. M. Reigeluth (Ed.), Instructional-design theories and models: a new paradigm of instructional theory (Vol. 2, pp. 215-239). New Jersey: Lawrence Erlbaum Associates.

Jones-Garmil, K. (1997). *The wired museum: emerging technology and changing paradigms, (1997).* Washington, DC: American Association of Museums.

Jones, J., & Christal, M. (2002). *The future of virtual museums: On-line, immersive, 3D environments.* Created Realities Group.

Jong, M. S. Y., Shang, J., Lee, F., & Lee, J. H. M. (2010). An evaluative study on VISOLE—virtual interactive student-oriented learning environment. *IEEE Transactions on Learning Technologies*, *3*(4), 307–318. doi:10.1109/TLT.2010.34

José López, F., Martin Lerones, P., Llamas, J., Gómez-García-Bermejo, J., & Zalama, E. (2018). Semi-automatic generation of bim models for cultural heritage. *International Journal of Heritage Architecture: Studies, Repairs, and Maintenance.* doi:10.2495/ha-v2-n2-293-302

Jöud, A., Sandholm, A., Alseby, L., Petersson, G., & Nilsson, G. (2010). Feasibility of a computerized male urethral catheterization simulator. *Nurse Education in Practice*, *10*(2), 70–75. doi:10.1016/j.nepr.2009.03.017 PMID:19443272

Jung, T., Dieck, M. C., Lee, H., & Chung, N. (2016). Effects of virtual reality and augmented reality on visitor experiences in museum. In Information and Communication Technologies in Tourism 2016. doi:10.1007/978-3-319-28231-2_45

Kaddoura, M., VanDyke, O., Cheng, B., & Shea-Foisy, K. (2016). Impact of concept mapping on the development of clinical judgment skills in nursing students. *Teaching and Learning in Nursing*, *11*(3), 101–107. doi:10.1016/j.teln.2016.02.001

Kaleci, D., Tepe, T., & Tüzün, H. (2017). Üç Boyutlu Sanal Gerçeklik Ortamlarındaki Deneyimlere İlişkin Kullanıcı Görüşleri (Users' opinions of experiences in three dimensional virtual reality environments). [Turkish Journal of Social Sciences]. *Türkiye Sosyal Araştırmalar Dergisi*, *21*(3), 669–689.

Kamarudin, M. F. B., & Zary, N. (2019, April). Augmented reality, virtual reality, and mixed reality in medical education: A comparative web of science scoping review. doi:10.20944/preprints201904.0323.v1

Kang, Y. W. (2019). The applications of digital reality in creative and oceanic cultural industries: The case of Taiwan. In K. C. C. Yang (Ed.), Cases on immersive virtual reality techniques (pp. 269-296). Hershey, PA: IGI Global.

Karaman, M. K., & Özen, S. O. (2016). A survey of students' experiences on collaborative virtual learning activities based on the five-stage model. *Journal of Educational Technology & Society*, *19*(3), 247–259.

Karaöz, S. (2003). An overview of clinical teaching in nursing and recommendations for effective clinical teaching. *Journal of Research and Development in Nursing*, *5*(1), 15–21.

Kardong-Edgren, S. S., Farra, S. L., Alinier, G., & Young, H. M. (2019). A call to unify definitions of virtual reality. *Clinical Simulation in Nursing*, *31*, 28–34. doi:10.1016/j.ecns.2019.02.006

Kardong-Edgren, S., Lungstrom, N., & Bendel, R. (2009). VitalSim® Versus SimMan®: A comparison of BSN student test scores, knowledge retention and satisfaction. *Clinical Simulation in Nursing, 5*(3), e105–e111. doi:10.1016/j.ecns.2009.01.007

Kargas, A., Loumos, G., & Varoutas, D. (2019). Using different ways of 3D reconstruction of historical cities for gaming purposes: The case study of Nafplio. *Heritage, 2*(3), 1799–1811. doi:10.3390/heritage2030110

Kaufmann, H., Schmalstieg, D., & Wagner, M. (2000). Construct3D: A virtual reality application for mathematics and geometry education. *Education and Information Technologies, 5*(4), 263–276. doi:10.1023/A:1012049406877

Kavanagh, S., Luxton-Reilly, A., Wuensche, B., & Plimmer, B. (2017). A systematic review of virtual reality in education. *Themes in Science and Technology Education, 10*(2), 85–119.

Keeler, A. (2015). *Gamification: engaging the students with narrative* (pp. 1–3). Edutopia; Retrieved from www.edutopia.org/blog/gamification-engaging-students-with-narrative-alice-keeler

Kenderdine, S. (2007b). The irreducible ensemble: Place-Hampi. In *Selected Proceedings, 13th Annual Virtual System and Multimedia Conference*, Brisbane, Lecture Notes in Computer Science: Springer Berlin/Heidelberg, pp. 58-67.

Kenderdine, S. (2013). *How will museums of the future look?* TEDx Talks. Retrieved from https://www.youtube.com/watch?v=VXhtwFCA_Kc

Kenderdine, S. (2013). Theatre, archaeology and new media. In S. Kenderdine (Ed.), Place-Hampi, Inhabiting the panoramic imaginary of Vijayanagara. Berlin Heidelberg, Germany: Kehrer Verlag, 223.

Kenderdine, S., Schreibman, S., Siemens, R., & Unsworth, J. (2015). Embodiment, entanglement, and immersion in digital cultural heritage. In S. Schreibman, R. Simens, & J. Unsworth (Eds.), A new companion to digital humanities, Chichester, UK.

Kenderdine, S. (2007a), Somatic solidarity, magical realism and animating popular gods: PLACE-Hampi where intensities are felt. In E. Banissi, & ... (Eds.), *Proceedings of 11th European Information Visualisation Conference, IV07*, July 3-7, Zurich, Switzerland: IEEE, 402-408. 10.1109/IV.2007.103

Kersten, T. P., Keller, F., Saenger, J., & Schiewe, J. (2012). *Automated generation of an historic 4D city model of Hamburg and its visualisation with the GE engine* (pp. 55–65). Berlin, Germany: Springer; doi:10.1007/978-3-642-34234-9_6

Kevin, F., & McCarthy, K. J. (2001). *A new framework for building participation in the arts*. Rand; doi:10.3102/0013189X030007010

Khalifa, Y. M., Bogorad, D., Gibson, V., Peifer, J., & Nussbaum, J. (2006). Virtual reality in ophthalmology training. *Survey of Ophthalmology, 51*(3), 259–273. doi:10.1016/j.survophthal.2006.02.005 PMID:16644366

KhannaA. (2019). *EyeSim*. Available at https://www.eonreality.com/portfolio-items/eyesim- ophthalmology/

Khanna, A., & Khanna, P. (2012). *Hybrid reality: thriving in the emerging human-technology civilization*. TED Books.

Khelemsky, R., Hill, B., & Buchbinder, D. (2017). Validation of a novel cognitive simulator for orbital floor reconstruction. *Journal of Oral and Maxillofacial Surgery, 75*(4), 775–785.

Khorshid, L., Eşer, İ., Sarı, D., Zaybak, A., Yapucu, Ü., & Gürol, G. (2002). Hemşirelik öğrencilerinde invaziv ve invaziv olmayan işlemleri ilk kez yapmaya bağlı korku semptom ve belirtilerinin incelenmesi (The examination of the fear symptoms and signs while performing first invasive and noninvasive nursing procedures in nursing student). [Journal of Anatolian Nursing and Health Sciences]. *Anadolu Hemşirelik ve Sağlık Bilimleri Dergisi, 5*(2), 1–10.

Khor, W. S., Baker, B., Amin, K., Chan, A., Patel, K., & Wong, J. (2016). Augmented and virtual reality in surgery—the digital surgical environment: Applications, limitations and legal pitfalls. *Annals of Translational Medicine, 4*(23), 454. doi:10.21037/atm.2016.12.23

Kiang, D. (2014, Oct. 14). *"Edutopia", Using gaming principles to engage students.* Retrieved from **www.edutopia. org/blog/using-gaming-principles-engage-students-douglas-kiang**

Kim, A. J. (2014). Innovate with game thinking, Amy Jo Kim, Jan. 15. Retrieved from http://amyjokim.com/blog/2014/02/28/ beyond-player-types-kims-social-action-matrix

Kim, A. J. (2014). *Innovate with game thinking.* Retrieved from http://amyjokim.com/blog/2014/02/28/beyond-player-types-kims-social-action-matrix

Kim, K., Hwang, J., Zo, H., & Lee, H. (2016). Understanding users' continuance intention toward smartphone augmented reality applications. Information Development, 32(2), 161–174.

Kim, S. L., Suk, H. J., Kang, J. H., Jung, J. M., Laine, T. H., & Westlin, J. (2014). Using unity 3D to facilitate mobile augmented reality game development. In *2014 IEEE World Forum on Internet of Things (WF-IoT)* (pp. 21–26). IEEE. doi:10.1109/WF-IoT.2014.6803110

Kim, Y., Kim, H., & Kim, Y. O. (2017). Virtual reality and augmented reality in plastic surgery: a review. *Arch Plast Surg. 44*(3), 179–187. Published online. doi:10.5999/aps.2017.44.3.179

Kim, Y. R., & Park, M. S. (2018). Creating a virtual world for mathematics. *Journal of Education and Training Studies, 6*(12), 172. doi:10.11114/jets.v6i12.3601

Kim, Y., Glassman, M., & Williams, M. S. (2015). Connecting agents: Engagement and motivation in online collaboration. *Computers in Human Behavior, 49*(1), 333–342. doi:10.1016/j.chb.2015.03.015

Kingsley, T. L., & Grabner-Hagen, M. M. (2015). Gamification: Questing to integrate content, knowledge, literacy, and 21st-century learning. *Journal of Adolescent & Adult Literacy, 59*(1), 51–61. doi:10.1002/jaal.426

Kinney, J. M., & Rentz, C. A. (2005). Observed well-being among individuals with dementia: Memories in the Making©, an art program, versus other structured activity. *American Journal of Alzheimer's Disease and Other Dementias, 20*(4), 220–227. doi:10.1177/153331750502000406 PMID:16136845

Kıran, B., & Taşkıran, E. G. (2014). Overview of nursing education and manpower planning in Turkey. Mersin University School of Medicine. *Journal of History of Medicine and Folk Medicine, 5*(2), 62–68.

Kızıl, H., & Şendir, M. (2019). Innovative approaches in nursing education. *International Journal of Human Sciences, 16*(1), 118–125. doi:10.14687/5437

Kluszczyński, R. W. (Ed.). (2012). Wonderful life. Laurent Mignonneau & Christa Sommerer. LAZNIA Centre for Contemporary Art, Gdańsk.

Kluszczyński, R. W. (Ed.). (2016). Patrick Tresset: Human traits and the art of creative machines. LAZNIA Centre for Contemporary Art, Gdańsk.

Koehl, M., Schneider, A., Fritsch, E., Fritsch, F., Rachedi, A., & Guillemin, S. (2013). Documentation of historical building via Virtual Tour: The complex building of baths in Strasbourg. *The International Archives of the Photogrammetry, Remote Sensing and Spatial Information Sciences, XL-5*(W2), 385–390. doi:10.5194/isprsarchives-XL-5-W2-385-2013

Kokkalia, G., Drigas, A., Economou, A., Roussos, P., & Choli, S. (2017). Paper-the use of serious games in preschool education the use of serious games in preschool education Spyridoula Choli. [IJET]. *International Journal of Emerging Technologies in Learning*, *12*(11), 15–27. doi:10.3991/ijet.v12i11.6991

Kolcu, G., Başaran, Ö., Sandal, G., Saygın, M., Aslankoç, R., Baş, F. Y., & Duran, B. E. (2017). Mesleki beceri eğitim düzeyi: Süleyman Demirel Üniversitesi tıp fakültesi deneyimi (Vocational skill education level: experience of the Süleyman Demirel University faculty of medicine). [Smyrna Medical Journal]. *Smyrna Tip Dergisi*, *3*, 7–14.

Konrath, S., O'Brien, E., & Hsing, C. (2011). Changes in dispositional empathy in American college students over time: A meta-analysis. *Personality and Social Psychology Review*, *15*(2), 180–198. doi:10.1177/1088868310377395 PMID:20688954

Korhan, E. A., Tokem, Y., Uzelli Yılmaz, D., & Dilemek, H. (2016). Hemşirelikte psikomotor beceri eğitiminde video destekli öğretim ve OSCE uygulaması: Bir deneyim paylaşımı (Video-Based teaching and OSCE implementation in nursing psychomotor skills education: Sharing of an experience). İzmir Katip Çelebi Üniversitesi Saglık Bilimleri Fakültesi Dergisi (İzmir Kâtip Çelebi University Faculty of Health Sciences Journal), 1(1), 35-37.

Korhan, E. A., Yılmaz, D. U., Ceylan, B., Akbıyık, A., & Tokem, Y. (2018). Hemsirelikte Psikomotor beceri ogretiminde senaryo temelli ogrenme: Bir Deneyim Paylasimi (Scenario based teaching in nursing psychomotor skills education: Sharing of an experience). Izmir Katip Celebi Universitesi Saglik Bilimleri Fakultesi Dergisi (İzmir Kâtip Çelebi University Faculty of Health Sciences Journal), 3(3), 11-16.

Kosowatz, J. (2017, May 1). *Mixed reality replaces cadavers as teaching tool.* Available at https://aabme.asme.org/posts/mixed-reality-replace-cadavers-as-teaching-tool

Krathwohl, D. R. (2002). A revision of Bloom's taxonomy: An overview. *Theory into Practice*, *41*(4), 212–218. doi:10.120715430421tip4104_2

Kraus, R. (2018, Oct. 25). A museum without walls: How the Met is bringing its ancient collection online. *Mashable.* Retrieved from https://mashable.com/article/the-met-museum-api/

Kuh, G. D. (2009). The national survey of student engagement: conceptual and empirical foundations, *New Directions for Institutional Research,* 141, pp. 5-20. doi:10.1002/ir.283

Kumar, B., & Khurana, P. (2012). Gamification in education: Learn computer programming with fun. *International Journal of Computers and Distributed Systems*, *2*(1), 46–53.

Kuzu-Kurban, N. (2015). Teaching in nursing and role of trainers. In S. Arslan & N. Kuzu-Kurban (Eds.), *Nurse Educator Becoming Process* (pp. 1–7). Ankara, Turkey: Anı Publications.

Kyaw, B. M., Saxena, N., Posadzki, P., Vseteckova, J., Nikolaou, C. K., George, P. P., ... Car, L. T. (2019). Virtual reality for health professions education: Systematic review and meta-analysis by the Digital Health Education collaboration. *Journal of Medical Internet Research*, *21*(1).

Kyaw, B. M., Saxena, N., Posadzki, P., Vseteckova, J., Nikolaou, C. K., George, P. P., ... Car, L. T. (2019). Virtual reality for health professions education: Systematic review and meta-analysis by the digital health education collaboration. *Journal of Medical Internet Research*, *21*(1). doi:10.2196/12959 PMID:30668519

Lancaster, R. J. (2014). Serious game simulation as a teaching strategy in pharmacology. *Clinical Simulation in Nursing*, *10*(3), 129–137. doi:10.1016/j.ecns.2013.10.005

Lau, K. W., & Lee, P. Y. (2015). The use of virtual reality for creating unusual environmental stimulation to motivate students to explore creative ideas. *Interactive Learning Environments*, *23*(1), 3–18. doi:10.1080/10494820.2012.745426

Laurel, B. (2004). *Design research: methods and perspectives*. Cambridge, MA: MIT Press.

Lave, J., & Wenger, E. (1991). *Situated Learning: Legitimate Peripheral Participation*. Cambridge, UK: Cambridge University Press. doi:10.1017/CBO9780511815355

Lee, E. A.-L., & Wong, K. W. (2014). Learning with desktop virtual reality: Low spatial ability learners are more positively affected. *Computers & Education, 79*, 49–58. doi:10.1016/j.compedu.2014.07.010

Lee, Y. Y., Choi, J., Ahmed, B., Kim, Y. H., Lee, J. H., & Son, M. G., ... Lee, K. H. (2015). A SAR-based interactive digital exhibition of Korean cultural artifacts. In *2015 Digital Heritage International Congress, Digital Heritage 2015*. 10.1109/DigitalHeritage.2015.7419591

Leite, W. L., Svinicki, M., & Shi, Y. (2010). Attempted validation of the scores of the VARK: Learning styles inventory with multitrait–multimethod confirmatory factor analysis models. *Educational and Psychological Measurement, 70*(2), 323–339. doi:10.1177/0013164409344507

Leone, S., Guazzaroni, G., Carletti, L., & Leo, T. (2010). The increasing need of validation of non-formal and informal learning. The case of the community of practice "WEBM.ORG". *Proceeding of IADIS International Conference on Cognition and Exploratory Learning in Digital Age* CELDA 2010, Timisoara.

Liang, H., Li, W., Lai, S., Zhu, L., Jiang, W., & Zhang, Q. (2018). The integration of terrestrial laser scanning and terrestrial and unmanned aerial vehicle digital photogrammetry for the documentation of Chinese classical gardens – A case study of Huanxiu Shanzhuang, Suzhou, China. *Journal of Cultural Heritage, 33*, 222–230. doi:10.1016/j.culher.2018.03.004

Liarokapis, F. (2002). *Augmented reality interfaces –architectures for visualising and interacting with virtual information*. (PhD thesis), University of Sussex, UK.

Liarokapis, F., Kouril, P., Agrafiotis, P., Demesticha, S., Chmelik, J., & Skarlatos, D. (2017). 3D modelling and mapping for virtual exploitation of underwater archaeology assets. *The International Archives of the Photogrammetry, Remote Sensing and Spatial Information Sciences, XLII-2*(W3), 425–431. doi:10.5194/isprs-archives-XLII-2-W3-425-2017

Limniou, M., Roberts, D., & Papadopoulos, N. (2008). Full immersive virtual environment CAVE TM in chemistry education. *Computers & Education, 51*(2), 584–593. doi:10.1016/j.compedu.2007.06.014

Lloyd., M., Watmough, S., & Bennett, N. (2018). Simulation-based training: applications in clinical pharmacy. *The Pharmaceuticals Journal-A royal pharmaceuticals society publication*.

Loizides, F., El Kater, A., Terlikas, C., Lanitis, A., & Michael, D. (2014). *Presenting cypriot cultural heritage in virtual reality: A user evaluation*. Lecture Notes in Computer Science Including Subseries Lecture Notes in Artificial Intelligence and Lecture Notes in Bioinformatics; doi:10.1007/978-3-319-13695-0

López, F., Lerones, P., Llamas, J., Gómez-García-Bermejo, J., & Zalama, E. (2018). A review of heritage building information modeling (H-BIM). *Multimodal Technologies and Interaction, 2*(2), 21. doi:10.3390/mti2020021

Lotto, L., Gentili, A., & Washington National Gallery of Art. (1997). Lorenzo Lotto: rediscovered master of the Renaissance;[exhibition dates: National Gallery of Art, Washington, Nov. 2, 1997-March 1, 1998... Galeries Nationales du Grand Palais, Paris, Oct. 12, 1998-Jan. 11, 1999]. Yale University Press.

Loumos, G., Kargas, A., & Varoutas, D. (2018). Augmented and virtual reality technologies in cultural sector: exploring their usefulness and the perceived ease of use. *Journal of Media Critiques, 4*(14). doi:10.17349/jmc118223

Lu, D.-F., Lin, Z.-C., & Li, Y.-J. (2009). Effects of a web-based course on nursing skills and knowledge learning. *The Journal of Nursing Education, 48*(2), 70–77. doi:10.3928/01484834-20090201-10 PMID:19260398

Luna Scott, C. (2015). *The futures of learning 3: What kind of pedagogies for the 21st century?.*

Macho, T. (1996). Vision und visage. Überlegungen zur Faszinationsgeschichte der Medien. In W. Müller-Funk & H. U. Reck (Eds.), *Inszenierte imagination. Beiträge zu einer historischen Anthropologie der Medien* (pp. 87–108). Wien, Austria: Springer-Verlag.

MacPherson, S., Bird, M., Anderson, K., Davis, T., & Blair, A. (2009). An art gallery access programme for people with dementia: You do it for the moment. *Aging & Mental Health, 13*(5), 744–752. doi:10.1080/13607860902918207 PMID:19882413

Madary, M., & Metzinger, T. K. (2016). Real virtuality: A code of ethical conduct. *Recommendations for Good Scientific Practice and the Consumers of VR-Technology. Front. Robot and AI, 3*(3). Retrieved from https://www.frontiersin.org/articles/10.3389/frobt.2016.00003/full

Madary, M., & Metzinger, T. K. (2016). Real virtuality: A code of ethical conduct. Recommendations for good scientific practice and the consumers of vR-technology. *Robotics and AI 3, 3.* doi:10.3389/frobt.2016.00003

Magli, P. (1995). *Il volto e l'anima. Fisiognomica e passioni.* Milano, Italy: Bompiani.

Malbezin, P., Piekarski, W., & Thomas, B. (2002). Measuring ARToolkit accuracy in long distance tracking experiments, *Poster session in 1ˢᵗ International Augmented Reality Toolkit Workshop*, Germany.

Malik, S. (2015, March). Impact of Facebook addiction on narcissistic behavior and self-esteem among students. *JPMA. The Journal of the Pakistan Medical Association, 65*(3), 260–263. PMID:25933557

Malinverni, E. S., Pierdicca, R., Paolanti, M., Martini, M., Morbidoni, C., Matrone, F., & Lingua, A. (2019). Deep learning for semantic segmentation of 3D point cloud. *International Committee of Architectural Photogrammetry, CIPA 27ᵗʰ International Symposium,* Avila, Spain.

Malraux, A. (1996). *Le musée imaginaire* [orig. 1947]. Paris, France: Gallimard; Retrieved from http://www.gallimard.fr/Catalogue/GALLIMARD/Folio/Folio-essais/Le-Musee-Imaginaire

Ma, M., Jain, L. C., & Anderson, P. (Eds.). (2014). *Virtual, augmented reality and serious games for healthcare 1* (Vol. 1). Berlin, Germany: Springer. doi:10.1007/978-3-642-54816-1

Mann, E. G., Medves, J., & Vandenkerkohf, E. G. (2015). Accessing best practice resources using mobile technology in an undergraduate nursing program. *Computers, Informatics, Nursing, 33*(3), 122–128. doi:10.1097/CIN.0000000000000135 PMID:25636042

Manovich, K. (2013). Multimedia versus metamedia. In S. Kenderine (Ed.), *Place-Hampi, Inhabiting the panoramic imaginary of Vijayanagara* (pp. 226–229). Berlin Heidelberg, Germany: Kehrer Verlag.

Mariani, G. (2018). The cultural and creative industries. Guillaume Mariani. Retrieved from https://www.guillaume-mariani.com/creative-industries/

Martín, S., Díaz, G., Cáceres, M., Gago, D., & Gibert, M. (2012, October). A mobile augmented reality gymkhana for improving technological skills and history learning: Outcomes and some determining factors. In *E-learn: World conference on e-learning in corporate, government, healthcare, and higher education* (pp. 260-265). Association for the Advancement of Computing in Education (AACE).

Marty, P. F., & Jones, K. B. (2009). *Museum informatics: people, information, and technology in museums.* New York: Routledge.

Massaro, D., Savazzi, F., Di Dio, C., Freedberg, D., Gallese, V., Gilli, G., & Marchetti, A. (2012). When art moves the eyes: A behavioral and eye-tracking study. *PLoS One*, *7*(5). doi:10.1371/journal.pone.0037285 PMID:22624007

Mastandrea, S. (2011). Il ruolo delle emozioni nell'esperienza estetica. *Arte, Psicologia e Realismo*, 48.

Matisse, H. (1972). *Henri Matisse. Scritti e pensieri sull'arte*. Torino, Italy: Einaudi.

McCarthy, C. J., & Uppot, R. N. (2019). Advances in virtual and augmented reality—exploring the role in health-care education. *Journal of Radiology Nursing*, *38*(2), 104–105. doi:10.1016/j.jradnu.2019.01.008

McConville, K. V. M., & Virk, S. (2012). Evaluation of an electronic video game for improvement of balance. *Virtual Reality (Waltham Cross)*, *16*(4), 315–323. doi:10.100710055-012-0212-7

McGonigal, J. (2011). *Reality is broken: Why games make us better and how they can change the world*. New York, NY: Penguin Press.

McLuhan, M. (1994). *McLuhan. Understanding media. The extensions of man*. Cambridge, MA: MIT Press.

Mehdizadeh, S. (2010, August). Self-presentation 2.0: Narcissism and self-esteem on Facebook. *Cyberpsychology, Behavior, and Social Networking*, *13*(4), 357–364. doi:10.1089/cyber.2009.0257 PMID:20712493

Mengoni, M., Germani, M., & Bordegoni, M. (2009). Virtual reality systems: a method to evaluate the applicability based on the design context. doi:10.1115/detc2007-35028

Mengoni, M., & Leopardi, A. (2019). An exploratory study on the application of reverse engineering in the field of small archaeological artefacts. *Computer-Aided Design and Applications*, *16*(6), 1209–1226. doi:10.14733/cadaps.2019.1209-1226

Menninghaus, W., Wagner, V., Wassiliwizky, E., Schindler, I., Hanich, J., Jacobsen, T., & Koelsch, S. (2018). What are aesthetic emotions? *Psychological Review*, *126*, ●●●. Retrieved from https://www.researchgate.net/publication/327779286_What_Are_Aesthetic_Emotions/link/5ba3e7c0a6fdccd3cb662478/download PMID:30802122

Micoli, L., Guidi, G., Angheleddu, D., & Russo, M. (2013). A multidisciplinary approach to 3D survey and reconstruction of historical buildings. In *2013 Digital Heritage International Congress (DigitalHeritage)* (pp. 241–248). IEEE. 10.1109/DigitalHeritage.2013.6744760

Mihelj, M., Novak, D., & Beguš, S. (2014). Virtual reality technology and applications.

Mills, A. J., & Durepos, G. (2013). Case study methods in business research (1–4). Thousand Oaks, CA: Sage.

Mills, A. J., Durepos, G., & Wiebe, E. (2010). Explanatory case study. In Encyclopedia of case study research. Thousand Oaks, CA: Sage.

Ministry of Culture (Taiwan). (2017). 2017 Taiwan cultural & creative industries annual report. Taipei, Taiwan: Ministry of Culture. Retrieved from http://cci.culture.tw/upload/cht/attachment/b131e555ec34a192be359838c9a4eb07.pdf

Minocha, S., & Reeves, A. J. (2010). Design of learning spaces in 3D virtual worlds: An empirical investigation of second life. *Learning, Media, and Technology*, *35*(2), 111–137. doi:10.1080/17439884.2010.494419

Minoli, G. (2014). *La Lista di Pasquale Rotondi, La storia siamo noi* – RAI. Retrieved from: https://www.youtube.com/watch?v=I5POv01SgBI

Mirzoeff, N. (2015). *How to see the world*. London, UK: Penguin Books.

Mitsuno, D., Ueda, K., Itamiya, T., Nuri, T., & Otsuki, Y. (2017). Intraoperative evaluation of body surface improvement by an augmented reality system that a clinician can modify. *Plastic and Reconstructive Surgery. Global Open*, *5*(8). doi:10.1097/GOX.0000000000001432

Mittelman, M., & Epstein, C. (n.d.). Meet me at MoMA - MoMA Alzheimer's Project. *MoMA*.

Mohammed-Amin, R. K., Levy, R. M., & Boyd, J. E. (2012). Mobile augmented reality for interpretation of archaeological sites. In *Proceedings of the second international ACM workshop on personalized access to cultural heritage - PATCH '12* (p. 11). New York, NY: ACM Press. 10.1145/2390867.2390871

Monahan, T., McArdle, G., & Bertolotto, M. (2008). Virtual reality for collaborative e-learning. *Computers & Education*, *50*(4), 1339–1353. doi:10.1016/j.compedu.2006.12.008

Monsky, W. L., James, R., & Seslar, S. S. (2019). Virtual and augmented reality applications in medicine and surgery-the fantastic voyage is here. *Anatomy & Physiology*, *9*(1), 313.

Morozzi, L., & Paris, R. (1995). *L'opera da ritrovare. Repertorio del patrimonio artistico italiano disperso all'epoca della seconda guerra mondiale*. Italia: Istituto Poligrafico dello Stato.

Mortara, M., Catalano, C. E., Bellotti, F., Fiucci, G., Houry-Panchetti, M., & Petridis, P. (2014). Learning cultural heritage by serious games. *Journal of Cultural Heritage*, *15*(3), 318–325. doi:10.1016/j.culher.2013.04.004

Muikku, J., & Kalli, S. (2017). *The IMD project VR/AR market report*. Retrieved from http://www.digitalmedia.fi/wp-content/uploads/2018/02/DMF_VR_report_edit_180124.pdf

Museum and The Web. (2015). Open cultural heritage data on the web. Retrieved from http://www.museumsandtheweb.com/mw2012/papers/radically_open_cultural_heritage_data_on_the_w

Nadkarni, A., & Hoffman, S. (2012). Why do people use facebook? Amsterdam, The Netherlands: Elsevier. *Personality and individual differences*, *52*(3), 243–249. doi:10.1016/j.paid.2011.11.007 PMID:22544987

Naismith, L., & Smith, M. P. (2009). Using mobile technologies for multimedia tours in a traditional museum setting. In M. Ally (Ed.), *Mobile Learning. Transforming the Delivery of Education and Training. AU Press*. Edmonton: Athabasca University; Retrieved from http://www.aupress.ca/books/120155/ebook/12_Mohamed_Ally_2009-Article12.pdf

Nancy, J.-L. (2000). *Il ritratto e il suo sguardo*. Milano, Italy: Raffaello Cortina Editore.

Napolitano, R. K., Douglas, I. P., Garlock, M. E., & Glisic, B. (2017). Virtual tour environment of Cuba's National School of Art. *The International Archives of the Photogrammetry, Remote Sensing and Spatial Information Sciences*, *XLII-2*(W5), 547–551. doi:10.5194/isprs-archives-XLII-2-W5-547-2017

Naspetti, S., Pierdicca, R., Mandolesi, S., Paolanti, M., Frontoni, E., & Zanoli, R. (2016). Automatic analysis of eye-tracking data for augmented reality applications: A prospective outlook. In Lecture Notes in Computer Science (including subseries Lecture Notes in Artificial Intelligence and Lecture Notes in Bioinformatics). doi:10.1007/978-3-319-40651-0_17

Nazik, E., & Arslan, S. (2011). The investigation of the relations between empathic skills and self-compassion of the nursing students. *Journal of Anatolian Nursing and Health Sciences*, *14*(4), 69–77.

Neguţ, A., Matu, S.-A., Sava, F. A., & David, D. (2016). Task difficulty of virtual reality-based assessment tools compared to classical paper-and-pencil or computerized measures: A meta-analytic approach. *Computers in Human Behavior*, *54*, 414–424. doi:10.1016/j.chb.2015.08.029

Nespeca, R. (2018). Towards a 3D digital model for management and fruition of Ducal Palace at Urbino. An integrated survey with mobile mapping. *SCIRES-IT - SCIentific RESearch and Information Technology*. doi:10.2423/I22394303V8N2P1

News, B. B. C. (2018). *Montreal museum partners with doctors to 'prescribe' art*. Retrieved from https://www.bbc.com/news/world-us-canada-45972348

Next Animation Studio. (2017, March 5). Next Animation Studio partners with national museum of prehistory. Retrieved from https://eprnews.com/next-animation-studio-partners-with-national-museum-of-prehistory-87380/

Nextplayground guardian. (2015, Nov. 3). Martell Singapore: Experience Martell air gallery. Nextplayground guardian, Retrieved from https://nextplayground.net/campaigns/martell-singapore-experience-martell-air-gallery/

Nicolae, C., Nocerino, E., Menna, F., & Remondino, F. (2014). Photogrammetry applied to problematic artefacts. In *International Archives of the Photogrammetry*. Remote Sensing and Spatial Information Sciences - ISPRS Archives; doi:10.5194/isprsarchives-XL-5-451-2014

Nielsen, J. (1994). *Usability engineering*. Elsevier.

Noble, S. (2019, March 25). *The 10 best augmented reality smartglasses in 2019*. Available at https://www.aniwaa.com/best-of/vr-ar/best-augmented-reality-smartglasses/

Nold, C. (2009). *Emotional Cartography. Technologies of the Self*, Retrieved from http://emotionalcartography.net

Norman, D. A. (2011). *Living with complexity*. Cambridge, MA: MIT Press.

Norris, L., & Tisdale, R. (2013). *Creativity in museum practice*. Left Coast Press.

North, M. M., & North, S. (2018). The sense of presence exploration in virtual reality therapy. *Journal of Universal Computer Science, 24*, 72–84.

Noya, N. C., García, Á. L., & Ramírez, F. C. (2015). Combining photogrammetry and photographic enhancement techniques for the recording of megalithic art in north-west Iberia. *Digital Applications in Archaeology and Cultural Heritage, 2*(2-3), 89–101. doi:10.1016/j.daach.2015.02.004

Noyudom, A.-N., Ketpichainarong, W., & Ruenwongsa, P. (2011). Development of a computer-based simulation unit on tracheal suctioning to enhance nursing students' knowledge and practical skills. In C. Denpaiboon, P. Pipitkul, A. Phitthayayon, S. Ondej, & S. Soranastaporn (Eds.), *Proceedings of the Thai Simulation (ThaiSim) 2011 3rd Annual International Conference* (pp. 65-76). Bangkok, Thailand: ThaiSim: The Thai Simulation and Gaming Association, Thonburi University.

O'Brien, H. L., & Toms, E. G. (2008). What is user engagement? A conceptual framework for defining user engagement with technology. *Journal of the American Society for Information Science and Technology, 59*(6), 938–955. doi:10.1002/asi.20801

O'Brien, H. L., & Toms, E. G. (2010). The development and evaluation of a survey to measure user engagement. *Journal of the American Society for Information Science and Technology, 61*(1), 50–69. doi:10.1002/asi.21229

Ochmann, S., Vock, R., & Klein, R. (2019). Automatic reconstruction of fully volumetric 3D building models from oriented point clouds. *ISPRS Journal of Photogrammetry and Remote Sensing, 151*, 251–262. doi:10.1016/j.isprsjprs.2019.03.017

Oettermann, S. (1997). The panorama. History of a mass medium. New York: Zone Book, 7.

Ökdem, Ş., Abbasoğlu, A., & Doğan, N. (2000). Nursing history, education and development. *Ankara Üniversitesi Dikimevi Sağlık Hizmetleri Meslek Yüksekokulu Yıllığı, 1*(1), 5–11.

Omale, N., Hung, W. C., Luetkehans, L., & Cooke-Plagwitz, J. (2009). Learning in 3-D multi-user virtual environments: Exploring the use of unique 3-D attributes for online problem-based learning. *British Journal of Educational Technology, 40*(3), 480–495. doi:10.1111/j.1467-8535.2009.00941.x

Öncü, S. (2014). *The CIPP model example in clinical skills education evaluation*. (Doctoral dissertation), Institute of Health Science, Ege University.

Onkka, K. H. (2018). *Precision OS allows surgeons to practice before taking on real surgery.* Available at https://healthiar. com/precision-os-allows-surgeons-to-practice-before-taking-on-real-surgery

Oppenheim, C. (1993). Virtual reality and the virtual library. *Information Services & Use, 13*(3), 215–227. doi:10.3233/ ISU-1993-13303

Orr, E. (2018). *Virtual reality as an effective medical tool.* Available at https://www.xr.health/virtual-reality-effective-medical-tool.html/

Ortiz, A. (2019). *Welcome to extended reality: Transforming how employees work and learn.* Available at https://www. ibm.com/blogs/insights-on-business/ibmix/welcome-to-extended-reality/

Osaba, E., Pierdicca, R., Malinverni, E., Khromova, A., Álvarez, F., & Bahillo, A. (2018). A smartphone-based system for outdoor data gathering using a wireless beacon network and GPS data: from cyber spaces to senseable spaces. *ISPRS International Journal of Geo-Information, 7*(5), 190. doi:10.3390/ijgi7050190

Osuagwu, O., Ihedigbo, C., & Ndigwe, C. (2015). Integrating virtual reality (VR) into traditional instructional design. *West African Journal of Industrial and Academic Research, 15*(1), 68–77.

Ott, M., & Pozzi, F. (2008, September). ICT and cultural heritage education: Which added value? In World summit on knowledge society (pp. 131-138). Berlin, Germany: Springer.

Ott, M., & Tavella, M. (2009). A contribution to the understanding of what makes young students genuinely engaged in computer-based learning tasks. *Procedia: Social and Behavioral Sciences, 1*(1), 184–188. doi:10.1016/j.sbspro.2009.01.034

Padilla-Meléndez, A., & del Águila-Obra, A. R. (2013). Web and social media usage by museums: Online value creation. *International Journal of Information Management, 33*(5), 892–898. doi:10.1016/j.ijinfomgt.2013.07.004

Palazzo Pianetti. Retrieved from https://en.wikipedia.org/wiki/Palazzo_Pianetti

Pan, X., & Hamilton, A. F. C. (2018). Why and how to use virtual reality to study human social interaction: The challenges of exploring a new research landscape. British Journal of Psychology, 109, 395–417.

Panofsky, E. (1955). *Meaning in visual art.* Chicago, IL: Chicago University Press.

Pantano, E., & Tavernise, A. (2009). Learning cultural heritage through information and communication technologies: a case study. [IJICTHD]. *International Journal of Information Communication Technologies and Human Development, 1*(3), 68–87. doi:10.4018/jicthd.2009070104

Pantelidis, P., Chorti, A., Papagiouvanni, I., Paparoidamis, G., Drosos, C., Panagiotakopoulos, T., . . . Sideris, M. (2017, Dec. 20). *Virtual and augmented reality in medical education, medical and surgical education - past, present and future,* IntechOpen, doi:. Available at https://www.intechopen.com/books/medical-and-surgical-education-past-present-and-future/virtual-and-augmented-reality-in-medical-education doi:10.5772/intechopen.71963

Pantelidis, V. S. (1993). Virtual reality in the classroom. *Educational Technology, 33*(4), 23–27.

Pasek, K., Golinkoff, R. M., Berk, L. E., & Singer, D. G. (2009). *A mandate for playful learning in preschool: Presenting the evidence.* New York, NY: Oxford University Press.

Passig, D., Tzuriel, D., & Eshel-Kedmi, G. (2016). Improving children's cognitive modifiability by dynamic assessment in 3D immersive virtual reality environments. *Computers & Education, 95*, 296–308. doi:10.1016/j.compedu.2016.01.009

Pattanasith, S., Rampai, N., & Kanperm, J. (2015). The development model of learning through virtual learning environments (VLEs) for graduate students, department of educational technology, faculty of education, Kasetsart University. *Social and Behavioral Sciences, 176*, 60–64.

Perkins Coie LLP. (March 2019) *Industry insights into the future of immersive technology.* Perkins Coie LLP and the XR Association VOLUME 3.

Pfandlera, M., Lazarovici, M., Stefan, P., & Weigl, M. (2017). Virtual reality-based simulators for spine surgery: A systematic review. *The Spine Journal,* ▪▪▪, 1529–9430. doi:10.1016/j.spinee.2017.05.016

Pierdicca, R., Frontoni, E., Pollini, R., Trani, M., & Verdini, L. (2017, June). The use of augmented reality glasses for the application in industry 4.0. In *Proceedings International Conference on Augmented Reality, Virtual Reality and Computer Graphics* (pp. 389-401). Cham, Switzerland: Springer. 10.1007/978-3-319-60922-5_30

Pierdicca, R., Paolanti, M., Naspetti, S., Mandolesi, S., Zanoli, R., & Frontoni, E. (2018). User-centered predictive model for improving cultural heritage augmented reality applications: An HMM-based approach for eye-tracking data. *Journal of Imaging.* doi:10.3390/jimaging4080101

Pietroni, E., Pagano, A., & Rufa, C. (2013). The Etruscanning project: Gesture-based interaction and user experience in the virtual reconstruction of the Regolini-Galassi tomb. In *2013 Digital Heritage International Congress (DigitalHeritage)* (pp. 653–660). IEEE. 10.1109/DigitalHeritage.2013.6744832

Pizzi, G., Scarpi, D., Pichierri, M., & Vannucci, V. (2019). Virtual reality, real reactions?: Comparing consumers' perceptions and shopping orientation across physical and virtual-reality retail stores. *Computers in Human Behavior, 96,* 1–12. doi:10.1016/j.chb.2019.02.008

Pletinckx, D., Callebaut, D., Killebrew, A. E., & Silberman, N. A. (2000). Virtual-reality heritage presentation at Ename. *IEEE MultiMedia, 7*(2), 45–48. doi:10.1109/93.848427

Polycarpou, C. (2018, Jan. 10). *The ViMM definition of a virtual museum.* Retrieved from https://www.vi-mm.eu/2018/01/10/the-vimm-definition-of-a-virtual-museum/

Poole, A., & Ball, L. J. (2006). Eye tracking in HCI and usability research. In Encyclopedia of Human Computer Interaction. doi:10.4018/978-1-59140-562-7.ch034

Prague (City of). (2018). Scale model of Pragues. Retrieved from http://www.langweil.cz/index_en.php

Qi, C. R., Su, H., Mo, K., & Guibas, L. J. (2017). PointNet: Deep learning on point sets for 3D classification and segmentation. In *Proceedings - 30th IEEE Conference on Computer Vision and Pattern Recognition, CVPR 2017.* doi:10.1109/CVPR.2017.16

Qi, C. R., Yi, L., Su, H., & Guibas, L. J. (2017). PointNet++: Deep hierarchical feature learning on point sets in a metric space. Retrieved from http://arxiv.org/abs/1706.02413

Qin, Z., Tai, Y., Xia, C., Peng, J., Huang, X., Chen, Z., ... Shi, J. (2019). Towards virtual VATS, face, and construct evaluation for peg transfer training of Box, VR, AR, and MR trainer. *Journal of Healthcare Engineering, 2019.* doi:10.1155/2019/6813719

Qualcomm. (2017). *Augmented and virtual reality: The first wave of 5G killer apps.* ©2017 ABI Research. Available at https://www.qualcomm.com/media/documents/files/augmented-and-virtual-reality-the-first-wave-of-5g-killer-apps.pdf

Quattrini, R., Pierdicca, R., Morbidoni, C., Malinverni, E. S. (2017-b). Conservation-oriented hbim. The bimexplorer web tool. *International Archives of the Photogrammetry, Remote Sensing and Spatial Information Sciences - ISPRS Archives, 42* (5W1), pp. 275-281.

Quattrini, R., Pierdicca, R., & Morbidoni, C. (2017-a). Knowledge-based data enrichment for HBIM: Exploring high-quality models using the semantic-web. *Journal of Cultural Heritage.* doi:10.1016/j.culher.2017.05.004

Quiroga, R. Q., & Pedreira, C. (2011). How do we see art: an eye-tracker study. *Frontiers in Human Neuroscience, 5*. doi:10.3389/fnhum.2011.00098 PMID:21941476

Radu, I. (2012, November). Why should my students use AR? A comparative review of the educational impacts of augmented-reality. In *2012 IEEE International Symposium on Mixed and Augmented Reality (ISMAR)* (pp. 313-314). IEEE. 10.1109/ISMAR.2012.6402590

Rae, J., & Edwards, L. (2016) Virtual reality at the British Museum: What is the value of virtual reality environments for learning by children and young people, schools, and families? *MW2016: Museums and the Web 2016.* Retrieved from https://mw2016.museumsandtheweb.com/paper/virtual-reality-at-the-british-museum-what-is-the-value-of-virtual-reality-environments-for-learning-by-children-and-young-people-schools-and-families/

Rae, J., & Edwards, L. (2016, January). Virtual reality at the British Museum: What is the value of virtual reality environments for learning by children and young people, schools, and families? In *Proceedings of MW2016: The Annual Conference Museums and the Web,* Los Angeles, CA.

Rahimian, F. P., Arciszewski, T., & Goulding, J. S. (2014). Successful education for AEC professionals: Case study of applying immersive game-like virtual reality interfaces. *Visualization in Engineering, 2*(1), 4. doi:10.1186/2213-7459-2-4

Ramasundaram, V., Grunwald, S., Mangeot, A., Comerford, N. B., & Bliss, C. (2005). Development of an environmental virtual field laboratory. *Computers & Education, 45*(1), 21–34. doi:10.1016/j.compedu.2004.03.002

Rawlings, C. (2013). Making the connection: social bonding in courtship situations. In The American Journal of Sociology, 118(6), 1596-1649.

Remondino, F. (2011). Heritage recording and 3D modeling with photogrammetry and 3D scanning. *Remote Sensing, 3*(6), 1104–1138. doi:10.3390/rs3061104

Remondino, F., & Rizzi, A. (2010). Reality-based 3D documentation of natural and cultural heritage sites—Techniques, problems, and examples. *Applied Geomatics, 2*(3), 85–100. doi:10.100712518-010-0025-x

Research methodology. (n.d.). Case study. Research methodology. Retrieved from https://research-methodology.net/research-methods/qualitative-research/case-studies/

ResearchAndMarkets.com. (2018, July 30). Global augmented reality (AR) & virtual reality (VR) market outlook to 2023 by devices, component, application, and geography: ResearchAndMarkets.com. Retrieved from https://www.businesswire.com/news/home/20180730005663/en/

Reyes, S. D., Stillsmoking, K., & Chadwick-Hopkins, D. (2008). Implementation and evaluation of a virtual simulator system: Teaching intravenous skills. *Clinical Simulation in Nursing, 4*(1), e43–e49. doi:10.1016/j.ecns.2009.05.055

Riassunto del libro. (2019, June 5) *La furia delle immagini*i. Retrieved from https://www.docsity.com/it/la-furia-delle-immagini-2/4631013/

Richey, R. C., Silber, K. H., & Ely, D. P. (2008). Reflections on the 2008 AECT definitions of the field. *TechTrends, 52*(1), 24–25. doi:10.100711528-008-0108-2

Ridel, B., Reuter, P., Laviole, J., Mellado, N., Couture, N., & Granier, X. (2014). The revealing flashlight: interactive spatial augmented reality for detail exploration of cultural heritage artifacts. *Journal on Computing and Cultural Heritage.* doi:10.1145/2611376

Rizzo, A., & Kim, G. J. (2005). A SWOT analysis of the field of virtual reality rehabilitation and therapy. *Presence (Cambridge, Mass.), 14*(2), 119–146. doi:10.1162/1054746053967094

Rizzo, A., Reger, G., Gahm, G., Difede, J., & Rothbaum, B. O. (2009). Virtual reality exposure therapy for combat-related PTSD. In P. J. Shiromani, T. M. Keane, & J. E. LeDoux (Eds.), *Post-traumatic stress disorder: Basic science and clinical practice* (pp. 375–399). Totowa, NJ, US: Humana Press; doi:10.1007/978-1-60327-329-9_18

Rizzolatti, G., & Fabbri-Destro, M. (2008). The mirror system and its role in social cognition. *Current Opionion in Neurobiology*, Retrieved from http://cogsci.bme.hu/~gkovacs/letoltes/mirror.pdf

Rizzolatti, G., & Craighero, L. (2005). Mirror neuron: a neurological approach to empathy. In J. P. Changeux, A. R. Damasio, W. Singer, & Y. Christen (Eds.), *Neurobiology of Human Values. Research and Perspectives in Neurosciences.* Berlin, Heidelberg: Springer; Retrieved from http://robotcub.org/misc/papers/06_Rizzolatti_Craighero.pdf doi:10.1007/3-540-29803-7_9

Robertson, A. (2018, Jan. 26). The best VR and AR from Sundance 2018, from haptic gloves to alien abduction. *The Verge,* Retrieved from https://www.theverge.com/2018/2011/2026/16919236/sundance-16912018-best-virtual-reality-augmented-vr-ar-new-frontier

Rosenberg, R., Baughman, S., & Bailenson, J. (2013). Virtual superheroes: Using superpowers in virtual reality to encourage prosocial behavior. *PLoS One*, •••, 8. PMID:23383029

Roy, E., Bakr, M. M., & George, R. (2017). The need for virtual reality simulators in dental education: A review. *The Saudi Dental Journal*, *29*(2), 41–47. Published online March 6, 2017. doi:10.1016/j.sdentj.2017.02.001

Ryan, M. D., & Hearn, G. (2010, August). Next-generation "filmmaking": New markets, new methods and new business models. Media International Australia, 136, 133–145.

Sachs, G. (2016). *Virtual reality and augment reality: Understanding the race for next computing platform.* The Goldman Sachs Group, Inc. Available at https://www.goldmansachs.com/insights/pages/technology-driving-innovation-folder/virtual-and-augmented-reality/report.pdf

Saidin, N. F., Halim, N. D. A., & Yahaya, N. (2015). A review of research on augmented reality in education: Advantages and applications. *International Education Studies*, *8*(13), 1–8. doi:10.5539/ies.v8n13p1

Sanchez, J. (n.d.). *Augmented reality in healthcare.* Available at https://www.plugandplaytechcenter.com/resources/augmented-reality-healthcare/

Sangregorio, E., Stanco, F., & Tanasi, D. (2008). The Archeomatica Project: Towards a new application of the computer graphics in archaeology. In *Eurographics Italian Chapter Conference* (pp. 1–5). Postfach 8043, 38621. Goslar, Germany: The Eurographics Association. doi:10.2312/LocalChapterEvents/ItalChap/ItalianChapConf2008/001-005

Sarıkoç, G. (2016). Use of virtual reality in the education of health workers. *Journal of Education and Research in Nursing*, *13*(1), 243–248.

Savini, M. (2015, April 15). Selfie, la rappresentazione di se stessi è affermazione dell'essere hic et nunc. *Wired.* Retrieved from https://www.wired.it/gadget/foto-e-video/2015/04/17/selfie-rappresentazione-se-stessi-affermazione-dellessere-hic-et-nunc/

Savini, M. (2018). *Arte transgenica. La vita è un medium.* Pisa, Italy: Pisa University Press.

Schaich, M. (2013). Combined 3D scanning and photogrammetry surveys with 3D database support for archaeology & cultural heritage. A practice report on ArcTron's Information System aSPECT 3D. In Photogrammetric Week '13.

Schall, A., Tesky, V. A., Adams, A. K., & Pantel, J. (2018). Art museum-based intervention to promote emotional well-being and improve quality of life in people with dementia: The ARTEMIS project. *Dementia (London)*, *17*(6), 728–743. doi:10.1177/1471301217730451 PMID:28914089

Schettino, P. (2013a). Rethinking the digital media process in museum, Design Principles and Practices: An International Journal — Annual Review, 7. Champaign IL, University of Illinois Research Park: Common Ground Publisher. pp. 1-18.

Schettino, P. (2013b). Home, sense of place and visitors' interpretations of digital cultural immersive experiences in museums: An application of the "embodied constructivist GTM digital ethnography in situ" method, *Digital heritage international congress (DigitalHeritage)*, Marseille. Oct. 28-Nov. 1, 2013. IEEE Proceedings. 1. pp. 721-124.

Schettino, P. (2013c). Emotions, words and colors: strategies to visualize and analyze patterns from visitors narratives in museums. In *Proceedings 2013 17th International Conference Information Visualisation (IV)*, London, UK. July 16-18, 2013. IEEE. pp. 551-554.

Schettino, P., & Kenderdine, S. (2011). Place-Hampi. Narratives of inclusive cultural experience. *Journal of Inclusive Museums, 3*(3), Common Ground Publisher. 141-156.

Schmidt, S., Bruder, G., & Steinicke, F. (2019). Effects of virtual agent and object representation on experiencing exhibited artifacts. *Computers & Graphics, 83*, 1–10. doi:10.1016/j.cag.2019.06.002

Schneider, A. (2006). *Appropriation as practice. Art and identity in Argentina*. New York: Palgrave MacMillan.

Schofield, G., Beale, G., Beale, N., Fell, M., Hadley, D., Hook, J., . . . Thresh, L. (2018, June). Viking VR: Designing a virtual reality experience for a museum. In Proceedings of the 2018 Designing Interactive Systems Conference (pp. 805-815). ACM. https://doi.org/10.1145/3196709.3196714

Schwartz, R., & Steptoe, W. (2018). The Immersive VR self: Performance, embodiment and presence in immersive virtual reality environments. *A Networked Self and Human Augmentics, AI, Sentience*. Retrieved from https://research.fb.com/publications/the-immersive-vr-self-performance-embodiment-and-presence-in-immersive-virtual-reality-environments/

Schweibenz, W. (1998). The "virtual museum": new perspectives for museums to present objects and information using the internet as a knowledge base and communication system. In H. Zimmermann, & H. Schramm (Eds.), *6th ISI, 34*, 185-200. Retrieved from https://www.semanticscholar.org/paper/The-%22Virtual-Museum%22%3A-New-Perspectives-For-Museums-Schweibenz/9e33a47afcc9ce8f64c71e85cfd9c28e1ade502a

Schweibenz, W. (1991). The virtual museum: new perspectives for museums to present objects and information using the Internet as a knowledge base and communication system. In H. Zimmermann, & H. Schramm (Eds.), *Proceedings of the 6th ISI Conference* (pp. 185–200), Prague, Konstanz, UKV.

Seam, A. (2019). *AT&T unlocks the power of edge computing: delivering interactive VR over 5G*. Available at https://about.att.com/innovationblog/2019/02/edge_computing_vr.html

Şengül, F. (2010). *The effect of nursing education models on the critical thinking dispositions of the students: A multi-center study*. (Master's Dissertation), Institute of Health Science, Çukurova University.

Şen, H. (2012). Hemşirelikte psikomotor beceri öğretiminde rehber ilkeler: Kalp masajı örneği (Guide principles of psychomotor skills teaching in nursing: Sample of chest compression). [Dokuz Eylul University Faculty of Nursing Electronic Journal]. *Dokuz Eylül Üniversitesi Hemşirelik Elektronik Dergisi, 5*(4), 180–184.

Serio, Di., Ibanez, M. B., & Kloos, C. D. (2013). *Impact of an augmented reality system on students motivation for a visual art course*. Computer and Education Society. doi:10.1016/j.compedu.2012.03.002

Seropian, M. A., Brown, K., Gavilanes, J. S., & Driggers, B. (2004). Simulation: Not just a manikin. *The Journal of Nursing Education, 43*(4), 164–169. PMID:15098910

Serrano, B., Baños, R. M., & Botella, C. (2016). Virtual reality and stimulation of touch and smell for inducing relaxation: A randomized controlled trial. *Computers in Human Behavior, 55*, 1–8. doi:10.1016/j.chb.2015.08.007

Shah, N. (2019). *The next big thing: Integrating AI into augmented and virtual reality.* Available at https://www.cygnet-infotech.com/blog/integrating-ai-into-augmented-and-virtual-reality

Shaw, J., & Kenderdine, S. (2011) Future narrative, discovery engines and making meaning in VR. *IEEE International Symposium on VR Innovation* 10.1109/ISVRI.2011.5759591

Shih, Y.-C., & Yang, M.-T. (2008). A collaborative virtual environment for situated language learning using VEC3D. *Journal of Educational Technology & Society, 11*(1), 56–58.

Shin, D. (2018). Empathy and embodied experience in virtual environment: To what extent can virtual reality stimulate empathy and embodied experience? Computers in Human Behavior, 78, 64–73.

Shin, D.-H. (2017). The role of affordance in the experience of virtual reality learning: Technological and affective affordances in virtual reality. Telematics and Informatics, 34, 1826–1836.

Shin, S., Park, J.-H., & Kim, J.-H. (2015). Effectiveness of patient simulation in nursing education: Meta-analysis. *Nurse Education Today, 35*(1), 176–182. doi:10.1016/j.nedt.2014.09.009 PMID:25459172

Shi, S. W., Wedel, M., & Pieters, F. G. M. R. (2013). Decision making : A model-based exploration using eye-tracking data. *Management Science, 59*(5), 1009–1026. doi:10.1287/mnsc.1120.1625

Short, M., & Samar, S. (2017). *Transforming healthcare and saving lives with extended reality (XR).* Available at https://www.accenture.com/us-en/blogs/blogs-extended-reality-for-enterprise-health-care

Sirilak, S., & Muneesawang, P. (2018). *A new procedure for advancing telemedicine using the HoloLens.* IEEE; doi:10.1109/ACCESS.2018.2875558

Smith, T., Nelson, J., & Maul, R. (2018). *Digital reality in life sciences and health care.* Available at https://www2.deloitte.com/content/dam/Deloitte/us/Documents/life-sciences-health-care/us-lshc-tech-trends-digital-reality.pdf

Smith, P. C., & Hamilton, B. K. (2015). The effects of virtual reality simulation as a teaching strategy for skills preparation in nursing students. *Clinical Simulation in Nursing, 11*(1), 52–58. doi:10.1016/j.ecns.2014.10.001

Smith, S. J., Farra, S., Ulrich, D. L., Hodgson, E., Nicely, S., & Matcham, W. (2016). Learning and retention using virtual reality in a decontamination simulation. *Nursing Education Perspectives, 37*(4), 210–214. doi:10.1097/01.NEP.0000000000000035 PMID:27740579

Smithsonian American Art Museum (SAAM). (2017). WONDER 360: Experience the Renwick Gallery Exhibition in Virtual Reality.

Smithsonian American Art Museum (SAAM). Retrieved from https://americanart.si.edu/wonder2360

Smithsonian. (2015). *Smithsonian brings historic specimens to life in free "skin and bones" mobile app.* Available at https://www.si.edu/newsdesk/releases/smithsonian-brings-historic-specimens-life-free-skin-and-bones-mobile-app

Solly, M. (2018). *Canadian Doctors Will Soon Be Able to Prescribe Museum Visits as Treatment.* Retrieved from https://www.smithsonianmag.com/smart-news/canadian-doctors-will-soon-be-able-prescribe-museum-visits-180970599

Solutions, M. (2017, Oct. 26). *Virtual reality and augmented reality in healthcare.* Available at http://moisaka.com/virtual-reality/

Sommerauer, P., & Müller, O. (2014). Augmented reality in informal learning environments: A field experiment in a mathematics exhibition. Computer Education, 79, 59–68.

Somyürek, S. (2014). Öğretim sürecinde z kuşağının dikkatini çekme: Artırılmış gerçeklik (Gaining the attention of generation Z in learning process: Augmented reality). [Educational Technology Theory and Practice]. *Eğitim Teknolojisi Kuram ve Uygulama, 4*(1), 63–80.

Sooai, A. G., Sumpeno, S., & Purnomo, M. H. (2016). User perception on 3D stereoscopic cultural heritage ancient collection. doi:10.1145/2898459.2898476

Sotiriou, S., & Bogner, F. X. (2008). Visualizing the invisible: Augmented reality as an innovative science education scheme. *Advanced Science Letters, 1*(1), 114–122. doi:10.1166/asl.2008.012

Sotirova, K., Peneva, J., Ivanov, S., Doneva, R., & Dobreva, M. (2012). Digitization of cultural heritage-standards, institutions, initiatives. In *Access to digital cultural heritage: innovative applications of automated metadata generation* (pp. 23–68). Plovdiv, Bulgaria: Plovdiv University; Retrieved from http://icom.museum/

Sparacino, F., Davenport, G., & Pentland, A. (2000). Media in performance: Interactive spaces for dance, theater, circus, and museum exhibits. *IBM Systems Journal, 39*(3.4), 479–510. doi:10.1147j.393.0479

Sparrow, L. (2016). Variations in visual exploration and physiological reactions during art perception when children visit the museum with a mobile electronic guide. In *Aesthetics and Neuroscience*. Scientific and Artistic Perspectives; doi:10.1007/978-3-319-46233-2_9

Stanco, F., Tanasi, D., Gallo, G., Buffa, M., & Basile, B. (2012). Augmented perception of the past. the case of Hellenistic Syracuse. *Journal of Multimedia, 7*(2). doi:10.4304/jmm.7.2.211-216

Stary, C. (2001). Exploring the concept of virtuality: Technological approaches and implications from tele-education. In A. Riegler, M. F. Peschl, K. Edlinger, G. Fleck, & W. Feigl (Eds.), Virtual reality: Cognitive foundations, technological issues & philosophical implications, (pp. 113-128). Peter Lang.

Stricker, D., Dähne, P., Seibert, F., Christou, I., Almeida, L., Carlucci, R., & Ioannidis, N. (2001). Design and development issues for archeoguide: An augmented reality-based cultural heritage on-site guide. In *International Conference on Augmented, Virtual Environments, and Three-Dimensional Imaging* (pp. 1–5). IEEE Computer Society. Retrieved from http://publica.fraunhofer.de/documents/N-5833.html

Stricker, D., & Daehne, P. (2001). Design and development issues for ARCHEOGUIDE: An augmented reality based cultural heritage on-site guide, *Proc. Of International Conference on Augmented Virtual Environments and three-dimensional imaging*, Mykonos, Greece.

Stroup, C. (2014). Simulation usage in nursing fundamentals: Integrative literature review. *Clinical Simulation in Nursing, 10*(3), 155–164. doi:10.1016/j.ecns.2013.10.004

Su, M. J. (2017, Nov. 7). Engaging audience through VR and AR technology in the National Museum of Natural Science. *The Liberty Times,* Retrieved from http://news.ltn.com.tw/news/life/breakingnews/2246155

Suess, A. (2014). *Art gallery visitors and Instagram*. University of Arts London. Retrieved from https://www.academia.edu/12086365/Art_Gallery_Visitors_and_Instagram

Sylaiou, S., Liarokapis, F., Kotsakis, K., & Patias, P. (2009). Virtual museums, a survey and some issues for consideration. *Journal of Cultural Heritage, 10*(4), 520–528. doi:10.1016/j.culher.2009.03.003

Sylaiou, S., Mania, K., Karoulis, A., & White, M. (2010). Exploring the relationship between presence and enjoyment in a virtual museum. *International Journal of Human-Computer Studies, 68*(5), 243–253. doi:10.1016/j.ijhcs.2009.11.002

Taçgın, Z. (2017). Ameliyathanede Kullanılan Cerrahi Setlerin Öğretimine Yönelik Bir Sanal Gerçeklik Simülasyon Geliştirilmesi ve Test Edilmesi[Development and evaluation of a virtual reality simulation to teach surgical sets used in the operating room]. Doctoral Thesis, Marmara University.

Tagaytayan, R., Kelemen, A., & Sik-Lanyi, C. (2018). Augmented reality in neurosurgery. *Archives of Medical Science*, *14*(3), 572–578.

Tamke, M., Evers, H. L., Zwierzycki, M., Wessel, R., Ochmann, S., Vock, R., & Klein, R. (2016). An automated approach to the generation of structured building information models from unstructured 3D point cloud scans. Retrieved from http://www.re-ad.dk/ws/files/60642021/IASS2016_1248_An_automated_approach_to...pdf

Tanhan, F., & Alav, Ö. (2015). Siber kimliklerin kişiliğe yansıması: Proteus etki (Tanımı, nedenleri ve önlenmesi) (The effect of ciber personalities on personality: Proteus effect (Definition, causes and prevention). *Online Journal of Technology Addiction & Cyberbullying*, *2*(4), 1–19.

Teferra, D., & Altbachl, P. G. (2004). African higher education: Challenges for the 21st century. *Higher Education*, *47*(1), 21–50. doi:10.1023/B:HIGH.0000009822.49980.30

The first hybrid neurosurgical simulator based on physical and augmented reality. (n.d.). Available at https://upsim.upsurgeon.com/discover/the-first-hybrid-neurosurgical-simulator-based-on-physical-and-augmented-reality-.kl

The Green Way. (2019). Past, present, and future meet on The Greenway! Retrieved from https://www.rosekennedygreenway.org/

The MET. (n.d.). The Met 360° Project. Retrieved from https://www.youtube.com/watch?time_continue=2020&v=h2019OTCFAmbmA

The Tellos Alliance. (2019), *The Tellos Alliance virtual radio is the future, the future is here*, Retrieved from https://www.telosalliance.com/Radio-Solutions/Virtual-Radio

The ultimate guide to understanding augmented reality (AR) technology. (n.d). ©RealityTechnologies.com Diversified Internet Holdings LLC. Available at https://www.realitytechnologies.com/augmented-reality/

Time Out. (n.d.). Martell Air Gallery: Zoe – The art of the alchemist. Time Out, Retrieved from https://www.timeout.com/singapore/art/martell-air-gallery-zoe-the-art-of-the-alchemist

Topuksak, B., & Kublay, G. (2010). Florence What has changed from Florence Nightingale to present in nursing education? Modern nursing education in Europe and Turkey (Nightingale'den Günümüze Hemşirelik Eğitiminde Neler Değişti? Avrupa ve Türkiye'de Modern Hemşirelik Eğitimi). *Maltepe Üniversitesi Hemşirelik Bilim ve Sanatı Dergisi (Maltepe University Journal of Nursing Art and Science)*, 298-305.

Torisu, T. (2016). *Sense of Presence in Social VR Experience*. Retrieved from http://www.interactivearchitecture.org/sense-of-presence-in-social-vr-experience.html

Tota, A. (1999). *Sociologie dell'arte. Dal museo tradizionale all'arte multimediale*. Rome, Italy: Carocci.

Trescak, T., Esteva, M., & Rodriguez, I. (2010). A virtual world grammar for automatic generation of virtual worlds. *The Visual Computer*, *26*(6-8), 521–531. doi:10.100700371-010-0473-7

Trindade, J., Fiolhais, C., & Almeida, L. (2002). Science learning in virtual environments: A descriptive study. *British Journal of Educational Technology*, *33*(4), 471–488. doi:10.1111/1467-8535.00283

Tröndle, M., Greenwood, S., Kirchberg, V., & Tschacher, W. (2014). An integrative and comprehensive methodology for studying aesthetic experience in the field: Merging movement tracking, physiology, and psychological data. *Environment and Behavior*, *46*(1), 102–135. doi:10.1177/0013916512453839

Tsai, S. L., Chai, S., & Chuang, K. H. (2015). The effectiveness of a chronic obstructive pulmonary disease computer game as a learning tool for nursing students. *Open Journal of Nursing*, *5*(7), 605–612. doi:10.4236/ojn.2015.57064

UK Creative Industry Council (CIC). (2018, November). UK creative industries-value. UK Creative Industry Council (CIC), Retrieved from http://www.thecreativeindustries.co.uk/resources/infographics

Unver, V., Basak, T., Watts, P., Gaioso, V., Moss, J., Tastan, S., & Tosun, N. (2017). The reliability and validity of three questionnaires: The student satisfaction and self-confidence in learning scale, simulation design scale, and educational practices questionnaire. *Contemporary Nurse*, *53*(1), 60–74. doi:10.1080/10376178.2017.1282319 PMID:28084900

Urry, J. (2001). *The tourist gaze. London* (2nd ed.). Thousand Oaks, CA: Sage.

Vaccari, F. (2011). *Fotografia e inconscio tecnologico*. Torino, Italy: Einaudi.

Vanlaere, L., & Gastmans, C. (2007). Ethics in nursing education: Learning to reflect on care practices. *Nursing Ethics*, *14*(6), 758–766. doi:10.1177/0969733007082116 PMID:17901186

Vaughn, J., Lister, M., & Shaw, R. J. (2016). Piloting augmented reality technology to enhance realism in clinical simulation. *Computers, Informatics, Nursing*, *34*(9), 402–405. doi:10.1097/CIN.0000000000000251 PMID:27258807

Vayanou, M., Ioannidis, Y., Loumos, G., Sidiropoulou, O., & Kargas, A. (2019). Designing performative, gamified cultural experiences for groups. *Extended Abstracts of the 2019 CHI Conference on Human Factors in Computing Systems - CHI EA '19*, 1–6. doi:10.1145/3290607.3312855

Vayanou, M., Ioannidis, Y., Loumos, G., & Kargas, A. (2019). How to play storytelling games with masterpieces: From art galleries to hybrid board games. *Journal of Computers in Education*, *6*(1), 79–116. doi:10.100740692-018-0124-y

Virno, P. (2003). Quando il Verbo si fa Carne. Linguaggio e Natura Umana. Torino, IT: Bollati Boringhieri.

Virno, P. (2004). *A Grammar of the Multitude: For an Analysis of Contemporary Forms of Life*. Los Angeles, CA: Semiotext(e) Foreign Agents Series. Retrieved from http://www.generation-online.org/c/fcmultitude3.htm

Virtanen, J.-P., Kurkela, M., Turppa, T., Vaaja, M. T., Julin, A., Kukko, A., ... Hyyppa, H. (2018). Depth camera indoor mapping for 3d virtual radio play. *The Photogrammetric Record*, *33*(162), 171–195. doi:10.1111/phor.12239

Virtual Health Clinic. (n.d.). Society of american gastrointestinal and endoscopic surgeons (Sage). Available at https://www.sages.org/virtual-hernia-clinic/

Wagner, D., Schmalstieg, D., & Billinghurst, M. (2006, November). Handheld AR for collaborative edutainment. In *International Conference on Artificial Reality and Telexistence* (pp. 85-96). Berlin, Germany: Springer.

Wagner, C. (2008). Learning experience with virtual worlds. *Journal of Information Systems Education*, *19*(3), 263.

Wagner, D., Schmalstieg, D., & Billinghurst, M. (2006). *Handheld AR for collaborative edutainment* (pp. 85–96). Berlin, Germany: Springer; doi:10.1007/11941354_10

Wang, Y., Sun, Y., Liu, Z., Sarma, S. E., Bronstein, M. M., & Solomon, J. M. (2018). Dynamic graph CNN for learning on point clouds. Retrieved from http://arxiv.org/abs/1801.07829

Wang, S., Parsons, M., Stone-McLean, J., Rogers, P., Boyd, S., Hoover, K., ... Smith, A. (2017). Augmented reality as a telemedicine platform for remote procedural training. *Sensors (Basel)*, *17*(10), 2294. doi:10.339017102294

Wang, X., Laffey, J., Xing, W., Ma, Y., & Stichter, J. (2016). Exploring embodied social presence of youth with Autism in a 3D collaborative virtual learning environment: A case study. *Computers in Human Behavior*, *55*, 310–321. doi:10.1016/j.chb.2015.09.006

Wedel, M., & Pieters, R. (2008). A review of eye-tracking research in marketing. *Review of Marketing Research*. doi:10.1108/S1548-6435(2008)0000004009

Weilenmann, A., Hillman, T., & Jungselius, B. (2013). Instagram at the museum: communicating the museum experience through social photo sharing. In *Proceedings of the SIGCHI Conference on Human Factors in Computing Systems - CHI '13* (p. 1843). New York, NY: ACM Press. 10.1145/2470654.2466243

Weiner, Y. (2018). *39 ways AR can change the world in the next five years*. Available at https://medium.com/thrive-global/39-ways-ar-can-change-the-world-in-the-next-five-years-a7736f8bfaa5

Wheeler, L. J. (2018) *North Carolina Museum of Art receives two American Alliance of Museums Awards*. Retrieved from https://ncartmuseum.org/images/uploads/blog/2018_AAM_Awards_release_FINAL.pdf

White, R., & Evan, C. (2002). *Clinical teaching in nursing* (2nd ed.). Springer.

White, W., & Liarokapis, F. (2004). *ARCOLite-an XML based system for building and presenting virtual museum exhibitions using Web3D and augmented reality. Proc. Theory and Practice of Computer Graphics* (pp. 94–101). Bournemouth, UK: IEEE Computer Society.

Whitney. (2017). Jordan Wolfson. Retrieved from https://whitney.org/exhibitions/2017-biennial#exhibition-about

Wiecha, J., Heyden, R., Sternthal, E., & Merialdi, M. (2010). Learning in a virtual world: Experience with using second life for medical education. *Journal of Medical Internet Research*, *12*(1), e1. doi:10.2196/jmir.1337 PMID:20097652

Witmer, B. G., & Singer, M. J. (1998). Measuring presence in virtual environments: A presence questionnaire. *Presence (Cambridge, Mass.)*, *7*(3), 225–240. doi:10.1162/105474698565686

Wittkover, R. (1987). Allegory and the migrations of symbols, New York: Thames and Hudon, 11.

Wolters Kluwer Health. 9AD, Summer (2017, May 15). *65% of nursing education programs adopting virtual simulation*. Retrieved from http://healthclarity.wolterskluwer.com/nursing-education-programs-virtual-simulation.html

Wright, T., de Ribaupierre, S., & Eagleson, R. (2017). Design and evaluation of an augmented reality simulator using leap motion. *Healthcare Technology Letters*, *4*(5), 210–215. doi:10.1049/htl.2017.0070

Wu, D., Weng, D. & Xue, S. (2016). Virtual Reality System as an affective medium to induce specific emotion: A validation study. *Electronic Imaging*, 1(6).

Wu, F., Liu, Z., Wang, J., & Zhao, Y. (2015, March). Establishment virtual maintenance environment based on VIRTOOLS to effectively enhance the sense of immersion of teaching equipment. In *2015 International Conference on Education Technology, Management and Humanities Science (ETMHS 2015)*. Atlantis Press. 10.2991/etmhs-15.2015.93

Wu, H. K., Lee, S. W. Y., Chang, H. Y., & Liang, J. C. (2013). Current status, opportunities and challenges of augmented reality in education. *Computers & Education*, *62*, 41–49. doi:10.1016/j.compedu.2012.10.024

Yang, K. C. C. (Ed.). (2018). Multi-platform advertising strategies in the global marketplace. In Advances in marketing, customer relationship management, and electronic services (AMCRMES) book series. Hershey, PA: IGI Global.

Yang, K. C. C., & Kang, Y. W. (2018). Integrating virtual reality and augmented reality into advertising campaigns: History, technology, and future trends. In N. Lee, X.-M. Wu, & A. El Rhalibi (Eds.), Encyclopedia of computer graphics and games. New York, NY: Springer. doi:10.1007/978-3-319-08234-9_132-1

Yang, K. C. C. (2019). Reality-creating technologies as a global phenomenon. In K. C. C. Yang (Ed.), *Cases on immersive virtual reality techniques* (pp. 1–18). Hershey, PA: IGI Global.

Yeditepe, B. B. (2015). Digital games: Design requirements and player psychology. *AJIT-e, 6*(19), 7–21. doi:10.5824/1309-1581.2015.2.001.x

Yin, C., Han-Yu, S., Hwang, G. J., Hirokawa, S., Hui-Chun, C., Flanagan, B., & Tabata, Y. (2013). Learning by searching: A learning environment that provides searching and analysis facilities for supporting trend analysis activities. *Journal of Educational Technology & Society, 16*(3), 286.

Yoshimoto, M. (2003, December). The status of creative industries in Japan and policy recommendations for their promotion. *NLI Research,* 1-9.

Zheng, S., Zhan, Z., & Zhang, Z. (2004). *A flexible and automatic 3D reconstruction method.* Istanbul, Turkey: ISPRS.

Zhou, Y., Ji, S., Xu, T., & Wang, Z. (2018). Promoting knowledge construction: a model for using virtual reality interaction to enhance learning. *Procedia Computer Science, 130*, 239–246. doi:10.1016/j.procs.2018.04.035

Ziv, A. (2005). Simulators and simulation-based medical education. In J. Dent, & R. M. Harden (Eds.), A practical guide for medical teacher (pp. 211-220). London, UK: Elsevier.

Ziv, A., Small, S. D., & Root-Wolpe, P. (2000). Patient safety and simulation-based medical education. *Medical Teacher, 22*(5), 489–495. doi:10.1080/01421590050110777 PMID:21271963

Zweifach, S. M., & Triola, M. M. (2019). Extended reality in medical education: Driving adoption through provider-centered design. *Digital Biomarkers, 3*(1), 14–21. doi:10.1159/000498923

About the Contributors

Giuliana Guazzaroni is a Technology Enhanced Learning Ph.D. She has developed EMMAP (Emotional Mapping of Museum Augmented Places) an interactive format for Museums, Archaeological Parks, Art Galleries etc. The Presidential Medal of the Italian Republic awarded her researches. She has used E-Learning environments, integrating learning objects with mobile devices, to create unique learning experiences where the participant interacts in a place, at the same time, authentic and augmented by the use of different media. She studies and develops Virtual or Augmented Reality systems useful in treating mental health, including VR 360 movies. She has published scientific articles on the themes of E-Learning, Augmented and Virtual reality, Virtual and augmented learning environments, Virtual and Augmented Reality in Mental Health Treatment. She has a degree in Foreign Languages (Università di Macerata), a master degree in Technologies and Methodologies of E-Learning (Università di Verona) and a Ph.D in Engineering Sciences, Curriculum E-Learning (Università Politecnica delle Marche).

* * *

Maria Cristina Acciarri works on research projects at the Neurological Clinic at Marche Polytechnic University, Ancona, Italy; she also participates as sub-investigator in clinical trials and collaborates at the Multiple Sclerosis Center of the Neurological Clinic of United Hospital of Ancona. Previously, she graduated in Medicine in 2014 and she specialized in Neurology in December 2018 at Marche Polytechnic University, Ancona, Italy.

Damiano Antonino Angelo Aiello received his master's degree in Building Engineering and Architecture from the University of Catania (Italy) in 2018. During his studies, he got two Erasmus+ traineeship scholarships to carry out a professional experience at DNA ARCHITECTS, an architecture firm in Barcelona (Spain), and a visiting research experience at CIMS Lab, a Carleton University research centre in Ottawa (Canada) dedicated to the advanced study of innovative, hybrid forms of representation. In 2019 he was hired as external collaborator at the Politecnico of Milan to develop VR and AR experiences and he is currently collaborating with the University of Catania on the exhibition design of MuRa (Museo della Rappresentazione) and on digitization and virtualization projects of Sicilian and European Cultural Heritage. He works, writes and presents widely on issues of digital surveying techniques, 3D modelling, digitization of Cultural Heritage and Virtual Reality.

Renato Angeloni is a Ph.D student at the Department of Civil and Building Engineering and Architecture of Marche Polytechnic University, Ancona. He graduated in Building Engineering and Architecture in 2015, with a thesis on 3D digital survey and augmented reality titled "The Roman Theatre of Fanum Fortunae: from the laser scanning survey to the reconstruction of a scientific model and new techniques of fruition". Research interests include laser scanning, photogrammetry, augmented reality and immersive virtual reality. Scientific production includes research papers about cultural heritage 3D surveying, survey data integration and fruition, focusing on the possibilities to enrich these data offered by different digital tools.

Cecilia Bolognesi is associate professor at Politecnico di Milano (Italy). During her career she hold several courses in Representation of Architecture and Digital Skills, actually being scientific coordinator of the 3d Modelling courses in the school AUIC of Politecnico itself, dealing with subjects from BIM environments to Virtual to Augmented ones. She has been leader group for Politecnico in financed researches from Ministery of Industry and Development regarding digital crafts and museum digitalization. She is author of several papers and speaker in International conferences regarding digital transformation of architecture and cultural heritage. She is part of a group coordinating a H2020 project on BIM and digital environment in construction.

Paolo Bonvini graduated at Istituto Universitario di Architettura di Venezia (IUAV) with full marks and honour, 1985. PhD in Architectural and Urban Design at Dipartimento di Architettura e Urbanistica dell'Università "G. D'Annunzio" di Chieti, Facoltà di Architettura di Pescara, 1997. Work as Teaching Assistant at Architecture Faculty of University of California at Berkeley, 1994. Post-graduated scholarship for research activity at Technical University of Delft, The Netherlands. 1988-89. Assistant Professor in Architectural and Urban Design since 2008 at DICEA, Department of Civil and Building Engineering and Architecture, Polytechnic University of Marche. He lectured in various international universities as BUCEA, Beijing, China, Huè Sciences University, Vietnam, NTNU Trondheim, Norway, FADU, Buenos Aires, Argentina. Since 1986 he cooperated with some architectural firms as: arch. Danilo Guerri (Ancona), arch. Giancarlo De Carlo (Milano), arch. Umberto Riva (Milano), arch. Henk Hopman (Delft, The Netherlands). With his own firm he took part in various national and international architectural competitions, obtaining various prizes and acknowledgments. In 1986 he got the "H.C. Andersen" Prize from Accademia Nazionale di San Luca, Rome; in 2008 the "Premio Marche Architettura 2008", "Architecture for public services", and in the 2009 the First Prize "Premio Innovazione e Qualità Urbana 2009", category "City and Architecture".

Giorgio Cipolletta is a transdisciplinary artist and media-theorist. In 2012 he obtained a PhD in Information and Communication Theory at the University of Macerata where he is adjunct professor of Visual Art and Technology. He is member of the media editorial staff of Noema / mediaversi / Riviste di Scienze sociali. He works as freelancer layout designer for the University press of Macerata (eum). He writings appeared in many academic journals (Flusser Studies, Heteroglossia) and his first book is Metrobodily passages. For an aesthetics of transition, eum, Macerata 2014. He has won many international poem prizes. Besides, he's showed his multimedia installations and performances in many national exhibitions (Corpus 2012, Chaos 2013, Bookquake 2017, Mea Culpa, 2018, Soundscapes from Earth 2018). He is founding partner and vice-president of Crash (Creative Art Shocking, 2014).

Paolo Clini is Full Professor at Univpm. PhD in 1997 at Florence University, in 2002 he obtained the diploma to the European Masters in History of Architecture at the University of Rome III with a study entitled "The drawings of the Basilica of Fano in "De Architectura" of Vitruvius, under the guide scientific of Professor Pierre Gros. He is member of the PhD school in "Engineering Science" at UNIPM, since 2010 he is Chairman of the "Vitruvian Research Center". Its interest concern analysis and historical architecture representation with digital technologies. Focused on digitization and survey, he is coordinator and scientific supervisor of more than 100 survey campaign for architectural and archaeological heritage, in Italy, East Europe and North Africa. He is co-author of more than 130 technical papers and six books. He is a member of several conference committee and collaborates in editorial board of scientific journals.

Enrico Cori, PhD in Business Management, is full professor of Business Organization at the Polytechnic University of the Marche (Ancona, Italy). He previously served as research fellow and assistant professor at the University of Pisa. He is currently involved in the following research fields: organizational traits and competence dynamics in the family SMEs, organization and management of music festivals, strategic and organizational issues of digitization processes in the cultural heritage.

Nesrin Özdener Dönmez completed her BS and MS at Marmara University, Atatürk Education Faculty, Physics Education Department and her PhD at the same faculty and the same university. Between 1989–1998 she worked at Physics Education Department of Atatürk Education Faculty. She has been teaching at Computer and Instructional Technologies Department since 1998. She works as a Professor since 2017. Her research areas include educational software design and simulations.

Aldo Franco Dragoni is in charge as Associate Professor at the "Università Politecnica delle Marche" where he teaches "Foundamentals of Computer Sciences", "Artificial Intelligence" and "Special Purpose Operating Systems". His scientific interests concerned several aspects of the Artificial Intelligence (AI) area, from the classic knowledge-based approaches to more advanced hybrid systems that integrate symbolic reasoning with neural networks. Recently he started a research activity in "Real Time Systems" and opened a new application area for AI techniques that he called "NetMedicine", which means every Health-related activity which is carried on through the Internet. Aldo devoted much interest also in the study of distributed information systems, under the realistic hypothesis that they can be affected by limited degrees of correctness and completeness. He tried to evaluate, on statistical basis, the global performances of a group whose members adopt the same local strategies for belief revision, the same policies for communication and the same criteria for partner selection. Recently he focused his attention to AI techniques that can perform in real-time and he also began to consider "e-Health" as an application area for AI. He served as Program Committee and Reviewer for several International Conferences and Journals about AI.

Fabio Fraticelli is Post-Doc Research Fellow in Organizational Science at Università Politecnica delle Marche (Ancona - Italy) and Scientific director of TechSoup Academy. He received his Ph.D in Business Administration from University of Pisa in 2012. Starting from an ethnographic study carried out at the National Park Service (USA) between 2010 and 2012, in recent years he has developed an intense research program focused on innovation management, IT-acceptance and digital transformation. On these issues, he has published contributions in national and international journals and books, as well as doing action-research project in several profit and non-profit organizations. As an academic and scientific director of

TechSoup Academy, today his main research interest regards the understanding of organizational forms and antecedents that enhance digital transformation, especially in the non-profit sector.

Emanuele Frontoni is a Professor of computer science with the Universit\'a Politecnica delle Marche, Italy. He received the Ph.D. degree in intelligent artificial systems the Department of Information Engineering (DII), Universit\'a Politecnica delle Marche, in 2006. His Ph.D. thesis was on ``vision-based robotics''. His research focuses on artificial intelligence and computer vision techniques applied to robotics, internet of things, e-health, and ambient assisted living. He is a member of the ASME MESA TC, GIRPR, and AI*IA.

Marco Gallegati is currently Professor of Economic Policy at the Department of Economics and Social Sciences of the Polytechnic University of Marche. He received his PhD in Economics in 1997 from the University of Ancona and has been visiting scholar at the University of California at Santa Cruz, the New School University of New York and the Bank of Finland. He has been involved in the realization of several national (MURST, COFIN) and European EU FP-7 research projects (Pohlia, Finnov, Ness, Mathemacs, Rastanews, Symphony and Finmap). His research interests include economic applications of wavelet analysis, especially business cycles, early warning and composite leading indicators, and climate change. He has published many papers in refereed international journals in economics, finance and statistics, the special issue New macro perspectives in the Journal of Economic Behavior and Organization, and the book Wavelet applications in economics and finance with Springer.

Danilo Gambelli is Associate Professor at the Department of Agricultural, Food and Environmental Sciences of the Polytechnic University of Marche. He is presently lecturer at the Department of Agricultural, Food and Environmental Sciences for the courses in the field of Economics, Agricultural Economics and Environmental Economics. In 2018 he attains the National Scientific Qualification as Ordinary professor, disciplinary grouping "Agricultural Economics and rural appraisal ". The main areas of research are organic farming, rural development, farm microeconomics and methodological aspects concerning applied economics analysis, particularly those integrating qualitative and quantitative data. He is author or co-author of more than fifty national and international publications, and is a research member in numerous European and national research projects in the field of organic farming, rural development and environmental analysis.

Ali Geris is a Research Assistant at Department of Computer Education & Instructional Technologies at Manisa Celal Bayar University. Also he is a Ph.D. candidate in CEIT at Marmara University. Current studies focuses on virtual reality, mixed reality, e-learning and mobile learning.

Giuliana Geronimo, PhD History and New Technology at Bologna University. She is co-founder of Streamcolors srl a Milan Digital Art Studio specialised in real-time software development and in the production of interactive solutions, immersive experiences, videos, VR and video games for worldwide clients museums and brands.

Salvatore Giannella is a former editor of the magazines Europeo and Genius, and from 1986 to 1994 of Airone, a monthly magazine dealing with nature and civilisation. For Chiarelettere he published "Voglia di cambiare", about excellence in Europe, and "Operazione Salvataggio", dedicated to the unsung heroes who saved works of art from wars.

Carlo Gioventù started his professional activity creating video games in 1993, publishing his first product "Pray for Death" with Virgin Interactive, a 3D graphics teacher since 1999 at the Macerata Academy of Fine Arts and since 2003 at the Academy di Brera in Milan. Many of his graduates have found employment with Weta, UbiSoft, Pacific Digital, Image Engine and others. He worked in 3D scanning companies, 3D prototyping, advertising graphics and founded the MenteZero Cultural Association for multimedia arts research in 2010. In 2012 he managed a production of an animated series pilot with a team of 20 students in the first experience, the pilot was successfully presented in Annecy in the same year. He specializes in visual programming in Unreal Engine by himself, producing Indie products and professional Gamification Applications for important companies in the sector. He has exhibited and lectured at various events throughout the country including the Venice Biennale He made the special effects of two multi-award-winning feature films abroad and in Italy: the Sculpture and Sfashion by director Mauro John Capece He is currently engaged in the production of a videogame project concerning interactive museography made with Unreal Engine 4.

Yowei Kang (Ph.D.) is Assistant Professor at Bachelor Degree Program in Oceanic Cultural Creative Design Industries, National Taiwan Ocean University, TAIWAN. His research interests focus on new media design, digital game research, visual communication, and experiential rhetoric. Some of his works have been published in *International Journal of Strategic Communication*, and *Journal of Intercultural Communication Studies*. He has received government funding to support his research in location-based advertising and consumer privacy management strategies.

Antonios Kargas holds a Bachelor degree in economics from University of Athens, a Master degree and a Ph.D. degree from the Department of Informatics and Telecommunications in the same University. Since 2007 he works as a research associate for the University of Athens, participating in several National and European funded projects. He is a Research Fellow in University of Athens (teaching Organizational Structures and Human resource Management), in Hellenic Open University (teaching Cultural Economics) and in University of Peloponnese (teaching Special Issues in Data Management). He has more than 15 publications in journals and conferences in the field of entrepreneurship, leadership, organizational culture, cultural economics and technological management in cultural sector.

Nikoletta Karitsioti is a Ph.D. Candidate in International Political Communication. She holds a Bachelor Degree in Philosophy and a Master degree in International Relations and Politics with expertise in Governance. She has participated as a major researcher in the Research Unit of Southeast Europe (SEE Research Unit -SEER-Unit) in University of Peloponnese and the Research Unit of the International Relations Institute. Since 2012, she works as a Communication Manager and has taken part in various European funded projects. She is experienced in planning, organizing and supporting the projects' communication and dissemination activities. At the same time, she writes articles in news - websites and newspapers on International Relations and Communication issues.

Ajinkya Kunjir completed Bachelor in Computer Engineering from M.E.S College of Engineering, Pune, India in 2017. Actively pursuing Masters Degree in Computer science at Lakehead University, Thunder Bay, Ontario, Canada. My research Interests include Data Mining, Machine Learning, Big Data and BCI.

Alma Leopardi graduated in Mechanical Engineering at Marche Polytechnic University, Ancona, Italy, in 2016. In November 2016 she started the PhD course in Industrial Engineering at the Department of Industrial Engineering and Mathematical Sciences (DIISM) at Marche Polytechnic University. Her research interest includes: new fruition and interaction technologies, customer experience, reverse engineering. Her research activity concerns the development of innovative interactive methods and tools, for the management and use of cultural heritage through the construction of virtual prototypes. The research focused on the study and comparison of different interaction and visualization technologies, able to enhance digital cultural heritage effectively based on the context and purpose of use.

Eva Malinverni graduated in Architecture at the Polytechnic of Milan, PhD in Cartography and Topography, currently Full Professor of Geomatics at the Faculty of Engineering of the Marche Polytechnic University in Ancona. His research is applied to different fields of Geomatics addressing both Cultural Heritage and the Landscape. From remote sensing to numerical and thematic mapping with the development of automatic analysis and classification techniques; from aerial digital photogrammetry to close range techniques, to obtain graphic representations, realistic three-dimensional models and orthogonalized images, from the use of digital tools for GNSS positioning to lidar/mobile acquisition for descriptions with increasingly complex levels of detail, up to the management of documentation acquired in the GIS/(H)BIM. The research activities that are always applied to the solution in an innovative way of complex problems. She, as associated to ITABC-CNR in Rome, is part of several research groups that deal with surveys on archaeological areas such as Chan Chan (Unesco site in Peru) or The land of Nineveh in Iraqi Kurdistan, and many others. She was a member of the Management Committee and active participant to the WG1 in the COST action "Cyberparks", combining the geomatic knowledge with the modern ICT techniques. Now she participates in the COST action "Arkwork" to deal the archeological data dissemination. She participates in ISPRS conferences, IGARSS-GRSS symposium, ICA and ICC workshops and at EARSeL special working groups. She is the author of more than 172 publications, 49 of these are in SCOPUS with 262 total citations and H-index 9.

Raissa Mammoli is a Ph.D. student and she is part of DiStori Heritage research group in the Dept. DICEA at Polytechnic University of Marche. Her research focuses on architectural and cultural heritage (AH-CH), analysis and developments of digital libraries and HBIM applications aimed at communication and management of architecture. She carries out applications experiences in traditional direct and instrumental survey methodologies. During the PhD course, she also deals with teaching assistance in the following courses: drawing and modeling buildings and architectural surveys, assisting students during practical exercises.

Serena Mandolesi is Postdoctoral Research Fellow at the Department of Materials, Environmental Sciences and Urban Planning of the Polytechnic University of Marche. In 2018 she attains the National Scientific Qualification as associate professor, disciplinary grouping "Agricultural Economics and rural appraisal".Her activity is concentrated on the study of agro-food marketing and neuromarketing with particular interest in food innovations, dairy and meat supply-chains and acceptance of edible insects as food; and of environmental sustainability (e.g. analysis of photovoltaic impact, deep-sea ecosystems). Studies conducted are based on the application of quali-quantitaive research methodologies such as: Q methodology, Means-End Chain analysis (MEC) and Eye-tracking technology.

Prabha Mathew is working as Guest Lecturer at Bishop Cotton Women's Christian College M.Tech. (Computer Science), M.Phil., MCA Over 11 years of Academic Experience Area of Interest: Data Mining, Software Engineering.

Maura Mengoni is Associate Professor in Methods and Tools of Industrial Engineering at the Polytechnic University of Marche, teaching courses in Virtual Prototyping (VP), and Design Methods for Product Data Management. Her main research activities concern with method and tools of industrial engineering, including cutting-edge technologies based on Affective Computing, Artificial Intelligence (AI) and VP to pursue Customer-centric Innovation. She is responsible of a research team, made of 10 persons and of the Virtual Reality Lab. She is author of more than 160 International publications and participated to more than 70 national and international research projects. She became in 2007 scientific advisor of the CO-ENV consortium, that carries out research and development activities in the field of codesign for 21 Large and SMEs, in 2010 Board Member of the Hyperlean Academic Spin-off and in 2017 co-founder and President of the EMOJ Spin-off that leads innovation in the field of AI. She also contributed and is owner of 3 national and European patents. She contributed to the foundation of the Italian technological Clusters TICHE, E-living and Marche Manufacturing. In the last years she has carried out research activities on the field of Digital Heritage with the aim to apply Reverse Engineering and Rapid Prototyping techniques to the conservation, management and promotion of cultural heritage. She has also explored the potentialities of Virtual Reality and novel multisensory Human-Machine Interfaces to empower the connection between the user and the digital artefact. Recently she is applying Emotional Analytics and AI techniques to improve and create engaging museum experiences. In 2019, she has become member of the scientific board on x-Reality Technologies of the Italian Cluster of Cultural Heritage and coordinates three important national projects about emotions in museums and culture.

Christian Morbidoni is a researcher at the Department of Information Engineering, Università Politecnica delle Marche, Ancona, Italy, where he obtained his PhD in Computer Science in 2006. His research interests include Semantic Web and Knowledge Representation/Management, and the application of related technologies in Digital Humanities and Cultural Heritage. Other active research areas are Information Retrieval and Extraction, Recommender Systems, Machine Learning and Deep Learning.

Biancamaria Mori, from her university years at the multimedia department of the Accademia di Brera, she established a collaboration with the Game Design courses of the Polytechnic and the State University of Milan. She collaborates with MenteZero, realizing artistic projects and courses on gaming. She specialized in applied gamification, with GameArt Gallery's Neoludica exhibits at the Venice Biennale and at Villa Bottini at Lucca Comics in collaboration with UbiSoft Italia, she is a speaker at numerous conferences including "Dialoghi d'Aragona", "Inside Videogames" and others, talking about the potential of the videogame medium for business and art. She is the author of gamification projects for important Italian companies.

Romina Nespeca is research fellow (ICAR 17) in DICEA, Department of Civil Engineering and Architecture, in the Polytechnic University of Marche - UNIVPM. Her doctoral thesis is "Point Cloud as Informative System. From integrated survey to digital documentation of Cultural Heritage". She qualified as Associate Professor in November 2018. During her study, she acquired skills and knowledge in relation to survey, documentation and representation. Her researches are specifically oriented to the data integration in information systems for archaeology and historical architecture. In particular, she works about the treatment of the point cloud for integrated surveys, for the restoration, conservation and visualization of Cultural Heritage. She has collaborated on many research activities. She participated in many national and international conferences related to these issues. She attended training courses for learning specific skills, continuing to remain up to date on technological innovations.

Marina Paolanti received the Ph.D. degree in Information Engineering the Department of Information Engineering (DII) at Università Politecnica delle Marche, in 2018. Her Ph.D. thesis was on "Pattern Recognition for Challenging Computer Vision Applications". She currently has a post doc position with DII. Her research focuses on Deep Learning, Machine Learning, image processing, and Computer Vision.

Roberto Pierdicca received the Ph.D. degree in Information Engineering the Department of Information Engineering (DII), Universit\'a Politecnica delle Marche, in 2017. His Ph.D. thesis was on ``Senseable spaces: from a theoretical perspective to the application in augmented environments''. He currently has a post doc position with DICEA Dipartimento di Ingegneria Civile, Edile e Architettura, Università Politecnica delle Marche. He's author of more than 50 international papers and member of national and international research projects.

Maria Paola Puggioni received the Master Degree in Architecture in 1985 and worked as professional Architect till 1992. From 1992 she is professor of "Tecnologia delle Costruzioni", "Progettazione", "Tecnologie e tecniche di rappresentazione grafica", "Gestione e sicurezza nel cantiere" at the ITET G.B.Carducci – G. Galilei in Fermo. Since November 2017 she is in the PhD School at Polytechnic University of Marche, Dipartimento di Ingegneria dell'Informazione - DII under the supervision of Prof. Emanuele Frontoni.

Ramona Quattrini joined the Dept. DARDUS at the Università Politecnica delle Marche, as a Ph.D. student in Engineering-Architecture. She obtained her PhD in 2008, now she is temporary assistant professor in the Dept. Construction, Civil Engineering and Architecture (DICEA). She qualified as Associate Professor in August 2017. Her research focuses on architectural and cultural heritage (AH-CH) survey and critical analysis, multiplatform digital libraries for smart access to knowledge and preservation. She works in the field of digital CH knowledge, analysis and monitoring, which she contributes in more than 70 publications. She has been serving, as scientific or technical responsible, in International Conferences and research projects based on competitive funding. She is Steering Committe delegate in the Interreg IT-HR REMEMBER (REstoring the MEmory of Adriatic ports sites. Maritime culture to foster Balanced tErritorial growth).

Patrizia Schettino works for AGID, Presidenza del Consiglio dei MInistri, Italy, as user experience researcher and digital media specialist. After a Masters in Design, Multimedia and Visual Communication at Politecnico in Milan, she worked as multimedia designer in Milan and Paris and taught at NABA, in Milan. She was an eLearning consultant for the European Network ERIC (European Resources for Intercultural Communication), and was involved as a graphic designer and instructional designer in 12 eLearning projects supported by the Swiss Virtual Campus in Switzerland. As visual artist, she has participated in several film festivals and exhibitions in Italy (POLI.design, Triennale, Milan, 1999; International Photography Award Viaggio in Basilicata, travelling exhibition 2006 and 2007; Potenza Film Festival, Potenza, 2006; Young Movie Festival, Potenza 2007 and 2009; and the Lucania Film Festival, Pisticci, 2006 and 2010, Biennale di Bari, 2018-2019). She has been visiting researcher at the Department of Information Studies and Interactive Media (INFIM), University of Tampere, the iCinema Center, University of New South Wales (UNSW), Sydney, the Immigration Museum, Melbourne, and the School of Museum Studies, University of Leicester, supported by a grant from the Swiss National Science Foundation. She has a PhD in Communication Science, Università della Svizzera italiana, and her PhD thesis is one of the first qualitative study about immersive media for cultural heritage. She has 20 year experience on digital media for cultural heritage.

Paolo Sernani is a post-doc research fellow at the Information Engineering Department of "Università Politecnica delle Marche", Ancona, Italy. He received the Ph.D. degree in Information Engineering in 2015 with a thesis entitled "Design and virtualization of intelligent systems for the management of assistive environments". Currently, his main research interests include multi-agent systems, expert systems, and deep learning, especially applied to cross-disciplinary research fields, such as ambient intelligence, ambient assisted living and augmented reality.

Mauro Silvestrini is a Full Professor of Neurology and Director of the Neurological Clinic at Marche Polytechnic University, Ancona, Italy where he is also the Deputy Head of the Faculty of Medicine. Previously, he has served as Assistant Professor of Neurology, Tor Vergata University of Rome, Italy and as Associate Professor of Neurology, Marche Polytechnic University, Ancona, Italy. Currently, he is in charge of neurology teaching in graduate courses, postgraduate and PhD schools. Research interests include cerebrovascular disorders and dementias. Scientific production includes about 300 research papers published on international peer-reviewed journals and his present H-Index is 40. He has received research funding from European (European Community) public national institutions (National Council of Research and the Ministry of Education, University and Research) and local institutions (University of Rome Tor Vergata and Polytechnic University of Marche). From March 2018 he is the elected president of the Italian Stroke Organization.

Massimo Tamberi is presently Professor of Economic Policy at the Department of Economics and Social Sciences of the Polytechnic University of Marche and is the Editor of the Working paper series Quaderni di Dpartimento. He has been visiting scholar at Stanford University several times under the supervision of Moses Abramovitz. His research interests include Italian economic development, international economics, specialization indexes, and export product diversification. He has published many papers in international economic journals and edited the book Geography, Structural Change and Economic Development with Edward Elgar.

Sevil Hamarat Tuncalı completed the bachelors' degree in nursing at the Dokuz Eylul University, Faculty of Nursing. She afterwards worked in Cardiovascular Intensive Care Unit for 3 years and chief of nursing department for a year. Currently, she is a graduate student in the Department of Fundamentals of Nursing at Izmir Katip Celebi University in İzmir, Turkey. She is interested in simulation in nursing education, and educational technology in nursing education.

Nazime Tuncay has Bachelor degree on Mathematics and Computer Education, Masters Degree on Applied Mathematics and Computer Science, PhD degree on Computer and Instructional Technology Education. Her PhD thesis is about the virtual platforms and she has constructed several virtual platforms to deliver her courses there. She has worked on various institutions as an instructor since 1999 and is keen on self development. Dr. Nazime Tuncay has also delivered distance education courses via virtual platforms and over Radio for many years. She has coauthored 6 books and more than 50 articles about Distance Education, Virtual Reality, Reality, Mobile Education, Special Education, Statistics, Computer Science, Mathematics and Instructional Technology.

Kenneth C. C. Yang (Ph.D.) is Professor in the Department of Communication at the University of Texas at El Paso, USA. His research focuses on new media advertising, consumer behavior, and international advertising. Some of his many works have been published in *Cyberpsychology, Journal of Strategic Communication, International Journal of Consumer Marketing, Journal of Intercultural Communication Studies, Journal of Marketing Communication*, and *Telematics and Informatics*. He has edited or co-edited three books, *Asia.com: Asia encounters the Internet* (Routledge, 2003), *Multi-Platform Advertising Strategies in the Global Marketplace* (IGI Global, 2018), and *Cases on Immersive Virtual Reality Techniques* (IGI Global, 2019).

Derya Uzelli Yılmaz completed Bachelor's, MSc and PhD degree in nursing at the University of Ege at Turkey. She also worked as a nurse for 5 years with clinical experience. Currently, she works as an assistant professor in the department of Fundamentals of Nursing at Katip Çelebi University in İzmir, Turkey. She interested in simulation in nursing education and educational technology in nursing education.

Yusuf Yılmaz is currently a researcher lecturer in the Department of Medical Education at Ege University, İzmir, Turkey. Dr. Yılmaz is also the coordinator of the Ege Media Education and Course Tools Unit. He earned his BS and MS in computer education and instructional technology from Dokuz Eylul University, and PhD in computer education and instructional technology from Middle East Technical University in 2018. His research focuses on faculty development, blended learning, e-learning, m-learning, technology integration in medical education, and virtual patients.

Index

Purchase Print, E-Book, or Print + E-Book

IGI Global's reference books are available in three unique pricing formats:
Print Only, E-Book Only, or Print + E-Book.

Shipping fees may apply.

www.igi-global.com

Recommended Reference Books

ISBN: 978-1-5225-5912-2
© 2019; 349 pp.
List Price: $215

ISBN: 978-1-5225-8176-5
© 2019; 2,218 pp.
List Price: $2,950

ISBN: 978-1-5225-7811-6
© 2019; 317 pp.
List Price: $225

ISBN: 978-1-5225-7268-8
© 2019; 316 pp.
List Price: $215

ISBN: 978-1-5225-7455-2
© 2019; 288 pp.
List Price: $205

ISBN: 978-1-5225-8973-0
© 2019; 200 pp.
List Price: $195

Do you want to stay current on the latest research trends, product announcements, news and special offers?
Join IGI Global's mailing list today and start enjoying exclusive perks sent only to IGI Global members.
Add your name to the list at **www.igi-global.com/newsletters.**

Publisher of Peer-Reviewed, Timely, and Innovative Academic Research

www.igi-global.com   Sign up at www.igi-global.com/newsletters   facebook.com/igiglobal   twitter.com/igiglobal   linkedin.com/igiglobal

Ensure Quality Research is Introduced to the Academic Community

Become an IGI Global Reviewer for Authored Book Projects

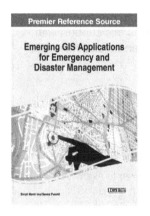
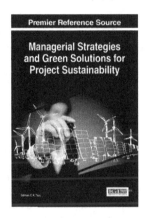

The overall success of an authored book project is dependent on quality and timely reviews.

In this competitive age of scholarly publishing, constructive and timely feedback significantly expedites the turnaround time of manuscripts from submission to acceptance, allowing the publication and discovery of forward-thinking research at a much more expeditious rate. Several IGI Global authored book projects are currently seeking highly-qualified experts in the field to fill vacancies on their respective editorial review boards:

Applications and Inquiries may be sent to:
development@igi-global.com

Applicants must have a doctorate (or an equivalent degree) as well as publishing and reviewing experience. Reviewers are asked to complete the open-ended evaluation questions with as much detail as possible in a timely, collegial, and constructive manner. All reviewers' tenures run for one-year terms on the editorial review boards and are expected to complete at least three reviews per term. Upon successful completion of this term, reviewers can be considered for an additional term.

If you have a colleague that may be interested in this opportunity,
we encourage you to share this information with them.

IGI Global Proudly Partners With eContent Pro International

Receive a 25% Discount on all Editorial Services

Editorial Services

IGI Global expects all final manuscripts submitted for publication to be in their final form. This means they must be reviewed, revised, and professionally copy edited prior to their final submission. Not only does this support with accelerating the publication process, but it also ensures that the highest quality scholarly work can be disseminated.

English Language Copy Editing

Let eContent Pro International's expert copy editors perform edits on your manuscript to resolve spelling, punctuaion, grammar, syntax, flow, formatting issues and more.

Scientific and Scholarly Editing

Allow colleagues in your research area to examine the content of your manuscript and provide you with valuable feedback and suggestions before submission.

Figure, Table, Chart & Equation Conversions

Do you have poor quality figures? Do you need visual elements in your manuscript created or converted? A design expert can help!

Translation

Need your documjent translated into English? eContent Pro International's expert translators are fluent in English and more than 40 different languages.

Hear What Your Colleagues are Saying About Editorial Services Supported by IGI Global

"The service was very fast, very thorough, and very helpful in ensuring our chapter meets the criteria and requirements of the book's editors. I was quite impressed and happy with your service."

– Prof. Tom Brinthaupt,
Middle Tennessee State University, USA

"I found the work actually spectacular. The editing, formatting, and other checks were very thorough. The turnaround time was great as well. I will definitely use eContent Pro in the future."

– Nickanor Amwata, Lecturer,
University of Kurdistan Hawler, Iraq

"I was impressed that it was done timely, and wherever the content was not clear for the reader, the paper was improved with better readability for the audience."

– Prof. James Chilembwe,
Mzuzu University, Malawi

Email: customerservice@econtentpro.com   www.igi-global.com/editorial-service-partners

www.igi-global.com

Celebrating Over 30 Years of Scholarly
Knowledge Creation & Dissemination

InfoSci®-Books

A Database of Over 5,300+ Reference Books Containing Over 100,000+ Chapters Focusing on Emerging Research

GAIN ACCESS TO **THOUSANDS** OF REFERENCE BOOKS AT **A FRACTION** OF THEIR INDIVIDUAL LIST **PRICE**.

InfoSci®-Books Database

The **InfoSci®-Books** database is a collection of over 5,300+ IGI Global single and multi-volume reference books, handbooks of research, and encyclopedias, encompassing groundbreaking research from prominent experts worldwide that span over 350+ topics in 11 core subject areas including business, computer science, education, science and engineering, social sciences and more.

Open Access Fee Waiver (Offset Model) Initiative

For any library that invests in IGI Global's InfoSci-Journals and/ or InfoSci-Books databases, IGI Global will match the library's investment with a fund of equal value to go toward **subsidizing the OA article processing charges (APCs) for their students, faculty, and staff** at that institution when their work is submitted and accepted under OA into an IGI Global journal.*

INFOSCI® PLATFORM FEATURES

- No DRM
- No Set-Up or Maintenance Fees
- A Guarantee of No More Than a 5% Annual Increase
- Full-Text HTML and PDF Viewing Options
- Downloadable MARC Records
- Unlimited Simultaneous Access
- COUNTER 5 Compliant Reports
- Formatted Citations With Ability to Export to RefWorks and EasyBib
- No Embargo of Content (Research is Available Months in Advance of the Print Release)

*The fund will be offered on an annual basis and expire at the end of the subscription period. The fund would renew as the subscription is renewed for each year thereafter. The open access fees will be waived after the student, faculty, or staff's paper has been vetted and accepted into an IGI Global journal and the fund can only be used toward publishing OA in an IGI Global journal. Libraries in developing countries will have the match on their investment doubled.

To Learn More or To Purchase This Database:
www.igi-global.com/infosci-books

eresources@igi-global.com • Toll Free: 1-866-342-6657 ext. 100 • Phone: 717-533-8845 x100

www.igi-global.com

Printed in the United States
By Bookmasters